The DATA Bonanza

**WILEY SERIES ON PARALLEL
AND DISTRIBUTED COMPUTING**

Editor: Albert Y. Zomaya

A complete list of titles in this series appears at the end of this volume.

The DATA Bonanza

Improving Knowledge Discovery in Science, Engineering, and Business

Edited by

Malcolm Atkinson
Rob Baxter
Michelle Galea
Mark Parsons
University of Edinburgh, Edinburgh, UK

Peter Brezany
University of Vienna, Vienna, Austria

Oscar Corcho
Universidad Politécnica de Madrid, Madrid, Spain

Jano van Hemert
Optos PLC, Dunfermline, UK

David Snelling
Fujitsu Laboratories Europe Limited, Hayes, UK

Library of Congress Cataloging-in-Publication Data:

Atkinson, Malcolm.
    The data bonanza : improving knowledge discovery in science, engineering,
and business / Malcolm Atkinson, Rob Baxter, Michelle Galea, Mark Parsons,
Peter Brezany, Oscar Corcho, Jano van Hemert, David Snelling.
        pages cm
    ISBN 978-1-118-39864-7 (pbk.)
  1. Information technology. 2. Information retrieval. 3. Databases. I. Title.
    T58.5.A93 2013
    001–dc23
                                        2012035310

Printed in the United States of America.

10 9 8 7 6 5 4 3 2 1

To data-to-knowledge highway engineers, everywhere.

Contents

Contributors

M. ATKINSON,   School of Informatics, University of Edinburgh, Edinburgh, UK

A. ASCHENBRENNER,   State and University Library Göttingen, Göttingen, Germany

J. AUSTIN,   Department of Computer Science, University of York, York, UK

R. BALDOCK,   Medical Research Council, Human Genetics Unit, Edinburgh, UK

R. BAXTER,   EPCC, University of Edinburgh, Edinburgh, UK

P. BESANA,   School of Informatics, University of Edinburgh, Edinburgh, UK

T. BLANKE,   Digital Research Infrastructure in the Arts and Humanities, King's College London, London, UK

J. BLOWER,   Reading e-Science Centre, University of Reading, Reading, UK

R. COOK,   Environmental Sciences Division, Oak Ridge National Laboratory, Oak Ridge, Tennessee, USA

O. CORCHO,   Departamento de Inteligencia Artificial, Universidad Politécnica de Madrid, Madrid, Spain

T. DAMOULAS,   Department of Computer Science, Cornell University, Ithaca, New York, USA

D. FINK,   Cornell Lab of Ornithology, Cornell University, Ithaca, New York, USA

C. FRITZE,   State and University Library Göttingen, Göttingen, Germany

M. GALEA,   School of Informatics, University of Edinburgh, Edinburgh, UK

A. GEMMELL,   Reading e-Science Centre, University of Reading, Reading, UK

O. HABALA,   Oddelenie paralelného a distribuovaného spracovania informácií', Ústav informatiky SAV, Bratislava, Slovakia

K. HAINES,   Reading e-Science Centre, University of Reading, Reading, UK

L. HAN,   School of Computing, Mathematics & Digital Technology, Manchester Metropolitan University, Manchester, UK

J. VAN HEMERT,   Optos plc, Dunfermline, UK

L. HLUCHÝ, Oddelenie paralelnèho a distribuovanèho spracovania informàciì', Ústav informatiky SAV, Bratislava, Slovakia

W. HOCHACHKA, Cornell Lab of Ornithology, Cornell University, Ithaca, New York, USA

M. HOLLIMAN, Institute of Astronomy, University of Edinburgh, Edinburgh, UK

A. HUME, EPCC, University of Edinburgh, Edinburgh, UK

M. JARKA, Comarch SA, Warsaw, Poland

S. KELLING, Cornell Lab of Ornithology, Cornell University, Ithaca, New York, USA

T. KITCHING, Institute of Astronomy, University of Edinburgh, Edinburgh, UK and Mullard Space Science Laboratory, University College London, Dorking, UK

A. KRAUSE, EPCC, University of Edinburgh, Edinburgh, UK

R. MANN, Institute of Astronomy, University of Edinburgh, Edinburgh, UK

P. MARTIN, School of Informatics, University of Edinburgh, Edinburgh, UK

W. MICHENER, DataONE, University of New Mexico, Albuquerque, New Mexico, USA

A. MOUAT, EPCC, University of Edinburgh, Edinburgh, UK

K. NODDLE, Institute of Astronomy, University of Edinburgh, Edinburgh, UK

I. OVERTON, Medical Research Council, Human Genetics Unit, Edinburgh, UK

M. PARSONS, EPCC, University of Edinburgh, Edinburgh, UK

W. PEMPE, State and University Library Göttingen, Göttingen, Germany

A. RIETBROCK, School of Environmental Sciences, University of Liverpool, Liverpool, UK

K. ROSENBERG, Cornell Lab of Ornithology, Cornell University, Ithaca, New York, USA

C. ŠILVA, Department of Computer Science, Polytechnic Institute of New York, Brooklyn, New York, USA

A. SPINUSO, School of Informatics, University of Edinburgh, Edinburgh, UK; Royal Netherlands Meteorological Institute, Information and Observation Services and Technology–R&D, Utrecht, The Netherlands

D. SNELLING, Research Transformation and Innovation, Fujitsu Laboratories of Europe Limited, Hayes, UK

C. SUN LIEW, School of Informatics, University of Edinburgh, Edinburgh, UK; Faculty of Computer Science and Information Technology, University of Malaya, Kuala Lumpur, Malaysia

B. SIMO, Oddelenie paralelnèho a distribuovanèho spracovania informàciì', Ústav informatiky SAV, Bratislava, Slovakia

V. TRAN, Oddelenie paralelnèho a distribuovanèho spracovania informàciì', Ústav informatiky SAV, Bratislava, Slovakia

L. TRANI, School of Informatics, University of Edinburgh, Edinburgh, UK; Royal Netherlands Meteorological Institute, Information and Observation Services and Technology–R&D, Utrecht, The Netherlands

L. VALKONEN, School of Informatics, University of Edinburgh, Edinburgh, UK

G. YAIKHOM, School of Informatics, University of Edinburgh, Edinburgh, UK; School of Computer Science and Informatics, Cardiff University, Cardiff, UK

Foreword

This book is a systematic approach to help face the challenge of data-intensive computing and a response to the articulation of that challenge set out in *The Fourth Paradigm*, a collection of essays by scientists and computer scientists that I co-edited. It also recognizes the fact that we face that challenge in the context of a digital revolution that is transforming communities worldwide at Internet speed.

This book proposes a strategy for partitioning the challenge, both in the ways in which we organize and in which we build systems. This partitioning builds on natural foci of interest and the examples show that this approach works well in the context of groups and organizations. The technological strategy reflects the evolving pattern of provision driven by business models and the flourishing diversity of tools and applications that enable human innovation.

We all face the need to separate concerns every time we face a data-intensive problem. This is key to making data-intensive methods routinely available and to their easy application. This leads to the recognition of effective working practices that need supporting with better 'datascopes' that are easily steered and focused to extract the relevant information from immense and diverse collections of data. The book calls for the introduction of "intellectual on-ramps" that match the new tools to well-understood interfaces, so that practitioners can incrementally master the new data-intensive methods.

This book calls for recognition that this notion of intellectual on-ramps is worthy of study. Data-intensive computing warrants an appropriate engineering discipline that identifies effective ways of building appropriate highways from data to required knowledge. It is a call to arms for a serious attempt at initiating the professionalization of this discipline.

We are very much at the start of the digital revolution. The growth in digital data will not abate, and in certain areas it will probably accelerate. There is much to be gained by exploiting the opportunities this bonanza of data brings but the extraction of insights and knowledge from 'Big Data' will also certainly transform our organizations and society. Responding effectively to these changes requires the availability of ready-made tools and reusable processes together with practitioners with the skills to deploy them precisely and safely. This book frames an approach as to how these tools, processes, and skills may be developed. Such a systematic approach is now urgently needed as the opportunities are rapidly outgrowing our capabilities to assemble and run data-intensive campaigns.

This book provides a vocabulary to facilitate data-intensive engineering by introducing key concepts and notations. It presents nine in-depth case studies that show how practitioners have tackled data-intensive challenges in a wide range of disciplines. It also provides an up-to-date analysis of this rapidly changing field and a survey of many of the current research hot-spots that are driving it. For all these reasons, I believe that this book is a welcome addition to the literature on data-intensive computing.

TONY HEY

Redmond, Washington
July 2012

Preface

The world is undergoing a digital-data revolution. More and more data are born digital. Almost every business, governmental, and organizational activity is driven by data and produces data. Science, engineering, medicine, design and innovation are powered by data. This prevalence of data in all that we do is changing society, organizations, and individual behavior. To thrive in this new environment requires new strategies, new skills, and new technology. This book is the first to expound the strategies that will make you adept at exploiting the expanding opportunities of this new world.

This book identifies the driving forces that are provoking change and proposes a strategy for building the skills, methods, technologies, and businesses that will be well adapted in the emerging data-wealthy world. This strategy will change the way in which you spend your organization's (country's, company's, institution's, and profession's) resources. You will invest more in exploiting data, even if that means spending less on creating, capturing or archiving it, as today most data are underused or never used, even though they frequently *contain the latent evidence that should be leading to innovation, knowledge and wisdom*. After reading this book, you will expect an understandable path from data, via analysis, evidence and visualization, to influential outputs that change behavior. When this is not happening, your organization is underperforming and is at risk. You will come to expect that all of those with whom you deal should be competent at getting good value from data.

This book will change your skills by developing your ingenuity in discovering, understanding, exploiting, and presenting data. You will acquire a compendium of tools for addressing every stage in the data life cycle. It will change education— everyone needs survival skills for the data-wealthy world. All professionals and experts need experience and judgement for their part of the path from data to discovery, innovation, and outcomes.

This book will initiate the development of professionals who will engineer tomorrow's data highways. These highways will be designed to meet carefully analyzed and anticipated needs, to interwork with existing data infrastructure, to accelerate the journeys of millions from data to knowledge. These knowledge discovery highways will make it easy for people to get data from wherever they are stored and promptly deliver understandable information to wherever it is needed.

Who Should Read this Book

This book will be valuable to a wide range of information strategists, decision makers, researchers, students, and practitioners, from domains such as computer science (data mining, machine learning, statistics, databases, knowledge-based systems, large-scale computing), e-Science, and to workers in any discipline or industry where large-scale data handling and analysis is important.

The ideas presented are relevant to and draw on: data mining, knowledge discovery in databases, machine learning, artificial intelligence, databases and data management, data warehousing, information systems, distributed computing, grid computing, cloud computing, ubiquitous computing, e-Science (including a wide range of scientific and engineering fields dealing with large data), modeling and simulation.

This Book's Structure

This book consists of 24 chapters grouped into six parts; they are introduced here.

Part I: Strategies for success in the digital-data revolution   Part I provides an executive summary of the whole book to convince strategists, politicians, managers, and educators that our future data-intensive society requires new thinking, new behavior, new culture, and new distribution of investment and effort. This part will introduce the major concepts so that readers are equipped to discuss and steer their organization's response to the opportunities and obligations brought by the growing wealth of data. It will help readers understand the changing context brought about by advances in digital devices, digital communication, and ubiquitous computing.

Chapter 1: The digital-data challenge   This chapter will help readers to understand the challenges ahead in making good use of the data and introduce ideas that will lead to helpful strategies. A global digital-data revolution is catalyzing change in the ways in which we live, work, relax, govern, and organize. This is a significant change in society, as important as the invention of printing or the industrial revolution, but more challenging because it is happening globally at Internet speed. Becoming agile in adapting to this new world is essential.

Chapter 2: The digital-data revolution   This chapter reviews the relationships between data, information, knowledge, and wisdom. It analyses and quantifies the changes in technology and society that are delivering the data bonanza, and then reviews the consequential changes via representative examples in biology, Earth sciences, social sciences, leisure activity, and business. It exposes quantitative details and shows the complexity and diversity of the growing wealth of data, introducing some of its potential benefits and examples of the impediments to successfully realizing those benefits.

Chapter 3: The data-intensive survival guide   This chapter presents an overview of all of the elements of the proposed data-intensive strategy. Sufficient detail is presented for readers to understand the principles and practice that we recommend. It should also provide a good preparation for readers who choose to sample later chapters. It introduces three professional viewpoints: domain experts, data-analysis experts, and data-intensive engineers. Success depends on a balanced approach that develops the capacity of all three groups. A data-intensive architecture provides a flexible framework for that balanced approach. This enables the three groups to build and exploit data-intensive processes that incrementally step from data to results. A language is introduced to describe these incremental data processes from all three points of view. The chapter introduces 'datascopes' as the productized data handling environments and 'intellectual ramps' as the 'on ramps' for the highways from data to knowledge.

Chapter 4: Data-intensive thinking with DISPEL   This chapter engages the reader with technical issues and solutions, by working through a sequence of examples, building up from a sketch of a solution to a large-scale data challenge. It uses the DISPEL language extensively, introducing its concepts and constructs. It shows how DISPEL may help designers, data-analysts, and engineers develop solutions to the requirements emerging in any data-intensive application domain. The reader is taken through simple steps initially, this then builds to conceptually complex steps that are necessary to cope with the realities of real data providers, real data, real distributed systems, and long-running processes.

Part II: Data-intensive knowledge discovery   Part II focuses on the needs of data-analysis experts. It illustrates the problem-solving strategies appropriate for a data-rich world, without delving into the details of underlying technologies. It should engage and inform data-analysis specialists, such as statisticians, data miners, image analysts, bio-informaticians or chemo-informaticians, and generate ideas pertinent to their application areas.

Chapter 5: Data-intensive analysis   This chapter introduces a set of common problems that data-analysis experts often encounter, by means of a set of scenarios of increasing levels of complexity. The scenarios typify knowledge discovery challenges and the presented solutions provide practical methods; a starting point for readers addressing their own data challenges.

Chapter 6: Problem solving in data-intensive knowledge discovery   On the basis of the previous scenarios, this chapter provides an overview of effective strategies in knowledge discovery, highlighting common problem-solving methods that apply in conventional contexts, and focusing on the similarities and differences of these methods.

Chapter 7: Data-intensive components and usage patterns   This chapter provides a systematic review of the components that are commonly used in knowledge discovery tasks as well as common patterns of component composition. That is, it introduces the processing elements from which knowledge discovery solutions are built and common composition patterns for delivering trustworthy information. It reflects on how these components and patterns are evolving in a data-intensive context.

Chapter 8: Sharing and re-use in knowledge discovery   This chapter introduces more advanced knowledge discovery problems, and shows how improved component and pattern descriptions facilitate re-use. This supports the assembly of libraries of high level components well-adapted to classes of knowledge discovery methods or application domains. The descriptions are made more powerful by introducing notations from the semantic Web.

Part III: Data-intensive engineering   Part III is targeted at technical experts who will develop complex applications, new components, or data-intensive platforms. The techniques introduced may be applied very widely; for example, to any data-intensive distributed application, such as index generation, image processing, sequence comparison, text analysis, and sensor-stream monitoring. The challenges, methods, and implementation requirements are illustrated by making extensive use of DISPEL.

Chapter 9: Platforms for data-intensive analysis   This chapter gives a reprise of data-intensive architectures, examines the business case for investing in them, and introduces the stages of data-intensive workflow enactment.

Chapter 10: Definition of the DISPEL language   This chapter describes the novel aspects of the DISPEL language: its constructs, capabilities, and anticipated programming style.

Chapter 11: DISPEL development   This chapter describes the tools and libraries that a DISPEL developer might expect to use. The tools include those needed during process definition, those required to organize enactment, and diagnostic aids for developers of applications and platforms.

Chapter 12: DISPEL enactment   This chapter describes the four stages of DISPEL enactment. It is targeted at the data-intensive engineers who implement enactment services.

Part IV: Data-intensive application experience   This part of the book is about applications that shaped the ideas behind the data-intensive architecture and methods. It provides a wealth of examples drawn from experience, describing in each case the aspects of data-intensive systems tested by the application, the DISPEL-based methods developed to meet the challenge, and the conclusions drawn from the prototype experiments.

Chapter 13: The application foundations of DISPEL   The early development of DISPEL was influenced and assisted by research challenges from four very different data-intensive application domains. This chapter reviews these four domains in terms of their particular needs and requirements and how, as a suite, they provide an effective test of all key dimensions of a data-intensive system. It reviews the data-intensive strategy in terms of these applications and finds support for the approach.

Chapter 14: Analytical platform for customer relationship management   This chapter demonstrates that the data-intensive methods and technology work well for traditional commercial knowledge discovery applications. Readers are introduced to the application domain through a scene-setting discussion, which assumes no prior knowledge, and are then taken through the process of analyzing customer data to predict behavior or preferences.

Chapter 15: Environmental risk management   This chapter presents applications in the context of environmental risk management. The scenarios involve significant data-integration challenges as they take an increasing number of factors into account when managing the outflow from a reservoir to limit the effects downstream.

Chapter 16: Analyzing gene expression imaging data in developmental biology   This chapter describes the application of data-intensive methods to the automatic identification and annotation of gene expression patterns in the mouse embryo. It shows how image processing and machine learning can be combined to annotate images and identify networks of gene functions.

Chapter 17: Data-intensive seismology: research horizons   Seismology has moved from focusing on events to analyzing continuous streams of data obtained from thousands of seismometers. This is fundamental to understanding the inner structure and processes of the Earth and this chapter investigates the data-intensive architecture necessary to enable the analysis of large-scale distributed seismic waveforms.

Part V: Data-intensive beacons of success   This part introduces a group of challenging, sophisticated data-intensive applications, which are starting to shape and promote a new generation of knowledge discovery technology. The chapters show that science, engineering, and society are fertile lands for data-intensive research. This part is targeted at novel application developers who like to include visionary aspects in their research.

Chapter 18: Data-intensive methods in astronomy   Astronomy has been at the forefront of the digital revolution as it pioneered faster and more sensitive digital cameras, and established a new *modus operandi* for sharing and integrating data globally. These are yielding floods of data, and opening up new approaches to exploring the cosmos and testing the physical models that underpin it. This chapter describes two examples that exemplify the data-intensive science now underway.

Chapter 19: Interactive interpretation of environmental data   A crucial step in any science is to explore the data available; this will often stimulate new insights and hypotheses. As the volumes of data grow and diverse formats are encountered, the effort of handling data inhibits exploration. This chapter shows how these inhibitory difficulties can be overcome, so that oceanographers and atmospheric scientists can easily select, vizualise and explore compositions of their data.

Chapter 20: Data-driven research in the humanities   Researchers in the arts and humanities are using digitization to see new aspects of the many artifacts and phenomena they study. Digital resources allow statistical methods and computational matching to be employed, as well as the full panoply of text processing and collaborative annotation. In this chapter, researchers show their plans for a Europe-wide data infrastructure to facilitate this new research.

Chapter 21: Analysis of engineering and transport data   Analysis of vibration data from aero-engines, turbines, and locomotives, 'listening to the engine', can reveal incipient problems and trigger appropriate remedial responses. To do this safely for large numbers of operational engines is a major data-intensive challenge. This chapter reports on ten years' progress and its spin-offs into analyzing medical time series.

Chapter 22: Determining the patterns of bird species occurrence   In this chapter, the ornithologists describe the challenge of estimating the populations of birds as they migrate and of inferring the factors affecting species numbers. It takes a great deal of sophisticated data analysis to extract and visualize the relevant information and much ingenuity to discover and use the data required from other disciplines.

Part VI: The data-intensive future   This part presents a summary of the state of the industry and research, the observed trends and the current 'hot-spots' of data-intensive innovation. It provides a framework for reviewing the current activity and anticipated changes it will bring about. It offers a rich set of pointers to the literature and Web sites, built over the 15 months of the data-intensive research theme at the e-Science Institute. This should help readers select and find highly relevant further reading.

Chapter 23: Data-intensive trends This chapter summarizes the learning about data-intensive methods and their potential power. It then analyzes some of the categories of data-intensive challenge and assesses how they will develop.

Chapter 24: Data-rich futures This chapter dangerously attempts some 'crystal gazing'. It looks first at technological factors and current research that should be observed by those who wish to further develop data-intensive strategies. It explores some of the economic factors that will shape a data-rich future and concludes with a view on the social issues that will emerge. We call on those with influence to strive for professional standards in handling data, from their collection to the actions based on their evidence.

How to Read this Book

There are two pieces of information that we wish to offer readers in order to help them get the most benefit from this book: the choice of routes through the book and conventions used in the book. We consider each of these in turn.

1. The primary story line of the book develops in the conventional way by reading the parts and the chapters in order, up to the end of Part IV. It begins with scene setting to establish a conceptual framework. It then addresses the methods and engineering needed to put the ideas into practice before successful applications in a wide range of domains. Many readers will want a selected-reading route that matches their needs; the following map and suggested routes will encourage them to plan their reading.
2. Research strategists, scientists and managers, who may be less interested in technical detail should follow Chapters 1 to 3→Part IV→Part V→Part VI.
3. Data-analysis experts should try Part I →Part II→Chapter 10→Chapter 11→ Part IV→Part VI.
4. Those building data-intensive systems should read Part I→Part III→Part IV→ Part VI.
5. Domain experts, who are looking for ideas that may pay off with their specialist data could read the applications first, Part V→Part IV→Chapters 1 to 3. We hope there are enough signposts that you can adjust your route easily to follow new interests.

The conventions concern the structure and the representation of certain items. As the map shows, there are six parts; each one begins with a preamble intended to orient readers who start in that part, and to relate that part to the other parts of the book. Appendix A provides a glossary, where we hope you will find useful definitions of terms used frequently in the book. Terms used infrequently may be traced via the index. Each chapter concludes with the references cited in that chapter. References to Web sites are shown as URLs in line with the text if they are short and in footnotes if they are long. The `http://` prefix is omitted.

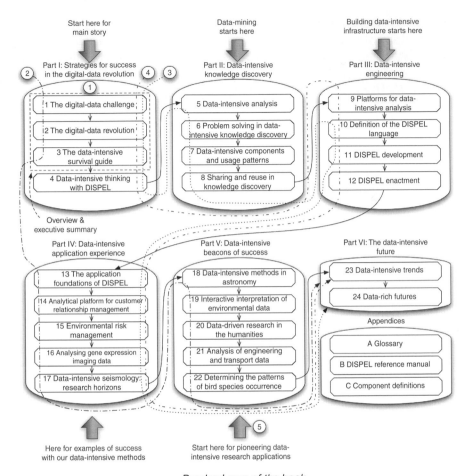

Readers' map of the book.

There are many programming examples, mostly represented in DISPEL. A consistent highlighting convention has been used for these, which we believe helps legibility. These are also available on the Web site (see following text), so that you can view them in your favorite editor. There are often corresponding diagrams, showing the data-flow graph that the program would generate. These pick up the same color conventions. The language DISPEL is introduced in Chapters 3, 4 and 10; the language definition is in Appendix B. The components that are used in the examples are provided from standard libraries of components; these are described in Appendix C.

Web Site with Additional Material

A Web site at www.dispel.lang.org holds material intended to help readers of this book; these include pages covering the following topics.

- An overview and table of contents of the book.
- A collection of success stories.
- Teaching material including presentations to be used in conjunction with chapters in the book.
- Copies of the program examples from the book, so that they may be used by readers.
- The libraries of components used in the book, with corresponding descriptions in a local registry.
- The DISPEL reference manual.
- Links to other sites including many of those referenced from the book, the associated open-source project and new developments.

This Web site will be updated and contributions from others will be welcome.

Acknowledgments

Many people have contributed to this book through discussions and visits over the past 6 years; we thank them all and limit the explicit list to those who worked directly on the book.

Funders   The primary funder of the editorial process was the European Commission's Framework Program 7's support for the ADMIRE project (www.admire-project.eu), grant number 215024. The tour of the USA by Atkinson and De Roure, to study their use of data (bit.ly/c0G2rn), and Atkinson's work on the book was funded by the UK's Engineering and Physical Sciences Research Council (EPSRC) Senior Research Fellowship to undertake the UK e-Science Envoy role, grant EP/D079829/1. The initial workshop on data-intensive research (bit.ly/bQpu5h), where many of the commitments for contributions to the book were made, and the one-year data-intensive research theme (bit.ly/cygimA), were funded by the e-Science Institute, EPSRC grant EP/D056314/1. The work to further develop this book, the technology and the methodology described, is partially funded in the University of Edinburgh by the EPSRC NeSC Research Platform (research.nesc.ac.uk) grant EP/F057695/1, and in Universidad Politècnica de Madrid by the Spanish Ministry of Science and Technology under grant TIN2010-17060. Baxter would also like to acknowledge the direct support of EPCC at the University of Edinburgh, and support from the UK's Software Sustainability Institute under EPSRC grant number EP/H043160/1.

Helpers   A big thank you to Jo Newman, who was a continuous support to the editors of the book, impeccably arranging many meetings and tele-communications, as well as thorough proof reading, checking copyright information, and communicating with all of the contributing authors. Kathy Humphry read nearly every chapter and gave good advice on each one of them.

In addition to being contributing authors, we must thank Ivan Janciak, in the University of Vienna, who made life much easier for all of us by setting up convenient macros for building the book; Paul Martin and Gagarine Yaikhom, of the Universities of Edinburgh and Cardiff respectively, for setting up the system for typesetting DISPEL highlighting its structure; and Amrey Krause and Chee Sun Liew of the University of Edinburgh, who set up the system for validating DISPEL text used in the book. Chee Sun Liew also did a great deal of LaTeX wrangling to shape the book into its final form. Ivan Janciak, Alexander Wöhrer and Marek Lenart of the University of Vienna reviewed several book chapters and helped improve the quality of figures and the formatting of the text.

We would also like to thank our colleagues Martin Šeleng and Peter Krammer from the Institute of Informatics of the Slovak Academy of Sciences for their excellent work on the data mining scenarios of the environmental risk management application, and our dear friends at the Slovak Hydro-Meteorological Institute and the Slovak Water Enterprise for their invaluable help with designing the pilot scenarios and providing real input data for them. A big thank you must go to the EPCC software engineering team for making large swathes of the prototype data-intensive platform work: Ally Hume, Malcolm Illingworth, Amrey Krause, Adrian Mouat and David Scott, with a special mention for our integration, test and build-meister Radek Ostrowski.

We heartily thank all of the open-source developers on whose work we built; all those who helped and confirm that all the remaining errors are the responsibility of the editors, led by myself.

MALCOLM ATKINSON

Edinburgh, UK
April 2012

The Editors

Malcolm Atkinson PhD is Professor of e-Science in the School of Informatics at the University of Edinburgh in Scotland. He is also Data-Intensive Research group leader, Director of the e-Science Institute, IT architect for the ADMIRE and VERCE EU projects, and UK e-Science Envoy. Atkinson has been leading research projects for several decades and served on many advisory bodies.

Rob Baxter PhD is EPCC's Software Development Group Manager. He has over fifteen years' experience of distributed software project management on the bleeding edge of technology. He managed the European ADMIRE project, rated "excellent" in its final review and plays a prominent role in the EUDAT, iCORDI and PERICLES projects—all large-scale scientific data infrastructures.

Peter Brezany PhD is Professor of Computer Science in the University of Vienna Faculty of Computer Science. He is known internationally for his work in high performance programming languages and their applications. He has led several projects addressing large-scale data analytics.

Oscar Corcho PhD is an Associate Professor at the Facultad de Informática, Universidad Politécnica de Madrid, and he belongs to the Ontology Engineering Group. His research activities are focused on Semantic e-Science and Real World Internet.

Michelle Galea PhD has over 15 years experience in the public sector, banking and academia, addressing the challenges of managing data from strategic and research perspectives. She is a research associate in the School of Informatics, University of Edinburgh.

Jano van Hemert PhD is the Imaging Research Manager and Academic Liaison at Optos, which is a global company providing retinal diagnostics. He is an Honorary Fellow of the University of Edinburgh and a member of The Young Academy of Scotland of the Royal Society of Edinburgh.

Mark Parsons PhD is EPCC's Executive Director and Associate Dean for e-Research at The University of Edinburgh. He has wide-ranging interests in distributed and high performance computing and is a leading contributor to the European PRACE research infrastructure.

David Snelling PhD is a Senior Research Fellow and manager of the Research Transformation and Innovation team at Fujitsu Laboratories of Europe. He is a primary architect of the Unicore Grid and a member of the European Commission's Expert Groups on Next-generation Grids and Cloud Computing, W3C, OGF, DMTF and OASIS standards organizations.

Part I

Strategies for Success in the Digital-Data Revolution

We provide an overview and introduction to each of the six parts of the book. This is an introduction to Part I, which itself gives a complete introduction to the current data-rich environment in which we find ourselves today. It is intended to be a synopsis of the whole book as well as being its introduction. It is helpful as an overview for technology leaders and research strategists who wish to better understand what data-intensive methods can do for them or their organization. It should also help those who are supporting users of data-intensive methods, for example, those who provide Cloud infrastructure for these applications. All readers who intend to dive more deeply into the book will find it a valuable orientation, setting the scene for later parts and steering readers with specific interests to relevant chapters.

The book has been written at a time when there is a great deal of contemporary interest in data and in the best methods of obtaining insight from data. It is based on a decade of experience of data-intensive research. In the last decade there has been a flurry of papers pointing out the advent of the growing wealth of data and of the substantial challenge of exploiting that wealth successfully. An early example, *The Data Deluge: An e-Science Perspective* by Tony Hey and Anne Trefethen [1], focused on the challenge of data volumes. Although *those* data volumes are no longer challenging, the growth of data has outrun the increase in capacity and power of data handling technology.

The DATA Bonanza: Improving Knowledge Discovery in Science, Engineering, and Business, First Edition.
Edited by Malcolm Atkinson, Rob Baxter, Michelle Galea, Mark Parsons, Peter Brezany, Oscar Corcho, Jano van Hemert, and David Snelling.

By the end of the last decade, there was growing recognition that the abundance of data was a widespread phenomena, spanning most domains of science, business and government. Jim Gray recognized the new way of thinking this enables and named it *The Fourth Paradigm*. The book of that name, in honor of Jim Gray's memory, by Tony Hey et al. [2], provides a compelling collection of essays showing the potential power of data in more than a dozen disciplines.

In the same year, the US government adopted a report, *Harnessing the power of digital data for science and society*, by an Interagency Working Group on Digital Data that spanned nearly every branch of government [3]. This recognized the potential of data and initiated a programme to make it as widely used as possible for the benefit of research and society. A corresponding report, *Riding the Wave*, set the data-intensive research agenda for Europe [4]. In February 2011, *Science* devoted a special issue to data (volume 331, issue 6018, pages 639–806) showing that though there are many demonstrable successes in scientific and medical research, the use of data is still fraught with challenges.

This book addresses those challenges by deliberately combining a vision of a future where a well-polished ecosystem of data-services, data-analysis tools, and professionally adopted data-intensive methods makes it far easier to exploit the growing wealth of data. Exploiting data effectively is now recognized as a key issue for many industries, for commerce, for government, for healthcare and for research. There are many other publications addressing related issues. They report how individuals or large teams with the required skills, and often with much effort, extract gems of knowledge from the new wealth of data. This book recognizes that the ever growing number of cases where such knowledge discovery is needed cannot be met by throwing that level of skill and effort at every case. The skill base cannot be grown at a rate which matches growth in demand, and the effort has to be reduced to deliver timely results economically. To address this issue, we raise the level of discourse, partition the intellectual challenge, and propose both sharing and automation.

Published in 2009, *Beautiful Data*, edited by Segaran and Hammerbacher [5], provides 20 examples of how data can be used effectively. Elegant solutions with a wide variety of data yield information that is then presented carefully to achieve intended effects on its beholders. A reference that should be consulted for inspiration, the following books give more help with understanding applicable principles.

The book, *Scientific Data Management: Challenges, Technology and Deployment*, edited by Shoshani and Rotem [6], provides a collection of strategies from experienced practitioners on how to build technology, to handle very large volumes of data, to organize computations that analyze and visualize those data, and to specify and manage the processes involved. It takes a file-oriented and high-performance computing viewpoint for the most part, looks predominantly at applications in the physical sciences and is replete with good solutions in that context. These are revisited in Parts IV and V of this book.

In the same year, *World Wide Research*, edited by Dutton and Jeffreys [7], examined the digital-data revolution from the viewpoint of the Arts and Humanities.

Their primary concern was the transformative impact of the Internet on their communities of researchers. A key ingredient is the new ability to create, curate, and share data, with a significant impact on research, and the mores guiding researchers.

The contemporary work, *Beautiful Visualization*, edited by Steele and Iliinsky [8], focuses on *going the last mile* with data, presenting the information in forms so well adapted to the recipients and intended purpose that it is natural to interpret it correctly.

All four books set the scene for this book. They contribute compelling examples of the high value and power of using data well, and they present detailed practical techniques that can be harnessed to take data and to convert it into reliable knowledge that can be safely acted on. They also show the ingenuity and detailed work currently necessary to achieve this; the insights, creativity, and perseverance of professionals will always be critical to success but we hope that our vision will make their work far easier. We envisage the automation of many of the technical details that currently limit the number of successes.

Two books announce a rich environment for implementing this vision: *Data Mining*, edited by Witten et al. [9], and *Data Analysis with Open Source Tools*, by Janert [10]. They offer two extensive collections of readily available elements that will be used in exploring and exploiting data. We have made extensive use of some of these elements to validate our vision. They reappear in Parts II and IV of this book. Today, tools for larger-scale data, such as Massive Online Analysis (MOA) (moa.cs.waikato.ac.nz), are emerging. These would be elements in future systems.

As always in computing, the digital environment is changing rapidly; indeed, we argue that the current intertwined set of changes constitutes a significant *digital revolution*. An aspect of this is that the choices of technology and the dominant business models are changing; for example, *Distributed and Cloud Computing: From Parallel Processing to the Internet of Things* [11] shows how data-intensive computing can now be accomplished in the Cloud. No book can be wholly insulated from such changes, but we have tried to do two things: to recognize the changes, explain them and indicate why they are important drivers in our story, and to deliver principles as well as practical details with the belief that these principles have long-term value.

Chapter 2 provides examples of the current data, showing its scale and complexity, as well as the global efforts to collaborate in making the best use of the data. It shows how these early days of the digital revolution are reshaping our world, both social and business behavior, an idea also explored by Dutton and Jeffreys [7] and manifest in the applications shown in Hey et al. [2], Segaran and Hammerbacher [5] and Steele and Iliinsky [8]. Steering these changes to the benefit of science and society by having governmental decisions lead the way is an explicit goal of the Interagency Working Group on Digital Data [3].

Chapter 3 rehearses a strategy for rapidly increasing our capabilities and agility in the exploitation of data, based on the recognition of how to partition the challenges, both in the human and technical dimensions. This provides a foundation for understanding the rest of the book and concludes with a guide for those who wish to then focus on a particular aspect of this strategy.

This part's final chapter, Chapter 4, introduces *data-intensive thinking*. It begins with the elementary stages of first addressing a knowledge discovery challenge and introduces a language and diagrammatic notation to facilitate thinking about these issues. It uses that notation and a running example to initiate consideration of the technological challenges of full-scale knowledge discovery processes showing the variety of issues encountered and the basic tactics for overcoming them.

Taken together, the four chapters in this part will give their readers an appreciation as to why they should exploit the burgeoning data bonanza, an awareness of the evolving context of the digital revolution, an introduction to a strategy and vision as to how to proceed, and a tutorial on how to think about data-intensive challenges.

REFERENCES

1. A. J. G. Hey and A. E. Trefethen, *The Data Deluge: An e-Science Perspective*, In, Berman, F, Fox, G C and Hey, A J G (eds.) *Grid Computing - Making the Global Infrastructure a Reality*. Ch. 36, pp. 809–824. John Wiley & Sons, Ltd, 2003.

2. A. J. G. Hey, S. Tansley, and K. Tolle, *The Fourth Paradigm: Data-Intensive Scientific Discovery*. Microsoft Research, 2009.

3. Interagency Working Group on Digital Data, "Harnessing the power of digital data for science and society: report to the Committee on Science of the National Science and Technology Council," tech. rep., Executive office of the President, Office of Science and Technology, Washington D.C., USA, 2009.

4. High-Level Expert Group on Scientific Data, "Riding the wave how Europe can gain from the rising tide of scientific data," tech. rep., European Commission, 2010.

5. T. Segaran and J. Hammerbacher, *Beautiful Data: The Stories Behind Elegant Data Solutions*. O'Reilly, 2009.

6. A. Shoshani and D. Rotem, *Scientific Data Management: Challenges, Technology and Deployment*, Computational Science Series. Chapman and Hall/CRC, 2010.

7. W. H. Dutton and P. W. Jeffreys, *World Wide Research: Reshaping the Sciences and Humanities*. {MIT} Press, 2010.

8. J. Steele and N. Iliinsky, *Beautiful Visualisation: Looking at Data Through the Eyes of Experts*. O'Reilly, 2010.

9. I. H. Witten, E. Frank, and M. A. Hall, *Data Mining: Practical Machine Learning Tools and Techniques (Third Edition)*. Morgan Kauffman, 2011.

10. P. K. Janert, *Data Analysis with Open Source Tools*. O'Reilly, 2011.

11. K. Hwang, J. Dongarra, and G. C. Fox, *Distributed and Cloud Computing: From Parallel Processing to the Internet of Things*. Morgan Kaufmann, 2011.

1

The Digital-Data Challenge

Malcolm Atkinson

School of Informatics, University of Edinburgh, Edinburgh, UK

Mark Parsons

EPCC, University of Edinburgh, Edinburgh, UK

This chapter is intended to interest all readers and to set the scene for the rest of the book. It reviews the current, rapidly growing wealth of data and our abilities to take best advantage of the potential knowledge that this data bonanza offers.

1.1   THE DIGITAL REVOLUTION

There is evidence all around us that the world is going through the early stages of a digital revolution; it is more stressful than the Industrial Revolution, as it is impacting virtually every nation simultaneously. From digital photographs to digital music and from electronic tax returns to electronic health records, this revolution is affecting all of us in many aspects of our lives. Global access to data is changing the ways in which we think and behave. This is seeding change in global collaborations and businesses powered by shared data.

The DATA Bonanza: Improving Knowledge Discovery in Science, Engineering, and Business, First Edition.
Edited by Malcolm Atkinson, Rob Baxter, Michelle Galea, Mark Parsons, Peter Brezany, Oscar Corcho, Jano van Hemert, and David Snelling.

This is a far more stressful revolution than those brought about by the previous advances in communication: speech, writing, telecommunications, and broadcasting, and by the Industrial Revolution, because it is so rapid and, unlike previous revolutions, it is penetrating every corner of the globe simultaneously, thanks to the Internet. Survival in a revolution depends on rapid and appropriate adaptation to the changes it brings. The successful survivors will be those people, organizations, and nations who are most adept at adapting to change.

Today's global challenges are urgent and intellectually demanding; making the best use of the world's growing wealth of data is a crucial strategy for addressing them. Data are the catalysts in research, engineering, business, and diagnosis. Data underpin scholarship and understanding. Data fuel analysis to produce key evidence for business decisions and supply the information for compelling communication. Data connect computational systems and enable global collaborative endeavors.

The digital revolution is transforming global economies and societies with ever-increasing flows of data and a flood of faster, cheaper, and higher-resolution digital devices. Research is being accelerated and enabled by the advances in automation, communication, sensing, and computation. To reap the benefits, the public and private sectors need novel infrastructure and tools that are as convenient, pervasive, and powerful as the Web 2.0 environment. While the Web facilitates communication for business and personal use, the new data-intensive infrastructure will facilitate the analysis of enormous volumes of data from a wide range of sources. This will empower new ways of thinking about the decisions that individuals and society face. The questions that the users will ask of data and the capabilities of the data-intensive facilities will coevolve as the new power stimulates new approaches to the challenges—both large and small—we face in our lives. Enabling that widespread access for every individual, group, and organization to explore data in the search for better knowledge will have profound effects.

These changes in the use of data will require radical changes in our working behavior and infrastructure provision. We advocate a collaborative endeavor to achieve this potential, exploring the new types of behavior, methods, computational strategies, and economies of provision. Data should be used fluently in research (be it business or academic), investigation, planning, and policy formulation to equip those responsible with the necessary information, knowledge, and wisdom. *The present cornucopia of data is underexploited.* Many people are aware of this; few understand what to do. The purpose of this book is to help the readers understand how to navigate this digital revolution and benefit from it in all aspects of their lives.

1.2   CHANGING HOW WE THINK AND BEHAVE

Ever since humans invented writing at the beginning of the Bronze Age, around 7000 years ago, we have created persistent data. Before the advent of the computer, data were transferred from generation to generation in the form of written, or latterly printed, books or other documents. Since the advent of the digital computer, and, in particular, since the start of the third millennium, the amount of recorded data has exploded. All of the books and documents written by man over the past 7000 years represent a tiny fraction of the data stored on computers at present.

Digital data are now a universal glue; they carry radio-frequency identification (RFID) messages, represent cartographic and satellite images, form SMS and email messages, encode mobile phone traffic, facilitate social networks, such as Facebook and Twitter, and enable the transactions of everyday life: booking a hotel, paying an account, planning a journey, and arranging to board an aircraft. Indeed, the rapid flow of data between individuals and organizations has changed the form of these interactions; at present, people expect to make detailed choices from offers shaped for them and get almost instantaneous responses when they interact with utilities, businesses, and government. Data capture our personal images in digital cameras and videos, carry films through each stage of production and transmission to market, represent books and newspapers, and are increasingly the medium of broadcasting. Data are the primary product of medical-imaging systems, satellite observations, astronomic surveys, microscopes, and experiments in nearly every field of science. Data capture inventories, accounts, plans, and conducted processes. Data are used to represent documents from initial drafting to final publication and production; today more and more are published in digital form. Data are the result of all simulation model runs and of many design studies. Data are the medium and product of social computation.

Managing the data deluge and using it to our advantage, whether that be for geopolitical planning purposes or a more mundane task such as buying a new car, requires significant changes in our behavior and in the information and communication technology (ICT) infrastructures that support the curation, management, and provision of the data we need. As data volumes increase exponentially, incremental changes will no longer be sufficient. We need to establish new working practices and new models of computing and infrastructure provision if we are to see the benefits of these huge quantities of data and the opportunities they bring.

Digital data are changing the way we think and how we behave. With information always available at our fingertips, for instance, through Google or Wikipedia, we are not necessarily better informed. We live in a world of instant information— far too much information for us to cope with. Many people believe the information that is presented without questioning its veracity; they only use a minuscule percentage of the data available when making decisions. Two issues must be addressed: better presentation of high quality aggregations of the data and accessible clarity about that presentation's origins and validity.

The goal is to accelerate and facilitate *knowledge discovery* from the growing wealth of data. For this, every step from finding and gaining access to the data, through information extraction to knowledge delivery, must be technically well supported. These steps should be as accessible to the individuals as Web 2.0 searches are at present. But the precision must be trustworthy and well understood, and the knowledge must be delivered to each person in a form that suits their needs. There are still many other issues to consider in any knowledge discovery project, the largest of these almost certainly being the social issues related to data ownership and how people react to requests for projects to use "their" data. Such socioeconomic considerations are not within the scope of this book, but readers should be aware of the complexity of the challenges posed by them—see, for example, Section 1.6 of [1]. Effective security mechanisms are needed to underpin these social contracts.

1.3   MOVING ADROITLY IN THIS FAST-CHANGING FIELD

The future will contain many innovations in our day-to-day behavior and the technology that supports it. Some data will remain specific to a community, business, or facility; some will be constrained by ethical and legal considerations. Many individuals and organizations will make use of information produced by large swathes of society.

The fundamental challenge that this book addresses is how to succeed in an age where individual people or organizations can no longer cope using manual methods of transforming data into information, to understand issues and to make decisions. Those who learn to move adroitly and embrace the new technologies that are being developed to support the analysis of data are those who will thrive in the digital age.

In addition to showing how these new technologies can benefit individual people or organizations, in this book, we propose a path intended to lead to more collaborative behavior, which will also drive and draw on innovation in other data-intensive contexts. For example, many data producers, be they separate organizations or separate divisions within a large organization, could deposit data in *shared data clouds* that would also be populated with reference and legacy data. When undertaking research to inform scientific enquiry or making business decisions, users will then deposit data and pose questions that compose and compare data from any contributing source. Legal and ethical regimes will become even more important to guide and control this use, balancing the concern for privacy with society's and the individual's needs for the best-quality decisions.

1.4   DIGITAL-DATA CHALLENGES EXIST EVERYWHERE

It is a common misconception that we are in the middle of the digital revolution. We are almost certainly only at the beginning. The sudden growth of digital-data collections is outstripping our ability to manually cope with the opportunities the creation of these collections bring. Obvious examples of large data collections are the enormous indexes of Web search and derived data created by online search engines such as Google. Companies such as eBay and Amazon handle prodigious volumes of data to support their global business with very large numbers of companies and individuals dependent on their services, but they do not present external users with opportunities to extract business information from their wealth of data, which is an in-house asset. Some of the largest data collections are being created and being made widely available in the scientific domain. Examples of types of scientific data collections include the following:

- the streams of sensor data from an extensively instrumented natural environment,
- the set of all gene sequences for all organisms with their annotations,
- spatiotemporal images of biological systems from within the cell, via organs and individuals, to ecosystems, and
- meteorological and oceanographic records.

Some datasets are already very large and contain multiple petabytes of data.[1] Many are interconnected, as data in one collection references related items in other collections.

In the business context, although to date the quantities of data are usually somewhat smaller than those addressed by science, the digital-data challenges are often more complex, involving the management of complex hierarchies of trust and security in order to access, integrate, and derive business information. For instance, in the coming few years, a prerequisite for any large business will be the creation of a data cloud shared across the organization from sources as diverse as operations, manufacturing, human resources, finance, and sales. The use of this data cloud in conjunction with the growing bodies of public and purchasable data will be a key business tool driving decision making. A better grasp of the changing business context will allow companies to respond to new opportunities and difficult trading conditions, enabling them to survive downturns and be ready to respond when economies improve. As the value of data sharing is seen to drive business success, it will extend beyond individual organizations and include trusted third parties such as key suppliers. This will be a profound change in the way that businesses respond to digital-data-driven information.

Likewise, in the scientific research space, having a data cloud shared by environmental and Earth-systems scientists, economic and social scientists, medical researchers and diagnosticians, engineers and physical scientists, and biological and life scientist's will facilitate the interdisciplinary compositions of data and open up research questions that would be infeasible otherwise.

In practice, at present, those who own or can access data cannot ask such questions because the data sources are organized for one class of questions and each collection is isolated, that is, without explicit and reliable links to support comparison or augmentation from other sources.

1.5 CHANGING HOW WE WORK

We face many challenges in this new era of data-intensive computing; the following examples often reinforce one another:

1. coping with the increasing volume and complexity of data, and the increasing rate of data or document deposition;

---

[1]A petabyte is 10^{15} or 1,000,000,000,000,000 bytes. See Appendix A for the glossary of terms.

2. accommodating the rapid growth in the number of people who want to make use of emergent data services and their rising expectations;

3. balancing the pressures to accommodate new requirements and information structures with the requirement to protect existing investment and limiting the costs.

With the advent of data-intensive computational strategies (discussed later), a much larger class of questions about large or complex data can be answered economically. The scientific domain has been the first domain to see the opportunities that the analysis of large or complex datasets can bring. At present, several large instruments, observatories, and reference data collections are each beginning to use computational systems optimized for data-intensive operations. These changes in working practices are being driven by the scientific research community. Just as the Internet was initially developed by the scientific community, business and other user communities will rapidly identify the benefits and adapt data-intensive technology for their own purposes. This will become a dominant data management strategy used by both business and science over the next decade. Succeeding will mean changing how we work, moving from manual to automatic methods, and accepting that we can no longer survive by doing it all ourselves.

The data-intensive cloud computing experts and database experts have, in the past decade, become adept at handling more and more forms of computational query and analysis by using carefully chosen computing hardware and software architectures. The latest strategies include new inventory-based forms of consistency between data centers [2] and use human input to fill gaps needed to answer a query [3]. We propose that researchers embrace the opportunity brought about by these and other technical advances to blaze a path toward the vision of easily accessed and composed data that they can fluently exploit for their work. This will involve the development of new types of behavior, frameworks, methods, and computational systems. Each step will deliver new capabilities, boosting knowledge and informing decisions.

However, producing new technology and adopting new methods of working are not enough. To succeed, we need to develop the skills needed in every walk of life to extract knowledge from data. Viewed as a whole, these problems are daunting, perhaps insurmountable. To succeed, we must adopt a *divide-and-conquer* approach and partition the challenges we face.

1.6   DIVIDE AND CONQUER OFFERS THE SOLUTION

This book explains how knowledge discovery can be simplified by partitioning the conceptual and design challenges—an approach that works well in virtually all data-intensive contexts. We show how each data-intensive community can be partitioned into three groups of experts. First, the *domain experts* who try to better understand how to use the data in their domain. Second, the *data analysis experts* who try to develop ways of representing and visualizing data and who create and refine the algorithms that extract information from that data. Third, the *data-intensive engineers* who develop the tools and systems required for data-intensive computing.

1. *Domain experts*: These experts work in the particular domain where the knowledge discovery from their data takes place. They pose the questions that they want to see their data answer, such as, "How can I increase sales in this retail sector?", "What are the correlations in these gene expression patterns?", or "Which geographic localities will suffer most in times of flooding?". They are aware of the meaning of the data that they use. They are presented with data-intensive tools, optimized and tailored to their domain by the following two groups of experts. Many of the technical and operational issues are hidden from them.

2. *Data analysis experts*: These experts understand the algorithms and methods that are used in knowledge discovery. They may specialize in supporting a particular application domain. They will be supported with tool sets, components, and workbenches, which they will use to develop new methods or refactor, compose, and tune existing methods for their chosen domain experts. They are aware of the structures, representations, and type systems of the data they manipulate.

3. *Data-intensive engineers*: These experts focus on engineering the implementation of the data-intensive computing platform. Their work is concerned with engineering the software that supports data-intensive process enactment, resource management, data-intensive platform operations, and language implementations. They deliver libraries of components, tools, and interfaces that data analysis experts will use. A data-intensive engineer's role includes organizing the dynamic deployment, configuration and optimization of the data's movement, and storage and processing as automatically as possible. They also provide well-organized libraries of common data-handling and data-processing components.

We return to the task of understanding how to support all three categories of data-intensive expert in Section 3.2. Partitioning users is only one aspect of dividing the problem. We must also divide each data-intensive task so that computational issues can be conquered. All too often, knowledge discovery projects run into difficulties because the focus of the project team is only on one aspect of the computational issues and others are ignored. In this book, we describe how the computation should be partitioned into three levels of abstraction in order to deliver effective user experiences. These levels are introduced here and developed in Chapter 3.

1. *Tools* are used to create the data-intensive processes to analyze the data and to create prepackaged solutions to particular data-intensive knowledge discovery tasks.

2. *Language* is needed to clearly express the queries and manipulations required to explore the various data sources during knowledge discovery.

3. *Enactment* sits below the language and tools and is controlled using the tools and programmed using the language.

Of crucial importance is the realization that partitioning the computational challenges into these layers and partitioning those involved in knowledge discovery projects into the three roles described above allows the overall data-intensive challenge to be broken down into manageable pieces. These data-intensive partitions, both people focused and computation focused, mean that each application's domain, for example, business, commerce, healthcare, or biology, can innovate and respond independently with relatively little knowledge of the underlying methods and technology.

Solutions in each application's domain build on a common expanding infrastructure being built by the data analysis experts and the data-intensive engineers, who work to increase the power of the libraries of compatible data-processing elements, of the predefined patterns for composing common solution elements, and of the data-intensive platforms that are available to all application domains, obviating the need for bespoke solutions on every occasion. This means that data analysis developers get data-handling power from data-intensive engineering, and data-intensive engineers are able to invest in good, well-optimized solutions that are used multiple times. This achieves a transition, moving from the present practice of large and highly skilled teams making heroic efforts to extract knowledge from data, to an environment where individuals skilled in their domain can use knowledge discovery methods directly.

1.7   ENGINEERING DATA-TO-KNOWLEDGE HIGHWAYS

As the digital revolution progresses, people will need to make data journeys; getting data from wherever it may be, in whatever form it is, combining, transforming, and analyzing the data, to produce information-bearing derivatives. Those derivatives have to be transformed into just the right form to communicate the relevant knowledge and be delivered to the right person at the right time, so that person may act on the new knowledge. To facilitate many people making many such journeys, we need data-to-knowledge highways. Traditional highway engineers have expertise in identifying what new highways should be built, working out where they should go to and how they should connect with the existing network of transport infrastructure, how they should be built with minimum cost and disruption, and how they should be operated sustainably. At present, we need to nurture a new breed of *data-to-knowledge highway engineers*. They will develop professional methods and skills including the following:

1. analysis of existing data-to-knowledge journeys and future requirements to see where and when new data-to-knowledge highways should be built;

2. design of those highways so that they serve the maximum number of useful data paths, from identified clusters of source data to identified clusters of knowledge delivery destinations;

3. organization of data-highway construction, calling on the data equivalent of civil engineers, namely, database providers, network providers, storage providers, computation providers; visualization services; and interconnections with all manner of other data and communication services;

4. establishment of the guidance and control mechanisms, "data GPS and traffic lights," to enable data-to-knowledge journeys to start and finish wherever they need, traveling effortlessly by taking full advantage of the evolving data-to-knowledge infrastructure.

All of the three foci of expert interest (domain expertise, data analysis expertise, and data-intensive engineering) have to be satisfied by a data-to-knowledge highway. Consequently, data-to-knowledge highway engineers have to understand all three points of view, take a holistic view, and balance the interests of these three categories of professional data-to-knowledge highway user. An operational data-to-knowledge highway should have the following properties:

1. Domain users are happy because the on and off ramps match their journeys and extra lanes prevent congestion.

2. The data analysis experts are impressed by and exploit the way bridges and bypasses optimize their regular routes.

3. The data-intensive engineers are engaged in optimizing the total traffic, building and scheduling the vehicles, and reshaping the surrounding infrastructure to take maximum advantage—they may also be pioneering better technology for the next data-to-knowledge highway.

This book is taking the first steps toward understanding just how a data-to-knowledge highway should be built, and the first steps in shaping the methods and skills of the profession that will build those highways. We envisage a future where such data-to-knowledge highways support millions of knowledge discoveries a day that exploit the full wealth of available data.

REFERENCES

1. I. H. Witten, E. Frank, and M. A. Hall, *Data Mining: Practical Machine Learning Tools and Techniques* (Third Edition). Morgan Kauffman, 2011.

2. D. Kossmann, T. Kraska, and S. Loesing, "An evaluation of alternative architectures for transaction processing in the Cloud," in *SIGMOD Conference*, pp. 579–590. ACM, 2010.

3. A. Feng, M. J. Franklin, D. Kossmann, T. Kraska, S. Madden, S. Ramesh, A. Wang, and R. Xin, "CrowdDB: query processing with the VLDB crowd," *Proceedings of the VLDB*, vol. 4, no. 12, pp. 1387–1390, 2011.

2

The Digital-Data Revolution

Malcolm Atkinson

School of Informatics, University of Edinburgh, Edinburgh, UK

As they experience the global digital-data revolution, people are changing their behavior. The digital-data revolution is, itself, a reflection of these changes as people, organizations, and technology coevolve, influencing each other in multiple waves and cycles of interaction. The new wealth of data makes new behavior and new thoughts possible. Innovators pioneering these new data-enabled strategies discover the need for new methods and the technologies to support them, provoking the creation of new tools and businesses. These in turn stimulate further changes. The many intertwined loops and waves of invention generate the turbulence of a revolution—as Darwin explained, only the agile who adapt quickly thrive during times of rapid change.

This chapter explores the changes already evident in the early stages of the digital-data revolution. We aim to provoke readers into thinking how they, their organizations, and their society should respond—it will be readers' insights, ingenuity, and creativity that will determine the future in their data-intensive world.

The intertwining changes affect all walks of life and intellectual disciplines as illustrated by the following examples:

The DATA Bonanza: Improving Knowledge Discovery in Science, Engineering, and Business, First Edition. Edited by Malcolm Atkinson, Rob Baxter, Michelle Galea, Mark Parsons, Peter Brezany, Oscar Corcho, Jano van Hemert, and David Snelling.

- Changes in the available data provoke new management, sharing, and archiving policies.
- Changes in the ways in which data are used stimulate exploitation opportunities and concern about their impact.
- Emerging data-intensive support for decision and policy making changes the behavior of experts, politicians, planners, and managers.
- Development of new data analysis methods changes the behavior of professional analysts and raises people's expectations as to what they can achieve.
- Provision of data analysis services triggers new data-intensive engineering and both provider and consumer businesses.
- Changes take place in organizational behavior as people and organizations become ever more dependent on their data.
- Changes are effected in the laws and ethics of data use, as society, both national and international, tries to balance risks with benefits.

The remainder of the chapter analyzes these changes from a number of viewpoints, providing examples and quantitative information wherever possible.

2.1 DATA, INFORMATION, AND KNOWLEDGE

In this book, "data" are any digitally encoded information that can be stored, processed, and transmitted by computers. Data accessibility may be controlled or open. There is an almost endless variety of sources and uses of data as the following examples illustrate:

- Personal data, including images, video sequences and recordings, any of the files on your computers, (old) DVDs, and the contents of other detached data storage devices.
- Collections of data from business processes, instruments, observatories, surveys, and simulations.
- Results derived from previous research and earlier surveys.
- Data from engineering and built-environment design, planning, and production processes.
- Data from diagnostic, laboratory, personal, and mobile devices.
- Streams of data from sensors in the built and natural environments.
- Data transmitting, and from monitoring, digital communications.
- Data transferred during the transactions that enable business, administration, healthcare, and government.
- Digital material produced by news feeds, publishing, broadcasting, Internet games, and entertainment.
- Documents in public collections and held privately, the texts and multimedia "images" in Web pages, wikis, blogs, emails, and tweets.

- Digitized representations of diverse collections of objects, for example, images of a museum's curated objects.

When data are in a form that triggers consistent or intended human thoughts, we can call them *information*. Generally speaking, some processes are required to present data as information. Digital decoding to sound, in a voice over Internet protocol (VOIP) or digital-radio transmission, is a case where the information and data are related in a previously organized way; in such cases, the extraction of information is productized and replicated easily—you can just go out and buy a digital radio or television.

Often, interesting information is latent in data in subtle and undiscovered ways, and it takes ingenuity to extract and use it. For example, the records of interactions of mobile telephones with the cellular networks' transmitters can reveal changes in people's movement patterns that could provide information for optimizing public transport in a city [1, 2]—a step toward developing a better understanding of cities and their inhabitants [3]. Ingenuity is needed, as well as care over privacy issues, before useful and operationally valuable information can be extracted.

The information is often obtained as the first step in a path that seeks to move from *data* to *information* to *knowledge* to *wisdom*. Where "knowledge" can be characterized as a combination of data and a model, such that humans understand the model and its relationship to the data, that is, they *understand* the model and data. Often, this will mean that they are able to use the model to make predictions and inform decisions.

"Wisdom" can result from repeated experience of using such knowledge, so that the humans involved have a well-developed judgment as to when to apply their knowledge. This path from data to wisdom is not a simple one; there are many false trails and much iteration. Intelligent deployment of experience, knowledge, creativity, and perseverance is needed before the successive goals are gained.

Today's collections of data could not be read by a human in a lifetime. For example, it would take many lifetimes to read the hundreds of millions of observations of stars and galaxies in a sky survey, each with more than 200 properties. Using statistical and data mining techniques, astronomers and cosmologists can extract comprehensible parameters that are crucial to understanding how the Universe works. Indeed, at present, astronomers combine data from multiple sky surveys to test hypotheses and discover new properties of our Universe—see Chapter 18.

Those patterns for extracting relevant comprehensible information from small or large bodies of data can be observed repeatedly. They are applied in all walks of life. For example, deciding how rapid and serious a pandemic will be, choosing the most effective advertisements to show a person who submitted a particular search request, recommending suitable opponents in an online game, and understanding and improving communication within a company. The list is endless and growing rapidly as more data become available. For several decades, statisticians, data miners, text miners, and image-processing specialists have been developing skills for discovering and presenting information hidden in the data.

We call these experts in extracting latent information from data *data analysis experts*. Invariably, they have to work together with *domain experts*, who understand a particular field of application very well, to decide which information to target, and to decide how best to seek it. The domain experts and data analysis experts, *working together*, will incrementally choose data sources, formulate questions to be answered, and devise strategies for answering them. This iterative process is both skill and knowledge intensive, that is, it requires extensive knowledge of the domain, the data sources and the available methods, and the skill to apply or extend methods successfully. The combination of these skills and knowledge cannot be expanded fast enough to match the growing wealth of data-enabled opportunities. For example, it is neither possible to rapidly equip all existing domain experts with additional data analysis skills, nor to quickly train sufficient cohorts of new data analysis experts to satisfy every expanding application field.

The approach expounded throughout this book seeks to husband those skills by dividing the intellectual challenges and minimizing the extraneous technical clutter. We are not alone in seeking new approaches to these challenges—see, for example, the work of the Algorithms, Machines, and People Lab (amplab.cs.berkeley.edu) at UC Berkeley.

The information may not be comprehensible unless it is suitably presented. For example, a decade's worth of daily prices for a variety of stocks presented numerically would not be understood by someone trying to choose where to invest. Simply plotting the prices to denote the time series would still make comparison difficult, as shares have very different prices. However, normalizing each stock as a ratio of its price at a chosen moment (September 2005 in Fig. 2.1 taken from [4]) enables visual comparison. Additional skills and effort are needed to take the extracted information *the last mile* so that its users can act on it, that is, it is readily understood and will be interpreted correctly. Specialized organizations are emerging to do this in different fields; for example, the Earth Data Analysis Center (EDAC) (edac.unm.edu) has, for more than 45 years, transformed NASA data into forms needed for planning, civil engineering, agronomy, and so on.

2.2 INCREASING VOLUMES AND DIVERSITY OF DATA

The growing wealth of data is a consequence of four mutually reinforcing effects:

1. the progressive increase in the speed and capacity of digital data-capture devices, while their cost remains static or falls,
2. the sustained increase in the use of digital data as an agent for interchanges in commerce, administration, leisure, communication, healthcare, transport, engineering, and just about every other human activity,
3. the growing capacity and ubiquity of digital communication—both wired and wireless,
4. the increasing numbers of people who are connected, both with Internet access and those with mobile phone contracts.

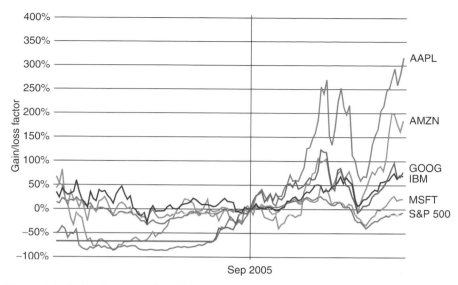

Figure 2.1 *Indexed presentation of the relative growth of selected technology share prices. Source: Heer et al. (2010) [4].*

2.2.1   More, Faster, and Cheaper Devices

The increases in speed and capacity of digital devices are well illustrated by the growth of mobile phones, digital cameras, and digital recorders. Their falling cost has led to ubiquity and a freedom to use them ever more frequently. Figure 2.2 shows the growth of mobile phone ownership from data produced by The International Telecommunications Union (ITU) [5]. It shows that, in 2011, 87% of the world's 7 billion population had a mobile phone and 35% used the Internet.

Similarly, the growth of digital-image sensors is sustained, with Gartner estimating the total volumes per year at approximately 4 billion, as shown in Figure 2.3 [6].

This combination of wide ownership of image capture devices and Internet connectivity has substantially changed human behavior. For example, in North Africa and the Middle East during the Arab Spring (2011), there was a widespread use of uploaded digital images to influence opinion and document atrocities.

In a similar manner, the immediate impact and effect of the magnitude 9 M_w Tōhoku earthquake in March 2011 and the subsequent tsunami were better recorded than any previous earthquake, as there were enormous numbers of tweets, posted digital images, and video records[1]. These can potentially be combined with the more formal records of seismographs and other scientific instruments, as Japan is well instrumented in its effort to improve the understanding of earthquakes, earthquake engineering, and emergency response. These spontaneous records plus official data offer a rich record for future researchers who want to analyze any aspect of these

---

[1]en.wikipedia.org/wiki/2011_Tohoku_earthquake_and_tsunami.

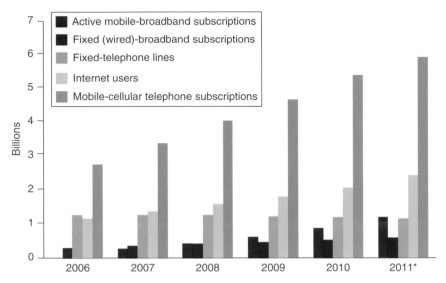

Figure 2.2   *Nearly 6 billion people had a mobile phone in 2011. Source: International Telecommunications Union (2011) [5].*

events. The diversity, the multiple formats, the numerous repositories, and the lack of established reference frameworks and standardized computational interfaces means that exploiting their full potential remains difficult.

Commensurate changes are happening for professional and specialized devices. For example, environmental and geosensors are becoming so cheap that they can be widely deployed, yet their sensitivity and data rates are increasing—see Chapter 17. To give a more specific example, we look at acoustic surveying for fossil fuel deposits. A seismic survey under an ocean, such as the Gulf of Mexico, is conducted using survey ships that tow 22 lines of seismometers, each 8 km long, with 80 instruments per kilometer (a total of 14,080 instruments) (Fig. 2.4). Each instrument is sampled 500 times per second, yielding 3 bytes per sample. This delivers a total of 17 MB/s. A typical survey will have 60 working days of continuous observation, yielding approximately 88 TB of data. A large survey will involve four ships for a year.[2] Specialist companies process these data—an example of business emerging to collect or analyze specific categories of data.

The advances in digital technology are also changing the way in which astronomy is performed—sky surveys are becoming the dominant observing method. The number of pixels obtained by each image of a modern telescope has risen to 1.6 gigapixels, and they are now used almost continuously every night for sky surveys. The next generation of radio telescopes will combine signals collected from a thousand dishes spread across thousands of kilometers and produce catalogs of tens of billions of astronomic objects (Chapter 18).

[2]Prof. Anton Ziolkowski, Geosciences, University of Edinburgh, January 2011.

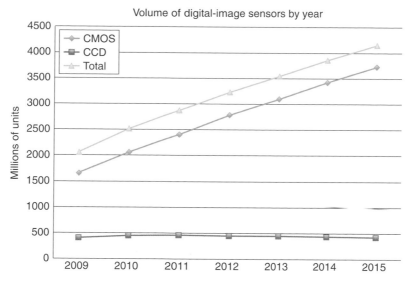

Figure 2.3 *Global growth of digital-image sensor units. Source: Based on Shimizu (2011) [6].*

Figure 2.4 *Towed array of seismometers: foreground illustration indicating the size of marine seismic acquisition spread. Source: Courtesy Petroleum Geo-Services over background map of Edinburgh on the same scale; Courtesy Google, DigitalGlobe, GeoEye, Getmapping plc, Infoterra Ltd., The GeoInformation Group, Map data.*

Medical images are similarly of ever-increasing resolution and being used more and more frequently in more and more hospitals for an increasing range of diagnoses and treatment plans. The speed of genetic sequencing is rising rapidly and the cost per sequence is falling commensurately as is illustrated in Figure 2.5. This will lead to rapidly increased use of sequencing, for example, in characterizing cells in a tumor or in understanding the population of organisms in a gut. These techniques will rapidly move from pioneering laboratories to routine clinical and

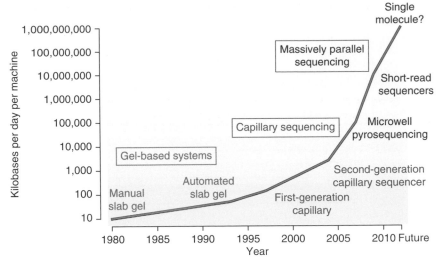

Figure 2.5 *The increasing power of DNA sequencers. Source: Reprinted by permission from Macmillan Publishers Ltd., copyright 2009, Nature [7].*

epidemiological applications. Both for diagnosis and research, such as drugs trials, it will become normal to combine the genotypical data obtained from sequencing with the phenotypical data obtained from images. Chapter 16 presents an example of such research.

Medical and veterinary imaging involves an increasing range of modalities for medical imaging: CT scanning, PET scanning, NMR scanning, endoscopy, optical imaging, retinal tomography, thermal imaging, and acoustic (ultrasound) scanning, as well as traditional X-ray. All of these are producing digital data and their results can be compared, integrated, and analyzed to see the progress of a condition, evaluate the effectiveness of an intervention, and study diseases or populations. Here, the challenges of data volumes and varieties of formats are compounded with the issues of privacy and ethical practices. With live subjects, the resolution and frequency of some images are limited by concerns about radiation dose or stress on the patient. However, the increasing use of imaging in autopsy is not limited by such concerns and very high resolution images may be used to determine the cause of death without dismembering a body [8], another example of the ways in which procedures are changing with the availability of data and computation over it.

The use of microscopy in biology and medicine to study and measure tissue and cells is rapidly advancing, as digital imaging and robotic techniques are deployed. The digital images grow in resolution and speed here as in all of the other applications. The robotics has two effects: it provides precision, for example, an image of the same 3D zone in a cell can be obtained repeatedly, and it provides high volume repetition, for example, obtaining a sequence of images of say 40 zones in a cell, 20 times per minute, with multiple laser illuminations, for several days to observe a cell's processes. Similarly, a modern pathology lab will use microscopes that generate histology images of $500,000 \times 500,000 \times 20 \times 4$ pixels, and the microscope may produce 200 images a day. To enable biologists and clinicians to take full advantage of such data, particularly if they need to automatically process thousands of images in a study, is a daunting data handling and computational (i.e., data-intensive) challenge. One open-source approach used by biologists is OMERO [9], but there are many commercial approaches to specific kinds of image, such as the work on ultra-wide-field retinal imaging by Optos (www.optos.com), which employs one of editors of this book.

As computers fall in cost and become more powerful, they are used to generate more and more data, from simulations, from analyses of other data, and from user-driven editing of extracts from existing data and text collections. Every system or user action on a computer and all of the interactions between services generate logs. These can then be analyzed to understand system and user behavior, to optimize provision, to detect intrusion and misuse, and to inform redesign and training [10]. There is evidence of coevolution. The rapid growth in connecting users and smart phones has generated markets and communities where a vast number of interests and businesses can all reach critical mass. The growth of these global communication-enabled activities provides more and more reasons for existing users to interact and more enticements for new users to join—a typical network effect. These growing businesses and growing user populations require growing data center and network capacity. Thus, the scale of the behaviors, systems, and communities that may be understood from analyzing the interaction events becomes ever more challenging. The benefit of gaining that understanding also grows at least at the same rate.

The fall in costs and the expanding need for high quality replicated processes has led to a massive increase in automated experimentation. A rapidly growing number of laboratory processes are being automated, increasing the use of such processes with a commensurate growth in the corresponding data. These are not just the chemical and mechanical procedures, but observational procedures such as generating populations of *Drosophila melanogaster* with particular genetic variations and classifying the behavior of thousands of pairs to yield statistical data on the relationship between genes and behavior [11]. The advent of automation and computer control of instruments and laboratory processes is yielding a much needed and rich stream of metadata describing the primary data, the processes, and the performance of the instruments.

As data storage devices fall in cost and rise in capacity, there is a tendency to preserve more and more data. This applies, whether the device is attached to the computer or is off-line, as in the case of most CDs and DVDs. A few of these are organized as formal archives and digital libraries, but the majority are relatively haphazard because of the organic growth of data collection and use.

This section has illustrated a few of the ways in which the explosion of digital devices is expanding the supply of data. It would require an encyclopedia to document all of the innovations and the vast number of human and business responses that they stimulate.

2.2.2 Data as an Interchange Agent

In more and more walks of life, data is an interchange agent. For example, in film and music industries, the creative product is frequently represented by digital data, as it progresses through the stages of creation, postprocessing, production, and distribution. The cumulative entertainment data are a rich resource for those studying creativity and society, as well as those steering each entertainment industry. For example, the growing quantity of digitally recorded music in large-scale resources, such as the Internet Archive and their annotations using semantic Web technologies, is enabling researchers to ask questions about the propagation of creative ideas across each genre [12, 13].

In multiplayer computer games, the game state and each player's moves are exchanged as data. The history of all games is a resource for shaping competitions, matching competitors, and informing the design of later versions [14, 15]. In the Microsoft context alone, in 2010, there were 10 million online games per day for a community of 6 million players.

Bohn and Short [16] observed that, in 2008, in the United States, nearly 55% of the Internet traffic was interactive games, and that this taken with movie downloads and TV traffic accounted for more than 99% of the bytes transmitted. Radio streaming, VOIP, intercomputer traffic, and printing accounted for less than 1% of data transmitted. They estimate that, in the United States, there were 3.6 ZB delivered to domestic consumers in 2008.

To place that in context, the Internet users of North America constituted 12% of the world's Internet community at the end of 2011—nearly 45% were from Asia.[3] Estimating the data reachable via the Internet is extremely difficult; one estimate was 5 EB in 2010 with 200 TB indexed by Google (just 0.004%).[4]

In business, more and more transactions are mediated by the exchange of data. Customers fill in a succession of online forms to perform their bank transactions, buy products and services, to make reservations, and to raise questions about products and services. Businesses interact with businesses to buy and sell products and services, to implement financial and employment transactions, to monitor contracts, and to develop collaborative strategies. They interact with governments to comply with regulations. The cumulative data, within and across companies are a fount of information for strategists, planners, economists, and social analysts. Collections of these data are investigated as evidence for litigation. An example is the analysis of all of the email from Enron [17] or the investigations initiated in 2011 related to telephone hacking in the United Kingdom. A small subset of the communication is human–human communication by email. This was at 294 billion messages per day in 2010.[5] Major insights can be gathered if these can be coanalyzed with the other data traffic within the company and with external transactions. At present, this is a difficult task, both in trying to identify relevant data and in trying to construct a framework that allows them to be combined.

---

[3]from www.internetworldstats.com copyright 2001–2012, Miniwatts Marketing Group.
[4]see gorumors.com/crunchies/how-big-is-the-internet.
[5]see gorumors.com/crunchies/when-was-first-email-sent.

In every branch of engineering, engineers use data to design and specify components, organize their production and deployment, monitor and analyze their test and deployed performance, and diagnose the causes of their failures. In some engineering disciplines, for example, aircraft design and manufacture, it is a legal requirement that these data are kept *in usable form* for many decades. The streams of data from digital instruments on engines, vehicles, electrical distribution networks, buildings, and bridges, for example, can be analyzed to detect imminent crises; plan preventative maintenance; and identify opportunities to improve design, manufacture, operational procedures, and environmental impact (Chapter 21).

National and local governments organize more and more of their administration and services using data exchanges in a similar manner to businesses, for example, for the collection of tax revenue, administering welfare services, planning, monitoring implementation, and monitoring effects of policy. These include national censuses every 10 years, records of property, land use, agronomy, transport use, employment, and commerce. The recognition of the importance of these data has led to legislation about the data themselves. For example, in Europe, the INSPIRE directive introduces a wide-ranging set of standards concerning the representation of geospatial and temporal information in governmental and administrative data [18]. In the United States, in January 2009, the President made a commitment to making governmental data open and available for public use, review, and research [19].

The Linking Open Data (LOD) initiative is making it easier to find and interpret such data.[6] The W3C also host a catalog of catalogs showing where you can find LOD-compliant data,[7] also providing information such as whether the data are open, how mature the site is, and so on. It is interesting to see catalogs for global organizations, such as the United Nations; governments, such as the United Kingdom; for regions and counties, such as Northern Ireland and Kent; cities, such as Birmingham; and companies, such as the Guardian. By May 2011, the UK Government had already published approximately 7000 datasets from several departments (Cabinet Office, Department for Business, Innovation and Skills, Department for Communities and Local Government, Department for Environment, Food and Rural Affairs, Department for Transport, Department of Health, and UK Statistics Authority). The primary goal of making data open does not imply that they are easily understood. Often, spreadsheets explaining encoding and notes explaining collection methods have to be consulted before relevant data can be interpreted. Consequently, there is a rapid and welcome growth of organizations, for example, companies and volunteers, who extract relevant data and make them presentable, perhaps by offering an app for a smart phone or Web interface that adapts the information to current location, time, and known interests of its users. The W3C eGovernment interest group provides information about its monthly meetings at[8]; it is a good source for pointers to the latest information on progress. In principle, one day, computationally searching with sophisticated queries over LOD, working from the high level

---

[6]esw.w3.org/SweoIG/TaskForces/CommunityProjects/LinkingOpenData.
[7]opengovernmentdata.org/data/catalogues.
[8]www.w3.org/egov/wiki/Main_Page.

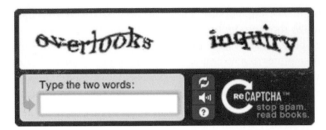

Figure 2.6   *Captcha challenge: subliminal social computing builds a machine-learning training set.*

catalogs or a known relevant data collection, should find all of the data relevant to an issue. The use of this strategy to search music collections [12] is a foretaste of that nirvana. In the United Kingdom, the Open Data Institute (ODI) is driving research to make that possible—building the semantic data highways.

Social networks and social computing both depend on large numbers of interchanges of data. For example, the progressive development of a personal presence on Facebook is achieved by many increments to an individual's personal data. The recommendation systems, for example, suggesting new friends depend on the analysis of all of the contemporary data. The progressive training of optical character recognizers in Captcha (www.captcha.net) collects misread data from optical recognition systems and presents them as half of each challenge presented to discriminate between humans and computers as shown in Figure 2.6 [20]. The human responses return data to the services using Captcha as a gatekeeper and data to provide machine-learning examples for training better character recognizers. This example of social computing, where millions of people willingly contribute their expertise, is successful because it has an excellent user interface and intrudes very little into the discrimination task, and the user is rewarded by being recognized as a human and allowed to proceed. The inventor of Captcha, Luis von Ahn, has used games as rewards to gain information about picture recognition and is now inducing people to train Web-page translation systems in exchange for language lessons—try duolingo.com [21].

In every branch of science, data have become a key agent for collecting the signals from instruments, simulations, and integrations of these sources. The models of complex systems, such as the functioning biological cell, an organ in an organism, the evolutionary history of life, the ecology of every geographical and biological environment, the earth's climate and oceans, the observed universe, are all built by compiling collections of data. These collections vary from the work of an individual researcher to the collaborative work of teams with similar interests to the data maintained by professional curators working in global collaborations over decades. Each collection behaves as a shared, globally accessible virtual notice board, written to by all of the data collectors and read by an open-ended community of future users. As a collection grows, more investment in organizing structure, maintaining quality, and ensuring disciplined use is needed—the work of data curators. Often, researchers need to extract information from multiple data collections to make discoveries.

Other domains of research are also using data in more and more imaginative ways. Sociologists and economists have always used the derivatives from governmental data in combination with data collected by specific studies. At present, they have extended their sources of data to include derivatives from the logs of news feeds; tweets and blogs; and the changing content of Web services, such as Flickr, YouTube, Facebook, and thousands of others. They also use simulations, for example, multiagent modeling calibrated from census data, to evaluate policy choices and project population statistics forward through time [22].

In the humanities, collections of digitized artifacts, digitally recorded conversations, digitized art and music, and digitized texts are adding to the more traditional purpose-built data collections. For example, the global collaboration to assemble Holocaust data, where just one collection of images is more than half a PB, and another consortia assembling images of classical texts, such as papyri fragments— as reported in Chapter 20.

In this section, we have seen a range of examples of data enabling human and organizational activity by carrying information between them, across space, and through time. It is another rapidly evolving aspect of the digital revolution that would be hard to fully catalog with today's tools. The LOD initiative has this as its ambitious goal.

2.2.3 Ubiquitous Digital Communication

There are two intertwined developments increasing the data involved in digital communication:

1. technical changes, and
2. social changes.

The growing use of digital encoding, in radio and television broadcasting, telephony, and event signaling has generated major data flows. The changes in protocols, particularly "store-and-forward," and transmission technology, have greatly increased the capacity of networks to move data. The growing ubiquity of connectivity via wired and wireless mechanisms has combined with an increasing propensity to connect devices to the Internet. Thus, the number and the content of digital signals have greatly increased. The deployed equipment that delivers this communication capacity also keeps logs that are analyzed for diverse purposes, though privacy and confidentiality issues have to be negotiated first.

In a great many workplaces, as diverse as offices and delivery vehicles, digital communication is an essential part of work practices. In many nations, the average citizen now expects to gain Internet access at home, to use connected devices and mobile telephones almost everywhere, and to be able to obtain copies of previously broadcast radio and television programs. The use of SMS messages has risen way beyond expectations, as mobile phone users track topics by registering interest in events, as they organize arrangements with others without being synchronously available, and as monitoring devices report data. In many work and leisure contexts, a great deal of communication, decision making, and authoritative statements are communicated by email. Publication of blogs, instant messaging, pooled information in shared wikis, and VOIP with associated image streams, such as Skype, are enriching and diversifying these modes of communication. Experiments are underway in some cities, and even countries, of providing digital connectivity everywhere for free. Meanwhile, Yammer (yammer.com) provides the same bundle of rapid communication tools but encapsulated so that they can be used privately within an organization.

2.2.4   Summary of the Driving Forces

In Section 2.2, we have illustrated the mutually reinforcing forces of change: the rapidly growing numbers of digital devices, the increasing connectivity, and the human response to these opportunities. This is a coevolving digital environment with so many interactions that it is difficult to predict its form even a few years ahead. There are a wealth of opportunities emerging and many new businesses forming to exploit them. Many of these are specializing in collecting or interpreting particular kinds of data. Modern questions are complex with many interacting economic, social, environmental, and scientific issues. Integrative approaches that build on the specialized practices and that deliver relevant understandable and trustworthy results are a consequent requirement. However, they have to be agile and flexible to survive in the turbulence of the digital revolution. Inevitably, they will be underpinned by advanced data-intensive methods.

2.3   CHANGING THE WAYS WE WORK WITH DATA

2.3.1   Life Science Examples

As already indicated, global consortia in industry and academia build shared collections of data, with carefully curated structure to support their collaborations. The life sciences provide examples from both commercial and academic viewpoints.

For example, in 1971, X-ray crystallographers, trying to understand the structure and function of proteins, initiated this process by sharing the structure of seven proteins. Since then, this activity has grown dramatically and is now called *wwPDB* with the following mission:

> The founding members are RCSB PDB (USA), PDBe (Europe), and PDBj (Japan). The BMRB (USA) group joined the wwPDB in 2006. The mission of the wwPDB is to maintain a single Protein Data Bank Archive of macromolecular structural data that is freely and publicly available to the global community [23].

In March 2012, there were more than 80,000 structures available, and the wwPDB served more than 30,000 downloads in February 2012. The complexity of the collection has grown, as the engaged community has extended from X-ray

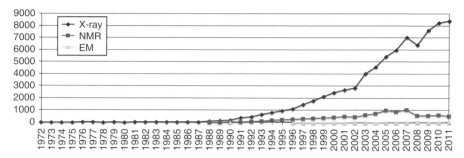

Figure 2.7 *Annual depositions into the Protein Data Bank. Source: Berman et al. 2003 [23]* *www.wwpdb.org.*

crystallographers to those using cryoelectron microscopy and nuclear magnetic resonance to collect structural data and to bioinformaticians using the collected data (Fig. 2.7). That community's practice has changed, to automatically deposit data when publishing structures, automatically search before investigating structures, and mine data to discover patterns and relationships as another path to understanding how proteins work. This depends on continuous investment in curators at the four sites as well as in the computational machinery to store, replicate, index, curate, analyze, and share the volumes of data [24, 25].

A concomitant development is the ever-increasing repository of published articles in PubMed and with local developments such as UK PubMed Central (UKPMC) [26]. These are harvested by text mining and used in combination with databases to extract data behind many biological discoveries. As an example, Andrey Rzhetsky develops ever more precise tools for text mining, and presenting very specific elements from the papers in PubMed [27, 28], uses them in conjunction with the databases to identify complex genetic mechanisms and their role in diseases [29, 30]. Similarly, Douglas Kell has recognized the importance of data-driven science for biology [31], developed text-mining strategies to better utilize the literature repositories [32], and delivered discoveries by combining these techniques with data mining from the data repositories; a few examples can be found in [33–37]. These strategies are bringing about two crucial changes in behavior: data driven science and revision of the value of publications. To quote Douglas Kell, "Three months in the lab can save a whole afternoon on the computer"[9]. In other words, to be successful, scientists need to use data-intensive methods to discover what is known before undertaking practical experiments. This does not detract from the eventual value of experiments to confirm understanding, but it just makes it more likely that effort is invested in informative experiments. The whole body of papers grows at a rate that exceeds researchers' ability to read, even if they focus narrowly. But information can be gleaned from large bodies of papers computationally and can be a key to advancing understanding. This posits a new way of considering the value of research, they may contain key facts that lead to many discoveries, yet not be

[9]blogs.bbsrc.ac.uk/index.php/2009/02/the-miners-strike-again accessed January 2013.

highly cited. They may also have contributed to the establishment or validation of evidence now in curated data repositories; it is hard enough to get the work of data curators recognized, let alone the sources on which they build, even when they are in the annotations in the database.

A similar story of evolving practice can be seen from the Human Genome Project (mid-1990s onward) of sharing data about genetic sequences to enable a global community of researchers to pool data and use them for their mutual benefit. The deposited data was initially only concerned with sequencing data from one composite sample of one species, *Homo sapiens*. At present, the collected data includes samples from multiple humans, a rapidly growing collection in the 1000-genome project to understand natural variability and its correlation with physiological variation, for example, vulnerability to particular diseases and response to particular drugs. The primary consortium curating these data is the International Nucleotide Sequence Database Collaboration, once again involving centers in the United States (GenBank at the National Center for Biotechnology Information, National Institute of Health), Japan (DNA Databank of Japan), and Europe (European Bioinformatics Institute) who interchange data daily to ensure preservation as well as serving their regional depositions and searches. By February 2012, the collection of sequences contained, nearly 10^{14} nucleotide bases from more than 194 million sequences, from 500,000 species [38]. Here again, the data's complexity grows as more mechanisms are added to coordinate the construction and use of annotations, both by the curators and by third party researchers.

These are just three examples of the very rapid growth in biological databases—in 2011, there were 1330 molecular biology databases [39]. Another indicator of changing behavior in these research communities is the progressive formulation of *rules of engagement*, which help all the participants contributing and using data to evolve appropriate behavior in these data-rich contexts. These explicit statements regarding the new data mores began under the Human Genome Project, and their fifth iteration was announced as the Toronto statement in September 2009. They are guidelines as to when data should be made public (Fig. 2.8). They balance the responsibilities of data creators, data users, data curators, publishers, and funding bodies, as they adopt the mores, so that credit, sustainability, and verifiability of research claims may be achieved. Many other communities are making similar collaborative and culture-shaping arrangements.

2.3.2 Earth's Systems Examples

Collaboration is a key to understanding Earth systems, such as the climate, oceans, the biosphere, and the Earth's crust. As these span the whole planet and as they interact, their study provides pressure to share data and to link data between systems that were previously studied in isolation. In each discipline, we see long-term collections of data to allow a study of their temporal and correlated behavior. This is a typical example where behavior is changing to meet the challenge. A global organization, Group on Earth Observations (GEO), was formed to provide a framework for developing the necessary agreements; it now (March 2012) has 64 members

Examples of prepublication data-release guidelines		
Project type	Prepublication data release recommended	Prepublication data release optional
Genome sequencing	Whole-genome or mRNA sequence(s) of a reference organism or tissue	Sequences from a few loci for cross-species comparisons in a limited number of samples
Polymorphism discovery	Catalogue of variants from genomic and/or transcriptomic samples in one or more populations	Variants in a gene, a gene family or a genomic region in selected pedigrees or populations
Genetic association studies	Genomewide association analysis of thousands of samples	Genotyping of selected gene candidates
Somatic mutation discovery	Catalogue of somatic mutations in exomes or genomes of tumour and non-tumour samples	Somatic mutations of a specific locus or limited set of genomic regions
Microbiome studies	Whole-genome sequence of microbial communities in different environments	Sequencing of target locus in a limited number of microbiome samples
RNA profiling	Whole-genome expression profiles from a large panel of reference samples	Whole-genome expression profiles of a perturbed biological system(s)
Proteomic studies	Mass spectrometry data sets from large panels of normal and disease tissues	Mass spectrometry data sets from a well-defined and limited set of tissues
Metabolomic studies	Catalogue of metabolites in one or more tissues of an organism	Analyses of metabolites induced in a perturbed biological system(s)
RNAi or chemical library screen	Large-scale screen of a cell line or organism analysed for standard phenotypes	Focused screens used to validate a hypothetical gene network
3D-structure elucidation	Large-scale cataloguing of 3D structures of proteins or compounds	3D structure of a synthetic protein or compound elucidated in the context of a focused project

Figure 2.8 *Agreed publication guidelines for biological data, part of the Toronto statement. Source: Reprinted by permission from Macmillan Publishers Ltd., copyright 2009, Nature [40].*

(www.earthobservations.org). GEO has established the Global Earth Observation System of Systems (GEOSS) project to link together many existing Earth observation projects. Figure 2.9 gives an impression of the spread of these organizations, many of which are international consortia, so the location of their headquarters is used. Unfortunately, space does not allow us to show their considerable diversity. This organizational behavior is needed to provide a forum for agreeing on interchange formats, standard metadata, and mechanisms for comparing and validating data. Perhaps even more importantly, it stimulates engagement and persuades participants to actively interoperate so that the interdisciplinary research has the shared data and models that it needs. Many of the data and data-collecting organizations were originally national or regional, and hence the activity requires governmental engagement to broaden remits and to reset priorities. Chapter 19 provides examples of accessing the climatological and oceanographic aspects of these shared data and Chapter 22 gives an example of analysis using the ornithological niche among these data.

The Intergovernmental Panel on Climate Change (IPCC) plays a similar role in enabling global collaboration by establishing a framework and incentives to encourage collaboration on a common cause, including data sharing and the interpretation

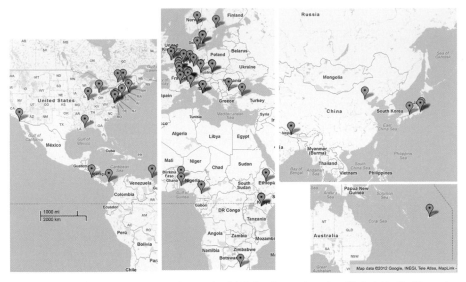

Figure 2.9   *Map of the 64 participants in GEO implementing the Global Earth Observing System of Systems (GEOSS). Source: copyright 2011 Google © 2011 Tele Atlas.*

of the results of simulations (www.ipcc.ch). The collections of data used to underpin simulations for each 5-year cycle have to be made available to the global climate research community, allowing sufficient time for their simulations to run forward from the agreed scenario starting conditions and for the papers that result processed through peer review so that they can then be used as a reliable input by the IPCC (Chapter 19).

2.3.3   Summary of Behavioral Responses

The preceding examples illustrate several emerging issues and responses:

- The growth in the rate of deposition of publications means that it is now impossible to read all relevant papers. Text mining extracts relevant and aggregate derivatives that may be consumed by humans or by data-mining processes.

- The growth in the number and content of data collections relevant to any research topic has had a number of consequences. Research communities and their funders have had to pool resources to afford the management, curation, and computational provisioning of these key data assets. This has led to global collaborations and many efforts to agree on common standards and interpretations. The availability of these data has introduced data-driven research as a crucial phase in many investigations. Long-term commitment to the provision of these key research assets requires new mores, that include proper attribution to the contributors and curators, become established. Funders and publishers need to underpin their persistence without inhibiting the growth of new data collections.

- The evident power of data-intensive methods in research and business stimulates expectations that similar benefits may be reaped in political decision making, healthcare, policy forming, and many other fields that affect people's daily lives. This has reinforced the push to make governmental data open and motivated the LOD movement, which seeks to accelerate the effective exploitation of a vast diversity of Web-accessible data.

- The increasing complexity of data from multiple sources exacerbates the difficulty of interpreting those data, as they are collected by a variety of mechanisms that change within the periods of interest covered by a research topic. Multinational and interdisciplinary bodies are emerging to help to establish frameworks without inhibiting innovation. In some cases, these are underwritten by legislation, such as the INSPIRE directive.

- The critical role of data in shaping research results increases the recognition that data should remain available to permit reanalysis, validation, and criticism of results. This leads to a requirement for firm foundations to record data provenance as well as archival technology to preserve data and to keep it accessible, as the computational platforms evolve.

- The challenges of the modern world require the synthesis of data from many fields, which are well illustrated in the preceding text for Earth systems. International collaborations and consortia may make progress possible, but they will not make the progress themselves. That is down to the individuals who become adept and creative at combining data and knowledge from diverse sources while maintaining intellectual control and direction. This capacity is rare at present. Our educational systems and subsequent professional development must change to generate such skills in a growing proportion of the world's population.

- In order to make these domain experts and data analysis experts as productive as possible, there is an increasing focus on removing (or at least hiding) technical and administrative hurdles from the path from data to knowledge. This has triggered research and commercial investment to deliver effective data-to-knowledge highways.

- The growing number of people wanting to exploit data effectively in their work, personal lives, and research provides a business opportunity. This includes building better services and tools with high quality and well-targeted presentation of results, the infrastructure for the data-to-knowledge highways, and the computational provisioning to support scalable operation of those highways.

REFERENCES

1. S. Phithakkitnukoon and C. Ratti, "Inferring asymmetry of inhabitant flow using call detail records," *Journal of Advances in Information Technology*, vol. 2, no. 2, pp. 1–11, 2011.

2. F. Calabrese, C. Ratti, M. Colonna, P. Lovisolo, and D. Parata, "Real-time urban monitoring using cell phones: a case study in Rome," *IEEE Transactions on Intelligent Transportation Systems*, vol. 12, no. 1, pp. 141–151, 2011.

3. M. Batty, *Cities and Complexity: Understanding Cities with Cellular Automata, Agent-Based Models, and Fractals*. The Massachusetts Institute of Technology (MIT) Press, September 2005.

4. J. Heer, M. Bostock, and V. Ogievetsky, "A tour through the visualization zoo," *Communications of the ACM*, vol. 53, no. 6, pp. 59–67, 2010.

5. The International Telecommunications Union, "ICT facts and figures," tech. rep., ITU, 2011.

6. H. Shimizu, *Forecast Analysis: Image Sensor Semiconductor Forecast, Worldwide, 2Q11 Update*, Market Analysis and Statistics G00214535. Gartner, Inc, 2011.

7. M. R. Stratton, P. J. Campbell, and P. A. Futreal, "The cancer genome," *Nature*, vol. 458, no. 7239, pp. 719–724, 2009.

8. K. L. Palmerius, M. Cooper, and A. Ynnerman, "Haptic interaction with dynamic volumetric data," *IEEE Transactions on Visualization and Computer Graphics*, vol. 14, no. 2, pp. 263–276, 2008.

9. C. Allan, J.-M. Burel, J. Moore, C. Blackburn, M. Linkert, S. Loynton, D. MacDonald, W. J. Moore, C. Neves, A. Patterson, M. Porter, A. Tarkowska, B. Loranger, J. Avondo, I. Lagerstedt, L. Lianas, S. Leo, K. Hands, R. T. Hay, A. Patwardhan, C. Best, G.J. Kleywegt, G. Zanetti, and J. R. Swedlow, "OMERO: flexible, model-driven data management for experimental biology," *Nature Methods*, vol. 9, pp. 245–253, 2012.

10. Y. Chen, A. Ganapathi, and R. H. Katz, "Challenges and opportunities for managing data systems using statistical models," *IEEE Data Engineering Bulletin*, vol. 34, no. 4, pp. 53–60, 2011.

11. J. A. Heward, P. A. Crook, T. C. Lukins, and J. D. Armstrong, "iBehave—application of supervised machine learning to behaviour analysis," in *Proceedings of the 6th Measuring Behaviour Conference*, 2008.

12. K. R. Page, B. Fields, B. J. Nagel, G. O'Neill, D. De Roure, and T. Crawford, "Semantics for music analysis through linked data: how country is my country?," in *eScience*, pp. 41–48, IEEE, 2010.

13. B. Fields, K. R. Page, D. De Roure, and T. Crawford, "The segment ontology: bridging music-generic and domain-specific," in *IEEE International Conference on Multimedia and Expo*, pp. 1–6, 2011.

14. Y. Bachrach, P. Kohli, and T. Graepel, "Rip-off: playing the cooperative negotiation game," in *The 10th International Conference on Autonomous Agents and Multiagent Systems*, pp. 1179–1180, 2011.

15. Y. Xu, X. Cao, A. Sellen, R. Herbrich, and T. Graepel, "Sociable killers: understanding social relationships in an online first-person shooter game," in *Computer Supported Cooperative Work*, pp. 197–206, ACM, 2011.

16. R. E. Bohn and J. E. Short, "How much information? 2009 Report on American Consumers," tech. rep., Global Information Industry Center, University of California, San Diego, CA, 2010.

17. L. Yao, S. Riedel, and A. McCallum, "Collective cross-document relation extraction without labelled data," in *Conference on Empirical Methods in Natural Language Processing*, pp. 1013–1023, 2010.

18. EU Parliament, "Directive 2007/2/EC of the European parliament and of the council of 14 March 2007 establishing an Infrastructure for spatial information in the European Community (INSPIRE)" *Official Journal of the European Union*, vol. 50, April 2007.

19. B. Obama, *Transparency and open Government*. Memorandum for Executive Departments and Agencies, January 2009.

20. L. von Ahn, M. Blum, and J. Langford, "Telling humans and computers apart automatically," *Communications of the ACM*, vol. 47, no. 2, pp. 56–60, 2004.

21. E. Law and L. von Ahn, *Human Computation*. Synthesis Lectures on Artificial Intelligence and Machine Learning, Morgan & Claypool Publishers, 2011.

22. N. Malleson and M. Birkin, "Towards victim-oriented crime modelling in a social science e-infrastructure," *Philosophical Transactions of the Royal Society A*, vol. 369, pp. 3353–3371, 2011.

23. H. M. Berman, K. Henrick, and H. Nakamura, "Announcing the worldwide protein data bank," *Nature Structural Biology*, vol. 10, no. 12, 2003.

24. K. Henrick, Z. Feng, W. F. Bluhm, D. Dimitropoulos, J. F. Doreleijers, S. Dutta, J. L. Flippen-Anderson, J. Ionides, C. Kamada, E. Krissinel, C. L. Lawson, J. L. Markley, H. Nakamura, R. Newman, Y. Shimizu, J. Swaminathan, S. Velankar, J. Ory, E. L. Ulrich, W. Vranken, J. Westbrook, R. Yamashita, H. Yang, J. Young, M. Yousufuddin, and H. M. Berman, "Remediation of the protein data bank archive," *Nucleic Acids Research*, vol. 36, pp. D426–433, 2008.

25. H. M. Berman, G. J. Kleywegt, H. Nakamura, and J. L. Markley, "The protein data bank at 40: reflecting on the past to prepare for the future," *Structure*, vol. 20, pp. 391–396, 2012.

26. J. R. McEntyre, S. Ananiadou, S. Andrews, W. J. Black, R. Boulderstone, P. Buttery, D. Chaplin, S. Chevuru, N. Cobley, L. Coleman, et al., "UKPMC: a full text article resource for the life sciences," *Nucleic Acids Research*, vol. 39, pp. D58–D65, 2011.

27. H. Shatkay, F. Pan, A. Rzhetsky, and W. J. Wilbur, "Multi-dimensional classification of biomedical text: toward automated, practical provision of high-utility text to diverse users," *Bioinformatics*, vol. 24, no. 18, pp. 2086–2093, 2008.

28. A. Rzhetsky, M. Seringhaus, and M. Gerstein, "Seeking a new biology through text mining," *Cell*, vol. 134, no. 1, pp. 9–13, 2008.

29. J. Liu, M. Ghanim, L. Xue, C. Brown, I. Iossifov, C. Angeletti, S. Hua, N. Negre, M. Ludwig, T. Stricker, H. Al-Ahmadie, M. Tretiakova, R. Camp, M. Perera-Alberto, D. Rimm, T. Xu, A. Rzhetsky, and K. White, "Analysis of Drosophila segmentation network identifies a JNK pathway factor overexpressed in kidney cancer," *Science*, vol. 323, no. 5918, pp. 1218–1222, 2009.

30. I. Iossifov, T. Zheng, M. Baron, T. Gilliam, and A. Rzhetsky, "Genetic-linkage mapping of complex hereditary disorders to a whole-genome molecular-interaction network," *Genome Research*, vol. 18, pp. 1150–1162, 2009.

31. D. B. Kell and S. Oliver, "Here is the evidence, now what is the hypothesis? The complementary roles of inductive and hypothesis-driven science in the post-genomic era," *Bioessays*, vol. 26, pp. 99–105, 2004.

32. D. Hull, S. Pettifer, and D. B. Kell, "Defrosting the digital library: bibliographic tools for the next generation Web," *Public Library of Science: Computational Biology*, vol. 4, p. e1000204, 2008.

33. P. Dobson and D. B. Kell, "Carrier-mediated cellular uptake of pharmaceutical drugs: an exception or the rule?" *Nature Reviews Drug Discovery*, vol. 7, pp. 205–220, 2008.

34. L. Kenny, D. Broadhurst, M. Brown, W. Dunn, C. Redman, D. B. Kell, and P. Baker, "Detection and identification of novel metabolomic biomarkers in preeclampsia," *Reproductive Science*, vol. 15, pp. 591–597, 2008.

35. P. Dobson, K. Lanthaler, S. Oliver, and D. B. Kell, "Implications of the dominant role of cellular transporters in drug uptake," *Current Topics in Medicinal Chemistry*, vol. 9, pp. 163–184, 2009.

36. D. B. Kell, "Iron behaving badly: inappropriate iron chelation as a major contributor to the aetiology of vascular and other progressive inflammatory and degenerative diseases," *BMC Medical Genomics*, vol. 2, pp. 63–82, 2009.

37. D. B. Kell, "Metabolomics, modelling and machine learning in systems biology: towards an understanding of the languages of cells. The 2005 Theodor Bücher lecture," *Federation of European Biochemical Societies Journal*, vol. 273, pp. 873–894, 2006.

38. G. Cochrane, I. Karsch-Mizrachi, and Y. Nakamura, "The international nucleotide sequence database collaboration," *Nucleic Acids Research*, vol. 39, pp. D15–D18, 2011.

39. M. Y. Galperin and G. R. Cochrane, "The 2011 nucleic acids research database issue and the online molecular biology database collection," *Nucleic Acids Research*, vol. 39, pp. D1–D6, 2011.

40. Toronto International Data Release Workshop Authors, "Prepublication data sharing," *Nature*, vol. 461, pp. 168–170, 09 2009.

3

The Data-Intensive
Survival Guide

Malcolm Atkinson

School of Informatics, University of Edinburgh, Edinburgh, UK

This chapter presents an overview of all of the elements of our proposed strategy. Sufficient detail is presented for readers to understand the principles and practice that we recommend. It should also provide a good context for readers who then sample later chapters.

It begins by summarizing the challenge of knowledge discovery in a data-rich world and then identifies three critical points of view. All three of these viewpoints have to be supported and each contributes to data-intensive solutions. A three-level data-intensive architecture facilitates this separation. The language DISPEL (data-intensive systems process engineering language) is introduced as the medium of computational and human communication in this data-intensive architecture. It supports communication among the three viewpoints, the incremental development of data-intensive solutions, and controlled coupling between the definition of tasks and their eventual enactment. This language is widely used in the rest of the book.

Sections on *datascopes* and *intellectual ramps* draw attention to two crucial aspects that have to be considered: the conversion of data-intensive methods into routine operational applications and the arrangements to enable practitioners to engage incrementally with new methods.

The DATA Bonanza: Improving Knowledge Discovery in Science, Engineering, and Business, First Edition.
Edited by Malcolm Atkinson, Rob Baxter, Michelle Galea, Mark Parsons, Peter Brezany, Oscar Corcho, Jano van Hemert, and David Snelling.
© 2013 John Wiley & Sons, Inc. Published 2013 by John Wiley & Sons, Inc.

Further development of the ideas in the subsequent chapters of this book will provide valuable practical information for those who wish to develop their data-intensive skills and strategies; this chapter, therefore, concludes with a map for readers who want to skip to chapters that match their specific interests.

3.1 INTRODUCTION: CHALLENGES AND STRATEGY

The challenges of the data bonanza emerging from the digital revolution, introduced in the preceding chapters, are summarized as follows:

1. How should we develop strategies that recognize and exploit the rapidly growing opportunities that the information latent in the growing wealth of data brings?
2. How can we invent and support effective methods and technologies that enable those strategies within the constraints of the realistically available skills and resources?
3. Almost every aspect of the organizations and infrastructures that collect, generate, handle, curate, and exploit data is experiencing rapid change; what are the best mechanisms for accommodating those changes?

The solutions for each society or a global community addressing data challenges must satisfy the following criteria:

1. All human activities that could benefit from improved use of the data should be able to find a path that leads to the new methods without unnecessary disruption of existing effective practices.
2. The methods and technologies should be easily shared within communities with common interests and, wherever possible, should be reused across existing organizational, disciplinary, and cultural boundaries.
3. Innovation should flourish *simultaneously* in every aspect of addressing the challenges, from the working practices to the underpinning technologies, across disciplines, across alternative business models and research practices, and at a wide range of scales.

The first of these criteria is necessary because existing investment in skills, methods, and organizations must be used wherever possible, and disruptive change fails to carry these assets forward. Furthermore, we have found that the professional users will only consider adopting new methods if there is an incremental path, which avoids excessive learning barriers. That path must also allow them to balance potential gain against the risks of lost time and opportunities while discovering how to apply the methods to their problems. We use the term *intellectual ramp* to describe a technically enabled path that minimizes the intellectual investment needed to gain portions of the potential benefits and reduces the risk of wasted time and lost opportunity. These intellectual ramps have to honor existing working practices, which includes users' currently preferred tools. Consequently, many such paths are needed to accommodate the diversity of users (Section 3.10).

The transferability of methods and technologies is important for three reasons. Methods and software that are widely used become progressively more robust and trustworthy, as they are honed through use—inevitable deficiencies are exposed and remedied and subsequent users are protected from these discovered problems if there is effective sharing. When colleagues or rivals are using the same methods and software, then they have good intuitions about how to interpret each other's results and inferences. As the methods often extract information from data that are then used to make significant, even life-critical, decisions, such scrutiny helps with trust and safety. Where technology can be reused by many communities, the cost of creating, evolving, and maintaining it can be amortized widely. However, these benefits should not be pursued to the extremes of a global monoculture with its inherent danger of lock-in to a suboptimal behavior. Human ingenuity and knowledge remain critical, both in devising the ways in which shared methods are used and in the creation of new methods and their implementations.

The turbulence of the digital revolution means that different groups are experiencing different rates of change in their data environment. Autonomous innovation allows those who find new opportunities or who are suffering from the inadequacy of their current methods, to respond with agility. To do this, they must be reasonably decoupled from the rest of the data-intensive community in aspects that are important to their innovation. Other innovators will introduce new technology or business practices when they spot opportunities delivered by changes in the socio-economic and technical contexts. The various forms of change may occur at any scale from coordinated global communities and businesses to the methods adopted by an individual.

When addressing the three categories of challenge, these three criteria may often conflict. The strategy set out in the following text and illustrated throughout the book is designed to minimize these conflicts. It does this by establishing the support for each category of expert, so that they each get a chance to contribute to solutions and to innovate new data-intensive strategies. The conceptual framework is intended to allow independent thinking in each context and also to allow collaboration and stimulation across the categorical boundaries. The technological architecture is shaped to facilitate that autonomy with communication when it is beneficial.

3.2 THREE CATEGORIES OF EXPERT

To provide appropriate paths for adoption and creation of new data-intensive methods, we recognize three categories of expert, each contributing to innovation in the use of data—these were first introduced in Section 1.6. Each category has characteristic skills and working practices that need to be engaged and supported. For sustained progress, all three categories of expert need to invent and adopt new methods. They need to be able to make progress independently as well as work together effectively.

Domain experts are specialists in some application domain, for example, a branch of engineering, a specialty in medicine, an aspect of finance, urban planning, social policy, or interpretation of ancient texts. They bring well-developed knowledge of their application domain, the phenomena of interest, the ways of characterizing and modeling those phenomena, the important questions, and the ways in which information should be presented to support their discipline's working practices. The domains may be divided into many schools or subgroups, each with their own modes of working, vocabularies, culture, perhaps endorsed by professional training, and established collaborative networks. Consequently, they bring domain-specific knowledge, skills, judgment, collaboration networks, and diversity.

Data analysis experts are specialists in extracting information from data—a process often called *knowledge discovery*. They will draw on statistical methods, machine learning, data mining, text mining, signal analysis, image analysis, and so on. They will have subgroups with repertoires of methods suitable for particular classes of problem and will have their favorite environments in which to develop and deploy algorithms, for example, R, MATLAB, Excel, Hadoop, or PostgreSQL. They will have an understanding of which methods are applicable in various circumstances, of how to transform questions so that those methods may be applied, and of how to estimate the trustworthiness of the results obtained. They too will have their own collaborative networks, cultures, and professional paths. We include in this category the experts in information presentation, that is, visualization experts, though they may be treated independently in some contexts. Data analysis experts bring method-specific knowledge, skills, judgment, collaboration networks, and diversity.

Data-intensive engineers are computer scientists, software engineers, information system architects, and hardware engineers who specialize in developing infrastructure and frameworks for data-intensive computations. As engineers, they will exploit the new opportunities brought by emerging technical and business innovations to deliver lower cost, more efficient, or more responsive systems in which data-intensive processes can be enacted. They will also use data-intensive methods to analyze workloads, identify recurrent patterns, and deliver more optimal data-intensive computational platforms. Invariably, they will be working with distributed computational systems. They will have subspecialities, for example, large-scale and reliable storage, load sharing, extremely large databases or file systems, array or image processing, low energy computing, RDF processing, and so on. They bring technology-specific knowledge, skills, judgment, collaboration networks, and diversity.

For the field of data-intensive applications to thrive, all three categories of expert have to be well supported, have to be encouraged to innovate in their own context, and have to be able to adopt and propagate new methods easily. The independence that enables innovation has to be balanced with a stability that promises a good return on the investment in adopting data-intensive methods. Although we separate these categories, we recognize the value of alliances and selective communication across the boundaries and that there are some exceptional experts and researchers who span these categories. We return to their significance after introducing an architecture and a notation.

Progress in the data-intensive field is also dependent on socio-economic factors. The experts will work together and successfully innovate, only if they feel that the benefits outweigh the risks. Leadership and beacons of other innovation successes are key factors underpinning discovery and new business (or research) models. Parts IV and V of this book offer many demonstrations of the power of the new methods and the variety of strategies for deploying them.

After presenting the main features of the architecture, we return to these three categories of expert to consider how they will work in the new data-intensive environment.

3.3   THE DATA-INTENSIVE ARCHITECTURE

In order to provide contexts in which each of the three categories of expert may flourish, we introduce a data-intensive architecture, as shown in Figure 3.1.

The upper layer, *the tool level*, is intended to support the work of both domain experts and data analysis experts. It will house an extensive and evolving set of portals, tools, and development environments, sufficient to support the diversity of

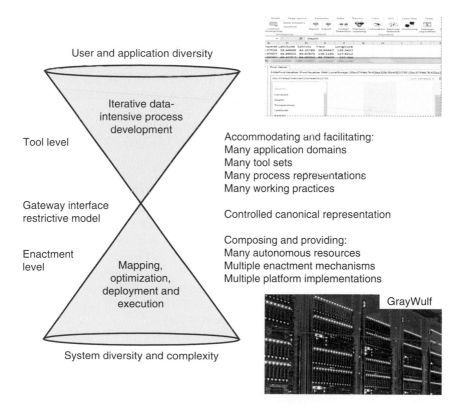

Figure 3.1   *The data-intensive architecture.*

both of these communities of experts. This layer is described in Chapter 11—see Figure 3.7 for a commercial example.

The lower layer, *the enactment level*, is intended to house a large and dynamic community of providers who deliver data and data-intensive enactment environments as an evolving infrastructure, called the *data-intensive platform*, that supports all the work underway in the upper layer. Most of the work of data-intensive engineers goes on here. There will also be some data analysis experts who develop generic, standard libraries optimized for a provider's enactment environment.

The crucial innovation is the neck of the hourglass, which is a tightly defined and *stable* interface through which the two diverse and dynamic upper and lower layers communicate. This gateway is *restrictive*, that is, it has a minimal and simple protocol and language that is ultimately controlled by standards, so that the upper and lower communities may invest, secure in the knowledge that changes in this interface will be carefully managed.

This interface is analogous to the HTTP and HTML interface that has powered the Web's technological and business successes. The HTTP and HTML interface has separated the enormous body of business and technical innovation that lies behind the interface to respond to all the diversity of Web requests (corresponding to the architecture's *enactment level*) from the equally significant body of tools and portals that generate those requests and handle the responses (corresponding to the *tool level*). Much of the rest of this book is concerned with communicating an understanding of what should and should not be in the equivalent data-intensive interface. That exploration is conducted by way of a specific prototype data-intensive system and a representative sample of applications (Part IV). The definitive form for that interface, suitable for standardization, has yet to be achieved. However, it is possible to demonstrate the power, potential, and feasibility of the proposed architecture.

The images on the right are tokens for the diversity in the upper and lower levels; the upper one is Microsoft's Excel DataScope (Sections 3.9 and 3.10) and the lower is the GrayWulf designed by Szalay et al. (Section 4.7.1).

3.4 AN OPERATIONAL DATA-INTENSIVE SYSTEM

We present here some of the features of the architecture, which the ADMIRE project[1] has used to conduct experiments, and thereby refine both the architecture and our understanding as to how it should be used. All the concepts introduced here are further described in Parts II and III of this book. Figure 3.2 shows the operational prototype, which introduces a new language, DISPEL, as the canonical form of communication through the gateway, fulfilling the equivalent role to that filled by HTML in Web architectures (Chapters 4 and 10).

The prototype operational system populates the tool level with an initial set of data-intensive process-authoring tools and provides an enactment level based on

---

[1] European Union Framework Programme 7 project "Advanced Data Mining and Integration Research for Europe" ADMIRE ICT 215024 www.admire-project.eu.

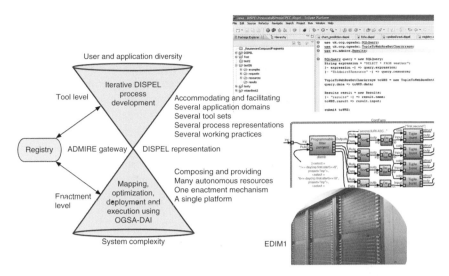

Figure 3.2 *An operational example of a data-intensive architecture.*

	Architectural level		
	Tool	Gateway and DISPEL	Enactment
Domain experts			
Data-analysis experts			
Data-intensive engineers			

Figure 3.3 *How the architecture supports the categories of expert.*

OGSA-DAI [1] (see Chapters 11 and 12, respectively). It introduces a *registry* to hold persistent descriptions of all of the components and services (Section 4.6 and Chapter 8). The registry enables distributed sharing of the definitions and semantic description of every component used, and thereby supports consistent views and use, both between the three levels of the architecture and across the distributed elements of an enactment and development platform.

Figure 3.3 summarizes the mapping of interests to the architecture. Communities of experts use the registry to pool information about components and to support collaboration, thereby building a shared knowledge base that spans from sources of data to forms of delivered results, and from domain-specialists' knowledge to the technologies underpinning enactment.

The domain experts who use this system contribute and use information about the sources, form, quality, and interpretation of data; about the processes they require; and about their choices of implemented algorithms. Where privacy or charging dictates, they may specify where their computations may be performed. They will use tools to develop descriptions, to embed their community's algorithms into components, to assemble components into enactment requests, and to submit requests repeatedly, varying parameters, data sources, and the workflow definitions.

The data analysis experts identify new analytic techniques and use tools to develop their implementation and to insert their descriptions into the registry. They recognize the operations used frequently by the domain experts they work with, and package these as patterns or portals. They interact with data-intensive engineers regarding the enactment services and participate in the coevolution of their libraries of components with the enactment level's implementation. They may work with data-intensive engineers to develop and refine libraries of components well tuned to the data-intensive platform's implementation and deliver support for bundles of data-intensive methods in which they are experts.

The data-intensive engineers play major roles in the design and implementation of the data-intensive platform and use DISPEL as the source of their workloads, and use the registry to pool their information, as well as to provide information for the other two categories of expert.

On the right-hand side of Figure 3.2, the images illustrate the kinds of data-intensive component dominant at each level. At the top level is a screenshot of a portal for editing and submitting DISPEL (Section 11.2.1), at the middle level is a typical graph of DISPEL elements implementing a more complex data-processing step (Section 4.7.3), and at the bottom is a machine, EDIM1, with a balanced architecture designed to run data-intensive tasks (Section 4.7.1).

3.5   INTRODUCING DISPEL

The language DISPEL is an experimental vehicle for exploring how the challenges and criteria summarized in Section 3.1 can best be met in the proposed architecture. It is particularly concerned with ensuring that all three categories of expert have the concepts and notations that enable them to work independently or collaboratively, as they address data-intensive challenges. How this is achieved will be explained as the concepts of DISPEL are introduced in the following text. A more technical introduction is provided in Chapter 4.

The design challenge for DISPEL is to enable separation of concerns above and below the gateway, encourage data-intensive thinking (Chapter 4), and be power-ful enough to communicate all necessary information through the gateway without becoming unnecessarily complex. It should prevent the flow of information that would couple the two levels in such a way as to inhibit their autonomous devel-opment. If details of the data-intensive platform are revealed at the tools level, they will be exploited in the formulation of data-intensive methods. This may yield a short-term performance gain, but it generates a much more serious long-term problem. As soon as the platform changes, the method will stop working. This leads to either a high maintenance load at the tool level or delays in introducing improvements at the enactment level. In addition, coupling between the tools and enactment level stops work being moved between platforms, introducing costs when porting methods to the new platform and inhibiting competition among platform providers. The DISPEL language needs to be suitable for human comprehension, though it may often be generated by tools. From the viewpoint of the tool level, it should support a wide diversity of tools and ways of working. From the perspective of the enactment level, it should leave open a diversity of enactment strategies and enactment service and data provider business models.

DISPEL draws inspiration from database query languages, workflow languages, and functional abstraction. It is syntactically similar to Java, but its innovative extensions have different semantics.

The most important aspect of DISPEL is the information that it carries, that is, the definitions of data-intensive processes. These processes are ultimately defined in terms of *instances* of *processing elements* (PE) interconnected by *connections* that carry *streams* of data. Often, parts of the specification will be *function* applications, which generate reusable patterns as *directed graphs* of *PE instances* interconnected by *connections*.

3.6 A SIMPLE DISPEL EXAMPLE

The following DISPEL request obtains data from a database, transforms it, and delivers the result; the details of how it does this can be found in Chapter 4. We use as a running example the scenario that data analysis experts have set up some PEs that perform major transformational steps in data-intensive processes required by domain experts who are geophysicists or seismologists using data from the archives of data streamed from large numbers of seismometers—a thorough treatment of this application can be found in Chapter 17. This first DISPEL example might correspond to the seismologists reviewing a sample of data and the effects of a Transformer PE designed for that data to check on the data selection and quality, and on the functionality of the Transformer they are using.

```
1   package book.examples.seismology {          //set working context
2     use dispel.db.SQLQuery;                    //import PE SQLQuery
3     use book.examples.seismo.Transformer;      //import PE Transformer
4     use dispel.lang.Results;                    //import PE Results
5
6     SQLQuery sq = new SQLQuery;                 // new instance of SQLQuery
7     Transform tr = new Transformer;            // new instance of Transformer
8     Results res = new Results;                  // new instance of Results
9
10    sq.data => tr.input;                        // set up data flow from sq to tr
11    tr.output => res.input;                     // set up data flow from tr to res
12    |- "uk.ac.bgs.earthquakes" -| => sq.source; // URI of source of data
13    |- "SELECT ... FROM ... WHERE ... " -| => sq.expression;  //query gets traces
14    |- "last 24 hours" -| => res.name;         //name of results for user
15
16    submit res;                                 // submit for enactment
17  }
```

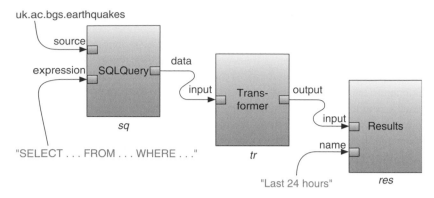

Figure 3.4   *The data-streaming graph from the first DISPEL example.*

Line 1 introduces a `package` name.[2] Lines 2–4 import predefined PEs and lines 6–8 make corresponding instances; this is done explicitly so that multiple instances of a PE may be used in the same DISPEL request. Line 10 connects the output stream of data from `sq` to the input of the `Transformer` instance `tr`. Lines 12–14 construct streams that are supplied to the specified PE instance's inputs. Lines 6–14 taken together construct the data-streaming graph shown in Figure 3.4, which is submitted for enactment by line 16.

`SQLQuery` is a typical PE in that it iterates, consuming values from its input streams and supplying resulting values to its output streams. That is, each time the `SQLQuery` instance `sq` is supplied with URIs (Web addresses) on input `source` and with SQL query expressions on `expression`, it produces a data stream on `data` that corresponds to the result of the query on the source. As values arrive on the `input` to `tr`, they are processed and corresponding values are emitted on `tr`'s `output` and sent as a stream along the connector to the `input` of `res`. All instances of `Results` deliver, to the client that submitted the DISPEL request, the values that arrive on their `input`, with the name supplied on their `name`. In this case, the name is `"last 24 hours"`, the data source is `"uk.ac.bgs.earthquakes"`, and the query expression is `"SELECT ... FROM ... WHERE ... "`. The results of each application of `sq` are lists, so that `tr` can process each list element separately if it wishes. When `sq` has no more input requests, it emits an end-of-stream and then shuts down. When `tr` receives this marker, it tidies up its processing and passes the marker on at the end of its `output` stream, this will then shut down `res` in a similar manner. This is the commonest form of process termination, others are explained later.

The DISPEL request would be produced using facilities in the tool level and then sent to a gateway that acts as the entry point to a data-intensive platform. If the gateway accepts the request, then it organizes the enactment in four phases. The first phase, DISPEL *language processing*, would parse and compile the DISPEL

---

[2]Several package names, such as this one, are used solely for the purpose of this book, to keep things simple.

request and then execute it to produce a data-streaming graph. The second phase, DISPEL *optimization*, transforms the graph into an equivalent graph that will process data faster on the available resources. The third phase, DISPEL *deployment*, places parts of the graph on different computers across the data-intensive platform as code ready for execution. The fourth and final phase, DISPEL *execution and control*, sets the data flowing and the code within PEs executing, and oversees the completion of all processing. This multiphase approach provides flexibility, mapping to heterogeneous platforms, colocation of computation with data, and automated adaptation to local changes.

3.7 SUPPORTING DATA-INTENSIVE EXPERTS

Here, we review how the combination of architecture and DISPEL language serves the needs of all three categories of data-intensive expert.

All of the *domain experts* work in the context of the tool level. The majority will not use DISPEL directly, but use it via their preferred tools or portals (Section 3.10). They will, of course, have strong views about the data and functionality they want, about the ways in which results should be presented, and sometimes about the algorithms and resources that should be used. In most cases, they will get the services they want by employing or influencing data analysis experts to set them up; such dedicated data analysis experts are often called *X-Informaticians*, where X is the domain, such as Astro, Bio, or Geo. Typical domain experts use portals to select predefined DISPEL requests and to provide parameters that control and guide a prepackaged data analysis process. They may use tools, such as graphical workflow editors, to compose predefined elements and to specify details. In both cases, they will indirectly, and possibly unknowingly, gencrate DISPEL requests that denote the data-intensive processes they want enacted. These are then submitted to gateways and enacted as described in the preceding text. Results should be streamed back to their portal or tool as soon as they are available, and the domain expert should be able to steer or cancel analyses before the enactment runs to completion.

A few computationally adept domain experts are also data analysis experts, and will also undertake the data analysis expert's role, ensuring the integration of their domain's requirements with the development of data analysis tools and services. In the majority of cases, enduring alliances between domain and data analysis experts achieve that recognition and refinement of goals, and then deliver against those goals through incremental development of components and processes.

All of the *data analysis experts* will use programming languages to specify algorithms that are eventually embedded in components such as PEs and use scripting or workflow languages to compose such components. Composition of predefined components is essential, in order to assemble elements of previous work, one's own work with that of colleagues and to facilitate rapid exploration of alternative strategies. When the data analysis challenges are data-intensive as they often are, a language such as DISPEL which is based on both data flow and functional abstraction, has many advantages. It facilitates composition in a way that is potentially highly optimizable on modern computing platforms and encourages a focus on high level patterns. However, data-intensive engineers may use a familiar scripting notation that is translated to the canonical language before being passed to the gateway.

Data analysis experts work at the tool level, using software development environments to create and refine components, both in DISPEL and in an algorithm specification language that may vary from mathematics to C, that is, they create processing elements in any language to match an agreed application-programming interface (API), or they can create them in terms of existing processing elements using DISPEL. It is vital to support the diversity of approaches taken by these experts. They are essential, as they populate the environment with a rich collection of components, organized as libraries, and accessed via the registry.

These experts will become fluent in DISPEL (or its successors) and will use the notation for understanding and discussing data-intensive processes. They will use the functional abstractions to embed facilities in domain-experts' tools and portals so that they can develop new solutions and accommodate change without having to revisit those tools. They will use functions to describe repeatedly used patterns and the mappings between high level (composite) processing elements and their constituent components. Some data analysis experts will build libraries of components to make a class of data analysis methods available, while others will make libraries that serve a particular domain well. They will all draw on existing libraries of components, particularly the utility facilities and standard libraries that are part of a well-implemented DISPEL. They will interact with the data-intensive engineers, establishing the requirements for these libraries, improving the design of supported patterns, and exploring performance and cost issues. The DISPEL notation is intended to facilitate this interaction.

The *data-intensive engineers* are responsible for creating and maintaining the data-intensive platform, so their main interest is in the enactment level. They will receive information on requirements from the data analysis experts and only rarely from domain experts. They will understand their platform and the workloads using data-intensive techniques to extract information about properties of the actual workload, about their implementations of the four phases of enactment, and about how well they are using their equipment. They will use DISPEL to provide utility libraries of widely required components and will take a particular interest in specifying patterns in such a way that they can be mapped onto current resources.

3.8   DISPEL IN THE CONTEXT OF CONTEMPORARY SYSTEMS

The DISPEL language draws on ideas from a great many successful *scientific* workflow languages. A good survey of those can be found in [2] with a recent update in [3], which provides a taxonomy for comparing workflow systems. There are also many commercial workflow systems, with the business process execution language (BPEL) as a standard [4], as well as standards aimed at managing business processing in a variety of domains, for example, ebXML [5]. There are also specialized systems that target specific aspects of business, for example, RosettaNet [6] for supply chain management. The majority of commercial workflow systems are tuned to orchestrating business processes including human activity, whereas the scientific workflow systems are more orientated to controlling computations and managing data movement. They, therefore, almost invariably give a high priority to identifying and exploiting data dependencies. The KNIME system provides a commercially supported workflow and data analysis system, with multiple server platforms, a large repertoire of biological image processing functions, interworking with R and traditional analytics, such as those supported by Weka; it is also available for academic research (www.knime.org).

DISPEL shares many features with these scientific workflow languages, for example, an extensible set of data-processing elements that are interconnected by flows of data. Similar to many of these systems, it has graphical and textual tools for authoring workflows and is defined independently, so that there may be many different forms of enactment engine.

There are many scientific workflow languages evolving to address the new challenges of data-intensive computing, for example, the Athena Data Flow Language (ADFL) [7], the Apache Camel system [8], Pig Latin [9] for programming MapReduce architectures such as Hadoop [10], Swift [11], Triana [12], Microsoft's Trident [13], and the ZigZag language of Meandre [14], as well as those mentioned in the following text.

A common problem from our viewpoint is that many of these languages allow their users to say too much, in the sense that they can specify nitty-gritty detail, which exposes the implementation mechanisms. This removes the platform independence, which is the foundation of our strategy for providing separation of concerns, diversity, resilience to change, and optimization using local and up-to-date information. A full survey is impossible in the context of this book, as it would both require too much space and fall rapidly out of date. We return to the topic of how contemporary commercial developments and research should influence the future of DISPEL in Part VI.

As a language, DISPEL has several important features:

1. With DISPEL, exactly the same language in the same syntactic form is used for communicating with the enactment engine and with humans. This is significantly different from Taverna's [15] internal form SCUFL [16] represented as XML. Similarly, Kepler [17] uses an XML-encoded Modeling Markup Language (MoML) [18], and Pegasus [19] translates its high level language to DAGMan [20]. The difference is significant for two reasons: DISPEL permits the data analysis experts and the data-intensive experts to use it as a precise tool for *discussing* data-intensive computations, and it raises the level of abstraction at which responsibility is passed to the enactment engine, opening up many more options for implementation strategies, thereby ameliorating the impact of platform changes on existing workflows.

2. Processing elements in DISPEL automatically iterate over the incoming streams of data. This is because it is based on 8 years of experience with

OGSA-DAI [1], which in turn was designed as an open-ended generalization of the streaming operators in relational (distributed) query evaluators [21]. Other scientific workflows, such as Taverna, automatically iterate, but DISPEL differs from them in a significant detail. In most workflow systems, there is a consistent unit of iteration, often a file, and so data is passed along connections in these units and iteration consumes these units. DISPEL is agnostic about the dataflow's granularity; consequently, fine-grained units can be used when micro-operations are manipulating the data stream, ideally with data and code staying in fast caches, exploiting the same optimization as column-oriented database management system (DBMS) [22] and Vertica (www.vertica.com), and large units can be used between computationally expensive operations and across long-haul networks. This agnosticism about the scale of work and data-transport units gives a continuity of language and semantics over a very wide range of data-intensive applications. Kepler has recently developed a set of actions to support stream processing [23] well tuned to processing environmental sensor streams. Massive online analysis (MOA), a companion to Weka [24], is developing scalable analysis algorithms that incrementally process data wherever possible [25]. Optimized strategies for deploying such workloads on the public Cloud are developing [26].

In addition, processing elements in DISPEL only take streams, that is, DISPEL does not have a separate concept of parameters. This ensures that "parameters" in one iteration of a workflow design can evolve to be values derived from databases, portals, or other data with minimal and localized change. This is achieved through the introduction of stream literals.

3. Building on ideas from Taverna, DISPEL provides a three-level type system to deliver rich opportunities for describing all components and both the logical structure and meaning of the data flowing through connections. Many uses are made of the improved descriptive power—these may be found later in the book. Two examples are given here. Taverna proposed the idea of automatically inserted "shims" that automatically repair differences between incoming and expected data [27]. In DISPEL the structural and the semantic descriptions of data streams are used to automatically unpack, translate, and reassemble data [28]. In the tools and registry, these descriptions guide the selection of components and support validation of workflows. This builds on strategies for describing and sharing workflows pioneered in myExperiment [29]. Further work, in the Wf4Ever project (www.wf4ever-project.org) seeks to develop more sharing of workflows that retain their validity and interoperate between workflow languages.

4. The DISPEL language uses functions to describe and generate distributed computational patterns. Facilitating the reuse of patterns parameterized by any of the constructs in the language is an extremely powerful method of capturing, refining, and sharing a crucial aspect of data-intensive computation.

5. The evaluation model permits a wide range of distributed computation patterns [30], so that enactment can be deployed across heterogeneous platforms

without redundant communication and without multistep data movement—this provides performance, flexibility, and scalability (Chapter 12).

In summary, DISPEL is an experiment in developing a language with the primary aim of supporting collaboration in solving data-intensive problems by facilitating precise dialog about the processes required; both between humans and between humans and distributed computational systems. The human-readable (non-XML and exclusion of execution details) orientation of DISPEL makes it an ideal notation for discussing, publishing, teaching, and implementing data-intensive methods.

3.9 DATASCOPES

A step toward easing the path from data to knowledge is to provide familiar tools. These can benefit each category of expert. For domain experts, the tools that persist and are consistent are progressively better understood, and they become more adept at exploiting them. For the data analysis experts, they can also develop a better understanding of how to provide good analyses exploiting a tool's properties. For the data-intensive engineers, persistent tools give greater opportunity for tuning their implementation. However, none of these experts wants stasis. They all want to improve when the opportunity arises. This can be achieved by a category of evolving technologies that maintain a consistent fundamental behavior and structure. We term these long-lived mechanisms for knowledge discovery *datascopes*, as they let us see deeper into data. They will offer frameworks into which data analysis "stages" fit, which can be easily tailored and steered to address particular goals. Common frameworks and sharable families of stages will facilitate sustainability, sharing, and reuse.

Science, engineering, and medicine have all advanced through improving the instruments with which they gather *relevant* data, for example, the microscope in biology and geology; X-ray methods in mineralogy, biochemistry, and medicine; and telescopes in astronomy. Each advancement in instrumentation enables humans to "see" new things and derive new information. The advent of an instrument is not a final step, but the start of an adventurous path with discoveries and technical innovation driving each other. Consider the path from the telescope in Figure 3.5 to today's diversity of Earth and space-based instruments; for example, the Europe-wide synthetic aperture telescope directed by computationally injecting a phase lag across its receiving elements, some of which are shown in Figure 3.6[3]. As the same incoming signals can be correlated with phase lags corresponding to any direction above the horizon, the low frequency array multi-purpose sensor (LOFAR)

---

[3]See www.lofar.org. with 138 PB of data per day, yielding 240 TB of correlated data per day; storage costs mean that data is only available for a week; the observations over the 5-year survey will observe 10^9 astronomic sources, some as many as 10^4 times, yielding a catalog of $\approx 10^{13}$ rows, occupying 1.5 PB.

Figure 3.5   *The first astronomical telescope. Source: Edinburgh University Library, Special Collections Department [31].*

telescope can, in principle, look in all directions at once. The rate at which data can be processed limits this drastically. The contrast between these two telescopes 400 years apart dramatically illustrates how fast technology changes what we can do.

The early astronomers built telescopes to enable them to see what their unaided eyes could not see; this changed our understanding of the Universe profoundly and deeply affected the way we think. At present, the early explorers of data are building *datascopes* to discover knowledge they cannot perceive with the unaided mind. These data "observations" take many forms, for example, MapReduce technology on a global network of data centers used by Google to observe and understand the

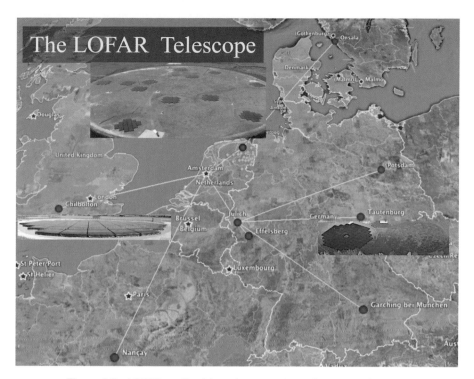

Figure 3.6 *LOFAR synthesizing a large-aperture microwave telescope.*

Web and the human activity the Web enables. Another example is the collection of astronomical queries supported on relational database technology and data-intensive hardware architectures built at Johns Hopkins University in collaboration with Microsoft [32].

A recent example is the embedding of data exploration and analysis in Microsoft Excel [33], as illustrated in Figure 3.7. The Excel DataScope provides a convenient mechanism for selecting data sources, composing functions to be applied to those data, inputting analysis-steering parameters, and graphically viewing results. The researcher using the DataScope directs the data analysis by selecting functions from the drop-down pallets in the data ribbon. This is familiar to any user of Excel and prompts incremental exploration of the power of the functions made visible on each pallet—this makes it an effective intellectual ramp—see the following text. When the data volume and computation warrants extra resources, the analysis is automatically shipped as a MapReduce application to the Microsoft Azure cloud. When the results are ready, the user is presented with a button to initiate a download.

In the example shown in the figure, the Excel DataScope ran K-means clustering on 5 million ocean sensor readings and returned the clusters in a data visualization tool that allows users to drill into the clusters. Here, the data lives in the cloud and the execution of the algorithm also takes place in the cloud in Microsoft Research's

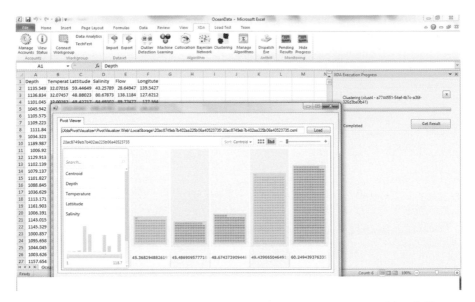

Figure 3.7   *A new datascope: the Excel Data-Scope data-exploration ribbon [33].*

MapReduce runtime. This is all transparent to the user, as they are simply pressing buttons in Excel.

Future datascopes will increase in data-resolving power and, similar to microscopes and telescopes, they will evolve to support systematic repetition and measurements of properties under scrutiny in the data. There will be growing expertise in their design and specialized systems will emerge to look for particular forms of information extraction. Their performance will improve and their operational costs will be reduced.

3.10   RAMPS FOR INCREMENTAL ENGAGEMENT

As explained in Section 3.1, it is necessary to provide well-supported paths that ease the adoption of data-intensive methods—we call these paths *ramps*. An *intellectual ramp* facilitates the process of learning about a new method such as its concepts, its power, its options, and how to use it on one's data. A *technological ramp* helps technologists install the mechanisms that support the new method in their computational context—facilitating the propagation of the new facilities.

Every expert is already busy. The demands of their jobs mean that they are always striving to stay at the forefront of their area of specialist skills and knowledge, always struggling to get results faster or more economically than their competition, and always monitoring their immediate field to assimilate all relevant developments. This applies to every category of expert; they are already undertaking intellectually demanding work, often close to the limits of their time and ability. Consequently, it is extremely difficult to persuade them to try new methods, as this requires allocating learning and setup time. They face a big risk that if it does not pay off; they will have fallen behind their competitors or failed to deliver on their existing commitments.

To overcome this, it is necessary to create *intellectual ramps* that permit a low cost entry to sample *the aspects of the method they choose* with minimum learning effort and disruption to existing skills and work patterns. A useful ramp is not just a prepackaged function, as that does not help experts understand and incrementally discover the power of the new methods, nor does it give them opportunity to invent new ways of using the emerging data and technology. Each ramp has to have the opportunity to keep exploring a little further with commensurate benefits and provide an intuitive environment that offers but does not impose the increments.

The Excel DataScope (Fig. 3.7) is an example that would work well for domain experts and data analysis experts who already do much of their work with Microsoft Excel. The data-exploration ribbon presents the set of data-exploration and analysis tools so that users can see that they exist and incrementally try them as and when they see the need. A characteristic of a good intellectual ramp is that it offers relevant and applicable operations on the selected data so that their users become aware of the new possibilities. The ramp should then offer low cost and lightweight experiments so that the users can get a feel for what those operations do and how much they cost. When a user is experimenting, the ramp should offer suitable samples for trial runs, for example, on a millionth of the data, on a thousandth, on a hundredth, and on a tenth. For this to be a useful ramp for the data analysis experts, it has to be convenient for them to introduce new libraries of operations. Similarly, the data-intensive engineers would want to add adapters for more data sources and tune the implementations of popular knowledge-discovery patterns.

An effective ramp differs from a well-packaged function that portals often present. In that case, the domain experts obtain the advantage of getting their work done quickly and efficiently, but in most examples, the functionality is fixed and the users only adjust parameters that have been chosen as variable by the portal designers. The advantage of this is that it can yield very significant productivity gains—it invariably accelerates adoption and greatly eases the task of learning how to achieve its specific purpose. However, such a tightly packaged facility does not usually expand the users' appreciation of the potential of the data and methods, whereas a ramp should do this.

A different "under-the-hood" embedding with similar incremental introduction to new functions would be needed for domain experts who normally worked with MATLAB[4] or any other problem solving tool. This requirement to couple with many established working environments is one of the reasons for providing functional capabilities in DISPEL—it should be relatively straightforward to call the same functions from different tool environments.

A few early pioneers will have taken risks and made enormous effort to explore the new data-intensive methods. Their pioneering is well reported, some are included

---

[4]www.mathworks.com

in Part V of this book, but the effort and risk are often understated. In many cases, the pioneering was only successful because a substantial team of other experts helped. As the demand from domain and data analysis experts rises, marshaling specialist teams to help becomes progressively more infeasible.

Pioneering is always necessary at the frontier, but many data-intensive methods are moving into a mature and established phase. They have to move beyond that stressful stage by being packaged and delivered in powerful datascopes that come with ramps to let their users incrementally adopt the new methods.

For a domain expert, it should be easy to "point" a datascope at the relevant data, to adjust the instrument to extract the required information, and to adjust the "eyepiece" and "camera" to see and capture the information in an optimal form. For the data analysis expert, it should be easy to install and change "stages" in the datascope, to preprogram it with patterns of target selection and information capture, and to investigate what is limiting its "resolving power." For the data-intensive engineer, it should be easy to monitor and refine the operational behavior of the datascope, for example, to connect it to new kinds of data source or provide its data-intensive platform with new forms of parallelism and replication.

Ramps for introducing datascopes should let data-service providers experience delivering their power while they are supported on a reference site or commercial service. Some providers may then choose to run their own copy, which in turn requires a ramp to be set up and manage the new data service.

We should, at this point, acknowledge the value of another category of experts who have a role to play; these are the educators, teachers, and trainers who can help people rapidly gain the new skills, introduce them to the new possibilities, and help them develop a conceptual framework for their future encounters with data-intensive innovations. These experts are prime users and often the inventors of intellectual ramps, as these eliminate the extraneous distractions of technical detail and inconsistencies that often prevent their students from gaining the required understanding—an example of this in the context of computational chemistry can be found in [34]. In the long term, the power of datascopes and the complexity of the knowledge discovery tasks will mean that, even with the best intellectual ramps, either formal training or informal learning from colleagues will be necessary.

3.11   READERS' GUIDE TO THE REST OF THIS BOOK

We now provide readers with a quick guide to the rest of the book, as they may want to leap ahead to motivating examples in Parts IV and V if their primary interest is in applications of data-intensive methods and return to the intervening chapters to fill in technical detail later. Those with a keen interest in the technology may prefer to read Parts II and III first. Part VI is our attempt to predict the future for decision makers and to provide a launchpad for researchers who want to contribute to the intellectual and technical momentum of data-intensive research.

PART II: DATA-INTENSIVE PROBLEM SOLVING

Part II introduces its readers to progressively more sophisticated knowledge-discovery strategies by way of a series of worked examples. The goal is to show would-be data analysis experts how the potential to partition a data-intensive challenge works out in practice. Familiar knowledge-discovery methods are revisited using the strategies espoused by this book. Later chapters then show how the approach provides extra power by delivering scalability and pattern reuse.

PART III: DATA-INTENSIVE ENGINEERING

Part III is intended for data-intensive engineers. It has two purposes: to show that the strategy adopted is feasible by describing crucial aspects of the architecture's implementation and to equip data-intensive engineers with the skills needed to exploit the strategy as well as to advance the quality of the implementations and services.

PART IV: DATA-INTENSIVE EXPERIENCE

Part IV recounts the experience of using the approach in four application domains: customer-relationship management, river and reservoir management, gene expression in developmental biology, and analysis of global seismic data sources. The domain experts and data analysis experts reveal how they used the ADMIRE prototype to explore a succession of knowledge-discovery challenges in their field. Readers will develop more insights into how to use the approach and methods; if they are interested in a similar field, the ideas may transfer very readily. If the reader works in a completely different discipline, these case studies should still stimulate creative thoughts about how to deploy data-intensive knowledge discovery in their own context. Data-intensive engineers who are looking for opportunities to innovate will find that the authors of these chapters usually conclude by mentioning unsolved challenges. Chief information officers and research strategists should find both Parts IV and V a valuable source of examples of the potential of data-intensive strategies. They will also find useful tactics for implementing those strategies.

PART V: DATA-INTENSIVE BEACONS OF SUCCESS

Part V provides five compelling examples of the power of data-intensive knowledge discovery strategies. They illustrate a wide range of approaches and illustrate the scale of the data-intensive challenges ahead. Drawn from the fields of astronomy, oceanography, climatology, environmental science, digital humanities, engineering, and ornithology, these examples confirm the pervasive impact of data-intensive methods. The authors report dramatic successes that should inspire similar successes in many commercial, governmental, and research contexts. Taken together, Parts IV and V illustrate a gamut of applications that a data-intensive service provider could integrate and support as a business model, whether in a commercial or research environment. Data-intensive engineers should read these two parts to gain an appreciation of the workloads their technological advances must support—there are a great many opportunities for innovation.

PART VI: THE DATA-INTENSIVE FUTURE

Part VI points to the future in a data-rich world. The first chapter looks again at the digital revolution. It develops a vision of the benefits and challenges ahead, considers the limits to data-intensive methods, and envisages the interplay between the data bonanza and society's response. This response includes revision of expectations, ethical assumptions, business models, and legislation. The second chapter is designed for those who will take up research into data-intensive methods from any of the expert categories. It will provide a framework for finding relevant current leading work based on the global activity in data-intensive research at the time of writing. It will pose current open research questions and will attempt to envisage the way they will be addressed.

Readers who want more technical foundations may continue with the following pages (Chapter 4). Readers who are interested in data mining may dive into Part II, while those interested in examples of data-intensive methods being used in a wide range of disciplines should read Parts IV and V.

REFERENCES

1. B. Dobrzelecki, A. Krause, A. Hume, A. Grant, M. Antonioletti, T. Alemu, M. P. Atkinson, M. Jackson, and E. Theocharopoulos, "Integrating distributed data sources with OGSA-DAI DQP and Views," *Philosophical Transactions of the Royal Society A*, vol. 368, no. 1926, pp. 4133–4145, 2010.

2. I. J. Taylor, E. Deelman, D. B. Gannon, and M. Shields, *Workflows for e-Science: Scientific Workflows for Grids*. Springer-Verlag, 2007.

3. E. Deelman, D. Gannon, M. Shields, and I. Taylor, "Workflows and e-Science: an overview of workflow system features and capabilities," *Future Generation Computer Systems*, vol. 25, no. 5, pp. 528–540, 2009.

4. D. Jordon and J. Evdemon, "Web services business process execution language, Version 2.0, OASIS standard," tech. rep., OASIS, April 2007.

5. ebXML Business Process Technical Committee, "ebXML Business Process Specification Schema Technical Specification (version 2.0.4)," tech. rep., OASIS, December 2006.

6. RosettaNet global supply chain standards organization, http://www.rosettanet.org/standards/rosettanetstandards/tabid/473/default.aspx, visited January 2013.

7. M. Tsangaris, G. Kakaletris, H. Kllapi, G. Papanikos, F. Pentaris, P. Polydoras, E. Sitaridi, V. Stoumpos, and Y. Ioannidis, "Dataflow processing and optimization on grid and cloud infrastructures," *IEEE Data Engineering Bulletin*, vol. 32, no. 1, pp. 64–74, 2009.

8. Apache Camel Open Software Project, "Apache Camel user guide, version 2.7.0," tech. rep., Apache Software Foundation, 2011.

9. C. Olston, B. Reed, U. Srivastava, R. Kumar, and A. Tomkins, "Pig Latin: a not-so-foreign language for data processing," in *SIGMOD Conference'08*, pp. 1099–1110, 2008.

10. T. White, *Hadoop: The Definitive Guide*. O'Reilly, 2009.

11. Z. Hou, M. Wilde, M. Hategan, X. Zhou, I. T. Foster, and B. Clifford, "Experiences of on-demand execution for large scale parameter sweep applications on OSG by swift," in *High-Performance Cloud Computing*, pp. 527–532, 2009.

12. D. Churches, G. Gombas, A. Harrison, J. Maassen, C. Robinson, M. Shields, I. Taylor, and I. Wang, "Programming scientific and distributed workflow with Triana services: research articles," *Concurrency and Computation: Practice and Experience*, vol. 18, no. 10, pp. 1021–1037, 2006.

13. Y. Simmhan, R. Barga, C. van Ingen, E. Lazowska, and A. Szalay, "Building the Trident scientific workflow workbench for data management in the cloud," in *International Conference on Advanced Engineering Computing and Applications in Sciences (ADVCOMP)*, IEEE, October 2009.

14. X. Llorá, B. Ács, L. S. Auvil, B. Capitanu, M. E. Welge, and D. E. Goldberg, "Meandre: semantic-driven data-intensive flows in the clouds," in *IEEE 4th International Conference on eScience*, pp. 238–245, IEEE Press, 2008.

15. D. Hull, K. Wolstencroft, R. Stevens, C. A. Goble, M. R. Pocock, P. Li, and T. Oinn, "Taverna: a tool for building and running workflows of services," *Nucleic Acids Research*, vol. 34, pp. 729–732, 2006.

16. T. Oinn, M. Addis, J. Ferris, D. Marvin, M. Greenwood, C. Goble, A. Wipat, P. Li, and T. Carver, "Delivering web service coordination capability to users," in *Proceedings of the 13th International World Wide Web Conference—Alternate Track Papers & Posters*, pp. 438–439, ACM, 2004.

17. B. Ludäscher, I. Altintas, C. Berkley, D. Higgins, E. Jaeger, M. Jones, E. A. Lee, J. Tao, and Y. Zhao, "Scientific workflow management and the Kepler system," *Concurrency and Computation: Practice and Experience*, vol. 18, no. 10, pp. 1039–1065, 2006.

18. E. A. Lee and S. Neuendorffer, "MoML—a modeling markup language in XML—version 0.4," tech. rep., University of California at Berkeley, March 2000.

19. E. Deelman, G. Singh, M.-H. Su, J. Blythe, Y. Gil, C. Kesselman, G. Mehta, K. Vahi, G. B. Berriman, J. Good, A. C. Laity, J. C. Jacob, and D. S. Katz, "Pegasus: a framework for mapping complex scientific workflows onto distributed systems," *Scientific Programming*, vol. 13, no. 3, pp. 219–237, 2005.

20. Condor Team, "Condor DAGMan Manual," tech. rep., University of Wisconsin-Madison, 2008.

21. M. Antonioletti, M. P. Atkinson, R. M. Baxter, A. Borley, N. P. C. Hong, B. Collins, N. Hardman, A. C. Hume, A. Knox, M. Jackson, A. Krause, S. Laws, J. Magowan, N. W. Paton, D. Pearson, T. Sugden, P. Watson, and M. Westhead, "The design and implementation of Grid database services in OGSA-DAI," *Concurrency and Computation: Practice and Experience*, vol. 17, no. 2–4, pp. 357–376, 2005.

22. S. Manegold, M. L. Kersten, and P. A. Boncz, "Database architecture evolution: mammals flourished long before dinosaurs became extinct," in *Proceedings of the International Conference on Very Large Data Bases (VLDB)*, (Lyon France), August 2009.

10-year Best Paper Award for Database Architecture Optimized for the New Bottleneck: Memory Access.

23. D. Barseghian, I. Altintas, M. B. Jones, D. Crawl, N. Potter, J. Gallagher, P. Cornillon, M. Schildhauer, E. T. Borer, E. W. Seabloom, and P. R. Hosseini, "Workflows and extensions to the Kepler scientific workflow system to support environmental sensor data access and analysis," *Ecological Informatics*, vol. 5, pp. 42–50, 2010.

24. I. H. Witten, E. Frank, and M. A. Hall, *Data Mining: Practical Machine Learning Tools and Techniques (Third Edition)*. Morgan Kauffman, 2011.

25. A. Bifet, G. Holmes, R. Kirkby, and B. Pfahringer, "MOA: Massive Online Analysis," *Journal of Machine Learning Research*, vol. 11, pp. 1601–1604, 2010.

26. G. Lee, B.-G. Chun, and R. Katz, "Exploiting heterogeneity in the public cloud for cost-effective data analytics," in *3rd Workshop on Hot Topics in Cloud Computing*, June 2011.

27. D. Hull, "Description and classification of Shims in myGrid," tech. rep., University of Manchester, 2006.

28. G. Yaikhom, M. P. Atkinson, J. I. van Hemert, O. Corcho, and A. Krause, "Validation and mismatch repair of workflows through typed data streams," *Philosophical Transactions of the Royal Society A*, vol. 369, no. 1949, pp. 3285–3299, 2011.

29. D. De Roure, C. Goble, and R. Stevens, "The design and realisation of the myExperiment virtual research environment for social sharing of workflows," *Future Generation Computer Systems*, vol. 25, pp. 561–567, 2009.

30. G. Hohpe and B. Woolf, *Enterprise Integration Patterns: Designing, Building, and Deploying Messaging Solutions*. Addison-Wesley, 2003.

31. J. Hevelius, *Selenographia: sive, Lunæ descriptio; atque accurata ... delineatio. In quâ simul cæterorum omnium planetarum nativa facies, variæque observationes ... figuris accuratissimè æri incisis, sub aspectum ponuntur ... Addita est, lentes expoliendi nova ratio.* Gedani : Autoris sumtibus, typis Hünefeldianis, 1647.

32. A. S. Szalay, G. Bell, J. vanden Berg, A. Wonders, R. C. Burns, D. Fay, J. Heasley, A. J. G. Hey, M. A. Nieto-Santisteban, A. R. Thakar, C. van Ingen, and R. Wilton, "GrayWulf: scalable clustered architecture for data intensive computing," in *Hawaii International Conference on Systems Sciences*, pp. 1–10, 2009.

33. R. Barga, D. Gannon, N. Araujo, J. Jackson, W. Lu, and J. Ekanayake, "Excel DataScope for data scientists," in *e-Science All Hands Meeting*, 2010.

34. C. Morrison, N. Robertson, A. Turner, J. van Hemert, and J. Koetsier, "Molecular orbital calculations of inorganic compounds," in *Inorganic Experiments*, pp. 261–267, Wiley, 2010.

4

Data-Intensive Thinking with DISPEL

Malcolm Atkinson

School of Informatics, University of Edinburgh, Edinburgh, UK

This chapter illustrates the range of issues that are considered when thinking about a data-intensive task. In doing so, it provides a technical introduction to DIS-PEL which requires some familiarity with computer languages and distributed computing. This should be sufficient for those who want to appreciate the DISPEL examples that appear throughout the remainder of this book. Those who want more insight into the design and implementation of DISPEL are referred to its *partial* definition in Chapter 10 and subsequent chapters, and to the DISPEL Reference Manual [1].

The purpose of DISPEL as a language for designing and implementing distributed data-intensive processes based on a data-streaming model was presented in Section 3.5 and Section 3.8 sets it in context. This chapter starts with introductory material and becomes progressively more technically challenging. For this purpose, we revisit the seismology example as a vehicle for introducing the principal concepts of data-intensive thinking and their representation in DISPEL. Both data analysis experts and data-intensive engineers should find compelling examples of how to partition data-intensive processes into tractable chunks. Three categories of types are provided to help each category of expert achieve correct implementations.

The DATA Bonanza: Improving Knowledge Discovery in Science, Engineering, and Business, First Edition.
Edited by Malcolm Atkinson, Rob Baxter, Michelle Galea, Mark Parsons, Peter Brezany, Oscar Corcho, Jano van Hemert, and David Snelling.
© 2013 John Wiley & Sons, Inc. Published 2013 by John Wiley & Sons, Inc.

The final sections of this chapter introduce the range of issues that data-intensive engineers need to tackle. They bring in additional issues that have been omitted previously for didactic clarity, showing how the effects of distribution, scale, heterogeneity, and failures can be addressed in data-intensive applications. The knowledge of all three categories of expert must be harnessed to address these issues and DISPEL is intended to facilitate that collaboration.

4.1 PROCESSING ELEMENTS

A *processing element* (*PE*) is the encapsulation of an algorithm that takes data from zero or more input connections and delivers data to zero or more output connections. PEs may be *primitive*, that is, implemented in some other language (such as Java, Perl, or Python), or composite, that is, implemented in DISPEL as a directed graph of PE instances linked by connections. A PE will normally consume values one at a time from its input connections and emit values one at a time on its output connections. This *autoiteration*, that is, automatically applying its operation to each value that arrives on an input, has the advantage that a PE only stores the minimum of data—although, clearly, a PE that sorts a list of values has to store those values before emitting them.

Users of DISPEL should be provided with well-organized libraries of predefined PEs that are fully described in the registry (Section 4.6). Developers working with DISPEL can extend these libraries by registering their own PEs and other components. They will be provided with tools for defining composite PEs and for wrapping existing code as PEs (Chapter 11). This is one of the opportunities for autonomous development. Data-intensive engineers and data analysis experts can build new libraries of PEs, encapsulating their latest methods and algorithms and can revise existing libraries. Computationally adept domain experts may generate primitive PEs by encapsulating their existing code in a harness made available in their chosen language to wrap their algorithms and deliver the data-plumbing interfaces expected by the data-intensive enactment platform. That existing code may come in many forms, for example, scripts in Python, MATLAB routines, and C code. Consequently, a production system needs a variety of PE-construction harnesses. Alternatively, PEs may be defined in terms of existing PEs using DISPEL; many examples follow.

When PEs, or any other predefined DISPEL components, are used, they must be explicitly imported by a `use` statement, for example,

```
package book.examples {
use dispel.db.SQLQuery;        //import SQLQuery
   ...   }
```

which would make the PE `SQLQuery` from the package `dispel.db` available. A small and frequently used set of PEs, for example, the PE `Results`, are to be found in `dispel.lang`; these can be used without being imported explicitly.

Some typical PEs are illustrated in Figure 4.1 and described in Table 4.1. PEs may hold state during an enactment, for example, a PE Count might hold the count of the number of values that have passed through it. To permit multiple occurrences of the same PE in one DISPEL graph, the construction of the graph

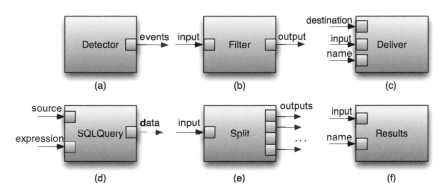

Figure 4.1 *Examples of typical processing elements described in Table 4.1.*

TABLE 4.1 Descriptions of processing elements in Figure 4.1

Figure	Name	Description
a	Detector	It has no inputs and one output, events. This will be bound to a sensor and will deliver a value on events whenever its kind of event occurs.
b	Filter	It has one input, input and one output, output. For each value received on input, it discards or emits it on output according to some internally encoded criterion. A more typical filter would have another input to specify the criterion.
c	Deliver	It has three inputs, destination, input, and name. Each value that is supplied to input is sent to the destination specified by a URI on destination with the name given on name using a protocol determined by the implementation of Deliver. Enactment may choose from several equivalent implementations to find an appropriate delivery protocol.
d	SQLQuery	Each time, an SQL query arrives on expression, the query is dispatched to the relational database specified by the URI on source and the result of the query is streamed as a list of tuples to data.
e	Split	It is a PE that enables parallel enactment, as it distributes the values arriving on input uniformly across the array of output connections outputs[ ]. The number of connections in outputs is deduced from the number of connections made to each instance of Split or set by an assertion.
f	Results	It delivers each value supplied to it on input with the corresponding name supplied on name to the client that submitted the DISPEL request. A user terminating a running enactment would cause all instances of Result to transmit *No more Data (NmD)* on their inputs.

of PEs is actually of PE *instances* interconnected by connections that carry data streams. The `new` operator generates an instance. For example,

```
package book.examples {
  use book.examples.Count;      //import Count
  Count count = new Count;      //make instance of Count
  ...  }
```

would create a new instance of `Count` and bind that to the local instance identifier `count`.

More properties of PEs are presented in terms of types in Section 4.5, in terms of their descriptions in Section 4.6, and in terms of their behavior in Section 4.7.2.

4.2 CONNECTIONS

Each connection carries a stream of data values from *one* source, an output of a PE instance, to an arbitrary number of destinations—inputs of other PE instances. Connections may carry data of any type. These data may have known structure that is transmitted along with the data by structure markers, such as *begin-list-marker* and *end-list-marker* or *begin-array-marker* and *end-array-marker* so that very large values may be passed incrementally. The atoms of data, which are passed along the stream, are as small or large as make computational sense, for example, an `Integer`, a `String`, an array of `Real` values, or a list of tuples.

The data-intensive platform takes full responsibility for buffering and optimizing the flow of values along each connection, for example, passing by reference when possible; or serializing, compressing, and encrypting when transmitting long haul. The system will automatically buffer, spilling to disk when this is unavoidable. These properties are mandatory so that composers of DISPEL requests do not need to know the relative speeds of PEs and available resources on the enactment platform. This prevents entanglement between the providers' technical solutions in the enactment layer, which may, for example, adjust resources to balance loads, and hence sustains their autonomy relative to the tool-level and user communities.

Once an enactment has activated a PE instance, it will hold resources allocated until it terminates. In a distributed system, it is important to ensure that these resources are eventually released. The normal release mechanism in DISPEL is a cascade of terminations driven by messages along connections.

A connection may have a finite or a continuous data stream, and these may be mixed within the enactment. When a PE instance determines that it has no more data for a connection, it should transmit *end-of-stream* (*EoS*) along that connection. When a PE instance has received an *EoS* on all of its inputs, it should

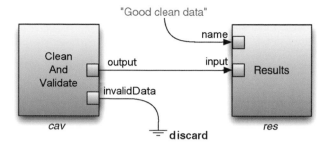

Figure 4.2 *Demonstration of connections for partitioned data.*

complete its processing, flush its outputs, transmit *EoS* on each of them, and then terminate.

When a PE instance determines that it does not need any more data from a particular input, it should transmit *No more Data* (*NmD*) back (i.e., in the reverse direction to the dataflow) along that connection. This should immediately stop the flow of data to that input. When all the destinations have signaled *NmD*, the source PE instance should stop generating output for that connection. When all its output connections have signaled "No more Data," the PE instance should organize the propagation of that message along all its input connections and then terminate.

There are standard connections to which an output can be connected: discard, errors, and warning.

```
1    Results res = new Results;
2    CleanAndValidate cav = new CleanAndValidate; //instance of CleanAndValidate
3    cav.output            => res.input;          //send clean data to Results
4    |- "Good clean data" -| => res.name;         //name those results
5    cav.invalidData       => discard;            //throw away uncleanable data
```

In the above fragment of DISPEL, line 3 would form a connection from the output of the PE instance cav to the input of the instance res. On line 4, it sets up a stream literal and provides that stream as an input to the res.name, and on line 5, it connects the output from cav.invalidData to discard. The operator => connects the output from the connection or stream expression on its left to the input of the connection on its right. The resulting graph is shown in Figure 4.2.

4.3 DATA STREAMS AND STRUCTURE

There are stream literal expressions for both finite and infinite streams. Line 4 in the preceding fragment of DISPEL illustrates an example of a *finite* stream with just one element of type String that will be delivered to a destination, such as res.name in this case. The symbols |- and -| denote start of stream and end of stream, respectively, in a stream literal. The expressions between these markers are the sequence of values delivered by the stream, the leftmost expression being the first to be delivered. For example,

```
|- "alpha", "beta", "delta", "gamma",  ... , "omega" -| => ape.input;
```

would deliver `"alpha"` and then `"beta"` and so on, up to `"omega"` to `ape.input`. The stream literal

```
|- repeat enough of "book.example.theDB" -|
```

denotes a continuous stream that supplies `"book.example.theDB"` as many times as it is needed.

As far as DISPEL is concerned, it is possible for any value to be transmitted along a connection, and any value that can be denoted in the DISPEL language to appear in a stream literal. This is deliberately open ended, as the potential values that may occur and their representations cannot be predicted. An implementation may choose any representation it wishes for the values as long as they are unchanged between transmission and receipt, and they must be delivered in the order they were transmitted. An implementation may have some practical limits on the transmittable values, but these should be minimized.

DISPEL provides *structural types* to describe a logical structure of the values that are passing through a connection or provided by a stream expression and *domain types* to describe the interpretation of those values in terms that are meaningful to the domain experts who use those values (Section 4.5).

The language DISPEL uses many traditional language constructs, such as `package` naming, the usual forms of iteration loops, conditional statements, block structures, and `case` statements. They replicate the Java syntax and semantics. As they are conventional, they are not described here but are in the reference manual [1].

4.4 FUNCTIONS

Functions in DISPEL provide a mechanism for algorithmically generating DISPEL graphs. This provides a number of benefits:

- A function can be used close to applications to parameterize a DISPEL request, for example, a tool or portal can solicit parameter values from domain experts for a frequently performed request. The request can then be formulated entirely as an expression applying the function with those parameters. This keeps the tool or portal interface stable, while other domain and data analysis experts, or data-intensive engineers, improve the function's implementation.

For example, a function getEarthquakes(region, after, before, magnitude) could provide access to a data-intensive process that consulted a number of databases and archives and delivered icons displayed on a map of the region denoting the earthquakes more powerful than magnitude in the period after to before with prepackaged drill-down data behind the icons. The seismologists maintaining this function could add or remove data sources, change the ways in which they deal with conflicting data in different sources, and revise the final transformation to geospatial data.

- A function can generate repetitive patterns, such as applying a graph of PEs to a number of data sources concurrently, before aggregating and digesting their combined output.

- Common patterns may be recognized and supported by functions that take PEs and other functions as parameters and generate graphs that implement those patterns. For example, a function that takes a data-mining classifier, Classifier, and an integer k could generate a k-fold cross-validation pattern that, given a supply of preclassified data, would divide it into k partitions and train the classifier on k − 1 of these, using each partition in turn as the remaining test set to evaluate the trained classifier. These evaluations would be fully parallel and then the resulting evaluations would be merged (Chapters 7 and 10).

Such pattern-generating functions enable developers to use patterns without cognizance of their implementation, while data-intensive engineers develop improved and alternative strategies for implementing these patterns. Some of these pattern implementations can be adaptive to the data being processed and to the available resources in the enactment context. For this reason, functions are evaluated after submission to a gateway, when the information for such decisions is available.

DISPEL developers can directly compose PEs to form graphs and then define them as composite PEs, which can be used in exactly the same way as other PEs. However, establishing functions to construct those graphs provides an encapsulated context for specifying and refining the decisions behind that assembly process. Therefore, composing and manipulating functions provides much greater opportunity for autonomous development and optimization than composing and manipulating composite PEs. Each of the expert categories will expect a repertoire of functions in the libraries that meets their common requirements. They will typically add new functions and improved versions of existing functions to this environment.

In the following section, these uses of functions are illustrated by showing the start of DISPEL function declarations and fragments of the kind of DISPEL process graph they produce. Chapter 10 provides information on how the bodies of such functions are written.

4.4.1   Examples of DISPEL Functions

In order to illustrate the use of functions, we return to the topic of supporting seismologists. Their functions also include selecting data from sources that contain *traces* from continuously recording seismometers, preparing that data by correcting for variations in instruments and trace-archiving arrangements by applying band-pass frequency filters and smoothing, and then correlating the traces from every pair of sensors (see Chapter 17 for a detailed description).

4.4.1.1 A Function Called from a Portal   The first example function wraps a process definition that will

1. select data from sources (list of URIs) for a specified period chosen by a seismologist,
2. preprocess those data into a standard form and with a specified derived signal,
3. perform an *all-meets-all* correlation of all the data obtained, and
4. store all the results with a user-specified name in a portal-specified store.

A portal or other tool might solicit these parameters and then submit the request. The declaration of this function would have the following form in DISPEL:

```
1  PE <Submittable> correlateAll (      //specify result must be like a Submittable PE
2    String[] dataSources;             //where to obtain seismic traces from
3    Time start, finish;               //the period for which traces are required
4    String resultsName )  {           //the name for these correlation results
5    ...  };
```

Line 1 indicates that the result must be a PE that complies with the PE type Submittable. Lines 2–4 declare the parameters. The implementation of correlateAll has been omitted. In a real version, there would be other parameters.

The request that the portal would send would take the form illustrated below: it is laid out to show the correspondence with the function's definition:

```
1  use book.examples.seismology.correlateAll;
2  submit new correlateAll(    //apply function and submit an instance of the PE it produces
3    new String[]{"uk.gov.bgs.northsea", "eu.org.orfeus.mediterranean"},
4    "20050101:000000", "20091231:235959",
5    "EuropeanPlateImage2005to2009sample1" );
```

Line 1 imports the previously defined correlateAll function, and line 2 makes an instance of the result of applying it (it produces a PE) and submits that instance for enactment. Line 3 identifies the data from two archives, line 4 selects a period of 5 years, and line 5 provides the name for the result data.

Figure 4.3 provides an example of the graph, with much detail suppressed, that might be generated by that submission and then enacted. The process element TracePreparer, which will be a composite process element set up by the seismology data experts, takes a stream of rules, specifying how to prepare the data

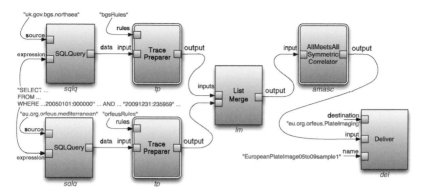

Figure 4.3 DISPEL process graph produced by correlateAll.

to accommodate the instrument and archival-storage variations. In a production system, these rules will be much more complex and will be stored in a database accessed by two more instances of SQLQuery so that the rules can be changed easily when a seismic archive changes its data representations or when the seismologists adopts new targets for the output of this step. The data destination will probably be specified by the portal provider so that results can be cached, for example, in a *data cart*, for inspection and later use.

4.4.1.2   The All-Meets-All Pattern
The correlator is a data-intensive and computational challenge—a great deal of data has to flow into it and out of it, and substantial computation is needed; for example, if there are 300 sensors in each region (600 in all), then there are $600 \times 600 \div 2$ pairs to be correlated. If there is one file per day, then each correlation processes two streams of 1725 files each and produces 1725 files, that is, 621,000,000 and 310,500,000 file writes, not to mention all the housekeeping and provenance tracking. Hence, this will be a focus of attention for data-intensive engineers, which we illustrate later in this chapter.

Over time, the detailed implementation of the correlateAll function would be steadily improved by the data analysis experts who are working with the domain experts, in this case, the seismologists. Those data analysis experts may use a function for organizing all-meets-all algorithms to generate the composite PE, AllMeetsAllSymmetricCorrelator. Such a function would be developed by data-intensive engineers and might have the following form—see Section 4.7 for further discussion:

```
PE <ListCombiner> makeAllMeetsAll (      //function that makes a PE like a ListCombiner
    Integer n;                            //Size of the matrix of ListCombiners
    PE <ListCombiner> TheCombiner;        //A PE that can perform the required correlation
    PE <ListCombiner> ResultAggregator;   //A PE to combine the results from each correlator
    ) {  ...   };
```

This function will produce a PE with two input streams, each containing lists of values in the expected form, that is, which satisfy the description of a ListCombiner (see Section 4.5). PEs with the type `ListCombiner` have an array of input connections and a single output connection. They take one list value from each input and combine them in some way—there will be many implementations with different semantics (three in this one fragment)—and yield a list on their output that represents that combination. They then repeat the process with the next set of inputs.

The function `makeAllMeetsAll` does this by making a graph that splits each of the input streams, so that each list value is divided into n sublists. It then constructs a graph to feed these sublists to a matrix of $n \times n$ instances of the PE supplied as the parameter `TheCombiner`. It will build a tree of instances of the `ResultAggregator` (assumed to combine just two inputs) to combine all the results from the n^2 instances of `TheCombiner`. This tree, `Agg`, will itself be built by a call to a tree-builder function, `makeMwayCombiner`, that has the following form:

```
PE <ListCombiner> makeMwayCombiner(Integer m, PE <ListCombiner> TheAgg) {  ...   };
```

The four functions, `correlateAll`, `makeAllMeetsAllSymmetricCorrelator`, `makeAllMeetsAll`, and `makeMwayCombiner`, illustrate the partitioning of the development effort to support the seismic-domain requirements. The data analysis experts would work closely with the seismologists to understand their requirements, data, working practices, and algorithms to refine the first two functions. The data-intensive engineers would hone the algorithms that perform the splits, so as to distribute data and computation optimally over available nodes (Section 4.7). This work by these engineers would be designed to be useful to a wide range of applications. Ineluctably, there would be discussion between the data analysis experts and the data-intensive engineers over the best form for functions delivering standard patterns and over the best performance attainable—DISPEL is designed to act as a vehicle for that discussion.

The output from the call

```
PE <ListCombiner> TestAMA = makeAllMeetsAll(3, TheComb, TheAgg);
```

is illustrated in Figure 4.4. The outer box is the composite PE generated by this call. It contains a `ListSplit` for each input, splitting each incoming list into three sublists. The sublists from the first input are fed to the first input of the comparators, `TheComb`, in each row, and the sublists from the second input are fed to the second input of each comparator in each column. All the outputs from comparators are fed to a tree of aggregators, `Agg`, which feeds the combined result to `output`. In this case, `Agg` would have been generated by a call of the form:

```
PE <ListCombiner> Agg = makeMwayCombiner(9, ResultAggregator);
```

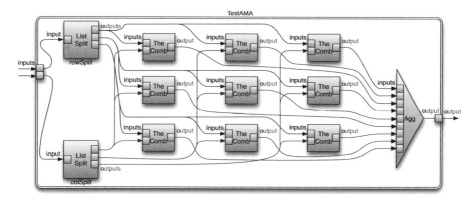

Figure 4.4   An all-meets-all graph from TestAMA = makeAllMeetsAll(3, ...).

4.4.1.3 Pattern Implementation   We now offer a glimpse of the implementation of a pattern by returning to the definition of correlateAll, which is an example of a self-join pattern with user-defined functions for the matching operation, SeismicTraceCorrelator, and for the result aggregator, SeismicResultStacker. It might contain the following DISPEL fragment:

```
1   Connection input;                    //single input for self-join autocorrelation
2   Integer matrixSize = 5;              // matrix is square of SeismicTraceCorrelators
3   ListCombiner theCorrelator = new makeAllMeetsAll(// make instance immediately
4     matrixSize,
5     ASeismicCorrelator,                //compares every pair of traces
6     ASeismicStacker );                 //assembles all correlations together
7   input => theCorrelator.inputs[0];    //feed input to both sides of the
8   input => theCorrelator.inputs[1];    //matrix of SeismicTraceCorrelators
```

This would build an AllMeetsAllSymmetricCorrelator and be a candidate implementation of makeAllMeetsAllSymmetricCorrelator. This, in turn, would be used in the implementation of correlateAll and uses the implementation of makeMwayCombiner shown in the preceding text, illustrating how they can all be revised independently. Figure 4.5 illustrates the graph that this DISPEL builds. Line 1 sets up the connection that will be the input data stream that receives a sequence of lists, each containing all the traces in a batch. In lines 7 and 8, these

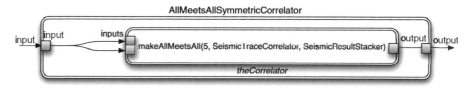

Figure 4.5   A functionally generated AllMeetsAllSymmetricCorrelator.

are fed to *both* the inputs of theCorrelator that was constructed in lines 3–6 to achieve the required "self-join" semantics. The implicit Tee to deliver the *one* input to *two* inputs has to ensure that the same sequence of values is delivered to each destination.

In Section 4.7, we look at how this might be optimized and how redundant comparisons can be avoided, before which some of the necessary machinery is introduced.

For those interested in the whole story, even though all the relevant DISPEL constructs have yet to be introduced, Figures 4.28–4.31, at the end of the chapter, show the implementations of makeMwayCombiner, makeAllMeetsAll, makeAll MeetsAllSymmetricCorrelator, and correlateAll functions, respectively.

4.5 THE THREE-LEVEL TYPE SYSTEM

Types are introduced for the usual reason of helping developers of data-intensive distributed processes get them correct. However, in DISPEL types are motivated by two other reasons: they act as a vehicle for extra descriptions of components and as a foundation for detecting and adapting to changes that might otherwise invalidate previously defined processes.

Three type systems are introduced, which serve three different purposes.

Language Types describe the allowed values in a DISPEL sentence so that consistency may be statically validated during compilation. This precedes evaluation of the sentence to generate the graph that represents the process and consequently precedes that process's enactment. These types, particularly those that define PE types, also provide the framework for other descriptions, including the other two categories of type.

Structural Types, introduced in DISPEL by the keyword Stype, define the structural composition and, therefore, the *logical format* of the data values in the stream passing through each connection. These are partially validated for consistency by traversing the graph produced during the DISPEL language-processing phase and propagating structural-type information. Dynamic checks and repairs may also be necessary because some operations generate outputs that have their type determined by incoming data; we call these *data-dependent types*. Delayed validation is also needed to accommodate *wild cards*: Any and rest, which are provided to accommodate change automatically and to permit applications to transmit private payloads. These dynamic checks are performed during execution by *validation PEs* inserted into the graph during the preceding enactment phases. The equivalence of structural types may be established by showing that the two structural-type expressions define the same set of values from which instances are drawn. Thus, the name of a structural type, though meaningful to a programmer, is not logically significant.

Domain Types, introduced in DISPEL by the keyword Dtype, also define the permitted set of values passing through a connection, but this time in terms that are pertinent to the domain experts. They capture the meaning of the data. Each application domain will have its own terms, often an agreed ontology, for that domain type.

Different domains may label the same information differently or use the same term with different meanings. The registry will store known relationships among domain types and these, in conjunction with information in referenced ontology sites, using the semantic Web and open linked data standards, will be used to partially validate the domain type consistency. This validation is achieved predominantly by traversing the graph produced during the DISPEL language-processing phase.

The same domain type may be represented by different structural types, for example, when recording water temperature, a TemperatureInDegreesCelsius might be represented by a Real or an Integer. Conversely, a given structural type will be used to represent a wide variety of domain types, for example, a Real may represent a TemperatureInDegreesKelvin or a RainfallInMetres. Domain types should include precision about their interpretation, for example, the units in use, and will be named according to the standard notations for the ontology.

Fragments of DISPEL illustrate the three type systems: first for each type category and then their combined use.

Examples of Language Types

```
1   Type Combiner is PE (              //define a PF type called Combiner
2     <Connection[ ] inputs> =>        //taking an array of inputs
3     <Connection output>              //producing one output
4   );
5   Type BinaryCombiner is Combiner with inputs.length = 2;    //only 2 inputs
6   Type SymmetricCombiner is Combiner with permutable inputs; //inputs interchangeable
```

Lines 1–4 define a language type called Combiner. All PEs that conform to Combiner have an array of input connections called inputs and a single output connection called output. Line 5 defines a subtype of Combiner that has exactly two inputs, while line 6 defines another subtype of Combiner that yields the same output irrespective of the order in which the data streams are connected to its inputs. Such descriptions allow optimizations in the handling of the PEs, as well as verification that they are being used correctly.

Examples of Structural Types   The following example illustrates how hypothetical data analysis experts supporting oceanographers might define a collection of structural types.

Line 1 uses the package construct to keep the identifiers used here from clashing with other identifiers. Lines 2–7 show how a tuple of Real values might be used to denote positions in three different frames of reference. The developers have naturally chosen identifiers, such as SphericalPosition and longitude to aid them in remembering how to interpret the data, but these identifiers are not "understood" by enactment systems, and so cannot substitute for domain types. Line 8 introduces the developers' own version of Time, hiding the default interpretation of Time provided ubiquitously by package dispel.lang, thereby arranging that the oceanographers'

```
1    package book.examples.oceanography { //illustrating Stype definitions
2      Stype Position is <Real x, y, z> with @description =
3        "A 3D rectilinear coordinate system with unknown origin, axes and units.";
4      Stype SphericalPosition is <Real radius, theta, phi> with @description =
5        "A spherical coordinate system with unknown origin, orientation and units.";
6      Stype GeoPosition is <Real latitude, longitude> with @description =
7        "A standard Earth-surface coordinate system with unspecified units.";
8      Stype Time is <Integer year, day; Real seconds> with @description =
9        "A time relative to some origin instant in unspecified units, "        +
10       "though the tuple-element names suggest units they are not actually " +
11       "formally specified.";
12     Stype Observation is <Time t; Geoposition p; Any measurement>
13       with @description =
14       "A three element tuple intended to denote an Earth surface observation.";
15     Stype ObservationTrack is [Observation] with @description =
16       "Sequence of Observation values denoting measurements taken along a path.";
17     Stype Survey is ObservationTrack[ ] with @description =
18       "An array of observation paths.";
19     register Position, SphericalPosition, GeoPosition,     //remember for future use
20            Time, Observation, ObservationTrack, Survey;
21   }
```

representation of `Time` is used in the definition of `Observation` on line 12. Line 15 defines an `ObservationTrack` as a list of values of type `Observation`, and line 17 defines a `Survey` as an array of values represented by `ObservationTrack`. Lines 19 and 20 arrange for all these structural types to be recorded in the registry. This example shows that values flowing along a data stream are potentially very large. Implementations have to handle such large data and there are two common options: the first is to use files for large values and to pass those values by passing the file names, relying on a shared file system or file transport protocols to actually move the data. The second is to stream a serialization of the value, embedding markers such as "start-row" and "end-row" to enable the structure to be reassembled, or passed on without reassembly, by PEs. The latter technique is used in our operational system.

A group of oceanographers and their data analysts would use widely adopted standard representations, such as NetCDF[1] or HDF5[2], to transmit data between their processes (Chapter 19). Consequently, a production version of data-intensive architecture would need support for such standards, with the ability to transfer and access them without unnecessary copying or data transformations. Similarly, emerging standards from the Open Geospatial Consortium (OGC)[3] would influence the form of structures such as `Observation`, and if they were working in Europe on a governmental project, they would also adopt the current set of INSPIRE directive standards (inspire.jrc.ec.europa.eu).

---

[1]www.unidata.ucar.edu/software/netcdf
[2]www.hdfgroup.org/HDF5
[3]www.opengeospatial.org

Examples of Domain Types The use of domain types is illustrated with examples that data analysis experts might set up to support brain-imaging domain experts studying or diagnosing the effects of stroke or the precursors of psychological disorders.

```
1    package book.examples.brainimaging {      //defining some domain types
2                                                //prefix short form nci refers to authority site
3    namespace nci "http://ncicb.nci.nih.gov/xml/owl/EVS/Thesaurus.owl#";
4
5    // These Dtypes are needed below, so get them from the registry.
6    use book.examples.brainimaging.{Depth, Settings};
7
8    Dtype Identifier represents "nci:Subject_Identifier"      //pseudomised identifier
9      with @description = "Encrypted secure two-way map human <-> med. record";
10   Dtype MedicalImage is Pixel[ ][ ] represents "nci:Medical_Image" //2D Pixel array
11      with @description = "Slice of image from any instrument";
12   Dtype Scan is <Time t; Depth d; Settings s; MedicalImage im>
13                          represents "nci:Scan"   //layer
14      with @description = "MedicalImage with instrument details and settings";
15   Dtype BrainScan is Scan[ ] represents "nci:Brain_Scan"    //stack of layers
16      with @description = "Stack of Scan allowing time lapse and setting changes";
17   Dtype LongitudinalStudy is [BrainScan]              //sequence of scans
18      with @description = "Repeated BrainScans of same individual anonymous";
19   Dtype CohortStudy is Set(<Identifier id; LongitudinalStudy ls>)
20      with @description =
21        "Set of subjects as LongitudinalStudy with privacy-protecting linkage id";
22   register CohortStudy;                        //save all of these for future use
23   }
```

A Dtype declaration introduces an identifier for the new domain type; it may then define that domain type in terms of other domain types and record how that internal identifier relates to external, often standard, terminology. Both kinds of definition are illustrated in the DISPEL example above. Line 3 introduces a short name, nci, for the longer prefix that shows where the externally referenced ontology is defined, and hence how to expand the identifiers such as Medical_Image into a full URI. Line 6 imports previously registered domain types. In addition, Pixel and Time are implicitly imported, as they are standard in DISPEL. When they are used, on lines 10 and 12, the context requires a domain type that is automatically substituted. Line 8 introduces Identifier into the DISPEL contexts and then records that it has the same meaning as Subject_Identifier in the referenced ontology. This mechanism enables the maintenance of relationships between external elements of the digital-data ecosystem, such as the Open Linked Data initiative (linkeddata.org), and the DISPEL specified processes. The arrangement for inward references to DISPEL domain types is described in the following text.

Line 10 introduces MedicalImage and defines it as a two-dimensional array of Pixel values. It also states that this concept represents the concept denoted by Medical_Image in the reference ontology. Lines 12–21 define Scan, BrainScan, LongitudinalStudy, and CohortStudy; the first two are a tuple structure and an array of other domain types, and represent two externally defined constructs. In contrast, the final two domain types are not mapped to external concepts.

The registration of `CohortStudy` on line 22 actually makes all these domain types available for future use, because when it is recorded in the registry, all the new definitions on which it depends are automatically preserved—this registration of all definitions on which a registered item depends spans the three type categories.

The registry also automatically constructs ontological URIs for each registered domain type, to enable inward reference to DISPEL defined concepts. Each URI is generated with the following pattern:

```
http://dispel-lang.org/resource/⟨package name⟩/⟨identifier⟩
```

where `http://dispel-lang.org/resource/` is the site of the DISPEL reference ontology; ⟨package name⟩ is a simple transformation of a package name, where each dot is replaced by a forward slash; and ⟨identifier⟩ is the identifier that has been registered. So in this case, `CohortStudy` would have the URI

```
http://dispel-lang.org/resource/book/examples/brainimaging/CohortStudy
```

As in the oceanographic case, a production version would need to accommodate the medical standard image formats, such as DICOM.[4] Similarly, the treatment necessary to achieve adequate privacy protection for subjects would need to be much more rigorous, as described by Rodríguez et al. [2].

Examples of Combining the Type Systems We now show the use of these types in combination by revising definitions of some PEs mentioned earlier. First, a type definition of the PE `SQLQuery`.

```
1    namespace db "http://dispel-lang.org/resources/dispel/db/";
2    Type SQLQuery is PE (          //a PE to apply a stream of queries to stream of DBs
3      <Connection locator terminator: String:: "db:DBURI" source;  //identifies each DB
4       Connection terminator: String:: "db:SQLQueryStatement" expression> => // query
5      <Connection: [<rest>]:: "db:TupleRowSet" data>          //results as lists of tuples
6    ) with lockstep(source, expression),         //a source required for each expression
7          rate(expression) = rate(data),       //a result list produced for each expression
8       @description =
9       "For each SQL query statement arriving on expression, SQLQuery "  +
10      "sends a query to the DB specified by source.  The result is "   +
11      "emitted as a list of tuples (possibly empty) on data.  It is "  +
12      "helpful to specify the Stype (and Dtype) of data if it is "     +
13      "predictable with an assertion against the new expression.";
```

Here, line 1 introduces an ontology for describing databases; line 2 starts the definition of the language type `SQLQuery`, where lines 3 and 4 define the input streams as a tuple of connections; and line 5 defines the one output stream, again as a tuple of connections; the `=>` separates the inputs from the outputs. The two input

---

[4] medical.nema.org

streams both have the structural type `String`, but they have different domain types: `source` is required to be a URI that refers to a database, and `expression` is an SQL query statement. The structural type of values on the result stream, `data`, have the structural type list of tuples, where `rest` permits any set of Stype, identifier pairs; as the contents of the tuple depends on the query and the schema. The domain type indicates that this is a relational result set. The *modifier* `lockstep` on line 6 indicates that the PE being described consumes a value on each of the inputs in the following list and processes them before consuming another value. Hence, here it states that each time `SQLQuery` consumes a value on `source`, it also consumes a value on `expression`; whereas, line 7 states that each time those values are read, a corresponding value, that is, list of tuples, is emitted on `data`. Lines 8–13 record a description that is held in the repository. It can be read when browsing the repository and can be displayed by tools offering `SQLQuery` for use.

The modifier `locator` indicates that analysis of values on this data stream may indicate where to place instances during optimization and deployment, and `terminator` indicates that this PE should stop when it receives an end-of-stream marker (*EoS*) on this input rather than waiting for *EoS* on all inputs. Developments in data-intensive engineering should seek to improve the quality of PE descriptions, so that the enactment phases can be better automated. However, a more precise description of the output data stream, `data`, cannot be achieved in the PE-type definition; it can, however, be refined by a tool or by a programmer with an assertion when an instance of `SQLQuery` is created, as illustrated below.

```
SQLQuery sq = new SQLQuery with data: //instance to get locations of seismic traces
    [<String fileStoreURI, filePath; Integer segmentStart, segmentLength>]::
    "seis:TraceFileSegments";
```

Here, the tuples in the list each have four elements, and these are to be interpreted as a list of segments to be extracted from the specified files.

Structural and Domain Type Propagation

Further information is needed to support the propagation of structural and domain types along the DISPEL graphs during validation; this is illustrated in the following examples.

Here, when defining the language type of `Split`, line 2 introduces a structural type, `ST`, that is a subtype of `Any` (i.e., any structural type), and line 3 introduces a similarly wide-ranging domain type. These are used in lines 4 and 5 to show that all the data streams in `outputs` have the same structural and domain types, which are the structural and domain types of the values flowing in on `input`, that is, it specifies that PEs of type `Split` leave the values that pass through them with their structural and domain types unchanged. Line 6 shows that the number of values is preserved.

Similarly, `ListSplit` is defined to take in lists of values of some structural and domain types via `input` and to emit lists containing the *same* values with the *same* structural and domain types. Both `Split` and `ListSplit` are used to divide incoming data so that it can be processed in parallel; they differ in that

```
1    Type Split is PE (        //distributes its input stream over the outputs
2      Stype ST is Any;                  //Stype of the input and outputs
3      Dtype DT is Thing;                //Dtype of the input and outputs
4      <Connection: ST:: DT input> =>   //input connection has some ST and DT
5      <Connection[ ]: ST:: DT outputs>  //all outputs have that ST and DT
6    ) with rate(input) = rate(sum(outputs[i])), //all values sent to 1 output
7        @description =
8          "Instances of Split distribute the values arriving on input across the " +
9          "array of connections, outputs. The distribution is implementation "    +
10         "determined, e.g. round-robin, random or responsive-to-demand."
11   ;
12   Type ListSplit is PE (   //distributes the values in each input list over outputs
13     Stype ST is Any;                  //Stype of the input and outputs
14     Dtype DT is Thing;                //Dtype of the input and outputs
15     <Connection: [ST]:: [DT] input> =>   //input has some [ST] and [DT]
16     <Connection[ ]: [ST]:: [DT] outputs> //outputs all have that [ST] and [DT]
17   ) with rate(input) = rate(outputs[i]), //1 list in implies 1 list on each output
18       listLength(input) = sum(listLength(output[i])), //no elements lost
19       @description =
20         "Instances of ListSplit distribute the elements of each list arriving " +
21         "on input across the array of connections, outputs. There is one list " +
22         "on each output per input list. The distribution is implementation "    +
23         "determined, e.g. round-robin, random or responsive-to-demand."
24   ;
```

Split distributes whatever values arrive across its outputs without utilizing their internal structure, whereas ListSplit requires that the incoming values have a list structure, and then uses that structure to distribute the values within the list, as illustrated in Figure 4.6. The interplay between structural and language types is necessary to capture these different semantics. Data-intensive engineers will provide a variety of implementations, for example, random, round robin, and responding to consumption rates, for such critical data-partitioning processing-element types, as they are the basis for distributing work within a data-intensive process. They should provide load distribution PEs for each of the Stype constructors and the corresponding PEs to reassemble data.

The next two fragments of DISPEL provide two more PE definitions to demonstrate more aspects of type transmission.

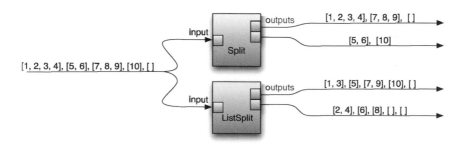

Figure 4.6 *Two forms of data-stream splitters.*

```
Type ListMerge is PE ( //Merge lists co-arriving on array of inputs and emit result on output
   Stype ST is Any;                             //Stype of the list elements
   Dtype DT is Thing;                           //Dtype of the list elements
   <Connection[ ]: [ST]:: [DT] inputs> =>       //Array of inputs each taking lists [ST]::[DT]
   <Connection: [ST]:: [DT] output>             //stream of lists [ST]::[DT]
) with lockstep(inputs[i]),                      //i implicitly iterates
     rate(inputs[i]) = rate(output),             //a list from each i forms 1 result list
     sum(listLength(inputs[i])) = listLength(output),  //all elements of lists preserved
     @description =
        "ListMerge takes a stream of lists in each inputs[i] and merges the "    +
        "lists that arrive together, copying unchanged the values from "         +
        "within the inputs[i] lists to form one output list for each "           +
        "co-arriving set of input lists. I.E. when all of inputs[i] are "        +
        "active, the first list from each inputs[i] are merged into one list. "  +
        "This repeats until an inputs[i] delivers EoS. Thereafter the "          +
        "remaining connections are merged, and so on, until all inputs "         +
        "have delivered EoS.  Of course, an NmD on output could stop "           +
        "processing earlier."
;
```

```
Type ListCombiner is PE ( //Combine lists co-arriving on array inputs, emit result on output
   Stype ST is Any;                             //Stype of the list elements
   Dtype DT is Thing;                           //Dtype of the list elements
   <Connection[ ]: [ST]:: [DT] inputs> =>       //array of inputs each taking lists [ST]::[DT]
   <Connection: [Any]:: [Thing] output>         //elements of unpredicted Stype and Dtype
) with lockstep(inputs[i]),                      //get a list from each active input
     rate(inputs[i]) = rate(output),             //and produce 1 result list from it
     @description =
        "ListCombiner takes the first list off each inputs[i] and combines the " +
        "elements of these lists to generate a list emitted on output."
;
```

Here, we see `ListMerge` is required to have `inputs` that have consistent structural and domain types and that it yields lists with those types on `output`. In contrast, the `ListCombiner` processing-element type also requires that all its inputs are of a consistent structural and domain type but places no constraints on the types of the elements of the lists emitted along `output`. Figure 4.7 illustrates this variation.

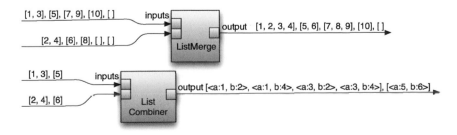

Figure 4.7 *Two forms of data-stream combiners.*

PEs compliant with type `ListMerge` can be safely used, where a PE compliant with `ListCombiner` is required. However, a PE where we only know it is compliant with `ListCombiner` cannot be used where a `ListMerge` is required, as it does not satisfy the structural and domain type propagation rules required. We say that `ListMerge` is a *subtype* of `ListCombiner` to describe the first relationship and that `ListCombiner` is *not a subtype* of `ListMerge` to describe the second relationship.

The actual PE shown in panel (b) of Figure 4.7 could be described more precisely by the `AllConsistentPairs` in the following DISPEL text; readers are referred to the full definitions in Appendix C for a yet more precise definition.

```
Type AllConsistentPairs is ListCombiner (       //Form list of all pairs from each pair
   Stype ST is Any; Dtype DT is Thing;          //of co-arriving lists
   <Connection[ ]: [ST]:: [DT] inputs>    =>    //with elements of types ST::DT
   <Connection: [<ST:: DT a, b>] output>        //producing lists of tuples of all pairs
   with inputs.length=2                         //constrain to two inputs
);
Type AllPairs is PE (                            //Form list of all pairs allowing
   Stype ST1, ST2 is Any; Dtype DT1, DT2 is Thing; //different element types in each list
   <Connection: [ST1]:: [DT1] input1;           //input1 has element types ST1:: DT1
    Connection: [ST2]:: [DT2] input2 >    =>     //input2 has element types ST2:: DT2
   <Connection: [<ST1:: DT1 a; ST2:: DT2 b>] output> //output lists of all pairs
);
Type AllIntegerPairs is PE (                     //Form list of all pairs of integers
   Dtype DT1, DT2 is Thing;                      //from co-arriving lists
   <Connection: [Integer]:: [DT1] input1;        //input1 element types Integer:: DT1
    Connection: [Integer]:: [DT2] input2 >   =>  //input2 element types Integer:: DT2
   <Connection: [<Integer:: DT1 a; Integer:: DT2 b>] output> //output lists of all pairs
```

Hence `AllConsistentPairs` is a subtype of `ListCombiner`. The other two PE type declarations describe similar, but not precisely the same, semantics. They name their inputs differently, and they allow different Stypes and Dtypes on their two input streams and specify how they combine in the output stream. These cannot be used anywhere `ListCombiner` is required, unless an assertion further constrains their behavior. Hence, they are not subtypes of `ListCombiner`. The processing-element type `AllIntegerPairs` has a particular Stype for each input, consistent with the Stypes in `AllPairs`. It is *not* a subtype of `AllPairs`, as it is more restrictive on its inputs, so if it were substituted in a location where `AllPairs` was valid but where the inputs were not of Stype `Integer`, an error would occur. Note that `AllIntegerPairs` allows its Dtypes to differ.

By establishing well-described processing-element types, including more of their properties than shown here, data-intensive engineers can inform the consumers of their products and services (data analysis and domain experts) of the PEs that handle the types they may use, validate DISPEL programs and the graphs they produce, and have information that is necessary for enacting and optimizing DISPEL requests. Later in this book, the reader will encounter further refinements of the notation for describing the behavior of PEs. This is a continuing endeavor to find a context-independent way of capturing knowledge about the PEs that can be used by developers, tools, and enactment. Nevertheless, this will never be a complete description. Their encapsulated algorithm has to be defined; either in terms of other DISPEL components or in another language. It is beneficial to automatically derive properties of these implementation algorithms, though this is not yet widely available, as the DISPEL system has to accommodate an open-ended set of processing-element implementation languages. Where they can be derived, such automatically inferred properties should be compared with any programmer-specified properties and recorded to save DISPEL programmers, the effort of providing all specification details.

The three type categories assist in allowing independent innovation that can be bound together by specific and localized mappings. The package-based and ontology-prefix mechanisms allow contemporaneous independent work with minimal risk of name clashes. The ontology prefix establishes links with the contemporaneous developments in any external, Internet accessible context. The automated URI generation similarly permits inward reference from these contexts to the DISPEL world. Such openness to interconnection is necessary for Web-scale distribution and for incremental introduction—a technological ramp!

4.6   REGISTRY, LIBRARIES, AND DESCRIPTIONS

The registry has three primary functions concerning information about DISPEL components:

1. Provision of persistent storage for any information about those components
2. Communication between the tools used for development and the subsystems implementing gateways and enactment
3. Communication and encouragement of sharing across the various communities creating and using data-intensive methods.

Uses of the Registry   Figure 4.8 shows the primary uses of the registry. It shows four workbenches, each comprising a collection of tools, including those

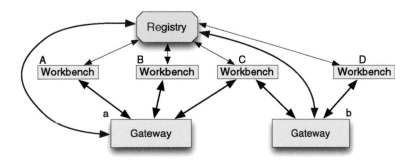

Figure 4.8   *The principal interactions with the registry.*

needed to browse and manage the registry's content (Chapter 11). Those tools interact with the registry to obtain descriptions of components. For example, a tool assisting a developer may send queries to retrieve descriptions of all the PEs that are capable of performing a specific transformation or analysis. Workers using the workbenches may directly edit information in the registry. For example, they may add information about their experiences using a PE. The interaction between tools in a workbench and the registry enables geographically dispersed workers at different workbenches to have their own tailored view and yet to share up-to-date information about the currently available DISPEL components and the logical computational context. For example, workbenches A and D are being used by two groups of domain experts. Workbench B is being used by Data analysis experts working with the domain experts using A. While workbench C may be supporting data-intensive engineers provisioning both application domains and the data analysis experts. The data-intensive engineers may also use the registry to contribute libraries of widely used or carefully tuned components and to share information about the physical computational context.

Use of the Registry by Workbenches   When users at any of the workbenches ask a tool to run a DISPEL request, it will be submitted to a gateway for processing and the gateway will return a response. During the processing of each DISPEL request (Chapter 12), the enactment subsystems will make requests to the registry: first, to verify that the request is consistent with all the relevant definitions in the registry, for example, to check that all items imported in `use` statements are defined and to collect those definitions to guide further processing; second, to obtain any components that it does not yet have. This means that the request is enacted in a way that is consistent with the information its originators used and that all the distributed parts of the platform needing these components load consistent versions. When new components are defined during the enactment, they may be registered in the registry using the `register` statement as shown below.

```
register makeAllMeetsAll, ListCombiner, Survey, CohortStudy;
```

This illustrates that all categories of DISPEL components can be registered; those in the example were defined in DISPEL examples in the preceding sections. During this statement, the DISPEL processor submits a description to the registry of each component and of any other unregistered components on which it depends. The gateways' interactions with the registry include enquiries to the registry to obtain relevant parts of the stored component descriptions, for example, when performing `use` statements or when checking for type consistency in a DISPEL graph.

Annotation of Components in the Registry Developers may add further
information to be saved with the registered components, as illustrated in the following DISPEL fragment.

```
register AllPairs with @creator = "Oscar Corcho", @organisation = "es.upm",
  @description =
  "Takes lists on two streams and generates a lexically ordered list of "   +
  "tuples with all of the elements from input1 as element a of a tuple and " +
  "all of the elements from input2 as element b of a tuple. The first "     +
  "element of input1's list will be paired with all of the elements from "  +
  "input2's list and then the next element of list 1 will be processed "    +
  "until all pairs have been generated. NB the size of the output list "    +
  "is the product of the sizes of the pair of input lists. AllPairs "       +
  "will then process the next pair of lists.";
```

In this case, we see that the @key = String expressions have been used to add
a creator, that is, creator's organization, and a short description of the PE being
registered. The same effect can be obtained by adding annotations when defining a
DISPEL element and then registering that element, as illustrated by the following
DISPEL.

```
Type AllPairs is PE (                            //Form list of all pairs allowing
  Stype ST1, ST2 is Any; Dtype DT1, DT2 is Thing; //different element types in each list
  <Connection: [ST1]:: [DT1] input1;             //input1 has element types ST1:: DT1
   Connection: [ST2]:: [DT2] input2 >   =>        //input2 has element types ST2:: DT2
   <Connection: [<ST1:: DT1 a; ST2:: DT2 b>] output> //output lists of all pairs
) with                                           //annotate with
    @creator = "Oscar Corcho",                   //authorship as per Dublin Core
    @organisation = "es.upm",                    //author's organisation
    @description =                               //and short description
    "Takes lists on two streams and generates a lexically ordered list of " +
    "tuples with all of the elements from input1 as element a of a tuple "  +
    "and all of the elements from input2 as element b of a tuple. "         +
    "The first element of input1's list will be paired with all of the "    +
    "elements from input2's list and then the next element of list 1 will " +
    "be processed until all pairs have been generated. NB the size of the " +
    "output list is the product of the sizes of the pair of input lists. "  +
    "AllPairs then processes the next pair of lists."
;
register AllPairs;
```

In order to effectively support collaborative behavior among subgroups within a
community that is working together, but protect them from distracting information
generated by other subgroups, it is necessary to provide controlled access, proper
attribution of contributions, clearly recorded provenance, and selective viewing of
the shared material. Strategies for addressing such requirements are exemplified by
myExperiment [3]. The ideas have been translated to the data-intensive platform
by providing a Web-based platform on top of the registry, which allows selection
and viewing using user-defined tags. Communities can organize their components

using tags consistently. For instance, seismologists may tag all their items with *seismology* and slowly introduce more tags to organize collaboratively their components, as their libraries become bigger, adding tags such as *BGS*, *ORFEUS*, and *VERCE*.[5] Furthermore, researchers may annotate the components with comments on the quality of results the components produce, on limits of their application, or give their endorsement to components that prove satisfactory. Automated tagging may record how much and where components are used.

Information in the Registry   To meet both the human and system needs, many aspects of each component are recorded. This is illustrated by showing some of the information that is recorded about each PE as follows:

1. a unique name made unique through the `package` naming system;
2. a short description, so that tools can tell users what they do;
3. an ontology-based classification of their purpose;
4. a precise description of their input and output connections;
5. the consistency and propagation rules for Stypes and Dtypes;
6. their known relationships in the subtype hierarchy;
7. their patterns of data consumption and production;
8. their termination behavior and error modes;
9. information useful for placing instances and optimizing enactment (Chapter 12).
10. information about version relationships that may be used by automated change adapters.

These 10 items are the tip of the descriptive iceberg, as they each require detail, for example, of the relationships between all the types mentioned and the representations used. As another example that each of the tools on the workbench in Figure 4.9 would use is the classification ontology to make recommendations to domain experts and would require data describing graphical presentations, for example, the image to use for display and the attachment points for connections and to support data analysis experts. Similarly, tools that were supporting data-intensive engineers would offer information about performance and past behavior of components.

The other architectural details of workbenches shown in Figure 4.9 and their interactions with the registry are discussed in Part III.

Libraries and Packages   Much of the power of any language comes from the libraries of components that have been carefully designed to cover common requirements. Good libraries also insulate developers and workflows (here DISPEL requests) from the particular idiosyncrasies of the current computing context.

---

[5]Referring to www.bgs.ac.uk, www.orfeus-eu.org and www.verce.eu respectively.

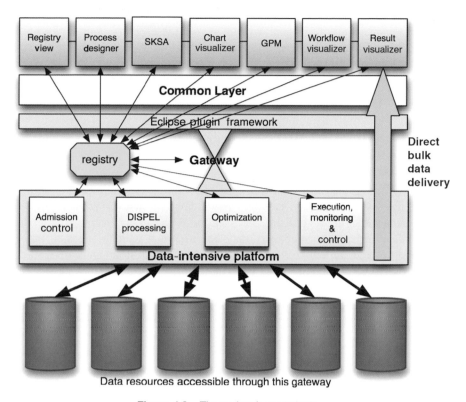

Figure 4.9 *The registry's central role.*

One of the roles of the registry is to describe these libraries, capturing and presenting the clustering of components that are intended to work together, describing the overall purpose of each library, and delivering an intellectual ramp that will enable users to incrementally discover, explore, and master the libraries and their components. As with all such ramps, it is crucial that users are encouraged to discover each facility—just when they first need it—in whatever order their work imposes. As users acquire islands of knowledge from using parts of several libraries, they need information about other components that relate to what they know and help finding out how to use these in conjunction with their existing work. The tools for browsing the registry and for composing DISPEL requests will submit queries to the registry to discover suggestions of alternative, related, or compatible components, in order to facilitate each users' incremental acquisition of knowledge about data-intensive knowledge discovery processes (Chapter 7).

An important category of library is those that interface with existing facilities and provide interoperability with contemporaneous work by other communities. For example, many data-intensive workers will need access to collections of algorithms, such as the linear algebra package, LAPACK,[6] and a statistical package such as R.[7] The achievements, skills, and investments of these other communities are an essential ingredient; consequently, efficient bridges to their work must be made available from any data-intensive platform. These intercommunity bridges will be accessed via specific libraries and will depend on carefully engineered underpinning to cross-call and exchange data with their software.

4.7 ACHIEVING DATA-INTENSIVE PERFORMANCE

Many data-intensive application goals are hard to achieve because of the combined complexity of the data and their analysis; this complexity may derive from the phenomena that generate data, from the historic and regional variations of data collection, from satisfying diverse uses, or from the desire to discover and understand very subtle effects. This complexity may be combined with the need to process very large volumes of data, for example, to expose very infrequent but significant events in a crowd of mundane ones or to gain sufficient statistical evidence.

The ability to partition the invention and description of data-intensive processes illustrated above is a key to addressing this complexity. However, it is all for nothing if the target data-intensive platform cannot economically enact these processes sufficiently quickly. There is, therefore, considerable pressure to consider efficiency issues. This section introduces some of the engineering strategies for achieving efficiency; they fall into three groups:

1. the implementation of data-intensive platforms,
2. the specification and implementation of data-intensive components, and
3. the choices made when composing components.

These topics are briefly reviewed to show their scope; they are revisited later in this book, and as Chapter 23 reports, are the subject of much ongoing research. Performance may be measured in different ways: for example, getting an answer as quickly as possible, running a sustained data-intensive workload with minimum energy, or getting the best answer possible for a fixed cost [4]. In whatever manner performance issues are framed, the following desiderata will be relevant.

4.7.1 Efficient Data-Intensive Platforms

4.7.1.1 Balanced Data-Intensive Hardware   A data-intensive platform has to be shaped to match its data-intensive workloads, as Jim Gray and Alex Szalay recognized [5] when designing GrayWulf [6] shown in Figure 4.10. They recalled Amdahl's laws for obtaining a balanced hardware architecture, where the goal is to balance the rate of data transfers with the rate of computation, so that *for the typical*

[6]www.netlib.org/lapack
[7]www.r-project.org

Figure 4.10   *GrayWulf: A data-intensive machine.*

anticipated workload, the data-transfer bandwidths, the memory capacity, and the CPU all reach maximum capacity at the same time. Putting this another way, none of the major components should sit idle while waiting for another component to deliver its part of the work. Amdahl's laws characterize that balance in terms of Amdahl numbers with definitions such that the ideal values are close to 1.0. For example, in order that processors are not starved of data and can also save results as fast as they produce them, Amdahl required 1 bit of I/O per CPU cycle; that is, an Amdahl number of 1.0 for the ratio of I/O bandwidth to CPU power.

In practice, by 2005, the Amdahl number had fallen to very much less than 1.0 in typical commodity or high performance systems,[8] as shown in Table 4.2 taken from [6]. This was generating problems for delivering the query workload against the Sloan Digital Sky Survey [7]; analysis showed that for most of the time processors were idle but consuming power while waiting for data. Hence, Szalay and Gray were motivated to design and build GrayWulf using commodity components.

The GrayWulf example is just one particular strategy to dealing with one of the aspects of achieving a balanced architecture. At the time of GrayWulf, eBay was achieving an Amdahl I/O ratio of 0.8, probably by investing in much more expensive storage systems, whereas Google was addressing that challenge by having a massively distributed system, so that key indexes and hot data were already memory resident.

---

[8]SC1 and SC2 were chosen from the SuperComputing top 500 list of the day.

TABLE 4.2   Comparing Current Amdahl Input/Output Ratios[a]

System	CPU Count	GIPS	Disk I/O [MB/s]	Amdahl I/O Ratio
GrayWulf	416	1,107	70,000	0.506
Beowulf	100	300	3,000	0.08
Desktop	2	6	150	0.2
Cloud VM	1	3	30	0.08
SC1	212,992	150,000	16,900	0.001
SC2	2,090	5,000	4,700	0.008

[a] After [6].

4.7.1.2 *Data-Intensive Software*

The next critical platform issue is adapting software to obtain data-intensive performance; examples of some key strategies appear as follows:

- Minimize data copying and translation, as they gobble scarce memory bandwidth. This has implications for operating systems, device drivers, file systems, and database systems. It is particularly difficult to achieve while implementing the bridges between different software communities' algorithm libraries.
- Reduce and localize data transport, for example, move data-reducing operations close to data sources, compress data for long-haul movement and storage, eliminate unnecessary data from transfers, and once data have been moved to a processor, apply multiple operations to them.
- Eliminate unnecessary data operations, for example, when loading scientific data into a database, switch off transactional mechanisms, as the data remains available to complete the installation after a failure. It would be better still to leave data where they are and map their file structures into the database or other data-intensive context.
- Use heterogeneous processors and storage devices and carefully deploy different operations to the variant to which they are best suited.
- Cache data in local RAM or disks, and cache intermediary results, so that data movement and reprocessing are avoided.
- Replicate data and distribute operations to share the load and parallelize data processing and transport.
- Incorporate into the data models' types of data, for example, arrays and structured files that are required by the existing external systems or established working practices.

Modern data-intensive platforms employ carefully optimized combinations of such techniques. Some of the techniques are in conflict, for example, minimizing data translation and compressing data. Consequently, data-intensive engineers have to measure systems and workloads—a data-intensive task in its own right—in order to optimize. There are many aspects of the system to consider, such as capital and operational costs, speed of response, throughput, energy consumption, data capacity, and computational power. Giving these different relative priorities leads to significantly different data-intensive platforms.

4.7.1.3   *Example Data-Intensive Platforms*

Examples that illustrate the variety of data-intensive applications and platforms appear in Parts III, V, and VI of this book. They include the accommodation of arrays and directly mapped files in SQL-Server and SciDB (www.scidb.org), the use of column storage in MonetDB (monetdb.cwi.nl) to deliver data directly from files in the formats that computational components require, the subtle forms of data splitting to achieve fast array processing in RASDAMAN [8], the exploitation of Cloud architectures in the Open Science Data Cloud [9], the use of Microsoft Azure to implement the Excel Data Scope introduced in Section 3.10, and the Microsoft SQL Server Parallel Data Warehouse, which also exploits Azure.[9]

4.7.1.4   *Automated Optimization Strategies*

Once a request for the enactment of a data-intensive process has been received, it has to be transformed and mapped to selected parts of the data-intensive platform. This involves analyzing the request and determining whether it can be run, whether it is best run on the local platform, or better delegated to another, or whether it should be partitioned and each part delegated to platforms that better matches its balance of resource requirements. These transformation and optimization tasks are based on four sources of data:

1. Descriptions of the components that were developed as they were created; these were illustrated in Section 4.5
2. Information gathered about the behavior of the components from previous enactments—see Chapter 12
3. Descriptions of the available hardware and software elements comprising the data-intensive platform
4. Annotation provided by the author of an enactment request or by tools that have manipulated it.

The goal of data-intensive engineering is to improve the quality of optimization by fully automated processes. At present, in many spheres of data-intensive work, the optimization is achieved by the authors of the request adding a great deal of detail in order to handcraft the mapping to the platform. This will continue in a few special cases, such as when pioneering development of a new data-intensive platforms or when preparing a data-intensive process that is already extremely demanding but has to be run very frequently, so the investment in skilled labor for their construction and maintenance is warranted. In the majority of cases, that handcrafting approach has to be replaced by automation for the following reasons:

[9]www.microsoft.com/sqlserver/2008/en/us/parallel-data-warehouse.aspx

- There is little chance of sufficient numbers of people being able to develop the necessary knowledge and skills.
- The complexities of a data-intensive platform may be concealed for commercial reasons.
- The investment in hand tuning is usually made at the start of an application's life for its *initial* target platform, and then, as the choice of platform changes and as the platforms evolve, what was once an optimization becomes a pessimization—reoptimization by hand is difficult and rare.

With *dynamic* automated optimization, that is, optimization that takes place at the start of or during an enactment, it is potentially feasible to respond to contemporaneous workloads to minimize conflict for scarce resources and to adjust plans when platform components do not perform as expected.

Chapter 12 illustrates one strategy for achieving this automation. In the context of databases, years of research and development has shown that translation from query requests to optimized query plans can be automated very effectively. Today's query optimizers produce far better mappings than handcrafted optimization, partly because they can exploit complex platforms and can gather operational statistics, and partly because they achieve the separation noted as necessary above. In many cases, for example, PostgreSQL (www.postgresql.org), SQL Server, MonetDB, and SciDB, they accommodate *user-defined functions* and so provide a framework for open-ended sets of types and operations. It is an open question whether continuing to build on the database experience will be the best route to automated optimization—it has a head start compared with strategies based on optimizing MapReduce or workflows [10]. Whatever the route, it has to yield an open-ended architecture, so that the many contemporaneous technologies, valuable legacy investments, such as data archives and established code suites, and large numbers of new data types, formats, and algorithms can be brought into the framework. This will require innovation in digital bridge building—efficient, flexible links between independent systems with adequate descriptions of the externally linked systems.

Reliability and availability (always on) also have to be provided by the data-intensive platform. For short-running enactments, replication of data and servers, which are then used for retries after a failure, delivers much of what is needed. Even in these cases, care has to be taken to clear up after a failed enactment. This will include making certain space reserved for data and intermediate results are recycled, and that metadata, such as provenance records, are left in a tidy and consistent state. When long-running enactments are required, it is desirable when recovering from a failure to use as much as possible of the work that has been accomplished. This is often implemented by recording provenance data incrementally, and then using that to shape the resumption request.

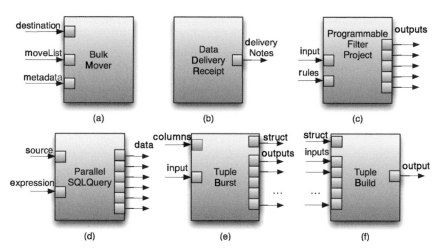

Figure 4.11 Examples of enhanced process elements described in Table 4.3.

4.7.2 Efficient Data-Intensive Components

The performance achievable by optimally mapping data-intensive requests to a platform is limited by the quality of the components it uses. The following list gives some categories of enhanced data-intensive components, Figure 4.11 illustrates some of these, and Table 4.3 briefly explains how those components can deliver benefits.

- PEs that are interacting with the external computational environment can incorporate optimizations based on encoding properties of that environment. For example, they can present data in the formats required by libraries built by other communities, they can do transfers in sympathy with the data paths and block sizes of external systems, or they can conserve bandwidth by delivering data directly to where they are needed.
- PEs that implement statistical, data-mining, text-mining, and similar functions can be based on new algorithms that reduce the number of passes over the data or provide incremental improvement of accuracy; these stop computing when a target accuracy has been reached.
- Functions that are implementing a pattern should adapt the pattern according to the supplied parameters, the properties of the data, and the computational context.
- Combinations of PEs generated by functions can exploit parallelism.
- Store-management PEs should enable data to be replicated, distributed, and clustered, as they are installed and support multiple simultaneous uses of active data.

TABLE 4.3 Descriptions of Enhanced Processing Elements Shown in Figure 4.11

Figure	Process Element	Description
a	BulkMover	This PE arranges high performance bulk data movement. Each move is triggered by the arrival of a list of data to be moved on moveList. Each item to be moved is described by a tuple, for example, the source and the filename. For each tuple on moveList, there is a value on metadata. BulkMover is particularly valuable on the many occasions when there is no distributed-file system spanning the source and destination locations.
b	DataDelivery-Receipt	When an external mechanism, such as BulkMover, results in new data available in the storage system that an instance of DataDeliveryReceipt is monitoring, it will emit a list of the new data available.
c	Programmable-FilterProject	A list of rules will be read first from the initializer rules; each rule is a tuple, the selector has a String value that is a script to select a subset of the possible values, the corresponding projector element is similarly a coding that computes the output value from selected incoming values for this rule. The ith rule determines the values emitted on outputs[i]. This allows multiple uses of data while they are in the processor's cache.
d	ParallelSQLQuery	The inputs to this PE are the same as they are for SQLQuery, but the output list of tuples is now a parallel stream of lists of tuples. If the database queried is parallel, then reassembling the results only to split them again is avoided.
e	TupleBurst	This PE requires an incoming stream of tuples on input and a list of String values on columns. It generates a list of tuples on struct to record the structure of the set of values on outputs, such that list element i describes the identifier, Stype and Dtype which was previously associated with the data flowing through outputs[i]. The mapping of tuple elements to streams is the tuple element with an identifier that matches the ith String in columns list. Nonmatched tuple elements are ignored.
f	TupleBuild	This PE performs the inverse of TupleBurst, as it rebuilds the tuple according to the recipe delivered by struct, taking one value at a time in lockstep from each of the data streams in inputs and emitting the reconstructed tuple on output.

- PEs that handle references to data should reduce data traffic and may allow data movement to be scheduled in ways that make best use of available data channels.
- PEs that incorporate flow control can prevent overload and let domain experts steer data-intensive processes toward valuable results.

4.7.2.1 Examples of Higher-Performance Processing Elements

The PE pair `BulkMover` and `DataDeliveryReceipt` are not necessarily used together. An instance is that `BulkMover` may be sending data to some other system, for example, to an archival store or a visualization system. Similarly, new data may arrive by any means, for example, the import of bulk data by transporting disks. These two PEs provide an abstract view of these processes, so that data-intensive engineers can choose an appropriate high capacity data movement and storage mechanism for their context and workload. When data arrive, the descriptions via `deliveryNotes` will include sufficient information to access the data and may include metadata, such as that supplied on the `metadata` connection on `BulkMover`.

The PE `ProgrammableFilterProject` illustrates one strategy for performing multiple operations on data, as it streams though a processor. The rules may be extracting different aspects of the data, or different samples, and a wide range of computations may be involved in generating the `outputs`.

The parallel query mechanism `ParallelSQLQuery` exposes a mechanism of parallel processing that is almost certainly going on in any scalable DBMS that the PE accesses. By bringing this parallelism out directly, it may allow the use of multiple data channels taking subsets of the results to the next stage of processing on a number of different nodes, to which the relevant stages of the total process have been farmed. This is illustrated later, after some preparatory material, in Figure 4.13.

The pair `TupleBurst` and `TupleBuild` are an example of a mechanism for stripping out extraneous data that is equivalent to column storage in databases. The individual streams may flow through their own series of PEs with each stream potentially on a different processor. This avoids competition for caches, threads, and RAM as each stream is processed. Figure 4.13 shows the pair being used as a projection mechanism.

4.7.2.2 Example of a Conditional Pattern

Other components must also be well adapted to scaling and to exploiting properties of the data and processing context. The following DISPEL fragment illustrates how a `makeAllMeetsAllSelfJoin` might save processing if the function applied is symmetric, that is, $f(x, y) = f(y, x)$ for all x and y, where f is the function that the supplied PE, `TheCombiner`, evaluates for each pair of supplied values in the input list.

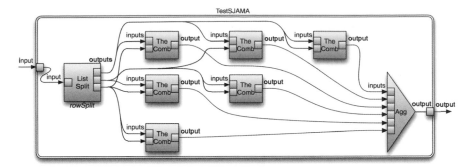

Figure 4.12 *An all-meets-all pairs graph with a symmetric function.*

```
PE <ListCombiner> TestAMA = makeAllMeetsAll(3, TheComb, TheAgg);
```

Then the result of the call

```
PE <ListCombiner> TestSJAMA = makeAllMeetsAllSelfJoin(3, TheComb, TheAgg);
```

with `TheComb` a symmetric function would be as shown in Figure 4.12, which can be compared with the nonsymmetric case in Figure 4.4. With larger n, the saving is substantial. The result can be used as an `AllMeetsAllSymmetricCorrelator`, as shown in Figure 4.5.

4.7.3 Efficient Data-Intensive Processes

The three categories of expert bring a fount of knowledge about their data, the processes that are being applied, and the sensible units of work. The domain experts will know about the volumes and rates of data they will obtain from their instruments, reference archives, and simulations. The data analysis experts will be able to characterize the computational costs of the operations they provide and describe the relative scales of inputs and outputs for their PEs. The data-intensive engineers know about the actual computational costs (bandwidth, storage, and CPU) and relationships between inputs and outputs for the operations they have encapsulated in standard PEs. They also know how their functions, implementing common processing patterns, are intended to be used; they will have designed them to balance and distribute workloads. They observe workloads on their operational data-intensive platform and derive characteristics of previous requests and the operational behavior of the platform's subsystems, patterns, and PEs.

It is crucial to enable this combined wisdom to be expressed in the formulation of data-intensive requests. However, these requests may then be used repeatedly for many years without revision; for example, they are activated from a portal whose developers are now focused elsewhere. Consequently, there is a delicate balance to be achieved in providing mechanisms for using this wisdom at a strategic level, while leaving tactical freedom for the automated optimizers to adapt well to changing circumstances. So, it is necessary that the designers of requests that will be run often, or will involve a substantial amount of data handling and computation, choose PEs that are potentially efficient and arrange their requests with enough structure and description for the optimizer to have an opportunity to create and steer the enactment efficiently. When the PEs are described sufficiently well and the logic of their composition is well defined, it will be possible to automatically replace DISPEL subgraphs with logically equivalent faster subgraphs, but the current state of the art can only make limited transformations. The two examples below characterize the kind of request today's experts would develop and prepare the ground for a discussion on suitable architectural arrangements for applications that involve long-running tasks.

4.7.3.1 Example of Parallel Data Access to Seismic Archive   We return to the seismology example set out at the start of Section 4.4.1. Recall that the task is to select seismic traces from multiple archives according to criteria provided by a seismologist, to prepare them, and then to compute, integrate, and present the result of correlating all pairs of traces. Figure 4.13 contains a DISPEL fragment that might be found inside the function correlateAll, which was introduced in that section. Figure 4.14 illustrates the kind of DISPEL graph this would build; readers are advised to look at the DISPEL text as well as the graph when reading the following narrative. These fragments omit the use statements and other code, which would bring into scope definitions of the identifiers used but not defined.

Lines 2 and 3 define the provenance metadata Stype that will be sent to the correlation site. An instance of PSQLQuery is used to send a query to the ORFEUS (www.orfeus-eu.org) metadata database to obtain the locations of all the parts of all files relevant to the seismologist's request (lines 4–13). As the DISPEL writer anticipated large volumes of work, the parallel PE was used; where it is not available, the serial SQLQuery could have been used followed by a ListSplit. The query was prepared by supplying a function with an array, stations, containing a list of all seismometers to be included and the time range (line 12). The list of seismometers could have been derived by some earlier function interpreting information, such as regions selected on a map and supplied by the seismologists.

SQLQuery is used to obtain the rules for cleaning up data and putting them in a standard form (lines 15–19). By obtaining the rules in this way, the DISPEL author has introduced a buffer against changes in ORFEUS's archive standard or in the required target standard; only the stored rules would need to be updated in the event of such changes— the DISPEL request would work unchanged. These rules could contain access control information. The rules emerge in the standard result-set form of a list of tuples, ListToStream is used to convert to a stream of tuples, and TupleBurst then projects the rules from the tuples (lines 20–24).

The multi-input merge tree, merger, is constructed to collect results from the parallel processing (line 25). The loop connects up par parallel instances of

```
1      ...
2      Stype TraceMD is <String fURI, fpath; Time startT, endT; Integer size, quality;
3                        String stationID, traceID>;         //tuple describes trace segment
4      Stype TraceLocations is [<String fURI, fpath; Integer startByte, length;
5                               String stationID, traceID>];
6      Integer par = 4;                                       //number of parallel streams
7      PSQLQuery psqlq = new PSQLQuery with                   //gets trace segments from DB
8                        data.length = par,                   //in par parallel data streams
9                        data as :TraceLocations;             //lists of places traces stored
10     Stream metadataURI = |- "org.orfeus-eu.trace-metadata" -|;  //URI of metadata DB
11     metadataURI => psqlq.source;                           //set metadata DB URI to query
12     String getFileData = makeDataExtractQuery(stations,startTime,endTime);//query
13     |- getFileData -| => psqlq.expression;                 //supply query to find traces
14                       //now get the rules for preparing traces from ORFEUS
15     SQLQuery sqlq = new SQLQuery with data as
16                    :[<ProgramScript:: "seis:TracePreparationRule" rule>]; //rules
17     metadataURI => sqlq.source;      //get rules to standardise traces from ORFEUS
18     |- "SELECT StandardTracesRule.RULES FROM ...  WHERE ...  = 'ORFEUS'" -| =
19                                                            sqlq.expression;
20     ListToStream l2s = new ListToStream with output as :<ProgramScript rule>;
21     sqlq.data => l2s.input;                  //transform list to stream
22     TupleBurst tb1 = new TupleBurst;         //project out the rules from each tuple
23     |- repeat enough of ["rule"] -| => tb1.columns;    //just one column
24     l2s.output => tb1.input; tb1.struct => discard;    //don't need the structure
25     Merge merger = new makeMwayMerge(par, BinaryMerge) with output: TraceMD;
26                       //set up parallel application of the preparation rules
27     for (Integer i = 0; i<par; i++) {                     //for each stream from the DB
28       TraceStandardiser ts = new TraceStandardiser;
29       psqlq.data[i] => ts.todoList;    //each tuple a trace segment to fetch and process
30       tb1.outputs[0] => ts.rule;       //standardisation rules for data prep
31       ts.output => merger.inputs[i];   //collect all resulting trace descriptions
32     };
33                       //form into batches for delivery and correlation
34     StreamToList s2l = new StreamToList with input as:TraceMD, output as:[TraceMD];
35     Integer batchSize = 200;              //chop stream into batches for delivery and correlation
36     |- repeat enough of batchSize -| => s2l.length;      //of specified size
37     merger.output => s2l.input;           //the merged stream of results
38                       //set up reliable data delivery mechanism
39     BulkMover bm = new BulkMover;         //get bulk data mover to deliver to site
40     |- repeat enough of "uk.ac.ed.edim1.dataloader" -| => bm.destination;
41     s2l.output => bm.metadata;            //supplying provenance metadata
42                       //request despatch of each batch of deliveries
43     TupleBurst tburst = new TupleBurst with input as:[TraceMD], outputs.length = 2;
44     TupleBuild tbuild = new TupleBuild with inputs.length = 2,
45                                          output as :[<String fURI, fpath>];
46     |- [ "fURI", "fpath" ] -| => tburst.columns; //pick out delivery list
47     s2l.output => tburst.input;           //supply list of tuples to project
48     tburst.struct => tbuild.struct;       //copy over structure description
49     tburst.outputs => tbuild.inputs;      //transfer both wanted columns
50     tbuild.output => bm.moveList;         //supply list of data to move
51     ...
```

Figure 4.13   *Example of parallel processing with file proxies.*

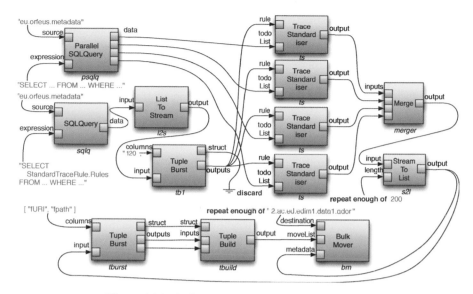

Figure 4.14   *An illustration of parallel data preparation.*

TraceStandardiser, almost certainly a composite PE, and supplies each with one of the streams of output from the PSQLQuery PE and the current standardization rules (lines 26–32). The input is a low volume per tuple description of the data to be extracted and standardized. This illustrates a method of reducing the data moved. The TraceStandardiser instances, each take their own stream, read the files in that stream, cleaning and standardizing the data, and store the result files in some storage location that they use. This means that if they have been deployed on separate nodes, they will exploit the disk and network bandwidth of each node. Each time they complete a file, they emit its description on output. That description should probably be written to a provenance and progress-tracking database—for simplicity, that is not shown here.

The combined output of tuples describing completed files is formed into lists of a specified batch size by StreamToList (lines 26–29). The **DISPEL** developer had reason to believe that this is an appropriate size for onward transfer—see the following example. The full descriptions are sent as metadata describing the batch and the relevant elements of the description are extracted to provide BulkMover with a list of files to move (or copy) (lines 38–49).

The **DISPEL** request's author has added annotation to show the structural types and, in two cases, the domain type of the data being processed. For example, by defining the Stype of the metadata (lines 2 and 3) and using it in assertions about the data on output streams (lines 25, 34, and 43), the author has provided helpful documentation and a fixed point for the type-consistency validator.

There is a problem about the two parameters controlling factors related to scaling: par = 4 (line 6) and batchSize = 200 (line 35). Both of these need to adapt to variations in the properties of the underlying data-intensive platform and to changes in the volumes of data and in the ways in which seismologists use the facility. The current, explicitly "hard-wired" values reflect the state of the art in most of today's general-purpose production systems. Ideally, such structure-shaping parameters would be set automatically in the pattern-generating code, for example, by calls to functions that interrogated the underlying platform properties, current workloads, and historical operational records to dynamically provide appropriate values on each occasion. As we see in Part VI, achieving this with any generality is still a matter for research.

The request's designers have also chosen to merge after the trace-preparation stage, presumably because they think this will read and write many files and that the rest is just manipulating the small volume of metadata and requires few resources. In fact, the BulkMover will need to read all the files and ship them in some way, for example, over the network. So it might have been better to have continued in parallel right up to and including data shipment. A goal of process-element description is to be able to automatically correct this mistake by transforming the graph so that it remains parallel. This is currently beyond the state of the art but appears to be within reach.

In the interim, DISPEL plays a key role as a medium for precise discussion among the many experts involved in an application. As some of these decisions become automated, others will emerge as requiring discussion. Hence, the requirement for a succinct legible language that can be translated into enactable forms will continue for the foreseeable future.

4.7.3.2 *Example of Preparing for the Seismic Correlation*   We now move to the next stage of processing these seismic data. The seismologists have chosen to keep the prepared files, so that they can reuse them. But the previous request has also initiated the copying of batches of these files to the Edinburgh Data-Intensive Machine (EDIM1) and hidden the protocol used for transport, almost certainly a reliable file transfer protocol,[10] which will wait for resources and retry for any incomplete transfers until they are complete. It has also hidden algorithms that the loader will use to distribute and possibly replicate data across the nodes of the EDIM1. We envisage that the loader will notify running instances of DataDeliveryReceipt when each batch has arrived.

This arrangement enables a strategy for organizing the all-meets-all correlation in several different ways. All of these seek to make the best use of data once it is loaded onto a cluster or into a node's memory. The data that is to be compared is in files, but the work will again be organized by a flow of proxies for the files that both identify their content and provide a mechanism for finding out where the data-loading end of BulkMove put them. This leads to a definition for the PE that performs seismic correlation as shown in the following DISPEL fragment.

---

[10]See for example www.globusonline.org.

```
use book.examples.seismology.{
                TraceMD,        //Stype of metadata giving provenance on delivery
                CorrTraceMD,  //Stype of metadata describing correlation trace
                PreparedTraceDescription, //Dtype of prepared trace description
                CorrelationTraceDescription}; //Dtype of a result description

   Type SeismicCorrelator is PE(   //type of symmetric seismic correlator PE
      <Connection[ ]: TraceMD:: PreparedTraceDescription
                    with length=2, permutable inputs > =>
      <Connection: CorrTraceMD:: CorrelationTraceDescription output>
   ) with lockstep(inputs), rate(inputs[i]) == rate(output);
```

This already corresponds to having made one of the decisions about how to organize an all-meets-all computation over large volumes of data. As a reminder, the goal is to calculate all the values of $f(x, y)$, where $x \in X$, $y \in Y$. The choices depend on understanding the properties of sets X and Y—this understanding normally comes from the domain experts, but it may come from analyzing previous enactments.

For example, if X and Y are small enough to fit in RAM, a rapid and simple cross-product algorithm is possible. This may still be spread over a number of nodes if evaluating f demands significant CPU. Conversely, there is no gain from deploying more nodes than the capacity of the network or disk channels to bring in prepared traces and deliver the results. The sweet spot needs to be determined for each application on each data-intensive platform, ideally automatically.

4.7.3.3 *Example of Clustering the Seismic Data*   A more typical case is that the data is so large that local disk storage should be used. If X and Y will both fit on disks attached to a node, then it may be worth loading both into a local disk storage and then running a cross-product algorithm. If each node in the cluster shares common storage, there is no need to consider where to place the data, but if each node has its own disk storage, then the distribution of the data across the nodes will affect performance. For example, if $f(x, y)$ only has a result for some of the pairs, then it is desirable to cluster the x and y for these on the same node. Here, we see the need of both domain experts, to advise on how to cluster the data, as they would for relational tables in the Microsoft SQL-Server parallel data warehouse[11] and for data-intensive engineers who would know the properties of the data-intensive platform being used.[12]

If each node has its own disks, it may be better to load one set, say X onto a suitable number of nodes, and then stream the other set, Y, through all the nodes. This continues to work if one of the sets is small enough to be totally loaded onto the set of nodes. Then the other set can be too large to store, or even be a continuous stream, as it can be streamed past the stored set. Such a scenario would

---

[11] www.microsoft.com/sqlserver/2008/en/us/parallel-data-warehouse.aspx
[12] As far as possible, these properties and their effect on the clustering should be computed automatically.

occur, when looking for a set of known individuals, the smaller set, X, in the data streams, Y, from many security cameras, for example.

None of these strategies works for the seismic correlation example, as here we have a self-join structure, $f(x_i, x_j)$ where $x_i \in X$ and $x_j \in X$ and $i \neq j$. The size of the set could be large, say daily traces for several years from 600 seismometers, making for 10 years: $600 \times 365 \times 10 \times 0.1$ GB files, that is, 219 TB of data. As the correlation is symmetric, that is, $f(x_i, x_j) = f(x_j, x_i)$, the analysis only need address all pairs such that $x_i \in X$, $x_j \in X$, and $i < j$—this again draws on domain knowledge and should be captured in the DISPEL request or an all-meets-all pattern function that it uses. The correlation can ignore signals that differ in time by more than the wave propagation time between the stations. For this reason, traces will only be correlated with data from the same day, the very end of the preceding day or the start of the following day. Hence, traces should be clustered on delivery by date of the observation, for example, if d is the number of days since the start of the period, p is the number of days in the period, and n is the number of nodes over which the data is to be deposited, then $\lfloor \frac{d \times n}{p} \rfloor$ is the node number on which files for day d should be deposited. This domain-driven decision has to be communicated to the delivery end of the BulkMover. To load data as rapidly as possible, the DISPEL request in Figure 4.13 should be engineered to process the extraction in the order of the seismometer numbers, so that all nodes are loading the data from that seismometer, and then the next, whereas if the output from that request were in date order, each node would be a bottleneck in turn. This illustrates the challenge of thinking holistically about the whole process and not just one part at a time.

4.7.3.4 *Example of Handling the Correlation Output*   In an application such as this, handling the output is even more challenging. For the above example input, the output would be 600×300 files per day of the sample period, that is, $180,000$ files and approximately 18 TB of data—65.7 PB for the whole period. These files are combined to produce a derivative, a process called *stacking* in this domain's parlance, before delivering the final output. It is clear that they cannot be stored indefinitely and that either requests much smaller than this example must be the operational norm or that the intermediate data should be used as they become available and then discarded. It is common to underestimate the challenge of handling intermediate data, though there is well-developed work to discard them as soon as they will no longer be used in the Pegasus workflow systems [11].

4.7.3.5 *Example of Allocating Evaluation Close to Data*   Once data have been clustered, the evaluation of f has to be distributed so as to minimize the network traffic between nodes. In our example above, for a cluster with local storage on each node, fURI will identify the file system and hence the node. If we generate a partial cross product on each node described by $x_i, x_j \in X$ and $i < j$ with two further restrictions: $x_i \cdot$fURI is on this node and both traces refer to the same day, that is, day($x_i \cdot$startT)=day($x_j \cdot$startT). Only one of the two traces is required to be on the node, because clustering is ineluctably advisory, as disks

failing or filling will disrupt perfect placement. The access to the ends of adjacent-day data will require network traffic for traces on the boundary of the cluster of days.

Now that each node is predominantly processing local data, it is also desirable to make the best use of each file once read. This might be done by generating the restricted cross product so that it is sorted on one of the file identifiers and relies on the operating system's caching. If access to x_j has a risk of being nonlocal, then that may be the slower read, and it would be worth sorting on x_j·fpath.

4.7.3.6 *Decision to Store the Correlation Output Temporarily* Before sketching a solution that takes these points into consideration, we will discuss how to handle the output from each SiesmicCorrelator and the factors affecting the number of nodes to deploy on the task. If the output from each correlation was only used once by the Stacker, then it would be best to stream the correlation trace as a stream of bytes (a serialized representation of Stype Trace) directly to the stacker (instance of Stacker) and incur no disk traffic apart from buffer spilling. There may, however, be reasons for writing such values to disk, for example, to enable quality monitoring and reliability (Section 4.8) or to accommodate legacy code in the stacker that was written for files. The cost of modifying the stacker call to take streamed data rather than a file is much less than the cost of writing such large volumes of data to disk, but it cannot be introduced until the domain experts trust the new code. These disk reads and writes are not logically necessary for any of these purposes and may be a significant overhead but with the current state of the art, they are common, and we use them in our running example.

4.7.3.7 *Choosing the Number of Correlation Nodes* The number of nodes used for the correlation is determined by balancing three factors:

1. providing an adequate work rate, that is, having sufficient bandwidth to nodes and disks and enough CPU capacity and memory to cope with the data arrival rates and not to exceed the correlation-output consumption rates;
2. providing sufficient *local* disk storage for storing inputs that need to be stored, in this case, X;
3. providing enough storage to hold a sufficient buffer of the intermediate results, in this case, all the values of $f(x_i, x_j)$ that have yet to be dealt with by the stacker, the recovery system, or the quality control sampling system.

The stacker improves accuracy by averaging multiple day's traces for each pair and by adjusting the interlaced network of wave paths to move toward a consistent parametric model of the observed segments of the crustal plates. The method used is discussed in Chapter 17 and is not elaborated here; suffice to say that the definition and resource allocation for the stacker should be balanced with the correlation design and resources so that the average rate of production of the correlator output is as close as possible to the rate of consumption of the stacker.

```
1    use book.examples.seismology.{
2                    SeismicCorrelator,     //type of seismic correlation PE
3                    TraceMD,               //Stype of metadata giving provenance on delivery
4                    CorrTraceMD,           //Stype of metadata giving provenance of result
5                    PreparedTraceDescription,   //Dtype of prepared-trace description
6                    CorrelationTraceDescription}; //Dtype of a correlation result
7    Stype TracePair is <TraceMD first, second>;     //two prepared traces to be correlated
8    Dtype PairToCorrelate is <PreparedTraceDescription first, second>; //their Dtype
9            //PE that listens for batches of traces to arrive and initiates their correlation
10   Type Responder is PE( < > =>
11     < Connection: TracePair:: PairToCorrelate output > ); //pairs to correlate
12            //PE that farms out these correlations to nodes with traces stored on them
13   Type CorrFarm is PE(
14     < Connection: TracePair:: PairToCorrelate input > =>
15     < Connection: CorrTraceMD:: CorrelationTraceDescription output > );
16            //PE that processes the resulting correlations, stacking, caching and sampling
17   Type CorrHandler is PE(
18     < Connection: CorrTraceMD:: CorrelationTraceDescription input > => < > );
19     ...        //definition of functions makeResponder, makeCorrFarm and makeCorrHandler
20        //function to make a pipeline that continuously handles each trace batch on arrival
21   PE <Submittable> makeCorrelationPipeline( PE <SeismicCorrelator> SC ) {
22     Responder arrivalResponder = new makeResponder( );       //acts on arrivals
23     CorrFarm correlator = new makeCorrFarm( SC );            //does correlation
24     CorrHandler useCorrelations = new makeCorrHandler( );  //handles results
25     arrivalResponder.output => correlator.input;            //deliver work to do
26     correlator.output => useCorrelations.input;            //deliver results to handle
27   };
28   register makeCorrelationPipeline;                         //preserve all new definitions
```

Figure 4.15 *DISPEL arranging data clustering for distributed correlation.*

4.7.3.8 *Phases of the Seismic Correlation Process*   Figure 4.15 shows a fragment of DISPEL that would generate the distributed correlator and Figure 4.16 shows the DISPEL graph that the call

```
PE <Submitable> CorrPipeline = makeCorrelationPipeline( SCX );
```

would produce.[13] Three process-element types are introduced to denote the three phases of correlating the seismic traces to allow the implementation of each phase to be thought about separately.

Phase 1, Responder, is triggered by the bulk-data delivery system signaling that a batch of data has arrived. The type, Responder, is defined on lines 10 and 11 and its instance is constructed by calling makeResponder (line 22)—the DISPEL text for makeResponder is given in Figure 4.17 with the corresponding DISPEL graph in Figure 4.18.

---

[13]This would normally be several separate DISPEL requests to define and register the PEs, then one each to define the three functions that generate their implementations and, finally, the request to put them together. Readers will also notice that DISPEL fragments, rather than complete requests are being presented for didactic purposes, for example, the **package** structure, some **use** statements, and some registration statements are being omitted.

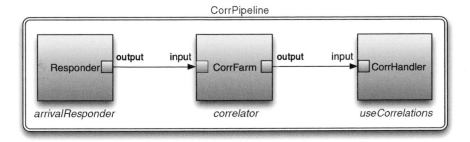

Figure 4.16 *The DISPEL graph showing three phases of correlation.*

```
1    PE <Responder> makeResponder( ) {        //make PE to respond to batches of data arriving
2     DataDeliveryReceipt ddr = new DataDeliveryReciept with:[TraceMD] deliveryNotes;
3     Pause pause = new Pause;                 //enable user or system to stop stream flow
4     ddr.deliveryNotes => pause.input;        //apply that flow control immediately on arrival
5     SQLInsert sqli = new SQLInsert;          //set up DB access to insert progress records
6     Stream progressDB = |- repeat enough of "eu.verce.progprov" -|; //& provenance
7     progressDB => sqli.source;               //supply stream to initialiser source to fix DB choice
8     pause.output => sqli.data;               //once flow permitted record safe arrival
9     String insertq1 = "INSERT #columns# INTO Arrived VALUES ( #list# );"; //update
10    |- repeat enough of insertq1 -| => sqli.expression; //update pattern to fill out
11    ProgrammableFilterProjectDistinct pfpd =
12                    new ProgrammableFilterProjectDistinct with :[Integer] outputs;
13    pause.output => pfpd.input;              //the full list of the arrived batch to obtain a list of
14    |- <selector="true"; projector="day(input.startT)"; eq="Integer.equals"> -| =>
15                    pfpd.rules;  //the distinct days included in the batch
16    MakeINQuery makinq = new MakeINQuery with sets.length=1;//and use after IN in query
17    pfpd.outputs[0] => makinq.sets[0];    //supply list of distinct days to query maker
18    String sfwPattern = "SELECT fURI, path, start, end, ... " + //pattern for query
19      "FROM Arrived AS arr WHERE day(arr.start) IN ( #list0# );"; //over all traces
20    |- repeat enough of sfwPattern -| => makinq.template;//that are for same day
21    SQLQuery sqlcom = new SQLQuery with :[TraceMD] data;//prepare to apply filled query
22    progressDB => sqlcom.source;            //using the same provenance and progress database
23    makinq.queries => sqlcom.expression;   //and the synthesised IN query
24    ProgrammableJoin mkpairs = new ProgrammableJoin; //makes list of pairs
25    pause.output => mkpairs.a;              //pairing each entry from the newly arrived batch
26    sqlcom.data => mkpairs.b;               //with traces from this and previous batches
27          //using the following rule that avoids self-correlation and symmetric duplicates
28    String rule = "day(a.startT)==day(b.startT) && a.stationId<b.stationId";
29    |- rule -| => mkpairs.test;             //lower-numbered station first
30    return Responder( < > => <output = mkpairs.pairs> ); //return the composite PE
31  }
```

Figure 4.17 *The DISPEL function to make the process respond to data arriving for correlation.*

Phase 2, `CorrFarm`, is supplied by `Responder` with all the pairs of traces to be correlated. The type, `CorrFarm`, is defined on lines 13–15, and its instance is constructed by calling `makeCorrFarm` (line 23). The DISPEL text for `makeCorrFarm` can be found in Figure 4.19 with the corresponding graph in Figure 4.20.

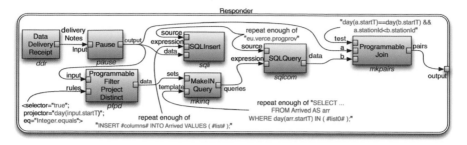

Figure 4.18   The DISPEL graph of Responder handling newly arrived data.

```
1   namespace db "http://dispel-lang.org/resources/dispel/db/";
2   use dispel.core.RuleFP;   //Stype of programmable filter PE's rules
3   ...                       //other use statements, etc.
4   PE <CorrFarm> makeCorrFarm( PE <SeismicCorrelator> TheSC ) {
5     Type URIDayRange is < String:: "db:FileSystem" fURI; //source of traces
6                       Integer minDay, maxDay >;   //for this period
7     URIDayRange[ ] dayMap = getDayMap( );   //access bulkloader's data-placement map
8     Integer nc = dayMap.length;             //number of data clusters or nodes
9     ProgrammableFilterProject distrib = new ProgrammableFilterProject
10          with :<TraceMD a, b> outputs, outputs.length=nc;
11    Merge merger = new makeMwayMerge( nc, BinaryMerge ) with output: CorrTraceMD;
12    Stream distribRule = SoL;                //start list of selector tuples
13    Stream sortRule = |- repeat enough of
14                          "(data.second.fURI,data.second.fpath) ASCENDING"-|;
15    Stream columns = |- repeat enough of ["first", "second"] -|;
16    for (Integer i=0; i<nc; i++) {           //for each data cluster
17      URIDayRange udr = dayMap[i];           //get placement description
18      RuleFP rulefp = new < selector = IntegerToString(udr.minDay) + //start day
19              " <= day(input.a.startT) && day(input.a.startT) <= " +
20              IntegerToString(udr.maxDay),              //end day
21              projector = "<first=input.a; second=input.b>" >;//pair to correlate
22      distribRule += |-rulefp-|;             //add rule for this data cluster
23      Sort sort = new Sort;                  //sort to re-use second trace while loaded
24      distrib.outputs[i] => sort.input;      //per cluster of data
25      sortRule => sort.rule;                 //always on the second trace
26      ListToStream l2s = new ListToStream;   //remove list structure now sorted
27      sort.output => l2s.input;
28      TupleBurst tburst = new TupleBurst with:TraceMD outputs[i],outputs.length=2;
29      l2s.output => tburst.input;            //send to be split into two trace descriptions
30      columns => tburst.columns;             //first to outputs[0]
31      tburst.struct => discard;              //no reconstruction expected
32      TheSC tsc = new TheSC with inputs.length=2,locator udr.fURI;//locate with data
33      tburst.outputs => tsc.inputs;          //couple pair of outputs to pair of inputs
34      tsc.output => merger.inputs[i];        //combine all the results
35    };
36    distribRule += EoL;                      //finished list of distribution selectors
37    distribRule => distrib.rules;            //distribute to farm of correlators
38    return CorrFarm( <inp = distrib.input> => <outp = merger.output> );
39  }
```

Figure 4.19   The DISPEL function to construct a farm of correlators.

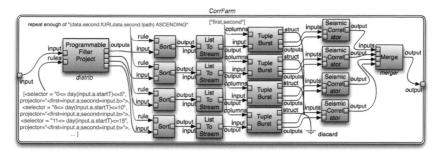

Figure 4.20   *The DISPEL graph of CorrFarm performing the correlation.*

```
1   PE <CorrHandler> makeCorrHandler( PE <SeismicStacker> TheStacker ) {
2      Connection correlations: CorrTraceMD:: "seis:CorrelationTraceDescription";
3      SeismicStacker stacker = new TheStacker; //will integrate all the correlations
4      correlations => stacker.input;
5      StreamToList makeBatch = new StreamToList;
6      Integer batchSize = 100;              //tuneable parameter number in batch
7      |- repeat enough of batchSize -| => makeBatch.length;
8      correlations => makeBatch.input;
9      Stream progressDB = |- repeat enough of "eu.verce.progprov" -|;//also provenance
10     SQLInsert reportDone = new SQLInsert;   //insert correlation result metadata as a
11     progressDB => reportDone.source;        //record of what has been done and for access
12     String newCorrelations = "INSERT #columns# INTO Correlated VALUES (#list#);";
13     |- repeat enough of newCorrelations -| => reportDone.expression;
14     makeBatch.output => reportDone.data;    //list forms unit of Tx update (append)
15     Sample sampler = new Sample;            //sample for inspection
16     correlations => sampler.input;          //from the correlation results
17     Real proportionWanted = 0.001;          //sampling rate is tuneable
18     |- proportionWanted -| => sampler.ratio;
19     StreamToList s21 = new StreamToList;     //handle samples in batches (lists)
20     Integer sampleBatch = 10;               //batch size is tuneable
21     |- repeat enough of sampleBatch -| => s21.length;
22     sampler.output => s21.input;            //form batches of samples as lists
23     TupleBurst tburst = new TupleBurst with outputs.length=2;
24     |- [ "fURI", "fpath" ] -| => tburst.columns;
25     l2s.output => tburst.input;             //select columns naming files
26     TupleBuild tbuild = new TupleBuild with inputs.length=2;
27     tburst.struct => tbuild.struct;         //copy the structure across
28     tburst.outputs => tbuild.inputs;        //build two-element file specification tuples
29     BulkMover bm = new BulkMover;           //prepare to deliver to visualiser & QA
30     |-repeat enough of "eu.seis.samples" -| => bm.destination;
31     tbuild.output => bm.moveList;           //list of files per batch to move
32     s21.output => bm.metadata;              //their metadata: annotation & provenance
33     return CorrHandler( < input = correlations > => < > );
34  }
```

Figure 4.21   *The DISPEL function to make a process handle a correlator's results.*

Phase 3, CorrHandler, takes the stream of metadata reporting what CorrFarm has done and arranges for those results to be used. The Type, CorrHandler, is defined on lines 17 and 18 and its instance is constructed by calling makeCoreHandler (line 24). The DISPEL text for makeCorrHandler is in Figure 4.21 and the corresponding graph is given by Figure 4.22.

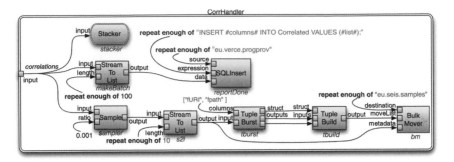

Figure 4.22 *The DISPEL graph of CorrHandler handling the result data.*

4.7.3.9   *Phase 1 of the Seismic Correlation Process*   The DISPEL in
Figure 4.17 produces the graph for responding to a list of traces arriving to be
correlated. The DISPEL corresponds to reading the graph from left to right, that
is, in the direction of the dataflow. The traces will need to be correlated with all
relevant traces that have already arrived and with the other traces in this new batch.
The DataDeliveryReceipt PE provides a new list each time a batch of data arrives.
The delivery process will have assigned incoming data to nodes according to the
specified clustering rule, replacing the fURI and fpath in the complete metadata
describing the trace, TraceMD (line 2). The Pause PE provides a means of stopping
and optionally resuming the processing. It behaves similar to a tap that can be
switched on and off by the user, system monitors, and operations administrators.
When it is open, it has no effect on the data flowing through it.

The next task in this implementation is to record that this data has arrived
in the progress and provenance database by an insert of a list of values into the
Arrived table (lines 5–10). The ProgrammableFilterProjectDistinct PE is then
used to obtain a list of Integer days without duplicates, so that a query can be
constructed to obtain the metadata for all the traces that occur on any of the days
represented in the newly arrived batch. Because of the preceding insert update, this
will include all the newly arrived traces (lines 11–23). The ProgrammableJoin PE
is used to generate a list of all the newly possible pairs that comply with $x_i, x_j \in X$
and $i < j$ and $\text{day}(x_i \cdot \text{startT}) = \text{day}(x_j \cdot \text{startT})$ introduced above, here encoded in
rule (line 28). On lines 14 and 15 and on 28 and 29, we depend on the input
connections being labeled initializer. Line 30 connects the internal structure
with the abstract definition of Responder and returns the implementation.

4.7.3.10   *Phase 2 of the Seismic Correlation Process*   In Figure 4.19,
the order in the DISPEL text again approximately follows the left to right flow of
data, which can be seen in Figure 4.20. The type URIDayRange records the URI to
which the traces for a range of days will be stored *if everything has gone to plan*. If
some traces have been stored elsewhere because of full or failed disks, for example,
the process will work but it will just run a little slower. Line 7 uses a function,
getDayMap, that will access a database to discover the configuration, that is, how

the traces were clustered onto the separate stores, defined with different URIs. If the clustering has been changed, and more than one cluster of traces is on a given store, that store's fURI will appear more than once in dayMap—the algorithm will still work, but the load may be less evenly distributed. The instance distrib of ProgrammableFilterProject will deliver a stream of work as a succession of lists of pairs to each of the nc parallel paths of the farm of correlators according to the rules in distribRule, with one entry per cluster of traces.

The loop from line 16 to 35 deals with one cluster of traces per iteration. It first makes the rule for recognizing members of that cluster and appends it to DistribRule (lines 18–22). It then sets up the Sort PE with the input sent by distrib and the sortRule, which is intended to make the best use of traces that may be more expensive to fetch (lines 23–25). The list was needed to bound the sort and now it is discarded (lines 26 and 27). A stream of tuples, each with a first and second element of Stype TraceMD, flows into the TupleBurst PE and is split into two streams of TraceMD values (lines 28–31).

This has all led up to the construction of the critical component of this farm element, the instance tsc of the supplied correlator, TheSC. It does the heavy work of accessing the two input traces, described by the two TraceMD values, and of computing the correlation trace. It then stores that result trace somewhere and builds its description as a CorrTraceMD value and sends that onto the merger (lines 32–34). As it accesses a great deal of data, it is clearly best located close to that data; the function's designer has passed that information on to the deployment system by associating the locator assertion with the instance and by supplying the URI that the dayMap states is the preferred home for these data. This will probably influence the eventual location of the other PEs in that farm element—in Figure 4.20, there are four farm elements; a much larger number would frequently be necessary.

4.7.3.11 Phase 3 of the Seismic Correlation Process

In Figure 4.21, the order in the DISPEL text again approximately follows the left to right flow of data as shown in Figure 4.22. This phase has three branches: the main branch applying the Stacker (lines 3 and 4), the recording of progress and provenance in the database (lines 5–14), and the despatch of samples and their metadata using the bulk data movement technology (lines 15–32). These three branches are indicated on the graph by the Connection correlations (line 2) being labeled for each branch. The use of the BulkMover again enables data to be moved between storage regimes are quite different, with entirely independent administration, naming, and resource allocation schemes. It completely hides the actual mechanism used for moving the data, so that the process definition still works when a different protocol becomes appropriate.

The study presented here of this example has adequately demonstrated the complexity that emerges, as larger volumes of data are processed across heterogeneous distributed systems. The complexity coming from the heterogeneity of the resources, data, and computational systems is challenging, but it can be handled by systematically using naming schemes and components that balance performance against independence from the details of the computational data and administrative context. The complexity is also addressed by judicious use of mechanisms for partitioning the intellectual and technical challenges.

Although we have exposed a wealth of examples of the need for multiscale thinking, considering both the balance in work rates and resource requirements of all stages of the knowledge discovery process, this particular example has not been completely covered. For example, we have acknowledged that we have not analyzed the `Stacker` that has to consume a substantial volume of intermediate results. Furthermore, we have considered neither how and where those intermediate values should be stored nor how we manage their removal once they are not needed.

Once an example such as this is running well, it stimulates the creative processes among the domain experts, in this example, the seismologists. They will start to want new knowledge, such as the way wave propagation speeds will change with time. They will want new data presentations, such as video sequences of the crust showing these temporal effects. Then they will want to study how these relate to other observed geophysical processes, such as, volcanic eruptions, major earthquakes, or hot spots—the full panoply of EPOS's remit.[14]. *The data analysis experts and data-intensive engineers will never fall idle!* Their "customers" will always want better data-to-knowledge highways.

4.8   RELIABILITY AND CONTROL

As the previous section has hinted, an additional challenge is to provide the users of data-intensive processes with a means of monitoring and controlling their progress. For long-running processes, this is very important, both to reassure the users and to allow them to stop or steer a process that would otherwise be unproductive. Once the processes become continuous, for example, when monitoring geophysical and environmental systems, such oversight and control becomes essential. Where tunable parameters shape a data-intensive process, as illustrated above, the control system should allow them to be adjusted by experts and data-intensive engineers until they can be set autonomically by the data-intensive platform. Those providing the platforms for data-intensive processes use the same tools to assess their platforms' operational performance and to diagnose problems with their work.

The preceding section also showed that a request can easily involve very substantial resources. As it uses distributed and heterogeneous data-intensive platforms, localized partial failures are inevitable. With short-running requests, it is acceptable simply to start again, provided that a consistent state is restored and allocated resources are recovered. With longer-running processes, the probability of encountering a failure inevitably rises. A restart strategy that starts from scratch may never achieve completion and would become prohibitively expensive. Therefore, strategies must be developed that resume after and recover from failures. This requires enough information to determine what work has been successfully achieved and

[14]www.epos-eu.org

can be safely used, what work is so incomplete that it should be discarded and redone, and what claimed resources need releasing before resumption. The traditional transactional approach to this is infeasible because it depends on making copies of data, and the volumes here prohibit that. Instead, *progress* is recorded transactionally, and domain knowledge is used to understand what are sensible units of progress and where recovery is feasible. Hence, this once again involves support for collaborative design and implementation from all three categories of experts.

4.8.1 Connecting Users with Computations

As a result of our design choices, a suitable data-intensive application architecture emerges, in which databases are used to meet the above requirements and to provide the *contact points* for the collaboration—a sketch of such an architecture is shown in Figure 4.23. The upper region of the diagram, *Seismic Portal*, represents an envisaged portal for domain experts, in this case, seismologists. The lower region denotes the *data-intensive platform* with several logical subdivisions of data under its control. These would typically be distributed and some would be autonomous, in which case the control is at best partial.

The main portal would allow the seismologists to input parameters and select or contribute algorithms, in order to form and submit a DISPEL request ①, such as those presented in preceding sections. (The encircled numbers refer to the similarly numbered data paths in Figure 4.23). The resulting data-intensive processes will use data and rules from the *Configuration* database, which allows data analysis experts and data-intensive engineers to influence the process enactment. This may only take effect when the process is submitted to the gateway, or those two categories of expert may have portals through which they can influence a running enactment. Such run-time control of enactment requires that the request contains mechanisms for obtaining modified parameters, just as an SQLQuery instance picked up transformation rules in Figure 4.13. If the domain experts wish to adjust operational parameters, for example, the quality-assurance sampling rate in Figure 4.21 line 17, this can also be arranged by letting them update control parameters in that database (through a portlet not shown here) and arranging that the DISPEL request solicits values from this source periodically, for example, after every 1000 data values have been processed.

4.8.1.1 Stop and Resume Controls   If seismologists wish to stop processing temporarily, they may click a button on the *Pause* portlet. This would send a signal to all the instances of the PE Pause in the current enactment by submitting request ②. Those instances would be placed at critical control points (as shown in Figure 4.17, line 3) and would stop the dataflow and hence processing, perhaps while the seismologist reviews the quality of the results obtained so far. A further click or another button would send a DISPEL request that caused resumption. A more sophisticated *Pause* portlet might allow the dataflow to be turned off and on separately at various different places in the graph. A *Stop* button should also be

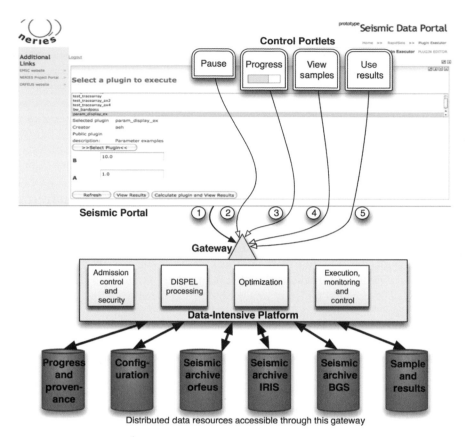

Figure 4.23 *Architecture for controlling data-intensive processes.*

provided, which triggers a termination of running enactments, for occasions when a domain expert decides that an errant process cannot be steered to a useful outcome. This may save substantial computing costs compared with uncontrolled batch processing. It would need to drain the data-intensive platform of useful results and commit all progress data and then clean up, recovering allocated resources.

4.8.1.2 Progress Indicators

For long-running enactments, it is helpful to let domain experts see some indicator of progress, shown here in simplified form as a *progress bar* in the *Progress* portlet. The progress record might be much more sophisticated, for example, a tower of discs denoting traces at each location on a map, which progressively changes colors as each stage of processing is achieved for the corresponding source data. A good implementation strategy depends on the primary request, ①, containing PEs that write progress records at each stage to the *Progress and Provenance* database, as illustrated in Figures 4.17, 4.19, and 4.21. The *Progress* portlet submits a DISPEL request ③ that periodically, for example, every 5 s, performs queries on the *Progress and Provenance* database, processes the results to calculate progress parameters, and then sends them as a result for display in the *Progress* portlet. As applications develop, these progress portlets become sophisticated "dashboards" with many aspects of progress and quality being derived and shown. This is warranted for repeatedly used or long-running, data-intensive processes.

4.8.1.3 *User-Controlled Visualization*

Visual inspection is a powerful quality control and diagnostic technique; its early application can save wasted time and futile expenditure of resources. Hence, a *View Samples* portlet is invariably useful, which allows domain experts to choose which samples to view and to set selection and viewing parameters. Each time they do this, a DISPEL request (④) is submitted to access the relevant data from the *Sample and Results* database, perhaps annotated with provenance information from the *Progress and Provenance* database. This was anticipated in the running example by the sampling in Figure 4.21, lines 15–32.

Ultimately, domain experts want to visualize the results as well as use them for processes that consume the derivative data. For short-running, data-intensive processes, this might be directly arranged in the initial request (①). However, in many cases, those experts will return to view the results when they are notified that substantial processing has been achieved or the entire task has been completed. In that case, they will employ the *Use Results* portlet to submit a DISPEL request (⑤) that discovers which results are ready by consulting the *Progress and Provenance* database and then marshals, transforms, and despatches those results and their provenance data to a viewing or analysis system.

This example of composing five logical channels of communication with the data-intensive platform and of augmenting the primary data, here three *Seismic Archives*, with other databases is typical of the more sophisticated application structures that develop, as the three categories of expert work together to support a sustained and demanding requirement. Inevitably, it evolves and becomes more complex. Keeping the descriptions of the various data-intensive processing stages separate and well organized helps to make that evolution sufficiently agile to satisfy the domain experts without generating infeasible demands on the data analysis experts and data-intensive engineers.

4.8.2 Reliability and Recovery

So far, for simplicity, the examples and discussion have assumed that everything works. In real systems, with real data and real users trying to reach new goals, this is rarely true. To perform both cleanup and recovery after a failure, it is necessary to have a record of what has been done to *persistent storage*, that is, to any recorded data that will not automatically be deleted and the resources recycled after some time-out.

A first step toward this, already present in some of the examples above, is to arrange the PEs that change persistent data provide a record of what they have done. It is also useful if PEs that interact with persistent storage provide error/success

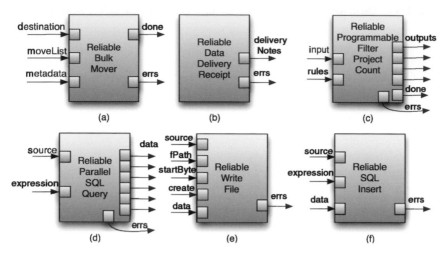

Figure 4.24 *Processing elements augmented to yield recovery data described in Table 4.4.*

status information that can be analyzed to determine the failure boundaries. These generated records also contain provenance data, as there is an overlap in the information required; they can then be written to storage by other PEs and used by later processes and data users to understand the data sources and the processing steps that produced the data. In many cases, a high level description of the required provenance records and recovery strategy would be used to generate the steps shown below to illustrate failure recovery. An expert would identify the relevant data units and processing boundaries and the tool doing that generation would insert the progress recording and "Have I already done this?" PEs, filling in all the details automatically.

Examples of PEs enhanced for reliability are shown in Figure 4.24 and their (new) features are described in Table 4.4. Data-intensive engineers would use these and analyze their diagnostic outputs when they are supporting long-running processes or working in a context where partial failures have to be considered.

4.8.2.1 Handling Errors During Seismic-Data Integration   As an

example, an augmented version of the data integration and despatch via the BulkLoader to the machine that will perform the actual correlation could record the traces successfully sent and any problems in the *Progress and Provenance database* (henceforth PaPDB). The DISPEL graph in Figure 4.25 shows how the data-intensive processes in Figures 4.13 and 4.14 can be extended to use the PaPDB to improve recovery and reliability.

The achievements of the bm instance of ReliableBulkMover in successfully shipping data, expressed as a sequence of ProgressReport tuples emitted via done, are recorded in the PaPDB by the did instance of ReliableSQLInsert. It is necessary that the tuples record some identification of the task, taskNumber, on behalf of

TABLE 4.4 Descriptions of Reliable Processing Elements shown in Figure 4.24

Figure	Process Element	Description
a	ReliableBulkMover	This performs in the same way as `BulkMover` but also reports on `done` a `ProgressReport` periodically and at the end an `Error` on `errs` for each data item it could not deliver.
b	ReliableData-DeliveryReciept	This provides the function of `DataDeliveryReciept` with an `Error` on `errs` for each delivered item that appears to have been corrupted in transit.
c	ProgrammableFilter-ProjectCount	This behaves as `ProgrammableFilterProject` and also reports periodically on `done` a tuple with three elements denoting progress, such that the ith element of `outputCounts` is a count of how many values have been emitted on `outputs[i]`. Two other fields of the tuple: `inputCount` and `ignoredCount` give the number of values received on `input` and the number of those that did not result in any output. An `Error` is emitted on `errs` if any of the rules generate an error.
d	ReliableParallel-SQLQuery	This behaves as `ParallelSQLQuery`, but it emits a `SQLError` on `errs` if errors occur.
e	ReliableWriteFile	This writes to the file store, `source`, a file with path, `fPath`, and with the content corresponding to the list of vectors of bytes on `data`, each transfer starting at the byte offset given by the integer in the corresponding list position on `startByte`. If the file does not exist, it is created if the value on `create` is true. If a write cannot be completed, an `Error` is emitted on `errs`.
f	ReliableSQLInsert	This has the same function as `SQLInsert`, but it emits `SQLError` on `errs` if an error occurs.

which the process is running and enough information to identify which original trace in which archive each delivered item came from. The `ReliableBulkMover` will normally have a semantics, where it does not claim success until it has a delivery acknowledgment from the data's destination. It would perform a suitable number of retries before it admits defeat on `errs`. The instance `bmerred` records these admissions of failure.

When a request arrives, it needs in some way to contain a `taskNumber`, so that the logic does not redo the work already accomplished for this task. However, if a new task, for example, with modified preparation rules, is starting, a new `taskNumber` will ensure that steps are reperformed. The insertion of the check `NotYetDone` introduces logic that checks for each trace segment arriving on `todo`

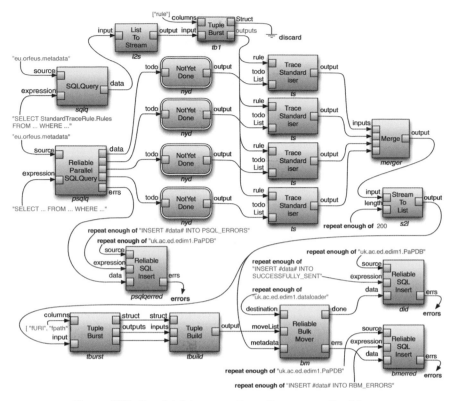

Figure 4.25 *Parallel data preparation with recovery after failures.*

whether it has been done already by consulting the table SUCCESSFULLY_SENT into which did recorded the successes. It removes things already done from the list and emits the remainder on its output for preparation processing and delivery as before. Thus, if work has been partially accomplished, a resubmission of the same task request should get more of it done. The resumption may be initiated by an automatic process, for example, by one that spots incomplete work as a gateway starts up or by an interface provided to domain experts and data-intensive engineers. This interface would include an option to discard the partially completed work. The TraceStandardiser PEs will do their own error handling; for example, they will report errors that arise during reading and writing the trace files or during the execution of the preparation rules.

A data-intensive engineer, or any other user for that matter, can examine the tables, PSQL_ERRORS and RBM_ERRORS, written by psqlqerred and bmerred, respectively, to assess whether errors have occurred. A portlet or workbench tool could help with this display and analysis. Summaries of what has been achieved and recorded errors can appear on the "dashboard," with a "drill-down" capability to allow deeper investigation via the recorded provenance data. Ultimately, automatic analysis of these records could generate DISPEL requests to fix or compensate for the errors and to update the tables with a record of the repair.

The error reports from instances of `ReliableSQLInsert` are all connected to the default error-handling stream `errors`. How it handles errors, for example, by displaying them on a dashboard, is implementation defined.

The record of achievements in `SUCCESSFULLY_SENT` can be analyzed by the region in which the trace was recorded or by time, in order to provide specific progress indicators on the distributed data collection and preparation.

4.8.2.2   Handling Errors During Phase 1 of Seismic Correlation   This phase was implemented in the DISPEL graph shown in Figure 4.18; the corresponding version augmented for recovery is shown in Figure 4.26. Two changes have been introduced. The instance `psqlarrivals` of `ReliableSQLInsert` records the arrival of each batch of prepared traces; comparisons between this and the `SUCCESSFULLY_SENT` will reveal data losses. The instance `pnyd` of `PairNotYetDone` removes from the list of pairs passed to the correlation farm any that have already been completed. Hence, retries after a failure will not redo work already completed. This depends on completion records being written after work has been completed and preserved. Once again, these records may be needed for provenance tracking and will be used to show progress toward task completion.

4.8.2.3   Recording Completed Work in the Third Phase of Seismic Correlation   The handling of completed seismic correlations was undertaken by an instance of `CorrHandler` as shown in Figure 4.22. Figure 4.27 shows the `CorrHandler` PE augmented with a recording step that provides the data for `pnyd`. This is accomplished by another `ReliableSQLInsert` instance, `stacked`, which records which of the correlation results have actually been used. This depends on modifying the type and implementation of `Stacker` (renaming it `ReliableStacker`) so that it yields such progress records. Alternatively, the recording of what has been

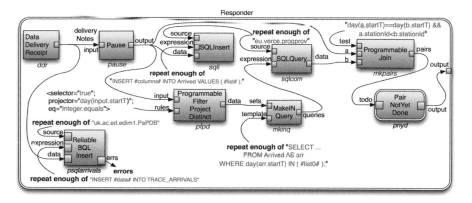

Figure 4.26   *Responding to data arrival with recovery after failures.*

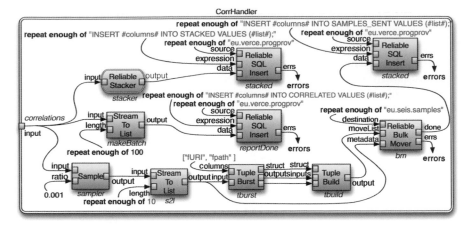

Figure 4.27 Handling correlation result data with recovery support.

used could be implemented inside Stacker, which would also save changing the PE type. The handling process has been further annotated into several other tables. This ancillary data to track progress and provenance can become large and the database operations to insert these records can become the speed-limiting factor. There is a design trade-off between the insertion traffic and the precision of provenance and recovery.

The accumulated information in SUCCESSFULLY_SENT, TRACE_ARRIVALS, CORRELATED, STACKED, and SAMPLES_SENT can be used by other data-intensive processes organized by data-intensive engineers to assess quality of processing, detect data losses, and recycle storage. These tables may also be analyzed in conjunction with performance records (Chapter 12), to understand the factors affecting performance and to focus on improvements in the critical places. The choice of the relational model for this provenance tracking is a matter of preference; others may choose log files, XML databases, or RDF stores.

4.9 THE DATA-TO-KNOWLEDGE HIGHWAY

This chapter has taken the reader on a rapid journey from a tutorial introduction of the basic features of DISPEL to the kind of language that is needed to describe and request sophisticated data-intensive processes. It has given a glimpse of the complexities and data scales that emerge even in apparently straightforward paths to discovering more knowledge from data. In doing so, it has introduced many of the "landmarks" seen on a typical journey along a highway from data to knowledge. Later parts of the chapter have introduced the reader to some of the "civil engineering" that must go on behind the scenes to make those journeys effective, efficient, and reliable.

```
/*
First of the examples of four functions from Section 4.4.1 to show complete
implementations. See Chapter 10 for DISPEL notations. This one makes a PE that takes
m inputs and combines them into a single output. */

package book.examples {
  use dispel.core.ListCombiner;            //any process combining list into a list
  PE <ListCombiner> makeMwayCombiner(      //result is an m way ListCombiner PE
    Integer m;                             //number of input streams supplying lists
    PE <ListCombiner> BC )                 //a BinaryCombiner compliant with ListCombiner
  {                                        //should check BC.inputs.length == 2
  if (m == 1) then  {                      //special cases terminate recursion
    BC bc = new BC;                        //use a single BC with empties on other stream
    |- repeat enough of [ ] -| => bc.inputs[1];   //infinite supply of empty lists
    return ListCombiner( <Connection inputs[0] = bc.inputs[0]> =>
                         <Connection output = bc.output> );
  };
  if (m == 2) then {                       //combining TWO inputs is just what
    return BC;                             //BC, the supplied PE, does
  };
  Connection[ ] inputsTmp = new Connection[m];      //will be the inputs
  Integer half = m/2;                      //divide and recurse to build tree
  Integer otherHalf = m-half;              //size of other tree branch
  ListCombiner FirstTree = makeMwayCombiner(half, BC);      //make one branch
  ListCombiner SecondTree = makeMwayCombiner(otherHalf, BC); //make other branch
  ListCombiner ft = new FirstTree;         //create first branch's subtree
  ListCombiner st = new SecondTree;        //create other branch's subtree
  ListCombiner base = new BC;              //use a BC to combine two subtrees
  Integer deposit = 0;                     //position in inputs
  for (Integer i = 0; i<half; i++) {       //connect first tree to first half of inputs
    inputsTmp[deposit] => ft.inputs[i];
    deposit++;
  };
  for (Integer i = 0; i<otherHalf; i++) {  //connect second tree to second half of inputs
    inputsTmp[deposit] => st.inputs[i];
    deposit++;
  };
  ft.output => base.inputs[0];             //connect output of first tree
  st.output => base.inputs[1];             //connect output of second tree
  return ListCombiner(<Connection inputs = inputsTmp>  =>    //result's inputs
                      <Connection output = base.output>)     //result's output
                      with inputs.length = m;    //assert number of inputs
  };
  register makeMwayCombiner;               //preserve and share definition for re-use
}
```

Figure 4.28 *Implementation of ListCombiner tree pattern used in examples earlier in the chapter but postponed until all aspects of DISPEL had been introduced (for a fuller introduction to DISPEL see Chapter 10 and Appendix B).*

The initial examples of PEs and their assembly into data-intensive data-streaming processes were straightforward. This introduced the concepts *PEs*, *processing-element instances*, *data streams*, and *connections*.

Then *functions* were introduced as a means of generating repeatedly required patterns, composing processing-element instances with connections and literal streams and delivering their results packaged as *composite PEs*. Parameterizing these functions with PEs or functions that yield PEs allows the composition of patterns. For

```
/*
Second of the examples of four functions from Section 4.4.1 to show complete
implementations. See Chapter 10 for DISPEL notations. This one makes a PE that
takes two inputs supplying streams and makes an n by n matrix of TheComb to
apply its process to every pair of values, taking one from each co-arriving list. */

package book.examples {
  use dispel.core.{ListCombiner,        //any PE that combines lists
                ListSplit};             //any PE that splits lists into sublists
  use book.examples.makeMwayCombiner;   //makes an m-input list combiner

  PE <ListCombiner> makeAllMeetsAll (   //make a PE to apply an f to every pair
  Integer n;                            //Size of the matrix of TheComb instances
  PE <ListCombiner> TheComb;            //PE that contains f
  PE <ListCombiner> TheAgg;             //a binary aggregator
  ) {
    ListSplit rowSplit = new ListSplit with outputs.length = n; //split first list
    ListSplit colSplit = new ListSplit with outputs.length = n; //split second list
    PE <ListCombiner> Agg = makeMwayCombiner(n*n, TheAgg);    //aggregates n^2 lists
    Agg agg = new Agg with inputs.length = n*n;               //for n^2 results
    Integer deposit = 0;                //next Agg inputs stream to use
    for (Integer row=0; row<n; row++) {         //construct n rows
      for (Integer col=0; col<n; col++) {       //of n columns
        TheComb tc = new TheComb with inputs.length=2;  //of f(x,y) in TheComb
        rowSplit[row] => tc.inputs[0];          //first sublist is x
        colSplit[col] => tc.inputs[1];          //second sublist is y
        tc.output => agg[deposit];              //collect the results
        deposit++;
      };
    };
    return ListCombiner (                       //prepare result
      <inputs[0] = rowSplit.input; inputs[1] = colSplit.input> =>
      <output = agg.output> );          //inputs rows and columns
  };                                    //output aggregation of all results

  register makeAllMeetsAll;             //preserve and share definition for re-use
}
```

Figure 4.29   *Implementation of all-meets-all pattern introduced in Section 4.4.1.2.*

example, the all-meets-all pattern was presented and parameterized with an operation to combine each pair of values. That combination pattern might itself use the all-meets-all pattern if the composition rule was complex and the values were large. Although not shown here, such pattern generation functions could use information about the target environment to produce more optimal implementations. The all-meets-all scenario explored here is at the heart of many implementations of relational join operations and is well explored in that context. It is also amenable to a MapReduce implementation, the function being applied during the map phase and the merge being incorporated in the reduction phase.

The mapping process can also use information provided by all three categories of expert. This is facilitated by a three-category type system that allows description of pertinent properties as the language is processed in preparation for enactment

```
/*
Third of the examples of four functions from Section 4.4.1 to show complete
implementations. See Chapter 10 for DISPEL notations. This one makes a PE that takes
one input, a stream of lists of seismic traces, and organises a cross-correlation
of all pairs of traces by using the all-meets-all pattern. */

package book.examples {
  use dispel.core.ListCombiner;              //used to embed the correlator function
  use book.examples.makeAllMeetsAll;         //applies function to all pairs
  use book.examples.seismology.{TraceMD,     //seismologists' trace metadata Stype
              CorrTraceMD};                   //correlation trace provenance metadata

  namespace seismo "http://dispel-lang.org/resources/book/examples/siesmology/";

  Type AllMeetsAllSymmetricCorrelator is PE (      //declare result type
    < Connection: [TraceMD]:: ["seismo:PreparedTraceDescription"] input > =>
    < Connection: [CorrTraceMD]::["seismo:CorrelationTraceDescription"] output >
  );

  PE <AllMeetsAllSymmetricCorrelator> makeAllMeetsAllSymmetricCorrelator(
    PE <ListCombiner> SeismicTraceCorrelator;    //correlates two lists of traces
    PE <ListCombiner> SeismicResultStacker)      //combines two lists of correlates
  {
      PE <ListCombiner> Correlator =             //make matrix to parallelise
          makeAllMeetsAll(5, SeismicTraceCorrelator, SeismicResultStacker);
      Correlator theCorrelator = new Correlator with inputs.length=2;
      Connection inputTraces;                    //incoming stream of lists of traces
      inputTraces => theCorrelator.inputs[0];    //sent to both correlator inputs
      inputTraces => theCorrelator.inputs[1];    //to obtain self-correlation
      return AllMeetsAllSymmetricCorrelator(     //construct result PE type
        < input  = inputTraces> =>               //with input from inputTraces
        < output = theCorrelator.output> );      //with output from correlator
  };

  register makeAllMeetsAllSymmetricCorrelator;   //keep and share for re-use
}
```

Figure 4.30 *Implementation of a self-join pattern introduced in Section 4.4.1.*

and separate description of consistency properties required as an enactment streams data. This latter role was divided into structural information, which can be thought of as an abstraction of formats, and semantic information about the interpretation of data of relevance to the domain specialists. These three elements of description promise a framework for significant help during workflow editing, improved validation of workflows, automated adaptation to preserve the meaning of a workflow, and optimization based on many factors derived from multiple sources.

The ongoing example of performing a correlation of all of a potentially large set of seismic traces provided a means of exploring progressively more sophisticated approaches. There could have been a very simple example that just retrieved the traces and fed them into a single SeismicCorrelator PE. The farming of the correlation tasks was first considered as an all-meets-all pattern, and some of the issues about choosing the scale of parallelization were explored. As distribution and larger scales were introduced, new forms of parallelism, integrated with

```
/* Fourth of the examples of four functions from Section 4.4.1 to show complete
implementations. See Chapter 10 for DISPEL notations. This one makes a PE that
implements the actions behind a seismic traces noise correlation portal.   */

package book.examples {
  use book.examples.seismology.{ AllMeetsAllSymmetricCorrelator,
          makeAllMeetsAllSymmetricCorrelator, SeismicTraceCorrelator,
          SeismicResultStacker, TracePreparer, TraceMD };
  use dispel.db.SQLQuery;
  use dispel.core.{ ListMerge, Deliver };
  use dispel.util.{ timeToString, fillStringArgs};
  namespace seismo "http://dispel-lang.org/resources/book/examples/siesmology/";
                                        //function behind seismology correlation portal
  PE <Submitable> correlateAll (        //that provides the following parameters
            String[ ] dataSources;      //URIs of seismology archives to search
            Time start, finish;         //UCT of start and end of period of interest
            String resultsName ) {      //seismologist's name for the results
   String queryTemplate =               //Prepare SQL query to find traces
    "SELECT T.filePath, T.segmentStart, T.segmentLength "     +
    "FROM TraceCatalogue AS T "                               +
    "WHERE T.START_TIME AFTER $1$ AND T.END_TIME BEFORE $2$; ";
   String[ ] params = new { timeToString(start), timeToString(finish) };
   String query = fillStringArgs(queryTemplate, params);//replace $n$ with params[n-1]
   Stream qs = |- query -|;                   //only running once so stream of query once
   String getRules =                          //Prepare SQL query to find rules
    "SELECT RULES.PREPARE_RULES AS rules FROM RULES; ";
   Stream grs = |- getRules -|;               //form stream of that query
   Integer n = dataSources.length;            //Make data extract and prep for each source
   ListMerge lm = new ListMerge with inputs.length = n;
   for (Integer i=0; i<n; i++) {
     SQLQuery sqlq = new SQLQuery with: [TraceMD]::obtain trace metadata from archive
                                 ["seismo:ArchivedTraceDescription"] data;
     qs => sqlq.expression;  |- dataSources[i] -| => qs.source;
     SQLQuery getr = new SQLQuery with: [<String rules>] data;  //obtain rules ditto
     grs => getr.expression; |- dataSources[i] -| => grs.source;
     TracePreparer tp = new TracePreparer;   //cleans and standardises traces
     qs.data => tp.input;                     //supply traces' metadata to be prepared
     grs.data => tp.rules;                    //supply rules applicable for same archive
     tp.output => lm.inputs[i];               //feed into merge of prepared traces
   };                                         //Make Trace Corellator
  AllMeetsAllSymmetricCorrelator amasc =      //set up correlator instance
    new makeAllMeetsAllSymmetricCorrelator(SeismicTraceCorrelator,
                                 SeismicResultStacker);
   lm.output => amasc.input;                  //deliver metadata lists of prepared traces
   Deliver del = new Deliver;                 //set up result delivery system
   amasc.output => del.input;                 //send results from correlator
   |- "eu.org.orfeus.PlateImaging" -| => del.destination;   //to standard destination
   |- resultsName -| => del.name;             //with seismologist's specified name
   return Submitable( < > => < > );           //result has no input or output
   };
   register correlateAll;                     //save and share for re-use
}
```

Figure 4.31   *Implementation of a portal-function pattern introduced in Section 4.4.1.1.*

databases at the data source, were considered. This led to a restructuring of the process into a sort-and-merge pattern with multiple phases that were characterized as PEs that would normally be developed independently. This independent treatment was demonstrated as controls and feedback mechanisms were introduced to each phase, represented as a composite PE, in turn. This demonstration of independent development continued, as error handling and recovery were considered. Along the way, a characteristic application architecture emerged.

This shows us that the data-to-knowledge journey involves intertwining paths.

- As the path from data to knowledge is explored, scale and complexity challenges often emerge.
- Incrementally, constructing and refining components are natural responses to meeting those challenges.
- The types provide a scaffold for progressively improving the descriptions of components.
- A language and a registry enable the three communities of experts to collaborate effectively, helping each other on the journey from data to knowledge.

Addressing each of these aspects for every knowledge-discovery task is unacceptably difficult at present, as there are too many such tasks to address piecemeal. As the wealth of data grows, as expectations of good intelligence gathering from data rise, and as the population of would-be knowledge discoverers expands, the piecemeal approach becomes ever more infeasible. The only sustainable strategy is an evolving digital-data ecology well supported by R&D investment and a growing industry to deliver its benefits. It will contain a mixture of tools, services, PEs, data sources, and data-intensive platforms. When these are organized so that the journey from data to knowledge is as smooth as current understanding permits, we call these "*Highways from data to knowledge.*" Much needs to be done to understand how best to build those highways. We hope that readers will read on and garner good ideas from our experience relevant to their goals and then contribute either as critical users demanding better highways or as engineers delivering better highways.

REFERENCES

1. Language and Architecture Team, ADMIRE project, "DISPEL: data-intensive systems process engineering language users' manual (version 1.0)," tech. rep., School of Informatics, University of Edinburgh, 2011.
2. D. Rodríguez, T. Carpenter, J. I. van Hemert, and J. Wardlaw, "An open source toolkit for medical imaging de-identification," *European Radiology*, vol. 20, pp. 1896–1904, 2010.
3. D. De Roure, C. Goble, and R. Stevens, "The design and realisation of the myExperiment virtual research environment for social sharing of workflows," *Future Generation Computer Systems*, vol. 25, pp. 561–567, 2009.

4. CIDR 2011, in *Fifth Biennial Conference on Innovative Data Systems Research, Asilomar, CA, USA, January 9–12, 2011, Online Proceedings*, www.crdrdb.org, 2011.

5. G. Bell, J. Gray, and A. S. Szalay, "Petascale computational systems: balanced cyber-infrastructure in a data-centric world," *IEEE Computer*, vol. 39, no. 1, pp. 110–112, 2006.

6. A. S. Szalay, G. Bell, J. vanden Berg, A. Wonders, R. C. Burns, D. Fay, J. Heasley, A. J. G. Hey, M. A. Nieto-Santisteban, A. R. Thakar, C. van Ingen, and R. Wilton, "GrayWulf: scalable clustered architecture for data intensive computing," in *Hawaii International Conference on Systems Sciences*, pp. 1–10, 2009.

7. V. Singh, J. Gray, A. R. Thakar, A. S. Szalay, J. Raddick, B. Boroski, S. Lebedeva, and B. Yanny, "SkyServer traffic report—the first five years," tech. rep. MSR-TR-2006-190, Microsoft Research, December 2006.

8. P. Baumann, "Array databases and raster data management," in *Encyclopedia of Database Systems* (T. Özsu and L. Liu, eds.), Springer, 2009.

9. R. L. Grossman, Y. Gu, J. Mambretti, M. Sabala, A. S. Szalay, and K. P. White, "An overview of the open science data cloud," in *High-Performance Cloud Computing*, pp. 377–384, 2010.

10. M. Stonebraker, D. Abadi, D. J. DeWitt, S. Madden, E. Paulson, A. Pavlo, and A. Rasin, "MapReduce and parallel DBMSs: friends or foes?" *Communications of the ACM*, vol. 53, no. 1, pp. 64–71, 2010.

11. E. Deelman and A. L. Chervenak, "Data management challenges of data-intensive scientific workflows," in *IEEE/ACM International Symposium on Cluster, Cloud and Grid Computing*, pp. 687–692, 2008.

Part II

Data-Intensive Knowledge Discovery

Part I of this book described a number of challenges that face those wanting to harness the power of data for their own or their organization's benefit, and a number of ideas for overcoming them. It focused on providing an overview of what data-intensive methods can do for organizations or individuals, and was addressed to a wide range of readers, from technology leaders and research strategists, to users that have to face data-intensive problems, to technology providers that support these users.

This part is mainly addressed to data-analysis experts and those who want to know how data-intensive thinking is provoking changes in the way in which we have approached knowledge discovery so far. The introduction of heterogeneity in data sources and the need to deal with bulkier, less structured, and more dynamic data sources generate the need to adapt the techniques to be used, and sometimes, and more importantly, the approach to problem solving. This may mean that models are updated more frequently and are more adaptive to changes in the data sources. This may also require different computational models to deal with the added computational requirements.

Therefore, we aim to provide readers with a more thorough description of the principles and problem-solving strategies that will guide them in this data-rich world, without going into the unnecessary details of the underlying enabling technologies. We will describe the usual steps followed in a typical data-intensive

The DATA Bonanza: Improving Knowledge Discovery in Science, Engineering, and Business, First Edition.
Edited by Malcolm Atkinson, Rob Baxter, Michelle Galea, Mark Parsons, Peter Brezany, Oscar Corcho, Jano van Hemert, and David Snelling.
© 2013 John Wiley & Sons, Inc. Published 2013 by John Wiley & Sons, Inc.

data-driven process, and compare this process with more conventional approaches. We will illustrate some of the key tasks in the process, which are organized according to a generic knowledge discovery process that is still valid in this context: understanding data, preparing it, analyzing it, generating data models, evaluating and deploying them, and visualizing the results.

It is important to note that we will not focus on specific methods or techniques to be used for each type of problem, but will instead provide some ideas on the range of available methods and techniques, from conventional to more recent ones. We will demonstrate how these methods and techniques should be organized in order to solve problems, with the aim of promoting the new way of thinking that data-analysis experts may practice in a data-intensive context.

Most of the literature in the area of knowledge discovery has focused on the description of specific methods, techniques and tools that can be applied in each phase of the knowledge discovery process (e.g., [1–3]), and not on providing a higher level of abstraction over the knowledge discovery processes themselves. The approaches closest to the one that we present here are CRISP-DM (*CRoss Industry Standard Process for Data Mining*, www.crisp-dm.org), CAT (*Clementine Application Templates*, now deprecated) and the SEMMA process (*sample, explore, modify, model, assess*[1]). However, they are not necessarily addressing the problems and solutions in the context of data-intensive knowledge discovery yet. We can safely say that at the time of writing this book there is a lack of guidance and material on knowledge discovery strategies in data-rich environments.

In terms of software support, the situation is better and improving, although there is still much work to be done in order to incorporate the new required algorithms and techniques into the common software tools used by data analysts; due to limitations in the current software or lack of availability of implementations, many data analysts resort to implementing their own versions for use with their preferred tool. A few tools are however being actively extended to deal with large scale and/or streaming data and these include Weka, with its Massive Online Analysis project (moa.cs.waikato.ac.nz), and RapidMiner with its Radoop extension (rapid-i.com).

Finally, this part will also reflect on the sharing and reuse strategies that can be put in place by knowledge discovery teams in order to increase their productivity. Such teams should be able to use and contribute to libraries of knowledge discovery components, something already present in the current state-of-the-art knowledge discovery tools (e.g., in the RapidMiner library [4], in myExperiment [5]), and usage patterns, which are less predominant in the current state of the art.

REFERENCES

1. I. H. Witten, E. Frank, and M. A. Hall, *Data Mining: Practical Machine Learning Tools and Techniques (Third Edition)*. Morgan Kauffman, 2011.

---

[1] www.sas.com/offices/europe/uk/technologies/analytics/datamining/miner/semma.html, verified January 2013.

2. D. Pyle, *Data Preparation for Data Mining*. San Francisco, CA, Morgan Kaufmann Publishers Inc., 1999.

3. N. Ye, *The Handbook of Data Mining*. Lawrence Erlbaum Associates, 2003.

4. I. Mierswa, M. Wurst, R. Klinkenberg, M. Scholz, and T. Euler, "Yale: rapid prototyping for complex data mining tasks," in *KDD '06: Proceedings of the 12th ACM SIGKDD International Conference on Knowledge Discovery and Data Mining* (L. Ungar, M. Craven, D. Gunopulos, and T. Eliassi-Rad, eds.), pp. 935–940. New York, ACM, 2006.

5. D. De Roure, C. Goble, and R. Stevens, "The Design and Realisation of the myExperiment Virtual Research Environment for Social Sharing of Workflows," *Future Generation Computer Systems*, vol. 25, pp. 561–567, 2009.

5

Data-Intensive Analysis

Oscar Corcho

*Departamento de Inteligencia Artificial, Universidad Politécnica de Madrid,
Madrid, Spain*

Jano van Hemert

Optos plc, Queensferry House, Dunfermline, UK

In this chapter, we show a set of prototypical scenarios that highlight the tasks that a data analysis team must deal with when approaching knowledge discovery problems. These problems are related to common activities of Telco Inc., a fictitious telecommunications company. Paul, a data analysis expert, and his team want to make use of the customer data that the company has stored over the recent years to enhance their understanding of their customer base. The analysts' goals are to find ways to provide a better service to Telco Inc.'s customers by offering them new deals and tariff packages (a strategy known as *up-selling*) and cross-selling additional products, by increasing their brand loyalty, so as to prevent them from moving to another competitor (a phenomenon known as *customer churn*), and ultimately, of course, maximize the company's profit. How the analyst and his team set about meeting these goals will be used as a running example throughout the rest of Part II, with the main objective of illustrating some of the key tasks that need to be performed in a typical data-driven process: understanding, preparing, and analyzing data; generating, evaluating, and deploying data models; and visualizing the results.

The example is presented as three scenarios of increasing complexity and scale. We start with a rather conventional scenario where a customer churn prediction

The DATA Bonanza: Improving Knowledge Discovery in Science, Engineering, and Business, First Edition.
Edited by Malcolm Atkinson, Rob Baxter, Michelle Galea, Mark Parsons, Peter Brezany, Oscar Corcho,
Jano van Hemert, and David Snelling.

model is built from the company's own data sources. Then we move to a more complex scenario where, following a company merger, the data sources of two companies have to be integrated, increasing levels of heterogeneity in the generation of the churn prediction model. Finally, we describe a scenario where less conventional techniques—graph analysis and stream mining—have to be applied in a more-heterogeneous and less-controlled scenario, with data originating not only from company databases but also from streams of social network information, such as microblog feeds.

We attempt to keep the three scenarios simple enough, in terms of data sources used and analyses performed, to make their treatment in the later chapters straightforward. This contrasts with what would be done in a "live" business context, as the real-world use case described in Chapter 14 illustrates in the domain of telecommunications. Nevertheless, we will see how our example covers a number of the knowledge discovery activities identified in Chapter 7, including characterization, classification, prediction, cluster analysis, evolution analysis, data-stream mining, graph mining, and so on. Our overall goal in this chapter is to set the scene for a classic knowledge discovery challenge, so that the problem-solving strategies and standard knowledge discovery design patterns to be described in the following chapters can be better understood.

5.1   KNOWLEDGE DISCOVERY IN TELCO INC.

Paul has been promoted recently to a customer manager position in Telco Inc., a fictitious telecommunications company. In this new role, his team is responsible for understanding what makes the company's customers stay, and perhaps, more importantly, why they leave. Such understanding will then be used by the company to predict customer churn and, most importantly, to establish successful well-informed strategies to prevent it (e.g., through up-selling and cross-selling).

Some years ago, achieving this goal would have required Paul to talk to a large number of people, including customer relationship phone operators, mobile phone resellers, and other experts. However, given the large amount of data about each customer that the company has been accumulating over the years—personal details, pricing plans, call records, and so on—Paul decides that he will base his decisions exclusively on those data. Therefore, he will need to understand the available data, filter them, and process them suitably to understand the behavior of his customers and thus hopefully prevent them from moving to another operator. Fortunately, all the required data are available in the company's databases, including information about users, types of tariffs, call records, contracted services, and so on. However, some of these databases are quite large, and in some of them, the information is unreliable because of duplicate records, missing information, identity resolution problems, and so on. Furthermore, some of the information that they contain may not be in a suitable format for use in this particular way—the databases were designed to facilitate billing, not for predictive analytics. This means that Paul will need to preprocess the data, selecting the most appropriate attributes, generating appropriate summaries, and applying suitable data analysis algorithms. All this will also need to be done iteratively, where the filters and the algorithms applied will change and adapt according to evolving requirements.

Several months later, Telco Inc. merges with another company, which also stores similar types of information about their customers. In fact, it may be the case that some of these customers are shared, as some of them may have moved from one company to other in the past or may have active phone accounts with both companies (e.g., for their personal and work mobile phones). Obviously, as the two companies' databases have been created separately and by different development groups, they are organized differently (different degrees of detail in the information that they contain, different data quality, etc.). Merging these systems requires a large effort of alignment and integration between them, both for operational purposes (to continue recording call details from customers, for billing, etc.) and for knowledge discovery purposes (understanding the behavior of different sets of customers or of shared customers that have phones with the two companies). Therefore, the complexity of running Paul's data analysis algorithms increases, and given the larger number of records that these algorithms now have to deal with, their performance may be adversely affected. For this reason, Paul needs to think about the characteristics of the algorithms used, to analyze whether they can still be applied in a reasonable time, and find alternative ones if necessary.

While these two knowledge discovery tasks may seem rather demanding and challenging, they are relatively standard, state-of-the-art types of data analyses, and made by most competitors. In order to get ahead of the company's competitors, Paul is considering the possibility of trying to connect mobile phone customer records available in the company databases with information from the social networks of each customer, and the relationships between calls that they make to each other. This would allow the company to offer special deals for groups of people (e.g., very cheap calls among all the members of a group who normally interact together, or when a relevant event is about to happen). Additional analyses of these data sources may allow the company to know almost instantaneously about any positive or negative sentiments about itself and about its competitors (known as *sentiment analysis*), especially if coming from its own customers. This is an example of an exploratory analysis, where heterogeneous private and public sources of information (customer and call databases, Twitter accounts, Facebook networks, etc.) need to be aligned. Data analysis experts such as Paul will need tools to be able to perform this kind of integration and analysis of such disparate sources in a more flexible and innovative way. The range of data analysis tasks that have to be performed in this case will extend to more advanced techniques in data stream and graph analysis, techniques well beyond those needed in the previous scenarios.

The rest of this Part will describe how Paul and his team will work in this data-intensive environment, taking into account the emerging business and data-driven requirements. We leave the details of how all these are implemented to Part III.

5.2 UNDERSTANDING CUSTOMERS TO PREVENT CHURN

In this scenario, the analysts' primary goal is to predict which customers will leave Telco Inc. for a rival. A secondary goal is to model those customers, to understand better the reasons why a customer decides to leave, to provide a way of predicting whether a customer might be about to leave, and thus to identify customers to whom timely offers might provide just enough incentive for them to stay.

5.2.1 Building a Churn Prediction Model

Let us first take a look at the data that we will use in this example. As noted previously, these data are simplified in the interest of keeping the example easy to follow. Real telecommunications companies have much more complex data structures, as they have to keep track, for example, of a changing landscape of tariff plans, as described in Chapter 14. Furthermore, many more attributes may exist about a given customer, their phones, and their phone usage.

Our data are organized as two large, main tables and some other auxiliary ones, illustrated in Figure 5.1. The first main table (CDM_CUSTOMERS_T) contains information about customers and is linked to their tariff plans. The combined tables contain a unique identifier for each customer, their current tariff plan (note that name mappings and joins are needed, for example, the tariff plan is in CDM_CONTRACTS_T as TARIF_PLAN_VARIANT_ID), the start date of this plan, the minimum duration of the plan, the total time the customer has been with this company, and, most importantly, whether they are still with the company. The second main table

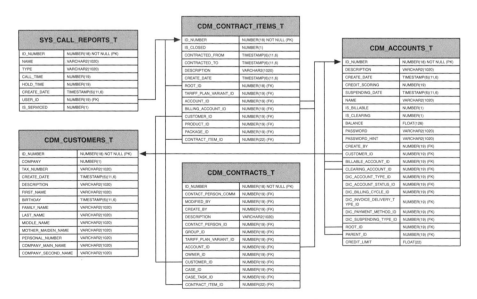

Figure 5.1 *Data structure diagram for tables about customers.*

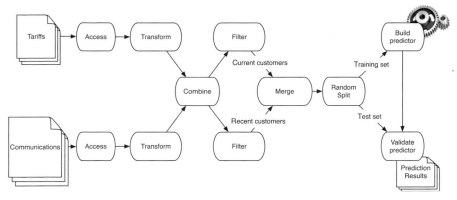

Figure 5.2 *Dataflow diagram that shows a straightforward approach to the construction of a prediction model for customer churn based on communication and tariff data.*

(SYS_CALL_REPORTS_T) consists of "communications" undertaken by all customers. Each row in this table contains a unique customer id, the type of communication (e.g., text, speech, voice mail, and data), the number called, the target network, the time and date of the call, the length of the call, and the cost of the call. The other tables provide additional information about the accounts of the company customers and contracts and their items.

Paul's hypothesis is that these data contain sufficient information to model why customers leave the company, and thus to predict when they might, before they do. In this example, we will use classification trees, a common approach used in the classification of data.

The full set of tasks is shown in Figure 5.2. The first step is to provide access to the tables. We will assume that these are stored in a relational database with external access enabled for people in Paul's team to send queries and to extract the results of those queries. This may not be the case in many knowledge discovery scenarios, where access to data has to be performed using specialized application program-ming interfaces (APIs) Web services, and so on, as we will see in Section 5.4. A set of queries are necessary to build the data model for performing the classification task. These queries take communication data for each customer and transform and integrate these as needed. For instance, a query may calculate the average length of calls made by a customer over a recent period, or a distribution of call frequency over the days of the week. These data are used to augment the customer data and build up a large physical table (following a data-warehousing approach) that contains many descriptive attributes for each customer. This attribute table will be used as an input for the next step of prediction model building.

The next stage is to perform a filtering step that selects the two subsets of data that we are interested in: recent customers who have left the company and current customers who have stayed with the company over the same period of time. The size of both subsets should be roughly the same, so as to avoid bias in the final results. This is generally regarded as good practice, even though classification trees, our chosen classification technique in this example, are normally able to handle imbalances of positive and negative examples. The balanced dataset that results from merging both subsets will form the input to our modeling step.

Once we have this rich dataset about each customer, we are ready to create a model to describe their behavior. We will use a classification tree to classify the augmented customer dataset into customers who have stayed and customers who have left, based on the properties that were generated during the data access and transformation steps. Following normal practice, we split the dataset into two distinct subsets: the training set, used to create the model, and the test set, used to validate the model's accuracy. The selection of the data records that go into each dataset is done randomly, again so as to avoid any bias introduced by the ordering in the original database.

The classification tree is generated with an appropriate classification tree-building algorithm (e.g., ID3 [1], C4.5 [2], CHAID [3], MARS [4], etc.). The selection of such algorithm will depend on several factors. For instance, one important factor is whether the attributes are numerical or categorical, as different algorithms are suitable for different types of data. A possible resulting classification tree for our example would be the one presented in Figure 5.3. As we can see, the most relevant attribute is related to the time until the end of the contract; 90% of customers with more than 2 weeks till the termination of their contract will stay with the company. If they are in the last 2 weeks of the contract, the next attribute to consider is whether they have themselves contacted a competitor (which can be known, as we have the list of calls made by the customer). In that case, the classification tree informs us that two-thirds of those who have contacted a competitor are prone to leave our company. Then we consider age, as younger people are more prone to leaving the company than less-young people, and hence should be contacted. In this manner, we can continue walking down the tree to classify a customer.

Then the predictive quality of the resulting tree is validated. For that, we execute it with all the items in the test set, which contain all attributes, and we tally the number of times it correctly classifies customers. This is used to determine the accuracy of the model.

5.2.2 Deploying the Prediction Model and Presenting Results

Paul has derived a prediction model from the available data, and he is happy with the prediction accuracy, so he can move on to the deployment phase. Here, the outcome of the previous process (the prediction model represented by the classification tree of Fig. 5.3) is used to predict whether an existing customer is likely to move to another company. The resulting list of predictions must then be filtered appropriately so that it can be sent to the customer care and marketing departments.

Figure 5.4 shows the dataflow for the execution of the prediction model. The process starts, as in the previous example, by accessing data from the main tables,

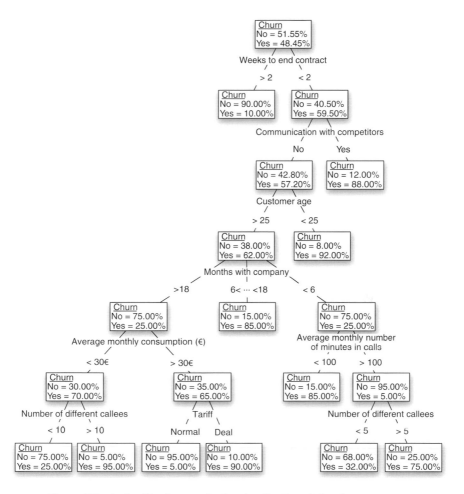

Figure 5.3 *A classification tree for the classification of churning customers.*

but also adds in the general customer details, as customers flagged as "likely to churn" will need to be contacted to offer them new deals (the filtering step for this dataset removes recent customers). Once the raw data have been read, they must again be transformed and joined to yield a uniform list that can be used as input for the "Apply predictor" step, which brings in the classification model learned from the training data.

A very important element in the whole knowledge discovery process is that of presenting the results of the prediction appropriately, so that all the stakeholders involved can get useful information according to their interests. The results of this step are used in several ways. On the one hand, descriptive summaries and reports are generated for the company managers, including the graphical representation of the classification tree, percentages of customers falling in each node, and so on,

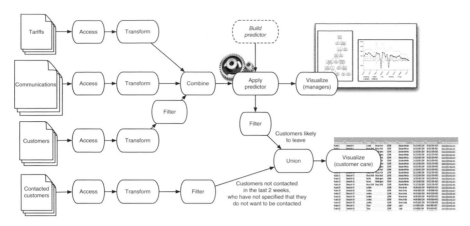

Figure 5.4   *Dataflow diagram that applies the prediction model over the list of customers.*

so that they can have a better characterization of the company's customers. On the another hand, the customers who are likely to churn are filtered progressively (there is no need to contact those for whom there is no evidence that they will leave the company, and it is not good practice to contact those who have been contacted within the last 2 weeks, or who have decided not to be contacted). This information will be used by the customer care manager on duty to assign these records to calling agents, which are responsible for "walking the last mile."

5.3   PREVENTING CHURN ACROSS MULTIPLE COMPANIES

The previous section showed how Paul and his team addressed a classic data analysis challenge using data available in their company. However, what happens if Telco Inc. merges with one of its rivals, PhoneCo, which has also a large international presence across the world? In this case, a similar analysis will need to be performed over new data, which may require changes to the filtering conditions applied to data, to the queries run over datasets, the classification methods used, and so on. There is also the important aspect of scale that arises from this new scenario: how much "bigger" might the analysis task get with these new data and added complexity? The typical size of any of these companies would be that of a few hundred million customers, presence in tens of countries in different continents, and a few billion calls every day.

5.3.1   Building a Churn Prediction Model from Heterogeneous Data

Paul now needs to perform the same kind of analysis (detecting when a customer is likely to move to another company) but must extend the analysis to a second set of databases from PhoneCo. Initially, this task may look simple, but Paul has to overcome some new problems:

- the preprocessing steps used in the original system (including the data access, transformation, and combination tasks from Fig. 5.2) have to be adapted for the new databases. The objective is to generate the same set of attributes for each customer record, so that these data can be used to build and validate the same kind of classifier;
- the computational performance of the data analysis system reduces dramatically with the inclusion of new data sources, because the number of items to deal with doubles, considering that the new company has a similar number of customers.

There may be also some legal problems associated with the fact that one company is now aiming at using data from another one (even if they merged), when customers may not have signed any agreement about transferring their data from one company to another. However, for the purpose of our explanation, we will consider that this has been already sorted out through the corresponding legal departments of both companies.

Let us assume that the databases from the PhoneCo company have their data stored in three large main tables instead of two. As in the first scenario, one table contains customer details and information about their tariff plans. It contains a unique identifier for each customer (current or recent) and their history of tariff plans. Some of these tariff plans are very similar across companies, and others are company specific. Besides, the identifiers used in this table are uncorrelated to those used in the corresponding table at Telco Inc. This means that two customers, each belonging to each company, may be identified with the same identifier in both tables or that different identifiers may be used to refer to the same customer, if that person has phones with both companies. The second table stores details of calls *initiated* by all customers. Each row in this table contains a unique customer id, the number called, the target network, the time and date of the call, the length of the call, and the cost of the call. The third table stores details of calls *received* by all customers, with a similar structure to the previous one, except for the cost.

As described before, the hypothesis is that the combined data from the two companies contain sufficient information to characterize why customers leave the company, and thus to predict in advance when they might. Paul's hypothesis now has an added assumption that even if the schemas and structure of the new data sources are different, a single classifier can be used for this purpose. An alternative would be to use two independent classifiers, but Paul expects to get a better understanding of his customers, and a better classification accuracy, with the singleton approach, as he now has more information with which to build a model. He may, for instance, be able to identify relations between more customers, as some of the calls made or received by Telco Inc. customers may have been with PhoneCo customers. Once again, Paul will use classification trees to create the classification model.

Paul's first decision is to use the same data model as before to characterize the new customers; thus, every customer will be described by the same set of attributes. This means that there is no need to adapt the access, transformation, and integration tasks that he used for the original Telco Inc. data. However, given that the tables used by PhoneCo are different, these tasks have to be adapted with new queries and new transformations, while keeping the same overall sequence of access, transformation, and combination steps. For instance, in the PhoneCo data, the calls initiated and received by customers are in separate tables and contain slightly different information. After this process, two large tables (one for each company) will have been generated and will contain descriptive attributes for each customer. These tables can be integrated by resolving the relationships between customers' calls in both companies, which generates a final single table.

It is important to note that appropriate mechanisms have to be applied here in order to avoid merging two originally independent records coming from the databases of the two companies when these two records refer to two different customers, although they share the same internal identifiers in both places. Furthermore, identity resolution mechanisms may be applied here to try to identify whether a single customer belongs to both companies and hence whether their records may be merged. There are potential residual errors in both directions, the same individual still may have unmatched identities in the two companies and some mergers may combine separate people with similar attributes. A responsible company would have mechanisms for handling such errors promptly, for example, they have kept enough data to avoid a false identity merge.

The rest of the process is the same as before, as shown in the lower part of Figure 5.5.

5.3.2 Deploying the Prediction Model and Presenting Results

Having built a new prediction model, Paul can move on to the deployment phase. In this scenario, the combined data means that the computing capacity required for the analysis is much larger, and the previous hardware setup may not be powerful enough to apply the newly created classifier over the larger amount of data that now has to be handled. Hence, Paul may need to contact a team of data-intensive engineers to solve the issues associated with the computational challenges that this new scenario generates. Despite this, the high level deployment scheme does not change much (Fig. 5.6): the new data sources are now included, the same set of access, transformation, filtering, and combination operations are performed, and the classifier is applied on the union of all these data sources. This is an excellent illustration of the separation of concerns enabled by this approach: as a data analysis expert, Paul can concentrate on his tasks without having to worry about the lower-level implementation details; these he can safely leave to the data-intensive engineers, and this will be dealt with in Part III of this book.

The complexity of the dataflow graph seems to increase significantly with two companies involved together with the data volumes that have to be handled. For every additional company that is added, we would require adding similar steps to

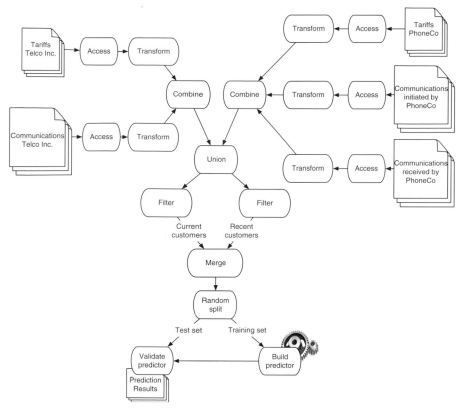

Figure 5.5 *Dataflow diagram that shows data integrated from two companies in order to construct a prediction model over combined communication/tariff data.*

the graph, and the data volumes would continue to grow, becoming increasingly more difficult to handle.

5.4 UNDERSTANDING CUSTOMERS BY COMBINING HETEROGENEOUS PUBLIC AND PRIVATE DATA

Having dealt effectively with the challenges of the merger and delivered useful tools to his marketing and customer care departments, Paul wants to go further in obtaining added value from the exploration and exploitation of data, keeping in mind the same business goal of understanding better the company customers and predicting whether they are likely to leave the company, so as to prevent churn. Now, Paul wants to identify trends in the communication behaviors of company customers, and he wants to do this using not only the private data stored by the company but also data from other communication media, such as Twitter, where explicit information such as mentions, retweets, and networks of followers and

Figure 5.6   *Dataflow diagram that shows data integrated from two companies in order to apply the prediction model over the combined list of customers.*

followees can be easily obtained (e.g., using the Twitter public API). This will enable the identification of communication trends across a combined set of media, and thus enable the company to react more quickly to these trends by offering special deals to customers and groups of customers, potentially increasing brand loyalty and perhaps attracting new customers.

As a side effect of this strategy, information available in the public blogosphere may allow detection of trends on the opinion about the company (known as *opinion mining* or *sentiment analysis*) from customers and noncustomers, on which the company has to react quickly in order to avoid losses.

In these examples, private data about customers are combined with publicly available data. The overall aim of this combination is to identify better those relationships between customers, which could not be obtained from the private data alone. This characterization needs to consider the dynamic nature of the data under consideration so that it can identify trends almost instantaneously (e.g., people communicating about an event happening in an hour's time or negative comments being spread quickly on the blogosphere). As a result of this, better pricing plans or immediate deals may be devised, not only for individuals but also for user groups (e.g., by generating communication plans for whole groups, it may be possible to convert some of the members of the group from their existing network supplier to the company). Furthermore, the company's marketing department may also react more quickly to negative comments, especially if they are posted by its customers.

This endeavor is technically more challenging than the previous ones in terms of the greater complexity and scale of the data to be handled. First, the data sources are more heterogeneous and less structured, unlike the previous cases where the data were controlled by the organization making use of them and where data schemas shared some similarities across both companies. The additional data sources, for instance, contain no information about pricing plans or costs of the interactions (which are free), and they are not available in the same structured format and accessible with the same mechanisms (e.g., as relational databases that can be queried using SQL) but are largely in the form of graphs of followers and followees, direct messages between users, and short texts (e.g., fewer than 140 characters if in Twitter), which are accessible through specialized APIs. Second, the volume of data to be handled will be much larger: interactions through online networking sites are typically "bulkier" than those through phone calls. Third, the data sources are inherently dynamic, and this has to be considered in the analysis and deployment process, especially in the case of characterizing users and identifying events or extracting opinions. Fourth, and most importantly, given the interest in dealing with groups instead of individuals, and in reacting almost immediately to communication and information trends detected in user groups, new data analysis methods are needed: techniques related to graph analysis, perhaps, for detecting communication "hubs" in the group (group leaders), data-stream analysis to account for the fact that communication between users comes as a continuous stream of data from external and internal data sources, and specialized text-mining techniques for dealing with the content of short text messages.

Finally, very important ethical and legal issues related to data privacy in this context may also arise, especially considering the international nature of telecommunications companies, with different national laws in place about data protection. In principle, private data held by the company is controlled under the agreements established in the supplier contract between each customer and the company and overseen by the corresponding telecommunications regulators, and public data on the blogosphere (e.g., available as microblogs, blogs, etc.) is publicly provided by users, and access to it is freely available by open APIs. The main difficulty here would lie in connecting the customer identifiers in the company databases with the corresponding usernames that these customers have online. Although this may provoke concerns around information privacy, it is not unrealistic to think that a large number of customers will provide public information about their mobile phone number on their social networking profiles or Web company profiles. In fact, they may even provide it directly to the phone company if asked for it in the context of a marketing campaign. Such privacy and ethical issues are discussed in [5].

5.4.1   Building Models with Public and Private, Structured and Nonstructured Data

Paul has identified new data sources that he wants to include in the data analysis process, as described above and shown on the upper-right side of Figure 5.7. As in the previous cases of structured data sources, some access and transformation steps have to be applied in order to obtain the necessary data (graphs of followers and followees, graphs of direct messages between customers, and texts where the company is mentioned). In this context, the cleaning steps are much more important than in the previous cases: the information that can be obtained from online sites is normally much less structured or controlled and much of it may need to be removed before proceeding to the next steps. The methods of data access are also different: these data are not available as relational data sources, which can be queried using SQL sentences but through specialized APIs.

In addition to these changes to the original process, a new data-integration step becomes necessary in this new scenario to join data coming from the different data sources, so that all communications can be treated similarly even if some of them are phone based and others are message based. Besides, joining these heterogeneous data may allow identifying that the same online username can be applied to two different customer ids from the original Telco Inc. and PhoneCo databases (e.g., the same person has two different mobile phone numbers, one for business and another for personal use). In other words, these additional data may be useful in improving identity reconciliation, which was not dealt with previously.

Hence, there are new transformations that must be applied before the original analysis process can take over, as shown in Figure 5.7 (for clarity of the diagram, we only show data from one company). After these transformations have been applied, however, the process remains very similar in respect of the criteria for building the churn-prediction model: the augmentation of data sources with derived attributes, the creation of a data model, and the validation of this model.

Paul has two additional objectives: characterizing customers by clustering them into groups, and detecting opinions about the company. Therefore, new tasks have to be performed.

The first, the characterization of customers by clustering them into groups, can be addressed following an unsupervised data analysis approach. This means that the classes in which customers will be classified are not known *a priori* (i.e., the customers are not labeled as in the previous examples) and the objective is to find hidden structures in these unlabeled data. It is important to note that this task is valid for the previous scenarios, as the communication graphs could be also generated from the information on calls, and especially when the data from more companies are being joined. Paul has decided to do it now, as he assumes that the inclusion of external sources, where new communication patterns can be established, may be even more fruitful in terms of characterizing customers and retaining them for the company.

Several techniques exist for this purpose, and Paul decides to select cluster analysis, which is an exploratory data analysis tool that sorts different objects into groups in a way that the degree of association between two objects is maximal if they belong to the same group and minimal otherwise. Several algorithms exist for this purpose (hierarchical clustering [6], k-means [7], expectation maximization [8], etc.), which can be selected depending on the characteristics of the data sources to be handled. Once the algorithm is selected and the appropriate parameters are chosen, the cluster model is built, as shown in Figure 5.7.

The second objective is focused on detecting opinions from current and recent customers in public data sources such as microblog sites (e.g., Twitter). From a

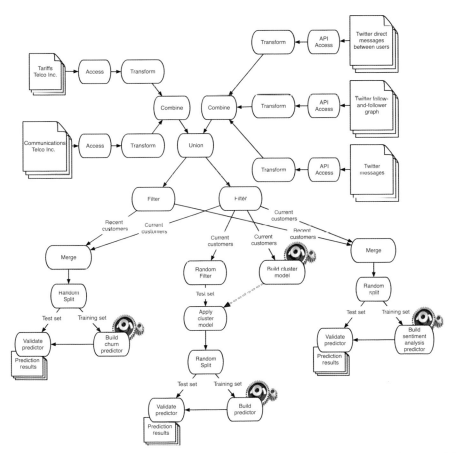

Figure 5.7 *Dataflow diagram that shows data integration of one company plus a social networking site in order to construct a prediction model over combined communication/tariff data, and in order to characterize user communication graphs by clustering.*

high level perspective, the dataflow is exactly the same as we had before, when we were focusing on preventing churn. It is a form of supervised learning, and hence we have labeled records (in this case, possibly annotated by humans) that can be used to train our prediction model. We take positive, negative, and neutral examples (i.e., positive, negative, and neutral comments posted on Twitter) and build the prediction model according to that. Obviously, the techniques that are used for model building are very different from those used in the case of churn prediction, as access and transformation tasks are mainly focused on analyzing texts. However, the overall model building and evaluation phases remain the same, as shown in Figure 5.7.

5.4.2 Deploying the Models

The deployment of the churn prediction and opinion-mining models obtained from this scenario is very similar to the earlier ones. There is only one fundamental difference in this deployment, which was not considered in the previous scenarios (even if our high level representation of the process at Fig. 5.8 does not show fundamental differences with respect to the previous cases). In the simpler cases, we may well assume that the model is applied to a static set of data at regular intervals (e.g., every night), hence following a data-warehouse philosophy. This is done because although the data on which decisions are being based are very dynamic (new calls are being made everyday and details from customers can change often as well), it is normally enough to build the models and execute them over real data from time to time. The objective is to provide relevant information to customer agents and managers the next morning, or at every new shift. In the new scenario, Paul wants to react more quickly to trends, by taking advantage of the dynamic nature of the data sources (and mainly of highly dynamic ones such as Twitter). Therefore, the deployment of the prediction model has to be based on the consumption of data streams, instead of assuming that all data are materialized and accessible. This does not mean that there will not be data caches across the deployment model, but according to our separation of concerns, this is not something that Paul's team should be taking care of.

Real-time data processing is even more relevant when it comes to detecting trends in opinions or sentiments from customers, as it is extremely important to react quickly, especially in the case of negative comments, which may spread very quickly and heavily damage the image of the company, provoking major losses. In this case, it is essential to consider data sources as streams of data that have to be analyzed continuously, as they get published. The presentation of results is also important in this case. Depending on the results obtained from executing the prediction model and the rate of positively or negatively classified exemplars, it may be relevant to send urgent notifications to managers (e.g., by automated phone calls or SMSs). Finally, there is a need for new means of visualizing information and providing reports that can be used by company managers. For example, Figure 5.9 shows a visualization of sentiment analysis information about different

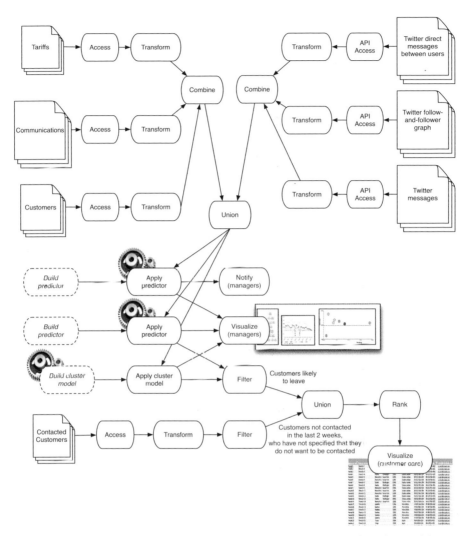

Figure 5.8 *Dataflow diagram for the deployment of the prediction and clustering models over the company's and Twitter data.*

telecommunications providers, extracted from the public comments where the company and its competitors are mentioned. The horizontal axis shows a timeline of several days in which a number of companies are analyzed, and the vertical axis provides the values of a function, which aggregates opinions about them (the higher the value, the more positive the opinion).

Finally, in the case of the characterization of user groups, the main result obtained from the model generation phase is clusters of users who are strongly related together with some of the characteristics that define their relationships.

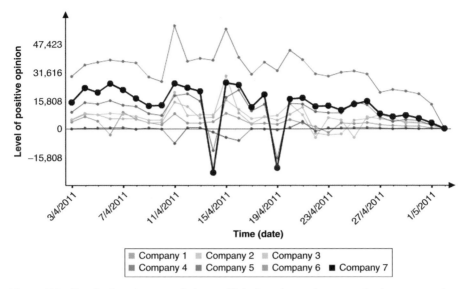

Figure 5.9   *Result of sentiment analysis over Web data about telecommunications companies.*

These groups need to be analyzed afterward and decisions taken about how to address them effectively, something that is done manually by the marketing department. Therefore, during the deployment phase, it may be enough to classify users according to the clustering model obtained previously, as shown in Figure 5.8. This could be useful for the customer care department as an additional piece of information that the customer care agent can use when calling a customer to offer up-selling or cross-selling alternatives. Another alternative may be to consider the clustering model as a model that can change continuously with the new information that can be received in real time about customers (e.g., new followers or followees, new messages or calls between customers, etc.). In this case, the difference between the model-building and deployment phases blurs, and we can talk of a dataflow where clusters and cluster membership are generated dynamically. Some specialized stream mining techniques can be useful for this purpose [9].

5.5 CONCLUSIONS

In this chapter, we have presented a set of scenarios that introduce different types of data analysis problems of increasing complexity, which could be handled by a team of data analysts in a telecommunications company. In the interest of understandability, we have kept the examples simple, omitting many of the deep details that normally appear in real-life scenarios, but at the same time, making sure that they demonstrate many issues that must be dealt with. With these scenarios, we try to provide the basis for explaining a large number of the strategies (Chapter 6) and components (Chapter 7) that are required by data analysts both in conventional data analysis projects and in nonconventional data-intensive ones.

REFERENCES

1. J. R. Quinlan, *Discovering Rules by Induction from Large Collections of Examples.* Expert Systems in the Micro-Electronic Age, Edinburgh University Press, 1979.
2. J. R. Quinlan, *C4.5: Programs for Machine Learning.* Morgan Kaufmann, 1993.
3. G. V. Kass, "An exploratory technique for investigating large quantities of categorical data," *Journal of the Royal Statistical Society, Series C, (Applied Statistics),* vol. 29, no. 2, pp. 119–127, 1980.
4. I. Imam and R. S. Michalski, "Learning decision trees from decision rules: a method and initial results from a comparative study," tech. rep., Reports of the Machine Learning and Inference Laboratory, MLI 93-6, School of Information Technology and Engineering, George Mason University, May 1993.
5. I. H. Witten, E. Frank, and M. A. Hall, *Data Mining: Practical Machine Learning Tools and Techniques (Third Edition).* Morgan Kauffman, 2011.
6. L. Pitt and R. E. Reinke, "Criteria for polynomial-time (conceptual) clustering," *Machine Learning,* vol. 2, pp. 371–396, 1988.
7. J. MacQueen, "Some methods for classification and analysis of multivariate observations," in *Proceedings 5th Berkeley Symposium on Mathematical and Statatistical Probabability,* University of California, 1967.
8. A. Dempster, N. Laird, and D. Rubin, "Maximum likelihood from incomplete data via the EM algorithm. With discussion," *Journal of the Royal Statistical Society, Series B,* vol. 39, no. 1, pp. 1–38, 1977.
9. C. C. Aggarwal, J. Han, J. Wang, and P. S. Yu, "A framework for clustering evolving data streams," in *Proceedings of the 29th International Conference on Very Large Data Bases,* pp. 81–92, VLDB Endowment, 2003.

6

Problem Solving in Data-Intensive Knowledge Discovery

Oscar Corcho

*Departamento de Inteligencia Artificial, Universidad Politécnica de Madrid,
Madrid, Spain*

Jano van Hemert

Optos plc, Queensferry House, Dunfermline, UK

This chapter aims at providing data analysis experts with an overview of the most common strategies in knowledge discovery, highlighting those steps or blocks of steps that are most likely to appear in common problem solving in conventional and data-intensive contexts, as well as giving examples that can be replicated in a range of problems in different domains. While trying to cover some of the most common strategies, we will not aim at being exhaustive in all the types of problems that a data analysis expert may need to address. That would convert this chapter into a long reference book on knowledge discovery strategies, which is out of our intended scope. In fact, it is in any case difficult to be exhaustive in providing strategies, given the wide range of domains and types of problems to be addressed in a data-intensive context, some of which will be seen in Parts IV and V. We will not focus on either specific methods or techniques to be used for each type of problem but

The DATA Bonanza: Improving Knowledge Discovery in Science, Engineering, and Business, First Edition.
Edited by Malcolm Atkinson, Rob Baxter, Michelle Galea, Mark Parsons, Peter Brezany, Oscar Corcho,
Jano van Hemert, and David Snelling.
© 2013 John Wiley & Sons, Inc. Published 2013 by John Wiley & Sons, Inc.

will provide some ideas on the range of available methods and techniques, from conventional to most recent ones, and how they should be organized in order to solve these problems, with the aim of contributing to the new way of thinking that data analysis experts should have in a data-intensive context.

We structure this chapter using the three scenarios from Chapter 5. We describe the activities that Paul has to perform as a data analysis expert, not from the detailed point of view of how algorithms are configured or fine-tuned but with the objective of presenting them from a higher level of abstraction, so that the problem-solving strategies that Paul uses in his work in such a data-intensive context can be better understood.

This will include discussions on the selection, exploration, and understanding of the data sources to be used; their preparation, cleaning, and filtering; the building of the data model (normally including data mining, integration, processing, and trans-formation processes); the evaluation of the model's accuracy and/or precision; the execution of the data model; and the interpretation and presentation of the results. We highlight that these multiple knowledge discovery tasks are done routinely in an iterative manner until the data analysis expert is satisfied with the results; the tasks may be reconsidered again if there are relevant changes in the business context, in the data sources, or in the data modeling techniques, among others.

In summary, we provide the common substrate that data analysis experts must know in order to address systematically their knowledge discovery problems in a data-intensive context. Inexperienced data analysis experts will find the chapter useful for understanding and systematizing knowledge discovery, problem-solving procedures beyond individual steps and components for conventional to data-intensive problems. More experienced data analysis experts may find this chapter useful to develop their understanding of how the data-intensive context influences conventional data analysis strategies.

All our descriptions will be accompanied by additional material (databases, models, etc.) that can be used by readers interested in understanding better the steps taken and their intermediate results for our running scenarios.

6.1   THE CONVENTIONAL LIFE CYCLE OF KNOWLEDGE DISCOVERY

In this section, we describe the problem-solving strategy that Paul's team follows in order to provide a knowledge discovery solution for the first of the presented scenarios. We use the term *conventional* to refer to this scenario, as it shows a rather traditional approach to knowledge discovery in terms of the amount of data available in the data sources, in terms of how data are handled, in terms of how models are run periodically, and so on.

The diagram in Figure 5.2 shows a straightforward dataflow that could be fol-lowed for constructing a prediction model for customer churn, based on data about the communications between customers and their tariffs. Now, we focus on under-standing more clearly the intention behind some parts of that dataflow, and how they would be normally organized in similar types of problems. For this, we place

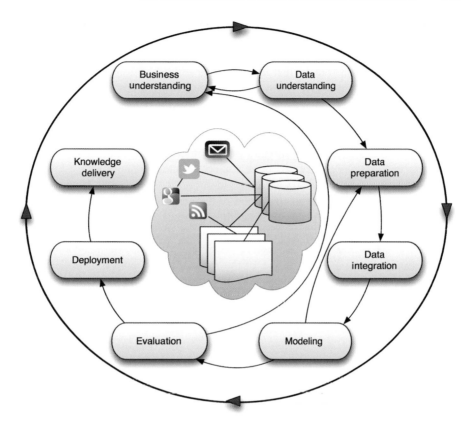

Figure 6.1 Phases of the knowledge discovery process (inspired by www.crisp-dm.org).

these activities in the context of the general knowledge discovery process, which is summarized in Figure 6.1. This process is based on earlier proposals for data mining, such as CRISP-DM (*CRoss Industry Standard Process for Data Mining*, www.crisp-dm.org), which identifies the cyclic set of phases or activities through which a data analysis project normally goes. The activities identified in this process are those of *business understanding*, *data understanding*, *data preparation*, *data integration*, *modeling*, *evaluation*, *deployment*, and *knowledge delivery*. The arrows between these activities identify the most common types of loops that normally happen in this process. In Figure 6.1, we illustrate what is done in each of them and how they are related to that dataflow.

One of the first activities undertaken in the context of this process is related to *business understanding*. In this initial phase, the objective of the team of data analysis experts is to understand what is expected from their data analysis work. As a result of this activity, they will normally compile a list of business-oriented requirements, so that they can convert that knowledge into a data analysis problem definition. It seems quite clear what the business motivation in Paul's problem is focusing on. Understanding the company's business helps Paul's team to determine the main economic consequences of customer churn in the company and the main reasons that customers leave or enter into contracts with the company; and lets them identify the data sources that are available within the company, which could be used to detect whether an existing customer may be about to leave the company. As a result of this phase, Paul's team will have identified the main databases that contain information about customers and that may be used to detect their potential churn. For simplicity, we have already assumed that these databases were composed of two large tables with information about customers and the calls made by them. (They are available as part of this book's supplementary material).

Once the first set of business needs are identified (determine whether a current customer may be leaving the company and the reasons why this may happen, so that the customer-care department can contact the customer with offers of better deals), the team moves into the *data understanding* activities. The data understanding activities allow the team to understand better the contents of the data sources that are made available to them and, at the same time, allow the identification of common patterns, errors, gaps, noise, and so on, present in them. These also allow them to determine which types of techniques will have to be applied in the next phases of the process in order to build and deploy data models that can provide solutions to the identified problems.

Normally, the first task to accomplish here is the collection of the data to be used. This can be done by contacting the company's IT department to obtain access to the company's databases. Once this is done, the team has to get familiar with the data, identify data quality problems, discover first insights into the data, or detect interesting subsets to form hypotheses for hidden information. The team will first explore the data schema, in order to identify how data is structured, which are the most important tables in the structure, how they are related, and how the different features are encoded in them. Then they will try to detect whether there are any quality problems in those data sources (e.g., by looking for cases where a customer is making calls when it has been marked as "gone from the company," or for records where some data values are missing). Some of the most typical data quality problems are shown in the two tables in Figure 6.2, where there are users who are calling two persons at the same time and do not have that possibility according to their contract, users who are making calls before being registered in the company (this may be because some telephone numbers are recycled, different contracts for the same user, etc.). The team will also check some of the statistical properties of the data in the dataset, such as the average duration and cost of calls, calling frequency, correlations between attributes such as calls, duration, age, and so on.

At this point, it may also become clear that the data sources that are available do not suffice to support the business case. It could also be the case that the business case has to be revised, taking into account the data available.

The next step is normally *data preparation*, the objective of which is to transform the initial raw data into a format that can be fed into the modeling tools, taking into account the quality properties that have been identified earlier and the characteristics

SYS_CALL_REPORTS_T

ID_NUMBER	NAME	TYPE ▼	CALL_TIME	USER_ID	
3349218348		Telco Inc	01/07/2011 15:00	443423412	▲
3349218349		Telco Inc	01/07/2011 15:01	443423414	
3349218350	John X.	PhoneCo	01/07/2011 15:01	443423412	
3349218351	Mary F.	PhoneCo	01/07/2011 15:01	443423412	
3349218352	Oscar C.	PhoneCo	01/07/2011 15:05	443423415	
3349218353		Telco Inc	01/07/2011 15:06	443423413	▼

CDM_CONTRACT_ITEMS_T

ID_NUMBER	IS_CLOSED	ACCOUNT_ID ▼	CONTRACTED_FROM	CUSTOMER_ID	
443423412	1	4342342341	01/05/2011 17:00	43423411212	▲
443423413	0	3423412344	05/07/2011 19:00	23123123121	
443423414	0	5452123442	05/03/2011 19:00	43423411212	
443423415	0	1234343322	05/04/2011 12:00	23123111231	
443423416	1	4123434332	05/06/2009 19:00	43222123322	
443423417	0	4234123432	04/12/2008 11:00	87623823123	▼

Figure 6.2 Some typical data quality problems.

that are considered to be relevant for building the data model. These activities of data preparation are normally performed multiple times, sometimes in no prescribed order, and include the selection of tables, records, and attributes; the removal of noise by cleaning the original data sources; and the transformation of data according to a specific set of rules. Normally, they are driven by the data modeling techniques selected for model building.

In our context, the first steps that were identified in Figure 5.2 correspond to the data-preparation phase and fall under the Access and Transform nodes in the data flow. There is no single manner of making this data preparation, and many different techniques can be applied in this step (e.g., tools such as RapidMiner provide more than one hundred techniques for data preparation), but, in general, it will consider many of the following activities (see [1], for example, for a deeper discussion of existing data preparation techniques):

- Selection of the relevant attributes for the classification task, for instance, removing attributes that are not important for this classification, such as much of the personal information about customers.
- Selection of the relevant records to be used for the classification task, for instance, removing records of poor quality or dropping customers who have left the company over a specific period of several months.
- Replacing missing values in records, for instance, average or random values may be used for the date of birth of a customer if not present in the database. It must be noted that this will affect the quality of the resulting model if not done appropriately.
- Detection and removal of outliers, according to the statistical distributions of some of the selected attributes, for instance, if a specific call for a customer

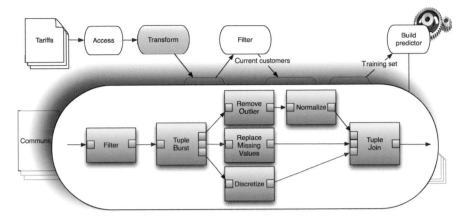

Figure 6.3   *Details of the possible dataflow for the Transform node in our scenario.*

shows that the customer was talking on the phone for over 300 min, this may be either an error or a genuine outlier considering usual values for call duration.

- Normalization (or denormalization) of the values of a given attribute, for instance, the duration of calls.
- Transformation of numerical values into categorical values, and vice versa, depending on the characteristics of the modeling algorithms to be used, for instance, customers may be classified according to their age groups.
- Aggregation of data attributes, for instance, taking communication data for each customer and transforming these to summaries over these calls (e.g., queries that calculate the average length of calls made by a customer over a recent period or calculate a distribution of frequency of calls over the days of the week).

An example of a potential dataflow for the Transform component in the dataflow of Figure 5.2 is shown in Figure 6.3. Here, the Transform component that was shown in our high level diagram consists of an initial Filter, which may be used to remove some specific records, then a TupleBurst that sends columns from the same tuples over three different connections so that they can be treated in parallel, a RemoveOutlier followed by a Normalize of some attribute values, a ReplaceMissingValues, and a Discretize, which are finally reassembled using a TupleJoin. This dataflow can be implemented using DISPEL.

At this stage, the data can be fed into the *data modeling* phase, whose result will be a model or a set of models that provide solutions for the data analysis task at hand. In this example, there is no need to perform any *data integration*, as the databases originate from a single source and are already connected. The need for integration will be present in the second and third scenarios. In this data modeling phase, there are a range of modeling techniques that can be selected and applied.

A good amount of work has to be done in the selection of their parameters, so that they are calibrated to obtain optimal values. The description of these techniques is out of the scope of this chapter and book, and good reference material can be found in the existing literature on machine learning [2–4]. In the context of our running example, Paul is running one of the most basic types of classification algorithms, based on the use of a classification tree, which will determine, given data about a set of customers, who will leave the company and who will not. Such classification algorithms are normally available off the shelf in common data analysis tools (e.g., Weka, RapidMiner, and R) and are well known to data analysis experts. When there is a need for a new algorithm or for a new implementation of an existing one, this has to be constructed and made available on the data analysis platform. In Part III of this book, we describe how to make these available in our data-intensive platform.

After an initial quality check of the obtained models, which may be made informally by the data analysis expert by manually inspecting the models and their results with a few samples, the next phase to be carried out is their *evaluation*, so that their quality can be assessed thoroughly and systematically before proceeding to their deployment. In this phase, the data analysis expert must review the steps executed to construct the models and the quality of the obtained models (also known as *performance*).

This evaluation will drive the decision as to whether the obtained models properly achieve the business objectives that were set at the beginning of the process and allow well-founded decisions to be taken.

As in the previous phase, different techniques can be used to evaluate the obtained models. In our case, Paul's team has decided to build classification trees that will allow prediction as to whether a customer will end their contract or not. A common evaluation of classification algorithms is to use a test set, for which the classes are already known (customers that end their contracts or not), and test how many individuals are correctly classified in each case, obtaining a confusion matrix, which aggregates the number of correct predictions and misclassifications. Figure 6.4 shows such a matrix for our scenario, considering a test set of records of 10,000 customers, with a proportion of 5000 who ended their contracts and another 5000 who continued being customers. We can see that approximately 90% of the customers who actually move to another company (4513) are classified correctly. Hence, approximately 10% of the customers ending their contracts would not be identified as such, and they would not be called by the customer care representatives, which may mean that they would be lost. We can also see that approximately 40% of those who did not actually move to another company are incorrectly classified (2066), which means that they would be probably called by the customer care department even if they were not thinking about ending their contracts. Another 60% would be correctly classified as loyal customers.

The appropriateness of the obtained classification model depends on the context in which it is going to be used. In this context, the results that we have presented may be considered good, as the precision of the classifier for true positives (customers to end their contracts who are correctly classified as such) is probably the

Prediction outcome

		Yes	No
Actual value	Yes	4513 True positives	487 False negatives
	No	2066 False positives	2934 True negatives

Figure 6.4   *A confusion matrix for our scenario — the result of the evaluation of our classification tree.*

most important parameter to maximize, and it may be difficult to obtain a 100% precision without falling into an overfitting problem. It could also be the case that false positives (customers who are not thinking of ending their contracts but are contacted by customer care, probably with some deals) are very relevant; then the percentages obtained are not so good in this case. In any case, an experienced data analysis expert will perform multiple runs of the classifier with different parameters, and then calculate an ROC curve to understand the relationship between sensitivity (rate of false negatives) and specificity (the rate of false positives), so as to make an informed decision on what parameters to use.

The previous test is a simple one to conduct. More elaborate tests may use *n*-fold validation techniques (where model building and model evaluation are intertwined in the process, as explained in Chapter 10). These techniques normally provide more precise results and prevent overfitting. Besides, stratification techniques can be used to ensure the representativeness of each of the test sets. Again, as described in the model-building phase, the objective of this book is not to provide detailed descriptions of the techniques that have to be used at each phase, and we will not go further into describing such evaluation techniques. When the evaluation results suggest that the quality of the models is not good enough yet, the team will need to revisit the earlier phases to ensure that model construction was adequately performed and run evaluations again until they are satisfied with the results obtained.

The next activity in the knowledge discovery process is the *deployment*, where the obtained model (the classification tree, in our case) is prepared to be used periodically (e.g., every day or at every shift in the customer care department) with the company databases. In the case of a classification tree, this means that the model is converted into a set of executable rules that allow determining, for each customer analyzed, whether they will potentially leave the company or not. This will be the basis for the generation of reports that will be used to inform the different stakeholders (e.g., company managers and members of the customer care department), so that they can take appropriate actions, as discussed later. The deployment of the model has to also consider data access, transformation, and combination tasks that are similar to the ones that were used for the generation of the model. While the main objective of the deployment activity is to make the classification tree actionable so as to classify customers, other activities will be included in the deployment, such as filtering those that will probably leave (we do not want to contact those that are not classified as such), avoiding contacting the same person several times in a reduced period of time, and so on. In other words, additional filtering, combination, and integration activities may be needed at this point, as is shown in Figure 5.3.

The final activity according to the process shown in Figure 6.1, is the one devoted to *knowledge delivery*. This is tightly integrated with the deployment activity. The objective is now to visualize the knowledge that has been gained in such a manner that the main stakeholders in the process can understand the results. This means, in the case of the company managers, that they will get a set of reports or a dashboard where they can not only visualize the classification tree that has been generated but also summaries of the number of customers who are prone to leaving, statistics and trends on the customers' behaviors, and so on, all of which can be obtained from the deployment that has been performed. This can be seen at the bottom of Figure 5.3. For the customer care department, this means that a ranked list of customers to be contacted should be produced, so that they can provide those to their customer care agents who have to make calls to customers. Enough data should be provided for them to understand the main reasons why they are calling those customers, so as to be able to follow the corresponding protocols, and this data has to be prioritized so that the efficiency of the process (measured in terms of the number of customers who remain loyal to the company) remains as high as possible. To get enough data for these reports, several activities have to be performed, where some data integration and combination would be needed, and also some filtering should be performed in order to avoid contacting a customer who has been already contacted short time ago.

As a summary of how all these phases are related to the work done by Paul's team, Figure 6.5 shows a combined figure with a mapping between the dataflow diagrams that were shown in Figures 5.2 and 5.4 and the knowledge discovery activities that we have described in this section. Obviously, some of the tasks performed for some activities, such as those of business and data understanding, are not reflected in this figure.

6.2 KNOWLEDGE DISCOVERY OVER HETEROGENEOUS DATA SOURCES

Now, we focus on the second scenario presented in Chapter 5, where new data sources have to be incorporated into the modeling and deployment phases because of the merger of the two companies. As we have already explained, the work to be done in terms of modeling does not change too much with respect to what Paul's team already did previously, as their hypothesis is that the same modeling strategy will be useful for the combination of the two sets of data sources. This does not

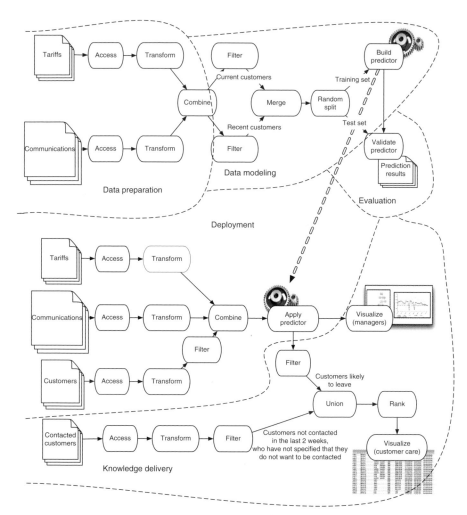

Figure 6.5 *Relationship between modeling and deployment steps and the conventional phases of a knowledge discovery project.*

mean that this is the only strategy to be followed, as other existing strategies that may allow, for instance, the generation of two separate models, one per company, and then the voting between the results of both in each case. Furthermore, in terms of deployment, the changes are mainly related to the fact that the computing infrastructure used so far was insufficient to handle the new amount of data being considered. This is out of the scope of this part of the book, and we defer discussion on how this would be dealt with to Part III of this book. Therefore, many of the explanations that we have already provided for the previous scenario still hold.

We now review the steps taken by Paul's team in each of the data analysis steps, focusing on the differences with respect to the previous scenario.

The first activity to be performed by Paul and his team is related to *business understanding*. The business motivation remains the same as described previously: understanding customers and discouraging them from leaving either of the two companies by knowing enough about their behavior so as to offer them appropriate deals. The result of this phase is, not surprisingly, similar as well: a set of objectives and indicators for the knowledge discovery process and the identification of the databases from both companies, which are subject to be used to detect potential customer churn. The simplified database for the company Telco Inc. was already described in the previous section, and the one for company PhoneCo was also described briefly in Chapter 5 with three large tables containing customer details, calls initiated by the company customers, and calls received by them. As this database was developed by a different team, the fields inside each table are not completely overlapping with those of the first company.

Once the data sources are identified, the next task to be performed is that of *data understanding*. Again, the IT department of the second company has to be contacted in order to obtain access to the databases, and a set of activities performed to get familiar with the data, to understand their quality, to identify interesting subsets, and so on. One particular interest that Paul's team has is that of determining whether it is possible to identify those users who are duplicate in both databases (i.e., customers who have phone contracts with both companies, for example, for their personal and work phones, and customers who left one company to start with the other).

In this case, data understanding can benefit from the use of data access functions (e.g., running SQL queries, with or without aggregation, on the data sources), running principal component analyses, singular value decompositions, and so on, on the data to reduce the size of attribute sets, obtaining statistics about the nominal and numeric attributes in the datasets, looking for correlations between attributes, finding the proportion of missing values, detecting outliers, and so on. All these analyses will allow better understanding of the new data source in isolation and also in combination with the one analyzed previously.

The next activities are those of *data preparation* and *data integration*, which are generally intertwined, that is, a part of the data preparation techniques may be applied over the original data sources and another part may be applied over the data sources already integrated, and some data-integration techniques may be applied over the original data sources and some of them over the already-prepared ones.

In terms of *data preparation*, the techniques to be used are not different from those already described in the previous section. As part of the intertwining with data integration, it may be the case that different access controls have to be negotiated for the data sources, where data may need to be extracted from different forms of storage (text files, binary files, relational databases, Web sites, etc.). We will see some more examples in the following scenario.

As for *data integration*, which was not necessary in our first scenario, the most common tasks are normally related to overcoming schema heterogeneity among the different datasets (by means of obtaining a common reference data model, as has been done in our case), detecting duplicates (also known as *co-reference resolution*), detecting sets of values for specific attributes that result from the combination of the values obtained from the different data sources, and so on.

In Figure 5.5, the integration activity is performed on the central Union step. These activities are not normally provided with much off-the-shelf support in existing data analysis tools, but specific tools can be used for this purpose (e.g., the Open Information Integration suite [openii.sourceforge.net], OGSA-DAI [5]).

Once the four initial activities are performed, the rest of them (*data modeling*, *evaluation*, *deployment*, and *knowledge delivery*) follow the same procedure described in the previous section, as illustrated in Figure 6.6. The number and types of techniques to be used in each case are the same (classification and regression, clustering and segmentation, association and item-set mining, etc., for modeling, validation, performance measurements, and statistical significance tests for evaluation). Deployment activities are more complex, as several data sources from different organizations have to be accessed, and in the case of large datasets, it may be better to move parts of the computation closer to the data in order not to have to move large amounts of data between different organizations. However, as already mentioned, this should not be the concern of data analysis experts, given the separation of concerns that we are trying to achieve.

6.3   KNOWLEDGE DISCOVERY FROM PRIVATE AND PUBLIC, STRUCTURED AND NONSTRUCTURED DATA

Besides adding unsupervised data analysis methods (clustering), the last scenario from Chapter 5 also introduced new dimensions to the type of knowledge discovery that Paul's team was addressing. First of all, now they do not only need to consider structured and controlled relational databases from the companies involved, but also other less-structured (textual) and uncontrolled data sources, with a different access model (accessible through APIs). Second, these data sources are huge and highly dynamic,[1] and this dynamicity has to be considered not only for deployment but also for the data preparation, integration, and modeling phases, since our models for sentiment analysis or clustering should be updated much more frequently so as to react more quickly to new events or to changes. All of these aspects impose a rethinking of some of the problem-solving strategies followed in the previous scenarios. Now we will describe the steps taken by Paul's team in the context of this new scenario.

During the *business understanding* phase, the work is mainly focused on understanding whether the exploratory work that is being done by Paul really makes sense from a business perspective. Several years ago, such a frequent update of supervised and unsupervised models would not have made sense, for two main reasons: one of them is technological, given the high computational demand of some

---

[1] As of April 2011, global Twitter updates account for more than 100M per day, and mentions of a single company in the telecommunications domain can go up to 1M Twitter updates per month.

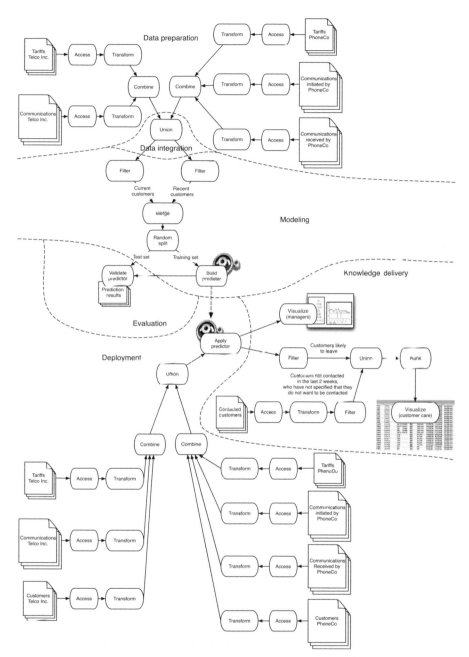

Figure 6.6   *Relationship between modeling and deployment steps and the conventional phases of a data analysis project with heterogeneous data sources.*

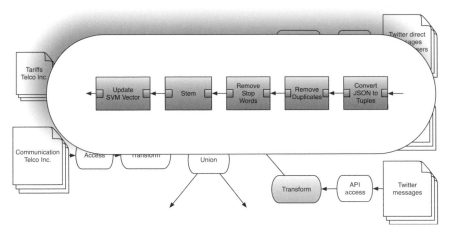

Figure 6.7 *Details of the possible dataflow for the Transform node associated to Twitter messages in our scenario.*

of these activities, the model building phase took a long time and it did not make sense to be performing it so frequently; second, the assumption was that customer profiling could be rather static, in the sense that once a classification model was created, this could be used for a long time with a high accuracy, since there was little risk that customers would be changing their behavior and views. However, nowadays the abundance of data sources that can provide information to character-ize users and the immediateness of decisions to be made, especially in aggressive commercial settings like those of telcos, make the situation of dynamic, almost continuous reconfiguration of models quite common. Therefore, this exploratory work may make sense for this problem and domain.

The next steps are those of *data understanding* and *data preparation*, for which Paul's team has already done much work with the company databases. Now they have to understand the additional data sources that they are incorporating, which includes the direct messages between Twitter users and the social network graph that is established between followers and followees in it, together with the access mechanisms that this platform provides to access their data (that is, their APIs). The techniques to be applied in this case differ from those applied in the previous scenarios, since the type of data and the form of access to this data are different. On the one hand, techniques to access this Web-based data (e.g., through REST services) have to be used. On the other hand, a good bunch of techniques exist and have to be applied in order to understand how to process, and to actually prepare and transform, these data sources in the following phase; these range from tokenizers, to filtering of stopwords, stemmers, n-Gram generators, and so on. Finally, much of this information will be transformed into graphs, so that they can be efficiently analyzed later. Figure 6.7 shows how the transformation step for this new type of data source can be handled in the case of analyzing texts.

The work to be done during the *data integration* phase is also challenging, in the sense that very different data sources have now to be interlinked: records coming from structured relational databases, semistructured data resulting from the analysis of the tweet texts, and graph-based information about users. Connecting all these together is challenging, and a lot of uncertainty can result from the lack of information that will exist in some cases. Hence, appropriate strategies have to be applied, for instance, for the management of missing values.

The *data modeling* phase can be performed next, and again there are differences in the techniques that can be used, even if the dataflow diagram that was presented in Figure 5.7 had many similarities with those of the previous scenarios. In the case of customer churn classification, or sentiment analysis, the techniques to be used for building the predictors should be able to handle data streams. For example, we can use techniques such as UFFT (Ultra Fast Forest of Trees) [6], and Hoeffding Trees [7]. These techniques are able to handle properties such as concept drift, which means that the statistical properties of the target variable, which the model is trying to predict, change over time in unforeseen ways. This causes problems to traditional means of generating classification trees, for instance, because the predictions become less accurate as time passes. The same applies to the building of the clustering model, where several techniques adapted for the management of data streams can be applied (as described in [8]).

For the *evaluation* of the models generated, we have two different techniques to follow, as one of them is supervised (the classification tree) and the other is unsupervised (the clustering model). At the same time, there are some differences with respect to how evaluation was done before, as now we are dealing with stream-based models that are updated dynamically, that is, while in batch learning, where we used finite training sets, cross-validation was one of the standard methods to evaluate the obtained model, this technique is only valid for datasets of restricted size, generated by stationary distributions, and assuming that examples are independent [9]. In a data-stream context, where data are potentially unbounded, the distribution-generating examples and classification models evolve over time, cross-validation is not directly applicable, and one of the alternatives that can be used is to set aside an independent test set, which is applied to the current classification model at regular time intervals, to monitor the evolution of learning as a process with the disadvantage that the estimates may be affected by the order of the examples. In any case, the strategy shown in Figure 5.7 is still valid in its diagrammatic representation with the idea that the validation activities are done at regular time intervals. As for the clustering model, we have already explained in Chapter 5 that there were also several options for evaluation by either computing errors in terms of the distance to the centroid of each cluster or training and using a classifier to act as an evaluation tool.

The *deployment* of the generated models requires an underlying platform that supports the data-streaming model across the entire dataflow. This will be the main focus of Part III, where the ingredients needed for a data-intensive platform will be explained in detail.

Finally, these results have to be delivered, as part of the *knowledge delivery* phase. As we explained in Chapter 5, this will include the generation of more comprehensive and dynamic reports for company managers as well as lists with extra information about customer characterization for the customer care department. It will also include sending notifications to managers when special situations are identified, which require their immediate attention.

6.4   CONCLUSIONS

In this section, we have reviewed the overall phases in which data analysis tasks can be performed, and we have illustrated them with examples coming from the three scenarios described in Chapter 5. We have shown that both conventional and less-conventional knowledge discovery processes follow similar problem-solving strategies with a number of phases that are present in most of them (business understanding, data understanding, data preparation, data integration, modeling, evaluation, deployment, and knowledge delivery), and where the differences among them are mainly related to the specific details of how data are accessed, transformed, and integrated; how models are generated and evaluated; and how they are deployed and results are delivered to the corresponding stakeholders in the process.

However, although there are many commonalities in the way of attacking problems, we have shown that the introduction of heterogeneity in the data sources and the need to deal with bulkier, less-structured and more-dynamic data sources generates the need to adapt the techniques to be used, and sometimes the approach to problem solving. This may mean that models are updated more frequently and are more adaptive to changes in the data sources, which requires different computational models to deal with the added computational requirements.

The availability of libraries of problem solving strategies, as well as of components that allow abstracting away from the underlying technical details of the operations to be performed (e.g., accessing a data source through SQL queries or by calling an API) is key in order to ensure that such problem solving can be performed in an efficient manner by an experienced data analysis expert.

In the following chapters, we will see how all these techniques and strategies are normally structured, depending on their data analysis objective and on the data sources that are used, and how they can be described formally, so as to promote sharing and reuse between data analysts and domain experts.

REFERENCES

1. D. Pyle, *Data Preparation for Data Mining.* San Francisco, CA: Morgan Kaufmann Publishers Inc., 1999.
2. C. M. Bishop, *Pattern Recognition and Machine Learning (Information Science and Statistics).* Springer, 2007.

3. E. Alpaydin, *Introduction to Machine Learning (Adaptive Computation and Machine Learning)*. The MIT Press, 2004.

4. I. H. Witten, E. Frank, and M. A. Hall, *Data Mining: Practical Machine Learning Tools and Techniques (Third Edition)*. Morgan Kauffman, 2011.

5. B. Dobrzelecki, A. Krause, A. Hume, A. Grant, M. Antonioletti, T. Alemu, M. P. Atkinson, M. Jackson, and E. Theocharopoulos, "Integrating distributed data sources with OGSA-DAI DQP and views," *Philosophical Transactions of the Royal Society A*, vol. 368, no. 1926, pp. 4133–4145, 2010.

6. J. Gama and P. Medas, "Learning Decision Trees from Dynamic Data Streams," *Journal of Universal Computer Science*, vol. 11, no. 8, pp. 1353–1366, 2005.

7. B. Pfahringer, G. Holmes, and R. Kirkby, "New options for Hoeffding trees," in *AI 2007: Advances in Artificial Intelligence* (M. Orgun and J. Thornton, eds.), vol. 4830 of Lecture Notes in Computer Science, pp. 90–99, Springer, 2007.

8. S. Guha, N. Mishra, R. Motwani, and L. O'Callaghan, "Clustering data streams," in *Proceedings of the 41st Annual Symposium on Foundations of Computer Science, IEEE Computer Society*, pp. 359–366, 2000.

9. J. Gama, P. P. Rodrigues, and R. Sebastião, "Evaluating algorithms that learn from data streams," in *Proceedings of the 2009 ACM Symposium on Applied Computing*, pp. 1496–1500, ACM, 2009.

7

Data-Intensive Components and Usage Patterns

Oscar Corcho

Departamento de Inteligencia Artificial, Universidad Politécnica de Madrid, Madrid, Spain

The objective of this chapter is to provide an overview of the most common components that are used in the knowledge discovery process.

Readers will gain appreciation of the variety of components available to support knowledge discovery, and how these components can be organized into libraries according to the role and the kind of data that they process, the type of computations that they make, or the type of outputs that they produce. We will also analyze the ways in which these libraries are evolving in the data-intensive world with new components emerging, which contain new algorithmic approaches to handle continuous data and to trade accuracy against cost as data volumes increase, and with new patterns of use adapted to the preparation of data, modeling, and evaluation with the new type of data sources.

The DATA Bonanza: Improving Knowledge Discovery in Science, Engineering, and Business, First Edition.
Edited by Malcolm Atkinson, Rob Baxter, Michelle Galea, Mark Parsons, Peter Brezany, Oscar Corcho, Jano van Hemert, and David Snelling.
© 2013 John Wiley & Sons, Inc. Published 2013 by John Wiley & Sons, Inc.

If we start by taking a look back at the generic knowledge discovery process illustrated in Figure 6.1, and the various dataflows that were presented in previous chapters, we can see that knowledge discovery processes commonly follow these steps:

1. For each data source, extract the relevant data and transform it into a form suitable for the next stage.
2. Integrate the resulting data from these multiple sources into a coherent body.
3. Deal with any residual cleaning, normalization, and partitioning issues in that coherent data body.
4. Run sampling and machine learning or statistical analysis algorithms on that output.
5. Validate the results of step 4.
6. Interpret the results of step 5, perhaps using it on a larger or remaining body of data prepared as in steps 1–3.
7. Formulate visualizations, notifications, and reports using the output from step 6, and send them with sufficient speed to the places where they are needed.

The following sections are structured according to these stages of the knowledge discovery process, from dealing with the source data to bringing new information to the knowledge of people or systems, which may need to react to it. We start by describing the basic components that can be used at each stage. Then we move into more advanced usage patterns (for sampling, validation, bootstrapping, etc.). And we pay special attention to data dynamicity and its impact on the evolution of these components and usage patterns in a data-intensive context. Our objective is to present a representative sample sufficient for readers to recognize the kinds of components that they will encounter and the ways in which these are evolving.

7.1 DATA SOURCE ACCESS AND TRANSFORMATION COMPONENTS

The usual starting point of any knowledge discovery process is that of extracting data from one or several sources. This is the role of data-access components, which are widely supported in data analysis tools and platforms. Data-access components cover a broad spectrum of data formats, including traditional files, databases, data warehouses, Web-based sources, and data streams, among others. While providing data retrieval functions, they also provide, normally, search and storage functions and some form of access control.

Access permissions and security arrangements have to be established before using any data. Normally, this first involves human agreements to comply with the data-use policies, and vetting to establish the trustworthiness of both parties. Data-access components are then needed to implement these mutual commitments.

Normally, the data sources are at a variety of sites within and outside the data-analysis team's organization. Hence, components are needed to access remote addresses, often specified as URIs (Uniform Resource Identifiers) or EPRs (End-Point References), to establish identity, negotiate access permissions, ensure the required levels of encryption on data transfers, and comply with privacy requirements, for example, by average samples, injecting noise, or "pseudomization." In the case of DICOM files containing an MRI brain scan, for example, a component is needed to ensure that both the metadata and the image are altered to prevent loss of privacy without loss of information for further analysis, and this would need to satisfy the relevant ethics committees. These examples illustrate the diverse issues and the kinds of components that those arranging data access have to deal with.

The types of *data-access components* that we can normally use depend on the format in which the data are available. The following is a characterization of the most typical formats:

- *Files.* Files may be in binary or text formats. The binary formats usually correspond to an established standard, such as HDF5 for climate data, and come with a repertoire of access components to extract features in corresponding in-memory formats. DICOM, widely used for medical imaging, includes a broad spectrum of metadata with the image, and the subsequent analysis may require extracts of this metadata and the image. Text formats may be highly structured, for example, an XML file compliant with a known schema, or they may be semistructured (the conventions loosely or tightly adopted by some community) or natural language. Collections of components will be developed by specialists, translating relevant features from these textual forms. In few cases, the text will be already close to the form required, for example, as comma-separated variables, and simple extraction and transformation components will suffice. The basic operations for opening, reading, reading parts of, and writing files will be in the standard repertoire but may differ for binary and text files. The additional operations for handling and interpreting the content of files, such as matrix extraction, performing a wavelet decomposition of images, computing a Fourier transform of a time series, extracting classes of noun phrases relevant to a topic from a text, and so on, require highly specialized knowledge. Hence, expert groups will form to compose the specialized components to yield standard forms required in the next stages. As problems are partitioned, they can work in their own access and transformation contexts and provide composite processing elements (PEs) that match the requirements of that context.
- *Databases.* A database management system consists of a collection of interrelated data and a set of programs to manage and access them. The programs provide mechanisms to define the structure (schema) of the database, for storing data, for accessing them, and for ensuring the consistency and security of the database. In the following, we characterize the most relevant database types *in terms of their data model.*

- Relational databases are collections of tables, each of which is assigned a unique name, consists of a set of attributes (columns or fields), and usually stores a large set of tuples (records or rows). Their query and access operations are encoded in SQL.
- XML databases allow data to be stored in XML format, a standardized quasihierarchical structure approved by the W3C, which is well designed for intermachine communication. Their query operations are encoded in XQuery (and in older systems XPath) and their update operations in XUpdate.
- Object-oriented (OO) databases use objects to model entities and directly encode relationships as references. This approximately aligns with the models in object-oriented programming languages such as Java. They are accessed using OQL.
- Object-relational databases represent a compromise design. They represent entities by extending the types, called *domains* in relational databases, and relationships with foreign keys. They are accessed using SQL with extensions associated with the introduced domains.
- Column-oriented databases are similar to relational databases but store their content by column rather than by row. Their query and access operations are also encoded in SQL.
- RDF databases, also known as *triple stores*, are designed to store semantic information about Web entities in the form of RDF, which is a language standardized by the W3C. They are optimized for the storage and retrieval of many short statements called *triples*, in the form of subject–predicate–object. They are accessed using SPARQL.
- Data warehouses are repositories of information collected from multiple sources stored under a unified schema. They are constructed via a process called *extract-transform-load* (ETL), which includes extraction of data from operational databases, data cleaning, transformation, and integration steps. They are usually organized in relational form and accessed by SQL augmented with statistical and data-mining operations to support business intelligence applications.
- Scientific databases are often based on relational technology. However, they are adapted to storing primary scientific data that is added from other sources so that transactions are not only redundant but also unacceptably costly. Additional data types are supported, such as multidimensional arrays, images, and time series. They are updated by loaders or by mapping *in situ* files and accessed by augmented forms of SQL. The augmentation includes queries over the additional data types and user-defined functions (UDFs) for selection, projection, join, and aggregation in particular domains. Examples include RASDAMAN [1], MonetDB [2], and SciDB [3].
- File Stores and Digital Libraries. Major collections of data are often organized in these systems, which integrate databases to record their structure and metadata with file systems optimized for rapid parallel ingest and

access. They may have standard APIs, but they usually also provide an API optimized for their community of users. Examples include dCache www.dcache.org, D4Science [4], and iRODS [5, 6]. Many reference sites are organized in this way, for example, Medline[1], at the US National Institute of Health for all medical publications; wwPDB www.wwpdb.org all three reference sites for the structures of biological molecules; and BADC badc.nerc.ac.uk, at the STFC Rutherford Appleton Laboratories, for UK atmospheric research data.

A database typically supports some form of a query language, for example, SQL (relational), XQuery and XPath (XML), OQL (OO), or SPARQL (RDF). Databases can also be *distinct because of their contents*: temporal databases typically store relational data that include time-related attributes; sequence databases store sequences of ordered events, with or without a concrete notion of time; time-series databases store sequences of values or events obtained over repeated measurements of time; spatial databases contain spatial-related information similar to satellite image data; spatiotemporal databases store spatial objects that change with time; text databases contain word descriptions, for example, long sentences or paragraphs, for objects; and multimedia databases store image, audio, and video data for applications such as video on demand.

A range of components are needed to interact with each of these variants of databases. In many cases, we need specialized components for each kind of activity (e.g., query and update) and for each query language variant. For instance, in the case of relational databases, each of SQLServer, PostgreSQL, DB2, mySQL, Oracle, tends to use different dialects of SQL and different encodings of values. Thus, the teams formulating access and transform PEs not only need to choose appropriate components but also have to understand the relevant SQL dialect and the schema of their target data. Partitioning helps to make this feasible. The SQL is sufficiently powerful that it is, in principle, possible to precisely select the appropriate data and perform most of the transformations in the query. Similar principles apply when formulating the access and transform components for the other forms of database, though these will not always provide as much transformational power.

The ability to augment the databases with extra types and with user-defined functions (*UDFs*) increases the capacity to ship transformational, and even subsequent processing steps, to the data. Here, those formulating Access and Transform operations have to balance two issues. Shipping work close to the data often reduces the cost of data movement (data derivatives are usually smaller) and exploits the highly honed optimizations of DBMS. On the other hand, an agreement with a data provider may require or impose restraint on the amount of work shipped to that provider's site.

Where the database contains scientific data types or where the extension afforded by object-relational types have been exploited, there will often be

---

[1]www.ncbi.nlm.nih.gov/pubmed

highly specialized and complex formats stored in the DB or mapped into its remit. Typical examples are standard geospatial objects, images, sound recordings, and so on. Most major DBMS, such as SQLServer and PostgreSQL, already have these built in.

Then the Access and Transform team, taking into account the above issue, may use the DBMS's facilities to extract the raw data and feed them into the specialized content-processing components that were introduced earlier under *Files*.

- *Web sources*. The World Wide Web is regarded as a global information space, which is based on linked Web pages, to facilitate interactive access for humans. Web pages are often unstructured and lack a schema, making it hard for computers to extract and link embedded data. The linked open data campaign uses RDF to describe data accessed via the World Wide Web with agreed standards to facilitate cross references and integration.

  The components that mediate access to Web sources include components to organize Web crawling and directly digest HTML, components to activate forms corresponding to queries and then to scrape the response screens for data to convert into relational results, and encapsulations of the wide variety of APIs. Access coding teams will become experts in the parameters to steer these components but will normally have to pass on the data to a series of transform-building components. These will start with components specialized for the data sources and then pass on the data to components that are also used with data from files and databases. When linked data resources are accessed, the subsequent processing may require a mix of metadata derived from the RDF and primary data from the described resources. Components for RDF processing and for data transformation may be used in parallel until a consistent combinable form has been achieved.

- *Data Streams* are becoming ever more prevalent, given the increase in dataflows from ubiquitously deployed digital devices monitoring many aspects of the natural and built environment (e.g., environmental sensor networks) and from the logging and monitoring of human activity (e.g., text streams from microblogging sites such as Twitter). Their principal characteristic is that they need to be treated as if they never terminate, so that useful information may be derived and acted on in a timely manner. Consequently, the components that enable their processing have to do event detection, feature detection, and statistical derivatives using techniques such as sampling through a moving window. Therefore, the typical query model for data streams is the continuous query model, where predefined queries constantly evaluate incoming streams, collect aggregate data, report the current status of data streams, and respond to their changes.

  Data stream access components may often be highly specialized to the sources of the data, as monitoring systems often transmit their data in a highly compressed form, which is domain specific, and have their proprietary APIs. There may be components that take query-like definitions of the features they wish to extract. Often, an application requires that these occurrences of a combination of features in the streams within a designated time window or sustained over a designated period should trigger an alarm. Consequently, the component repertoire will include both trigger generators and trigger responders. The latter may unleash a burst of analytic processing. A commercial example of such systems is Oracle's Event Processing system.[2]

Access components should hide the underlying technology used to store, search, and retrieve data. It should expose the means to store, search, and retrieve data in the corresponding format. For example, if the data consists of satellite images, the search could involve areas of the Earth's surface and time intervals, and the outputs could consist of a series of rectangular images over time. Another example could be saving data in spreadsheet cells, where the results may consist of processed data from a next-generation sequencing experiment. The procedure would involve the name and sheet of the spreadsheet with relevant column and row numbers, or preferably, via naming the columns and rows.

In a data-intensive environment, it is important to ensure that the result of a data-access component is turned into a stream of values that are well described and can be operated on by consecutive steps discussed in the following text. This should be done independently of the format of the data source (files, databases, Web sources, etc.). For instance, in the case of accessing a relational database, a database-access component (e.g., the SQLQuery PE introduced in Chapter 3) will take source URI as initializers, specifying the database that will be accessed, and SQL queries. The component will output streams of results of each query. This way, the input to the database access component, or any type of access component for that matter, can be formed by other components that stream these queries.

In the case of sensor data, the behavior may be a bit different, as sensors are broadly seen as instruments that are providing a continuous feed of data (i.e., they are already generating streams, and hence the previous transformation into streams is not needed). Many different kinds of sensors are live at present, including surveillance cameras, weather stations, seismometers, radar satellites, and traffic movement sensors. Also, many measurements are taken during the operation of computer systems, both directly from the hardware—the speed at which the fans are rotating—as well as software—the current computational load of the computer. Sensors are ideally suited to streaming access, as they provide a regular stream of data already. It could be that the data-access component of a sensor allows tweaking the stream, for instance, by lowering the rate of output data, changing the sampling or reporting rate, selecting the properties measured, or adjusting sensitivity and precision.

Similarly, many scientific instruments are now producing massive amounts of raw data in almost continuous streams. The well-known examples are particle accelerators, telescopes, next generation sequencing, and computer simulations. Access patterns will differ significantly from sensors, as these instruments require a different setup for each experiment. It is even likely that several different access components would exist for the same instrument. The most common tasks will

---

[2] www.oracle.com/technetwork/middleware/complex-event-processing

consist of processing raw data and the corresponding instrument-generated metadata into a form suitable for analysis then storing them until that analysis can be performed.

Once data have been accessed, that is, brought into the data-intensive processing environment through an `Access` PE, their translation to the form required by other components in the dataflow needs to be completed (i.e., the `Transform` PE has to be included in the dataflow).

We now review some of the characteristics of these *data transformation components*, again without the aim of being exhaustive, given the large number of transformations that can be performed. Among the data transformation components that can be used in this process, we can include the following:

- Generic administrative components such as `Split`, `Merge`, `TupleBurst`, `TupleBuild`, `ArrayBurst`, and `ArrayBuild`.
- Standard operations akin to the operations found inside a database query processor such as `Filter`, `Project`, `Join`, `CrossProduct`, `GroupBy`, and `MultipleSelectProject`.
- Operations that do structured transformations such as `FormList`, `DeList`, `ArrayToList`, `ListToArray`, `IntegerToString`, and `CSVToTupleList`.
- Operations that handle a particular category of data, such as time series `Filters` to select frequency ranges, or text `Filters` to remove stop words and perform stemming.

The set of possible components is almost unbounded and hence descriptions are needed to organize, find, and use the components, as will be described in Chapter 8. The power of components, especially in this context, can be greatly enhanced by making them "programmable." For example, an `ArithmeticProject` component could take an expression that specifies a transformation applied to each incoming value that generates an outgoing value. Thus, the same component could be used to translate between any incoming and outgoing units, perform coordinate system transforms, and so on.

A large repertoire of transformation components provides composable translation steps to achieve the overall effect. As the composition uses streaming, multistage transformations can be economically computed. Expensive transformation can be easily parallelized by splitting the stream with a `Split` component, performing the transform on each branch and then merging the stream with an appropriate `Merge` operation. The transforms of parts of an incoming stream, for example, elements of a tuple and tiles of an array or image, can be processed in parallel (column-wise) by a suitable `Burst` and `Build` operation at either end of the transformation processing pipelines.

7.2 DATA INTEGRATION COMPONENTS

The outputs from the implementations of the `Transform` processing element should have progressed as far as possible towards a consistent format, representation and semantics for each input to integrate. For example, all the units for a particular measurement should be the same across the entire set of streams generated from a set of heterogeneous data sources (e.g., temperature sensors deployed in close geographical locations, where all temperatures are transformed into Celsius).

Integration then proceeds as a series of Union, Intersection (e.g., with priority list), Difference (e.g., with exception lists), and Join components. However, the components used to perform these operations have to be sophisticated (programmable) versions of these operators as the notion of "equality" is domain and context dependent. The operational behavior of these components is important in the context of stream-based, data-intensive contexts, as data streams are inherently ordered in terms of when the data items arrive into the different dataflow components. Hence, this order may impose important restrictions on them (e.g., when joining information from two data streams that are not ordered according to the same parameter, in which case special techniques have to be applied, or when trying to compute aggregates over a data stream). Special techniques and algorithms are being created for this purpose. Although they are not the scope of this book, some examples can be found in the success stories in Parts IV and V.

An example of this type of data integration may be, for instance, to decide whether a PlaceName refers to the same place in two inputs. It may be necessary to consult a gazetteer to discover whether different spellings because of time (e.g., Istanbul and Constantinople) or because of culture (Köln or Cologne) refer to the same place. But it would also be necessary to check other attributes such as geographicPosition or Country to avoid false coincidences, such as Washington in County Durham, UK, being confused with Washington, a state in the United States.

In many cases, establishing connections between independently sourced records is a very challenging task, and a large amount of literature exists in the area of co-reference resolution in databases that can be brought in for this purpose for the implementation of these data integration components, for example, trying to decide whether two documents refer to the same person in the historical record or in medical and social administration records. People do not spell their names consistently, do not always use the same address, nor provide accurate information. Those entering the data often make mistakes. A plethora of techniques, often tuned to the origins of the data, and the target decision quality can be found encoded in components to handle such errors.

7.3 DATA PREPARATION AND PROCESSING COMPONENTS

As with data transformation components, the list of data preparation components is long and it is difficult to make it exhaustive. There is also a large amount of literature in the form of books, scientific papers, and technical manuals that deals with such types of components and explains when, why, and how they should be applied in a knowledge discovery process, depending on the type of input data that they have to handle and the type of data-mining model that is going to be generated. These components are similar both in conventional and data-intensive cases, although their implementations may be different in order to cope with the different scale of data in each case.

Basically, these components can be divided into the following nonexhaustive list of types:

- data-cleansing components such as `Remove Outlier`, `Replace Missing Values`, `Replace Infinite Values`, and `Discretize`;
- filtering components such as `Sample` and `Remove Duplicates`;
- sorting components such as `Randomize`, `Sort`, and `Shuffle`;
- aggregation components such as `Aggregate`;
- attribute set reduction components such as `Principal Component Analysis`, `Singular Value Decomposition`, `Fourier Transformation`, and `Remove Correlated Attributes`.

7.4   DATA-MINING COMPONENTS

Typically, we can identify two main high level goals of data mining: prediction and description. These can be achieved using a variety of data-mining methods, for example, association rules, sequential patterns, classification, regression, clustering, change and deviation detection, and so on. While descriptive mining characterizes the general properties of a dataset, predictive mining performs inference on it in order to make predictions. Another important characteristic is the one that differentiates supervised from unsupervised techniques. In the former, we know "*a priori*" the classes that we want to obtain, and we have some exemplars already classified according to those classes, so that we can use them for training our models. In the latter, we do not know *a priori* the classes in which items can be classified.

Although the field of data mining is quite mature and many techniques are quite stable, new data-mining methods are also being developed, for example, evolution analysis, data-stream analysis, graph mining, spatial data mining, and so on, in order to address newer types of problems, most of them in the data-intensive context.

In the following, we describe some of the most common data-mining methods.

7.4.1   Mining Frequent Patterns, Associations, and Correlations

Frequent patterns are patterns that occur frequently in a dataset. Different kinds exist, including itemsets, subsequences, and substructures. A frequent itemset commonly refers to a set of items that appear together frequently in a transactional dataset, such as bread and butter in a shopping transaction. A frequent subsequence represents a reoccurring pattern of one item followed by another and then another, such as PC followed by printer followed by ink cartridges. If a subsequence occurs frequently, it is called a *frequent sequential pattern*. A substructure points to different structural forms such as graphs, trees, or lattices. They may be combined with itemsets or subsequences. If a substructure occurs frequently, it is called a *frequent structured pattern*. Mining frequent patterns enables the discovery of associations and correlations within a dataset.

7.4.2   Classification and Prediction

Classification is a supervised process for finding a model to distinguish classes, which can be used to predict the class of those objects whose class membership is not known. The model is based on the analysis of a set of training data that includes objects whose class label is known. The model may be implemented as classification rules (if–then statements), decision trees, or neural networks.

A decision tree is a flow-chart-like tree structure where a node denotes a test on an attribute value, a branch represents an outcome of the test, and leaves represent classes. An example of such a tree was given in Figure 5.3. Decision trees can easily be transformed into classification rules, which could be part of an `ApplyClassificationTree` component.

A neural network used for classification is typically a collection of neuron like processing units with weighted connections between the units. The weights associated with connections represent the relevance that these connections have to activate the target neuron, and each neuron has an activation threshold above which they get activated.

While classification models predict categorical labels, prediction models can be used to predict continuous-valued functions. Missing or unavailable numerical data values, distribution trends, and class labels may be the prediction target. Regression analysis, a statistical method, is mostly used for numeric prediction.

Both methods, classification and prediction, may require a preparation step called *relevance analysis*. This method tries to identify attributes that do not contribute to the process and can therefore be excluded.

7.4.3   Concept Description: Characterization and Discrimination

Using these methods, a dataset can be associated with a set of concepts (e.g., a person about to leave a company, a hurricane), which in turn allows their description in summarized and yet precise terms. These concept descriptions can be generated in different ways by means of data characterization, which aims at summarizing the data associated with the corresponding concept according to their most general characteristics; by data discrimination, and by comparison of the described concept with a set of comparative concepts. The output format of such concept description can be graphical, including pie charts, bar charts, curves, multidimensional data cubes, as well as textual in rule form.

7.4.4   Cluster Analysis

Cluster analysis operates on data objects without a known class label. Objects are grouped into clusters by maximizing the intracluster similarity and minimizing the intercluster similarity, where the similarity metric between objects is provided as a parameter. Each resulting cluster can be viewed as a class of objects, from which rules can be derived. Hierarchical cluster analysis can also facilitate taxonomy creation, the organization of observations into a hierarchy of classes that group similar events together.

7.4.5   Outlier Analysis

Data objects of a dataset are outliers if they do not comply with the general behavior or model of the data. Outliers may be detected using distance measures and statistical tests based on a distribution or probability model for the data. In addition, deviation-based methods identify outliers by examining differences in the major characteristics of objects in a group.

7.4.6   Evolution Analysis

Evolution analysis describes trends for objects whose behavior changes over time. Although this may include the former mentioned methods on time-related data, they also include time-series data analysis, sequence or periodicity pattern matching, and similarity-based data analysis.

7.4.7   Data-Stream Analysis

The characteristics of data streams have been introduced before. Streamed data are often at a low level of abstraction, whereas analysts require higher and multiple levels of abstraction. Thus, multilevel and multidimensional online analysis and mining techniques are normally performed on them.

7.4.8   Graph Mining

Graphs are becoming increasingly important in modeling complex systems such as circuits, social networks, and chemical compounds. Frequent substructures are the first to be discovered in multiple graphs and can be used for characterizing graph sets and supporting similarity search in graph databases. Recent developments support the classification of chemical compounds and allow analysts to study structural protein families.

7.5   VISUALIZATION AND KNOWLEDGE DELIVERY COMPONENTS

These are the last steps identified in the introduction to this chapter and can be all grouped under a knowledge delivery step: delivering critical information to the right people at the right time in a presentation that they can understand. A wide variety of components are needed in order to perform this knowledge delivery appropriately, for example, via PEs that send results as a stream in the right proto-col, send a Web-event notification, send an SMS message, send an email, or send a tweet. The important challenge is to "go the last mile" sending the right infor-mation to the right people or systems in the correct form with the appropriate level of urgency. This is important in organizations that have to deal with emergencies or maintain a continuous high quality service. New Web 2.0 services are emerging to record and implement the final stages of delivery, handling alternative means of communication, finding substitutes within a group, and initiating escalation if there is no response within a critical time.

Delivery of results to users may require different forms of representation: rules, tables, crosstabs, pie/bar charts, and so on. These forms can be used to visualize diverse datasets, some interesting patterns constructed during knowledge discovery processes, or results as obtained from the application of data analysis techniques over data sources to support decision making. Various forms of data require spe-cific methods for presenting time-series data (e.g., index charts, stacked graphs, etc.), statistical distributions (e.g., Q–Q plots, scatter plots, parallel coordinates), and many others. Presentation of the interesting patterns requires more advanced techniques, frequently visualized as 3D plots.

We now discuss different types of presentation according to the different types of users of knowledge discovery systems.

7.5.1 Presentation for Data Analysis Experts

The first group are the data analysis experts who need the results represented in a very detailed form that enables them to correctly interpret and evaluate the results from the purely statistical and data-mining point of view. This involves deep understanding of semantics of the input data, quality of the used data, and detailed descriptions of mined models. The quality of the visualization tools has a strong influence on the representation of the results, so a different view on the results is required. These tools support interactive drill up/down, pivoting, slicing, and dicing, providing different perspectives to data. Advanced visualization techniques can present charts as a summary level. There are many visualization techniques for some popular data-mining methods such as decision trees, association rules, clustering, and neural networks, which are typically supported by data analysis software suites.

7.5.2 Presentation for Domain Experts

The second group are knowledge workers including managers and executives who are mostly concerned with clearly presented information already verified by the analysis experts. For these users, the discovered knowledge might be more under-standable when represented at a high level of abstraction. However, the decision makers have to have enough background knowledge so that they can recognize an impact of the results on the targeting targeted business. Therefore, for this kind of user, a graphical form of results is in high demand.

Events that require quick decisions are supported by triggering actions influencing the internal business processes.

The final presentation is crucial, for example, if the data has a geospatial coordinate, it is almost always worth providing a feed to standard geographic viewing systems, such as those provided by Google and Unidata. Chapter 19 illustrates this for oceanographic and climate data, Birkin et al. [7] shows its use for sociological data, and Batty [8] has shown its use for urban dynamics, Twitter surveys, and social reaction to economic events. In such cases, the data would be fed through components that transform it to comply with the Open Geospatial Consortium standard forms (now ISO standards and enshrined in the European INSPIRE directive). Transformation to map overlay form with viewing controls is well established. Similar well-established and well-honed mechanisms are needed for other forms of data if the results of data-intensive processes are to achieve their value by being properly interpreted to have their intended impact.

7.5.3   Presentation for Other Systems

Provenance data contain information about who commissions a data-intensive process, about its parameters and data sources, about time, and about the data obtained and the process steps used to obtain results. Provenance components can help in provenance data collection, organization, and summarization and can be written to a persistent provenance record. Some of these components are those that are used for manipulating and storing any form of data. Some of the primary PEs performing the data derivations will provide an additional output stream that emits provenance records as the PE accomplishes steps in the processing. Frequently, it is necessary to derive provenance data from data-intensive processes that use legacy PEs and that do not supply their own provenance data. In these cases, it is necessary to impose observer processes in the channels to carry data from one process step to the next. These observers transmit the observed data unchanged and also emit a record as to what has passed. These records can then be composed using standard PEs to generate the provenance record. Chapter 17 has a good example of this strategy in practice.

REFERENCES

1. P. Baumann, "Array databases and raster data management," in *Encyclopedia of Database Systems* (T. Özsu and L. Liu, eds.), Springer, 2009.

2. M. Ivanova, N. Nes, R. Goncalves, and M. L. Kersten, "MonetDB/SQL meets SkyServer: the challenges of a scientific database," in *Scientific and Statistical Database Management*, p. 13, DOI: 10.1109/SSDBM.2007.19 2007.

3. P. Cudre-Mauroux, H. Kimura, K.-T. Lim, J. Rogers, R. Simakov, E. Soroush, P. Velikhov, D. L. Wang, M. Balazinska, J. Becla, D. Dewitt, B. Heath, D. Maier, S. Madden, M. Stonebraker, and S. Zdonik, "A demonstration of SciDB: a science-oriented DBMS," in *Very Large Database conference*, VLDB Endowment, August 2009.

4. D4Science Data Infrastructure Ecosystem for Science, http://www.d4science.eu, 2013.

5. iRODS Integrated Rule-Oriented Data System, https://www.irods.org,2013.

6. M. Conway, R. Moore, A. Rajasekar, and J.-Y. Nief, "Demonstration of policy-guided data preservation using iRODS," in *Policy*, pp. 173–174, IEEE Computer Society, 2011.

7. M. Birkin, R. Procter, R. Allan, S. Bechhofer, I. Buchan, C. A. Goble, A. Hudson-Smith, P. Lambert, D. De Roure, and R. Sinnott, "Elements of a computational infrastructure for social simulation," *Philosophical Transactions of the Royal Society A*, 2010 vol. 368 no. 1925 3797–3812.

8. M. Batty, *Cities and Complexity: Understanding Cities with Cellular Automata, Agent-based Models, and Fractals*. The MIT Press, September 2005.

8

Sharing and Reuse in Knowledge Discovery

Oscar Corcho

*Departamento de Inteligencia Artificial, Universidad Politécnica de Madrid,
Madrid, Spain*

In the previous chapters, we have shown a number of strategies that can be used to get added value from data in our data-intensive world. We have described how the knowledge discovery process is an iterative process that can be divided into a set of phases where a number of tasks are performed, ranging from the understanding of the business and the data to its preparation, integration, analysis, and evaluation, and finally to the deployment of the models and the delivery of the obtained knowledge in appropriate formats. We have shown that data may belong to the organization applying this knowledge discovery process, and to other organizations or already available in the public domain and that formats and access mechanisms by which data is available are also highly heterogeneous.

The problem-solving strategies described in Chapter 6 have been written with the assumption that the development was done by a closely related group, Paul's team, which would have had no difficulty in establishing a common shared understanding of the data, the processes, and the goals of the process. However, it is often the case that people move in or out these data analysis teams, that new data analysis challenges arise (e.g., analyzing other data sources from the organization, or from the open world of the Web), and that new techniques are made available, which

The DATA Bonanza: Improving Knowledge Discovery in Science, Engineering, and Business, First Edition.
Edited by Malcolm Atkinson, Rob Baxter, Michelle Galea, Mark Parsons, Peter Brezany, Oscar Corcho,
Jano van Hemert, and David Snelling.

may be more appropriate for the tasks at hand (e.g., new data analysis algorithms for data streams or characterization algorithms with better performance). These are just some examples of situations that may require appropriate action in order to preserve the knowledge gathered by these groups, mainly in terms of know-how and lessons learned in the design and execution of these processes, together with the knowledge gathered about the appropriateness of the used techniques for the problems at hand. It also shows the importance of having good descriptions of traditional and novel data analysis techniques, so that domain experts and data analysis experts can determine more easily whether they can use them for their knowledge discovery purposes.

Furthermore, a large proportion of the data-intensive case studies that were mentioned in Part I and that will be described in Parts IV and V are related to scientific domains. In these domains, it is even more important to be able to share data-intensive components and usage patterns developed by groups of researchers, so that others in the scientific community can benefit from them. Consequently, the sharing and reuse of these components and patterns across scientists in a community is a good practice that provides mutual benefits.

In order to support these shareability and reusability requirements, good descriptions of data-intensive components and usage patterns have to be available. These descriptions range from formal descriptions, where the inputs and outputs of components, or the parameters of usage patterns, are described according to some formal language (e.g., following the DISPEL three-layered type system), to informal, although normally structured, descriptions of the types of problems where they have been applied, associated papers that describe the problems solved, developers who have made them available, information about their execution properties, etc.

In this chapter, we review the mechanisms that can be used for the provision, sharing, and use of such descriptions, using examples from our sample scenarios described in Chapter 5.

8.1 STRATEGIES FOR SHARING AND REUSE

If we consider the three scenarios introduced in Chapter 5 and the strategies and techniques used to solve them, we soon realize that many of the components used there (processing elements, functions, domain types) are shared across scenarios. This is not surprising, as the three scenarios have been presented in an incremental manner, making an initial knowledge discovery problem increasingly complex. However, if we consider other scenarios in the same or other domains, such as those described in Parts IV and V, we will realize that many of those components can be reused further. Categories of components that are frequently reused are typified by data access and integration processing elements (for accessing data, for joining and merging data, for sampling, etc.), data-mining processing elements (e.g., decision trees, clustering methods, etc.), generic domain types that refer to items present in several domains (images, text, persons, products, etc.), and even general strategies for problem solving, such as those presented in Chapter 7.

Therefore, most of the existing knowledge discovery tools and platforms provide libraries of these components, which are mainly populated with processing elements, and less with domain types and functions. For example, to name just a few, RapidMiner provides more than 400 elements in its default library, Meandre provides more than 100 elements, the ADMIRE platform provides around 100 processing elements, Weka provides around 200 elements, and MOA provides around 50 elements. Some of these tools and platforms also provide libraries of user-generated, data analysis processes, which can be downloaded and executed locally or remotely, and of general strategies, which can be used as templates for building common data analysis tasks. For instance, the process repositories supported by RapidMiner, which can be maintained locally or made available online, or the repository of workflows that a virtual research environment such as myExperiment maintains.

The common driver for the maintenance of such libraries in these tools and platforms is the promotion of reusability and shareability. There are three mutually reinforcing benefits from this. First, it increases the agility and efficiency of data analysis teams, as they can easily plug components into processes. Second, it allows improving quality and trust in the components, as these get honed by multiple users that test and extend their capabilities. And third, it reduces costs as the maintenance is amortized over more platforms, users, and uses. This affects the basic components (processing elements), which are necessary in order to be able to construct solutions for the data analysis problems and without which these tools and platforms would not make sense. One could not imagine a data analysis tool that did not provide a basic set of data analysis processing elements. Appropriate libraries also shape the workflows and strategies that are adopted to solve classes of problems, and thus, they provide data-intensive engineers with better opportunities to tune their platforms.

However, there are different scales at which reusability and shareability of data analysis components and processes can be performed[1]:

- *Predefined component libraries.* Tools such as Weka belong to this group. In this group, tools provide a predefined library of components, which can be used to execute data analysis tasks and create data analysis processes (e.g., with the Weka Knowledge-Flow functionality). In some cases, sample processes are also provided through the tool or directly in a Web site so that they can be downloaded, reused, and tailored to the problem at hand. The same applies to sample datasets, which can be used mainly for educational purposes. If data analysts want to share the processes that they have developed for a specific task, the script for this process has to be uploaded as a file to a Web site of their own, for example, and they have to describe it in a Web page or in a forum, so that others get to know about it and can reuse it, if they wish, by downloading the corresponding files and opening them in their editor.

[1]The assignment of tools and platforms to each level reflects their current status at the time of writing and may change in the future. In fact, the frontiers between these levels are not strictly defined.

- *Predefined component libraries and simple upload options in their online repositories.* Tools such as RapidMiner belong to this group. In this group, tools also provide a predefined library of components, and sample datasets and prototypical processes to ease the learning curve of practitioners. However, they go one step further by giving more support to users to share and reuse processes. Data analysis processes can be uploaded and obtained from online repositories. Besides, they support the sharing and reuse of problem-solving strategies, by allowing the creation and use of templates and building blocks (e.g., encoding the usual structure for *n*-fold cross validation in a building block, which can later be easily used by a data analyst, by simply replacing the required parameters). Processing elements and processes are normally described in a textual form, and basic validation utilities are provided to check the validity of the processes.

- *Social-network-enabled virtual research environments.* Platforms such as myExperiment belong to this group.[2] In this group, tools are accompanied by online platforms that act as virtual research environments for practitioners who can share their process scripts across their social networks, comment and rate them, find other related processes from known and unknown colleagues, get recommendations, etc. They can also pack all the elements used in a process (workflows, data sources, related publications, etc.) as research objects, to ease their sharing and reuse. All these functionalities associated with the social networking aspects of the environments stimulate the growth of the contributor and user communities, and the uptake of popular (presumed of proven value) components. Provenance recording also encourages proper attribution as a reward for creators and improvers of components.

- *Platforms with rich annotations and descriptions.* The **ADMIRE** tools and platform belong to this group, as does the myExperiment platform. In this group, the benefits for shareability and reusability across communities, which are brought in by Web2.0 platforms, are complemented with additional domain-type-based annotations, which are applicable to the inputs and outputs of processing elements, to the description of datasets used, to the encapsulation of processes as functions, and to the workflows represented by **DISPEL** scripts, at a higher level of granularity. These domain type annotations facilitate the evaluation of **DISPEL** scripts at design time, and the discovery of processing elements, datasets, and functions. The explicit recording of relationships between components also develops a relationship graph, which tools can navigate, as they assist the users of processing elements, datasets, or functions. The adoption of a rich notation, **DISPEL**, is an approach to improving the description of components incrementally, from all viewpoints. All categories of experts can find anchors for their aspects of annotation. They can then build tools that exploit and augment these annotations. We hypothesize that this knowledge base about data-intensive components, if organized to protect and reward

---

[2]RapidMiner already provides some plug-ins to support browsing myExperiment workflows.

contribution, will reach a critical mass that empowers very effective and potentially automated recommendation, rather than pruning invalid designs.

In the following sections, we describe the basic ingredients that allow support for reusability and sharing in the most advanced level. This is done by providing the vocabulary to be used to specify the metadata attached to data analysis components and processes. This growing and evolving vocabulary is defined by means of a network of ontologies, which combine the following:

- data analysis ontologies for data analysis experts, which allow the description of data analysis processes and components from the point of view of the methods, techniques, and algorithms that these experts use;
- generic ontologies for domain experts, data analysis experts, and data-intensive engineers, which provide support for the inclusion of descriptive generic metadata to all these resources (e.g., authorship information, licenses, etc.);
- domain ontologies for domain experts, which allow the description of inputs and outputs of processing elements according to the domain-type layer of the three-layered type model presented in Chapters 4 and 10;
- and domain-independent vocabularies of modifiers for data-intensive engineers, which allow the description of the operational behavior of components and which can be used during optimization, as described in Chapter 12.

These descriptive structures are the start of a vital endeavor to describe components sufficiently well that (i) their users understand their potential capabilities and limitations, (ii) the tools can become proficient at supporting their use and filling in detail, and (iii) the data-intensive platforms can autonomically adapt processes as contexts change. The current capabilities described in the following text give a flavor of this anticipated future.

8.2 DATA ANALYSIS ONTOLOGIES FOR DATA ANALYSIS EXPERTS

Data analysis ontologies are domain-independent vocabularies that support the broad description of the data analysis tasks undertaken in the knowledge discovery process. This description is formulated in terms of the types of methods that have been used, the techniques and algorithms applied, the phases of the knowledge discovery process that they belong to, and so on.

Several efforts have been made to construct ontologies addressing these description needs, some of them focused on the whole knowledge discovery process [1] and some others more narrowly focused on data mining [2–6]. The concept hierarchies in these ontologies normally mimic the structure of processing elements in the data analysis libraries associated with commonly used data analysis tools (e.g., RapidMiner, Weka, R, etc.). For example, Figure 8.1 shows an excerpt of the Rapid-Miner library, which is the basis for the Data Mining Ontology described in Hilario

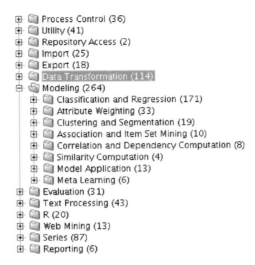

Figure 8.1   *High-level organization of the RapidMiner library of processing elements.*

et al. [2] They describe the most common types of parameters that allow characterizing, in a generic manner, the processing elements in the library. In this manner, they aim at facilitating the organization of content in these libraries, providing a structure that can be easily understood and used by data analysis experts.

Figure 8.2 shows the concept hierarchy associated with the classification algorithms of one of these data analysis ontologies, where classification algorithms are divided into three major families: generative, discriminative, and discriminant function algorithms, and these are further classified into more specific types of algorithms. Another ontology in this group is the data analysis ontology that has been developed in the context of **ADMIRE** and which is available at www.dispel-lang.org/ontology/DataMiningOntology.

Even though these ontologies exist, it must be noted that the description and organization of components in most of these tools are still done rather informally. That is, components are not described or structured according to these ontologies but organized in a folder-based manner and mainly described using quasinatural language text. Although these informal descriptions serve their purpose for data analysis experts, there are some disadvantages from the lack of formal ontology-based descriptions. For example, the fact that multiple classification of components into a set of categories is not normally allowed, given the single-classification model imposed by folder-based structures. Similarly, properties of the groups of processing elements are not provided, and terminology used is not unified by an authority site. This lack of a consistent ontological foundation may provoke problems if data analysis workflows are to be exchanged between tools, between independent groups or across disciplines.

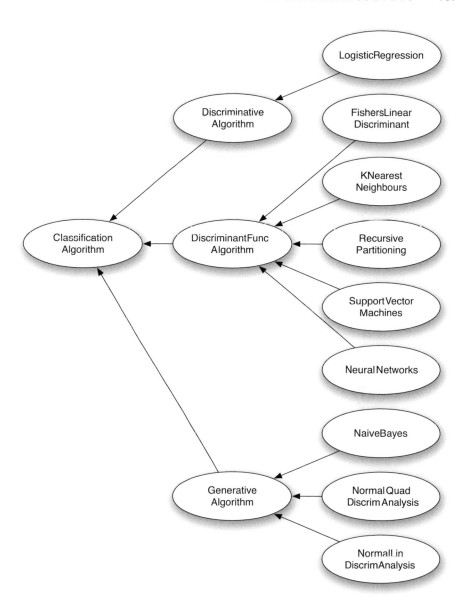

Figure 8.2 *Excerpt of the concept hierarchy of a data analysis ontology. Source: Adapted from www.e-lico.eu.*

An example of how these ontologies can be used to describe a processing element is provided later, in the DISPEL language. The following is a fragment of the DISPEL code that corresponds with the definition and registration of one of the processing elements that belongs to the default library of the ADMIRE platform (BuildClassifier). This is a fairly generic processing element that builds a classifier. Obviously, this processing element can be (and is) further specialized into other processing elements, such as `BuildDecisionTreeClassifier` or `BuildDecisionTreeClassifierWithID3`. This processing element has several input connections for the data that is used to build the classifier, the definition of the nominal values, the identifiers of columns that are relevant for the classification, the field that acts as the class, and several options, and an output connection that generates the classifier. These input and output connections are typed according to the structural and domain type systems allowed in DISPEL and registered in the library with several properties. Among these properties, we can highlight, as it is related to the type of annotations described in this section, the one specified by `@type` on line 18, which establishes that this is a `"datamin:Classifier,"` according to the data analysis ontology.

```
1   namespace datamin "http://www.dispel-lang.org/ontology/DataMiningOntology#" ;
2   namespace kdd "http://www.dispel-lang.org/ontology/kdd#" ;
3   namespace dispel "http://www.dispel-lang.org/ontology/lang#" ;
4   namespace db "http://www.dispel-lang.org/ontology/db#" ;
5
6     Type BuildClassifier is PE(
7     <Connection:[<rest>]::"db:TupleRowSet" data;
8       Connection:[String]::["dispel:String"] nominalValues;
9       Connection:[String]::["datamin:ColumnIndex"] columnIndices;
10      Connection:Integer::"dispel:Integer" classIndex;
11      Connection algorithmClass;
12      Connection:[String]::["dispel:String"] options> =>
13    <Connection:Any::"datamin:Classifier" classifier>);
14
15  register BuildClassifier with @creator = "Oscar Corcho",
16    @organisation = "es.upm",
17    @description = "Creates a classifier from an example set",
18    @type = "datamin:Classifier",
19    @belongsToKDDPhase = "kdd:DataModelling";
```

With this description, we are now able to retrieve this processing element when we are looking for processing elements that can be used during the data-modeling phase, and also when we are looking directly for a type of classifier.

8.3   GENERIC ONTOLOGIES FOR METADATA GENERATION

The previous example showed that data analysis ontologies provide the vocabulary required to describe the data analysis properties of processing elements (and functions, although these were not described above), which can then be registered. These descriptions can be supplemented with additional information of a more organizational nature, which records the provenance of the registered components (the author, the organization to which the author belongs, the textual description of the component, the date when it was created and modified, version information, etc.). In fact, much of this information might be added automatically to the `register` statement by the tool that the DISPEL developer is using.

Several ontologies can be used for this purpose. The most widespread one is Dublin Core (dublincore.org/documents/dces/), a simple ontology that comprises a set of 15 properties, which can be used to annotate any resource. These properties are `contributor`, `coverage`, `creator`, `date`, `description`, `format`, `identifier`, `language`, `publisher`, `relation`, `rights`, `source`, `subject`, `title`, and `type`. Some of them were already used in the previous example (`creator`, `description`) and are accepted and used by the **ADMIRE** platform.

Other general purpose ontologies that are used similarly, together with Dublin Core, are the Creative Commons ontology (creativecommons.org/ns), which allows specifying the rights associated to the element that we are registering in the library, or the myExperiment Annotation Ontology (rdf.myexperiment.org/ontologies/annotations/), which allows adding tags, comments, ratings, and reviews to these elements. Some examples of their usage are shown in the following **DISPEL** fragment.

```
1    with @cc:requires="cc:ShareAlike", @cc:requires="cc:Attribution";
2
3    with @meannot:uses-tag="classifier", @meannot:uses-tag="decisionTree";
```

8.4 DOMAIN ONTOLOGIES FOR DOMAIN EXPERTS

Finally, domain ontologies are one of the most important types of ontologies to be considered in this effort to support shareability and reusability of processing elements, functions, and types. Domain ontologies provide definitions related to a domain of expertise and serve as the basis for the **DISPEL** domain-type system, as described in Chapters 4 and 10. These are the annotations that are valuable especially for domain experts, as they capture the meaning of the data that is being moved across connections between processing elements or as parameters in functions. Besides, they represent the agreement of a domain community on the vocabularies to be used to annotate and exchange information in their discipline.

Different levels of domain ontologies will be used in this context. The first layer of domain ontologies is that of ontologies that are generic across domains and contain terms that are shared by all those domains. Examples of such terms are Image, Person, Product, etc. Large efforts have been invested in the context of the ontology-engineering discipline to provide such types of common-sense, generic, or upper-level ontologies, as these types of ontologies are normally referred to. Examples of such ontologies are Cyc [7], SUMO [8], and DOLCE [9], which cover spatial and temporal relations, causality vocabularies, actions, social units, etc. Some of these ontologies are thoroughly described in Gomez-Perez et al [10]. Classes from these ontologies are the ones that are (or would be) most commonly used in the predefined libraries of data analysis tools and platforms, as many of the data analysis methods and algorithms can be applied to a large number of domains.

As an example, the **ADMIRE** platform provides two base ontologies that contain many of those terms imported from such upper-level ontologies. These ontologies are available at www.dispel-lang.org/ontology/DISPEL (a generic ontology that contains terms such as `"dispel:Image"` and `"dispel:Product"`) and www.dispel-lang.org/ontology/db (a generic ontology that contains terms related to relational databases, such as `"db:Schema,"` `"db:Table,"` `"db:Column,"` and `"db:PrimaryKey,"` and which is heavily used to describe those processing elements related to data access and integration activities). In the example shown in Section 8.2, some of these terms were used: `"db:ColumnIndex,"` `"db:TupleRowSet,"` `"dispel:String,"` and `"dispel:Integer."`

The second layer is composed of domain-specific ontologies that can be organized within domains and can serve to identify whether a processing element or function can be applied to a specific domain, as it is fine-tuned for it. These ontologies do not need to be constructed specifically for data analysis tasks. Instead, they are normally imported from widely used ontologies in their respective domains. Some examples are the NGOSS ontologies for telecommunication companies [11], the GoodRelations ontology for product and service offering [12], the SWEET suite of ontologies in the case of environmental science (sweet.jpl.nasa.gov/), the Gene Ontology in the case of genetics [13], and ICD in the case of diseases (www.who.int/classifications/icd/en/). Processing elements and functions described with these ontologies are normally specialized for the domain and organized in domain-specific libraries, as they are fine-tuned to deal with information from a specific domain (for instance, a text analysis processing element that is fine-tuned to deal with scientific articles from PubMed, or with the usually badly formed text from tweets).

A final layer of domain and task-specific ontologies may be used in some cases when there is a need to make use of domain types that are very specific for the task that the domain and data analysis experts are trying to solve. These ontologies are not normally very reusable, in the sense that they are very specific for the task that they have been built for, but are connected to the widely used domain ontologies mentioned above. An example of such an ontology would be a specialization of the GoodRelations ontology to describe the specific service offerings that are made by our telecommunications company, which are only used by them and hence, not shared in the community.

8.5   CONCLUSIONS

In this chapter, we have explained why the reuse and shareability of all the types of components that are used in knowledge discovery processes can be useful to improve efficiency and productivity. We demonstrated that improved descriptions of components may greatly facilitate their reuse by experts engaged in problem solving, by tools assisting in the many facets of data-intensive applications throughout the knowledge discovery process, and by the enactment systems optimizing and organizing data-intensive processes in a changing environment.

We illustrated the variety of descriptions that are needed for processing elements—this would be extended to functions and types. This metadata is organized as libraries of components (also known as *registries*).

At present, experts familiar with the libraries may get by without the descriptions, tools, and automation. As the volume of data-intensive applications grow, with the corresponding growth in the component libraries and numbers of staff engaged in the work, this will no longer be sustainable.

The drive for better descriptions, from the technical consistency rules to the licenses controlling sharing and attribution of contributions, is intended to stimulate safe and reliable "markets" of shared data-intensive components. This will have benefits in the agility of designing and modifying knowledge discovery processes, of improving their trustworthiness and reliability, and of reducing their costs.

We have also shown that these descriptions can be layered according to different types of vocabularies, which focus on different aspects of the description of components. From generic descriptions that are not related to data analysis tasks, such as those that can be provided with the Dublin Core or Creative Commons vocabularies, to generic descriptions about the types of data analysis models used or specifying the phases in which processing elements can be applied. The range includes domain-specific descriptions of parameters, inputs and outputs, that provide a fine-grained description of those elements that are useful not only to data analysis experts but also to domain experts.

In more general terms, the objective of this part of the book has been to show through a set of descriptive examples the main tasks that data analysis experts have to perform in order to solve their knowledge discovery problems, the usual components and strategies they use in a data-intensive world, and, finally, the tools that can be used in order to increase efficiency and productivity by means of sharing and reusing components and strategies. The treatment has not been exhaustive in the types of methods that can be used and are normally available in tool and platform libraries, nor detailed as to when and where these methods can be applied, as this is beyond the scope of this part of the book.

This part of the book has taken the reader through many stages from the viewpoint of a data analysis expert. We have demonstrated that they can consider data-intensive processes from their statistical and logical viewpoint without distraction by the technical detail of making this work on a particular data-intensive platform. That is only valid if the responsibility is shouldered by data-intensive engineers, as they design, build, and operate those enactment platforms, which is the topic of the next part of the book.

REFERENCES

1. M. Zakova, P. Kremen, F. Zelezny, and N. Lavrač, "Planning to learn with a knowledge discovery ontology," in *Proceedings of the Second Planning to Learn Workshop*, pp. 29–34, 2008.

2. M. Hilario, A. Kalousis, P. Nguyen, and A. Woznica, "A data mining ontology for algorithm selection and meta-learning," in *Proceedings of the ECML/PKDD09 Workshop on Third Generation Data Mining: Towards Service-oriented Knowledge Discovery*, pp. 76–87, 2009.

3. P. Brezany, I. Janciak, and A. M. Tjoa, "Ontology-based construction of grid data mining workflows," in *Data Mining with Ontologies - Implementations, Findings, and Frameworks*, Ch. 10, pp. 182–210, Information Science Reference (an imprint of IGI Global), 2008.

4. P. Panov, S. Dzeroski, and L. Soldatova, "OntoDM: an ontology of data mining," in *Proceedings of the International Conference on Data Mining Workshops, 2008*, pp. 752–760, IEEE Computer Society, 2008.

5. M. Cannataro and C. Comito, "A data mining ontology for grid programming," in *Proceedings of the 1st International Workshop on Semantics in Peer-to-Peer and Grid Computing, in conjunction with WWW2003*, pp. 113–134, 2003.

6. A. Bernstein, F. Provost, and S. Hill, "Toward intelligent assistance for a data mining process: an ontology-based approach for cost-sensitive classification," *IEEE Transactions on Knowledge and Data Engineering*, vol. 17, no. 4, pp. 503–518, 2005.

7. D. B. Lenat and R. V. Guha, *Building Large Knowledge-based Systems: Representation and Inference in the CYC Project*. Reading, MA: Addison-Wesley, 1990.

8. I. Niles and A. Pease, "Towards a standard upper ontology," in *Proceedings of the international conference on Formal Ontology in Information Systems*, pp. 2–9, ACM, 2001.

9. A. Gangemi, N. Guarino, C. Masolo, A. Oltramari, and L. Schneider, "Sweetening ontologies with DOLCE," in *Proceedings of the 13th International Conference on Knowledge Engineering and Knowledge Management. Ontologies and the Semantic Web*, EKAW '02, pp. 166–181, Springer, 2002.

10. A. Gomez-Perez, O. Corcho, and M. Fernandez-Lopez, *Ontological Engineering: with Examples from the Areas of Knowledge Management, e-Commerce and the Semantic Web. First Edition (Advanced Information and Knowledge Processing)*. Springer, 2004.

11. Y. Liu, W. Lv, and J. Kang, "GENp2-4: towards the NGOSS SID ontology based on description logics," in *Global Telecommunications Conference*, pp. 1–5, IEEE Computer Society, 2006.

12. M. Hepp, "GoodRelations: an ontology for describing products and services offers on the Web," in *Proceedings of the 16th international conference on Knowledge Engineering: Practice and Patterns*, pp. 329–346, Springer, 2008.

13. M. Ashburner, C. A. Ball, J. A. Blake, D. Botstein, H. Butler, J. M. Cherry, A. P. Davis, K. Dolinski, S. S. Dwight, J. T. Eppig, M. A. Harris, D. P. Hill, L. Issel-Tarver, A. Kasarskis, S. Lewis, J. C. Matese, J. E. Richardson, M. Ringwald, G. M. Rubin, and G. Sherlock, "Gene ontology: tool for the unification of biology. The Gene Ontology Consortium," *Nature Genetics*, vol. 25, no. 1, pp. 25–29, 2000.

Part III

Data-Intensive Engineering

Part I of this book discussed the evolving landscape of data-intensive computing and the challenges that organizations and individuals face in extracting knowledge and, eventually, value from data. Part II delved deeper into the analysis processes needed to perform data-oriented computations. These processes included not just analysis techniques, patterns, and approaches to deal with widely distributed and unstructured data, but also strategies for adapting the higher level development processes to deal with dynamic and changing data sources.

Part III, this part, is targeted at technical experts, mostly data-analysis experts and data-intensive engineers, expecting to develop components or complex applications in DISPEL and those considering developing platforms supporting the data-intensive architecture outlined here. There may be some domain experts, who will find this discussion interesting, but like the automobile it is not necessary to understand the engine to drive the car; this part is for those that want to understand and work on the data-intensive platform. While most of the focus so far has been on knowledge discovery, the architecture outlined is of a general nature and should be considered by practitioners across a wide range of (data-centric) specialities, for example the programming paradigms such as Hadoop [1], mapreduce [2], and related technologies. We expect data-analysts from many disciplines to make effective use of the data-intensive platform and to contribute its expanding capabilities, including general technologies of data-intensive distributed computing, such

The DATA Bonanza: Improving Knowledge Discovery in Science, Engineering, and Business, First Edition.
Edited by Malcolm Atkinson, Rob Baxter, Michelle Galea, Mark Parsons, Peter Brezany, Oscar Corcho, Jano van Hemert, and David Snelling.
© 2013 John Wiley & Sons, Inc. Published 2013 by John Wiley & Sons, Inc.

as scalable index generation, image processing, text analysis, and sensor stream monitoring.

At the time of writing, there were already a plethora of tools available to the data-intensive engineer and, no doubt, over the coming few years more will emerge. These tools are of direct interest to all users of data-intensive analysis, but those seeking to create a platform will need to incorporate the capabilities of most of these tools in some form or another into their platform. The following represents a partial snapshot of the tools available: Hadoop [1], mapreduce [2], RapidMiner[1], WEKA [3], Stig[2], Noflo[3], Storm[4], Kepler [4], KNIME[5] LarKC[6], DataCaml[7], S4[8], and Orange[9].

Many of the above are presented as complete solutions and do in fact provide solutions either in specific contexts or even in a general sense. The key to creating a complete platform, as envisioned here, is the provision of a comprehensive but not a duplicated set of capabilities. If we first deconstruct the technologies involved in such a platform, we can then piece together a solution. The following categories can be identified and many of the technologies above include one or more of these deconstructed categories.

1. Data-analysis technologies such as data-mining algorithms, warehousing strategies, complex analytics, and so on provide the intelligent components, which in this architecture are packaged as processing elements and accessed through DISPEL, which we introduced in Chapter 4 and cover in more detail in Chapter 10.

2. Data-flow handling appears in the above in many and varied forms, including static data stores, small packet distribution systems such as found in Complex Event processing (CEP) solutions, and data streaming solutions. The DISPEL approach most closely resembles the data streaming strategy, but is capable of emulating either the warehouse or the CEP approach.

3. Heterogeneous data management is clearly the norm in the domain of data-intensive computing. The processing element concept in DISPEL encapsulates this technology as well.

4. Development tools tend to be the selling point of many existing platforms, due to their user facing focus. The architecture presented here is not tied to any particular approach of development, although development tools feature prominently in what follows.

[1] rapid-i.com
[2] stigdb.org
[3] github.com/bergie/noflo
[4] stormmq.com
[5] www.knime.org
[6] www.larkc.eu
[7] anil.recoil.org/2011/06/18/datacaml-with-ciel.html
[8] docs.s4.io
[9] orange.biolab.si

5. In all cases, a language of some sort is required in order to describe the intended computation. In many cases, a simple scripting language or extension thereof is used. While these have the advantage of shorter learning curves, they fall short of the expressive power of a purpose designed language such as DISPEL.

6. The richness of available libraries plays a significant role in the success of data analysis platforms. Appendix C presents a basic set of required library components.

7. Lastly, the execution platform itself must provide a collection of monitoring and management services in order to provide capabilities and insight not just into the data analysis but also into the effectiveness of the enactment itself.

The challenge to the data-intensive engineer is therefore not in finding tools, but in bringing them together into a coherent platform of use to the data-intensive application developer. This part provides a roadmap for this process. Starting with a look at the data-intensive context and reprising the hourglass that highlights the separation of concerns in data-intensive knowledge discovery, we then look at the programming language DISPEL as a guide to what capabilities a platform needs to have and how to describe them. The final two chapters in this part discuss the development tools, needed to create DISPEL, and the enactment platform on which the computation takes place.

REFERENCES

1. T. White, *Hadoop: The Definitive Guide*. O'Reilly, 2009.
2. J. Dean and S. Ghemawat, "MapReduce: simplified data processing on large clusters," *Communications of the ACM*, vol. 51, no. 1, pp. 107–113, 2008.
3. I. H. Witten, E. Frank, and M. A. Hall, *Data Mining: Practical Machine Learning Tools and Techniques (Third Edition)*. Morgan Kauffman, 2011.
4. B. Ludäscher, I. Altintas, C. Berkley, D. Higgins, E. Jaeger, M. Jones, E. A. Lee, J. Tao, and Y. Zhao, "Scientific workflow management and the Kepler system," *Concurrency and Computation: Practice and Experience*, vol. 18, no. 10, pp. 1039–1065, 2006.

9

Platforms for Data-Intensive Analysis

David Snelling

Research Transformation and Innovation,
Fujitsu Laboratories of Europe Limited, Hayes, UK

This chapter looks at the context of tools and platforms for data-intensive engineering and sets the context for the following chapters, which look in greater detail at each aspect of platforms for data-intensive engineering. Figure 9.1 shows the scope of data-intensive computing relative to distributed computing and knowledge discovery. The key properties of data-intensive computing are that the focus is on data as much as computation and that the data in question are distributed. The data-intensive platform described here is specialized to address these aspects.

In order to engineer such a platform, a number of connected tasks must be orchestrated to create the overall platform, namely, we describe the DISPEL language, the Lingua Franca of the platform, the development tools used to create DISPEL sentences (programs), and the processes involved in enacting a data-intensive computation. Together, these form the blueprint for an abstract data-intensive platform, instances of which can be constructed to meet the specific needs of a community.

The DATA Bonanza: Improving Knowledge Discovery in Science, Engineering, and Business, First Edition.
Edited by Malcolm Atkinson, Rob Baxter, Michelle Galea, Mark Parsons, Peter Brezany, Oscar Corcho, Jano van Hemert, and David Snelling.

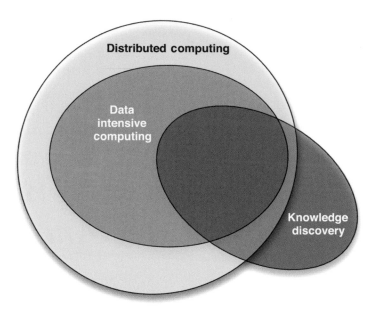

Figure 9.1   *Diagram frames data-intensive computing in the context of generalized distributed computing and knowledge discovery.*

9.1   THE HOURGLASS REPRISE

As introduced in Chapter 3, the hourglass analogy for the architecture separates the complexities of supporting diverse applications from the various strategies for providing data-intensive, distributed computer services. Both are complex and evolving rapidly, so a stable interface is required to permit independent innovation. This interface, the neck of the hourglass, is a gateway through which DISPEL requests are passed. DISPEL is intended to have sufficient expressive power to satisfy all of the requirements of data-intensive engineers. Part III is about that gateway and the strategies for handling the requests submitted to it. The two key parts are the DISPEL language and the data-intensive platform.

In the *Top Bulb*, see Figure 9.2 and Part II, there is a creative zone in which human judgment and reasoning are required. Business decisions need to motivate the questions asked and these drive the creative process of identifying the workflow and corresponding DISPEL program needed to address these business questions. The *Top Bulb* is where concepts are dynamic and ever changing and, therefore, the humans in this space need support from tools. Traditionally, people will stick to the tools they know, such as spreadsheets, Weka, RapidMiner, and Taverna. Therefore, we will need to provide, as part of the overall environment, "Ramps" to enable rapid development of applications and components and libraries of reusable shared components, as described in Chapter 8. These aspects of the platform are discussed in Chapter 11—DISPEL Development.

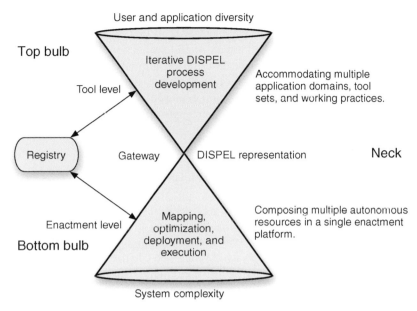

Figure 9.2 *Hourglass architecture separating the complex contexts of users and providers.*

In the *Neck* of the hourglass, creativity should not be present. Here, we need a stable means of discourse between the developers and the enactment platforms. At some time in the future, we would expect the protocols and languages defining the *Neck* to be standardized. For data-intensive computing, the DISPEL language acts as the stable means of discourse, that is, its design is intended to explore and expose the information content required to pass through the *Neck*. As a formal language, it provides a stable view both up and down from the *Neck* of the hourglass; however, identifying the right level of abstraction for the language is one of the key challenges. In particular, care must be taken not to expose the exigencies of current technologies to the upper-level's communities or data analysts and domain experts.

In the *Bottom Bulb*, we again need creativity. The complexities of mapping a DISPEL sentence onto distributed, physical computational resources and data sources require many types of expertise and significant levels of automation, such as optimization. This domain, similar to the *Top Bulb*, is also evolving. The rapid changes in technology and pressures from the world of business mean that the way in which the *Bottom Bulb* is realized will change over time. This highlights, as we illustrated in Parts I and II, why the *Neck* must be stable. The creativity applied in the *Bottom Bulb* is not only technological in nature but novel business models can drive significant changes in the realization (e.g., the need to classify and react to events almost immediately). The historical success of the notion of compilation has been used to motivate the approach recommended here. As technologies change, compilation technologies tend to evolve with them, thus providing a stable interface at the *Neck*. It should also be realized that in the *Bottom Bulb*, human intervention should be avoided. In systems management, we call this idea *autonomic computing*, and it should form a foundational aspect of any realization of the platform.

In the later chapters of Part III, we describe the approach taken to create one such realization of a data-intensive platform and identify key issues that the platform should address. However, this realization represents only one possible approach and the reader should be aware that other approaches are also possible and will likely be realized over time.

9.2   THE MOTIVATION FOR A PLATFORM

The creation of such a platform is only possible if all of the actors involved see a selfish, business-driven motivation for proceeding to use, develop, or deploy the platform. The three actors in this context are *domain experts*, *developers*, either of the platform itself or the data analysis libraries, see Chapter 8 (the later are usually either data analysis experts or data-intensive engineers), and *service providers*, who deploy the platform and data resources associated therewith.

The *domain experts'* business perspective is one of the needs to understand answers to domain-specific questions without having to invest significant effort into the development of either analysis schemes or their realizations. They need working environments in which information is presented in domain-specific terminology, using familiar tools and with a user interface that is easy to use. These interfaces need to encapsulate the complexity of analysis methods and allow frequent reapplication of the data analysis process, including minor changes to parameters or search terms and queries. It should also be possible to modify running analyses to steer the direction of the analysis, to interrupt the process, or even to terminate the process.

The *developers* who provide these tools seek a business where application development effort can be amortized across many enactments, by either the same or different customers. This applies whether the developer has created an entire domain-specific platform for a particular class of domain expert or has developed a single component that might be used in many application scenarios. Successful implementation strategies will incorporate many library components, possibly contributed by a community of developers. Therefore, developers of data-intensive platforms need to provide collaboration support. The architecture outlined in the following text supports this through a rich description registration framework for storing and maintaining components.

The *service provider* will usually represent a data provider and will be interested in getting as many users as possible for these data. The motivation may be financial, such as with a direct "data-as-a-service" offering, but government data providers may simply be interested in promoting better use of existing data sources, so the immediate financial motivation may not always be present or yet apparent, such as when using Twitter streams. There may also be a provider that acts as an integration and aggregation source for a number of data sources. Significant computational resource providers will also have similar motivations. As the business models and technologies evolve, the costs of the data-intensive engineering will be reduced by colocating the data with computation and by reaping the benefits of scale [1].

9.3 REALIZATION

The realization of a DISPEL-based environment for data-intensive computing includes a number of aspects beyond a programming language. The overall environment, referred to here as a *data-intensive platform*, includes the DISPEL language; an application development environment (including libraries of processing elements, functions, and data types); the transformation engine that compiles a DISPEL sentence and processes it to create data-processing graphs; and an enactment engine that optimizes those graphs, deploys them, executes them in a controllable framework that permits interaction with the end user, and finally terminates them and cleans up the environment.

In Chapters 10 and 11, we describe the DISPEL programming language and the environment for developing DISPEL programs. Chapter 12 outlines the *complete* processing of requests specified as DISPEL sentences. We call this whole process a DISPEL enactment, which is achieved by four phases of processing:

1. DISPEL *language processing* comprises compilation of the DISPEL sentence, acquisition of descriptions of the imported DISPEL entities from the registry, and validation, annotation, and production of the defined DISPEL entities. These entities include graphs of processing elements connected via data streams (called *connections*), function definitions and types. Selected definitions and descriptions may be recorded for reuse in the registry.
2. DISPEL *optimization* transforms abstract graphs produced by the previous phase; mapping processing elements, data sources, etc. to suitable concrete instances and carrying out optimizations that yield equivalent graphs with lower cost.
3. DISPEL *deployment* arranges the dynamic creation or acquisition of the computational resources in appropriate places that are needed for the execution of the graph produced by the previous phase. This includes the delivery of relevant code and constants to those resources, the set up of connections and the preparation for monitoring the next phase.
4. DISPEL *execution and control* starts the deployed process elements, monitors execution, streams data and monitoring information to specified targets, and ensures termination and clean up of the resources that have been allocated.

REFERENCES

1. J. Gray, "Distributed computing economics," Tech. Rep. MSR-TR-2003-24, Microsoft Research, 2003.

10

Definition of the DISPEL Language

Paul Martin

School of Informatics, University of Edinburgh, Edinburgh, UK

Gagarine Yaikhom

School of Informatics, University of Edinburgh, Edinburgh, UK; School of Computer Science and Informatics, Cardiff University, Cardiff, UK

This chapter is intended for those wanting a working understanding of the DISPEL language, its capabilities, and its fundamental components. Later chapters deal with details of DISPEL program development and execution. Further details can be found with the DISPEL reference manual [1], and Section 3.8 has placed it in the context of other systems.

The *data-intensive systems process engineering language* (DISPEL) is a high level scripting language used to describe abstract workflows for distributed data-intensive applications. These workflows are compositions of processing elements (PEs) representing data analysis or knowledge discovery activities (such as batch database querying, noise filtering, and data aggregation, as described in Chapter 6) through which significant volumes of data can be streamed in order to manufacture a useful knowledge artifact. Such PEs may themselves be defined by compositions of other, more fundamental computational elements, which may each have their

The DATA Bonanza: Improving Knowledge Discovery in Science, Engineering, and Business, First Edition.
Edited by Malcolm Atkinson, Rob Baxter, Michelle Galea, Mark Parsons, Peter Brezany, Oscar Corcho, Jano van Hemert, and David Snelling.
© 2013 John Wiley & Sons, Inc. Published 2013 by John Wiley & Sons, Inc.

own internal workflows. Users can construct workflows using existing PEs or can define their own, registering them for later use by themselves or their peers.

DISPEL is based on a streaming-data execution model used to generate dataflow graphs that can be mapped onto computational resources hidden behind designated gateways. DISPEL is used to specify new workflow patterns and submit workflows to the gateway. This gateway constructs, validates, optimizes, and executes concrete distributed workflows that implement submitted DISPEL specifications. The gateway may have access to numerous ways to implement the same abstract workflow under different circumstances, but this is hidden from the average user who instead selects PEs based on well-defined logical specifications. Thus, workflows can be constructed without particular knowledge of the specific context in which they are to be executed.

10.1   A SIMPLE EXAMPLE

DISPEL uses a syntactic notation similar to that of Java [2]. A representative example of DISPEL is shown in Figure 10.1, demonstrating the registration of new workflow components. In this example, reusable definitions are defined (abstract type `SQLToTupleList` and constructor `lockSQLDataSource`), which are then used to derive new PE types, (`SQLOnA` and `SQLOnB`), which are in turn exported to the registry.

```
 1   package book.examples.dispel {
 2     /* Import existing PE from the registry and define domain namespace. */
 3     use dispel.db.SQLQuery;
 4     namespace db "http://dispel-lang.org/resource/dispel/db";
 5
 6     /* Define new PE type. */
 7     Type SQLToTupleList is
 8       PE( <Connection:String::"db:SQLQueryStatement" expression> =>
 9           <Connection:[<rest>]::"db:TupleRowSet" data> );
10
11     /* Define new PE function. */
12     PE<SQLToTupleList> lockSQLDataSource(String dataSource) {
13       SQLQuery sqlq = new SQLQuery;
14       |- repeat enough of dataSource -| => sqlq.source;
15       return PE( <Connection expression = sqlq.expression> =>
16               <Connection data       = sqlq.data> );
17     }
18
19     /* Create new PEs. */
20     PE<SQLToTupleList> SQLOnA = lockSQLDataSource("uk.org.UoE.dbA");
21     PE<SQLToTupleList> SQLOnB = lockSQLDataSource("uk.org.UoE.dbB");
22
23     /* Register new entities (dependent entities will be registered as well). */
24     register SQLOnA, SQLOnB;
25   }
```

Figure 10.1   A DISPEL script that registers new process elements.

```
1   package book.examples.dispel {
2     /* Import existing and newly defined PEs. */
3     use book.examples.dispel.SQLOnA;
4
5     /* Construct instances of PEs for workflow. */
6     SQLOnA    sqlona  = new SQLOnA;
7     Results   results = new Results;
8
9     /* Specify query to feed into workflow. */
10    String query = "SELECT * FROM AtlanticSurveys" +
11                   " WHERE AtlanticSurveys.date before '2005'" +
12                   " AND AtlanticSurveys.date after '2000'" +
13                   " AND AtlanticSurveys.latitude >= 0";
14
15    /* Connect PE instances to build workflow. */
16                          |- query -| => sqlona.expression;
17                          sqlona.data -> results.input;
18    |- "North Atlantic 2000 to 2005" -| => results.name;
19
20    /* Submit workflow (by submitting final component). */
21    submit results;
22  }
```

Figure 10.2 *A DISPEL script that uses the definitions registered in Figure 10.1.*

In the second example, shown in Figure 10.2, the definitions from the previous example are used in an executable workflow. The new PE SQLOnA is retrieved by importing it from the registry and an instance of SQLOnA is constructed. The new instance sqlona is then fed an SQL expression that it can use to query the data source at "uk.org.UoE.dbA". The output from sqlona is then passed to an instance of the Results PE. This final instance exists to pass the output to an appropriate client-side interface (e.g., a terminal interface or other visualization tool).

Now that the workflow is ready, it can be submitted to a local gateway for execution. In this case, only results needs to be explicitly submitted—the gateway will also submit all other components connected to that instance by dataflow connections.

Clearly, this example workflow is rather trivial; however, within the two example scripts given, instances of all the core DISPEL constructs can be found. These constructs are explored in more detail.

10.2   PROCESSING ELEMENTS

PEs are user-defined computational activities that encapsulate algorithms, services, and other data transformation processes—as such, PEs represent the basic computational blocks of any DISPEL workflow. The DISPEL platform provides a library of fundamental PEs corresponding to various data-intensive applications as well as a number of more specific PEs produced for selected domains. Just as importantly, however, DISPEL provides users with the capability to produce and register new

PEs by either writing new ones in other languages or creating compositions of existing PEs.

10.2.1   Processing Element Characteristics

PEs that are available on the DISPEL platform are described in a *registry*. Each PE has a unique name within the registry. This name helps the enactment platform to identify a specific PE and is also used to link the PE with any available implementations. While generating this unique name, which is part of the metadata stored in the registry, the DISPEL parser takes into account the context in which the PE is defined.

In addition to the PE name, the registry contains for each PE the following specification:

- Brief description of its intended function as a workflow component
- Precise description of expected input and output data streams
- Precise description of its iterative behavior
- Precise description of any termination and error reporting mechanisms
- Precise description of type propagation rules from inputs to outputs
- Precise description of any special properties that could help the enactment engine to optimize workflow execution.

Some of these characteristics are fixed on registration with the registry (e.g., expected behavior), whereas some are configurable on instantiating an instance of a PE for use in a workflow (e.g., some optimization properties and certain aspects of type propagation). All of these characteristics are described according to the ontologies described in Chapter 8.

Almost all PEs take input from one or more data streams and produce one or more output streams accordingly. Different types of PEs provide different *connection interfaces*—by describing the connection interfaces available to a given type of PE, we provide an abstract specification for that type, which can be used to construct new PEs. The *internal connection signature* of a PE takes the following form:

```
PE( [Declarations]
    <Input_1,  ... , Input_m> => <Output_1,  ... , Output_n> )
    [with Properties]
```

Each input or output is a declaration of a `Connection` or a declaration of a `Connection` array (Section 10.2.4). For example, the following is the type signature of the PE `SQLQuery`:

```
PE( <Connection:String::"db:SQLQueryStatement" terminator expression;
    Connection:String::"db:DBURI" locator source> =>
    <Connection:[<rest>]::"db:TupleRowSet" data> )
```

From this, it can be inferred that the SQLQuery PE has three connection interfaces: two input (expression and source) and one output (data). It can also be inferred that expression accepts database queries stored as strings, source accepts an initial universal resource identifier likewise stored as a string, and data produces lists of tuples of undisclosed format as results. Finally, it can be inferred that source provides information that can be used to locate a data source (which can then be taken into account when assigning execution of an instance of SQLQuery to a specific service or process) and that when the stream connected to expression terminates, the instance of SQLQuery can itself be terminated (see Section 10.2.5 to know more on connection modifiers).

In addition, it is possible to extend the internal connection signature of a PE with additional type declarations and PE properties—examination of such type declarations is deferred to the DISPEL reference manual, while PE properties are briefly discussed in Section 10.2.5.

10.2.2 Processing Element Instances

Before a PE can be used as a workflow component, an instance of that PE must first be created. A PE can be instantiated many times, and each of these instances is referred to as a *processing element instance*, or PEI.

A PEI is the concrete object used by the enactment engine while assigning resources. It is created from a PE using the new keyword as follows:

```
SQLQuery sqlq = new SQLQuery;
```

In this case, SQLQuery is a PE and sqlq is its PEI.

While creating PEIs, a programmer can respecify any PE properties that are still modifiable. For example, during the following instantiation of SQLQuery, the programmer explicitly specifies more concretely the data stream format for the communication interface data, which is the output interface specified for all instances of SQLQuery:

```
SQLQuery sqlq = new SQLQuery
  with data as :[<Integer i, j; Real r; String s>];
```

The assertion, with data as :[<Integer i, j; Real r; String s>], only applies to the connection interface named data of the PEI named sqlq. This assertion does not affect the original definition of the SQLQuery PE. It is also possible to impose new connection modifiers and specify the size of arrays of connections—for instance, the following defines a combiner with exactly three permutable inputs:

```
Combiner combine = new Combiner with permutable inputs, inputs.length = 3;
```

Using with allows PE instances to be significantly modified for particular scenarios— for recurring scenarios, however, it will often be better to define a new PE type with the properties desired.

10.2.3   Defining New Types of Processing Element

It is possible to define new types of PEs by modifying existing types. For example,

```
Type SymmetricCombiner is Combiner with permutable inputs;
```

This use of with is as above but applies to all instances of the new PE type rather than just to a single instance. It is also possible to define entirely new types of PEs by describing its internal connection signature. For example,

```
Type SQLToTupleList is PE( <Connection expression> => <Connection data> );
```

Such PEs are referred to as *abstract* PEs if there exists no implementation for these PEs which can be used by the enactment platform to implement workflows that use them. Abstract PEs cannot be instantiated. Therefore, it becomes necessary to make these PEs implementable by use of special PE functions. The following function describes how to implement an instance of SQLToTupleList:

```
PE<SQLToTupleList> lockSQLDataSource(String dataSource) {
  SQLQuery sqlq = new SQLQuery;
  |-repeat enough of dataSource-| => sqlq.source;
  return PE( <Connection expression = sqlq.expression> =>
             <Connection data      = sqlq.data> );
}
```

PE functions return descriptions of how a PE with a given internal connection signature can be implemented using existing PEs. The notation PE<*Element*> designates the type of all subtypes of PE *Element*, which is shorthand for its internal connection interface—without this notation one might expect that the above function would return an instance of SQLToTupleList (which it does not), rather than an implementable subtype.

Using such a PE function, an implementable variant of a given abstract PE can be defined which can then be instantiated freely:

```
PE<SQLToTupleList> SQLOnA = lockSQLDataSource("uk.org.UoE.dbA");
SQLOnA sqlona = new SQLOnA;
```

Implementable PEs that are not primitive PEs (i.e., PEs described by function templates rather than PEs with prior registered implementations) are often referred to as *composite* PEs, as they are commonly defined using compositions of other implementable PEs, primitive or otherwise.

10.2.4 Connection Interfaces

A connection interface is described by a declaration of language type `Connection`. A basic connection interface requires only an identifier; an interface can also be annotated, however, with the expected structure and domain type of any data streamed through it and with any number of connection modifiers (Section 10.2.5), as appropriate.

Connection interfaces are defined within PE type declarations:

```
Type AbstractQuery is
  PE( <Connection:String::"db:SQLQueryStatement" expression> =>
      <Connection:Any::"db:Result" data> );
```

Connection interfaces can be assigned other `Connection` types as part of the return value of PE constructor functions:

```
PE<AbstractQuery> makeImplementableQuery( ... ) {
  Connection input;
  Connection output;
  ...   // Body of function ...
  return PE( <Connection expression = input> =>
             <Connection data      = output> );
}
```

Connection interfaces within a PE are defined as being input interfaces or output interfaces, based on the internal connection used within that PE. Certain connection modifiers are only applicable to input interfaces or only to output interfaces—to apply a connection modifier to an interface of the wrong kind is an error.

Connection interfaces can be further defined for particular subtypes of PE or for particular instantiations of PEs:

```
Type ListVisualiser is Visualiser with locator input as :[Any];
```

```
ListVisualiser visualiser = new ListVisualiser
  with input as :[Integer]::"bexd:PopulationList";
```

Such refinements can only be used to create a valid subtype of the original `Connection` declaration. Connection interfaces can also be defined in arrays (`Connection[]`):

```
Type TupleBuild is
  PE( <Connection:[<String columnName, typeSpec>] struct;
       Connection[]:[Any] lockstep inputs> =>
       <Connection:<rest> output> );
```

Any structural or domain type information is assumed to apply to each individual interface in the array. Connection modifiers may have different meanings, however, when applied to arrays than when applied to individual interfaces (Section 10.2.5). The size of a connection array should be defined upon creating an instance of any PE with such an array:

```
TupleBuild build = new TupleBuild with inputs.length = 4;
```

10.2.5   Connection Modifiers

Connection modifiers are used to indicate particular aspects of a PE or PEI's internal connection signature, which either:

- affect how the PEI interacts with other components in a workflow or
- provide information to the enactment platform as how to best implement a workflow containing such a PEI.

They are applied to either the declaration of a connection interface within an abstract PE definition or the redefinition of an interface during the instantiation or subtyping of an existing PE. For example,

```
Type SQLQuery is
  PE( <Connection:String::"db:SQLQueryStatement" terminator expression;
       Connection:String::"db:DBURI" locator source> =>
       <Connection:[<rest>]::"db:TupleRowSet" data> );
```

```
Type LockedSQLQuery is SQLQuery with initiator source, requiresStype data;
```

```
LockedSQLQuery query = new LockedSQLQuery
  with preserved("localhost") data as :[<Integer key; String result>];
```

Some of the modifiers available in DISPEL are described at the end of the section. The input interfaces expression and source of PE type SQLQuery are modified with terminator and locator, respectively. A subtype of SQLQuery called LockedSQLQuery is then defined, which assigns an additional modifier initiator to source as well as requiresStype to output interface data. Finally, a specific instance of LockedSQLQuery is created wherein data is further modified with preserved; the structural type of data is also refined as required by the earlier modification of data with requiresStype. Thus, the internal connection signature of query is

```
PE( <Connection:String::"db:SQLQueryStatement" terminator expression;
     Connection:String::"db:DBURI" locator initiator source> =>
   <Connection:[<Integer key; String result>]::"db:TupleRowSet"
      requiresStype preserved("localhost") data> );
```

Connection modifiers are applied during either the declaration of a Connection interface or Connection array as defined in Section 10.2.4 or during the refinement or instantiation of a PE using with as demonstrated above. Multiple modifiers can be applied at once by declaring them successively:

```
Type EncryptedQuery is SQLQuery
  with encrypted("caesar-cipher") preserved("localhost/secured") data;
```

Some modifiers take parameters. These parameters are listed in parentheses immediately after the modifier keyword:

```
Type AbstractLearner is
  PE( <Connection model; Connection training;
       Connection after(model, training) test> =>
     <Connection results> );
```

Most connection modifiers are applicable to both input and output connection interfaces; however a few are only applicable to inputs or outputs exclusively (or have different meanings when applied to an input or output as with encrypted). In addition, most connection modifiers can be applied to arrays of connections and to individual connections—there also exist, however, a subset of modifiers that are only applicable to arrays (generally concerning the relationship between individual interfaces within the array). The complete set of connection modifiers available in DISPEL are described in detail in the DISPEL reference manual.

In addition to modifiers applied to individual connection interfaces and arrays of interfaces, additional properties applicable to the PE type definition as a whole or to arbitrary subsets of connection interfaces can be defined. These can be appended to either the declaration of a connection interface within an abstract PE definition or the redefinition of an interface during instantiation of subtyping, just as for connection modifiers. For example,

```
Type DataProjector is
  PE( <Connection:String::"db:DBURI"              source;
      Connection[]:[Integer]::"bexd:Vector"   vectors> =>
      <Connection:[<rest>]::"bexd:Projection"  projection>
      with lockstep(source, vectors) );
```

```
SQLQuery query = new SQLQuery with lockstep(source, expression);
```

PE properties are attached using the `with` directive, and their effects often overlap with those of connection modifiers. As with modifiers, the properties available are described in detail in the **DISPEL** reference manual and are also summarized in part as follows:

after is used to delay the consumption of data through one or more connections. [*Requires a list of predecessors*]

compressed is used to compress data streamed out of the modified connection or to identify the compression used on data being consumed when applied to an output or an input interface, respectively. [*Requires a compression scheme*]

default is used to specify the default input streamed through a connection should input be otherwise left unspecified. [*Requires a stream expression; input only*]

encrypted is used to encrypt data streamed out of the modified connection or to identify the encryption scheme used on data being consumed when applied to an output or an input interface, respectively. [*Requires an encryption scheme*]

initiator is used to identify connections that provide only an initial input before closing and allowing all other inputs to proceed. [*Input only*]

limit is used to specify the maximum number of data elements a connection will consume or produce before terminating. [*Requires a positive integer value*]

locator is used where the modified connection indicates the location of a resource to be accessed by the associated PEI (which might influence the distribution of the workflow on execution). [*Input only*]

lockstep indicates that a data element must be streamed through every interface in the modified array before another element can be streamed through any of them. [*Connection arrays only*]

permutable indicates that a given array of inputs can be read from in any order without influencing the outputs of the PEI. [*Input connection arrays only*]

preserved indicates that data streamed through the modified connection should be recorded in a given location. [*Requires a URI or goes to a default location*]

requiresDtype dictates that on instantiation, the specific domain type of the modified connection must be defined.

requiresStype dictates that on instantiation, the specific structural type of the modified connection must be defined.

roundrobin indicates that a data element must be streamed through each interface in the modified array in order, one element at a time. [*Connection arrays only*]

successive indicates that each interface of the modified array must terminate before the next one is read. [*Connection arrays only*]

terminator causes a PEI to terminate on the termination of the modified connection alone (rather than once all inputs or all outputs have terminated).

The enactment platform that actually executes a submitted DISPEL workflow may have at its disposal many alternate implementations of a given PE specification. The use of connection modifiers and PE properties can serve to restrict and modify (via wrappers) the use of certain implementations. It may also be the case, however, that some implementations tacitly impose certain connection modifiers themselves (e.g., assuming all inputs are in lockstep) that may not be explicitly referenced by the abstract PE specification, resulting occasionally in workflow elements consuming or producing data in an unexpected manner. In essence, the more precisely a PE is defined in DISPEL, the more confidence the user can have that the workflow will execute precisely as intended.

10.3 DATA STREAMS

DISPEL uses a streaming-data execution model to describe data-intensive activities. All of the PEIs in a workflow application interact with one another by passing data. Data produced by one PEI is consumed by one or more other PEIs. Hence, to make the communication between PEIs possible, DISPEL allows users to define external connections between PEIs. These connections channel data between interdependent PEIs as streams via their connection interfaces.

Every data stream can be deconstructed as a sequence of data elements with a common abstract structure, which can then be validated against the structure of data expected by a given interface. PEIs will consume and produce data element by element according to the specification of its immediate PE type, defined on instantiation of the PEI. In DISPEL however, the specifics of data production and consumption are generally hidden, delegating the tasks of buffering and optimization to the enactment platform.

10.3.1 Connections

In DISPEL, there exist two types of connections: *internal* and *external*. Internal connections are defined in the specification of PEs and have already been encountered in Section 10.2.1 and elaborated in succeeding sections. An internal connection links any number of input connection interfaces to any number of output connection interfaces, but only one such connection can exist within a given PE:

```
PE( <Connection:String::"db:SQLQueryStatement" terminator expression;
     Connection:String::"db:DBURI" locator source> =>
   <Connection:[<rest>]::"db:TupleRowSet" data> )
```

An external connection is established by linking an output connection interface of one PEI to an input of another PEI. Assume the existence of two PEs, `Producer` and `Consumer`, with the following PE type definitions:

```
Type Producer is
  PE( <> => <Connection output; Connection[] outputArray> );
Type Consumer is
  PE( <Connection input; Connection[] inputArray> => <> );
```

Now assume two PEIs, designated `producer` and `consumer`:

```
Producer producer = new Producer with outputArray.length = 3;
Consumer consumer = new Consumer with inputArray.length  = 3;
```

To refer to the communication interfaces of a given PEI, we use the dot operator (`.`). The left-hand side of this operator must be a reference to a PEI, and the right-hand side must be a reference to an interface. For example, we refer to the input interface of the consumer PEI as `consumer.input`; similarly, the output interface of `producer` as `producer.output`. A connection can be established using the connection operator (`=>`) as shown below:

```
producer.output => consumer.input;
```

Any given output connection interface can be connected to multiple input connection interfaces; all data transported are replicated across all connections. It is not permissible to connect multiple output connection interfaces to a single input interface however; if a merger of outputs is desired, then a suitable PE must be provided to act as intermediary in order to resolve precisely *how* multiple outputs should be merged.

In the case of composite PEs defined by PE constructor functions, the internal connection defined by the internal connection signature of the PE will be implemented by a set of internal "external" connections linking together a set of internal PEs. These may themselves have their internal connections implemented by connections between further internal PEs, if they are also composite. For example, take a composite PE of abstract type `SQLToTupleList` constructed using the simple wrapper function `lockSQLDataSource`:

```
PE<SQLToTupleList> lockSQLDataSource(String dataSource) {
  SQLQuery sqlq = new SQLQuery;
  |-repeat enough of dataSource-| => sqlq.source;
  return PE( <Connection expression = sqlq.expression> =>
               <Connection data       = sqlq.data> );
}
```

In this case, the internal connection signature of SQLToTupleList is implemented by connecting input expression to the expression input of an internal instance of SQLQuery (a primitive PE) while output data is connected to the data output of that same internal instance. A slightly more complex case is demonstrated by function makeCorroboratedQuery:

```
PE<CorroboratedQuery> makeCorroboratedQuery(Integer sources) {
  SQLQuery[]      sqlq   = new SQLQuery[sources];
  ListConcatenate concat = new ListConcatenate
       with input.length = sources;
  Connection   expr;
  Connection[] srcs = new Connection[sources];

  for (Integer i = 0; i < sources; i++) {
          expr => sqlq[i].expression;
       srcs[i] => sqlq[i].source;
    sqlq[i].data => concat.inputs[i];
  }

  return PE( <Connection expression = expr;
              Connection sources    = srcs;
              <Connection data       = concat.output> );
}
```

In this case, the internal connection signature of CorroboratedQuery (assumed here to be much the same as the signature of SQLQuery albeit with an array of data source inputs sources rather than a single input source) is implemented by:

- connecting input expression to every input expression of an array of SQLQuery instances;
- connecting each input in interface array sources to the input source of a different instance of that same SQLQuery array;
- connecting each output expression of every instance of the SQLQuery array to a different input of an instance of ListConcatenate, a PE that combines lists from multiple inputs into a single list;
- connecting output data to the output of the ListConcatenate instance.

This produces a composite PE for querying databases which collates results from multiple sources.

Thus, all workflows, even when constructed using composite PEs, can be decomposed into a graph of connections between primitive "black-box" PEs showing the complete flow of data from beginning to end.

10.3.2 Stream Literals

Typically, a PEI processes data stream elements that it receives via its input connection interfaces, consuming input through each interface one element at a time. Each data element is designed to be as small as possible, in terms of raw data volume, as long as it still makes computational sense to the receiving PEI. A single data element could be an integer value, a string, a tuple of related values, a single row of a matrix, or something else entirely.

The enactment platform is responsible for the buffering of the data units that are flowing through the communication objects within a workflow. It is also responsible for optimizing the mapping of PEIs to resources in order to minimize the communication costs—for example, opting to pass data by reference when data units are communicated between PEIs, which have been assigned to the same computational resource; serialization and compression of data for long-haul data movement; or buffering to disk when specifically requested or when buffer spill is unavoidable.

When the values of the data units for a given stream are known *a priori* or can be evaluated as an expression at instantiation, they can be specified within a DISPEL script itself. Consider, for example, PEs that only communicate with specific data sources. In DISPEL, these *a priori* specifications are referred to as *stream literals*. Stream literals are identified within the script by the use of the stream literal operators |- and -|. These operators enclose an expression that when evaluated during instantiation generate a stream entity that can be connected to a PEI via one of its input interfaces. For example,

```
|- "Hello", "World" -| => consumer.input;
```

If it is necessary to repeatedly produce the same data within a stream for the benefit of the consuming PEI, the `repeat` construct can be used within the stream literal expression. For example,

```
|- repeat 10 of "Hello" -| => consumer.input;
```

In this case, the string literal `"Hello"` will be passed to the `input` interface 10 times. When it is uncertain how many times a given literal must be repeated, the `enough` keyword can be used. For example,

```
|- repeat enough of "Hello" -| => consumer.input;
```

In this case, the string literal `"Hello"` will be passed to `input` as many times as required by `consumer`.

10.4   TYPE SYSTEM

Compared to other dataflow expression languages, DISPEL introduces a sophisticated type system for validation and optimization of workflows. Using this type system, gateways are not only capable of checking the validity of a DISPEL script (e.g., for incorrect syntax) but also validate the connection between PEs (e.g., for incorrect connections where the type of output data produced by a source PE does not match the type of input data expected by a destination PE). Furthermore, this type system exposes the lower-level structure of the streaming data that is being communicated through valid connections, so that workflow optimization algorithms implemented beyond the enactment gateways can refactor and reorganize PEs and their various interconnections in order to improve performance.

The DISPEL language uses three-type systems to validate the abstraction, compilation, and enactment of DISPEL scripts:

1. The *language-type system* statically validates at compile time whether or not the operations in a DISPEL script are consistently typed. For instance, the language type checker will check whether the parameters supplied to a function invocation match the type of the formal parameters specified in the function's definition.

2. The *structural-type system* describes the format and low level (automated) interpretation of values that are being transmitted along a connection between two PEIs. For example, the structural-type system will check if the data flowing through a connection is a sequence of tuples as expected or a sequence of arrays instead.

3. The *domain-type system* describes how domain experts interpret the data that is being transmitted along a connection in relation to the application. For instance, the domain-type system could describe whether the data flowing through a connection is a sequence of aerial or satellite image stripes, each stripe being represented as a list of images.

Figure 10.3 illustrates some of DISPEL's type constructs. Language types, structural types, and domain types are defined, respectively, using Type (line 10), Stype (line 6), and Dtype (line 7) statements. Since domain types are associated with ontological definitions, we use the namespace keyword (line 3) to refer to existing ontology locations where the term definitions can be found.

Structural and domain types, once defined, can then be attributed to connection interfaces. Structural types are attached to Connection declarations using the ":" connector, while domain types are attached (usually immediately after a structural type) using the "::" connector. Direct references to ontology elements as domain types are always enclosed inside double quotes (see lines 12, 16 and 18), while aliases created by Dtype statements use standard identifier notation (see lines 14 and 17). Complex structural types may permit domain typing of constituent elements (see lines 16 and 17). Specification of structural and domain types is optional, but

```
 1   package book.examples.dispel {
 2     /* Define domain namespace. */
 3     namespace bexd "http://dispel-lang.org/book/examples/dispel";
 4
 5     /* Define structural and domain type aliases. */
 6     Stype InitType is <Integer firstValue, step>;
 7     Dtype Taggable represents "bexd:CountableObject";
 8
 9     /* Define new PE type. */
10     Type TagWithCounter is
11       PE( // Define input connection interfaces 'init' and 'data'.
12           <Connection:InitType::"bexd:IterationControl"
13               initiator init;
14           Connection:Any::Taggable data> =>
15           // Define output interface 'output'.
16           <Connection:<Integer::"bexd:OrderedSequence" tag;
17                        Any::Taggable value>
18                        ::"bexd:PreserveOrder" output> );
19
20     /* Register new entity. */
21     register TagWithCounter;
22   }
```

Figure 10.3   *An example of the DISPEL type system in use.*

provides valuable information to the gateway when implementing a workflow and assisting the user in verifying the correctness of code.

Owing to limited space, we shall not discuss here many of the details of the type system—for instance, the type constructors, propagation rules, type checking, and so forth. These details are available in the DISPEL users' manual [1]. Some discussion of subtyping has been included here, however, to alert readers to some of DISPEL's more useful capabilities.

10.4.1   Processing Element Subtyping

A PE is a subtype of another PE if instances of the initial PE in a workflow can be replaced by instances of the subtype without invalidating the workflow. Thus, the subtype PE must have certain properties as follows:

- It must have the same abstract configuration of interfaces as that of the other PE—the same number of input interfaces and output interfaces, each with the same name. If arrays of interfaces are specified in the parent-type PE, then there must exist equivalent arrays in the subtype PE.
- The structural and domain types of each output interface on the subtype must be themselves subtypes of the structural and domain types used by the equivalent interface on the parent type, as defined in Sections 10.4.2 and 10.4.3. This ensures that if an instance of the parent type is replaced by an instance of the subtype, then all outbound connections will remain valid, as downstream

PEs will be expecting an equal or greater range of inputs than the subtype will produce.

- The structural and domain types of each input interface on the *parent* type must be themselves subtypes of the structural and domain types used by the equivalent interface on the *sub*type. This ensures that if an instance of the parent type is replaced by an instance of the subtype, then all inbound connections will remain valid, as the subtype PE will be expecting a wider range of inputs than would have been handled by the parent type.

- Connection modifiers are *not* factored into subtype and parent-type relationships—the user is free to use whatever modifiers are desired with the accompanying risks to streaming.

For logical purposes, every PE is also a subtype of itself (i.e., PE subtyping is reflexive). It should be noted that subtype relationships are determined *solely* by the (extended) internal connection signatures of PEs. The actual functionality of a PE is not considered. The justification for this resides in the nature of the workflow model around which DISPEL is designed—as far as DISPEL is concerned, each PE is a black box that consumes and produces data in a particular manner and that determines how relationships between PEs are evaluated. Consider the type specification of PE SQLQuery:

```
Type SQLQuery is
  PE( <Connection:String::"db:SQLQueryStatement" terminator expression;
      Connection:String::"db:DBURI" locator source> =>
      <Connection:[<rest>]::"db:TupleRowSet" data> );
```

PE SpecialisedSQLQuery is a subtype of SQLQuery with a more specialized output interface, as it produces a DictionarySet, which is a specialized version of a TupleRowSet where the values are represented in key/value pairs:

```
Type SpecialisedSQLQuery is
  PE( <Connection:String::"db:SQLQueryStatement" terminator expression;
      Connection:String::"db:DBURI" locator source> =>
      <Connection:[<Integer key; String value>]::"db:DictionarySet" data> );
```

Likewise, PE FlexibleQuery is a subtype of SQLQuery with a more permissive input interface; in this case, the query need not be in the form of a string:

```
Type FlexibleQuery is
  PE( <Connection:Any::"db:SQLQueryStatement" terminator expression;
      Connection:String::"db:DBURI" locator source> =>
      <Connection:[<rest>]::"db:TupleRowSet" data> );
```

However, PE `AugmentedSQLQuery` is not a subtype of `SQLQuery`, having a more permissive output, which might produce data unsupported by downstream workflow elements expecting output from an `SQLQuery` instance:

```
Type AugmentedSQLQuery is
  PE( <Connection:String::"db:SQLQueryStatement" terminator expression;
      Connection:String::"db:DBURI" locator source> =>
      <Connection:[Any]::"db:TupleRowSet" data> );
```

Likewise, PE `CorroboratedQuery` is not a subtype of `SQLQuery`, despite otherwise being a derivative of it, because it has an array of interfaces where `SQLQuery` has a single connection:

```
Type CorroboratedQuery is
  PE( <Connection:String::"db:SQLQueryStatement" terminator expression;
      Connection[]:String::"db:DBURI" locator sources> =>
      <Connection:[<rest>]::"db:TupleRowSet" data> );
```

While two independently created PEs can exhibit a subtype relationship, the most common way by which a PE subtype is created is by the use of a `Type`/`with` construct (as described in Section 10.2.3):

```
Type SpecialisedSQLQuery is SQLQuery
  with data as :[<Integer key; String value>]::"db:DictionarySet";
```

Note, however, that not all PEs derived from other PEs are subtypes—the refinement of input interfaces, for example, will actually create a parent type relation.

The range of subtypes of a given PE *Element* is designated by the notation `PE<Element>`. Subtype relations are principally made use of by PE constructor functions in their parameters or their return types. A PE function returns a subtype of a given abstract type and can also take subtypes of an abstract PE type as a parameter. For example,

```
PE<ParallelProcessor>
makeParallelisedProcess(PE<Processor> Element) { ... }
```

In this case, `makeParallelisedProcess` returns a subtype of the `ParallelProcessor` abstract PE constructed using instances of any subtype of the `Processor` PE. It is essential that any subtype of `Processor` be insertable into a workflow that expects a `Processor` PEI at any particular point. Likewise, it is essential that the PE created using `makeParallelisedProcess` can be used anywhere where an implementation of `ParallelProcessor` is expected.

10.4.2 Structural Subtyping

A structural type ST' is a subtype of another structural type ST ($ST' \sqsubseteq ST$) if both types have homomorphic abstract structures and the structural information provided by ST' is at least as detailed as that of ST. To this end, the following rules apply:

- $\forall\ ST.\ ST \sqsubseteq Any.$
- $\forall\ ST.\ ST \sqsubseteq ST.$
- $[ST'] \sqsubseteq [ST]$, if and only if $ST' \sqsubseteq ST$.
- $ST'[\ ] \sqsubseteq ST[\ ]$, if and only if $ST' \sqsubseteq ST$.
- $< ST'_1\ id'_1\ ;\ \dots\ ;\ ST'_m\ id'_m > \sqsubseteq < ST_1\ id_1\ ;\ \dots\ ;\ ST_n\ id_n >$ if and only if $m = n$ and, after sorting identifiers according to a standard scheme, $id'_i = id_i$ and $ST'_i \sqsubseteq ST_i$ for all i such that $1 \leq i \leq n$.
- $< ST'_1\ id'_1\ ;\ \dots\ ;\ ST'_m\ id'_m > \sqsubseteq < ST_1\ id_1\ ;\ \dots\ ;\ ST_n\ id_n;$ **rest** $>$ if and only if $m \geq n$ and there exists a permutation of identifiers $id'_1, \dots, id'_m$ such that $id'_i = id_i$ and $ST'_i \sqsubseteq ST_i$ for all i such that $1 \leq i \leq n$.

These rules are applied recursively on all known substructures of a given structural subtype. The greatest common subtype ST' of two structural types, ST_1 and ST_2, is simply a structural type for which:

- $ST' \sqsubseteq ST_1$ and $ST' \sqsubseteq ST_2$.
- There does not exist another subtype ST'' such that $ST'' \sqsubseteq ST_1$, $ST'' \sqsubseteq ST_2$, and $ST' \sqsubseteq ST''$ unless $ST' = ST''$.

Structural subtyping is important for the identification of subtype relationships between PEs. It is also important that the enactment platform when validating workflows is able to determine whether or not the structure of data passing through a connection is a subtype of the structure expected by the connection interfaces at either end of that connection.

10.4.3 Domain Subtyping

A domain type DT1 is only known to be a subtype of another domain type DT2 if:

- such a relationship is described within the two types' underlying ontology (as referenced by a namespace statement);
- there exists a prior statement Dtype DT1 is DT2, which has the effect of declaring that DT1 is a DT2; or
- there exists a sequence of Dtype statements relating DT1 to DT2, such that a subtype relation can be inferred by transitivity.

Otherwise, DISPEL infers that certain domain types are subtypes of other domain types based on how those types are used within workflows unless given evidence to the contrary—essentially, without a sufficiently well-defined ontology for a whole workflow, DISPEL will infer an *ad hoc* ontology mapping for domain type elements, as it validates a submitted workflow and will simply check for consistency. This permits robust default behavior in scenarios where a complete ontological description of a workflow's dataflow is not available.

Such inferences are based on domain type assertions made on refinement or instantiation of PEs and on external connections created between connection interfaces with different domain type annotations. In the first case, any domain type refinement made is assumed to demonstrate a subtype relationship between the new and prior domain types. For example,

```
Type Modeller is
  PE( <Connection:[Real]::"kdd:DataFeatures" data> =>
      <Connection::"kdd:DataModel"          model> );
  ...
Modeller modeller = new Modeller with data as ::"bexd:Coordinates";
```

In this case, an adapted instance of Modeller is created, which changes the domain type of output interface data from "kdd:DataFeatures" to "bexd:Coordinates," from which it can be inferred that there exists a possible subtype relation between the two domain types (though it is not yet clear *which* domain type is the subtype). Note that this inferred relation crosses ontologies (kdd and bexd).

The second case is illustrated below—the domain type of the output interface model is required to be a subtype of the input interface classifier on the other side of the connection operator:

```
Type Classifier is
  PE( <Connection:[Real]::"kdd:DataFeatures" data;
      Connection:[Real]::"kdd:Classifier"   classifier> =>
      <Connection:Boolean::"dispel:Boolean" class> );
  ...
Classifier classifier = new Classifier;
  ...
modeller.model => classifier.classifier;
```

In this case, "kdd:DataModel" is inferred to be a subtype of kdd:Classifier (which may or may not be confirmed or disputed by the kdd ontology).

These inferred subtype relationships are combined with subtype relationships drawn from existing ontologies referenced by the PE components imported from the registry and checked for contradictions. Only if an inconsistency is found will the DISPEL parser fail to validate a DISPEL workflow on grounds of invalid domain type use.

10.5 REGISTRATION

The registry is the knowledge base of the entire platform. This is where all of the information concerning PEs, functions, and other user-defined types are stored. For an application to be executable within the platform, all of the relevant information must first be made available to the registry (see Chapter 8). This is because when a gateway receives a workflow application (submitted as a DISPEL script), it communicates with the registry to resolve dependencies, expand pattern abstractions, and retrieve type information before the workflow is passed to the enactment system.

When a DISPEL script is submitted for enactment, the underlying workflow graph described by the script is expanded using definitions provided by the registry and then used to select suitable implementations of components from available sources. Execution of those components is then delegated to various available resources; the enactment platform will attempt to optimize this process by accounting for the location and interconnectivity of resources, drawing on any additional information provided by the DISPEL script in the form of connection modifiers (such as `locator`) and general PE properties.

DISPEL provides constructs for two-way communication between the DISPEL parser in the gateway and the registry service interfaces. These are `register` for exporting DISPEL entities to the registry and `use` for importing entities from the registry.

10.5.1 Exporting to the Registry

Example 10.1 illustrated the `register` directive, the critical parts of which are reproduced below:

```
package book.examples.dispel {
   ...
  Type SQLToTupleList is PE(  ...  );
  PE<SQLToTupleList> lockSQLDataSource(String dataSource) {  ...  };
  register lockSQLDataSource;
}
```

In the DISPEL code segment above, a function is specified that produces a PE, that directs queries to a specific data source; this function can now be used to generate a multitude of application domain-specific PEs with their own respective data sources. Since it is prudent to save recurring patterns for reuse, this function can be registered with the registry using the `register` construct:

```
register Entity_1, Entity_2,  ...  ;
```

As described in Chapter 8, it is also possible to register elements with additional annotations. This is done by adding `with` to the register statement:

```
register SQLToTupleList, lockSQLDataSource
  with @author = "Anonymous", @description = "  ...  ";
```

During registration, the DISPEL parser automatically collects all of the dependencies and stores this information with the entity being registered. In doing so, the registry guarantees that any new registration is complete (extending or replacing tagged content as appropriate) and reproducible when exported from the registry.

Consider the function `lockSQLDataSource` as defined in Figure 10.1. It depends on `SQLQuery`, an existing PE type. When registering function `lockSQLDataSource`, the registry will only make a note that `lockSQLDataSource` depends on `SQLQuery`. However, if there is a dependency where the required entities are not already in the registry, the DISPEL parser will automatically register all of the entities defined within the same package before registering the entity. For example, in the script segment in the previous section, the definition of `SQLToTupleList` will be registered automatically before `lockSQLDataSource` is registered, even though `SQLToTupleList` is not explicitly registered by the script.

10.5.2   Importing from the Registry

The platform relies on the registry for the evaluation of DISPEL scripts. This is done by importing definitions from the registry using the `use` directive. To illustrate this construct, reconsider the example in Figure 10.1. In this example, function `lockSQLDataSource` depends on the PE, `SQLQuery`. To import `SQLQuery` so that it is available to the gateway during the construction of the workflow defined by `lockSQLDataSource`, the `use` construct must be applied as shown here:

```
use dispel.db.SQLQuery;
```

```
use dispel.core.{ListSplit, ListMerge};
```

Each `use` statement must identify one or more DISPEL entities to be imported, prefixed by a qualified package name, a mechanism used by the platform for name resolution (Section 10.6). To import multiple entities from various packages, a DISPEL script can have multiple `use` statements. In the above examples, the first statement imports the entity named `SQLQuery` from the `dispel.db` package, whereas the second statement imports `ListSplit` and `ListMerge` from the `dispel.core` package. Every entity that is used by a script must be defined in the same package as the dependent entity, be imported from the registry before they can be used to compose a workflow, or be defined in the special `dispel.lang` package.

10.6   PACKAGING

During registration and use, the platform must protect declarations, definitions, and instantiations of DISPEL components from conflicts with unrelated but similarly named components. To avoid component interference, DISPEL uses a packaging methodology similar to that of Java. Registration of related components are grouped inside a package using the `package` keyword. This is illustrated in the following example:

```
package book.examples.geography {
  Stype Cartesian is <Real x, y, z>;
  Stype Polar is <Real radius, theta, phi>;
  Stype Geographical is <Real latitude, longitude>;
  register Cartesian, Polar, Geographical;
}
```

Here, three structural types are being registered, which may be used for representing geographical positions. As they are defined within a package named book.examples.geography, they will be managed separately from other similarly named definitions within the registry. If a user wishes to use all of these structural types, they must include the following in their DISPEL script:

```
use book.examples.geography.{Cartesian, Polar, Geographical};
```

Multiple packages are allowed in a single DISPEL script but should not be nested.

10.7 WORKFLOW SUBMISSION

A workflow must be submitted for execution in order to produce results. Every resource in the environment is controlled by a gateway. The gateway hides these resources, instead providing appropriate interfaces for accessing them. These interfaces are in turn hidden from the user and must be invoked from within the DISPEL script. This is done using a `submit` command. For example,

```
use book.example.math.PrimeGenerator;
use book.example.math.makeSieveOfEratosthenes;

PE<PrimeGenerator> SieveOfEratosthenes = makeSieveOfEratosthenes(100);
SieveOfEratosthenes sieve = new SieveOfEratosthenes;
submit sieve;
```

On receiving a `submit` command, the gateway will check that the workflow is valid. This is done by expanding the workflow patterns and by checking the validity of the connections between PEIs for type safety. Once the workflow is deemed executable, the gateway initializes the computational activities encapsulated within the PEs by assigning them to the available resources. Finally, the connections between these computational activities are established in accordance with the workflow by allocating data transport channels to connections. The `submit` command has the following syntax:

```
submit instance_1, instance_2,  ... ;
```

Each workflow is a connected graph of one or more PEIs. This graph can be submitted using the `submit` command referencing an instance within the graph. For example,

```
PE <PrimeGenerator> SoE100 = makeSieveOfEratosthenes(100);
SoE100 sieve100 = new SoE100;
submit sieve100;
  ...
PE<PrimeGenerator> SoE512  = makeSieveOfEratosthenes(512);
PE<PrimeGenerator> SoE1024 = makeSieveOfEratosthenes(1024);
SoE512  sieve512  = new SoE512;
SoE1024 sieve1024 = new SoE1024;
submit sieve512, sieve1024;
```

It is possible to submit multiple disjointed workflow graphs simultaneously using a single `submit` command. This is shown in the above example, where soe512 and soe1024 are submitted using a single `submit` command. Finally, there can be multiple `submit` commands within a single DISPEL script.

10.7.1 Processing Element Termination

In a distributed stream processing platform, termination of computational activities must be handled appropriately to avoid resource wastage. If unused PEIs are not terminated, then they will continue to claim resources allocated to them while the PEI was active. In the platform, a PEI is terminated when either all the inputs from its sources are exhausted or all the receivers of its output have indicated that they do not want any more data:

- The first case occurs when all of the input interfaces of the PEI have received an `EoS` (end-of-stream) token or an input interface designated `terminator` (Section 10.2.5) has received an `EoS` token. In this case, the PEI will finish processing pending data elements and, when done, will send any final results through its output interfaces. The PEI will then send an `EoS` token to all of its output interfaces and a `NmD` (no-more-data) token through any still-active input interfaces. This will trigger a cascading termination effect in all PEIs, which depend on the terminated PEI.
- The second case occurs when a PEI receives a `NmD` token back through all of its output interfaces, or when it receives a `NmD` token back through any output interface designated `terminator`, signifying that no more data is required. In this case, the PEI will convey the message further up the workflow by relaying a `NmD` token back through all of its input interfaces and an `EoS` token

through any still-active output interfaces. This will likewise create a cascading termination effect.

Cascading termination through the propagation of termination triggers helps the platform reclaim resources for enactment of other DISPEL scripts.

10.8 EXAMPLES OF DISPEL

In this section, we present two examples to help the reader understand the use and power of DISPEL, building on examples already given in Parts 1 and 2. The first, the *Sieve of Eratosthenes*, is a streaming implementation of a familiar computational problem—the generation of prime numbers. The aims here are to (i) present an easy-to-follow example of stream-based processing, (ii) provide a complete example so that the whole execution cycle can be visualized, (iii) describe a few common programming patterns, (iv) demonstrate that DISPEL is a general purpose programming language, and (v) show the use and function of distributed termination necessary in data-intensive computing.

The *k*-fold cross-validation example goes on to present the full power of DISPEL and demonstrate the use of functional abstraction in a well-known real-world example. This example also demonstrates that the actual graph can grow, in both size and complexity, well beyond that which can be managed without the abstractions provided by DISPEL.

10.8.1 The Sieve of Eratosthenes Example

The *Sieve of Eratosthenes* is a simple algorithm for finding prime numbers. The algorithm works by counting natural numbers and filtering out numbers that are composite (not prime). We start with the integer 2 and discard every integer greater than 2 that is divisible by 2. Then, we take the smallest of all the remaining integers, which is definitely prime, and discard every remaining integer divisible by that prime (in this case 3). We continue this process with the next integer and so on until the desired number of primes have been discovered.

10.8.1.1 Workflow Design   The Sieve of Eratosthenes can be implemented as a pipeline pattern described by a DISPEL function. Using a PE function, it is possible to implement the pipeline for an arbitrary number of primes. This pipeline pattern will take the form shown in Figure 10.4.

10.8.1.2 Workflow Specification   The principal component of the Sieve of Eratosthenes pipeline is the filtering component used to determine whether or not a given integer is divisible by the last encountered prime. The PE `PrimeFilter` and the overall `PrimeGenerator` PE are declared in the following DISPEL script which also registers these types for use in the enactment process (Fig. 10.5).

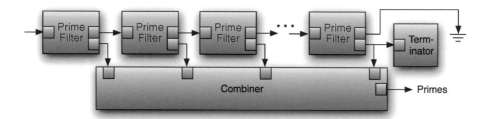

Figure 10.4   *The pipeline for the Sieve of Eratosthenes.*

```
1    package book.examples.math {
2
3      namespace bexm "http://dispel-lang.org/book/examples/math";
4
5      /* PE for generating prime numbers. */
6      Type PrimeGenerator is PE (<> =>
7        <Connection:Integer::"bexm:PrimeNumber" primes> );
8
9      /* PE for accepting a prime and forwards only relative primes. */
10     Type PrimeFilter is PE (
11       <Connection:Integer::"dispel:Integer"    input> =>
12       <Connection:Integer::"bexm:PrimeNumber" prime;
13        Connection:Integer::"dispel:Integer"    output>
14     );
15
16     register PrimeFilter, PrimeGenerator;
17   }
```

Figure 10.5   *Types needed for the Sieve of Erathosthenes as a workflow.*

A primitive PE (implemented in a language other than DISPEL) conforming
to the `PrimeFilter` interface would be an instance of `PrimeFilter` that reads a
stream of integers from its input connection, `input`. The first such integer is output
immediately through the connection `prime`, which also defines its future behavior.
Each successive integer is then divided by this initial value; if evenly divisible,
then the integer is composite and is ignored. Otherwise, the integer is output via
connection `output`.

In order to implement the sieve, all that is necessary is to connect instances of
`PrimeFilter` in series, `output` to `input`. The values sent on the `prime` connection
for each PE instance can be streamed from the pipeline as the sieve's output—this
can be done with a `Combiner` PE, a generic component for conflating an arbitrary number of inputs into a single stream. Thus, Figure 10.6 shows the function
`makeSieveOfEratosthenes`.

Function `makeSieveOfEratosthenes` describes an implementation of
`PrimeGenerator`. An abstract PE `PrimeGenerator` takes no input, producing only
a stream of prime numbers. The function makes an array of `PrimeFilter` PEIs, as

```
1    package book.examples.math {
2
3      use dispel.lang.Terminator;              // Receives a single input and terminates.
4      use dispel.core.Combiner;                // Merges inputs into single stream.
5      use book.examples.math.PrimeFilter;      // Primitive filter PE definition.
6      use book.examples.math.PrimeGenerator;   // Prime generator PE definition.
7
8      /* Function for constructing Sieves of Erathosthenes. */
9      PE <PrimeGenerator> makeSieveOfEratosthenes (Integer count) {
10
11       PrimeFilter[] filter   = new PrimeFilter[count];
12       Combiner      combiner = new Combiner
13           with roundrobin inputs, inputs.length = count;
14       Terminator terminate = new Terminator;
15
16       /* Initialise sieve stages. */
17       for (Integer i = 0; i < count - 1; i++) {
18         filter[i] = new PrimeFilter with terminator output;
19       }
20       filter[count - 1] = new PrimeFilter with terminator prime;
21
22       /* Construct internal workflow. */
23       for (Integer i = 0; i < count - 1; i++) {
24         filter[i].output => filter[i + 1].input;
25         filter[i].prime  => combiner.inputs[i];
26       }
27       filter[count - 1].prime  => combiner.inputs[count - 1];
28       filter[count - 1].output -> discard;
29       filter[count - 1].prime  => terminate.input;
30
31       /* Generate input until NmD (no more data) token received. */
32       |- 2 to infinity -| => filter[0].input;
33
34       /* Return all prime numbers generated. */
35       return PE ( <> => <Connection primes = combiner.output> );
36     }
37
38     /* Register PE function. */
39     register makeSieveOfEratosthenes;
40   }
```

Figure 10.6 *The Sieve of Erathosthenes as a workflow pattern encapsulated in a PE function.*

well as an instance of Combiner. Note that Combiner is instantiated with one input for each PrimeFilter PE and modifies its inputs with the roundrobin modifier. The effect of this is that each connection in array inputs will only consume a value after a prime has been read through every preceding interface in the array, which ensures that the stream of primes output by an instance of the sieve will be in order regardless of how components of the sieve are distributed across resources during enactment.

Each instance of PrimeFilter (except the last) is instantiated with the modifier terminator on the output connection, while the final instance of PrimeFilter is instantiated with the modifier terminator on the prime connection. When the last prime is sent to the Combiner, it is also sent to the Terminator PE. This utility PE will simply terminate on receipt of any input. Since the prime connection

```
1    package book.examples.math {
2
3        use book.examples.math.PrimeGenerator;
4        use book.examples.math.makeSieveOfEratosthenes;
5
6        /* Construct instances of PEs for workflow. */
7        PE <PrimeGenerator> SoE100 = makeSieveOfEratosthenes(100);
8        SoE100   sieve100 = new SoE100;
9        Results results   = new Results;
10
11       /* Construct the top-level workflow. */
12       |- "Prime numbers" -| => results.name;
13               sieve100.primes => results.input;
14
15       /* Submit workflow. */
16       submit results;
17   }
```

Figure 10.7   *An execution script for generating the first 100 primes in the Sieve of Erathosthenes.*

from the final `PrimeFilter` PE is annotated with the modifier `terminator`, this PE will terminate. As it does so, it starts a reverse cascade terminating the remaining `PrimeFilter` PEs.

To elaborate, when the `Terminator` PE terminates, it will send a `NmD` (no more data) token back to the previous instance via its `output` connection, which being denoted as `terminator` will cause the previous instance to terminate, which will start a backward termination cascade. As each instance terminates, each connection to the `Combiner` will receive the `EoS` (end of stream) token that will lead to the eventual termination of the `Combiner`, and so the termination of the whole sieve. This common pattern exists in many different workflows. Also, termination is defined and managed at the platform level rather than as one of application domain concerns. This contrasts strongly with traditional approaches to distributed termination.

The Sieve of Eratosthenes for 100 prime numbers can now be executed as shown in Figure 10.7.

This stream-based implementation of the Sieve of Eratosthenes demonstrates the use of reusable patterns to create general purpose solutions in a distributed environment from initiation to termination.

10.8.2   The *k*-Fold Cross-Validation Pattern

In statistical data mining and machine learning, *k-fold cross validation* is an abstract pattern used to estimate the classification accuracy of a learning algorithm. It determines that accuracy by repeatedly dividing a data sample into disjoint training and test sets, each time training and testing a classification model constructed using the given algorithm before collating and averaging the results. By training and testing a classifier using the same data sample divided differently each time, it is hoped

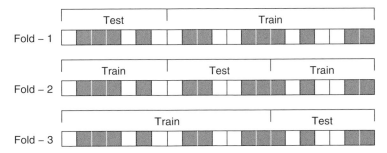

Figure 10.8 *Threefold cross-validation on a data sample with 21 elements.*

that a learning algorithm can be evaluated without being influenced by biases that may occur in a particular division of training and test data.

The basic structure of a k-fold validation workflow pattern is very simple. First, a random permutation of the sample dataset is generated, which is then partitioned into k disjoint subsets. A classifier is trained using the given learning algorithm and then tested k times. In each training and testing iteration, referred to as a *fold*, all sample data excluding that of one subset, different each time, is used for training; the excluded subset is then used to test the resulting classifier. This entire process can be repeated with different random permutations of the sample data. Figure 10.8 illustrates how a data sample might be divided for a threefold cross-validation process.

10.8.2.1 *Constructing a k-Fold Cross Validator*   To specify a k-fold cross-validation workflow pattern that can be reused for different learning algorithms and values of k, it is best to specify a PE function that can take all necessary parameters and return a bespoke cross-validator PE on demand. Such a PE can then be instantiated and fed a suitable data corpus, producing a measure of the average accuracy of classification.

Figure 10.9 shows a PE function `makeCrossValidator`. This function describes an implementation of `Validator`, an abstract PE, which given a suitable dataset should produce a list of results from which (for example) an average score and standard deviation can be derived:

```
Type Validator is
  PE( <Connection:[<rest>]::["kdd:Observation"] data> =>
      <Connection:[Real]::["kdd:Score"]          results> );
```

The function `makeCrossValidator` requires four parameters:

`Integer k` specifies the number of subsets into which the sample data should be split and the number of training iterations required—in other words, k is the k in k-fold.

```
1    package dispel.datamining {
2      // Import abstract types.
3      use dispel.datamining.Validator;
4      use dispel.datamining.TrainClassifier;
5      use dispel.datamining.ApplyClassifier;
6      use dispel.datamining.ModelEvaluator;
7      use dispel.core.DataPartitioner;
8      // Import PE constructor function.
9      use dispel.datamining.makeDataFold;
10     // Import implemented type.
11     use dispel.core.ListMerge;
12
13     // Produces a k-fold cross validation workflow pattern.
14     PE<Validator> makeCrossValidator(Integer k,
15                               PE<TrainClassifier> Trainer,
16                               PE<ApplyClassifier> Classifier,
17                               PE<ModelEvaluator>  Evaluator) {
18       Connection    input;
19       // Data must be partitioned and re-combined for each fold.
20       PE<DataPartitioner> FoldData = makeDataFold(k);
21       FoldData          folder  = new FoldData;
22       ListMerge         union   = new ListMerge with inputs.length = k;
23
24       // For each fold, train a classifier then evaluate it.
25       input => folder.data;
26       for (Integer i = 0; i < k; i++) {
27         Trainer    train    = new Trainer;
28         Classifier classify = new Classifier;
29         Evaluator  evaluator = new Evaluator;
30
31         folder.training[i] => train.data;
32           train.classifier => classify.classifier;
33            folder.test[i] => classify.data;
34           classify.result => evaluator.predicted;
35            folder.test[i] => evaluator.expected;
36           evaluator.score => union.inputs[i];
37       }
38
39       // Return cross validation pattern.
40       return PE( <Connection data = input> =>
41                  <Connection results = union.output> );
42     }
43
44     // Register PE pattern generator.
45     register makeCrossValidator;
46   }
```

Figure 10.9 *PE function* makeCrossValidator.

PE<TrainClassifier> Trainer is a PE type, instances of which can be used to train classifiers—it must encapsulate the learning algorithm to be tested and be compatible with the TrainClassifier PE.

PE<ApplyClassifier> Classifier is a PE type, instances of which take test data and a classifier model and produce a prediction. Any classifier must be an implementable version of the ApplyClassifier PE.

PE<ModelEvaluator> Evaluator is a PE type, instances of which take observation data and accompanying predictions and assigns a score based on the accuracy of those predications. The evaluator must be an implementable version of the ModelEvaluator PE.

In this case, there are three instances where a PE type is passed into a PE function in order to create an arbitrary number of instances of that PE within its internal workflow. Each must be compatible with (i.e., have internal connection signatures subsumed by) a given (possibly abstract) PE:

```
Type TrainClassifier is
  PE( <Connection:[<rest>]::["kdd:Observation"] data> =>
      <Connection:Any::"kdd:Classifier"        classifier> );
```

TrainClassifier consumes a body of training data in the form of a list of tuples and produces a classification model. Any PE implementation of TrainClassifier must encapsulate a learning algorithm and must know how to interpret the data provided—this includes knowing which feature a classifier is to be trained to predict. Thus, any such PE would probably be a bespoke construction generated by a function immediately before the creation of the cross validator.

```
Type ApplyClassifier is
  PE( <Connection:[<rest>]::["kdd:Observation"] data;
       Connection:Any::"kdd:Classifier"        classifier> =>
      <Connection:[<rest>]::["kdd:Prediction"]  result> );
```

ApplyClassifier consumes a body of data in the form of a list of tuples and a classification model, producing a list of tuples describing classification results.

```
Type ModelEvaluator is
  PE( <Connection:[<rest>]::["kdd:Observation"] expected;
       Connection:[<rest>]::["kdd:Prediction"]  predicted> =>
      <Connection:[Real]::["kdd:Score"]         score> );
```

ModelEvaluator consumes a body of observations (test data) alongside an accompanying body of predictions (classifications), producing a score between 0 and 1 rating the accuracy of classification.

The workflow described by function makeCrossValidator begins by splitting its input using a FoldData PE, created using subfunction makeDataFold.

10.8.2.2 Producing Data Folds for the Cross Validator   A k-fold cross validator must partition its input data into k subsets and construct training and test datasets from those subsets. Figure 10.10 shows a PE function makeDataFold.

```
1    package dispel.datamining {
2      // Import implememed types.
3      use dispel.core.RandomListSplit;
4      use dispel.core.ListMerge;
5
6      // Produces a PE capable of splitting data for k-fold cross validation.
7      PE<DataPartitioner> makeDataFold(Integer k) {
8        Connection   input;
9        Connection[] trainingData = new Connection[k];
10       Connection[] testData     = new Connection[k];
11       // Create instance of PEs for randomly splitting and recombining data.
12       RandomListSplit sample = new RandomListSplit with results.length = k;
13       ListMerge[]     union  = new ListMerge[k];
14
15       // After partitioning data, form training and test sets.
16       input => sample.input;
17       for (Integer i = 0; i < k; i++) {
18         union[i] = new TupleUnionAll with inputs.length = k - 1;
19         for (Integer j = 0; j < i; j++) {
20           sample.outputs[j] => union[i].inputs[j];
21         }
22         sample.outputs[i] => testData[i];
23         for (Integer j = i + 1; j < k; j++) {
24           sample.outputs[j] => union[i].inputs[j - 1];
25         }
26         union[i].output => trainingData[i];
27       }
28
29       // Return data folding pattern.
30       return PE( <Connection data       = input> =>
31                  <Connection[] training = trainingData;
32                   Connection[] test     = testData> );
33     }
34
35     // Register PE pattern generator.
36     register makeDataFold;
37   }
```

Figure 10.10 *Pattern generator* makeDataFold.

This function describes an implementation of DataPartitioner, an abstract PE, which given a suitable dataset should produce an array of training datasets and an array of test datasets:

```
Type DataPartitioner is
  PE( <Connection:[<rest>]::["kdd:Observation"] data> =>
      <Connection[]:[<rest>]::["kdd:Observation"] training;
       Connection[]:[<rest>]::["kdd:Observation"] test> );
```

The function makeDataFold requires just one parameter, count, specifying the number of folds of the input data to create. The function itself uses two existing PE types: RandomListSplit, which randomly splits its input into a number of equal subsets (or as close to equal as can be managed), and `TupleUnionAll`, which combines its inputs (each carrying lists of tuples) into a single tuple list. In the workflow described by the function, an instance of `RandomListSplit` is used to partition all incoming data, and each partition is placed into all but one training set (different for each partition) using an instance of `TupleUnionAll`; each partition is also taken as its own test dataset. All training datasets and test datasets are then sent out of the workflow.

Using `makeDataFold`, the function `makeCrossValidator` can construct a PE that will prepare training and test data for cross validation.

10.8.2.3 *Training and Evaluating Classifiers*   For each "fold" of the cross-validation workflow pattern, one training set is used to train a classifier via an instance of the provided `Trainer` PE. This classifier is then passed on to an instance of the provided `Classifier` PE, which uses it to make predictions on the test dataset corresponding to the training set (i.e., the single partition of the original input data *not* used for training). Finally, the generated predictions are sent along with that same test data to an instance of the provided `Evaluator` PE that assigns a score to the classifier based on the accuracy of its predictions.

The scores for every fold of the workflow pattern are then combined using an instance of `ListMerge`, an existing PE that constructs an (unordered) list from its inputs.

Figure 10.11 demonstrates the *k*-fold cross validation in use. PEs compatible with `TrainClassifier`, `DataClassifier`, and `ModelEvaluator` are provided, which are then used to implement a new PE `CrossValidator`. This PE can then simply be connected to a suitable data source (in this case, an instance of `DataProducer`), and a place to put its results (in this case, simply an instance of `Results`, however, one can imagine a PE that takes input from several cross validators, each testing a different learning algorithm, which then maps the average result for each algorithm in a graph with standard deviations noted).

10.9 SUMMARY

This chapter has presented the DISPEL language in enough detail for the reader to understand the aims and abilities of the language. A deeper understanding is provided by the DISPEL reference manual [1].

DISPEL is a powerful programming language, while at the same time providing a high level of abstraction to ease the development of data-intensive applications. Much of the complexity and detail of a computation is embedded in the PEs themselves, which are created by specialists in their own domains. DISPEL functions and the registry provide further capabilities to abstract development for the user— for example, a function may encapsulate a complex composition of other constructs so that the resulting PE(s) can be directly used without knowledge of their underlying structure. The registry, empowered by the structural and domain type system, provides the ability to validate a DISPEL script in terms of more than simple syntax

```
 1   package book.examples.kdd {
 2     // Import existing PEs.
 3     use book.examples.kdd.DataProducer;
 4     use book.examples.kdd.TrainingAlgorithmA;
 5     use book.examples.kdd.BasicClassifier;
 6     use book.examples.kdd.MeanEvaluator;
 7     // Import abstract type and constructor.
 8     use dispel.datamining.Validator;
 9     use dispel.datamining.makeCrossValidator;
10
11     // Create a cross validator PE.
12     PE<Validator> CrossValidator = makeCrossValidator(12, TrainingAlgorithmA,
13                                       BasicClassifier, MeanEvaluator);
14     // Make instances of PEs for workflows.
15     DataProducer    producer  = new DataProducer;
16     CrossValidator  validator = new CrossValidator;
17     Results         results   = new Results;
18
19     // Connect workflow.
20     |- "uk.org.UoE.data.corpus11" -| => producer.source;
21                       producer.data => validator.data;
22                    validator.results => results.input;
23            |- "Classifier Scores" -| => results.name;
24
25     // Submit workflow.
26     submit results;
27   }
```

Figure 10.11 *An example submission of a workflow using k-fold cross validation.*

and provides a wealth of opportunities for optimization, which are further enabled by the available modifiers.

In Chapter 11, we will discuss the tools that a DISPEL platform might be expected to provide as aids to the development of DISPEL applications. These tools need to span the many possible uses of a data-intensive platform, including construction of DISPEL programs using a traditional syntax aware editor or interactive graphical editors. Likewise, there will be a number of tools required in the development phase to support debugging and tuning of applications. Finally, tools to support the final visualization and analysis of data are required. Chapter 11 presents an example collection of these tools.

In Chapter 12, we present the processing, optimization, and enactment of a DISPEL program.

REFERENCES

1. Language and Architecture Team, ADMIRE project, "DISPEL: Data-Intensive Systems Process Engineering Language users' manual (version 1.0)," tech. rep., School of Informatics, University of Edinburgh, 2011.

2. J. Gosling, B. Joy, G. Steele, G. Bracha, and A. Buckley, "The Java Language specification: Java SE 7th Edition," Tech. Rep. JSR-000901, Oracle, 2012.

11

DISPEL Development

Adrian Mouat

EPCC, University of Edinburgh, Edinburgh, UK

David Snelling

Research Transformation and Innovation,
Fujitsu Laboratories of Europe Limited, Hayes, UK

Application developers in data-intensive computing should find in this chapter an outline of the features that will convince them that they could use this type of development environment productively. On the other side of the partnership, data-intensive engineers should acknowledge the potential for building useful frameworks and be able to identify features that would distinguish their implementation from others, for example, high quality development environments, extensive and well-organized libraries, and full application life-cycle support tools. The organization of this chapter includes three sections covering the application-development environment, the importance and structure of libraries for the platform, and the tools needed for the complete life cycle of data-intensive applications. We highlight the expected capabilities of any development platform and emphasize those extensions that are particular to data-intensive application development platforms.

11.1 THE DEVELOPMENT LANDSCAPE

The provision of high quality development environments is critical to the success of any computational platform. The ability to develop, test, and deploy applications

The DATA Bonanza: Improving Knowledge Discovery in Science, Engineering, and Business, First Edition.
Edited by Malcolm Atkinson, Rob Baxter, Michelle Galea, Mark Parsons, Peter Brezany, Oscar Corcho, Jano van Hemert, and David Snelling.

easily and efficiently for a given platform can make or break the platform as a whole. Current platforms for software development such as .NET [1] and Java [2] have sophisticated integrated development environments (IDEs) and a wealth of libraries and supporting software are available. The new wave of Android and iOS programmers also enjoy similarly advanced environments. These development platforms have created a landscape where software engineers have high expectations and, as a result, are able to be remarkably productive. New development platforms will be judged against this landscape. In what follows, we break the IDE concept down into data-intensive workbenches and data-intensive libraries.

The ADMIRE workbench is the primary development platform for DISPEL workflows used by data analysis experts and data-intensive engineers, and occasionally by domain experts. Data analysis experts include the software developers working on knowledge discovery projects and knowledge discovery experts who are tasked with implementing solutions for domain experts. Data-intensive engineers may use the workbench to investigate and optimize movement and computation of data or analyze the effectiveness of PEs (processing elements), functions, and patterns but will not be creating solutions for end users. It is important that data-intensive engineers are provided with the kind of comprehensive environment they are accustomed to, if data-intensive platforms are to achieve significant uptake.

Domain experts would normally expect to work at a level above the workbench, interacting with a portal or similar interface. However, during the development of DISPEL workflows, the domain-specific knowledge provided by domain experts is an essential ingredient in creating an effective and accurate solution. In particular, the domain expert could be expected to contribute to any domain-specific PEs, types, or functions such as those for processing domain-specific data (e.g., PEs for the conversion of seismology data formats). These domain experts should not be expected to become experts in DISPEL and should be allowed to work with whatever tools and languages are familiar to them as far as possible. For this reason, the workbench needs to support the creation of PEs in many different languages. Domain experts also benefit from graphical tools for studying and creating DISPEL workflows, which reduces the need for them to learn and understand DISPEL syntax.

Data analysis experts are the main users of the workbench. They require a platform that supports rapid development and evaluation of DISPEL workflows. They are expected to be very familiar with DISPEL and are best served by modern development environments that provide code completion, inline documentation, and other advanced features that aid productivity. In particular, it should be trivial for them to find and use the required types and PEs for their workflow. During development of workflows, data analysis experts will constantly need to evaluate their progress, getting early results and changing methods to suit the data. For this reason, the submission and monitoring of workflows and the retrieval and visualization of the results must be as straightforward as possible.

Data-intensive engineers require tools to help them analyze how data is moving about the system and how it can be improved. This requires the system to log information on the performance of PEs and data connections in order to be able to identify bottlenecks. Tools should be available, which allow data-intensive engineers to visualize the flow of data through the system and allow them to try substituting PEs for different versions (e.g., parallel) or encouraging the system to move data or processing to different nodes.

11.2 DATA-INTENSIVE WORKBENCHES

There are several core properties that a data-intensive workbench must provide. There needs to be convenient mechanisms for discovering and using components— the PEs, functions, and types provided. These should be backed up by easily accessible documentation and examples that are integrated into the workbench at several levels, for example, the workbench should propose PEs that can connect to the currently selected output and link to documentation for each of them. Creation of new components and their maintenance needs to be a first-class feature of the workbench. From inside the workbench, it should be possible to create new components and update components as well as find and use them.

As a concrete reference case, we use the ADMIRE workbench. This workbench, while a prototype, possesses many of the required features, albeit in some cases with less sophistication than might be expected at present. Where these real tools fall short of the ideal that we envisage, we will describe both the reality and the vision.

The ADMIRE workbench is based on the Eclipse [3] platform, which provides a professional, feature-rich IDE, to which plug-ins add additional data-intensive specific functionality, including the following:

- DISPEL aware text editor
- graphical DISPEL editor
- registry viewer and searcher
- processes view, which monitors running processes and supports retrieval of results
- visualization of plug-ins for viewing process output as charts, diagrams, or plain text
- semantic knowledge sharing assistant which integrates with the registry to suggest DISPEL documents and other resources related to the users domain
- diagnostic tools including workflow performance analysis.

Domain experts can further customize the environment to their domain, for example, by adding visualization plug-ins for their domain. A screenshot of the workbench can be seen in Figure 11.1.

11.2.1 DISPEL Editor

The DISPEL editor provides a familiar text editor for the creation of DISPEL code with several additions designed to help the developer, such as syntax highlighting

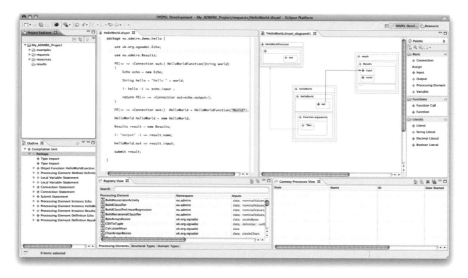

Figure 11.1   *The ADMIRE workbench.*

```
*k-fold1.dispel

    // Produces a k-fold cross validation workflow pattern.
    PE<Validator> makeCrossValidator(Integer k,
                                PE<TrainClassifier> Trainer,
                                PE<ApplyClassifier> Classifier,
                                PE<ModelEvaluator> Evaluator) {
        Connection     input;
        // Data must be partitioned and re-combined for each fold.
        PE<DataPartitioner> FoldData = makeDataFold(k);
        FoldData            folder   = new FoldData;
        ListBuilder         union    = new ListBuilder with inputs.length = k;

        // For each fold, train a classifier then evaluate it.
        input => folder.data;
        for (Integer i = 0; i < k; i++) {
          Trainer     train     = new Trainer;
          Classifier classify   = new Classifer;
          Evaluator   evaluator = new Evaluator;

          folder.training[i] => train.data;
```

Figure 11.2   *Using the DISPEL editor to develop a program.*

and checking. Syntax errors are marked with error symbols as soon as issues are detected.

The registry browser, described in Section 11.2.3, is normally used alongside the editor to provide information on available PEs, types, and other resources. The editor uses this information to provide code completion for PEs and their inputs and outputs.

Figure 11.2 shows the editor being used to develop a DISPEL program. The developer has misspelt the name of "Classifier" PE type causing the editor to mark the line as an error.

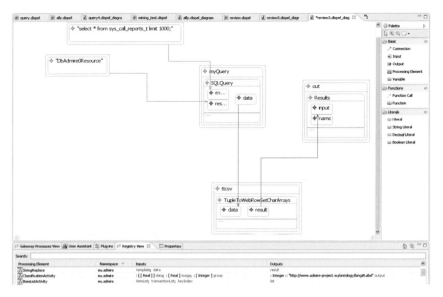

Figure 11.3 *Using the graphical editor to develop a workflow.*

It is important to bear in mind that the development of workflows within the data-intensive workbench takes place on two levels: the "higher" level of creating the actual DISPEL document, undertaken by the data analysis experts, and the "lower" level of implementing any PEs required by the workflow that are not yet available in the library. Creation of new PEs is generally undertaken by a data-intensive engineer. PEs can potentially wrap any sort of existing program from a Java library to a Web service. Development of these PEs may be performed outside the workbench using specialist tools or using features of the underlying platform not specifically aimed at workflow development. For example, a .NET-based PE might be developed in Visual Studio or a Java-based PE in the Java environment using the same Eclipse instance used to develop the DISPEL program.

11.2.2 Graphical Editor

The graphical editor allows DISPEL workflows to be created and edited through a GUI, which operates on the graph structure of the workflow. Changes made in the graphical editor are automatically reflected in the DISPEL editor and vice versa. The registry browser is used to select processing elements and resources to add to the graph. Figure 11.3 shows the graphical editor being used to create a workflow.

Given the power of DISPEL to describe extensive, complex workflows, the reader may wonder at the utility of a graphical editor. This style of workflow creation is very intuitive, as the workflows have a natural graph structure. The graphical editor is particularly appealing to new users who are saved the need to learn DISPEL syntax before they can start putting workflows together. Expert developers will still use the text editor, as it provides a faster and more concise experience. Also, application of advanced features of the DISPEL language in a graphical structure can become unintuitive and difficult.

The need for graphical editors for workflow is supported by the plethora of graphical tools for workflow environments, whether they are targeted at data-streaming models of programming or at more task-oriented models, for example, Taverna [4], Wings [5], Kepler [6], and Java CoG [7], and for a survey, see [8].

11.2.3   Registry Browser

The registry browser provides information on all library elements available in the framework, including processing elements, types, functions, and resources (such as databases). Definitions of these elements are stored in a central *registry* that can be searched by clients. The registry contains both syntactic and semantic information on processing elements, for example, the domain types of processing element connections (providing semantic information) are recorded as well as the names of the connections (syntactic information). The registry also contains links to actual implementations (source and/or binary) of processing elements and functions. More details on the registry can be found in Chapter 4.

To the DISPEL developer, the registry browser is similar to having an always up-to-date version of Javadoc, which can be searched or browsed by several terms, integrated directly within the workbench. Resources, such as publicly accessible databases, also form part of the information and can be located in the same way as computational libraries. Developers can register new functions, types, PEs, and resources directly through DISPEL code as described in Chapter 10. By default, descriptions of entries include the name of the entity, its package, and the types used in arguments and return values or as values in connections. Other common annotations include textual descriptions, version numbers, and keywords describing the domain of the PE. The workbench uses these descriptions to create a variety of useful methods for finding PEs when needed. For example, the workbench can pop-up a code completion style list of PEs that can attach to a given input or output connection, based on Stype and Dtype. Searching for PEs can be based on the name and package of the PE or keywords related to the application under development.

Figure 11.4 shows the registry browser being used to view the available processing elements. A developer can easily see the name and namespace of the processing elements, along with their inputs and outputs, including any available type information.

11.2.4   Process Viewer

The process viewer provides users with details on the progress of workflows submitted to the platform for enactment (Chapter 12) and allows them to retrieve results.

The structure of data-intensive computing, in general, and DISPEL in particular, creates a somewhat different user experience because of the way in which code

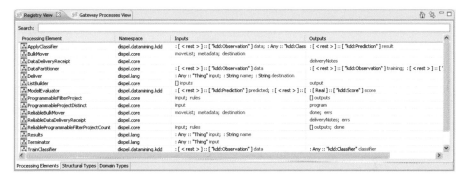

Figure 11.4 *Using the registry browser to view available processing elements.*

is processed. For example, when a DISPEL program is submitted to a gateway, it is compiled to a workflow graph and checked for structural and domain type compatibility; connections between PEs and functions are tested to see if they have compatible types, as described in Chapter 10. If an inconsistency is found, the gateway may attempt to insert a converter and/or an equivalent PE, which can convert or handle the input connection. For example, if a sensor is providing temperature in degrees Celsius, but a PE expects input in Kelvin, the gateway may be able to automatically insert a PE that converts between the two types. If no conversion PE is available for a nonmatching connection, compilation will fail and an error message will be returned to the user and presented in the process viewer.

Once deployed, a workflow may run for an extended period, days even, depending on the use case. The process viewer provides a mechanism for the user to track the progress of a number of running workflows, similar to the batch queue monitors of large-scale scientific systems.

Figure 11.5 shows the process viewer displaying the details of several workflows, both completed and in progress. The results of completed workflows can be viewed using the process viewer to launch one of the assistants described in the next section. The process viewer is also used to retrieve any error messages from failed workflows.

State	Name	ID	Date Started	Execution Time
COMPLETED	query.dispel	process-45cee26d-2211-40a4-adbe-041d4...	Thu May 26 17:02:01 BST 2011	0h 0m 2s
PROCESSING (Results Available)	astro.dispel	process-b6aaf70b-bd35-4dd4-ab1b-95f46...	Thu May 26 17:08:16 BST 2011	0h 4m 20s
results				
PROCESSING (Results Available)	astro.dispel	process-996ca49c-297d-4c5a-8f74-8544d...	Thu May 26 17:10:24 BST 2011	0h 2m 11s

Figure 11.5 *Process viewer showing status of workflows.*

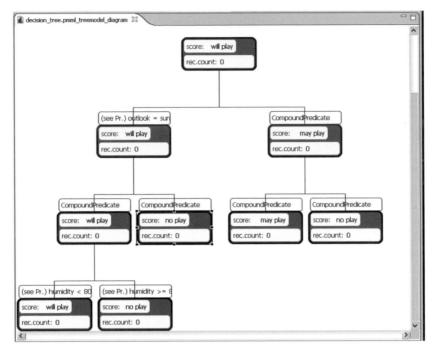

Figure 11.6   *Decision tree output, visualized from a specialized visualization assistant.*

11.2.5   Visualization Assistants

The results of workflows submitted for enactment can be viewed through various visualization assistants launched from the process viewer. These range from a simple text viewer to more complicated graph viewers and specialist viewers for particular types of data.

During development of workflows, developers will regularly submit partially completed workflows in order to verify that each stage is producing the expected results. Developers are likely to use several different visualizers during development of workflows to view output in various formats, which may or may not be used when running the finalized workflow. The workbench can suggest appropriate visualizers based on the type of the output connection, so for instance, a tree model visualization can be automatically displayed when a classifier produces a decision tree as its output, as shown in Figure 11.6.

Several plug-ins are also capable of displaying streaming results that are updated as more data are received. This is very useful for getting an immediate idea of the characteristics of the data without waiting for a workflow to complete or to see how the data change as the workflow progresses. The chart visualizer is perhaps the best example of this; it is able display several types of diagrams, including pie charts and bar graphs, which are updated dynamically.

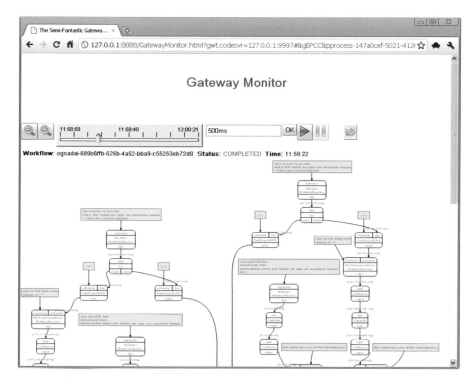

Figure 11.7 *Workflow monitor displaying the status of running workflow.*

Adding new visualizers to the workbench is straightforward, requiring developers to implement a very small Java interface. This means that developers can quickly add new visualizers tailored to their data models.

11.2.6 Diagnostic Tools

Testing is hard in any distributed computing environment, where executing applications require the use of several distributed machines. To mitigate this, applications are often developed piecemeal or broken into several parts that are each tested until the developer is confident that they work. Testing normally involves the use of small test datasets and dry runs, gradually increasing the dataset size until the developer is confident that the application can handle the full dataset. Running on the complete dataset will often require significant processing and storage resources and is likely to take hours or even days to complete.

Similarly, debugging of distributed workflows is difficult by its very nature. It is dependent on being able to pin down the location and timing of errors and propagate error messages back to the developer.

In order to ease this burden on the developer, high quality monitoring and debugging tools are required, such as the workflow monitor shown in Figure 11.7, which provides playback of running and completed workflows, showing the flow of data and any blocking that occurs. This can be used to identify the source of problems and bottlenecks. The workflow monitoring tool uses operational data collected for performance optimization (Section 12.3.1), which will facilitate the development of more sophisticated debugging and optimization tools.

11.2.7 Workbench Integration

The ADMIRE workbench, which provided the example tools described in this chapter, is made up of a group of cooperating Eclipse plug-ins. These plug-ins are designed to share information with other plug-ins and build on the functionality of each other. New plug-ins can easily be added to extend the functionality of the workbench. In particular, specialized domain areas are likely to have their own data types, which may require the creation of new visualization plug-ins to be viewed. Using the Eclipse update site functionality, developers can make any plug-ins they create easily available to other users to install. In general, a data-intensive workbench will be tied to other components of the platform. However, the role that the workbench plays in the architecture is also abstract and, therefore, DISPEL developers can expect workbenches to emerge, which are generic in nature or possibly specialized to a particular domain.

Within the data-intensive architecture, the workbench relies on a number of components that would appear in any implementation of the architecture.

- The registry holds all the information on the component library, without which it becomes impossible to build workflows unless the developer is aware of all the PEs they require and their exact syntax, and even then things will be much more difficult and slower.
- A gateway is needed to which DISPEL workflows can be submitted for execution. The workbench closely integrates with the gateway in order to display information on any submitted workflows and retrieve results or error messages.
- The repository is used as a central data store, holding the implementations of PEs as well as shared DISPEL code and other data.

The repository and the registry are the foundation for collaboration between developers. The registry provides a means for developers to find new components as well add their own, which can be obtained from the repository. The registry supports tagging of items with metadata, meaning that developers can quickly find components related to their domain area or simply find PEs and functions that produce output of the required type. The metadata need not be limited to the domain of the component but can also include details such as the license terms under which the component is released or what programming language was used to implement it.

In the future, one can imagine a scenario similar to Apple® App Store™ ecosystem, where developers can find components and data sources for nearly every need that is imaginable. Owners of valuable data could make their data accessible only on a subscription or metered basis. Similarly, creators of new PEs may have a simple version available for free but charge for the sophisticated version that can take advantage of multicore architectures to process data at a much higher rate.

11.3 DATA-INTENSIVE COMPONENT LIBRARIES

The component library itself lies at the heart of the platform. By having accessible, but powerful, methods for not just finding and using components, but also creating, organizing, extending, and refining them, the community can benefit from having a large, high quality library with components specialized to various domain areas. This effect can be magnified even further by facilitating collaborative behavior between developers, for example, supporting methods for sharing DISPEL and identifying common patterns and pitfalls.

The data-intensive computing library is made up of functions, PEs, and type definitions, grouped into packages covering various domains. These are the building blocks of any DISPEL-generated workflow. By joining together these blocks, it is possible to quickly build workflows involving complex data analysis that are capable of dealing with enormous amounts of data. Having a large library containing PEs for common data processing tasks, functions for implementing patterns, types for common data domains, and assessors for common datasets greatly reduces the amount of work required by developers. Only with the provision of a large and robust library, will the workbench become a useful, time-saving tool for developers.

Data-intensive computing is applicable to a wide range of domains, undoubtedly including many unforeseen, each of which requires its own specialist PEs, functions, and data sources on top of more generic functionality. For example, if someone wants to analyze data from a physics simulation, they would require the data sources providing access to the data, PEs containing algorithms required to analyze the data, and PEs for converting the data into the output format required, for example, an SVG chart.

Some of these entities are very specific to the given problem and could not be anticipated in advance, for example, the data sources. For example, a database with information on the zebrafish genome may be an open resource that is of interest to a large group of researchers. For this reason, it makes sense to add an entity to the library that provides access to it and which can be reused by others. Once a data-intensive developer has written the code for accessing this resource, they save it to a repository and add its location to the registry. By adding appropriate metadata tags to the registry entry, others can easily discover and use the data source.

A lot of functionality useful to data-intensive developers exists already in libraries, such as streaming data-mining algorithms and statistics operations. It should be possible to easily wrap such functions in PEs (where licenses, copyright, etc. allow). By wrapping the Java MOA [9] libraries, the platform quickly gains powerful streaming data-mining algorithms such as Hoeffding Trees [10].

The structure of these data-intensive libraries will evolve over time; however, there are a number of library categories or packages identified throughout this book. Appendix C presents this package structure and lists the contents of each package in the DISPEL that would be used to load the package into the registry.

11.4 SUMMARY

The workbench, in whatever form it takes, is a developer's entry point into the data-intensive world. We have described the characteristics of and abstract workbench exemplified by the ADMIRE workbench. However, it is from the diversity of data-intensive researchers, which the workbenches of the future will derive their requirements. The communities of developers and users will provide a market for workbench development in the form of either community open-source projects or commercial workbenches designed for specific communities.

However, the real value of a workbench will come from the access it provides to a rich component library. High quality libraries will be packaged with platforms for addressing generic capabilities tuned for that platform and community developed libraries, usually focused on a specific domain, will also emerge and evolve.

This chapter has taken the DISPEL language from Chapter 10 and shown the tools, in the form of a workbench, needed to create a DISPEL document, submit it for processing, interact with a running workflow, and analyze the results produced. In the final chapter of Part III, we describe the invisible part of the data-intensive architecture, the platform on which data-intensive computation takes place.

REFERENCES

1. Microsoft Corporation, "NET Framework," Programa de Computador, January 2002.
2. J. Gosling, B. Joy, G. Steele, and G. Bracha, *Java Language Specification, Second Edition: The Java Series* (Second Edition). Boston, MA: Addison-Wesley Longman Publishing Co., Inc., 2000.
3. R. C. Gronback, *Eclipse Modeling Project: A Domain-Specific Language (DSL) Toolkit.* Upper Saddle River, NJ: Addison-Wesley, 2009.
4. D. Turi, P. Missier, C. A. Goble, D. De Roure, and T. Oinn, "Taverna workflows: syntax and semantics," in *International Conference on e-Science and Grid Computing,* pp. 441–448, IEEE Computer Society, 2007.
5. Y. Gil, V. Ratnakar, E. Deelman, G. Mehta, and J. Kim, "Wings for pegasus: creating large-scale scientific applications using semantic representations of computational workflows," in *Proceedings of the 19th National Conference on Innovative Applications of Artificial Intelligence,* vol. 2, pp. 1767–1774, AAAI Press, 2007.
6. I. Altintas, C. Berkley, E. Jaeger, M. Jones, B. Ludascher, and S. Mock, "Kepler: an extensible system for design and execution of scientific workflows," in Proceedings of 16th International Conference on Scientific and Statistical Database Management, pp. 423–424, June 2004.

7. G. von Laszewski and M. Hategan, "Workflow concepts of the Java CoG Kit," *Journal of Grid Computing*, vol. 3, pp. 239–258, 2005.

8. V. Curcin and M. Ghanem, "Scientific workflow systems - can one size fit all?" in *Cairo International Biomedical Engineering Conference*, pp. 1–9, December 2008.

9. A. Bifet, G. Holmes, R. Kirkby, and B. Pfahringer, "MOA: massive online analysis," *Journal of Machine Learning Research*, vol. 11, pp. 1601–1604, 2010.

10. P. Domingos and G. Hulten, "Mining high-speed data streams," in *The Sixth ACM SIGKDD International Conference on Knowledge Discovery and Data Mining*, KDD '00, pp. 71–80, ACM, 2000.

12

DISPEL Enactment

Chee Sun Liew

School of Informatics, University of Edinburgh, Edinburgh, UK; Faculty of Computer Science and Information Technology, University of Malaya, Kuala Lumpur, Malaysia

Amrey Krause

EPCC, University of Edinburgh, Edinburgh, UK

David Snelling

Research Transformation and Innovation, Fujitsu Laboratories of Europe Limited, Hayes, UK

In the previous chapters, we have introduced the DISPEL (data-intensive systems process engineering language) language and presented an environment for developing DISPEL scripts and components. This chapter describes the processing of DISPEL requests. We call the overall process DISPEL *enactment*. We first present an overview of the four stages of the DISPEL enactment process and further describe each stage in the subsequent sections. This chapter is targeted at the data-intensive engineers who work on the implementation of the data-intensive platforms.

12.1 OVERVIEW OF DISPEL ENACTMENT

Recall from Chapter 9 that there are four stages in the enactment process of data-intensive computations. Any implementation of a data-intensive platform will probably implement these in some form of the following:

The DATA Bonanza: Improving Knowledge Discovery in Science, Engineering, and Business, First Edition.
Edited by Malcolm Atkinson, Rob Baxter, Michelle Galea, Mark Parsons, Peter Brezany, Oscar Corcho, Jano van Hemert, and David Snelling.

1. DISPEL *Language Processing* includes parsing and validating a DISPEL scripts and creating its corresponding dataflow graph—usually annotated with the information deduced during this phase.

2. *Optimization* includes selection of PEs (processing elements), transformation of the dataflow graph, substitution of PEs, identification of available resources, and the mapping of PEs to resources.

3. *Deployment* includes compiling the graphical representation into platform-specific executable graphs and setting up resource and dataflow connections.

4. *Execution and Control* includes instrumentation and performance measurement, failure management, results delivery, termination, and clean up.

These phases are shown in Figure 12.1. In this chapter, we outline these processes in detail. Section 12.2 deals with DISPEL language processing. Section 12.3 outlines the optimization process, Section 12.4 addresses deployment, and Section 12.5 outlines the execution and control phase.

This enactment framework provides a high level abstraction of data-intensive applications. This is achieved through a *separation of concerns*, where the software details are abstracted at various levels, for example, the application level, algorithmic level, and execution level. This framework uses a data-streaming execution model, abstracted using the DISPEL language for the higher-level expression of dataflow graphs. Using this abstraction, the framework validates and optimizes the execution of data-intensive applications. Every component in the framework uses this language to communicate data-related processes and their interrelationships. For instance, the enactment gateway, which is the interface for submitting data-intensive jobs, communicates with the registry to retrieve reusable components that the registry supplies in the form of valid DISPEL scripts and implementations of PEs.

Recall that DISPEL is an abbreviation for the *Data-Intensive Systems Process Engineering Language*. It is a scripting language that is processed by a DISPEL parser to generate dataflow graphs in the form of executable workflows. The primary function of DISPEL is to express how a data-intensive application uses PEs (for instance, that provide noise filtering algorithms) and how these elements communicate with each other. In other words, DISPEL is a language for expressing a directed graph, where PEs represent the computational nodes and the flow of data between PEs is represented by connections. Thus, DISPEL provides an abstraction technique for a data-streaming execution model. At the lower level, DISPEL also handles validation and provides the required model for carrying out workflow optimizations.

In this chapter, we use a real-world workflow from a life sciences use case, EURExpress, which is described in Part IV, Chapter 16 to describe the DISPEL enactment stages. This workflow retrieves data samples from a database splitting them into two sets: one set for training a classifier and the other for evaluating the trained classifier—following the k-fold cross-validation pattern described in Section 10.8.2. In the implementation, we have split this workflow into three DISPEL requests: data preparation, feature selection, and k-fold cross validation.

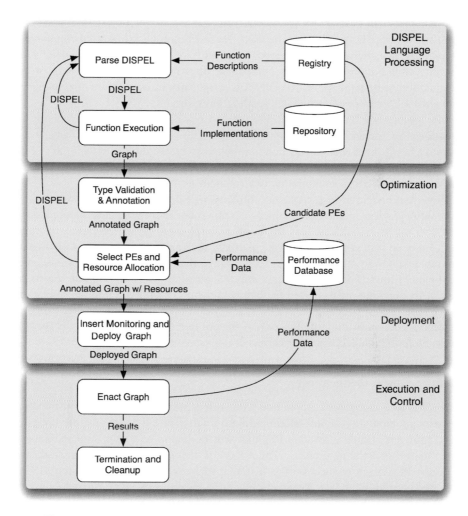

Figure 12.1   *Diagram showing the steps involved in processing DISPEL scripts.*

12.2   DISPEL LANGUAGE PROCESSING

12.2.1   Compilation

When a request is received by the gateway (Section 12.4.1), the DISPEL script is parsed and its syntax is validated, followed by type checks at the language level, for example, ensuring that values are assigned correctly to variables, and function parameters and return types are assigned and used properly.

Compilation is an iterative process as reusable components, such as functions, types, and composite PEs (e.g., those containing PEs), referenced in the DISPEL request must be retrieved from the registry. These imported entities are represented by their metadata descriptors (available from the registry) and DISPEL code and must be compiled before they can be used. Therefore, for each imported component, a compilation subprocess is triggered, the results of which are imported into the ongoing compilation process. If a component does not exist in the registry or the compilation of its implementation DISPEL script fails, a compilation error is raised and DISPEL processing terminates sending back results.

An important example of this iterative process results from the invocation of functions to create components of a workflow. For example, when the makeSieveOfEratosthenes function is invoked to create the PrimeGenerator, see Section 10.7, an array of PrimeFilter PEs is also created and must also be processed by the DISPEL compilation environment.

Note that primitive PEs, those not implemented directly in DISPEL, must have executable implementations available for deployment later in the enactment process. The data-intensive platform may import these implementations in a variety of ways. Some may be core components of the platform such as the Results PE. Others may be implemented in other languages such as Java that can be dynamically loaded at deployment time. These components may be precompiled, compiled on the fly as part of this process, or passed to the platform as a script for runtime interpretation, in the case of Perl for example. In the registry entry for a component, one property is often a URL indicating the location of the component in a repository. This helps to promote the availability and sharing of components.

12.2.2   Graph Generation

The result of a successful compilation process is a fully expanded graph of the data-intensive computation represented by the original DISPEL script. All the nodes of this graph are primitive abstract PEs that will be bound to actual implementations later in the enactment process. The edges of the graph represent the dataflow between PEs. Each connection has a source PE producing data and a list of sink PEs that consume the data. Because a given PE may appear many times in a graph, each node is given a unique identifier that will be used later to identify the actual deployed PE instance in the executed data-intensive computation. This identifier will be used for monitoring and diagnostics.

As the graph is validated, checks are made to ensure that implementations of the components exist that can perform actions as requested and that the descriptions of those components are compatible with the specifications in the request. If a nonexistent component is referenced in the request, for example, when attempting to connect to a PE that has no outputs, an error is raised and the DISPEL processing terminates.

PEs and connections in a DISPEL graph may carry additional information as annotations. An annotation is a property value that can be identified by a key. Annotations are used to convey type information and semantics, as outlined in the language definition, to the later stages of DISPEL processing.

Connections and PE inputs and outputs have structural (Stype) and domain (Dtype) types. The PE descriptor defines the types that an input can consume and the types that an output produces. These types can be further restricted for individual requests by annotations attached to connections in the DISPEL script. When these types are propagated across the graph at a later point (Section 12.3), this information allows type verification for compatibility by testing structural subtyping for Stype and by querying the type hierarchy in the registry and possibly resolving type clashes by inserting type converters, as described in Chapter 10.

The resulting graph carries all of the structural and domain type information and semantics that are provided by registered metadata as well as request-specific semantics. PE descriptors carry modifiers on their data connections that specify termination behavior, data consumption rate, type transient behavior, and others, as outlined in the language definition (Chapter 10). For example, modifiers may indicate the rate at which data are consumed or emitted by a PE, or the order in which data are read from the set of input streams. Other semantics, such as type assertions and non-default termination behavior of a PE, may also be defined using modifiers and communicated to the later phases of enactment via these descriptors.

During the compilation, data inputs marked as a locator are identified and their values are added to the annotations if they are included as literals in the request. These locator values are important parameters used by the optimization stage that prepares the DISPEL graph for deployment.

At the end of the compilation process, reusable components are registered with the registry directed by the register command. Submitted dataflow graphs are passed to the next stage, optimization (Section 12.3).

12.2.3 Registration

DISPEL entities must be registered before they can be reused. Using the register command (as described in Section 10.1), a component can be published in the registry.

When registering an entity, the DISPEL processor creates a metadata descriptor and places it in the registry. The DISPEL script representing the implementation of the component is stored for use when deploying a workflow.

The registration of a new reusable component may fail, for example, if another component with the same name already exists in the registry. The DISPEL processor attempts to register as many entities as possible and provides warnings for failed attempts.

12.3 DISPEL OPTIMIZATION

The output of the DISPEL *language processing* stage is a fully expanded and annotated DISPEL graph. The next step is to organize the distributed computations on the execution engines—computing resources used to deploy and execute the DISPEL graph. In general, a typical scientific workflow comprises complex computation steps on heterogeneous data and is enacted on distributed computing platforms. The performance of enacting such a workflow relies on various

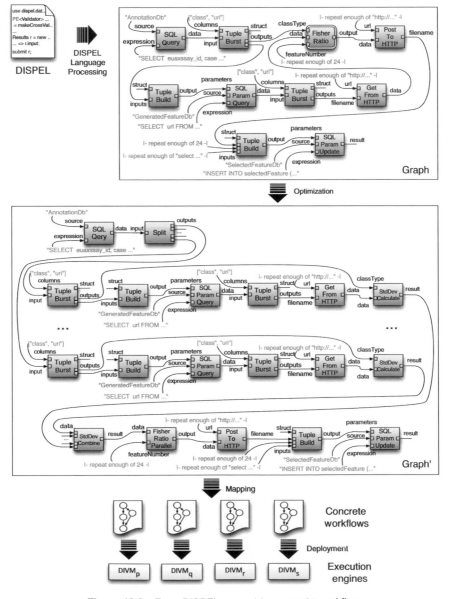

Figure 12.2 *From DISPEL request to concrete workflow.*

factors, for example, the selection of scattered data sources in the workflow may trigger a high communication cost of moving data between execution engines. Workflows need to be mapped onto the appropriate execution engines, in terms of workloads, computing paradigms, and resource availability, in order to achieve maximum efficiency.

Thus, it is a challenge to find a way of organizing the distributed computation that will deliver the same results within the application-dependent criteria at the least cost. Various cost functions may apply, for example, time to initial output, time to completed output on all delivery streams, or amount of energy used. This challenge is known as *multigoal optimization* (Section 12.3.3), where a set of *goals* is defined and is achieved through a series of *optimization approaches* within some predetermined *constraints*.

Let us say that we want to reduce the overall *makespan*—time difference between the start and end of the enactment—of enacting the graph shown in Figure 12.2. We can identify the most appropriate PE implementations for the enactment based on the enactment requests, data, and available execution engines. By identifying these factors and designing a structured system to capture relevant performance data, useful information can be extracted to further improve the enactment. Section 12.3.1 describes the rationale and implementation of the performance database (PDB) to capture such data.

Assume that the performance data collected from previous enactments show that it takes longer to process the training subgraph than it does to process the testing subgraph. Given enough computational resources, we can take another optimization approach: to split the training subgraph into parallel streams and enact them on multiple execution engines. Section 12.3.2 describes this parallelization as well as other graph transformations. The optimization process produces concrete work-flows that are ready for deployment on the execution engines, as discussed in Section 12.4.

To perform all of the processes above, the optimizer must first obtain information about:

1. the descriptions of components provided by the domain and data analysis experts (who designed and implemented them);
2. the performance of the component instances gleaned from observing previous enactments, for example, processing time per unit of data (unit cost), memory footprint, and so forth;
3. the descriptions of the data-intensive platforms, both hardware properties (e.g., number of computing nodes, bandwidth between their connections, etc.) and software properties (e.g., database engines, execution engines, etc.).

This requires a good understanding of where and how to collect such data, and how to transform these data into useful information for the later stages of optimization and deployment.

12.3.1 Performance Database

The PDB, a component of the optimization phase of compilation, is designed to gather information at the level of PE classes so that we can determine how each class and data stream behaves. For instance, information collected from a previous enactment can indicate whether co-locating certain PEs within the same execution

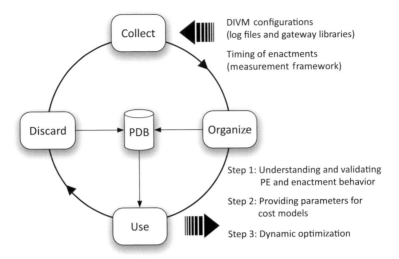

Figure 12.3 *Performance data life cycle.*

engine will result in poor performance because these PEs are competing for the same resources. The use of performance data collected from previous enactments is worthwhile for two reasons. Firstly, domain experts tend to repeat similar enactment requests to iterate their understanding or to process multiple similar data samples. Secondly, there are many fundamental PEs that are used across domains and consequently appear in many enactment requests, for example, SQLQuery and Split used in the **DISPEL** graph shown in Figure 12.2 are commonly found in any workflow that requires access to a database and to split the data stream into training and testing datasets during the data integration process.

We introduce a four-stage life cycle for performance data: *collect, organize, use,* and *discard,* as shown in Figure 12.3 to describe how the performance data are collected, transformed into information, used for optimization, and then discarded.

12.3.1.1 *Data Sources and Collecting Mechanism*   We define a data-intensive virtual machine (DIVM) as an abstraction for the computational environment (i.e., the layers of software and hardware) in which a processing element instance (PEI) runs during enactment. Understanding a *DIVM's configuration* is important because it allows us to discover whether two PEIs are sharing a common platform element and whether that in turn influences their enactment performance. This information is extracted from *system log files*.

As a typical operational environment is complex, deriving relevant information, for example, whether two PEIs are competing for the same CPU, is difficult. The DIVM abstraction is used to reduce the complexity by suppressing detail, so that queries against the PDB can discriminate such conflict criteria. This abstraction also has to reflect locality so that relative costs of inter-PEI communication can be estimated using the PDB.

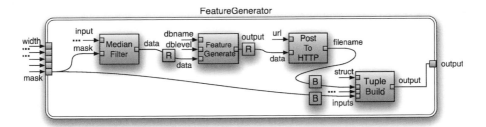

Figure 12.4 *Demonstration of* observer *PE in a fragment of a DISPEL process graph.*

The overall performance of an enactment is affected by the behavior of the PEIs, including how they are connected and on which DIVM they are deployed. In general, the tasks performed by PEIs include computation, communication, and I/O operations. These are performed at different rates depending on the assignment of PEIs to DIVM instances—remember the distributed data-intensive platform is normally made up of heterogeneous components.

The *Measurement framework* captures these enactment-performance data using a specific type of PE, named an *observer*. An observer receives data from input streams from a previous PE, applies a time stamp, and outputs the data to the following PE without altering the data. By placing observers on the data streams, detailed enactment information can be captured and used for making appropriate optimization decisions. In theory, we can have three types of observers, each with minimum impact on performance and a capability to capture performance data from a different perspective:

- *Type observer* is used to capture type information of the dataflow on any given data stream. Together with the semantic information of the workflows, the type information may be useful in estimating the data transfer cost and determining the ability to split a data stream and process in parallel. The type information should be collected before execution.

- *Rate observer* measures the data processing rate of data streams. When used in pairs, rate observers can capture the processing time per unit of data of a PEI. As shown in Figure 12.4, a rate observer is placed before FeatureGeneration to capture its input data rate during the enactment. Together with the output data rate measured by another rate observer, we can infer the processing rate of FeatureGeneration.

- *Buffer observer* is used to observe the buffer implementation of data streams. Buffers are used when there are variations in the data processing rate of any connected PEs. In Figure 12.4, buffer observers on the two input streams of TupleBuild determine the rates at which data arrive on each stream and from which we can infer the critical path of the workflow.

For the implementation of a data-intensive platform, the type observer is applied during the DISPEL language processing stage. When the DISPEL language processor walks the generated graph verifying that source assertions and destination requirements about the structure types of values in the data stream are compatible, the input and output structural type of every PEI in the request will be recorded. Both rate observer and buffer observer are implemented during the execution stage, observing the pipe buffer events generated by the data stream. During the enactment, the data producer of a data stream writes the data into the buffer while the consumer reads data from it. Both operations will trigger different events. Another two interesting events to record are blocking from read and write, for example if a fixed-size buffer is empty or full respectively.

The results collected from observers are sent to a *gatherer* that will insert these data into the PDB after the enactment is finished. To further reduce the overhead incurred during enactment, each gateway should have gatherers that run on separate execution engines to process the collected data on the fly and insert the derived and hence much-compressed performance data into the PDB. However, the platform should provide an option to keep all of the recorded events when data-intensive engineers are trying to trace the events that occurred for diagnostic purpose.

12.3.1.2 *Organizing Performance Data and Transforming into Information*   The tables in the PDB are divided into three categories according to how their data are collected (Fig. 12.5). The first type of table stores data harvested from log files, for example, `DIVMInstance` and `DIVMInstallation`. The second type of table stores data collected from the measurement framework, for example, `DataStream`. These two types of data are considered raw data. The final type of table stores derived data, for example, `PerfOfInstance`, which are preprocessed by gatherer on all of the events recorded. These data are used in the calculation of the unit cost for any given PE on the DIVM where enactment occurred.

The performance data gathered in the PDB are used in stages, as shown in Figures 12.1 and 12.3. For each stage, we formulate different sets of queries to access the PDB. The PDB data allow us to understand and validate hypotheses

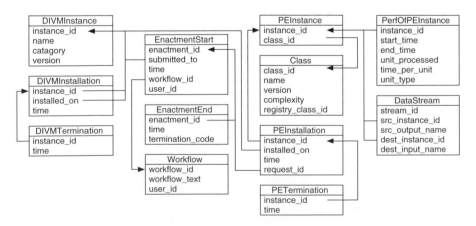

Figure 12.5   *Logical content of the PDB.*

about PEs and their enactment behavior, such as the type of dataflow in the data stream[1] and the processing rate of PEs on different execution engines, through queries such as the following:

```
SELECT AVG(PerfOfPEInstance.time_per_unit), MIN(PerfOfPEInstance.time_per_unit),
       MAX(PerfOfPEInstance.time_per_unit), COUNT(DIVMInstance.instance_id),
       DIVMInstance.instance_id
FROM PerfOfPEInstance, PEInstance, DIVMInstance, PEInstallation
WHERE PerfOfPEInstance.instance_id = PEInstance.instance_id
  AND PEInstallation.instance_id = PEInstance.instance_id
  AND PEInstallation.install_on = DIVMInstance.instance_id
  AND PEInstance.class_id = 'PEa'
  AND (DIVMInstance.instance_id = 'DIVM1' OR DIVMInstance.instance_id = 'DIVM2')
GROUP BY DIVMInstance.instance_id
```

The query will retrieve all of the previous execution records of a PEI on all of the DIVMs, filtered by $DIVM_1$ and $DIVM_2$, to find the more suitable DIVM on which to enact a PEI. This enables the optimizer to deploy PEs on the execution engines best able to support them in a heterogeneous environment. More queries and demonstration of the PDB use can be found in [1].

The size of the PDB is expected to grow rapidly. To sustain the performance of the PDB, a cleaning process is needed to remove outdated or less important data. The PDB is cleaned in two ways: (i) by removing data associated with deprecated versions of a PE and (ii) by removing data that are obsolete (e.g., pertaining to a discontinued DIVM or after a predefined number of days).

12.3.2 Graph Transformation

The graph generated in the DISPEL *language processing* stage will go through a series of transformations as a result of optimization. This process is conducted repeatedly until a final graph is produced, which is ready for the *deployment* stage (Fig. 12.2). In this section, we further examine four types of common transformations: *subgraph substitution*, *type conversion*, *parallelization*, and *reordering*.

During the optimization stage, the optimizer tries to identify candidate implementations for every abstract PE (nodes in the DISPEL graph). An abstract PE can be mapped to a single physically located PE instance, or, if it is a composite PE, to a group of implemented PEs. In the latter case, the PE node will be *substituted by a subgraph* of PE nodes. This process continues until all concrete PEs are processed. The FisherRatio PE used in the DISPEL example, shown in Figure 12.2, has two implementations: sequential and parallel. The parallel implementation is defined using a composition of three implementable PEs: (i) StandardDeviationCalculation, (ii) StandardDeviationCombine, and (iii)

---

[1]This may not be known a priori because the DISPEL scripts deliberately use Any and rest to suppress details, accommodate change, and support domain-specific formats. Once enactment is being considered, the optimizer needs to "look under the hood."

FisherRatioParallel. In this case, the FisherRatio PE is expanded into a sub-graph that comprises three implemented PEs.

DISPEL introduces a sophisticated type system to validate the connections between the PEs (Chapter 10). Together with the semantic description of the PEs stored in the registry, this architecture provides a powerful capability for *type conversion* in the DISPEL request, which inserts a *converter PE* into the graph to convert the data type [2]. For example, the metric for temperature stored in the data source is expressed in *Kelvin*, whereas the metric used in the data mining PEs is expressed in *Celsius*. In such a situation the optimizer finds a *converter PE* to be placed into the data stream to perform a Kelvin-to-Celsius conversion, which alters the DISPEL graph.

The optimizer improves the enactment performance by exploring *parallelization* opportunities. To speed up a slow-processing-rate subgraph, the optimizer looks for parallel-executable PEs and splits the data streams. This parallelization is categorized as data parallelism, where a data stream is split into multiple streams for parallel execution. As illustrated in Figure 12.2, a Split PE is added after the SQLQuery PE to split the data for parallel execution.

Reordering is about transposing the PEs' order based on a quality of service metric. It follows the approach in database optimization, where the reordering is guided by a set of rules based on relational algebra. For instance, placing a filtering operator before a projection operator may reduce the computation cost of performing these operators in reverse since the filtering operator reduces the amount of data to be processed by the projection operator. In order to support reordering PEs, the optimizer needs to obtain semantic information from the registry that shows whether these PEs are transposable.

12.3.3 Multiple Goal Optimization

The optimization challenge is to find a way of organizing the distributed computation that will deliver the same results within the application-dependent criteria at the least cost. In optimization, we define the *goal* and the *constraints*, then we choose the appropriate *strategies*. The goal is the main focus of the optimization at which improvement is aimed. The goal is achieved through a set of approaches. However, there are certain restrictions that limit the approaches, which are referred to as *constraints*. There are two common optimization goals: *time-based criteria* and *resource efficiency*. The time-based optimization is focused on the application perspective, especially on minimizing the response time or execution time. In contrast, the resource efficiency type of optimization looks at the resource perspective (computation, storage, network traffic, or energy). For instance, optimizing the system throughput seeks to get the most out of the data-intensive platform, reducing disk storage to accommodate more applications, or minimizing energy consumption.

To achieve these goals, the optimizer needs to understand appropriate and available optimization strategies, such as

- ameliorating performance bottlenecks by executing in parallel;
- distributing enactment to balance workload (load balancing among execution engines);
- minimizing data movement by co-locating large dataflows within the same region of a platform;
- clustering small tasks to reduce deployment and data movement costs;
- performing logical transformation (e.g., reordering PEs);
- dynamically selecting services (or PEs) based on availability and performance.

Some strategies may not be applicable to all computing models. For instance, if the goal is to increase resource efficiency and the limitation of storage space is a constraint, the common approaches taken in other workflow systems is to either remove data files at runtime (when they are no longer needed) [3] or to restructure the workflow (reduce the "width" and increase the "depth" of the workflow). However, these strategies are less applicable in the data-streaming model because all of the PE instances are very likely to be loaded before the enactment starts and overlap during the execution. The model already eliminates many intermediate files.

All of the approaches described earlier are performed before execution (during the mapping stage). The optimizer makes all of the decisions before the graph(s) are deployed. From the deployment stage onward, the optimizer does not interfere in the execution. The design of the data-intensive architecture is intended to enable the enactment of DISPEL on different data-intensive platforms and not every platform allows the alteration of PE instances during the execution. However, given the ability to control the state of PE instances and the data stream on the execution engines, dynamic optimization that looks at load balancing during runtime is achievable, but it will be platform dependent.

The optimizer needs to understand the list of constraints that it has to satisfy, such as accessibility restrictions. In principle, the PE implementation codes are stored in the repository and are loaded to the execution engines during the deployment stage. However, there are PEs that are mapped to proprietary implementations, which are only accessible at a specific gateway. Similarly, some confidential data sources are only available via specific gateways. Another reason that restricts the choice of mapping candidates is the processing capability. Some PE implementations are platform dependent and require a dedicated execution engine for their deployment.

12.3.3.1 Three-Stage Optimization Algorithm for Data-Streaming Model
Finding the scheduling candidates of PEIs on DIVMs involves exhaustive computation, especially for large workflows that comprise many PEIs. Some of the PEIs have a relatively small time to process a unit of data (i.e., unit cost), and the assignment of these PEIs onto any of the DIVMs may not impose a significant workload. Most of the PEIs have a relatively small unit cost and a few have much larger unit costs. Optimization, therefore, focuses on assigning these

expensive PEIs to DIVMs. They first have to be identified by defining a *performance threshold* that divides the PEIs into two categories based on their unit cost. The performance threshold needs to be determined from experiments and may be domain specific. We apply job-shop scheduling on these *heavy* PEIs with larger unit cost and use a *bead-sliding algorithm* (Section 12.4.1) to assign the remaining *light* PEIs. We also consider the locality of the PEIs besides the unit cost criterion. Some PEIs have to be enacted on selected site because of the accessibility or processing capability constraints.

This type of PEI is marked as an *anchor* and handled separately during the assignment process.

We summarize the assignment algorithm in the following steps:

1. Identify the *anchors* and assign them accordingly to the DIVMs
2. Apply job-shop scheduling to assign *heavy* PEIs
3. Apply bead-sliding technique to assign *light* PEIs.

12.3.3.2   *Partitioning the PEIs into Three Subsets*   The optimizer scans the set of PEIs and identifies the following two critical subsets to be allocated to DIVMs first:

1. The *Anchored PEI*. These are PEIs that have the `location` modifier (Section 10.2.5) and have been annotated with a stream literal expression defining data to which they are anchored.
2. The *Heavy PEI*. These are the PEIs not in the above set, which have been identified as having high unit processing costs, that is, that are above a defined *threshold*.

All of the remaining PEIs are categorized as *light* PEIs.

12.3.3.3   *Assigning Anchored PEIs*   The anchored PEIs can be assigned only to one of the DIVMs near their source data unless the DIVMs do not exist or are overloaded. In the latter case, they are treated similar to heavy PEIs with a data movement precursor job. The optimizer first attempts to assign these anchored PEIs. For each PEI in the anchored set, the optimizer discovers all of the instances of the required data and, for each of these, discovers all of the DIVMs close to the data and capable of accessing it. It then allocates each anchored PEI to one of these DIVMs, distributing load and reducing data movement.

12.3.3.4   *Assigning Heavy PEIs*   One of the important characteristics of the data-streaming model is that PEs are connected in a pipeline that allows task executions to overlap. PEs start to process as soon as they have received sufficient data from their predecessors and emit data as soon as their processing on a unit of input has finished. This overlapping behavior[2] of the PEIs' execution generates

---

[2]The overlapping behavior is intended to allow multiple PE steps to work on data while they are close to the processors in the execution engines' memory hierarchy.

a problem when calculating the total execution time of a DISPEL graph. One of the possible solutions is to model the *time to produce an element of the final result* and think of this as a *job-shop scheduling problem*. A job-shop scheduling problem is about scheduling a set of jobs J on M machines to achieve the minimum completion time.

We define a *job*, $\mathrm{Job}_{i,j}(k)$, as the processing of the PEI$_i$ to generate a data element on output j and k is an output element counter $\{1, 2, \ldots\}$, for example, $J_{\mathrm{MF,data}}(1)$ is the execution of MedianFilter to produce the first element on output data (Fig. 12.4). We then define a dependency graph between all of these jobs $J_{i,j}$ according to the dataflows along each connection. For instance, the processing of the first output element of TupleBuild, $J_{\mathrm{TB,output}}(1)$, is dependent on the output of $J_{\mathrm{Post,filename}}(1)$ and input Connection mask, which both have dependencies on other jobs.

The jobs will be scheduled to available DIVMs. When the scheduling requires moving data elements across DIVMs, it incurs additional *communication time*. To model the communication time, we consider the data movement as a separate job, which can only be executed in an abstract DIVM, *transport DIVM*. We propose a transport DIVM, $\mathrm{TM}_{s,d}$ to move an element of data from DIVM$_s$ to DIVM$_d$. For instance, assume that MedianFilter and FeatureGenerate are mapped to DIVM$_i$ and DIVM$_j$; accordingly, a data movement job $J_{\mathrm{MF,FG}}$ is added to $\mathrm{TM}_{i,j}$ to move the output element of $J_{\mathrm{MF,data}}(1)$ from DIVM$_i$ to DIVM$_j$ for $J_{\mathrm{FG,data}}(1)$. In terms of dependency, $J_{\mathrm{MF,FG}}$ must be scheduled after $J_{\mathrm{MF,data}}(1)$ and before $J_{\mathrm{FG,data}}(1)$ without any overlap.

Our optimization goal is to *minimize the time to produce a unit of result* (a unit of output element of the PEI). In other words, if $T(\mathrm{DIVM}_i)$ is the time spent in processing all of the jobs in DIVM$_i$, we want to minimize the $\max(T(\mathrm{DIVM}_i))$, for all $1 <= i <= n$. To achieve the optimization goal, our scheduling algorithm should (i) minimize the idle time of DIVMs and (ii) minimize the movement of data across DIVMs (minimizing the jobs on the abstract transfer DIVM).

The following is a list of known constraints:

- All of the jobs from the same PEI must be scheduled on the same DIVM.
- Precedence of data must be obeyed (jobs must be executed in order).
- All PEIs are allowed to overlap their execution, but this is NOT necessary.
- The jobs are not preemptive.
- Each DIVM executes one job at a time (even though each DIVM is scheduled to multiple PE instances during enactment).

12.3.3.5 Assigning Light PEIs

We see the DISPEL graph as *beads* connected with strings that correspond to a sequence of their dataflow interconnections, and the DIVMs as the *bowls* to store the beads, as illustrated in Figure 12.6. The assignment problem is the task of allocating beads into bowls. For each bead, we have to decide whether it should slide down into the left bowl or to the other direction into the right bowl. For *sliding* PEIs into DIVMs, the decision

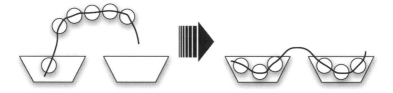

Figure 12.6   *Beads and bowls as analogy of PEIs and workflows.*

is affected by two criteria: *the volume of dataflow* of each stream connecting the PEI to its predecessors and successors, and *the workload* of each of the DIVMs. If there are multiple connections between these beads (i.e., PEI with more than one input/output), there may be several strings pulling them in different directions. In such a situation the string that has the biggest pull will be chosen because it is transferring the most data.

12.4   DISPEL DEPLOYMENT

At this point in the enactment process, the optimizer has created a well-annotated graph of the computation described by the original DISPEL script. If the graph needs to be executed across several gateways (which is assumed to be the normal case), the graph has to be decomposed into separate subgraphs for deployment at the sites specified by the annotations. The information included in the annotations includes the location of the execution engine that will perform that subgraph, the location of all data sources (databases or streaming sources), locations where temporary repositories for intermediate results will be located, and the assurance that the code needed for each PE is runnable at the execution engine identified for the PE. This graph (or rather set of graphs) is mostly platform independent. What remains to be done is to complete the deployment process, a largely platform-specific function. The deployment process involves obtaining and deploying executable code for the PEs, linking the data connections between PEs within an execution engine and across multiple engines, and establishing the monitoring and control infrastructure.

The compiler will have verified that an implementation of each PE is available to each execution engine that runs a given PE. However, there are a number of platform-specific ways in which this code can be deployed. A very simple implementation of the platform might require that the code associated with each PE be precompiled as part of the platform. This might be suitable in specialized scenarios, but, in general, a more flexible code deployment strategy will be expected. A highly flexible platform would maintain a repository of PE implementations (possibly centrally) and, during this deployment phase, distribute the PE code to the various gateways for dynamic loading into the execution engine. To some extent, the deployment strategy for code will depend on the implementation language of the PE itself. Java code, for example, can be linked with the platform itself, dynamically loaded as required, or indeed compiled on demand. Perl or other scripting languages are likely to be run interpretively in any case and, therefore, will use a more dynamic deployment strategy. A very flexible platform supporting multiple implementation languages will likely use several deployment strategies.

Clearly, one of the primary services provided by the platform is connecting the various PEs with dataflows, as specified by connections in DISPEL. Platforms have a wide variety of mechanisms available to implement this function depending on many design factors and the context in which a given connection is being deployed. The following are a few examples of strategies that could be taken and the contexts in which they might make sense:

1. In the simplest rendering of an execution engine, all PEs might run within the same JVM. In this case, connections could be implemented using something similar to Object Streams. These could be extended to provide various levels of buffering and monitoring.

2. A high performance data processing implementation might use a high performance network passing data along connections using network-specific protocols of libraries carefully tuned to that network, for example, MPI.

3. Similarly, a site that offered a number of different execution engines, some of which might be simple data sources such as detectors, the interconnection technology used to connect PEs representing these sources would need to account for the site's infrastructure capabilities.

4. When execution engines are located at different sites, the communication between the subgraphs may be over low bandwidth or even public networks and, therefore, data compression and encryption would need to be incorporated in these connections.

5. It is also possible that gateways on different sites might be provided by different implementations, in which case the implementations would need to incorporate a negotiation step into the deployment whereby they agree on a data exchange protocol standard to use.

The last, and in some way optional, aspect provided by the platform implementation as part of deployment is the monitoring infrastructure. The more information gathered by the infrastructure about performance, the more sophisticated the optimizer can become. Even simple implementations will find that a little monitoring information can aid in diagnostics and help spot performance bottlenecks. More complex implementations will also provide real-time visualization of the graph, as it is processed by a collection of execution engines.

12.4.1 The Role of Gateways

In distributed computing contexts, the gateway takes on an additional role beyond that described in the hourglass discussion (Fig. 9.2). When data processing is spread across multiple sites, the gateway provides additional infrastructure.

Firstly, the gateway can accept completely annotated DISPEL subgraphs that have been generated as part of the optimization and distribution process. These

DISPEL descriptions of subgraphs will typically be fully optimized already, but nonetheless, the gateway processes them as usual. Since these partitioned graphs will need to communicate with each other, these subgraphs will contain additional information (in the form of either annotations, additional PEs, or both) to facilitate the interconnections between subgraphs.

Secondly, the original gateway will serve as the user's point of contact with their running workflow. This gateway will need to collate information such as errors, performance data, and progress indicators from any other gateways to which it sent partitions of the original DISPEL graph. It is also through the initial gateway that the user will receive some of the results from the workflow, although where significant data volumes are concerned, the user may be referred to the gateway actually holding the data in question.

Thirdly, in production environments, the gateway will also provide security functions, such as overall authentication and authorization. This level of security is needed to control access to the site running the gateway. Further mechanisms are needed to manage fine-grained access to the data sources themselves, including record level access databases.

In the following section, we discuss the execution phase of enactment.

12.5   DISPEL EXECUTION AND CONTROL

At this stage in the enactment process, see Figure 12.1, the following have all been completed:

1. The DISPEL script has been compiled and run to generate an abstract graph.
2. The graph has been optimized in the context of available resources at several possible locations.
3. The collection of PEs (rendered in location-specific forms) has been deployed and resources allocated for their execution.

What remains is the execution of the data-intensive application itself. As the process of enactment has progressed as outlined above, the technology involved has become more and more precise. At this point, we are ready to execute the primitive instructions of the data-intensive application. Any implementation following this approach will need mechanisms to handle a number of key aspects of execution and control.

Up to this point, there has been nothing specific stated about how the data are passed from one PE to another or even what processing paradigm is used to implement the PEs themselves. The discussion so far has been limited to the definition of a kind of abstract machine for implementing data-intensive distributed computing (DIDC), which can be built using a number of different technologies. In the ADMIRE project [4], the implementation of the execution phase was based on the OGSA-DAI [5] distributed data integration platform. We will not discuss the details of this particular implementation here, but rather provide a description of the capabilities that any platform implementing DIDC would need to have. Given that there are many possible ways to render the platform, there are a number of issues that all platforms executing DIDC applications will need to address. These are discussed in the following sections.

12.5.1 Data Flow Control

The single, most fundamental aspect of the DIDC platform arises from the streaming dataflow model implicit in the whole approach. All processing follows a dataflow paradigm. In particular, computation only takes place when the data needed for the computation becomes available. This is in contrast to the traditional von Neumann model where the computing engine fetches the data as it moves through a computation described by a script. Thus, the management of data streams is foremost to the concept of DIDC. The notion of a data stream must be a first class object in any implementation. In fact, the approach taken to addressing data streams embodies the distinguishing characteristic of an implementation. Typical approaches might include event-driven systems where each DISPEL tuple would be treated as an event and processed in a manner similar to complex event processing systems [6]. A primitive implementation might be rendered as a collection of Unix processes connected by pipes. More sophisticated implementations would provide direct networked sockets between processes (with or without threading within the processes). Implementations targeted at widely distributed deployment might opt for Web-services-based protocols.

Once a basic paradigm is identified, the next issue to address is the initiation of the dataflow that drives the computation. The graphical nature of the DISPEL-described graph does provide for the existence of a *root* node or nodes that provide the initial stream of data that will in turn drive the computation. However, the distributed nature of the application may mean that the actual initiation data source is remote. In these cases, the implementation will need to identify the incoming data stream as the local point of initiation. Once computation begins, it must then be managed. There are two further aspects to managing dataflow, data marshaling (usually with buffers) and dataflow termination.

Data marshaling is needed as part of the platform itself, as even in the most precisely defined applications there will be instances when, because of resource constraints, for example, data will either build up at the output of one or the input of another PE. In Chapter 10, we described a number of language level mechanisms that provide hints to the management of dataflow. The platform should use the hints to improve the marshaling of data in and out of PEs running in the platform. For example, *emits* indicated the rate of output from a PE relative to its input. The notation *round-robin* indicates that data is taken from each input in turn. These annotations can help a platform better optimize the management of information flow in the system.

However, there will be times when buffering will be required and the platform must provide the ability to accommodate this. Even with buffering in place, it is important for platforms to provide other capabilities that could be used to prevent excessive buffering. This may be important when the various stages of a computation have widely varying execution times. In these cases, the platform may be able to notify the upstream PE that it should throttle back on the production of tuples. In a quality implementation, this function should not be visible to the user, but rather provided as a quality of service capability of the platform.

The reverse is also common in data-intensive applications. A given PE may be able to process much more quickly than the PE upstream from it and, therefore, be subject to starvation. While not a resource constrained problem, the potential for efficient use of resources is possible on platforms that acknowledge and exploit the possibility of starvation. For example, see the next section with respect to virtualization.

Closely related to overall termination, the termination on a given data stream needs to be handled by the platform. The hosting environment that controls the execution of PEs and, therefore, also manages the resources they consume needs to be informed when a data stream no longer is expected to deliver data to the connection. The transmission and receipt of these *EoS* (end of stream) tokens controls one-half of the termination model of DIDC. In the other direction, that is, upstream, termination conditions are also supported. In this case, the PE that has terminated (for whatever reason) will notify upstream PEs that it expects no more data. The propagation of this information and the anticipation of the changes in execution they imply need to be handled by the platform.

12.5.2 Processing Control

While DIDC is focused mostly on the data, it is not without a computational element. The role of the platform in this respect can be best summarized as one of resource management. The deployment phase pairs up computational elements (PEs and Connections) with specific resources associated with each gateway, but it is the platform that controls and manages their execution during processing of the data-driven workflow. The level of support offered by a platform will be one of the distinguishing features of the platform. The simplest platform resource manager will simply adopt the course-grained allocation provided in the deployment phase. This would have consequent issues of resources becoming overloaded or idle depending on other activity in the environment. A more sophisticated platform would support some type of dynamic resource allocation.

The extent to which a platform can be flexible with respect to these variations in load and resource utilization will greatly depend on the level of support provided by the final stage of the enactment process. In particular, a platform that supports dynamic binding of abstract PEs to their implementation will have much greater flexibility with respect to resource allocation. In some cases, this can be as powerful a capability as a further pass at optimization, albeit at a local level only. Platforms could even be permitted to substitute a parallel implementation for particular PEs without recourse to the user or developer. The benefits of using spatial as well as temporal optimization (trading time versus space in either direction) will create the potential for a market place where quality of service can be part of the decision making process.

The sensitivity of the platform to conditions in the execution environment and the state of execution of all the activities under its control will also provide opportunities for improved efficiency. In many cases, a particular PE will enter a temporary phase of starvation while it waits for additional input on one or more of its input connections. A this time, a platform should take advantage of the increase in resource availability to perform other, possibly unrelated work. Platform implementers are likely to exploit the value of virtualization in addressing this issue. Because of the specific nature of the DIDC environment, this virtualization need not be simply at the virtualized host or operating system level, but virtualization technology within the platform itself could provide greater benefit to the users than more brute force approaches.

In some cases, there will be factors beyond simple optimization that require the platform to respond through resource management. For example, a memory overload due to uncontrolled buffering might require the migration of the overloaded task (or another one sharing the same resource) to ameliorate the situation. Similarly, there may be changes in execution priority or quota limits that require the platform to respond to the situation dynamically. Again, as with virtualization, the unique nature of DIDC means that the implementers of the platform do not need to rely on operating system services to enable their platforms.

The nature of DIDC described here allows for platforms to carry out local optimizations that are highly specialized. One example is the ability to reuse precomputed data. A frequently requested partial result could be identified by the platform and reused on a subsequent occasion, thus saving the recomputation of the result. This capability is supported by the DIDC architecture described here through the registry and repository model. The accurate semantic description of results (partial or otherwise) allows platforms to participate in the same kind of reuse optimization that only the DIDC developers would normally undertake.

The structure and details of information needed in support of the optimization process are discussed in Section 12.3. However, it is the platform that must gather, maintain, and distribute this data to the distributed gateways performing the optimization phase of enactment. While this data are fairly specific, the data will be accompanied by platform (and possibly gateway)-specific accounting information.

In many cases, users will be interacting with the workflow, making decisions to continue, archive, or, in other ways, influence the execution of a workflow. The provision of this interactive element adds significant complexity to the platform's resource management strategy. Users may interact at specific times, meaning that the platform must "hold" the computation until requested by the user. Likewise, the user may "interrupt" the computation to alter running conditions or parameters. Both situations should be catered for by the platform.

In line with the separation of concerns adopted by the DIDC architecture described here, the platform developers can exploit the abstraction provided by the neck of the hourglass in Figure 9.2 and provide significant creativity to their rendering of the architecture. For example, the more flexible and well-instrumented platform will be able to include green assessments and carbon accounting in their resource summaries and, therefore, offer users the opportunity to choose a greener implementation of their application.

12.5.3   Termination, Error Management, and Cleanup

While less exciting than green resource management, the ability of the platform to deal with the fundamental issues of termination and failure are critical. Termination of a distributed, graph-based, data-driven computation is complicated to begin with. The possibility of failure makes this a real challenge to implementations. The termination criterion defined by the DIDC architecture can be summarized as follows.

The default termination behavior of a PE occurs when either all the inputs are exhausted or all the receivers of outputs have indicated that they do not want more data. In order to reach this condition across the whole graph, when all of a PE's inputs have received *EoS*, the PE completes the use of its current data, sends an *EoS* on all of its outputs, and then stops. Likewise, when all of a PE's outputs have received a "no more data" signal, the PE sends a "no more data" signal on all of its inputs and then stops. In this way, termination propagates across a distributed enactment based only on local decisions.

The above describes the default behavior. Termination conditions can be defined on PE descriptors (e.g., a PE terminates when any one of the input streams is exhausted). Thus, platforms will need to extend this default behavior to deal with the following special situations:

1. One PE in the graph may execute an explicit *Stop* operation.
2. A fault occurs in one of the PEs. The implementation will also need to distribute this fact back to the user.
3. Deadlock is detected, although this will be rare in the presence of throttled buffer management, because of the DAG (directed acyclic graph) nature of the graph.
4. Time-out may also be included in places within the enactment to detect silent failures.
5. The propagation of distributed termination in the presence of network failures.

12.5.4   The Future Role of Standards

As noted above, the rendered platform is, at present, very specific to one implementation. However, as data sources and data-intensive resources are already widely varied in terms of implementation technology, data format, communication protocols, and so forth, integration of all this potential will be nearly impossible in the long term without some form of standardization. There are several places where standards can play the greatest role and others where the benefits will not pay off in the short or medium term.

Access to the data sources themselves is an obvious initial target for use of standards. However, with the exception of database access languages such as SQL, there are no universally agreed standards for remote access to data resources. Some efforts, within closed domains such as Web services, do exist [7]. Implementations will need, for the time being, to provide effective tooling for wrapping and interfacing to these data sources using the data sources that the provider makes available.

In Chapter 10, the outlined dataflow control mechanisms provide another opportunity for standards. If the interaction between execution PEs can be agreed across implementations of DIDC platforms, then the potential for greater collaboration and/or expanded business models become possible. These standards will need to address the issues described above around flow control, compression, encryption, termination, and failure. In particular, standardizing the connection interface between different gateways implementing instances of the DIDC platform would address many of the interoperability issues inherent in this architecture.

Since the rendering on individual PEs has been designed to be independent of any particular execution language or platform, this area is unlikely to be a focal point for standardization. The exception would be the DISPEL language itself.

REFERENCES

1. C. S. Liew, M. P. Atkinson, R. Ostrowski, M. Cole, J. I. van Hemert, and L. Han, "Performance database: capturing data for optimizing distributed streaming workflows," *Philosophical Transactions of the Royal Society A*, vol. 369, no. 1949, pp. 3268–3284, 2011.

2. G. Yaikhom, M. P. Atkinson, J. I. van Hemert, O. Corcho, and A. Krause, "Validation and mismatch repair of workflows through typed data streams," *Philosophical Transactions of the Royal Society A*, vol. 369, no. 1949, pp. 3285–3299, 2011.

3. E. Deelman, G. Singh, M.-H. Su, J. Blythe, Y. Gil, C. Kesselman, G. Mehta, K. Vahi, G. B. Berriman, J. Good, A. C. Laity, J. C. Jacob, and D. S. Katz, "Pegasus: a framework for mapping complex scientific workflows onto distributed systems," *Scientific Programming*, vol. 13, no. 3, pp. 219–237, 2005.

4. M. P. Atkinson, J. I. van Hemert, L. Han, A. Hume, and C. S. Liew, "A distributed architecture for data mining and integration," in *Proceedings of the Second International Workshop on Data-aware Distributed Computing*, DADC '09, pp. 11–20, ACM, 2009.

5. B. Dobrzelecki, A. Krause, A. Hume, A. Grant, M. Antonioletti, T. Alemu, M. P. Atkinson, M. Jackson, and E. Theocharopoulos, "Integrating Distributed Data Sources with OGSA-DAI DQP and Views," *Philosophical Transactions of the Royal Society A*, vol. 368, no. 1926, pp. 4133–4145, 2010.

6. D. C. Luckham, *The Power of Events: An Introduction to Complex Event Processing in Distributed Enterprise Systems*. Addison-Wesley Professional, 2001.

7. M. Antonioletti, A. Krause, N. W. Paton, A. Eisenberg, S. Laws, S. Malaika, J. Melton, and D. Pearson, "The WS-DAI family of specifications for Web service data access and integration," *SIGMOD Record*, vol. 35, pp. 48–55, March 2006.

Part IV

Data-Intensive Application Experience

This part of the book is about applications, the applications that have helped to develop and shape the ideas behind the data-intensive computing architectures and the DISPEL language. It is aimed at the reader who understands best by example: the theory is all well and good, but show me what it actually *does*.

It is, of course, the desire to make better use of data that drives us. In this part we discuss four applications that were core to the development of DISPEL and the data-intensive architecture. Part V describes five further data-intensive research domains challenged by the same issues of scale and complexity, and the innovative solutions developed in each case. The introduction to Part I highlights a number of important books each of which further motivates the quest. Together these sources illustrate the myriad potential applications of digital data, and provide powerful motivation for the development of new research methods.

Like every other major development in computing, the DISPEL language and the data-intensive architecture have been designed to solve problems. Drawing on a number of scientific and business domains, the designers of the architecture and methods described in this book have made extensive use of data-intensive application scenarios to color the decisions and challenge the ideas behind the approach. This part introduces specific examples of data-intensive problems from the domains of environmental science, customer relationship management (CRM), developmental biology and seismology. We explain why they were chosen, and how data-intensive methods have been able to support new solutions, in some cases to existing problems, in others to entirely new challenges within a domain.

Chapter 13 introduces the four application domains key to the development of DISPEL and the data-intensive architecture, and defines a number of metrics against which we have been able to measure the effectiveness of the architecture and language in addressing real data-intensive challenges. Subsequent chapters look at each of the application domains in turn, beginning with analytical CRM in the telecoms domain (Chapter 14). Chapter 15 describes a series of new approaches to decision support in environmental risk management that have been enabled by the data-intensive architecture. Chapter 16 looks at some of the emerging data-intensive challenges in systems biology, illustrating the need for new methods to support the rapidly-increasing data volumes now prevalent in post-genomic life sciences. Chapter 17 presents some ground-breaking work in the field of seismology on how data-intensive methods can be useful tools in the analysis of earthquakes and other geophysical phenomena.

13

The Application Foundations of DISPEL

Rob Baxter

EPCC, University of Edinburgh, Edinburgh, UK

This chapter reviews the four application domain areas chosen as test beds for the development of the data-intensive architecture. It seeks to motivate the choices of the individual scenarios in terms of their abilities to challenge and shape the data-intensive architecture and DISPEL language. It also reviews our overall data-intensive strategy in terms of genuine application experience and finds a lot to recommend it as an overall approach to data-intensive problems.

13.1 CHARACTERISTICS OF DATA-INTENSIVE APPLICATIONS

Why choose these four domains? Data-intensive system designers need real data-intensive requirements if they hope to build an infrastructure that has the capability to solve real problems. The applications described here have all been instrumental in shaping the formation of the data-intensive architecture and language because they each exhibit key required features of data-intensive analysis. Broadly speaking, these applications demand systems that:

The DATA Bonanza: Improving Knowledge Discovery in Science, Engineering, and Business, First Edition.
Edited by Malcolm Atkinson, Rob Baxter, Michelle Galea, Mark Parsons, Peter Brezany, Oscar Corcho, Jano van Hemert, and David Snelling.
© 2013 John Wiley & Sons, Inc. Published 2013 by John Wiley & Sons, Inc.

- are scalable, in terms of an ability to deal with large volumes of data, large numbers of data sources, or both;
- are distributed, in being able to manage data sources and resources across network boundaries, and potentially across the Internet;
- support heterogeneity, in terms of allowing data from arbitrary sources to be drawn into the analysis—images, database records, simulation results files, sensor readings;
- support iterative exploration, because the process of knowledge discovery is not single pass but invariably involves a domain and data analysis experts iterating toward a solution through a process of continuous modeling, refinement, and testing;
- are extensible because data analysis experts will need to create their own processing elements to deal with domain-specific requirements.

The four application areas, then, were chosen to exercise different combinations of these demands that together enabled us to develop a comprehensive and effective approach to data-intensive analysis.

13.1.1   Analytical Customer Relationship Management

Any large modern business collects enormous amounts of data about its customers. From retail to financial services and telecoms to IT, large firms collect large amounts of data with the potential for providing extremely useful business intelligence—if only it could be found in the haystack of customer records.

Analytical customer relationship management (ACRM) aims to make use of these operational data to enable the measurement, analysis, and, ultimately, the optimization of customer relationships. An established field in business analytics, modern ACRM is struggling to manage the increasing tides of data, and thus provides a fruitful application area for new data-intensive methods.

ACRM can be characterized by numerous very large, privately held relational databases—typically many terabytes in size—which increase in size very rapidly as customer transactions are recorded. On top of this, the explosion of public data sources in social media networks is becoming of increasing interest to marketers in service-oriented and Web-facing firms, begging questions such as: how can we merge our records for a given customer's spending habits with what we can discover of their online habits? How can we merge streams of data from these disparate sources? How can we extract business intelligence from it all? Big databases, multiple dynamic sources, heterogeneity—all these dimensions provide effective challenges to any designer of data-intensive systems.

Chapter 14 describes the application of data-intensive methods to ACRM in the telecoms domain, demonstrating that not only can traditional knowledge discovery and business intelligence processes be supported by the new data-intensive architecture but also that it accelerates the development of methods and delivers agile data exploration. This chapter describes a real-life version of Paul's ongoing challenges at Telco Inc., introduced in Chapter 5.

13.1.2 Environmental Risk Management

In terms of our increasing awareness of our ever-changing planet, effective environmental modeling and disaster prediction are becoming more and more important and increasingly data driven. The necessity to combine and analyze data from multiple heterogeneous sources, potentially in real time, is a compelling application of data-intensive methods.

Traditional attempts to understand natural phenomena have relied on large-scale simulations of weather, river systems, and so on. The complexity of atmospheric physics and natural processes generally make this notoriously difficult, and in terms of supporting decision makers in charge of managing a major river system, for example, it may be that alternative approaches based on sifting historical and real-time data can offer more pragmatic solutions.

Applying this data analytic approach to risk management and decision support requires systems that can assimilate data from an extremely heterogeneous environment—databases, sensor streams, images from weather radar, and simulation data from numerical weather prediction applications. This complexity of sources provides a fascinating challenge for a data-intensive system: can one approach provide the flexibility, agility, and extensibility to generate workable solutions?

DISPEL-based techniques have been used to extend flood forecast simulations in Slovakia, providing domain experts at the Slovak Hydrometeorological Institute with access to new data sources and new knowledge discovery tools. Chapter 15 explores this use of data-intensive computing in the management of a river system that includes reservoirs and waterworks stations, and its use in predicting and managing river flood levels. It demonstrates very effectively the power of these techniques in capturing complex knowledge discovery processes in flexible and repeatable ways and proves the concept of the use of data analytic methods in environmental risk management.

13.1.3 Developmental Biology

With genetic sequencing techniques moving into the next generation, genetic data volumes are set to increase at an astonishing rate. The effective processing of these data has long ceased to be a manual task; automation is no longer merely desirable but essential.

The nature of biological digital data has diversified enormously in recent years, with high resolution images becoming a key format for capturing both research and clinical data. High resolution images pose particular challenges for a data-intensive systems architecture, requiring not only efficient methods of access but also significant computing resource "nearby" for image analysis algorithms to be executed quickly enough to keep the overall pipeline flowing.

Researchers from the Eurexpress project,[1] have been instrumental in guiding the development of DISPEL in support of the automation of the image processing

[1]www.eurexpress.org/ee verified January 2013

and data mining required to understand the development of the mouse embryo. In Chapter 16, we look at the challenges of annotating terabytes of image data with information about which anatomical features show the expression of a particular gene at a particular point in the development cycle, and the design of the DISPEL-based solutions that meet these challenges. The chapter begins by describing a classification approach for embryo images that was successfully implemented using the data-intensive architecture, and then moves on to a question currently being studied: can one use these methods to identify all pairs of coregulated genes?

13.1.4 Seismological Data Analysis

Seismologists at present collect terabytes of data per year from automated sensors that monitor every shiver and twitch of the Earth's crust. Extracting useful information from these data is a mammoth task, involving the cross-correlation of sensor readings from around the globe but is vital in the quest to provide better understanding of the risk of earthquakes or volcanic eruptions. The primary challenge here for a data-intensive architecture is the ability to manage and assimilate a very large number of data streams in real time.

The first prototypes of a powerful, flexible data assimilation framework for broadband seismology have been developed using the approaches advocated here, and the DISPEL language has been refined accordingly against one of the most challenging data-intensive application scenarios. Chapter 17 describes the approach, showing the different stages of data-intensive processing, fetching data from multiple archives and conducting analyses that use existing code and controls already familiar to seismologists.

13.2 EVALUATING APPLICATION PERFORMANCE

Table 13.1 summarizes our evaluation of the performance of the data-intensive architecture against the demands of the four applications. As an additional point of comparison, we include metrics gathered from an astronomy workflow developed for classifying quasars and discussed in greater detail in Chapter 18.

In performing these evaluations, we created a number of measurable metrics related to the requirements noted earlier and conducted experiments using data-intensive implementations of various scenarios from the four application domains.

The first two metrics define our measures for the scalability of the architecture in terms of the number of data processed, both byte-wise and object- or tuple-wise; the next two provide complementary measures of the distributed nature of the architecture. We choose to measure heterogeneity in terms of both the data and geography of the system—disparate data from multiple sites. The metric for iterative exploration is a qualitative answer to the question of working in real time with partial data results, and we measure the extensibility of the system by considering both the complexity of workflows developed and the reuse of existing patterns in each case.

TABLE 13.1 Evaluation Criteria Mapped to Use Cases (Including the Quasar Classification Example from the Astronomy Work Described in Chapter 18)

	Scalability		Distribution		Heterogeneity	RT?	Extensibility	
	V_d	D_d	N_S	N_P	$(x+y)$		ALP	N_W
Environmental risk	500 GB	1 M	10	10	6 + 3	No	Yes[a]	32
ACRM	1.5 TB	60 M	1	$4 \ldots N_M$[b]	3 + 3	Yes[c]	Yes[d]	10+
Gene annot.	170 MB	809	5	$4 \times k$[e]	5 + 3	No	Yes[f]	57
Seismology	20 TB	2.3 M	4	510	4 + 2	No	Yes[g]	20+
Astronomy	256 MB	65 M	2	10–20	1 + 2	No	No	19

Color indicates how well suited a use case is to evaluate a certain feature of the data-intensive architecture, as defined by the associated criterion (green is excellent, yellow is borderline, and red is poor).

Key (and threshold above which the case provides an effective test): V_d, data volume (>1 TB); D_d, data dimensions (>1 M tuples); N_S, number of data sources (>2); N_P, number of concurrent processes (>100); $x + y$, heterogeneous data sources + physical sites ($x + y > 5$); RT?, real-time processing required (qualitative); ALP, abstract language patterns used (qualitative); N_W, number of steps in the workflow (>20).

[a] Data filters.
[b] N_M, number of models trained.
[c] Real-time statistical sampling.
[d] Data filters; k-fold cross validation.
[e] k, number of folds in a k-fold cross validation.
[f] k-fold cross validation; directed acyclic graph.
[g] Pair-wise cross correlation.

- Data Volume. A dataset is considered to be large if the raw volume is greater than 1 TB. At present, it is not an easy task to move and process 1 TB of raw data in a distributed system. One gigabyte is a plausible size to transport and process on current systems but will still present problems in certain processing steps.

- Dimensions. A dataset is considered to be of a large dimension if it contains more than 1 million rows. From previous experiments, we know that this is a useful indicator for evaluating different streaming models and the robustness of the architecture in terms of memory models. The number of attributes per row has a product effect on the dimension.

- Data Sources. This evaluates the integration of data from two or more sources. The sources may be physically colocated but are logically separate, such as different databases that may or may not have similar schema, or a database and a file system.

- Concurrent Processes. This evaluates the potential of the architecture for the parallelization of processing elements, which may be computationally demanding or data intensive and which may require distribution over loosely coupled compute resources. One hundred or more processes are considered a significant challenge to the architecture. The parallelism is achieved as a product of pipelining and farming.

- Heterogeneous Data + Physical Sites. This is the integration of data that may be heterogeneous, such as data from databases with data from flat files and from one or more different physical sites. If x denotes the number of heterogeneous data sources, and y the number of different physical sites, then $x + y > 5$ is considered a good indicator of the architecture's performance in this regard.

- Real Time. This is relevant for end users—domain or data analysis experts—who may wish to observe partial results from a DISPEL request while it is still being processed. This is useful for evaluating streaming models, as the output of streams may be presented to an end user before all computations complete, providing an opportunity for steering, which can potentially save much wasted computation.

- Abstract Language Patterns. These are required to allow the use, and reuse, of common and complex data integration and mining patterns, such as all-meets-all, k-fold cross validation, and decision-tree building. They allow us to evaluate how well the architecture can handle the abstractions introduced by DISPEL, and, in turn, how well the separation of concerns is facilitated by the architecture.

- Steps in Workflow. This is the number of processing elements in the longest path from source data to output results in a DISPEL graph, with a number greater than 20 indicating that the capacity of the DISPEL enactment system is being challenged.

For quantitative criteria, the figure in parentheses noted in the table key indicates the point at which we may consider the architecture to be presented with a real challenge. For instance, a dataset is considered to be large and sufficiently challenging to the data-intensive architecture if the raw volume is larger than 1 TB. The color of each table cell is also an indication of the extent to which a feature of the architecture is tested by a use case—green is well tested, yellow is moderate, and red indicates a poor test.

The table demonstrates a reasonable degree of coverage. Each element of the architecture is well challenged and tested by at least two of the application use cases, with several elements tested by all or almost all of the cases. We thus consider the set of these application use cases to be a good test of the data-intensive architecture and an effective yardstick for the overall strategy.

13.3 REVIEWING THE DATA-INTENSIVE STRATEGY

Testing and evaluating the performance of the data-intensive architecture against these current real-world challenges allows us to review not only our particular prototype implementations but also our overall data-intensive strategy, as set out in Chapter 3. To recall, this strategy comprises the following:

- the partitioning of human concerns into three categories of experts;
- the division of technology into a data-intensive architecture with three principal levels and an integrating registry;
- the solution of knowledge discovery challenges by partitioning the problem and by composing both components and patterns to develop solutions.

In the following sections, we review the success of this strategy from each of these viewpoints and then conclude with a collation of the open questions the application experiments revealed. These are revisited in Part VI.

13.3.1 Partitioning the Role of Experts

Separating the concerns of the various experts involved in the development of each solution has proven to be a particularly effective approach. In each case, *domain experts* were engaged effectively in the solution design without having to learn new languages or terminology; they were able to apply their own domain knowledge within a context still familiar to them. The *data analysis experts* who undertook the bulk of the solution development adopted DISPEL very quickly and came to appreciate its power and utility as a tool to capture the required business context and create the right computational solution without needing in-depth knowledge of either of those spheres. The contracts defined by the DISPEL documents furthermore enabled the *data-intensive engineers* to focus on implementation details within the prototype enactment framework without needing to know the application context.

13.3.2   Data-Intensive Architecture

The successful separation of the experts' concerns provides hints as to the effectiveness of the architectural separation, in particular the use of DISPEL descriptions to capture domain knowledge and codify a contract between the analysts and engineers who develop the solutions.

DISPEL has proven a very powerful tool indeed. Across the four domains, application-specific solutions and interfaces were developed on a variety of platforms—integrated development environments, Web applications (both rich and simple), command-line tools—and in each case, the DISPEL description provided the canonical point of reference for the data analysis experts. To provide the necessary framework for developing and evaluating the applications, the research teams behind this book implemented a large-scale distributed test bed across five European countries, involving an eclectic mix of platforms, data resources, and computing machinery. Growing and shrinking this test bed, incorporating new elements, and retiring others without disrupting the work of the analysts proved very straightforward; the heterogeneity of detail was hidden very successfully behind the gateways, with DISPEL as the single allowed—and only required—medium of discourse.

13.3.3   Partitioning Solutions and Reuse

The concept of data-intensive workflow and the level of granularity defined by the concept of a processing element have enabled data analysis experts in the four areas to develop solutions in an incremental way. In each case, a natural and obvious partition of the designs into data gathering, data preparation, data integration, data analysis or mining, and delivery of results was both supported and encouraged by the architecture and tools. In a number of cases, generic DISPEL functions and patterns developed for one application and registered centrally were simply picked up and reused by data analysis experts from a different domain—the k-fold cross-validation pattern is a prime example.

13.3.4   Outstanding Issues

Our experiences with the application experiments detailed in this part lead us to state with some confidence that the strategy and architecture we advocate stands up well to the rigors of real-world, data-intensive challenges. The approach of separation and partition around a canonical language does indeed enables the rapid and effective development of solutions to some of the most challenging data problems facing us at present.

There are outstanding issues, of course. Those highlighted in particular by many, if not all, in the experiments are the following:

- Engineering sufficiently performant platforms. Creating platforms that can deal efficiently with data streams at rates of gigabytes per second is a key challenge for the data-intensive future and must be the primary goal of the emerging cadre of data-intensive engineers. The infrastructure used to prove the concepts described in this book was sufficient unto that task, but real-time, general purpose data-intensive production systems are still some way off.

- Greater support for the development of processing elements. The key to enabling domain experts and data analysis experts to work efficiently on solutions to their problems lies in making it easy to create and "drop in" new domain-specific processing elements and in providing them with rich libraries of generic processing elements from which to assemble solutions. Improving mechanisms for creating both processing elements and libraries would be a clear extension to the work described here.

- Support for a broader range of platforms and development environments. Domain experts and data analysis experts have their favorite tools and favorite ways of working. Any data-intensive platform must be able to work with whatever tools the experts are most comfortable with—be that Eclipse, R, MATLAB, Excel, or a rich Web application.

- Support for greater autonomy in the platform. The descriptive power of a system-wide registry with support for both structural and domain types, coupled with the capacity of the data-intensive architecture to record statistics about its use, offers the tantalizing possibility of much greater autonomy within a gateway, much greater leeway for a data-intensive system to make its own decision about where to execute a particular fragment of DISPEL, or which of the several implementations of *this* processing element should be chosen in *this* context.

14

Analytical Platform for Customer Relationship Management

Maciej Jarka

Comarch SA, Warsaw, Poland

Mark Parsons

EPCC, University of Edinburgh, Edinburgh, UK

This chapter describes the application of new data-intensive methods to "classical" business data mining.

Customer relationship management (CRM) systems form the backbone of many large businesses at present, especially those in the service and retail sectors. The CRM databases contain massive amounts of data on customer habits and patterns of spending, and analyzing these databases to provide business intelligence is an increasingly important plank in many firms' strategies.

This chapter describes two specific applications of the data-intensive architecture to CRM database analysis carried out by a team at Polish IT services firm Comarch SA. Specialists in CRM services to the telecoms sector, Comarch have used the

The DATA Bonanza: Improving Knowledge Discovery in Science, Engineering, and Business, First Edition.
Edited by Malcolm Atkinson, Rob Baxter, Michelle Galea, Mark Parsons, Peter Brezany, Oscar Corcho, Jano van Hemert, and David Snelling.
© 2013 John Wiley & Sons, Inc. Published 2013 by John Wiley & Sons, Inc.

data-intensive methods described here to demonstrate real advantage in working with large customer databases. They report that the capabilities offered by the data-intensive architecture to formulate reusable patterns has, for them, accelerated the exploration of both data and methods. The streaming nature of the architecture enabled them to invent new incremental algorithms that were better able to handle massive data volumes.

Readers are introduced to CRM analysis in the telecoms domain through a scene-setting discussion that assumes no prior knowledge (Sections 14.1 and 14.2). They are then taken through the process of analyzing customer data to predict whether and when customers may move to a new service provider—a phenomenon known as *customer "churn"* (Section 14.3). The second example (Section 14.4) shows how data can be used to understand how best to offer existing customers complementary services. Section 14.5 offers some thoughts on the effective exploitation of data-intensive methods for business intelligence in a production capacity, including considerations of problem scale, and the last section (Section 14.6) summarizes the key findings from our "classical" experiments in CRM data mining.

14.1   DATA ANALYSIS IN THE TELECOMS BUSINESS

Telecommunications firms collect enormous quantities of data each day, every day as a by-product of providing services to their customers; as a result, telecom firms possess some of the largest databases in the world. By-product or not, the highly competitive nature of the telecoms business provides compelling motivation for leveraging these data through the use of knowledge-based systems to support marketing decisions. As a consequence, telecoms was one of the first commercial areas to adopt data-mining methods to support the business.

Telecoms data are typically related to network status, call details, and the personal details of each customer. The complexity and size of the datasets very quickly made them unsuitable for manual analysis. The earliest attempts at improved decision support saw telecom firms deploy expert systems; however, the development process of such systems was, and still is, expensive and inefficient because of the difficulty of capturing sufficient expert knowledge for them to be effective. The promise of automatic and intelligent knowledge discovery directly from the data was one clear advantage offered by data mining, and this led to a rapid expansion in the availability and effectiveness of data-mining tools.

Telecom analysts apply data-mining techniques to several kinds of business problems. Customer data—call summaries and contract details, for example—can be used to build models for *churn prediction* or *fraud detection*. Similarly, mining data related to the status of the network helps companies to maintain it and plan for its expansion. The general aim is to derive useful models from historical data that can be used to predict future customer behavior, but realizing such models against a backdrop of steadily increasing data volumes requires a combination of more effective tools and highly skilled staff.

14.2   ANALYTICAL CUSTOMER RELATIONSHIP MANAGEMENT

There is a degree of misunderstanding concerning the meaning of the term *customer relationship management* (CRM). Very often, it is interpreted as a specific IT system (a "CRM system") that helps companies collect and organize information about customers. A broader and arguably more useful definition has been proposed by Francis Buttle [1]. Buttle describes CRM as a "core business strategy that integrates internal processes and functions, and external networks, to create and deliver value to targeted customers at a profit." In other words, the definition covers not only the IT systems that support it but also CRM in relation to overall business strategy.

Buttle describes four types of CRM: analytical, collaborative, operational, and strategic. In this chapter, we concentrate on *analytical customer relationship management* (ACRM), which is concerned with *"capturing, storing, extracting, integrating, processing, distributing, using, and reporting customer-related data to enhance both customer and company value"* [1]. To this list, the authors would add *cleaning, preparing, and delivering*. Taken together, this list describes the characteristics of a full end-to-end knowledge discovery process, well suited to solution through data-intensive methods.

14.2.1   Data Analysis Approaches for ACRM

In ACRM, data analysis, mining, and integration processes (collectively, "knowledge discovery" processes) are built around the particular business challenges that the company has set for itself. In this chapter, we focus on two major tasks that demonstrate the importance of ACRM for a telecoms company—*churn prediction* and *cross selling*. Churn prediction asks: is this existing customer likely to cease being a customer and move elsewhere, and if so, why? Cross selling tries to determine which additional products a given customer might be interested in. Both kinds of analyses have significant business benefits to the company in terms of increased profits and efficiency, particularly of marketing campaigns, but perhaps more importantly, they can help the company become more customer oriented.

Standard ACRM techniques such as these are not restricted to the telecoms domain but can be applied to any service-sector business that collects significant information about its customers, for example, financial services, IT, and utilities markets. Modern retail customer databases are also highly amenable to these kinds of analyses, especially the question of cross selling: do customers on a Friday evening *really* buy more beer if we stock it next to the nappies aisle?

14.2.2   Quality Concerns

In ACRM, the data analysis expert is tasked with delivering a useful predictive model to the domain expert. However, providing a classification model without some measure of its quality is only half the story—here is our model, but is it any good? By "measure of quality" here, we are clearly interested in the *probability of classifying a customer correctly* and to get a handle on the effectiveness of, say, a given churn model we need to test it against historical data containing customers known to have left ("churned") and customers known to have stayed loyal ("not churned").

In a model with two classes such as this, what is considered to be "good"? With two possible outcomes, statistically the worst model that we can get is the one that is 50% accurate. We could replace such a model with the flipping of a coin. Understanding the quality or effectiveness of binary classification models involves examining the true positive and true negative rates from tests against known data.

The *true positive rate* ("sensitivity," "hit rate," or "recall") in the case of a churn prediction model measures the proportion of customers who *did* leave the company and who were correctly classified as "churned." Sensitivity is degraded below a perfect 100% by the presence of false negatives—ex-customers the model failed to predict would leave.

The *true negative rate* or "specificity" is a complementary measure, capturing the number of loyal customers correctly classified as "not churned." Specificity is degraded below 100% by the presence of false positives—loyal customers incorrectly classified as "churned."

The perfect binary classifier, therefore, has a sensitivity of 1 and a specificity of 1. Neither measure alone is sufficient to assess the quality of a particular model: a classifier that always says "churned" no matter what the actual status of a given customer will have a sensitivity of 1—it never misses a churned customer—but is clearly not a useful test [2, 3].

The quality of a binary classifier can also be recorded as a *confusion matrix*, a 2×2 table that records true and false positives and negatives, as shown here:

		Predicted value	
		P	N
Actual value	P'	True positives	False negatives
	N'	False positives	True negatives

Measuring the accuracy of a predictive model requires that we test it against a set of data for which we know the outcomes (so we can compare the model's predictions with reality) and which is independent of the data used to train the model. If we have a lot of data, we can simply divide the full dataset into two parts: a training set and a test set (this, of course, reduces the amount of training data available). Alternatively, we can perform a k-fold cross validation [4], as described in Chapter 10. Whatever method we choose, understanding the quality of our model predictions is an essential part of the analysis process.

14.3 SCENARIO 1: CHURN PREDICTION

The basic premise behind churn prediction is that keeping an existing customer is much cheaper than finding a new one. Furthermore, loyal customers are likely to be more profitable [5].

Customer churn happens continuously in the telecoms industry, being the direct result of strong competition between companies. In a sort of continuous arms race, companies make better and better offers to potential clients, people who are more often than not already customers of other companies. The ultimate aim of churn prediction is to prevent customers so tempted from leaving; it is, therefore, not only about determining which particular customers may change company but also about understanding *why* they do, thus, allowing the company to prepare an appropriate pre-emptive counter-offer. This section describes the general ideas behind churn prediction and our experience of preparing an example of its application using DISPEL and the execution platform developed in the ADMIRE project.

14.3.1 Data Analysis Processes

The core of any ACRM task is to develop data integration and analysis processes that can, with the right data and a little luck, answer the relevant business question. In doing this, the data analysis expert will typically prepare solution workflows, first of all deciding what kind of results are needed. In our case of churn prediction, we are looking for a predictive model that can be handed to the domain expert in an easy-to-use form. The model should allow the domain expert to classify whether any particular customer is likely to churn or not.[1] These classification models can be based on a variety of algorithms (decision tree, neural network, naïve Bayes), but the analyst's goal is to deliver it to the domain expert as a business tool rather than a mathematical exercise.

In our specific ACRM deployment, there is no need to prepare special implementations of any algorithms; existing libraries of standard methods provide everything we need. The real challenge is to prepare an appropriate dataset to train and evaluate the model. Here, the data analysis expert has to deal with all kinds of issues: the necessary data are scattered across a number of physically separate databases and are in different formats, with missing values and possibly corrupted entries. It is in this preparatory phase of data cleaning, preprocessing, and integration that data-intensive methods really come into their own.

The data analysis expert starts by selecting and preparing a group of attributes or properties for the customer that experience has shown are potentially significant in the classification process for problems of this type. In our example, we can divide the attributes into the following four groups of properties that can be extracted from the databases:

---

[1]It is possible to extract more than two kinds of customers in terms of churning. In [5], the author describes *loyalists and apostles, hostages, defectors, and mercenaries.*

- Customer related—for example, age, gender;
- Contract related—for example, number of contracts, tariff plan transitions;
- Contact related—for example, the number of complaints or enquiries registered at the call center;
- Call related—for example, the number of outbound calls made in the evening.

Typically, some of these attributes can be extracted directly from the company databases, but some require initial transformations. In our churn prediction scenario, we choose to make as many transformations as possible on the database side, exploiting the power of the database management system (DBMS) to make the overall process faster. In some cases, particularly where data are derived from primitive resources such as flat files, a lot of work has to be done in the workflow to prepare the data. In our specific example, the most significant problem is preparing the values of the arguments appropriately for the classification algorithms, as the database type system is unfortunately (and not atypically) incompatible with the algorithmic library that we use.

Figures 14.1 and 14.2 represent the (simplified) conceptual design of the training process. To complete the design, the abstract activities are mapped to known processing elements, either through the use of a supporting tool such as the ADMIRE Workbench or written directly in the DISPEL language. By enacting the DISPEL requests, the data analysis expert adds more and more trained models to the company's knowledge discovery repository.

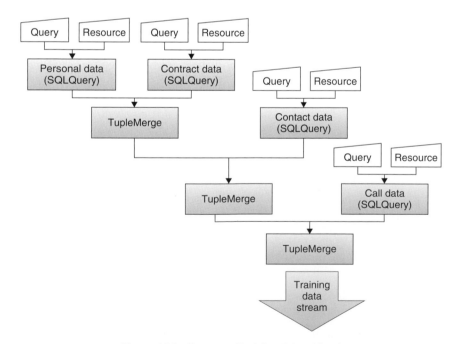

Figure 14.1 *Process of training data retrieval.*

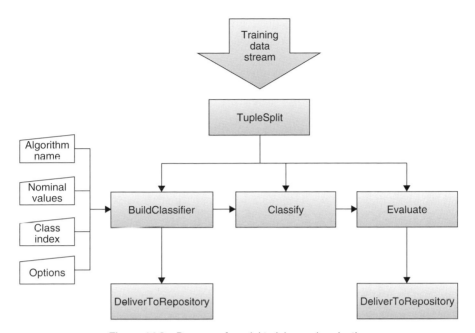

Figure 14.2   *Process of model training and evaluation.*

The four streams of data integrated in the first phase (Fig. 14.1) are horizontally split into two substreams (Fig. 14.2). To create a reliable model and provide an effective evaluation, the split is performed randomly so that the training data (first stream) and the test data (second stream) have similar qualities. The first substream feeds the `BuildClassifier` PE (processing element), which builds the model. For our purposes, the nature of the model is unimportant; what is important is that the output produced by this PE can perform "churned" or "not churned" class prediction on the test data. The argument `argumentClass` specifies the learning algorithm to use, and other options specify the parameters for that algorithm. For instance, we might specify a decision tree algorithm, and options may be maximum depth of the tree or the pruning level.

There are two outcomes from this workflow—a trained model and its confusion matrix. The model is passed to the `Classify` PE, which performs predictions on the second stream of data. The `Evaluate` PE compares the results of this prediction with the actual values and calculates the confusion matrix. Both the model and its confusion matrix are submitted to a central repository and can then be used by the domain expert, as explained in Section 14.5.

14.4   SCENARIO 2: CROSS SELLING

Cross selling is a type of marketing activity in which a company encourages existing customers to purchase products that they do not currently own but may find interesting. The key question asked is: given a customer's purchase history then what, from a portfolio of available products, is likely to be the next one they buy? Encouraging customers to buy additional products and services is an important route to increasing revenue per customer in any business, but in the high churn, cut-throat arena of telecoms, it is vital. Companies must be careful though; mismatched campaigns can have bad results-sending messages promoting completely unnecessary products and services will have a negative effect on the customer and may lead to their subsequent loss.

What we would like is a set of principles that describes a particular customer's past purchase decisions, and thus, hopefully predicts their future ones. In datamining terminology, what we seek are *association rules*, rules that suggest items that are likely to be purchased together. In a wider context, cross selling is not just about associating one product with another, but it is typically a more complex task of determining which customers buy which products, and in what order. In terms of data mining, for a given customer or set of customers we need to extract patterns from a historical list of purchases. A simple example rule could be: "If customer is aged between 20 and 25, and the customer recently bought a smartphone, the next purchase will be mobile Internet access."

14.4.1   Data Preparation and Transformation

The data used in the cross-selling scenario are derived from the same data sources as used in the churn prediction application, although in this case the data may require many more preanalysis transformations. This makes for a significantly more involved workflow.

Firstly, we need to prepare a list of purchased items and services appropriate for association rules mining algorithms. This activity is presented in Figure 14.3: data from the main *contracts* table are transformed into a Boolean matrix form. The contracts table contains each purchase in a single row and we must aggregate the contracts for each customer to produce the summary. The association rule mining algorithms can then produce rules such as those in Equation 14.1.

$$IF \ \text{BOUGHT\_SERVICE\_X} = TRUE$$

$$AND \ \text{BOUGHT\_SERVICE\_Y} = TRUE$$

$$THEN \Rightarrow \text{BOUGHT\_SERVICE\_Z} = TRUE \tag{14.1}$$

Ideally, we would aim to use as many features and properties of a customer as possible to produce rules. Some properties of a continuous nature—age, for example—will need to be transformed into a discrete representation to make them manageable (Fig. 14.4).

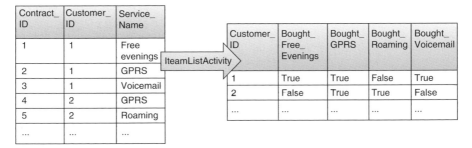

Figure 14.3 *Transformation of the contract database.*

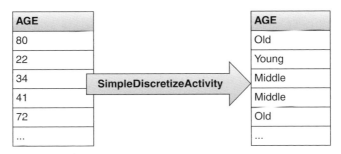

Figure 14.4 *Discretization of attribute values.*

14.4.2 Association Rule Quality Measures

As with classification models, association rules have measures of quality; but in this case, the measures are different. In our cross-selling application, we use *support*, *confidence*, *lift*, and *leverage*, as defined in Mobasher [6]. These values help to distinguish rules that describe data patterns that often appear from those that appear rarely in the dataset. Rules delivered together with measures can then be sorted in a more useful way, or those which discriminate below the data analyst's expectations of quality can be ignored.

14.4.3 Data Analysis Processes

Generally speaking, the design of the cross-selling process is similar to that of the churn prediction application: the data analysis expert derives rules from the training dataset and delivers them to a shared central repository from where the results can be accessed by domain experts using specific business applications. The difference is that we do not need to split the data into training and test datasets to evaluate the rules as evaluation figures are delivered along with association rules.

As before, we extract the data from two resources. The first contains personal customer data, which we discretize if necessary. The second contains data related to customer contracts, which we transform into matrix form. We merge these two data streams and send the result to the `BuildAssociator` PE, which outputs the sorted set of any rules discovered, plus related meta information (Fig. 14.5).

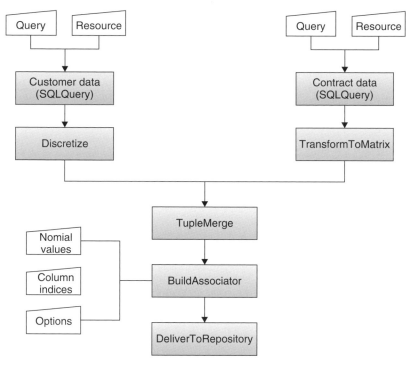

Figure 14.5 *Conceptual view of the cross-selling workflow.*

14.5 EXPLOITING THE MODELS AND RULES

Both churn prediction and cross-selling workflows deposit their results—models and rules—in a "knowledge repository" on central company servers. Domain experts—business analysts or sales personnel, for example—can then access the results through domain-specific user interfaces, which we term *portals*. These are typically Web-based interfaces, providing the necessary functionality for a manager or a call center worker to use the underlying models without necessarily being exposed to unnecessary detail.

The churn prediction portal allows a user to apply data-mining classifiers even to single customers to determine their (predicted) churn behavior. Data can be imported from comma-separated value (CSV) files or typed in manually. This application also displays a list of the available models that can be applied, together with model descriptions and visual representations that highlight which attributes influence the prediction most—in other words, which of the customer features have had the most impact on their leaving the company. Most of the classifier training algorithms are displayable as a tree.

Domain experts also have the opportunity to select more than one model at a time to predict customer behavior. In such a situation, every classifier used "votes"

```
1   PE(<Connection testData> => <Connection classifiedData>)
2       classifyTestData(String[] modelNames, Integer[] priorities,
3                       String repositoryParams){
4           MultiClassify classify = new MultiClassify;
5           for(Integer i = 0;i<modelNames.length;i++) {
6                   Deserialiser dsr = new Deserialiser;
7                   GetFromHTTP obtain = new GetFromHTTP;
8                   |- modelNames[i] -| => obtain.filename;
9                   obtain.data => dsr.data;
10                  |- url -| => obtain.url;
11                  dsr.result => classify.classifier[i];
12          }
13          priorities => classify.priorities;
14      return PE(<Connection testData=classify.data> =>
15                      <Connection classifiedData=classify.result>);
```

Figure 14.6   *MultiClassify DISPEL code.*

for a class for each customer, and the final value for each customer is the class with the highest number of votes. The domain expert can set a different weight for each model, giving it a stronger position while voting. This can be useful, for instance, where we trust one model more than the other—perhaps, it was trained on a more reliable or up-to-date dataset.

The process of applying a particular model (or models) to the customer group is described in a DISPEL document that is "hidden" behind the graphical user interface of the business portal. Development of domain-specific portals on top of DISPEL requests can be simplified by using advanced language elements such as functions or loops. As we hide much of the process logic inside the function, changes to the portal are limited only to binding input forms to DISPEL function parameters (and even this can be done automatically). Capturing the knowledge discovery process in DISPEL is thus a powerful way of facilitating reuse and reducing reinvention.

As an example, take the idea of classifiers voting. Through the business portal, the domain expert can select any number of models from the knowledge repository and give them weights. The implementation of this idea is handled entirely in DISPEL—see the listing in Figure 14.6.

For the portal to make use of entirely different models, it need only call the DISPEL function with different parameters; the core business logic is captured entirely within the DISPEL and the learned models are stored elsewhere in the ACRM system central repository (Fig. 14.7).

The association rule model generated by the cross-selling scenario uses the same deployment model of business portal and DISPEL logic behind the scenes. The domain expert using the portal can upload small datasets and find rules that match the data and discover suggestions of what to offer to a particular customer or set of customers. Such an application is designed to support employees working in call centers to improve the effectiveness of their selling.

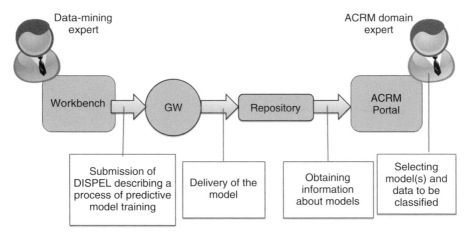

Figure 14.7   *Cooperation of data mining and domain experts in the ACRM application. Here GW denotes a* DISPEL *enactment gateway.*

14.5.1   The Challenges of Scale

By the very nature of data-intensive analysis, significant challenges arise when the size of the datasets used to train models becomes large. In our experiments, we observed that for datasets larger than a terabyte, the process of training was taking a length of time measurable in days. For a domain expert, waiting several days for a final model is unlikely to be acceptable.

In both churn prediction and cross selling, we focused on developing *stream* processing. In both workflows, the training processes worked on very large datasets, so our design had to address the two main problems of scale:

- *Memory Overload.* In a streaming environment, we do not have access to the whole database. We can also store only a limited number of data at one time in memory.
- *Long-Lasting Processing.* In standard analyses, the trained models are available only after the whole dataset is processed. However, for usability in the data-intensive world, it is important to be able to view partially trained models, that is, models based on parts of the dataset, to ensure that the overall process is still on track and generating useful results.

We deal with both problems by introducing state-of-the art incremental algorithms into the data-intensive workflows. For churn prediction, we make use of Hoeffding trees [7], and for cross selling we take advantage of the Moment algorithm [8]. Thus, in our application, we can perform both long-lasting and memory-hungry processes capable of producing partial results almost immediately; the user no longer has to wait several days until the end of processing. Moreover, with this solution, we can determine a maximum allowed amount of memory to be used and tailor the use of the infrastructure accordingly.

A necessary consequence of using incremental algorithms is poorer quality in the produced results. However, the evaluation processes in both cases provide consistent information about quality, and in many applications, slightly poorer quality is an acceptable trade-off for better operational performance.

It is important to note here that the data-intensive architecture supports this incremental approach to mining data streams at a fundamental level; swapping out in-memory algorithms for incremental ones requires little in the way of adjustment to the overall DISPEL workflow. This is a compelling endorsement of the data-intensive method.

14.6 SUMMARY: LESSONS LEARNED

DISPEL and the prototype data-intensive execution environment built by the ADMIRE project have been used with great success at Comarch to extend the ACRM application with churn prediction and cross-selling capabilities. The power of this approach to the "classical" task of knowledge discovery for CRM systems is already apparent. In summary, we highlight the following three key benefits that data-intensive methods enable:

- Simplified management of complex workflows; a single DISPEL document can capture every detail of the workflow in terms of data retrieval, transformation, data mining, and delivery.
- Enhancement of knowledge sharing by distinguishing three kinds of experts and sharing work between them, results can be innovative and lead to a more efficient approach. This is especially important in the telecoms domain where companies have many employees in various locations.
- Simplified application development and deployment, as the main computational engine is accessible as a Web service, the development of domain-specific applications is limited to creating a user interface that configures the request in DISPEL.

REFERENCES

1. F. Buttle, *Customer Relationship Management: Concepts and Tools*. Elsevier Butterworth-Heineman, 2004.
2. D. Altman and J. Bland, "Statistics notes: diagnostic tests 1: sensitivity and specificity," *British Medical Journal*, vol. 308, no. 6943, p. 1552, 1994.
3. B. Goldacre, *Bad Science*. Harper Perennial, 2009 (reprint).
4. F. Guillet and H. J. Hamilton, *Quality Measures in Data Mining*. Berlin Heidelberg, Springer-Verlag, 2007.
5. M. A. Lejeune, "Measuring the impact of data mining on churn management," *Internet Research*, 1991.

6. B. Mobasher, "Association rule mining with WEKA." http://maya.cs.depaul.edu/classes /ect584/WEKA/associate.html, verified August 2011.

7. P. Domingos and G. Hulten, "Mining high-speed data streams," in *The Sixth ACM SIGKDD International Conference on Knowledge Discovery and Data Mining*, KDD '00, pp. 71–80, ACM, 2000.

8. Y. Chi, H. Wang, P. S. Yu, and R. R. Muntz, "Catch the moment: maintaining closed frequent item sets over a data stream sliding window," *Knowledge and Information Systems*, vol. 10, pp. 265–294, October 2006.

15

Environmental Risk Management

Ladislav Hluchý, Ondrej Habala, Viet Tran, and Branislav Šimo
Oddelenie paralelného a distribuovaného spracovania informácií,
Ústav informatiky SAV, Bratislava, Slovakia

This chapter presents the motivation and challenges in applying state-of-the-art knowledge discovery technologies in the domain of environmental risk management.

Environmental risk management research is an established part of the Earth sciences domain, already known for using powerful computational resources to model physical phenomena in the atmosphere, oceans, and rivers [1]. In this chapter, we explore how the data-intensive processes mentioned above can be applied to benefit the experts who produce daily weather predictions, as well as rarely needed, but crucial and often time-critical risk assessments for emerging environmentally significant events. We illustrate the possibilities on a simple scenario from the hydrometeorological domain, and then describe how this scenario extends to provide meteorologists and hydrologists with new data and insights currently not routinely available. These examples illustrate the complexity of working with real data from multiple sources and lead to a series of "lessons learned" at the end of the chapter.

The DATA Bonanza: Improving Knowledge Discovery in Science, Engineering, and Business, First Edition.
Edited by Malcolm Atkinson, Rob Baxter, Michelle Galea, Mark Parsons, Peter Brezany, Oscar Corcho, Jano van Hemert, and David Snelling.
© 2013 John Wiley & Sons, Inc. Published 2013 by John Wiley & Sons, Inc.

15.1   ENVIRONMENTAL MODELING

The Earth sciences rely on a plethora of data sources to model, analyze, understand, and predict natural processes on a global scale. Earth observation satellites are perhaps the best-known example of environmental data sources [2]. These satellites alone produce more than 250 TB of data per day in the form of high resolution imagery, and this is only a part of the data collected about the Earth, its weather, its seismic activity, or its hydrological processes. Many other data sources, some traditional, some novel, all contribute to a continuously growing database that describes our world.

This vast data space is difficult to describe in its entirety, let alone navigate, search, order, and exploit. Some of the major challenges in tackling these problems are listed as follows:

- the (lack of) standardization of data formats and exchange protocols;
- The (lack of) standardization of metadata describing the quality, access policies, or validity of data;
- addressing intrinsically evolving data—topologies change with land use and development, weather changes constantly, ecosystems perish and new ones replace them;
- understanding the connections and correlations between various pieces of data from different sources;
- tracking the quality and provenance of data;
- accessing data in real time—perhaps the most complex problem, as various data sources, even if online and publicly available, need to be accessed by various methods: Web pages, Web-service-accessible databases, and files on FTP servers; these data sources have to be addressed one by one, and components that stream the data found in them in a common format need to be developed and maintained, as the relevant data source changes the structures and format of data and access services.

One of the main users of these data is the field of numerical weather prediction (NWP) [3]. The NWP models require both high CPU performance and large storage space, and meteorological services have been traditionally considered excellent clients for computer vendors. NWP is classified by length of prediction into nowcasting (up to 6 h), short-range prediction (up to 48 h), and medium-range prediction. Medium-range prediction ranges from 3 to 15 day-long forecasts and is produced by global atmospheric models in the main meteorological centers across the world.

In the specific case of meteorological predictions in Slovakia, for the past several years, there has been an operational implementation of the ALADIN local area model at the Slovak Hydrometeorological Institute (SHMI).[1] The model is run

---

[1]Please see www.cnrm.meteo.fr/aladin/ for a description of ALADIN and the people who use it.

four times per day (every 6 h at 00, 06, 12, and 18 UTC) and each time a 3-day forecast is computed. The operational suite consists of an assimilation process, forecast computation, postprocessing, and subsequent applications. The amount of data produced every 6 h is approximately 20–30 GB. The initial and boundary conditions for ALADIN are provided by METEO France.[2]

The ALADIN model is a classical prediction model based on fundamental physical principles: the conservation of energy, mass, and momentum. The predicted variables are temperature, surface pressure, horizontal wind components, specific humidity, cloud, water, ice, and other variables related to physical parameterizations.

15.2 CASCADING SIMULATION MODELS

Meteorology is closely linked to, and has great influence on, hydrology and hydraulics—the flow of water in river basins. As meteorology tries to understand and predict weather, including precipitation, hydrology (for which precipitation is a major influence) tries to understand the natural water cycle, from atmosphere to rivers, from rivers to sea, and back into the atmosphere. Advances in hydrology also allow us to employ hydraulics and to model hydrological processes on a smaller scale, sometimes even in a way suitable for the modeling and prediction of floods. Attempts have been made, not without success [4], to employ a whole cascade of simulations to predict the weather; then from this prediction, hydrological conditions over a limited geographical area are computed, and from these conditions, a detailed model of the flow of water in a river basin is created.

These cascading environmental simulation models typically require the assimilation, integration, and filtering of terabytes of data, coupled with massive supercomputing power near to hand. However, there are some problems in this domain that need a new method of data processing in order to become manageable and practically deployable in a production environment. Three such scenarios were chosen as pilots for the new approaches described in this book: the problem of meteorological nowcasting based on radar imagery, the prediction of flash floods on smaller rivers, and the cooperation between a waterworks management body and hydrometeorological experts in the protection of a civil population from local floods. The rest of this chapter describes how novel approaches to data exploitation can reap dividends in environmental risk management.

15.2.1 The Flood Forecasting Simulation Cascade

The Flood Forecasting Simulation Cascade (FFSC) is the name given to the distributed data management and processing architecture used in the experiments described here. Originally designed for flood forecasting, the application suite has expanded over recent years to become a broader suite of tools for environmental risk management.

[2]Meteo France, 1 quai Branly, 75340 Paris Cedex 07, France, http://www.meteofrance.com.

In a domain where centralized databases and large supercomputers are the usual tools, the FFSC takes a more novel approach to environmental knowledge discovery. Architecturally, it comprises the following:

- A set of data access elements, local to the respective databases and file storage systems where input data originates.
- A set of data filters, deployed in one or more data processing centers. These filters are developed, maintained, and deployed by information technology experts knowledgeable in environmental data management.
- A data mining model, deployed at a high performance computing center with sufficient computing power and managed by data analysis experts.
- A multifaceted and remotely accessible user interface, presenting different tools to different groups of users.

This fundamentally distributed architecture, depicted in Figure 15.1, benefits our application significantly because it allows us to handle different tasks at different locations in optimal ways as exemplified in the following.

- Input data are best stored where they can be effectively maintained by environmental management experts. The datasets are constantly updated not only with new data but also quite often with existing data that are modified in the light of new observations, corrected when faulty equipment is detected, and so on.
- Data processing has to be done by analysts who not only understand the data but also understand the complexities of the final data-mining process. The analysts need to prepare the data and facilitate their transition from a set of raw hydrometeorological values represented in different spatiotemporal meshes (in different coordinate systems) into a stream of uniform, normalized, repaired, filtered, and ordered tuples.
- The target data-mining model may need to handle tuples of arbitrary width (sometimes with hundreds of distinct items per tuple), and streams of millions of tuples. Such a task requires processing power not commonly found in a local data center of a meteorological or hydrological authority, and thus, the prepared data have to be streamed to a location where they can be processed speedily. Results are often needed within minutes, not hours, of an input data occurrence. The data-mining model itself may be too complex to be optimally handled by anybody other than a trained data-mining expert.

The three application scenarios themselves reflect this distributed architecture, being composed of distinct, often geographically distributed, services that process data. They are as follows:

- ORAVA—prediction of water levels and temperature on the Orava river;
- RADAR—short-term rainfall prediction based on the analysis of weather radar imagery;
- SVP—reservoir inflow forecast based on meteorological predictions.

15.3   ENVIRONMENTAL DATA SOURCES AND THEIR MANAGEMENT

The environmental domain makes extensive demands of data management and data processing. A significant portion of data input to weather prediction models (both physical and statistical) comes from observations. Only a fraction of these observations can be made remotely (satellite and radar observations are examples of remote weather sensing), and the bulk of the input data comes from local observations of air temperature, humidity, pressure, precipitation, and other parameters. Local observations tend to produce local data sources, and a large number of local observations leads to a large number of local data sources. Even in a context where there is a national weather management authority, several geographically dispersed data sources are needed for any integrated analysis. For example, in Slovakia, we might consider the following data sources:

- Meteorological observation databases owned by the SHMI[3];
- Weather radar observations conducted by the SHMI and stored in a separate data store;
- Hydrological observations conducted by branches of Slovak Water Enterprise (SWE),[4] and stored locally at the respective branches;
- Waterworks manipulation schedules, local to the management center of the respective waterworks (there are four such centers);
- Local observations by specialized personnel at airports and other installations, where weather is a major operational concern.

This list is not complete and the number of sources may be much larger. A traditional approach to data management in this environment is to establish a list of necessary data sources, perform negotiations with their owners, acquire the data (usually in a form of a static database image), assess its quality, prepare it, and then feed it to the model. This process is cumbersome, can take months, and is not suited for day-to-day environmental management operations.

A different approach is to use modern methods of distributed data management: establish a quality of service agreement, an online data integration process including all necessary data preparation and filtering, and make the process as automated as possible. The main difference is in treating the input data not as a suite of static data sets, but rather *as a group of converging data streams*: weather does not cease to exist at the moment a snapshot ends. While this approach is still a novelty for domain experts trained in a different context and accustomed to data transfer channels with much smaller bandwidths, it has been recognized as the future of environmental data distribution. Witness, for example, the pan-European INSPIRE Directive [5], mandating the use of service-oriented architectures and

[3]Slovenský hydrometeorologický ústav, Jeséniova 17, 833 15 Bratislava, Slovakia, http://www.shmu.sk.
[4]Slovenský vodohospodársky podnik, štátny podnik, Radničné námestie 8, 969 55 Banská Štiavnica, Slovakia, http://www.svp.sk.

TABLE 15.1   Nature, Current Size, and Approximate Rates of Increase of the Various Data Sources Used in the Environmental Risk Management Scenarios

Dataset	Source	Nature	Size (MB)	MB/year
NWP data	SHMI	Simulation	Arbitrary[a]	c. 20,000
Synoptic stations	SHMI	Sensor	50	1
Rainfall measurement	SHMI	Manual	100	< 1
Radar imagery	SHMI	Sensor	10,000	300
Waterworks	SWE	Manual	300	20
Hydrology stations	SHMI	Sensor	300	30

While training the various predictive models makes use of historical snapshots, the live system is designed to work with incoming streams of data from the various sources, some of which change slowly but significantly over the course of a year.
[a] can be regenerated as required.

a significant set of geospatial standards for environmental data publication and access.

The experiments described in this chapter are dependent on several input datasets, which we describe in detail in the following text and summarize in Table 15.1. We measure these datasets not only in terms of absolute size but also in terms of how quickly they are increasing. While many of the datasets comprise in large part a historical corpus of measurements, new observations and new simulations are being performed and added all the time. Training of any given predictive model [6, 7] will, of course, make use of historical data, but actual *use* of such a model will require the most up-to-date data available. This is a good illustration of the concept of "thinking in streams"—data are dynamic, not just static blocks.

We also explain why distributed data integration is so important to this approach. The whole picture of how data are acquired, processed, and mined can be obtained from Figure 15.1.

15.3.1   Numerical Weather Predictions

When we want to predict meteorological processes using weather prediction from physical meteorological models, we also need to train our models using computed weather data [8]. At first, this may seem odd—why use computed data from a physical model for the past, when we already have actual observations? The problem is that we want to mine *future data*, which is, of course, available only in simulated form. In data mining, it is important to train your model on a dataset whose properties are as close as possible to the properties of the data to be mined; thus, in our case, we have to use the simulation data for training. So we come to the paradoxical situation that we use less-precise data (simulation data) for the training of our models even though there are precise data (observations) already available.

The NWP dataset is by far the largest one we use here: one decade of data for model training is several hundred gigabytes in size. The quality of these data

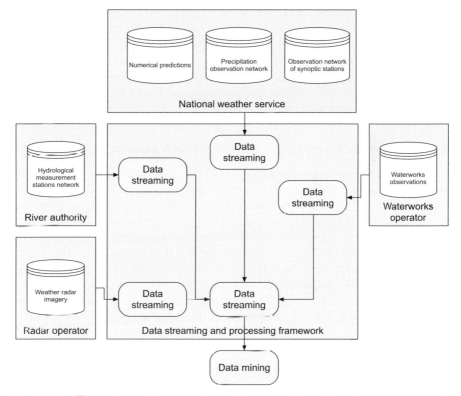

Figure 15.1 *The representation of our virtual data space with multiple data sources owned by multiple data providers and the background framework providing data streaming and processing capabilities. The filtered, integrated, cleaned, and repaired data are processed by data-mining algorithms that are designed and maintained by data analysis experts.*

depends on the source from which we obtain them, but as it is computationally generated, we can achieve almost perfect quality, without missing values and without the errors typically produced by faulty observations or transcription from written records into the computer. Of course, we assume that the meteorological model does not produce errors in its output (other than its naturally imprecise prediction of weather!).

15.3.2 Weather Observations — Synoptic Stations

Another source of meteorological data is actual past observations. Of these, the ones provided by a network of synoptic meteorological stations are the most detailed. These observations contain several meteorological parameters, including air temperature, humidity, accumulated precipitation, air pressure, wind speed and direction, and others, which may not be important for our application.

These data are provided by the SHMI, with a historical corpus of some tens of megabytes in size and a very modest rate of increase. As the sensor network that measures them is relatively new (and being regularly upgraded), the more into the past we go, the sparser the dataset becomes. The SHMI currently operates over 30 of these stations, with more to be deployed in the near future.

The data are of relatively good quality, considering that they are observed data. The synoptic stations network is automated, with data flowing into central computers using wireless data transfer. The stations require only minimal maintenance in order to provide precise measurements.

15.3.3   Weather Observations — Rainfall Measurement Stations

The SHMI operates an extensive collection of rainfall measurement stations (more than 600 nodes) in a nonautomated network using volunteer observers and very simple technology. This network is more mature than the synoptic sensor network, and data are available from past records, although record density varies over time. The measurements are made manually by volunteers and are provided once a day as 24-h cumulative rainfall. The historical size of this data collection is of the order of hundreds of megabytes. Their quality is inferior to the previously described datasets, as we must consider the possibility (or rather inevitability) of human error. The data are further processed, cleaned, and repaired at the SHMI before being made available, but they still need to be checked for gaps and erroneous values.

15.3.4   Radar Imagery

Modern methods of weather observation include meteorological radar, which are able to provide a basic picture of the meteorological situation over a large area in real time. The radar image contains information about the reflectivity of the atmosphere. Reflectivity is directly proportional to water content, so by appropriately transforming the reflectivity index obtained by radar scanning, we can estimate the amount of rainfall [9]. An array of meteorological radar stations is operated by the SHMI and its partners in central Europe, and the resulting data are available as a set of two-dimensional bitmaps containing both reflectivity indices and the computed cumulative rainfall.

Radar image data are large. The current collection, from only a few years of operation, already stretches beyond 10 GB and the expected rate of increase is measured in hundreds of megabytes per year. Their quality also varies significantly. This method of meteorological sensing, although very promising, is not suitable for further computer processing without significant cleaning and filtering.

15.3.5   Waterworks Observations

SWE is a major provider of data in the hydrological domain. This state-owned enterprise is the administrator of all major waterworks in Slovakia. It also performs regular observations of the hydrometeorological conditions at the waterworks, and these data include air and water temperature, the amount of water in a given reservoir, and the outflow from the reservoir. These data have typically been collected for the whole history of the respective waterworks—often over decades.

The quality of these data varies—they are recorded by human observers using basic meteorological tools and are thus not free from human error. There are also gaps in the data, and they must be filtered and cleaned in order to be used.

15.3.6 Hydrological Stations Network

Complementing the waterworks dataset by SWE, the SHMI manages a network of automated hydrological observation stations along all major rivers in Slovakia. The data from these observations provide us with current river depth, the amount of water flow, water temperature, and air temperature. This dataset covers over 10 years with a historical corpus that is hundreds of megabytes in size, with a steady rate of increase of tens of megabytes annually. The quality of the data unfortunately suffers from the complexity of the conditions under which the observations are made. Apart from containing time gaps and obviously spurious values, some of the data (taken at specific stations) need to be further processed to account for significant seasonal changes in certain environmental parameters which influence the actual observations. For example, the increased presence of vegetation during summer months may lead to increased water levels, while the amount of water flowing in the river remains constant.

15.4 SCENARIO 1: ORAVA

This scenario was originally defined by the Hydrological Service division of the SHMI. Its goal is to predict the water discharge wave and temperature propagation below the Orava reservoir, one of the largest reservoirs in Slovakia [10, 11].

This scenario covers a relatively small area of northern Slovakia (Fig. 15.3). The selected data that influence the scenario's target variables—the discharge wave propagation and temperature propagation in the outflow from the Orava reservoir to the Orava river—are shown in Table 15.2. The data are gathered from the hydro-meteorological sensor networks of several data providers. Figure 15.2 shows the layout of the sensors below the Orava reservoir. Orange dots represent the sensor network of SWE, which provides reservoir water temperature and discharge data. Red dots show part of the network of hydrological sensors operated by the SHMI. These sensors are stationed in the Orava river and its tributaries, and measure current river temperature and water level. The densest sensor network, depicted by green dots, is the network of precipitation measurement stations, providing hourly precipitation data. In addition to these, there are more complex synoptic sensor stations, depicted in yellow, which provide precipitation and other climatological measurements. What is not shown in the picture is the mesh of values provided by meteorological radar and by meteorological simulations.

As predictor variables in this scenario (shown in Table 15.2), we have selected rainfall and air temperature, the discharge volume of the Orava reservoir, and the

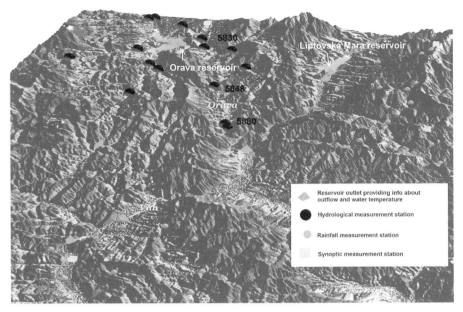

Figure 15.2   *A visualization of an actual network of hydrometeorological sensors in the northern part of Slovakia, around the Orava reservoir.*

TABLE 15.2   Schematic Depiction of the Predictor Variables and Targets in the Water Level and Temperature Prediction Scenario

Time	Rainfall	T_A	Discharge	T_R	H_{St}	T_{St}
$t-2$	R_{T-2}	F_{T-2}	D_{T-2}	E_{T-2}	X_{T-2}	Y_{T-2}
$t-1$	R_{T-1}	F_{T-1}	D_{T-1}	E_{T-1}	X_{T-1}	Y_{T-1}
t	R_T	F_T	D_T	E_T	X_T	Y_T
$t+1$	R_{T+1}	F_{T+1}	D_{T+1}	E_{T+1}	X_{T+1}	Y_{T+1}
$t+2$	R_{T+2}	F_{T+2}	D_{T+2}	E_{T+2}	X_{T+2}	Y_{T+2}

T_A denotes air temperature, T_R reservoir temperature, and T_{St} the temperature at the water station in question. H_{St} is the station height above the sea level.

temperature of water in the Orava reservoir. Our target variables are the water level and water temperature measured at a hydrological station below the reservoir. As can be seen in Figure 15.3, the station directly below the reservoir is number 5830, followed by numbers 5848 and 5880—these stations are the target sites for which predictions are made. If we run the data mining process at time t, we expect to know all sensor data up to this time (first three data lines in Table 15.2). The future rainfall and temperature values are obtained by running a standard meteorological model. The future discharge rate of the reservoir is given in the management schedule of the reservoir. The actual data-mining targets are the X and Y variables for times after time t.

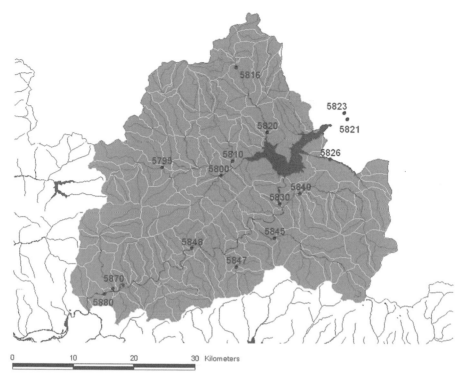

Figure 15.3 *The geographical area of the hydrological pilot scenario. Source: Image courtesy of the Slovak Hydrometeorological Institute.*

15.4.1   Solution Design

This scenario can be divided into three processes: data integration, training, and prediction.

The first process, shown in Figure 15.4, integrates the required data from the distributed data sources and saves the result to a file repository in the form of a stream of tuples. The process begins by extracting data about the relevant hydrological measurement station from a relational database (station water level, station discharge, station water temperature). These values are merged into the initial tuple, which is then expanded further as the process progresses by means of a simple Tuple merge operation (employed numerous times throughout the process). In parallel, we read data from the reservoir database (operated by a separate entity), and also access various parameters present in the computed weather data stored in the form of GRIB (GRIdded Binary) files [12].

The data from the reservoir need to be filtered by the operation Orava reservoir linear trend, which replaces missing values in the data by a linear interpolation. Also, any reading of a particular GRIB file is preceded by access to the GRIB metadata database, which holds information about the contents of the GRIB files. After integrating all of these data into a wide tuple, the tuple is filtered to remove

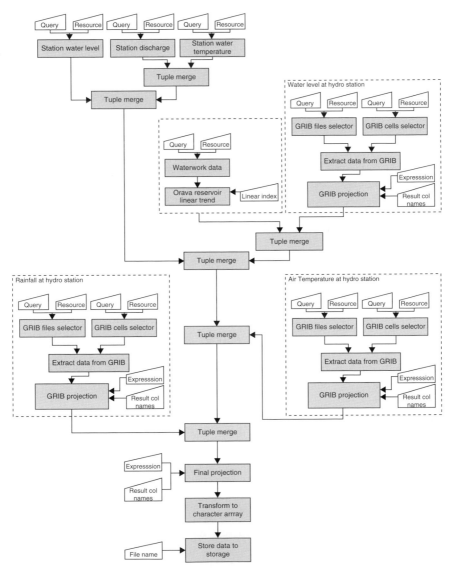

Figure 15.4 *A graphical representation of the data integration process in the ORAVA hydro-logical scenario predicting water level and water temperature.*

duplicate occurrences of some parameters (e.g., the date and time, which are used by `Tuple merge` to synchronize the data stream), and the result is stored in a file repository for later use.

The second process, shown in Figure 15.5, reads the integrated data from the stored file, deserializes it (the operation `Transformation to tuples`), and builds a linear regression classifier using parameters set and verified by a data-mining expert. The trained model is then serialized and stored back in the repository.

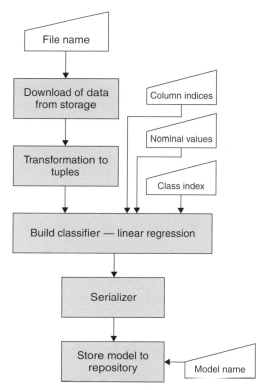

Figure 15.5 *Graphical representation of the model training process of the hydrological scenario.*

The final part of this scenario is the prediction process shown in Figure 15.6. This process expects to find already-integrated data in the file repository, as created by the integration process (Fig. 15.4). It also downloads the trained data-mining model, feeds the integrated data into the model, and then merges the original data with the predicted ones. This process may be used for both verification of the model (if we use past data for prediction) and for the actual prediction (if we use data containing future weather prediction).

This scenario illustrates very well the complexity of the data preparation and integration stages of the analysis process. The design of the model algorithm is actually a rather small part of the overall knowledge discovery process.

15.5   SCENARIO 2: RADAR

The usual methods of meteorological prediction, the kind we see daily in weather reports, are optimized for long-term prediction of up to 48 h and are not suitable for prediction of flash floods and nowcasting. These short-term problems are tackled in our second pilot scenario that aims to predict the movement of moisture in

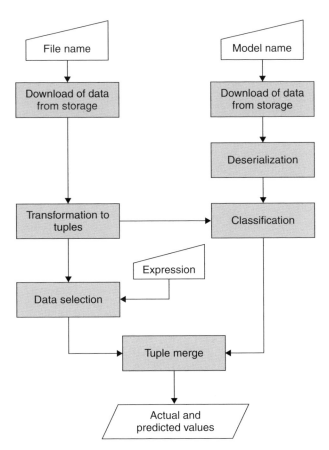

Figure 15.6 *Graphical representation of the prediction process of the hydrological scenario.*

the air from a series of radar images. Weather radar measures the reflective properties of air, which are transformed to potential precipitation before being used for data mining. An example of a preprocessed radar sample, with the reflectivity already mapped to millimeters of rainfall accumulated in an hour, can be seen in Figure 15.7.

This scenario uses both historical precipitation data (measured by sensors maintained by the SHMI) and weather predictions computed by a meteorological model. In addition, the SHMI has provided several years' worth of weather radar data, pretransformed to measure potential precipitation.

In NWP, the extrapolation of these observations in time has proved more accurate (up to several hours ahead) than the prediction of physics-based models. Thus, the purpose of this experiment is to investigate various approaches to extrapolating precipitation measurements in time. Our question is, can we obtain a very short-term prediction of precipitation using radar imagery and historical values of measured precipitation? Even 30-min warning of a possible flash flood can be valuable, if

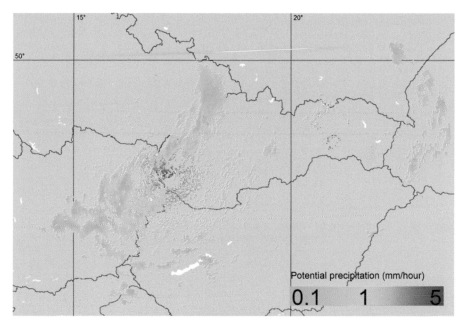

Figure 16.7 *An example of weather radar image with potential precipitation. Source: Source data courtesy of the Slovak Hydrometeorological Institute.*

it gives time for water services management to take preventative action or gives emergency services extra time to respond.

The inputs to the scenario are a time series of radar imagery (reflectivity and potential 15-min accumulated precipitation) and historical values of 24-h accumulated precipitation as measured by a ground sensor network. The outputs are a set of predicted values of precipitation for the whole territory of Slovakia. The predicted precipitation can be directly verified against the potential precipitation or against the ground-based sensors. A secondary output is the motion vector time series produced from the radar images.

The overall process of the scenario is as follows:

1. Read two successive radar images.
2. Find the motion vectors from a combination of these two images. The simplest method to compute motion vectors is to use moving frames with correlations computed within frames in between the images.
3. Repeat steps 1 and 2 to transform the radar image time series to motion vector time series.
4. Smooth motion vectors over some time period (30 min to 2 h).
5. Assume a linear translation of precipitation at time t with a smoothed motion vector computed over an interval with end at time t_e. We can compute a 15-min accumulated prediction up to 2 h ahead from time t (for every time t, we produce predictions $t + 15$, $t + 30$, $t + 45$, ... , $t + 120$ min).

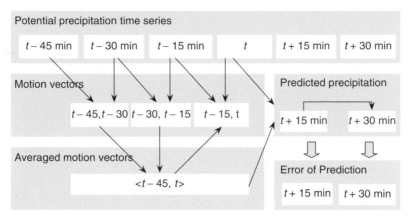

Figure 15.8 *Graphical representation of the short-term weather prediction scenario dataflow. Example of prediction at time t. Motion vectors are averaged using the last three motion vectors computed and then the prediction is computed using the precipitation at time t and the averaged motion vectors. Precipitation is computed up to 30 min with a 15-min step. The error of prediction can be directly computed using the potential precipitation time series.*

6. Compute the error of the predicted 15-min accumulated precipitation using the potential 15-min accumulated precipitation. In this way, we can compute a time series of errors for different prediction ranges.

An alternate approach is to use a data-mining technique with a model based on analogy. Here, we look for similar sequences of images and assume that the rainfall prediction is analogous to the one that has already occurred. This approach can probably be significantly improved by the proper calibration of radar images against ground-based observations as follows:

1. Train the model using the sequence of potential 15-min accumulated precipitation (or by some diagnostics based on precipitation).
2. Produce prediction of 15-min accumulated precipitation using the trained model.
3. Verify the predicted data against the potential 15-min accumulated precipitation (Fig. 15.8).

15.5.1 Solution Design

Figure 15.9 shows the graphical representation of the data integration and data training of the RADAR scenario. Radar data are stored in binary format (bitmaps, 1 byte for each pixel). The radar data are read in two steps: first, we select which files to read according to the required date and time (operation Select range files); second, we read the actual data from a predefined location (Read raw

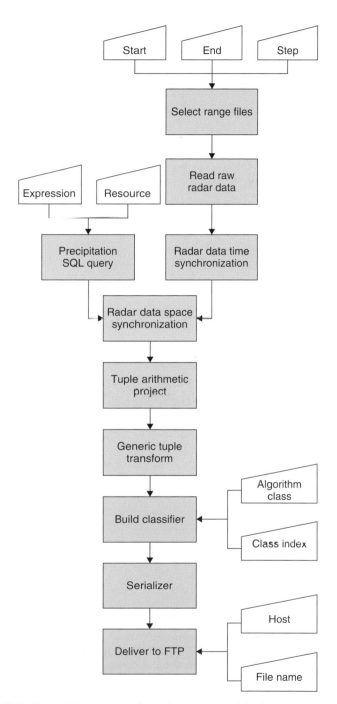

Figure 15.9 *The training process of the short-term precipitation prediction scenario.*

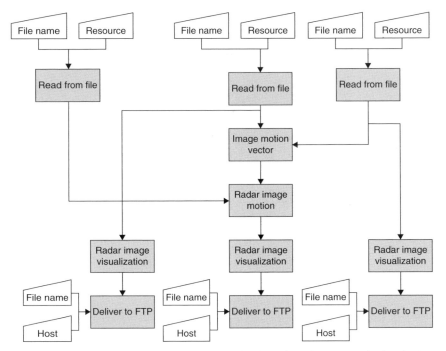

Figure 15.10   *The process of extraction and application of motion vectors in the short-term precipitation prediction scenario.*

radar data). Data from meteorological sensors are stored in and fetched from a relational database. The data are merged and synchronized by their date and time, then a classifier is built and stored in a repository for later use in the actual prediction process.

In the second part of this scenario, we first have to extrapolate the radar observations by extracting motion vectors from the observations we have. This process is shown in Figure 15.10. Two successive radar observations are read from the repository (Read from file, the motion vector describing the change that occurred between them is computed in Image motion vector, and then applied to the latter image to extrapolate it into the future with Radar image motion. This product is again stored in the repository. In this manner, we create predictions for a short time ahead—no more than 2 h, as after that the extrapolation becomes unusable.

The final part of this scenario then uses the trained model from the first step on the future radar images created in the second step and produces predictions of precipitation, as is shown in Figure 15.11.

15.6   SCENARIO 3: SVP

This scenario is the most complex of the three experiments described here. It uses a statistical approach to do what the original FFSC application did—predict

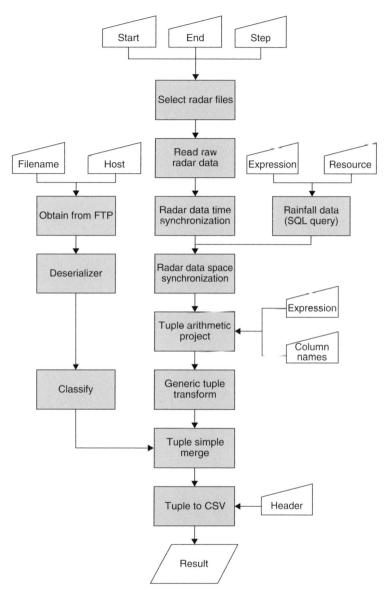

Figure 15.11 *Prediction process in the short-term precipitation prediction scenario.*

floods. Predicting floods using physical simulation models is extremely complex. Our thesis is that a statistical approach may prove more effective. It is certainly more robust than simulation in the face of incomplete input data.

For this experiment, we make use of 10 years of historical data from the Vah cascade of waterworks from SWE, 9 years of meteorological data (precipitation, temperature, wind) computed by the ALADIN model at the SHMI, and hydrological data from the river Vah (again from the SHMI). In addition, we have measurements of soil capacity for water retention, courtesy of the Institute of Hydrology of the Slovak Academy of Sciences.[5] We base our efforts on the theory that the amount of precipitation that actually reaches the river basin and contributes to the water level of the river is influenced by actual precipitation and its short-term history, by water retention capacity of the soil, and, to a lesser extent, by the evapotranspiration effect.

In our experiment, the aim is to predict water flow into the Orava reservoir at the head of the Orava river, the site of the first scenario as shown in Figure 15.2. This inflow is very important for waterworks manipulation and also is one of the basic factors for flood prediction downstream. Once the model for inflow to the reservoir is created, we can use its output for further models at downstream sites in the same way that we did in the first scenario.

15.6.1   Solution Design

Datasets with very similar structures are needed for the training and prediction steps of both models. Historical air temperatures and rainfalls at the Orava reservoir are obtained from the SWE waterworks data. Future values can be calculated by the ALADIN model. As data used in this scenario have different periods (from hourly for the air temperature to weekly for snow levels), data aggregation and interpolation must be applied to achieve the required time synchronization between datasets.

The data integration process is shown in Figure 15.12. Subsequently, in Figure 15.13, the data are filtered and snow information is interpolated (as snow cover measurements occur only once every 14 days). Invalid rows are removed, and two different models are trained—a linear regression model and a decision tree model. These are then stored in the repository for later use in the prediction phase.

The predictor and target variables are shown in Table 15.3. The target variable—water flow into the reservoir—is predicted using two models. The first, a snowmelt model, is used to predict the snow level on a given day using the temperature, rainfall, and snow level of the previous day. This is a linear regression model. The second, a runoff model, is used to predict the flow into the reservoir from the rainfall, snowmelt levels (from the previous model), and the flow from the previous day. This model uses a decision tree with the M5P training algorithm [13].

As a validation method, we use 20-fold cross validation. These two models are trained on 10 years of historical data and are stored in the repository. The prediction process is implemented by sequentially applying the classifiers—the snow model and flow model—for each predicted day.

Once again, our aim in this scenario is to provide a predictive model of river and reservoir levels to allow water services managers to take better decisions with respect to storage and release. Such models, validated against historical data, could prove valuable tools in the design of improved outflow and inflow schedules for

---

[5]Ústav hydrológie Slovenskej akadémie vied, http://www.ih.savba.sk/index.html.

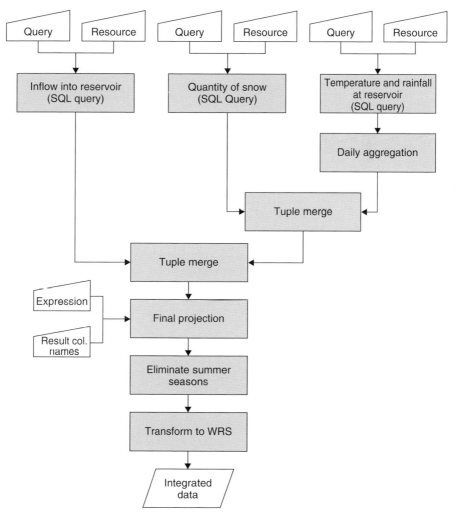

Figure 15.12 *The data integration process of the SVP inflow prediction scenario.*

water management stations not only on the Orava but also on any major river system.

15.7 NEW TECHNOLOGIES FOR ENVIRONMENTAL DATA MINING

The DISPEL language allows us to describe the processes in each of the three environmental risk scenarios at a high level of abstraction, independently of any low level concerns regarding the underlying enactment engines, databases, or any consideration of the distributed environment. Our experiments have made use of

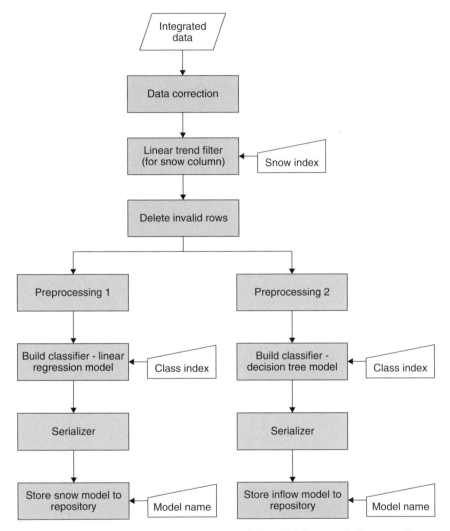

Figure 15.13 *The model training process of the SVP inflow prediction scenario.*

several interconnected gateways, which together provide all the necessary data, processing elements, and visualization tools that our scenarios require.

This novel approach allows us to easily extend the FFSC infrastructure to new data providers by deploying a gateway at the site of the new provider and registering it with the other gateways. Then, when a data analysis expert creates a DISPEL document that makes use of one of the capabilities provided by this gateway, it can be accessed and integrated automatically into the overall knowledge discovery workflow.

In addition, this approach allows us to use remote high performance, data-mining tools or to access other data storage facilities.

TABLE 15.3 Input and Target Variables in the SVP Inflow Prediction Process

Date	Temperature	Rainfall	Snow$_{prev}$	Snow	Inflow$_{prev}$	Inflow
$t-1$	$T(t-1)$	$R(t-1)$		$S(t-1)$		$F(t-1)$
t	$T(t)$	$R(t)$	$P(t)$	$S(t)$	$I(t)$	$F(t)$
$t+1$	$T(t+1)$	$R(t+1)$	$P(t+1)$	$S(t+1)$	$I(t+1)$	$F(t+1)$
$t+2$	$T(t+2)$	$R(t+2)$	$P(t+2)$	$S(t+2)$	$I(t+2)$	$F(t+2)$
$t+3$	$T(t+3)$	$R(t+3)$	$P(t+3)$	$S(t+3)$	$I(t+3)$	$F(t+3)$
$t+4$	$T(t+4)$	$R(t+4)$	$P(t+4)$	$S(t+4)$	$I(t+4)$	$F(t+4)$

This model provides a clear separation of responsibilities between data-intensive engineers, data analysis experts, and the domain experts of the application. The underlying infrastructure and gateway network is managed by the data-intensive engineers. The data analysis experts use DISPEL to create full knowledge discovery workflows, which *utilize* the infrastructure without needing to *understand* it. In turn, these workflows are used by the domain experts via specialized domain-specific portals, in a very similar manner to that described in Chapter 14.

Apart from separating the concerns of the involved stakeholders, this approach also separates the technology into fairly independent layers, and so a tuned DISPEL document will work even when the infrastructure changes significantly, provided that the infrastructure is still capable of providing all of the processing elements referenced by the document.

This approach also provides for a reasonable amount of fault tolerance. If one data center becomes unavailable, it may conceivably be replaced transparently by a different one, without the final users of our product ever knowing it happened. Some centers and gateways are, of course, irreplaceable in a given network (primary data storage centers, for instance), but data filters may be deployed at several locations to enhance redundancy. There may also be several high-performance computing (HPC) facilities available to a given user, so the temporary inaccessibility of one of them is no issue—the DISPEL description of the required data-oriented solution is entirely agnostic of such things.

15.8 SUMMARY: LESSONS LEARNED

Environmental data are important inputs to a host of daily simulation and prediction tasks, which are themselves important to our society and have a long history of development. As an alternative to large, expensive, and complex simulations, data analytics and distributed data integration may prove a useful new avenue of exploration.

A data analysis process may be designed, trained, verified, and deployed in a significantly shorter time, and with much less expertise at hand, than is necessary for a physical simulation model. Also, a data analysis process may be designed in a way that is less prone to failure due to inconsistent or faulty data and may degrade more gracefully, as the quality of the input data becomes poorer.

Using historic data to train the model, that is, using the response of the system to driving conditions on a prior occasion as a predictor, this approach does not require full discovery of all the mechanisms at work. It may fail when the driving conditions are far from those previously recorded, and hence, long-term observations and records are essential for this approach. Modeling is essential if the goal is to understand rather than manage. For example, a model would be needed to predict the likely impact on the flooding hazard of a proposed civil engineering activity that modified a river's profile and banks.

Thus, domain experts may benefit significantly from a statistical, data analytical approach, especially in experimental environmental management scenarios. Using this approach, we can extract, stream, mine, and present data in complex scenarios much more quickly than is customary in this field. A quick assessment of a given hydrometeorological situation, supported by actual data obtained from a data-mining model, may be crucial to proper decision making during the handling of a potential environmental disaster such as a major river flooding.

Apart from the increased speed of prediction, another benefit of our approach lies in the ability of data mining to cover situations for which there are no suitable physical models available, or where their configuration would be too costly. Several such scenarios have been proposed by hydrological and meteorological experts, and we have developed and deployed the tools and infrastructure necessary for their experimental evaluation.

The data-mining approach to environmental risk management naturally has its own disadvantages. While a classical mathematical simulation of a weather process may be designed in a way that makes it possible to predict weather extremes occurring only rarely, a data-mining model needs to be trained with all the possible scenarios we might expect it to predict. If a certain situation has not been observed and is therefore not included in the model training set, we cannot expect the model to be able to recognize such situations in new data and produce meaningful results.

Our experimental implementation of several hydrometeorological scenarios as distributed data integration and knowledge discovery processes has taught us several lessons:

- With the increased adoption of broadband Internet access by hydrometeorological authorities and with the increasing employment of personnel accustomed to using such infrastructure, it has become easier to negotiate online access to original, live databases holding weather data. The INSPIRE Directive aims to remove most obstacles to instant access to environmental data in the European Union [5].
- Distributed data integration is feasible in the hydrometeorological domain and may provide important benefits over the traditional CRISP-DM methodology.[6] With the ever-wider adoption of Web-based, service-oriented technologies and the (slowly) progressing development of the INSPIRE suite of technological

[6]CRoss Industry Standard Process for Data Mining, www.crisp-dm.org.

standards for environmental data management, it is also becoming easier to implement, as more tools and services are readily available.

- A high level, data-intensive processing language is crucial in deploying a successful cross-organizational knowledge discovery process. Without it, the complexities of managing a set of process components deployed in several different administrative domains may prove too cumbersome and time consuming for the activity to be maintainable over a longer period of time. With a high level process description, once it is in place and finalized, the day-to-day management of the process components may be more localized and the communication between different groups may become less crucial.
- Distributed data management scales well, both logically and geographically, and the processes developed using this architecture are easy to maintain—we can add to them without disturbing the existing flow of data, we can experiment with them using parallel streams, and we can add more data sources without having to consult existing ones. We can also develop the workflows in an incremental manner—if we change the process, we need to change only the relevant part of the workflow without having to start from scratch.

The suite of scenarios described in this chapter could also be applied in a different geographical area, on a different river or for a different reservoir, provided the data for the new area is made available and accessible through a DISPEL-aware gateway network. In practical terms, to add another application scenario, one has only to provide the data sources and a DISPEL description of the scenario's knowledge discovery process, together with any specialized processing elements that are not found in the current component registry. All of the infrastructure already developed and deployed can be effortlessly reused and incorporated into the new scenario.

It remains to be seen whether the approach is sufficiently robust that it will scale up to transnational hydrographic and environmental tasks, such as modeling the whole of the Danube river and its tributaries. The progress with INSPIRE makes this a tantalizing possibility, though there would also be many socioeconomic and political issues operating at that scale.

REFERENCES

1. M. Yokokawa, K. Itakura, A. Uno, T. Ishihara, and Y. Kaneda, "16.4-tflops direct numerical simulation of turbulence by a fourier spectral method on the earth simulator," *SC Conference*, vol. 0, p. 50, 2002.

2. P. K. Rao, S. J. Holmes, R. K. Anderson, J. S. Winston, and P. E. Lehr, *Weather Satellites: Systems, Data and Environmental Applications*. Boston, MA, American Meteorological Society, 1990.

3. B. Mason, "Numerical weather prediction," *Contemporary Physics*, vol. 27, pp. 463–472, 1986.

4. L. Hluchý, O. Habala, B. Simo, J. Astalos, V. Tran, and M. Dobrucky, "Problem-solving environment for flood forecasting," *Management of Environmental Quality: An International Journal*, vol. 15, pp. 268–275, 2003.

5. EU Parliament, "Directive 2007/2/EC of the European Parliament and of the Council of 14 March 2007 establishing an Infrastructure for Spatial Information in the European Community (INSPIRE)," *Official Journal of the European Union*, vol. 50, April 2007.

6. L. Hluchý, M. Šeleng, O. Habala, and P. Krammer, "Mining Environmental Data in Hydrological Scenarios," pp. 1988–2992, 2010.

7. L. Hluchý, O. Habala, M. Šeleng, P. Krammer, and V. Tran, "Using advanced data mining and integration in environmental risk management," in 2011 IEEE 9th International Symposium on Applied Machine Intelligence and Informatics (SAMI), pp. 49–54, January 2011.

8. J. Bartok, O. Habala, P. Bednar, M. Gazak, and L. Hluchý, "Data mining and integration for predicting significant meteorological phenomena," in *ICCS 2010—INternational Conference on Computational Science*, vol. 1 of Procedia Computer Science, pp. 37–46, Elsevier, 2010.

9. L. Hluchý, P. Krammer, O. Habala, M. Šeleng, and V. Tran, "Advanced data integration and data mining for environmental scenarios," in 2010 12th International Symposium on Symbolic and Numeric Algorithms for Scientific Computing (SYNASC), pp. 400–406, September 2010.

10. M. Ciglan, O. Habala, V. Tran, L. Hluchý, M. Kremler, and M. Gera, 'Application of ADMIRE data mining and integration technologies in environmental scenarios," in *Parallel Processing and Applied Mathematics, Part II*, vol. 6068 of Lecture Notes in Computer Science (R. Wyrzykowski, J. Dongarra, K. Karczewski, and J. Wasniewski, eds), pp. 165–173, Springer, 2010.

11. L. Hluchý, O. Habala, V. Tran, and M. Ciglan, "Hydro-meteorological scenarios using advanced data mining and integration," in Sixth International Conference on Fuzzy Systems and Knowledge Discovery, 2009. FSKD '09, vol. 7, pp. 260–264, August 2009.

12. World Meteorological Organization, "GRIB (GRIdded Binary) format," http://www.wmo.int/pages/prog/www/WMOCodes.html. Accessed 28th April 2011.

13. J. Quinlan, "Learning with continuous classes," in *Proceedings of the Australian Joint Conference on Artificial Intelligence*, pp. 343–348, Singapore, World Scientific, 1992.

16

Analyzing Gene Expression Imaging Data in Developmental Biology

Liangxiu Han

School of Computing, Mathematics & Digital Technology, Manchester Metropolitan University, Manchester, UK

Jano van Hemert

Optos plc, Queensferry House, Dunfermline, UK

Ian Overton

Medical Research Council, Human Genetics Unit, Edinburgh, UK

Paolo Besana

School of Informatics, University of Edinburgh, Edinburgh, UK

Richard Baldock

Medical Research Council, Human Genetics Unit, Edinburgh, UK

This chapter describes the application of data-intensive methods to the automatic identification and annotation of gene expression patterns in the mouse embryo.

Understanding the regulatory and developmental mechanisms for multicellular organisms requires detailed knowledge of gene interactions and expression. The

The DATA Bonanza: Improving Knowledge Discovery in Science, Engineering, and Business, First Edition.
Edited by Malcolm Atkinson, Rob Baxter, Michelle Galea, Mark Parsons, Peter Brezany, Oscar Corcho, Jano van Hemert, and David Snelling.
© 2013 John Wiley & Sons, Inc. Published 2013 by John Wiley & Sons, Inc.

availability of large datasets with both spatial and ontological annotation of the spatiotemporal patterns of gene expression in mouse embryos provides a powerful resource to discover the biological function of embryo organization. These datasets represent a significant challenge for automated analysis and here we present two analysis scenarios that test existing data-intensive systems.

The ontological annotation of gene expressions entails labeling images with terms from the anatomical ontology for mouse development. If the spatial genes of an anatomical component are expressed in an image, the image is then tagged as having that anatomical component. Currently, annotation is done manually by domain experts, a process that is both time consuming and costly. In addition, the level of detail is variable and, inevitably, errors arise from the tedious nature of the task.

Section 16.1 introduces ideas behind modern computational and systems biology, how the explosion of data in the postgenomic world has led to new possibilities and even greater challenges. The particular computational biology problem that we focus on here—annotating images of gene expression with the right anatomical terms—is described in more depth in Section 16.2, while an automated solution based on data-intensive methods is discussed in Section 16.3. Section 16.4 looks ahead to the biological significance and systems biology application of these approaches, and Section 16.4.1 describes a large-scale challenge and possible series of experiments with a novel data-intensive computational architecture.

16.1 UNDERSTANDING BIOLOGICAL FUNCTION

Computation has long been involved in the understanding of biological process and function. The history of computational biology includes the tackling of complex problems in understanding the detailed behavior of individual cells such as neuronal firing [1, 2] through to morphological shape [3] and pattern formation [4]. These and other pioneering studies have developed into the field of systems biology that covers the range from molecular and cellular biology through to the modeling of physiology and developmental processes such as shape formation and differentiation.

With the development of approaches to capture "omics" data, including genome, transcriptome, and proteome-wide measurements, the scientific field of bioinformatics has emerged. Primarily concerned with management, analysis, and visualization of biological data, this field has now "exploded," coupling high-throughput data capture with sophisticated modeling and data mining.

Organism-level data is of particular interest in showing detailed patterns of biological activity. At the organism level, whole organ data is typically captured by microscopy imaging for high resolution data (confocal, optical projection tomography, μMRI, μCT, multiphoton, etc.) or ultrasound for larger samples. This trend has been extended to very large-scale imaging at the ultrastructural scale of neural tissues to elucidate the detailed "connectomics" and synaptic organization of real neural networks. A dataset generated by block-face imaging using electron microscopy could have a resolution of a few tens of nanometers, and the size of a single three-dimensional image can extend to terabytes.

Analysis and mining of these data will depend on how aspects of the information content or signal can be annotated. This could be via mapping of the signal (or structure) onto, for example, anatomical ontologies, or by direct spatial mapping onto reference atlases. It is also likely that data-mining approaches can bypass the annotation step and use data features established by the training of classifiers in either supervised or unsupervised modes. These options will provide complementary views of the underlying data and deliver different analysis capabilities. In all, cases coupling the new systems approaches for modeling biology to large image data volumes will provide novel challenges to the underlying computer science and informatics because of the tight coupling between large volume data and high performance computing. Biology will provide very complex use cases for the field of data-intensive research that will certainly challenge current approaches.

In this chapter, we illustrate this with a "simple" example of the automation of the annotation of spatial patterns of expression of protein coding and microRNA genes in the developing mouse embryo.

One approach to understanding the role of the expression of a given gene and interactions between genes in the developmental processes of multicellular organisms requires monitoring the gene expression levels and spatial distributions on a large scale. Two high-throughput methods have been widely used to curate gene expression at different developmental stages of organisms, including DNA microarrays [5, 6] and RNA *in situ* hybridization (ISH) [7–9]. Microarray techniques, and more recently RNA sequencing, measure gene expression levels of a large number of genes for a tissue sample or cell, but at poor spatial resolution. RNA ISH uses specific gene probes to detect and visualize spatiotemporal information of particular target genes in tissues. The result of RNA ISH consists of images of sections of tissue stained to reveal the presence of gene expression patterns. To understand gene functions and the interactions between genes in depth, we need to transform the raw image data into detailed knowledge. One approach entails the labeling of images with ontological terms corresponding to anatomical components. For every anatomical component that shows expression in the image, the image is labeled with that anatomical component using an ontology that describes the developing mouse embryo.

Much effort has been devoted to the curation of gene-expression patterns in developmental biology. For example, the Eurexpress project [8] has built a transcriptome-wide atlas for the developing mouse embryo established by RNA *in situ* hybridization; it has so far collected more than 18,000 genes at one development stage of wild type murine embryos and has curated 4 TB of images. In this chapter, we use the large Eurexpress dataset of more than 350,000 images to explore two data-intensive research applications. The first concerns the automated annotation of spatial gene expression patterns; the second involves the analysis of image data to infer putative genetic interactions and control networks.

16.2 GENE IMAGE ANNOTATION

Most annotation is manually curated, although with the increasing automation of instruments to measure ISH, leading to a significant increase in data volumes, it is becoming increasingly difficult and inefficient for domain experts to entirely rely on manual annotation. Thus, we have developed an automatic method for the annotation of spatial gene expression patterns. Some existing studies have developed methods for annotating images from fruit fly [10–15] and adult mouse brain [16]. These annotations have provided potential opportunities for further genetic analysis. Here, we address gene expression for mouse embryos, a difficult challenge because of the variability of the data presentation and the complexity of the anatomy of this embryo.

Our image annotation solution uses a method that combines image processing and machine learning. We use image processing to preprocess images and feed the results to a machine-learning method to construct classification models for automatic annotation.

To cope with issues that arise in multianatomical components coexisting in images, we have designed a set of binary classifiers, one for each anatomical component. The main advantage is the strong extensibility of the framework.

We evaluate our method on image data from the Eurexpress study where we use it to automatically classify nine anatomical terms: humerus, handplate, fibula, tibia, femur, ribs, petrous part, scapula, and head mesenchyme. The accuracy of our method lies between 70% and 80% with few exceptions.

16.2.1 Data Description and Challenges

The Eurexpress project uses an automated process for ISH experiments on all genes of whole-mount mouse embryos at Theiler Stage 23.[1] The results are the images of embryo sections that are stained to reveal where mRNA is present—where genes are being expressed. These images are then annotated by human curators. The annotation involves selecting from 1,500 terms representing anatomical components, which are then used to label each image if and only if the image exhibits gene expression in the whole or part of that component. This manual annotation is very time-consuming and thus far has only involved the "simpler" regionally expressed patterns, that is, it has not covered expression over a large proportion of the embryo. This means that about 30% of the images are annotated with anatomical terms, about 50% are deemed "ubiquitous" or "no detected pattern," and about 20% are not annotated at all. For this study, the regional expression patterns that have been annotated are used to train the classifiers, which ultimately can be applied to all of the remaining images. The input to our method is a set of image files and annotations, the output will be a set of classifiers to enable the identification of all anatomical components that exhibit gene expression patterns for each image.

---

[1]Prenatal mouse development is divided into 26 Theiler Stages, after [17]. Stage 23 is illustrated at http://www.emouseatlas.org/Databases/Anatomy/Diagrams/ts23/, verified October 2011.

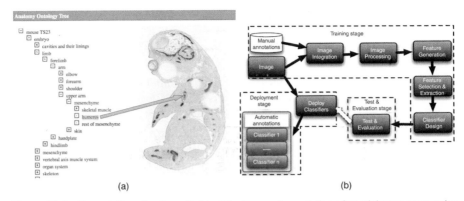

(a)   (b)

Figure 16.1 Formulation of automatic identification and annotation of spatial gene expression patterns. (a) Annotating an image using a term from the anatomy ontology for the developing mouse embryo. (b) High level overview of the method for automatic annotation of images from ISH studies. Source: Reprinted from [18] by permission of Oxford University Press.

This is a typical pattern recognition task. As shown in Figure 16.1a, first we need to identify the features of "humerus" in the embryo image and then annotate the image using the ontology terms listed on the left side.

We had to overcome three major challenges to automate the process of the annotation:

1. The images created from RNA ISH experiments include variations arising from natural variation in embryos and technical variation from processing and capturing material. The same anatomical components, therefore, may have variable shape, location, and orientation.

2. Each image for a given gene will, in general, be annotated with multiple anatomical terms. This means that features for multiple components coexist in the image, which increases the difficulty of discrimination. Hence, if two components often exhibit gene expression in the same image, it will be hard to discriminate between them.

3. The number of images associated with a given anatomy term is distributed unevenly. Some terms may be associated with many images and others with only a few.

16.3   AUTOMATED ANNOTATION OF GENE EXPRESSION IMAGES

To annotate images automatically, the following three stages are required. At the *Training stage*, the classification model has to be built using a training set of image datasets complete with human annotations. At the *Test & Evaluation stage*, the performance of the classification model has to be evaluated in terms of accuracy. Finally, when the performance is satisfactory, the *Deployment stage* involves applying the model to perform classification on images without annotation.

The training stage divides into a number of subtasks, as illustrated in Figure 16.1b.

Image Integration. Before we can perform machine learning, we need to integrate data from different sources. Manual annotations are stored in a database and the images are located in a file system. The result of this integration process is a set of images with annotations.

Image Processing. The dimensions of the images are variable. We apply median filtering and image rescaling to reduce image noise and rescale the images to a standard size. The output of this process is a set of standardized and denoised images. These images can be represented as two-dimensional arrays, $m \times n$.

Feature Generation. After image preprocessing, we generate features that represent different gene expression patterns in the images using a wavelet transform method. The features again are represented as two-dimensional arrays, $m \times n$.

Feature Selection & Extraction. Owing to the large number of features, the feature arrays must be reduced before we can construct a classifier. This can be done by either feature selection or feature extraction, or a combination of both. Feature selection selects a subset of the most significant features for constructing classifiers. Feature extraction performs a transformation on the original features to achieve dimensional reduction and obtain representative feature vectors for constructing classifiers.

Classifier Design. The main task is to annotate images with the correct anatomical terms. As gene patterns in images will typically express in several anatomical components, we must construct classifiers that can discriminate between patterns in different components. Here, we have formulated this multiclass problem as a two-class problem. Namely, we construct a set of binary classifiers where each classifier will aim to decide for one anatomical component whether that component exhibits gene expression. In other words, the result of such a classifier is either "detected" or "not detected" gene expression.

The test and evaluation stage will use the result from the training stage to validate the accuracy of classifiers. During this stage, k-fold cross validation is used for evaluating the classification performance (see Section 10.8.2 in Part III for a general discussion of the k-fold cross-validation pattern).

With k-fold cross validation, the sample dataset is randomly split into k disjoint subsets. For each subset, we construct a classifier using the data in $k - 1$ subsets and then evaluate the classifier's performance on the data in the kth subset. Thus, each record of the dataset is used once and only once to evaluate the performance of a classifier. If 10-fold validation is used, we can build 10 classifiers, each trained on 90% of the data and each evaluated on a different 10% of the data. This process is essential to guard against unlucky distributions of training and testing datasets and to prevent the overall classifier from overfitting its performance on one training set.

The deployment stage deals with the configuration of how the classifiers are deployed, that is, how classifiers are applied to add annotation to images that have not yet been annotated.

16.3.1 Data-Intensive Solution with DISPEL

The implementation of the automated annotation workflow provided an effective demonstration of the features of DISPEL discussed in Chapter 3, Section 3.8. Firstly, the data-intensive architecture enabled the data analysis experts to focus on designing their computations in DISPEL while leaving the enactment engine to deal with the complexity present in actual execution. This complexity included the retrieval of data from heterogeneous data sources (i.e., databases, file systems, repository), the deployment and execution on distributed enactment engines, and the storage of results back at the relevant data sources; all of these were successfully hidden from the analysis expert. Secondly, the DISPEL request uses an off-the-shelf k-fold cross-validation function to train and test the classifier. Altogether, three DISPEL requests were created to perform both training and testing stage: data preparation, feature selection, and k-fold cross validation.

As mentioned in Section 16.2.1, the raw images include both natural and technical variations, and each image is expected to be annotated with multiple anatomical terms (the same image will be used multiple times for training different classifiers). Thus, the first DISPEL request is for *data preparation*, which comprises the first three subtasks described in the previous section: image integration, image preprocessing, and feature generation. The generated features are stored in a file repository, while the metadata are stored in a features database. Images can be preprocessed independently, thus allowing parallel execution; the dataset is divided into multiple subsets based on the number of available execution engines.

At this point, all of the images are preprocessed and features are generated. The second DISPEL request, *feature selection*, is submitted to select the most significant subset of the features for constructing a particular anatomical classifier, defined by one of the parameters. Figure 12.2 (in Chapter 12) shows part of the workflow graph produced from this DISPEL request. We have two implementations for the FisherRatio PE (processing element): sequential and parallel. The parallel implementation splits the computation into two parts. The first part computes the median and standard deviation calculation on a given subset of the dataset (retrieved from the repository) using a StandardDeviationCalculation PE on each of the execution engines. The second part then combines all of these calculations using a StandardDeviationCombine PE and completes the Fisher Ratio computation using FisherRatioParallel PE. The result is returned to the repository.

The final DISPEL request trains and tests a classifier using the k-fold cross-validation function makeCrossValidator, found in the package dispel .datamining.kdd, as shown in Figure 16.2. We developed three application-specific PEs for this workflow: TrainClassifier, Classify, and Eval from the package book.examples.eurexpress. The gray box in Figure 16.3 shows instances of these PEs for each "fold" (see Chapter 10, Section 10.8.2 for the discussion of the

```
1    package book.examples.eurexpress {
2      use dispel.db.SQLQuery;
3      ...
4      use dispel.datamining.kdd.Validator;
5      use dispel.datamining.kdd.makeCrossValidator;
6      use book.examples.eurexpress.FeatureExtraction;
7      use book.examples.eurexpress.TrainClassifier;
8      use book.examples.eurexpress.Classify;
9      use book.examples.eurexpress.Eval;
10
11     // Specify query expression and data sources
12     String expression  = "select euxassay_id, case when " +
13                          "embryo_limb_forelimb_arm_upper_arm_mesenchyme_humerus" +
14                          " < 5 then 0 else 1 end from annotation";
15     String repository  = "http://admire4.epcc.ed.ac.uk:8080/AdmireRepository";
16     String annotationDbSource = "AnnotationDb";
17     String featureDbSource    = "GeneratedFeatureDb";
18     String selectionDbSource  = "SelectedFeatureDb";
19
20     // Create a cross validator PE.
21     PE<Validator> CrossValidator
22        = makeCrossValidator(10, TrainClassifier, Classify, Eval);
23
24     // Make instances of PEs for workflows.
25     SQLQuery annotationQuery = new SQLQuery;
26     ...
27     TupleBuild builder = new TupleBuild;
28     CrossValidator validator = new CrossValidator;
29     Results        results   = new Results;
30
31     // Connect workflow.
32     |- expression -| => annotationQuery.expression;
33     |- annotationDbSource -| => annotationQuery.source;
34     ... // extract significant features to construct dataset <features,class>
35     builder.output => validator.data;
36     validator.results => results.input;
37     |- "Classifier Scores" -| => results.name;
38
39     // Submit workflow.
40     submit results;
41   }
```

Figure 16.2 *A DISPEL request to run 10-fold cross validation for an anatomical component classifier.*

k-fold cross-validation function). The desired anatomical component to be classified is defined in line 13. Lines 15–18 define the sources of the data.

16.3.2   Image Processing

We first obtain training datasets by integrating both images and manual annotations using a database SQL query to specify which images will be included. These images are filtered and standardized to a uniform size suitable for the feature generation process. We use a median filter to remove noise from images [19]. The median filter is nonlinear, its advantage over the traditional linear filter being its ability to

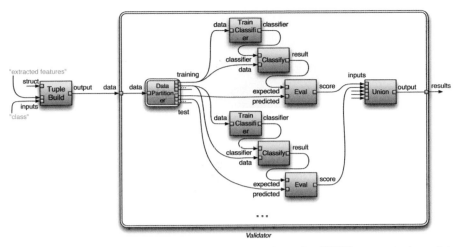

Figure 16.3 *Part of the DISPEL graph generated from the DISPEL request showed in Figure 16.2.*

eliminate noise values with extremely large magnitudes. The median filter replaces a pixel using the median of its neighboring pixels' values.

Given a two-dimensional image, the value of a pixel is represented as $f_0(m_0, n_0)$, a neighborhood of f_0 is represented as K and a pixel value in k is represented as $f(m, n)$. The median filter can then be expressed mathematically as

$$f_0'(m_0, n_0) = median\{f(m, n), (m, n) \in K\}$$

Figure 16.4 shows the result of an image (a) before and (b) after the median filter. The filtered image is much smoother than the original image.

In addition to the median filter, we also standardize the image dimensions so that the images can all be processed by the methods used in the feature generation step.

16.3.3 Feature Generation

To characterize multiple spatial gene expression patterns in embryo images, we use wavelet transforms to generate features. The wavelet transform is well known as a powerful tool for applications in signal and image processing [20, 21]. There are two major reasons for using the wavelet transforms here. Firstly, it provides a mathematical method for the hierarchical decomposition of functions to obtain a projective decomposition of the data into different scales, thereby extracting locality information. This contrasts with Fourier transforms that only yield global information in the frequency domain. Using wavelet transforms, an image can be decomposed into different subimages at subbands (different resolution levels). As the resolutions of the subimages are reduced, the computational complexity will be reduced.

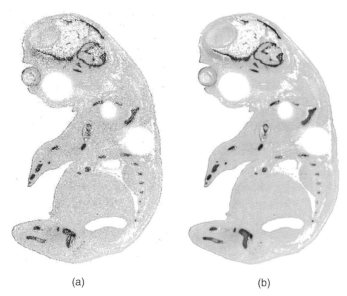

(a)   (b)

Figure 16.4 *An example to show the effect of a mouse embryo image (a) before and (b) after the median filter. Source: Reprinted from Reference 18 by permission of Oxford University Press.*

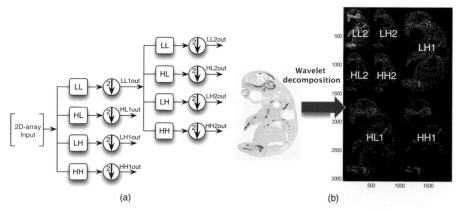

(a)   (b)

Figure 16.5 *An example of the process and result of wavelet decomposition. (a) Wavelet decomposition on a two-dimensional array. (b) Wavelet decomposition on an image. Source: Reprinted from Reference 18 by permission of Oxford University Press.*

The wavelet transform of a signal can be imagined as an input passing through a series of filters with down sampling applied at each stage to derive output signals based on scales (resolution levels). Figure 16.5a shows the filter representation using the wavelet transform on a 2D array input. The *LL* is a low–low pass filter that is a coarser transform of the original two-dimensional input, and a circle with an arrow means downsampling by a factor of 2; *HL* is a high–low pass filter that transforms the input along the vertical direction; *LH* is a low–high pass filter that transforms the input along the horizontal direction; and *HH* is a high–high pass filter that transforms the input along the diagonal direction. This process is applied iteratively, which leads to decomposition of the initial input signal into different subbands.

Mathematically, for a signal $f(x, y)$ with two-dimensional array $M \times N$, the wavelet transform is the result of applying filters at different resolution levels, calculated as follows:

$$W_\phi(j_0, m, n) = \frac{1}{\sqrt{MN}} \sum_{x=0}^{M-1} \sum_{y=0}^{N-1} f(x, y)\phi_{j_0,m,n}(x, y) \qquad (16.1)$$

$$W_\psi^i(j, m, n) = \frac{1}{\sqrt{MN}} \sum_{x=0}^{M-1} \sum_{y=0}^{N-1} f(x, y)\psi_{j,m,n}^i(x, y) \qquad (16.2)$$

where i is {horizontal, vertical, diagonal}, $W_\phi(j_0, m, n)$ is the low pass output and $W_\psi^i(j, m, n)$, respectively, represents the other three combinations of low and high pass outputs when the wavelet decomposition is performed along the vertical, horizontal, and diagonal direction. j_0 is a scale start point. $\phi_(j_0, m, n)$ and $\psi_{j,m,n}$ are wavelet basis functions. In this case, we use Daubecheis wavelet basis functions (db3) [22].

An example of a wavelet transform of an embryo image at the second resolution level is shown in Figure 16.5b. The image is decomposed into four subbands or subimages. The subbands *LH1*, *HL1*, and *HH1*, are the transformations of the image along horizontal, vertical, and diagonal directions with the higher frequency component of the image. After applying the filters, the wavelet transform of *LL1* is further carried out for the second level resolution as *LL2*, *LH2*, *HL2*, and *HH2*. If the resolution of the image is $3,040 \times 1,900$, the dimension of subimages are downsampled by a factor of 2 at the second resolution level and are, respectively, *LL2* (760×475), *LH2* (760×475), *HL2* (760×475), *HH* (760×475), *LH1* $(1,520 \times 950)$, *HL1* $(1,520 \times 950)$, and *HH1* $(1,520 \times 950)$. The number of coefficients from the total wavelet transform—these are the features—for this image is $3,040 \times 1,900 = 5,776,000$.

16.3.4 Feature Selection and Classifier Construction

Owing to the large number of high dimensional features generated in the previous subtask, it is necessary to select the most discriminating features before proceeding. We use Fisher ratio analysis [23] for feature selection and extraction. The Fisher ratio finds a separation space to discriminate features of two classes by maximizing the difference between classes and minimizing differences within each class.

We construct a classifier for each anatomical component and formulate our multiclass problem as a two-class problem; that is, for each anatomical component we create a training dataset that is divided into two classes: one class containing all of the samples that exhibit spatial gene expression in part of the anatomical component in question and the other containing all of the samples without any gene expression in that component. In this case, we use linear discriminant analysis (LDA) [23]. For a given two-class problem ($C_1\{x_1, \ldots, x_i, \ldots, x_n\}$ and $C_2\{y_1, \ldots, y_i, \ldots, y_m\}$), the linear discriminant function can be formulated as

$$f(X) = W^T X + w_0 \tag{16.3}$$

The goal is to find W (a weight vector) and w_0 (a threshold) so that if $f(X) \geq 0$, then X is in class C_1 and if $f(X) < 0$ then X is in C_2. The idea is to find a hyperplane that can separate these two classes. To achieve this, we need to maximize the target function denoted by

$$T(W) = \frac{|W^T S_B W|}{|W^T S_W W|} \tag{16.4}$$

where S_W is called the *within*-class scatter matrix and S_B is the *between*-class scatter matrix. They are defined, respectively, as

$$S_B = (m_1 - m_2)(m_1 - m_2)^T \tag{16.5}$$

where m_1 is the mean of $x_i \in C_1$ and m_2 is the mean of $y_i \in C_2$.

$$S_W = S_1 + S_2 \tag{16.6}$$

where $S_1 = \sum_{x \in C_1} (X - m_1)(X - m_1)^T$ and $S_2 = \sum_{y \in C_2} (Y - m_2)(Y - m_2)^T$.

16.3.5   Experimental Setup and Evaluation Metrics

Currently, we have built nine classifiers for nine gene expressions of the nine target anatomical components and have evaluated our classifiers using 809 images. As described in Section 16.3, we use k-fold cross validation to test our approach.

We adopt both sensitivity and specificity as evaluation metrics to measure the classification performance. *Sensitivity* is the true positive rate that represents the proportion of actual positives in the test dataset, which are correctly predicted (i.e., those images that have gene expression in the anatomical component). *Specificity* is the true negative rate that represents the proportion of negatives that are correctly predicted (i.e., those images that do not have gene expression given the anatomical component). If both specificity and sensitivity are high, we can say that the accuracy of classification is good (Section 14.2.2).

Table 16.1 shows the results of 10-fold validation for nine anatomical components in terms of specificity and sensitivity as averaged over the 10-fold with a confidence interval of 95% around the average (in brackets). The confidence interval for specificity and sensitivity can be calculated as *average* $\pm$ *confidence*. The results clearly show that the proposed method for automatic classification

TABLE 16.1 A Comparison of Accuracy of Our Proposed Method with Four Well-Known Machine-Learning Methods for the Classification on Nine Anatomical Components

Anatomical Component	Our Proposed Method		SVM		LSVM		ANN		CNN	
	Sp	Se	Sp	Se	Sp	Se	Sp	Se	Sp	Se
Humerus	0.79 (0.04)	0.76 (0.04)	0.84	0.67	0.50	0.49	0.90	0.51	0.97	0.07
Handplate	0.79 (0.03)	0.66 (0.09)	1.00	0.03	0.67	0.75	0.57	0.54	1.00	0.00
Fibula	0.72 (0.03)	0.72 (0.07)	0.97	0.07	0.73	0.72	0.79	0.56	1.00	0.00
Tibia	0.74 (0.05)	0.75 (0.08)	0.94	0.27	0.75	0.74	0.90	0.51	1.00	0.00
Femur	0.72 (0.03)	0.72 (0.08)	0.97	0.24	0.56	0.65	0.88	0.49	1.00	0.00
Ribs	0.75 (0.03)	0.55 (0.06)	0.79	0.51	0.12	0.90	0.73	0.56	0.77	0.52
Petrous part	0.73 (0.03)	0.79 (0.06)	0.99	0.11	0.27	0.86	0.80	0.63	1.00	0.00
Scapula	0.71 (0.04)	0.79 (0.09)	0.99	0.06	0.73	0.73	0.82	0.56	1.00	0.00
Head mesenchyme	0.58 (0.03)	0.80 (0.09)	1.000	0.01	0.30	0.86	1.000	0.00	1.00	0.00

The sensitivity (Se) is the true positive rate. The specificity (Sp) is the true negative rate, with 95% confidence interval reported in brackets for the results of our proposed method.

works well, with the specificity and sensitivity between 70% and 80% for most components. The exceptions are head mesenchyme, where it is difficult to identify whether gene expression is present, and ribs, where it is difficult to identify whether gene expression is *not* present. We postulate that this could be a result of the particular shape and distributed nature of these anatomical components.

16.3.6 Comparative Study with Other Machine-Learning Methods

To help assess the effectiveness of our approach, we have evaluated the other well-known machine-learning algorithms, including SVM (support vector machine) [24], LSVM (Lagrangian support vector machines) [25], ANN (artificial neural networks) [26], and CNN (convolutional neural networks) [27].

The SVM is a classification method that uses a maximum margin hyperplane from a set of hyperplanes in a high dimensional space to separate two or more classes by distancing the plane from the closest data point of all classes. The LSVM is a specific SVM based on an iterative approach with the aim to speed up training.

The artificial neural network (ANN) is a nonlinear classification method inspired by the operation of biological neural networks. The neural network process samples one by one and compares the results calculated by the neural network with the known classification of samples. The errors are then fed back into the network in order to modify parameters for the next iteration until the output gets closer to the known correct classification of samples. There is another class called *convolutional neural networks* (CNN), which are often used in facial recognition. They provide nonlinear algorithms for feature extraction in hidden layers built into the ANN, which consider local receptive fields, shared weights, and spatial subsampling to achieve a certain degree of shift and distortion invariance [27].

We have computed both the sensitivity and specificity when using SVM, LSVM, ANN, and CNN to perform the pattern recognition task. We optimized the parameter settings for these algorithms and then performed the same k-fold cross validation as performed for our method. The results are shown in Table 16.1. When compared with results from our method, we conclude that our method outperforms the other four methods, as it provides the most consistent results across the anatomical components as well as the most balanced results between sensitivity and specificity. Note that it is easy to get a high sensitivity by classifying many images as positive, but this will lead to a low specificity. The results from SVM for handplate and head mesenchyme are good examples of this kind of unwanted behavior. Although SVM and LDA both use hyperplanes to separate two classes, their performance can be vastly different between problem domains. This is because they adopt different optimal criteria to find their hyperplanes. With SVM, it proved difficult to reach convergence in our experiments. Similarly, with CNN, we have poorer classification performance compared with the others; and again, it proved difficult to reach convergence with CNN. The overall classification performance is compared in Figure 16.6 by multiplying the specificity and sensitivity results of each method.

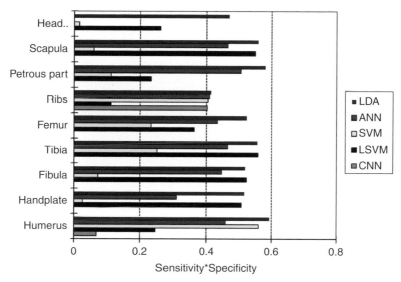

Figure 16.6 *The overall classification performance in terms of sensitivity × specificity (higher is better) of the five classification methods (LDA, SVM, LSVM, ANN, and CNN) for each anatomical component. Source: Reprinted from [18] by permission of Oxford University Press.*

16.4 EXPLOITATION AND FUTURE WORK

Genetic control of phenotype is mediated through an intricate mesh of interconnected networks rather than linear pathways [28, 29]. Many genes function in several subcellular processes (e.g., p53, GSK3β, IKKα, Gas2) [30-33], while some play seemingly opposite context-dependent roles, such as to both promote and suppress cancer progression (e.g., Notch, KLF4, TGFβ, WT1, SnoN) [34-38]. Network properties can predict disease outcome [39] and contribute to incomplete penetrance of mutations, for example, by thresholding stochastic fluctuations [40]. Therefore, network biology offers a credible, effective abstraction of living systems and a route toward new clinical tools [41-44]. We are applying machine learning to infer networks of gene functional associations and transcription factor physical interactions drawing on the Eurexpress/EMAP [45] ISH images introduced in Section 16.2. Many genes of unknown function are coordinately regulated in embryonic development [46]. Genome-scale datasets such as Eurexpress provide an unprecedented opportunity for probabilistic gene function mapping in order to address this knowledge gap [47].

Transcription factor (TF) physical interactions are fundamental for the regulation of gene expression and can be predictive of cell fate [48]. Indeed, TFs typically form complexes with chromatin modifiers and other TFs [49]. Current estimates indicate that less than a third of TF interactions have been identified [46]. Large-scale studies of *in vivo* transcription factor interactions face several difficulties, including transient association, context dependence, low TF concentrations, and a relatively small number of highly specific, reliable antibodies. Therefore, a data-driven, machine-learning approach is an attractive strategy to infer TF complexes and so develop understanding of combinatorial interactions in gene regulation. Morphogenetic plasticity in development and cancers is a key area of future interest. Cells in tumors and embryos share fundamental behavior, including proliferation, invasion, survival, and migration [48-50]. Indeed, embryonic signaling mechanisms are implicated in cancer progression, opening avenues for selective therapies [48, 49, 51-53]. EMAP/Eurexpress affords large-scale, high resolution analysis of spatial gene expression patterns in embryonic development and is, therefore, relevant to studying gene regulation in cancers. Developmentally important signaling molecules are conserved across species [54, 55] and conservation is associated with core cellular functions [56, 57]. Furthermore, common biological processes operate in cancers from different species [58, 59], comparative genomics has proven potential for oncogene discovery [60, 61], and genome sequencing indicates that drivers of cancer remain to be discovered [62-64]. Therefore, research at the interface between mouse development and human cancer promises clinical impact [50, 65].

16.4.1   Workflow for Learning Gene Interaction Networks from Imaging Data

Considering the above, an attractive goal is the creation of a data-intensive workflow to enable the automated learning of gene interaction networks from image data. The images will be input for supervised machine learning in order to define gene networks encoding (i) relationships in cell signaling and metabolism and (ii) transcription factor physical interactions. Gold standard data will be drawn from known interactions [48, 66]. The general workflow is summarized in Figure 16.7 and will be run independently for the prediction of different networks (i.e., (i) and (ii) above). The five main activities are outlined as follows:

> *Image Preprocessing.* This will include size normalization, denoising, and warping based on manually generated tie points. Size normalization and denoising have been described in Section 16.3. The warping [67] will improve the alignment of gene expression signals according to points of correspondence (tie points) already identified visually by the editorial office of the EMAGE mouse-embryo gene database.[2]
>
> *Wavelet Transform.* This has been described in Section 16.3.3.
>
> *Feature Ranking.* Wavelets will be treated as features and will be ranked according to the positive ("interacting") and negative ("noninteracting") training data. Metrics that are likely to prove useful for ranking are mutual information and Spearman's rank correlation coefficient.
>
> *Feature Selection.* A wrapper-based approach will be taken [68] over the training dataset. Different search strategies will be evaluated including best

---

[2]http://www.emouseatlas.org/emage/, verified October 2011.

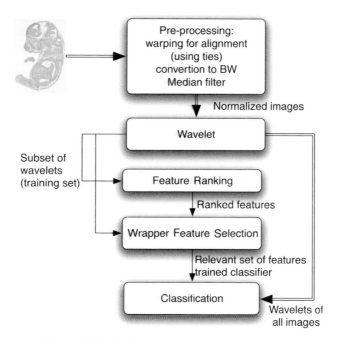

Figure 16.7 The image-to-gene networks workflow.

first-forward search and backward elimination. Prefiltering may prove useful to make tractable backward elimination. Different learning methods will be examined (e.g., Bayesian logistic regression, support vector machine, artificial neural network).

Network Inference. The final algorithm will be employed to infer an interaction score amongst all gene pairs, thresholding of this score will generate a high confidence network by maximizing the F-measure [69] and minimizing the false-positive rate over the training dataset. Finally, evaluation of the classifier and thresholded network will be performed on blind test data.

With the above in mind, the computational infrastructure must allow the workflow to be easily rerun with different configurations and afford comparison of results, including provenance. A preliminary small-scale study based only on Eurexpress text annotation data gave encouraging results, developing a classifier of transcription factor interactions that had 70% accuracy, estimated by fivefold cross validation with Bayesian logistic regression.

16.4.2 Computing Architecture

The workflow of Figure 16.7 will operate on 350,000 images in the full Eurexpress dataset to identify global gene interactions, although the transcription factor dataset is about an order of magnitude smaller. The scale of this work implies the use of a compute cluster. We are interested in studying an architecture aimed at data-intensive problems. The traditional approach assumes a scarcity of CPUs [70]: data are kept in a storage server, and they are transferred to the processing cluster when needed. When working on large dataset, this is not efficient: CPUs remain idle while waiting for the data.

With the goal of reducing the inefficiencies of traditional architectures when dealing with large datasets, we have developed a different architecture that couples storage units with inexpensive processing units. On the basis of ideas by Jim Gray and Alexander Szalay [71], this architecture colocates processes and data, avoiding the transfer of data over the network. While this architecture does not aim to replace high-performance computing resources, it might prove successful in redesigning the task distribution between storage and processing centers. This requires a review of the workflows currently used: the PEs that can be brought to the data must be identified.

The experiment has been run on a dedicated machine comprising low power consumption data nodes. Each node has 6.25 TB of storage capacity, a dual core Intel Atom CPU, and is connected through a gigabit Ethernet link. Figure 16.8 summarizes the alternative architectures. Forty nodes were used.

Data mining is executed on the results of correlations between the wavelets extracted from the images. Thus, the largest portion of the workflow is the preparation of the data toward the data-mining step: images are warped, cleaned, aligned, and their wavelets are computed. These steps can be done in a completely parallel and distributed manner. The alignment of the slices and the wavelet correlations are the most network intensive: the alignment of the slices between two genes requires the computation of the Hausdorff distance between all of the images of the two genes and the wavelets of each slice need to be correlated with the wavelets of the corresponding slices of all the other genes.

In our storage architecture, the images are stored on the different nodes. Deciding how to distribute the data among the storage node is usually a critical decision: a

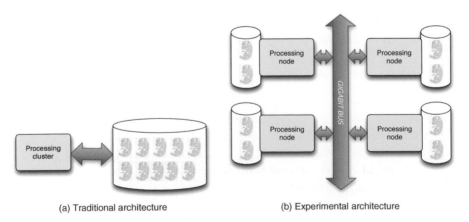

(a) Traditional architecture   (b) Experimental architecture

Figure 16.8   *Alternative architectures.*

good partitioning of the data can minimize the number of transfers between nodes. For example, when working on temporal data, such as with the seismological data described in Chapter 17, it is a reasonably efficient strategy to store on the same nodes data by time rather than by source: concurrent seismograms from different stations are likely to be compared and analyzed. In the case of the images of slices, each set of images belonging to a gene must be compared with all the other sets, so the location of the images does not influence the efficiency.

The alignment is a step that can be improved by separating it into two phases, one computed locally on the nodes whose output is a reduced amount of data to transfer between the nodes. The Hausdorff distance computes the distance between profiles: the profiles are computed locally and only the profiles (consisting of arrays of coordinates of points) are transferred between the nodes. This is obviously more I/O efficient than transmitting the images and computing the profiles where the distance is computed.

Given the number and size of the wavelets (each file is between 50 and 100 MB), it is not possible to store all the files on all the nodes. Each node asks for the wavelets from the other nodes one at a time. When one wavelet file is received, it is cached in memory and correlated with all the wavelets local to the node.

The results of the correlations are stored in a database: the data-mining algorithm is fed from the result of a query obtaining the results of the correlations.

16.5 SUMMARY

We have developed and evaluated a method for automatic identification and annotation of gene expression patterns in the images of ISH studies on mouse embryos.

Our method has several important features. The automatic identification and annotation of gene expression patterns are based on a flexible combination of image processing and machine-learning techniques and provide an efficient way for domain experts who handle large datasets. The method allows for the incremental construction of classifiers, as we have formulated the multiclass problem—what anatomical components exhibit gene expression in an image?—as a two-class problem—in this image, does a given anatomical component exhibit gene expression? One classifier is related only to one anatomical component and its result is, therefore, independent from other classifiers.

We evaluated our method on image data from the Eurexpress study, where we use it to automatically classify nine anatomical terms. The accuracy of our method lies between 70% and 80% with few exceptions. We show that other known methods perform worse and have much more variability in accuracy, both across anatomical components and between their sensitivity and specificity.

We also outline ongoing work to learn about networks of gene function and transcription factor physical interactions using computational systems biology approaches. These networks provide an attractive route to glean insights into the control and organization of cell behavior, with application to human disease. By doing this, much of the previous work on constructing data-intensive workflows and PEs would be eminently reusable.

The results presented are promising and encouraging. However, there are still several challenges related to the accuracy of automatic annotation and computational performance. With respect to the former, the accuracy of annotation on training datasets is a key to design unbiased classifiers. Currently, the annotation of our training dataset heavily depends on manual annotation from domain experts. During the development of the computational method, we found that the annotation performance can be further enhanced by a deep collaboration with domain experts. Moreover, the mouse embryo images generated via the RNA ISH have variable shape, location, and orientation. It is crucial to investigate advanced image registration. Regarding computational performance, the current experimental dataset is small and the prototype performance is tolerable. However, to put our proposed method into practice, with all of the images for all anatomical features, or all of the images for all genes, it is critical to find a solution to accelerate computational performance. The methods described in this book yield an effective architecture for large-scale and long-running, data-intensive computations, which will provide the right platform with which these emerging challenges in developmental biology can be addressed.

REFERENCES

1. D. Noble, "Cardiac action and pacemaker potentials based on the Hodgkin-Huxley equations," *Nature*, vol. 188, pp. 495–497, 1960.

2. O. F. Hutter and D. Noble, "Rectifying properties of heart muscle," *Nature*, vol. 188, p. 495, 1960.

3. D. Thompson, *On Growth and Form* (*Second Edition*). London, Dover, reprint 1942, 1992.

4. A. M. Turing, "The chemical basis of morphogenesis," *Philosophical Transactions of the Royal Society of London Series B: Biological Sciences*, vol. B 237, pp. 37–72, 1952.

5. M. Schena, D. Shalon, R. W. Davis, and P. O. Brown, "Quantitative monitoring of gene expression patterns with a complementary DNA microarray," *Science*, vol. 270, pp. 467–470, 1995.

6. P. O. Brown and D. Botstein, "Exploring the new world of the genome with DNA microarrays," *Nature Genetics*, vol. 21, pp. 33–37, 1999.

7. A. Visel, J. Ahdidan, and G. Eichele, "A gene expression map of the mouse brain," *A Practical Guide to Neuroscience Databases and Associated Tools*, Boston, MA, Kluwer Academic Publishers, 2002.

8. *Eurexpress: a Transcriptome Atlas Database for Mouse Embryo*, http://www.eurexpress.org/ee/, 2009 verified October 2011.

9. J. H. Christiansen, Y. Yang, S. Venkataraman, L. Richardson, P. Stevenson, N. Burton, R. A. Baldock, and D. R. Davidson, "Emage: a spatial database of gene expression patterns during mouse embryo development," *Nucleic Acids Research*, vol. 34, no. 1, pp. D637–D641, 2006.

10. G. Grumbling, V. Strelets, and T. F. Consortium, "Flybase: anatomical data, images and queries," *Nucleic Acids Research*, vol. 34, pp. D485–D488, 2006.

11. C. Harmon, P. Ahammad, A. Hammonds, R. Weiszmann, S. Celniker, S. Sastry, and G. Rubin, "Comparative analysis of spatial patterns of gene expression in *Drosophila melanogaster* imaginal discs," in *Research in Computational Molecular Biology* (T. Speed and H. Huang, eds.), vol. 4453 of *Lecture Notes in Computer Science*, pp. 533–547, Berlin/Heidelberg, Springer, 2007. DOI: 10.1007/978-3-540-71681-5_37.

12. J. Pan, A. G. R. Balan, E. P. Xing, A. J. M. Traina, and C. Faloutsos, "Automatic mining of fruit fly embryo images," in *Proceedings of the 12th ACM SIGKDD International Conference on Knowledge Discovery and Data Mining, (Philadelphia, PA)*, pp. 693–698, New York, NY, ACM, 2006.

13. J. Zhou and H. Peng, "Automatic recognition and annotation of gene expression patterns of fly embryos," *Bioinformatics*, vol. 23, no. 5, pp. 589–596, 2007.

14. S. Ji, L. Sun, R. Jin, S. Kumar, and J. Ye, "Automated annotation of Drosophila gene expression patterns using a controlled vocabulary," *Bioinformatics*, vol. 24, no. 17, pp. 1881–1888, 2008.

15. D. L. Mace, N. Varnado, W. Zhang, E. Frise, and U. Ohler, "Extraction and comparison of gene expression patterns from 2D RNA in situ hybridization images," *Bioinformatics*, vol. 26, no. 6, pp. 761–769, 2010.

16. J. P. Carson, T. Ju, H. C. Lu, C. Thaller, S. L. Pallas, M. C. Crair, J. Warren, W. Chiu, and G. Eichele, "A digital atlas to characterize the mouse brain transcriptome," *PLoS Comput Biology*, vol. 1, pp. 0290–0296, 2005.

17. K. Theiler, *The House Mouse: Atlas of Embryonic Development*. New York, Springer-Verlag, 1972.

18. L. Han, J. van Hemert, and R. Baldock, "Automatically identifying and annotating mouse embryo gene expression patterns," *Bioinformatics*, vol. 27, no. 8, pp. 1101–1107, 2011.

19. G. A. Baxes, *Digital Image Processing: Principles and Applications*. New York, Wiley, 1994.

20. E. Stollnitz, T. DeRose, and D. Salesin, *Wavelets for Computer Graphics* Morgan Kaufmann Publishers, Inc., 1996.

21. S. G. Mallat, *A Wavelet Tour of Signal Processing*. Academic Press, 1999.

22. I. Daubechies, *Ten Lectures on Wavelets*. S.I.A.M, 1992.

23. R. O. Duda and P. E. Hart, *Pattern Classification and Scene Analysis*. Wiley, 1973.

24. J. Shawe-Taylor and N. Cristianini, *An Introduction to Support Vector Machines and other Kernel-based Learning Methods*. Cambridge University Press, 2000.

25. O. L. Mangasarian and D. R. Musicant, "Lagrangian support vector machines," tech. rep., Dept. of Mathematics and Computer Science, University of Wisconsin, 2006.

26. G. German and M. Gahegan, "Neural network architectures for the classification of temporal image sequences," *Computers & Geosciences*, vol. 22, no. 9, pp. 969–979, 1996.

27. S. Lawrence, C. L. Giles, A. C. Tsoi, and A. D. Back, "Face recognition: a convolutional neural-network approach," *IEEE Transactions on Neural Networks, Special Issue on Neural Networks and Pattern Recognition*, vol. 8, no. 1, pp. 98–113, 2002.

28. A. Barabasi and Z. N. Oltvai, "Network biology: understanding the cell's functional organization," *Nature Reviews Genetics*, vol. 5, pp. 101–113, 2004.

29. M. B. Yaffe, "Signaling networks and mathematics," *Science Signaling*, vol. 1, p. eg7, 2008.

30. T. Bouwmeester, A. Bauch, H. Ruffner, P. Angrand, G. Bergamini, K. Croughton, C. Cruciat, D. Eberhard, J. Gagneur, S. Ghidelli, C. Hopf, B. Huhse, R. Mangano, A. Michon, M. Schirle, J. Schlegl, M. Schwab, M. A. Stein, A. Bauer, G. Casari G. Drewes, A. Gavin, D. B. Jackson, G. Joberty, G. Neubauer, J. Rick, B. Kuster, and G. Superti-Furga, "A physical and functional map of the human TNF-[alpha]/NF-[kappa]B signal transduction pathway," *Nature Cell Biology*, vol. 6, pp. 97–105, 2004.

31. K. K. Lee, M. K. Tang, D. T. Yew, P. H. Chow, S. P. Yee, C. Schneider, and C. Brancolini, "gas2 is a multifunctional gene involved in the regulation of apoptosis and chondrogenesis in the developing mouse limb," *Developmental Biology*, vol. 207, pp. 14–25, March 1999. PMID: 10049561.

32. M. L. Agarwal, W. R. Taylor, M. V. Chernov, O. B. Chernova, and G. R. Stark, "The p53 network," *Journal of Biological Chemistry*, vol. 273, pp. 1–4, 1998.

33. A. M. Arias, A. M. Browntand, and K. Brennan, "Wnt signalling: pathway or network?" *Current Opinion in Genetics & Development*, vol. 9, pp. 447–454, 1999.

34. Q. Zhu, A. R. Krakowski, E. E. Dunham, L. Wang, A. Bandyopadhyay, R. Berdeaux, G. S. Martin, L. Sun, and K. Luo, "Dual role of SnoN in mammalian tumorigenesis," *Molecular and Cellular Biology*, vol. 27, pp. 324–339, 2007.

35. B. D. Rowland and D. S. Peeper, "KLF4, p21 and context-dependent opposing forces in cancer," *Nature Reviews Cancer*, vol. 6, pp. 11–23, 2006.

36. L. M. Wakefield and A. B. Roberts, "TGF-[beta] signaling: positive and negative effects on tumorigenesis," *Current Opinion in Genetics & Development*, vol. 12, pp. 22–29, 2002.

37. P. Hohenstein and N. D. Hastie, "The many facets of the Wilms' tumour gene, WT1," *Human Molecular Genetics*, vol. 15, pp. R196–201, 2006.

38. F. Radtke and K. Raj, "The role of notch in tumorigenesis: oncogene or tumour suppressor?" *Nature Reviews Cancer*, vol. 3, pp. 756–767, 2003.

39. I. W. Taylor, R. Linding, D. Warde-Farley, Y. Liu, C. Pesquita, D. Faria, S. Bull, T. Pawson, Q. Morris, and J. L. Wrana, "Dynamic modularity in protein interaction networks predicts breast cancer outcome," *Nature Biotechnology*, vol. 27, pp. 199–204, 2009.

40. A. Raj, S. A. Rifkin, E. Andersen, and A. van Oudenaarden, "Variability in gene expression underlies incomplete penetrance," *Nature*, vol. 463, pp. 913–918, 2010.

41. K. Lage, K. Mollgard, S. Greenway, H. Wakimoto, J. M. Gorham, C. T. Workman, E. Bendsen, N. T. Hansen, O. Rigina, F. S. Roque, C. Wiese, V. M. Christoffels, A. E. Roberts, L. B. Smoot, W. T. Pu, P. K. Donahoe, N. Tommerup S. Brunak, C. E. Seidman, J. G. Seidman, and L. A. Larsen, "Dissecting spatio-temporal protein networks driving human heart development and related disorders," *Molecular Systems Biology*, vol. 6, 2010.

42. A. Ergun, C. A. Lawrence, M. A. Kohanski, T. A. Brennan, and J. J. Collins, "A network biology approach to prostate cancer," *Molecular Systems Biology*, vol. 3, 2007.

43. R. Laubenbacher, V. Hower, A. Jarrah, S. V. Torti, V. Shulaev, P. Mendes, F. M. Torti, and S. Akman, "A systems biology view of cancer," *Biochimica et Biophysica Acta (BBA)—Reviews on Cancer*, vol. 1796, pp. 129–139, 2009.

44. T. S. Deisboeck, "Personalizing medicine: a systems biology perspective," *Molecular Systems Biology*, vol. 5, March 2009.

45. L. Richardson, S. Venkataraman, P. Stevenson, Y. Yang, N. Burton, J. Rao, M. Fisher, R. A. Baldock, D. R. Davidson, and J. H. Christiansen, "EMAGE mouse embryo spatial gene expression database: 2010 update," *Nucleic Acids Research*, vol. 38, no. Database, pp. D703–D709, 2009.

46. N. Fossat, S. Pfister, and P. P. Tam, "A transcriptome landscape of mouse embryogenesis," *Developmental Cell*, vol. 13, pp. 761–762, 2007.

47. A. G. Fraser and E. M. Marcotte, "A probabilistic view of gene function," *Nature Genetics*, vol. 36, pp. 559–564, 2004. PMID: 15167932.

48. T. Ravasi, H. Suzuki, C. V. Cannistraci, S. Katayama, V. B. Bajic, K. Tan, A. Akalin, S. Schmeier, M. Kanamori-Katayama, and N. Bertin, "An atlas of combinatorial transcriptional regulation in mouse and man," *Cell*, vol. 140 no. 5, pp. 744–752, 2010.

49. E. Fedorova and D. Zink, "Nuclear architecture and gene regulation," *Biochimica et Biophysica Acta (BBA) - Molecular Cell Research*, vol. 1783, pp. 2174–2184, 2008.

50. F. C. Kellcher, D. Fennelly, and M. Rafferty, "Common critical pathways in embryogenesis and cancer," *Acta Oncologica*, vol. 45, no. 4, pp. 375–388, 2006.

51. P. A. Clark, D. M. Treisman, J. Ebben, and J. S. Kuo, "Developmental signaling pathways in brain tumor-derived stem-like cells," *Developmental Dynamics: An Official Publication of the American Association of Anatomists*, vol. 236, pp. 3297–3308, 2007. PMID: 18000980.

52. I. Malanchi, H. Peinado, D. Kassen, T. Hussenet, D. Metzger, P. Chambon, M. Huber, D. Hohl, A. Cano, W. Birchmeier, and J. Huelsken, "Cutaneous cancer stem cell maintenance is dependent on beta-catenin signalling," *Nature*, vol. 452, pp. 650–653, 2008. PMID: 18385740.

53. E. E. Bar, A. Chaudhry, A. Lin, X. Fan, K. Schreck, W. Matsui, S. Piccirillo, A. L. Vescovi, F. Dimeco, A. Olivi, and C. G. Eberhart, "Cyclopamine-Mediated hedgehog pathway inhibition depletes Stem-Like cancer cells in glioblastoma," *Stem cells (Dayton, Ohio)*, vol. 25, pp. 2524–2533, 2007. PMID: 17628016 PMCID: 2610257.

54. L. Wolpert and C. Tickle, *Principles of Development (Fourth Edition)*. OUP Oxford, 2011.

55. W. McGinnis and R. Krumlauf, "Homeobox genes and axial patterning," *Cell*, vol. 68, pp. 283–302, 1992. PMID: 1346368.

56. A. G. Fraser, R. S. Kamath, P. Zipperlen, M. Martinez-Campos, M. Sohrmann, and J. Ahringer, "Functional genomic analysis of c. elegans chromosome i by systematic RNA interference," *Nature*, vol. 408, pp. 325–330, 2000. PMID: 11099033.

57. S. A Chervitz, L. Aravind, G. Sherlock, C. A. Ball, E. V. Koonin, S. S. Dwight, M. A. Harris, K. Dolinski, S. Mohr, T. Smith, S. Weng, J. M. Cherry, and D. Botstein, "Comparison of the complete protein sets of worm and yeast: orthology and divergence," *Science*, vol. 282, pp. 2022–2028, 1998.

58. N. Schreiber-Agus, D. Stein, K. Chen, J. S. Goltz, L. Stevens, and R. A. DePinho, "Drosophila Myc is oncogenic in mammalian cells and plays a role in the diminutive phenotype," *Proceedings of the National Academy of Sciences of the United States of America*, vol. 94, pp. 1235–1240, 1997. PMID: 9037036.

59. R. S. Maser, B. Choudhury, P. J. Campbell, B. Feng, K. Wong, A. Protopopov, J. O'Neil, A. Gutierrez, E. Ivanova, I. Perna, E. Lin, V. Mani, S. Jiang, K. McNamara, S. Zaghlul, S. Edkins, C. Stevens, C. Brennan, E. S. Martin, R. Wiedemeyer, O. Kabbarah, C. Nogueira, G. Histen, J. Aster, M. Mansour, V. Duke, L. Foroni, A. K. Fielding,

A. H. Goldstone, J. M. Rowe, Y. A. Wang, A. T. Look, M. R. Stratton, L. Chin, P. A. Futreal, and R. A. DePinho, "Chromosomally unstable mouse tumours have genomic alterations similar to diverse human cancers," *Nature*, vol. 447, pp. 966–971, 2007. PMID: 17515920.

60. L. Zender, M. S. Spector, W. Xue P. Flemming, C. Cordon-Cardo, J. Silke, S. Fan, J. M. Luk, M. Wigler, G. J. Hannon, D. Mu, R. Lucito, S. Powers, and S. W. Lowe, "Identification and validation of oncogenes in liver cancer using an integrative oncogenomic approach," *Cell*, vol. 125, pp. 1253–1267, 2006. PMID: 16814713.

61. M. Kim, J. D. Gans, C. Nogueira, A. Wang, J. Paik, B. Feng, C. Brennan, W. C. Hahn, C. Cordon-Cardo, S. N. Wagner, T. J. Flotte, L. M. Duncan, S. R. Granter, and L. Chin, "Comparative oncogenomics identifies NEDD9 as a melanoma metastasis gene," *Cell*, vol. 125, pp. 1269–1281, 2006. PMID: 16814714.

62. I. Varela, P. Tarpey, K. Raine, D. Huang, C. K. Ong, P. Stephens, H. Davies, D. Jones, M. Lin, J. Teague, G. Bignell, A. Butler, J. Cho, G. L. Dalgliesh, D. Galappaththige, C. Greenman, C. Hardy, M. Jia, C. Latimer, K. W. Lau, J. Marshall, S. McLaren, A. Menzies, L. Mudie, L. Stebbings, D. A. Largaespada, L. F. A. Wessels, S. Richard, R. J. Kahnoski, J. Anema, D. A. Tuveson, P. A. Perez-Mancera, V. Mustonen, A. Fischer, D. J. Adams, A. Rust, W. Chan-on, C. Subimerb, K. Dykema, K. Furge, P. J. Campbell, B. T. Teh, M. R. Stratton, and P. A. Futreal, "Exome sequencing identifies frequent mutation of the SWI/SNF complex gene PBRM1 in renal carcinoma," *Nature*, vol. 469, pp. 539–542, 2011.

63. C. Greenman, P. Stephens, R. Smith, G. L. Dalgliesh, C. Hunter, G. Bignell, H. Davies, J. Teague, A. Butler, C. Stevens, S. Edkins, S. O/'Meara, I. Vastrik, E. E. Schmidt, T. Avis, S. Barthorpe, G. Bhamra, G. Buck, B. Choudhury, J. Clements, J. Cole, E. Dicks, S. Forbes, K. Gray, K. Halliday, R. Harrison, K. Hills, J. Hinton, A. Jenkinson, D. Jones, A. Menzies, T. Mironenko, J. Perry, K. Raine, D. Richardson, R. Shepherd, A. Small, C. Tofts, J. Varian, T. Webb, S. West, S. Widaa, A. Yates, D. P. Cahill, D. N. Louis, P. Goldstraw, A. G. Nicholson, F. Brasseur, L. Looijenga, B. L. Weber, Y. Chiew, A. deFazio, M. F. Greaves, A. R. Green, P. Campbell, E. Birney, D. F. Easton, G. Chenevix-Trench, M. Tan, S. K. Khoo, B. T. Teh, S. T. Yuen, S. Y. Leung, R. Wooster, P. A. Futreal, and M. R. Stratton, "Patterns of somatic mutation in human cancer genomes," *Nature*, vol. 446, pp. 153–158, 2007.

64. D. A. Haber and J. Settleman, "Cancer: drivers and passengers," *Nature*, vol. 446, pp. 145–146, 2007.

65. A. Moustakas and C. Heldin, "Signaling networks guiding epithelial-mesenchymal transitions during embryogenesis and cancer progression," *Cancer Science*, vol. 98, pp. 1512–1520, 2007. PMID: 17645776.

66. M. Kanehisa and S. Goto, "KEGG: kyoto encyclopedia of genes and genomes," *Nucleic Acids Research*, vol. 28, pp. 27–30, 2000. PMID: 10592173.

67. R. Baldock and B. Hill, "Image warping and spatial data mapping," in *Image Processing and Analysis A Practical Approach*, No. 219 in A Practical Approach, pp. 261–288, OUP Oxford, 2000.

68. R. Kohavi and G. H. John, "Wrappers for feature subset selection," *Artificial Intelligence*, vol. 97, no. 1–2, pp. 273–324, 1997.

69. C. J. van Rijsbergen, "Information retrieval," 1979.

70. R. L. Grossman and Y. Gu, "On the varieties of clouds for data intensive computing," *IEEE Data Engineering Bulletin*, vol. 32, no. 1, pp. 44–50, 2009.

71. A. S. Szalay, G. Bell, J. vanden Berg, A. Wonders, R. C. Burns, D. Fay, J. Heasley, A. J. G. Hey, M. A. Nieto-Santisteban, A. R. Thakar, C. van Ingen, and R. Wilton, "GrayWulf: scalable clustered architecture for data intensive computing," in *Hawaii International Conference on Systems Sciences*, pp. 1–10, 2009.

17

Data-Intensive Seismology: Research Horizons

Michelle Galea

School of Informatics, University of Edinburgh, Edinburgh, UK

Andreas Rietbrock

School of Environmental Sciences, University of Liverpool, Liverpool, UK

Alessandro Spinuso and Luca Trani

School of Informatics, University of Edinburgh, Edinburgh, UK; Royal Netherlands Meteorological Institute, Information and Observation Services and Technology R&D, Utrecht, The Netherlands

The seismology community is being offered an unprecedented opportunity to conduct data-driven research that will lead to fundamental changes in the way society manages the Earth and its resources. This arises from the increasing wealth of global seismic waveform data being captured and made available on a continuous basis. An essential foundation is an infrastructure that allows seismologists to harness this distributed data to build models that will further their understanding of the Earth's structure and processes. This chapter begins to explore the viability of such an infrastructure through the application of the prototype data-intensive platform for the processing of terabytes of distributed ambient noise data. In particular, this chapter discusses requirements such as managing heterogeneous sources of data

The DATA Bonanza: Improving Knowledge Discovery in Science, Engineering, and Business, First Edition.
Edited by Malcolm Atkinson, Rob Baxter, Michelle Galea, Mark Parsons, Peter Brezany, Oscar Corcho, Jano van Hemert, and David Snelling.

and the importance of satisfying domain experts' needs such as using existing, community-trusted analytic software.

17.1   INTRODUCTION

Recent earthquakes in Japan (2011), New Zealand (2011), Haiti (2010), and Chile (2010) demonstrate yet again that better models for forecasting the occurrence and impact of earthquakes are still necessary.

Seismologists analyze seismic waves generated by earthquakes and man-made energy sources, traveling through the Earth as elastic waves and recorded at the surface by seismometers measuring ground displacement. These signals—seismograms—contain a wealth of information about the sources that generate them. Seismograms collected to study the earthquake distribution in a specific region may also be used to analyze the Earth's structure and processes, for example, studies ranging from the Earth's upper crust to the core–mantle boundary. This multiuse attribute of seismic data makes them extremely valuable, and the seismological community has invested heavily in archiving these data and making them freely and easily accessible.

New advances in theory and data processing now allow seismologists to also use the background (ambient) noise in seismograms to investigate the Earth's structure. This literally means that every byte of seismic data recorded can be used to monitor Earth processes. Furthermore, the amount of recorded data is continuously increasing—Figure 17.1 shows the size of the archive of the Data Management Center (DMC) of the Incorporated Research Institutions for Seismology (IRIS),[1] that collates the data of several international seismological networks. From 1992, the archive followed an exponential growth curve, settling around 2008 into an approximately linear increase of some 21 TB per year. Traditionally, seismologists have studied all of the waveforms recorded by their observatories or all of the traces required for their research project. It is becoming increasingly obvious that this current approach will not be feasible in the future, and a paradigm shift in how we extract parameters and information from continuous streams of data is needed.

The seismological community is, at present, unable to fully exploit the wealth of available data. Although seismic data are recorded in open and standardized formats, the services that provide access to these data are not standardized across different institutes and countries. Tools are generally developed and used locally on data that is downloaded from central archives. They are driven from the command line without any universal guidelines for their use or any intuitive user interfaces to aid adoption by the wider community. Compute resources must be found locally by each researcher, which often prevents scale-up of experiments to the required amount of data. All this leads to problems in tracking resource and experiment provenance data, wasteful disk use, and potential mismatched versions of tools and preprocessed data. This in turn makes it more likely that opportunities are missed

---

[1]www.iris.edu, verified March 2012.

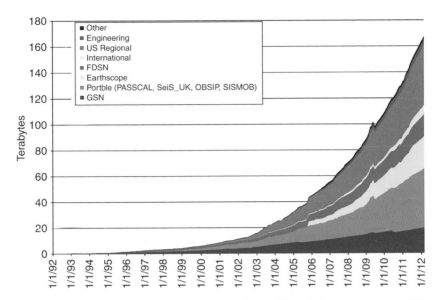

Figure 17.1   *Seismological data volumes of the IRIS DMC archive, as of 1 March 2012.*

for significantly advancing our understanding of the Earth through the comparison of results and the integration of models across the whole of the seismological field of research.

It is clear that the capabilities to capture more data and extract more valuable knowledge from data are growing. However, this generates a pressing requirement for a robust and adaptable data-intensive platform that allows us to do this efficiently, effectively, and in collaboration with colleagues in the wider seismological community. The processing of seismic data increasingly requires the use of high performance computing technology that is not always available either at a data center's facilities or within individual research groups. Thus, there is also a need for any data-intensive platform to provide an accessible facility of "software as infrastructure" capable of both "data-rich" and "cpu-rich" tasks, as well as the tools and capabilities for data and model sharing, information and knowledge extraction, data mining, processing, and visualization. Other crucial considerations include allowing a domain expert to focus on the data and the research questions (and not the underlying enabling technology), and facilitating the use of existing community-trusted software in the enactment of complex data integration and analysis tasks.

The next section introduces ambient noise processing and the key role it plays in several seismic applications. Section 17.3 describes the implementation of the ambient noise processing on the prototype data-intensive architecture, discussing how requirements such as the integration and processing of distributed data stored on heterogeneous systems was resolved, and the importance of capturing experiment provenance data during the enactment of workflows. In Section 17.4, we reflect on our experience of using the prototype architecture; in Section 17.5, we discuss possible extensions of both our seismology application and of the architecture; and in Section 17.6, we present our conclusions.

17.2   SEISMIC AMBIENT NOISE PROCESSING

The seismograms captured by seismology networks are an essential ingredient in seismic interferometry, which is the study of the interference of pairs of seismic signals. The signals may come from earthquakes, background propagating waves, laboratory, or other artificial seismic sources such as underground explosions. Seismic interferometry has several applications in science and industry, but in most cases, the core steps are the same: the pair-wise cross correlation of signals and their aggregation (stacking). The cross correlation of signals recorded at two different geographical locations yields an estimate of the Green's function, which is a waveform that would be observed at one of the locations if a signal source were placed at the other [1–3].

The postprocessing of the resulting stacked signals determines the final application [4], and one increasingly studied application area is *ambient noise tomography* (ANT).

ANT involves cross-correlating long time sequences of ambient seismic noise and extracting information about the Earth's crust and upper mantle from the estimated Green's function. ANT has mainly been applied to determine dispersion measurements of surface waves (*Rayleigh* or *Love* waves) in order to create tomographic maps [5–7]. However, surface wave information may also be used to learn about the Earth's interior (e.g., fluid content, composition, temperature) and advance our understanding of its processes [8].

Large-scale deployment of seismometers is planned and occurring around the world, including in the United States, China, and Europe, and research suggests that ANT is best applied to large arrays of seismometers [9], using time series of at least a year in length [10, 11]. These factors drive the need for an easy-to-use and effective data-intensive processing environment. To that end, we investigate the viability of the prototype data-intensive architecture by implementing a realistic task: the retrieval, preprocessing, cross correlation, and stacking of approximately 7 TB of data from two seismic data providers—the British Geological Survey (BGS)[2] and the ORFEUS Data Centre (ODC) of the European Seismological Commission.[3] This number is based on 5 years of data obtained from the ODC (2005–2010) and 3 years' data from the BGS (2008–2010). The ODC data are collected from a varying number of stations, from 150 stations in 2005 to 500 in 2010, and the BGS data are collected from 29 UK stations.

Specifically, we implement core steps of the ambient noise data processing procedure for obtaining surface wave dispersion measurements described in [12]. This

[2]www.bgs.ac.uk, verified March 2012.
[3]www.orfeus-eu.org/Organization/organization.html, verified March 2012.

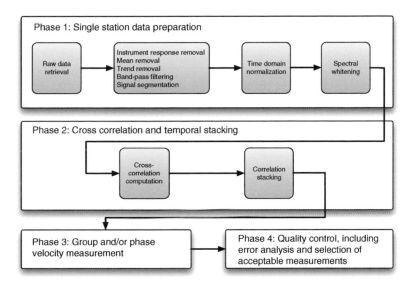

Figure 17.2 *Phases of the seismic ambient noise processing procedure. Source: After Bensen et al. [12].*

procedure consists of four phases: (i) single station data preparation, (ii) cross correlation and temporal stacking, (iii) measurement of dispersion curves, and (iv) quality control. The rationale for the order of the steps, and the specific techniques selected for each step, is provided in [12] and is beyond the scope of this chapter.

The ambient noise processing procedure is depicted in Figure 17.2, with more detail shown for the two phases implemented as part of our experimental scenario. The main purpose of the first phase is to prepare the recorded signals for cross correlation, by removing all evidence of events such as earthquakes or storms, and instrument irregularities. This leaves only ambient noise for processing. The second phase first cross correlates all possible pairs of seismic signals. The cross correlation is often performed on day-long segments; 5 years of signals from 100 stations split into such segments yield over 16 million pairs for cross correlation. The resulting cross correlations are then aggregated, or *stacked*, to correspond to longer time-series segments—on average, stacking over increasingly longer time series improves the signal-to-noise ratio.

In our experiments, we focused on the first two phases because our primary aim was to investigate the capabilities of the data-intensive architecture for the large-scale integration and processing of distributed data. However, as is discussed further in Section 17.5, the implemented workflow may be extended to include all phases in the ambient noise processing procedure, and further to implement different applications in different scientific domains. Other major considerations during the implementation of this scenario were the incorporation of the seismology community's existing software libraries in the enactment of the workflows developed, and the capturing of important provenance data for both replication of experiments and for recovery from error. These are discussed in the following section.

17.3 SOLUTION IMPLEMENTATION

In this section, we describe how we implemented the ambient noise processing scenario on the prototype data-intensive architecture.

17.3.1 Configuration of the Infrastructure

The current experimental test bed simulates the access to multiple data providers, hosting an instance of a data-intensive gateway. This scenario required the data-intensive architecture to deal with heterogeneous data and metadata, and with distributed data sources. This capability is needed because, despite embracing a common standard for raw seismological data called Mini-SEED [13], each institution has its own way of storing and managing data and metadata. Our solution must, therefore, adapt to different local access arrangements and metadata schemes. In our example, we have two different file systems holding the raw data, whereas for the station metadata (gain, response, frequency, etc.), we had to write workflow components to use either a database structure (SeisComP3 Database [14]) or a well-known ASCII format (RESP files [15]) stored in a file system structure.

An important issue to be taken into account in a data-intensive platform is the minimization of data transfers and shipments throughout the system; therefore, a key feature of the data-intensive architecture was the ability to move some of the processing steps close to the data. As shown in Figure 17.3, one possible solution configuration would comprise two gateways (*Gateway A* and *Gateway B*) mainly dedicated to data access and preprocessing and each deployed at its data center, whereas the third gateway (*Gateway C*) acts as front end and orchestrator, hosting the main processing activities.

17.3.2 Description of the Workflow

Ambient noise processing is usually performed in *time windows* applied to data from a predefined set of *seismic stations*. These are considered the main inputs, together with a number of domain-specific *parameters* that are provided to the system via portals or other types of interface, ultimately via a DISPEL document. In this context, the choice of the optimal time window length is relevant because it could affect the final result of the analysis. Ideally it is desirable, from a user's point of view, to be able to specify the duration of the overall period of interest as a single window. In order to address these requirements, we introduced a TimeSampler as the first element in our workflow. This PE (processing element) behaves in some sense as a clock for the system, chopping up the overall interval of analysis (in general, months or years) into subintervals (typically hours or days), thus giving the user the ability to adjust these parameters. By presenting intermediate results

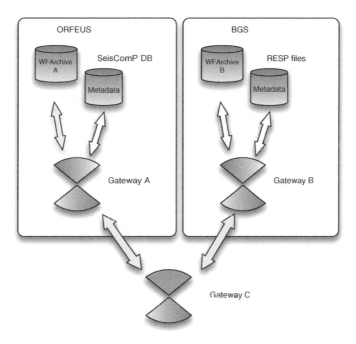

Figure 17.3   *System diagram of a possible ambient noise correlation infrastructure deployment.*

to the users, the system enables them to make dynamic parameter adjustments and thereby to steer the overall computation.

Figure 17.4 provides a high level view of the main blocks composing the ambient noise workflow, which integrates two geographically distinct data sources. The sampling phase generates a list of time windows $[T_1, \ldots, T_n]$, which from now on we can refer to as the single time T_i. Subsequently, the user's query, typically a list of stations $[S_1, \ldots, S_n]$, plus the time T_i, is sent in parallel to several DataAndMetadataExtraction modules. The main task of these modules is to interface with the data sources providing a direct-access layer and preparing a uniform output for the next steps. This addresses the heterogeneity in the data systems, handling the different data and metadata storage and management mechanisms, as shown in Figure 17.3. For this purpose, specific implementations have been created and then mapped onto a generic PE (WFRetrieve) whose specific implementation depends on the particular gateway at which it is deployed, thus providing a consistent and transparent interface to the seismic data and metadata.

Once data and metadata have been fetched from the archives, they can be streamed into subsequent PEs. In order to minimize data shipment, we moved some preprocessing steps, including *filtering*, *normalization*, *instrument response removal*, *whitening*, and *decimation*, close to the data themselves. These are recurrent operations that do not entail large computation and that contribute to reducing the dataflow. For each operation, an activity has been implemented making reuse of

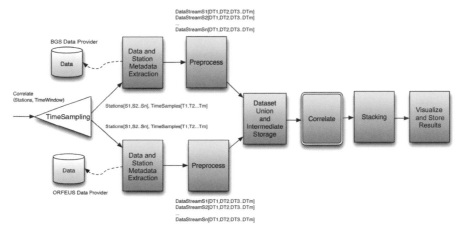

Figure 17.4 *The ambient-noise workflow using two seismic archives.*

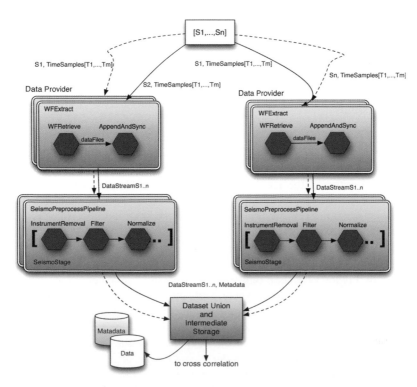

Figure 17.5 *Data extraction and preprocessing.*

```
1    /* Extracts and synchronizes time series based on the time window in input*/
2
3    PE<SeismoTrace> extractWFTimeSeries(String datares,String provenanceRes,
4      String channelCode, String station, String network)
5    {
6      Tee tee = new Tee;
7      ListConcatenate lc1 = new ListConcatenate;
8      WFRetrieve retrieve = new WFRetrieve;
9      WaveformAppendAndSync appsyn = new WaveformAppendAndSync;
10     SeismoMetadataTuple metastoreex1 = new SeismoMetadataTuple;
11     SeismoMetadataTuple metastoreex2 = new SeismoMetadataTuple;
12     |-provenanceRes |=>metastoreex1.resource;
13     |-provenanceRes-|=>metastoreex2.resource;
14     |-datares-| => retrieve.resource;
15     |-datares-| => appsyn.resource;
16     String cha="ch="+channelCode;
17     String sta="sta="+station;
18     String net="net="+network;
19     tee.output[0]=>lc1.input[0];
20     |-repeat enough of [cha,sta,net]-|=>lc1.input[1];
21     lc1.output=>retrieve.parameters;
22     retrieve.metadata=>metastoreex1.metastring;
23     retrieve.wflocations=>appsyn.input;
24     tee.output[1]=>appsyn.parameters;
25     appsyn.metadata=>metastoreex2.metastring;
26     metastoreex1.datasetid=>metastoreex2.stepbackid;
27     return PE(<Connection window=tee.input> =>
28     <Connection output=appsyn.output;Connection datasetid=metastoreex2.datasetid>);
29   }
```

Figure 17.6 *DISPEL code for retrieving seismic traces from distributed data sources.*

existing domain-specific libraries. Details of the implementation with an emphasis on the integration issues can be found in Section 17.3.3.

The WFExtract PE is a composite PE consisting of two main elements, the WFRetrieve PE and an AppendAndSync PE (Fig. 17.5), which are responsible for shaping the data stream based on the requested time window. Figure 17.6 shows how we implemented the extraction phase using DISPEL.

The preprocessing steps are then assembled in a pipeline structure such that at each step the stream is modified in some respect. This approach provides great flexibility and allows the data analysis expert to extend, change, and reshuffle the workflow by just rearranging the pipeline or plugging in new PEs. Figure 17.7 illustrates the function responsible for assembling the pipeline makeArrayPipeline—it accepts as parameters the generic SeismoStage PEs (line 3), which are in turn the result of three different functions shown at lines 25, 30, and 33.

At the end of the pipelines, we obtain preprocessed streams that are almost ready for cross correlation. However, some effort is still required to merge the streams together choosing the most appropriate traces. Because each data center is completely independent from the other, they could, for example, provide data that originated from the same station. Therefore, we must take into account the

```
1    /*Builds the preprocessing pipeline*/
2
3    PE <SeismoPipeline> makeArrayPipeline(PE <SeismoStage>[] TheStages) {
4      Integer len = TheStages.length;
5      SeismoStage[] stages = new SeismoStage[len];
6      PE<SeismoStage> Stage = TheStages[0];
7      stages[0] = new Stage;
8      for (Integer i = 0; i<len-1; i++) {
9        DeliverToNull tonull = new DeliverToNull;
10       PE<SeismoStage> Stg = TheStages[i+1];
11       stages[i+1] = new Stg;
12       stages[i].output => stages[i+1].input;
13       stages[i].datasetid => stages[i+1].stepbackid;
14       stages[i].metadata=>tonull.input;
15     };
16     return SeismoPipeline( <Connection input = stages[0].input;
17            Connection stepbackid = stages[0].stepbackid> =>
18              <Connection metadata = stages[len-1].metadata;
19              Connection datasetid=  stages[len-1].datasetid;
20              Connection residue =   stages[len-1].output> );
21     };
22
23   /*The current implementation includes the 3 following stages:
     instrument and mean removal, filtering and decimation, prewhitening*/
24
25   PE<SeismoStage> removeInstrumentMeanAndNormalize(
26     String station,String channel,String datares,String provenanceRes)
27   {
28   ...
29   }
30   PE<SeismoStage> filterAndDecimate(String provenanceRes){
31   ...
32   }
33   PE<SeismoStage> whiten(String provenanceRes){
34   ...
35   }
```

Figure 17.7 *DISPEL code for building the preprocessing pipeline.*

existence of duplicates and set up mechanisms for an optimal choice based on some quality parameters. In our case, we chose the copy with the least total "Number of Gaps" (NoG) present in the traces as the discriminating factor, which perhaps seems quite a rough measure in that it does not consider the duration of these gaps. Nevertheless, we assume that the data are prechecked by the data centers.

A merger PE, StreamHarvester, has been implemented to accomplish this task: after selecting the best n trace samples matching the initial query, the emerging data can be pushed further and eventually preserved in an intermediate storage system that is useful for recovery and successive re-elaboration of the workflow. This feature, coupled with the data provenance mechanism discussed later (Section 17.3.4), contributes to ensuring the reliability and repeatability of the overall process, improving the quality of the scientific results. We believe that in order to set up a robust and stable automated data processing procedure, it is vital to adopt proper data quality control measures. The traceability of the experiment together with quality monitoring is a good indicator for the validation and verification steps.

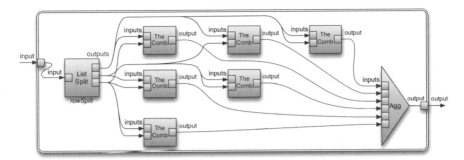

Figure 17.8   *The correlation phase of the workflow exploiting symmetry.*

We are now ready for the primary objective of our analysis: pair-wise cross cor relation of the preelaborated time series. A symmetric cross correlator, as shown in Figure 17.8, could fulfill the requirement. The description of a possible implementation of this pattern can be found in Section 4.4.1, among other examples of DISPEL functions.

It is important to notice, though, that from a data analysis expert's point of view, the correlation phase is similar to the DISPEL snippet in Figure 17.9. Here, the effort is mainly focused on expressing the functionality descriptively, without any knowledge of the underlying infrastructure. How this feature is then enacted depends on the specific deployment. The data-intensive architecture takes care of optimization considering the appropriate level of parallelism, and this point is discussed in Section 17.4.1.

The last part of our data analysis is summarized in Figure 17.10. After computing the cross correlations of the n streams coming from the preprocessing pipelines $[P_1, \ldots, P_n]$, they are made persistent in an appropriate storage space. Following the approach already discussed, each set $[XC_1, \ldots, XC_k]$ of correlations refers to a particular time T_i generated from the initial slicing into subperiods. It is actually common practice in this type of problem to partition the computation into small time periods. However, this requires an additional step before providing the results: in order to enhance the information by increasing the signal-to-noise ratio, the intermediate correlations are stacked to assemble the overall duration of interest.

The final results are presented as images showing the correlation functions between pairs of stations. Therefore, there is an immediate visual feedback for the seismologists that can be very helpful in adjusting and tuning the correlations while they are still running. In Figure 17.11, we show an example of different outcomes obtained by changing just one parameter in the correlation phase. Eventually, these images could be dynamically updated as new streams are computed and presented in a portal, providing a very useful monitoring system.

17.3.3   User-Defined Processing Elements

As described in Chapter 10, the building blocks of a DISPEL workflow are the PEs, the execution of which is optimized and parallelized throughout the nodes

```
1    /* Computes cross correlation between input1 and input2:
     the maximum delay is parametrized (timeShift)*/
2
3    PE<XCorrelationF> crossCorrelate(
4    String timeShift, String datares, String provenanceRes){
5       WFXCorrelator xcorr =new WFXCorrelator;
6       |-datares-|=>xcorr.resource;
7       |-repeat enough of ["tshift="+timeShift]-|=>xcorr.parameters;
8       return PE(<Connection input1=xcorr.input;Connection input2=xcorr.input2> =>
9         <Connection output=xcorr.output;Connection metadata=xcorr.metadata>);
10      };
11
12   ...
13
14   PE<XCorrelationF> XCorrelation =
15    crossCorrelate(timeShift, correlationRes, provenanceRes);
16    Integer n=stations.length;
17
18   for(Integer x=0;x<n;x++){
19     for(Integer y=x+1;y<n;y++){
20       PE(<Connection input> => <>) PlotterPE =
21       plotCorrelation(stations[x],stations[y],channel,processedRes);
22       XCorrelation xCorr = new XCorrelation;
23       PlotterPE plot=new PlotterPE;
24       WFXCorrelationStacker stacker=new WFXCorrelationStacker;
25       ...
26       xCorr.output=>stacker.input;
27       stacker.output=>plot.input;
28       plot.output=>rr.input;
29     }
30   }
31
```

Figure 17.9 *DISPEL code for performing the cross correlation of n streams.*

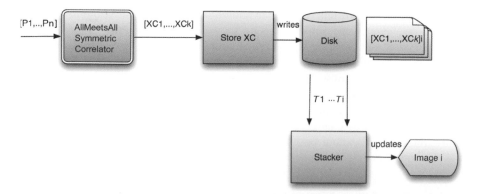

Figure 17.10 *Storage and stacking of the correlation results.*

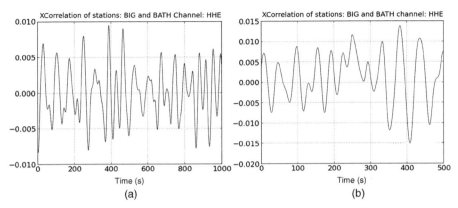

Figure 17.11 *Cross correlation using different maximum time delays (in seconds) (a) lshift = 500 s (b) tshift = 250 s.*

of the underlying data-intensive system. The prototype data-intensive architecture used in our experiments makes use of the OGSA-DAI data-stream processing technology [16].

An important aspect of our experimental scenario has been the dedicated integration of a domain-specific library of algorithms (ObsPy [17]) into OGSA-DAI activities to form the low level implementation of the seismological analysis PEs. This implementation choice was driven by a more general and important requirement of seismology scientists who expect to develop their analysis code using their favorite, trusted libraries, programming languages, and APIs.

To allow for the introduction of user-defined algorithms within our workflow engine, we have implemented a framework (Fig. 17.12) that abstracts over aspects related to the most basic and important needs of this genre of activities. These aspects concern: the configuration of the activity that has to execute a specific analysis code within a particular runtime environment (Python, C), the passage of the parameters and the data between these layers, the production of the metadata in an interoperable format (JSON [18]), and the deallocation of memory and other resources.

All of the light gray colored classes in the UML representation of Figure 17.12 are part of the framework. The `SeismoActivity` and the `SeismoResourceActivity`, which inherit from a core OGSA-DAI activity class and interface, are the activity classes that implement the PEs. A `SeismoActivity` accepts one *input* and a set of *parameters*. Once they are read, they are passed to a `userDefinedProcess` that takes care of organizing this information before passing it to an implementation of the `IExecutorWrapper` that is responsible for running the script performing the actual transformation on the data. Once the transformation has been applied, the result is returned to the wrapper and eventually to the `SeismoActivity`, where it gets written to the output connections.

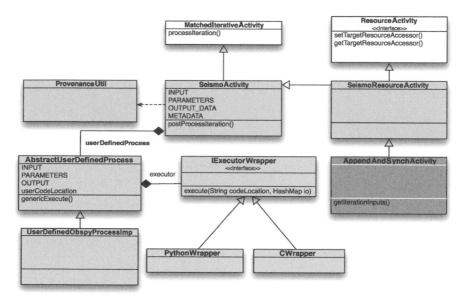

Figure 17.12 *A UML diagram describing the framework developed to enable the integration of a domain-specific library of algorithms within OGSA-DAI.*

Sometimes a specific task required us to extend the `SeismoActivity`. This might happen when the input is not a data stream but, for instance, a list of file references. Let us take as an example the `AppendAndSyncActivity`. Its function is to read a list of Mini-SEED files from a file system, then merge and slice the time series contained in the files according to a specific time window passed as a parameter. Ultimately, the activity converts the time series obtained into a data stream to be delivered through the `OUTPUT_DATA` connection. Notice that the `AppendAndSyncActivity` extends from `SeismoResourceActivity` (Fig. 17.12), which already provides all the required methods to its subclasses to enable access to a specific resource, a file system in this case.

The `PythonWrapper` is the key component which enables communication between OGSA-DAI and the underlying Python technology. This allows us to bring the continuously evolving library of algorithms being developed by seismology experts into the context of the data-intensive platform—the primary requirement of the framework's design.

After investigating the spectrum of the solutions already available to help such integration, we decided to implement the wrapper using JEPP [19], a library designed to embed CPython in Java within a heavily threaded environment, which is exactly what we have to achieve in our experiment. The exchange of information between the Java and Python environments is achieved through the passage of a `HashMap` containing the data that has to be processed and the parameters specified within the workflow. The same `HashMap` is then populated from the script, after its execution, with the processed data and metadata.

This small framework provided us with the ability to assign a behavior to a PE realized as a `SeismoActivity`, directly within the configuration system of the data-intensive prototype architecture. The adoption of the Spring technology [20] allowed us to configure the properties of such PEs just by editing an XML file, declaring a different configuration for each PE name, specifying which `IExecutor-Wrapper` to use and which analysis script to execute. In other words, different PE names can be bound to the `SeismoActivity` class, and the behavior is determined within the `SeismoActivity` at runtime by accessing the Spring context, thus obtaining the desired configuration depending on the name of the PE invoked.

17.3.4 Data Provenance

The increasing amount of data needed to perform the type of analysis required by this scenario led us to acknowledge the existence of all sorts of information about the creation process of the data streams that contribute to the final result that is obtained eventually by the aggregation and stacking of a large quantity of intermediate and partial results.

In using a workflow framework where several distributed services are used to accomplish complex computational tasks, it is interesting to understand how the results from such a computation were created. Storing and accessing provenance information allows for later examination of the derivation process. It tells the user the details of the data quality at a certain point of an experiment and can also be used to re-execute part of the workflow using partial results already available in intermediate archives.

Most of the scientific workflow systems (e.g., VisTrails, Taverna) [21] are aware that preserving execution data is extremely important when validating the obtained results, a fundamental requirement of any scientific computation. Current attempts to resolve problems related to information management infrastructure, workflow provenance, visualization, and database integration are aiming to converge on a single, interoperable framework, the Open Provenance Model [22, 23], for recording provenance data. The Open Provenance Model offers a higher level of abstraction with the aim of improving interoperability among workflow systems, leading toward a better understanding of the execution of a scientific computation that connects different tools, processing services, databases, and computational infrastructures.

However, because of time constraints, it was not possible for us to investigate too deeply if such an approach was suitable for a production-level workflow engine such as OGSA-DAI, designed for distributed analysis and processing of continuous data streams. The provenance-recording solution we adopted is thus particular to this application scenario and provides a starting point for further investigation.

In [24] we find a description of two main strategies in the recording of provenance data: the eager and lazy approaches. While the first is often based on the collection of annotations at each step of the processing and carrying them along until the end of the computation, the latter suggests that the processing of the provenance should happen only when needed. It assumes also that the provenance information of a certain result can be inferred by running a query on a database that is obtained as a transformation of a source database performed by the execution of the computational task.

Our choice for collecting provenance embraces several aspects of the lazy approach, leaving the workflow developer to choose at which point in the computational process it is relevant to store provenance metadata. Such knowledge is directly produced from the single analysis PE that performs a transformation on the data stream. When needed, this information is extracted by a set of dedicated provenance PEs, processed, and stored into a centralized relational database. In case of errors, these are also extracted from the analysis PEs and stored into the relational model. The provenance PEs can be connected together in order to keep track of the story of the metadata produced from the analysis PEs to which they are attached (Fig. 17.13). At the end of the computation, a query on the relational database can provide all of the relevant provenance information that led to a specific output result.

The kind of provenance information collected can be also considered as *retrospective provenance* [25], where we record not only information about the processing steps but also information related to the execution environment, in our case, the PEs' InstanceID and gateways' RequestID. These IDs, coupled with the data-intensive architecture's internal monitoring system, can be used to retrieve additional execution details that can help the validation process, for example, when recreating a certain data product.

In a distributed framework that seeks to allow process execution as close to the data as possible, retaining the knowledge about where the computation is happening can become extremely useful—for example, to detect and eventually address

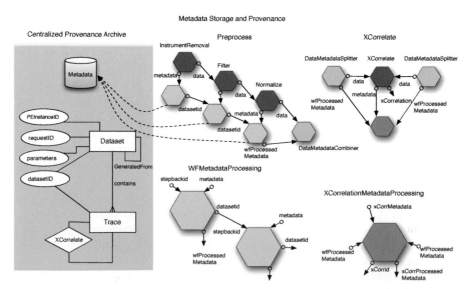

Figure 17.13 *A centralized approach to storing and processing the provenance of distributed PEs.*

weaknesses in a workflow that may be related either to a particular pattern of deployment across the infrastructure or to the quality of the data provided by one of the nodes feeding the stream.

To achieve this, we include a `RequestID` within the dataset's metadata, generated by the gateway itself and assigned to the subgraph of the workflow that is being executed. This allows data-intensive engineers to reconstruct the topology of each run of the workflow, enabling them, for example, to evaluate how a processing subgraph that is executed within a specific gateway is contributing to overall system performance or to any failure that might occur.

The entity relationship schema adopted to represent the `XCorrelation` process (Fig. 17.13) assumes that, during preprocessing, a sequence of the dataset's metadata is produced as the result of the transformation applied on the stream by the analysis PEs invoked with a particular set of parameters. The datasets are generally composed of one or more traces (time series) and each transformation on these time series produces a new dataset with a new set of traces. The `XCorrelation` relationship combines together two traces, producing the intermediate results, before passing them to the stacking phase of the workflow, which leads to the final result. Thus, the `XCorrelation` relationship retains the information needed to discover how all of the traces were processed, that is, the history of the transformations that were applied to them and the gateways that performed them.

Storing errors might also become important at this point, for example, when the final result presents fewer stations than the ones specified by the initial request. In such cases, tracing the `RequestID` of the subgraphs involved in the computation could provide the information needed to understand the point during the workflow at which the missing stations disappeared and why.

17.4 EVALUATION

In this section, we discuss our experience of using the prototype data-intensive architecture and the DISPEL language, highlight lessons learned, and discuss some aspects that we think should be addressed to improve the *intellectual ramps* of the framework.

17.4.1 Usability and Functionality

When we first started to work on our seismology application, the data-intensive framework was in an early stage of development and the scenario's requirements positively contributed to its shaping. In particular, while the DISPEL language was incrementally refined in its definition, the implementation was following the specs at a slower pace. This gave us the opportunity to focus and to push for the finalizations of those aspects of the language that had a major impact on our use case.

As we have seen in earlier chapters, the architecture proposes a three-layer paradigm, where each layer addresses a different, and to some extent independent, role—that of the domain expert, the data analysis expert, and the data-intensive engineer. In this context, we could place ourselves in the middle of the hourglass in Figure 3.1 as data analysis experts, acting as a point of interface between the domain experts and the data-intensive engineers. However, given the experimental and ongoing nature of the original **ADMIRE** project, we often had to deal in some depth with the concerns of the other two categories of experts, and therefore, not always completely appreciated the separation of concerns intended by the platform. We believe that this issue can be easily overcome once the framework is fully developed and mature, offering a complete and rich library of functions and types.

On the whole, however, the prototype architecture proved to be very straight-forward to use. The current release supported by an extensive set of tools and documentation should make life even easier. Crucial to a successful impact on the final scientific users, that is, the domain experts, is the improvement and further development of the registry. We believe that a large and comprehensive set of domain-specific PEs, supplied with the appropriate descriptions and usage patterns, will be one of the key features to attract new users. But this can be seen as an incremental process of collaboration and synergy among actors playing the different roles, and the framework successfully proved itself to be a perfect platform for implementing the three-layer approach while maintaining a certain independence.

Supplemented by a well-populated registry, **DISPEL** appears to be a very powerful and expressive language. Those accustomed to object-oriented programming could face a steep learning curve when approaching the streaming model for the first time, but once this learning period is passed, users will recognize the utility of **DISPEL**'s power in declaring and adopting reusable patterns—one can condense specific behaviors into a few lines of code that can be reused in different contexts, such as, for example, the aforementioned `makeArrayPipeline` function. The general approach to using this new language is quite smooth and exploitation of the more advanced features can be built up incrementally. We bear in mind that these were the early days of development of this platform and language, but we can foresee that with a certain degree of maturity, the role of the **DISPEL** programmer will be eased by an extensive range of available patterns.

Our application test bed provided the opportunity for the development of some common functionality needed by seismologists, and we spent a significant amount of effort in trying to integrate the domain-specific library described in Section 17.3.3. Developing the necessary PEs was a nontrivial task (the logic in our case was complicated), although there is extensive documentation and support available.

The integration of community libraries of algorithms into the data-intensive system is a good example of the complexity issues that we had to tackle. Such a scenario often requires the execution of code written, compiled, or interpreted in languages other than Java. We described how adopting JEPP allowed us to pass the single chunk of data to be processed directly from the Java environment to the CPython module and back. This choice was mainly motivated by our attempt to be as consistent as possible with the data-stream processing model implemented within the prototype architecture. An alternative could have been the creation of a file for each chunk of data. In this case, the reference to the file would need to be propagated from PE to PE and down to the Python algorithm, where the file would be read and a new file created after the processing, thereby breaking the streaming model.

The JEPP helped us to avoid this, but still a few workarounds were needed. First of all, the actual data transferred between the analysis PEs is a serialization of the ObsPy `Stream` object representing the data, rather then an interoperable data stream in Mini-SEED format. The choice of transferring the `Stream` object, serializing/deserializing it within the Python code, is forced by the lack of a feature in ObsPy to acquire Mini-SEED standard volumes from a memory buffer. The library expects to read the data only by passing a reference to a Mini-SEED file, thus breaking the streaming model, again exactly what we wanted to avoid.

The approach we have described to overcome this limitation binds the content of the data stream to the specific technology that is able to deal with it, requiring, for the sake of interoperability, the development of converter PEs in order to transform the Python object into either a Mini-SEED file or a Mini-SEED stream, and vice versa. In order to have a more flexible and interoperable solution, the ObsPy community has been solicited to consider this aspect in further developments of the library. On the other hand, JEPP appears to have issues in passing references to objects that are not Strings, Maps, or List of Strings to the Java environment. This limitation needs to be investigated further in order to allow the passage of Mini-SEED chunks of compressed binary data from the Python to the Java layers.

Processing a large quantity of data in small chunks is a major advantage of streaming data workflows: it reduces the memory footprint, optimizing the overall consumption of resources over time, and allowing a "process and forget" strategy to work. On the other hand, our scenario requires that a fixed sample of a certain amount of data is processed at each step of the computation, and this sample can sometimes be relatively large—around 10 MB. On the basis of the analysis of the fluctuation of the memory allocated from the Java virtual machine, we recognized that the memory deallocation of such large objects must be performed explicitly, to permit a better memory recovery by the garbage collection of the virtual machine. This suggests that the development of PEs requires particular attention to the allocation of memory resources when the amount of data processed at each iteration can be very unpredictable.

The development of the provenance PEs gave us the opportunity to understand some of the capabilities and limitations of the current prototype enactment system with regard to off-the-shelf database PEs. The system does not currently provide a generic activity to execute a list of SQL update/insert expressions on different tables in one transaction, with respect to, for instance, foreign key constraints. Our solution is to embed within the set of provenance PEs, the logic that performs the updates on the database consistently with such constraints.

Another interesting issue that we had to tackle is related to data encoding. The String serialization of our Python objects caused the SOAP communication among OGSA-DAI engines to fail. This is due to the introduction of some unexpected characters into the Web-service payload. To overcome this problem, we included in the framework, depicted in Figure 17.12, the encoding/decoding of the data String in its byte representation, which turns out to be SOAP friendly. As a remark, we think that, in general and in future, a PE developer should concentrate on data types and processing functionalities, rather than on encoding issues. These are problems that should be taken into account within the communication layer of the enactment engine, hence hidden away from the developer.

Generally speaking, the flexibility and adaptability of the data-intensive architecture—in particular with respect to its modularity and layered structure—allowed us to develop our application at an almost constant pace, thereby avoiding any critical bottlenecks. There are still some major aspects to be taken into account though, in order to move to a production level architecture. These are mainly related to the optimization phase that has to accomplish the data integration and analysis tasks by exploiting the underlying infrastructure in the most efficient way. For example, if we consider that the cross correlation of a large number of time series covering a long observation period can be a very long-running and computationally expensive operation, it is clear that an efficient and effective use of the compute resources together with proper recovery and fault tolerant mechanisms become crucial. Therefore, we believe that these are the key features on which effort should now be focused, in order for the platform to play a primary role in the scientific community. Some of this work will be addressed as part of a European Union funded project aimed at developing a data-intensive framework for the earthquake and seismology research community—this is discussed further in Section 17.5.

17.5   FURTHER WORK

The primary goal for developing this application scenario was to explore the added value that such an architecture could provide to the European seismological community as a whole.

Our overall experience has been a positive one, and more work on the data-intensive architecture is planned as part of a European Union project called VERCE[4]—Virtual Earthquake and Seismology Research Community in Europe. VERCE's aim is to enable the seismology community to significantly advance its understanding of the Earth's structure and wave sources in order to aid society in its management of natural hazards, energy resources, environmental changes, and national security concerns. VERCE's strategy is to provide the community with the tools necessary to fully exploit the underutilized wealth of available seismological data. Key to this strategy is a data-intensive computation framework and architecture adapted to the scale and diversity requirements of the community. We discuss here the key extensions that we believe are necessary to facilitate the community's scientific work and transform the prototype architecture into a production quality one.

One important requirement is to reduce the divide between the domain expert and the application platform by developing an intuitive, easy-to-use, and flexible

[4]www.verce.eu, verified March 2012.

interface. A simple application portal for this use case has been created, which allows a user to select the seismological stations and the time period for the data to be retrieved, integrated, and processed. This is a useful demonstration of a production quality tool with more functionality, designed with the seismologist in mind. As a first extension, the approach illustrated in Figure 17.12 could be developed to allow the dynamic deployment of user-defined PEs. This feature can open up interesting scenarios where a Web portal provides the user with an easy point of access to explore seismic data stored at data centers, together with an integrated production environment for developing, testing, deploying, and sharing seismic analysis tools. To achieve such a functionality, the data-intensive platform would need to be enhanced to support the efficient and dynamic validation and deployment of users' code across the platform.

The provenance data feature discussed in Section 17.3.4 may be further refined to facilitate dynamic and user-steered workflows. The information recorded during workflow executions could be used to build up a knowledge base that can be queried to extract behavioral and resource utilization patterns. With the appropriate interfaces and tools, we could provide users with views of the overall process and allow them to intervene and adjust the workflow if required. For instance, no default techniques or default parameter values exist for many of the ambient noise processing steps we have implemented; visualization of intermediary results and control over the execution of the whole process, would allow the seismologist to decide whether different parameter values and/or analytical techniques should be used instead. We could, therefore, aim to provide smart recovery mechanisms that enable users to resubmit and rerun partial pieces of workflow without losing relevant intermediate results. It would also be useful to explore whether some of the emerging new methods for the interactive visualization of data discussed in Chapter 19 could be integrated into our portal to enable seismologists to more fully exploit our wealth of data.

17.6 CONCLUSIONS

We have stated that the increasing volumes of seismological data and advances in theory and processing are forcing seismologists to rethink their scientific methodologies and practices. These data and new developments provide a real opportunity to significantly advance our understanding of the Earth. However, complex and/or large numbers of computations on large volumes of distributed data require a robust and adaptable data-intensive architecture, one that can accommodate and support the different types of users involved in defining, designing, and executing the data-intensive processing tasks.

In our work, we adopted a well-established seismological procedure and used it to explore both the existing and potential capability of a prototype data-intensive platform; although still in an embryonic state, the platform met the demands of our scenario and promises to cater for our future requirements.

We can quickly start to add value to our current scenario and the seismological community—an obvious first extension is the addition of PEs to implement the final two phases of the ambient noise data processing procedure described in [12] that is, the processing relating to the interpretation and presentation of the results for surface wave dispersion measurements. However, as previously mentioned, how we postprocess stacked cross-correlated signals determines the application— in [26] for instance, the cross correlation of seismic waveforms is used to estimate the stability of the timing system of a seismic network; in [27] the authors show how wave speeds obtained from ambient noise decreased before eruptions of the Piton de Fournaise volcano; while [28] suggests that application areas may extend beyond the Earth itself—the author cites works using cross correlation of ambient noise to establish time–distance helio seismology[5] [29] and to learn about the lunar regolith[6] [30]. The data-intensive architecture allows us to reuse PEs and patterns where appropriate to quickly create the required workflows.

It is also worth noting that another area in which seismic interferometry is increasingly applied is exploration geophysics, where the focus is often on the detection of the location of ore minerals and hydrocarbons such as crude oil and gas, and where the volumes of data are also significant (as has been shown in Section 2.2, a seismic survey seeking fossil fuel deposits can easily generate upward of 80 TB of data).[7] Also, a natural progression for future development might be to move from using archived data to real-time data streams—with a few adjustments to the current workflow, mainly related to the community analytical code library, we could start monitoring natural phenomena such as volcanoes.

Given an intuitive and effective interface to define, run, pause, redefine, and resume data integration and analysis workflows quickly, coupled with a production-quality, data-intensive platform, the possibilities are manifold. In our view, the prototype architecture we have investigated has the potential to advance science not merely by efficiently processing large volumes of distributed data but by providing scientists with the tools that enable and encourage them to explore new directions and research horizons.

Acknowledgments

The authors would like to thank the following for their valuable support and the provision of data: Brian Baptie and Richard Luckett, British Geological Survey; Torild van Eck, ORFEUS Data Centre; and Andrew Curtis and Ian Main, School of Geosciences, University of Edinburgh.

---

[5]The study of the structure and processes of the Sun's interior by measuring and analyzing the travel times of solar waves between any two points on the Sun's surface.

[6]The loose covering of dust and rock fragments on the surface of the moon.

[7]This increase in interest in processing ambient noise is evidenced by a special section on interferometry applications in a May 2011 issue of *The Leading Edge*, a journal of the Society of Exploration Geophysicists [31].

REFERENCES

1. R. Weaver and O. Lobkis, "On the emergence of the Green's function in the correlations of a diffuse field: pulse-echo using thermal phonons," *Ultrasonics*, vol. 40, no. 1–8, pp. 435–439, 2002.
2. M. Campillo and A. Paul, "Long-range correlations in the diffuse seismic coda," *Science*, vol. 299, no. 5606, pp. 547–549, 2003.
3. K. Wapenaar, E. Slob, and R. Snieder, "Unified Green's function retrieval by cross-correlation," *Physical Review Letters*, vol. 97, p. 234301, 2006.
4. A. Curtis, P. Gerstoft, H. Sato, R. Snieder, and K. Wapenaar, "Seismic interferometry—turning noise into signal," *The Leading Edge*, vol. 25, no. 9, pp. 1082–1092, 2006.
5. G. D. Bensen, M. H. Ritzwoller, and N. M. Shapiro, "Broad-band ambient noise surface wave tomography across the United States," *Journal of Geophysical Research*, vol. 113, no. B05306, 2008.
6. A. Y. Villaseñor, Y. Yang, M. H. Ritzwoller, and J. Gallart, "Ambient noise surface wave tomography of the Iberian Peninsula: implications for shallow seismic structure," *Geophysical Research Letters*, vol. 34, no. L11304, 2007.
7. X. Song, Z. Xu, X. Sun, S. Zheng, Y. Yang, and M. H. Ritzwoller, "Surface wave dispersion measurements and tomography from ambient noise correlation in China," in *Proceedings of the 31st Monitoring Research Review of Ground-Based Nuclear Explosion Monitoring Technologies*, 2009.
8. Y. Yang, M. H. Ritzwoller, F. C. Lin, M. P. Moschetti, and N. M. Shapiro, "Structure of the crust and uppermost mantle beneath the western United States revealed by ambient noise and earthquake tomography," *Journal of Geophysical Research*, vol. 113, no. B12310, 2008.
9. F. Lin, M. P. Moschetti, and M. H. Ritzwoller, "Surface wave tomography of the western United States from ambient seismic noise: Rayleigh and Love wave phase velocity maps," *Geophysical Journal International*, vol. 173, no. 1, pp. 281–298, 2008.
10. L. Stehly, M. Campillo, and N. M. Shapiro, "A study of the seismic noise from its long range correlation properties," *Journal of Geophysical Research*, vol. 111, no. B10306, 2006.
11. Y. Yang and M. H. Ritzwoller, "The characteristics of ambient seismic noise as a source for surface wave tomography," *Journal of Geophysical Research*, vol. 9, no. 2, 2008.
12. G. D. Bensen, M. H. Ritzwoller, M. P. Barmin, A. L. Levshin, F. Lin, M. P. Moschetti, N. M. Shapiro, and Y. Yang, "Processing seismic ambient noise data to obtain reliable broad-band surface wave dispersion measurements," *Geophysical Journal International*, vol. 169, no. 3, pp. 1239–1260, 2007.
13. "SEED Reference Manual v2.4, Appendix G: Data Only SEED Volumes (Mini-SEED)," IRIS - Incorporated Research Institutions for Seismology. http://www.iris.edu/manuals/SEED/_appG.htm. Accessed August 2012.
14. "SeisComP3," http://www.seiscomp3.org. Accessed August 2011.
15. "What is a RESP file?" http://www.iris.edu/KB/questions/69/What+is+a+RESP+file. Accessed August 2011.
16. M. Antonioletti, M. P. Atkinson, R. M. Baxter, A. Borley, N. P. C. Hong, B. Collins, N. Hardman, A. C. Hume, A. Knox, M. Jackson, A. Krause, S. Laws, J. Magowan,

N. W. Paton, D. Pearson, T. Sugden, P. Watson, and M. Westhead, "The design and implementation of Grid database services in OGSA-DAI," *Concurrency and Computation: Practice and Experience*, vol. 17, no. 2–4, pp. 357–376, 2005.

17. M. Beyreuther, R. Barsch, L. Krischer, T. Megies, Y. Behr, and J. Wassermann, "ObsPy: a Python toolbox for seismology," *Seismological Research Letters*, vol. 81, pp. 530–533, 2010.

18. "JSON." http://json.org. Accessed August 2011.

19. "Jepp—Java Embedded Python," http://jepp.sourceforge.net. Accessed August 2011.

20. "SpringSource," http://www.springsource.org. Accessed August 2011.

21. D. Hull, K. Wolstencroft, R. Stevens, C. A. Goble, M. R. Pocock, P. Li, and T. Oinn, "Taverna: a tool for building and running workflows of services.," *Nucleic Acids Research*, vol. 34, pp. 729–732, 2006.

22. T. Ellqvist, *Supporting Scientific Collaboration through Workflows and Provenance*, Linköping Studies in Science and Technology. Thesis 1427, 2010.

23. The Open Provenance Model, 2008, http://openprovenance.org/. Accessed August 2012.

24. W.-C. Tan, "Research problems in data provenance," *IEEE Data Engineering Bulletin*, vol. 27(4), pp. 42–52, 2004.

25. B. Clifford, I. Foster, M. Hategan, T. Stef-Praun, M. Wilde, and Y. Zhao, "Tracking provenance in a virtual data grid," *Concurrency and Computation: Practice and Experience*, vol. 20, no. 5, pp. 565–575, 2008.

26. C. Sens-Schönfelder, "Synchronizing seismic network with ambient noise," *Geophysical Journal International*, vol. 174, no. 3, pp. 966–970, 2008.

27. F. Brenguier, N. Shapiro, M. Campillo, V. Ferrazzini, Z. Duputel, O. Coutant, and A. Nercessian, "Towards forecasting volcanic eruptions using seismic noise," *Nature Geoscience*, vol. 1, pp. 126–130, 2008.

28. M. Ritzwoller, "Ambient noise seismic imaging," in *McGraw Hill Yearbook of Science and Technology 2009*, McGraw Hill Professional, 2009.

29. T. L. Duvall Jr., S. Jefferies, J. Harvey, and M. Pomerantz, "Time-distance helioseismology," *Nature*, vol. 362, pp. 430–432, 1993.

30. E. Larose, A. Khan, Y. Nakamura, and M. Campillo, "Lunar subsurface investigated from correlation of seismic noise," *Geophysical Research Letters*, vol. 32, no. L16201, 2005.

31. I. Vasconcelos, M. Haney, and M. Diallo, "Special section on interferometry applications," *The Leading Edge*, vol. 30, no. 5, pp. 502–567, 2011.

Part V

Data-Intensive Beacons of Success

The previous parts of this book document the broad and significant progress that data-intensive research has made in the past several years and the role of the DISPEL system in this process. This was well demonstrated by a number of selected advanced applications presented in the preceding book part.

This part of the book introduces a group of challenging, novel data-analytics (knowledge-discovery) applications, which are also starting to shape a new generation of other data mining and integration technologies. While they start from different viewpoints and use different technologies, the examples in the following five chapters reinforce the message in the preceding four parts. They show that data-intensive issues are pressing and challenging, and that their solution strategies take similar paths. As in the chapters of Part IV, they illustrate that science, engineering, environment, and society are fertile territories for data-intensive research. A brief characterization of the chapters in terms of the application domains are addressed as follows:

- **Astronomy** deals with phenomena beyond the Earth's atmosphere, especially, research into space bodies, their systems, various processes in the Universe and the Universe as a whole. Astronomy has a long history of data collection. The increasing capabilities and decreasing price of the digital devices used in signal processing, data analysis and data storage has transformed astronomy from an

The DATA Bonanza: Improving Knowledge Discovery in Science, Engineering, and Business, First Edition.
Edited by Malcolm Atkinson, Rob Baxter, Michelle Galea, Mark Parsons, Peter Brezany, Oscar Corcho, Jano van Hemert, and David Snelling.
© 2013 John Wiley & Sons, Inc. Published 2013 by John Wiley & Sons, Inc.

observational science into a digital and computational science. Especially, in the past 5 years, this domain has become increasingly dependent on the support of high performance computational infrastructures, because the new generation of high resolution telescopes produces enormously large volumes of data. One of the most challenging projects in the history of astronomy is "The Square Kilometre Array Telescope" – the largest and most sensitive telescope ever built. It will require very high performance computing engines and long haul links with a capacity greater than the current global Internet traffic. It will be able to survey the sky more than ten thousand times faster than ever before. The project is aimed at providing answers to fundamental questions about the origin and evolution of the Universe and to shed light on some of the Universe's greatest mysteries.

In Chapter 18, Kitching et al. describe two examples of data- and compute-intensive applications from astronomy. The first is a specific analysis, which centers on running classification algorithms on a dataset generated from two existing sky-survey databases; while the second is a description of a more general problem, that of extracting constraints on cosmological-model parameters by measuring weak gravitational lensing. Improving the accuracy and scope of such measurements is one of the main science drivers for the next generation of sky surveys. This pair of examples illustrates some of the challenges facing modern astronomy that require the development of new data-intensive methods and the availability of a computational infrastructure on which to run them. It is the rate of development of these methods which is likely to dictate the pace of astronomical discovery in the next two decades.

- **Environmental data and interactive research**. Environmental science is an interdisciplinary academic field that integrates physical and biological sciences, including but not limited to Ecology, Physics, Chemistry, Biology, Soil Science, Geology, Atmospheric Science, and Geography. Environmental scientists work on subjects such as the understanding of Earth processes, evaluating the alternative energy systems, pollution control and mitigation, natural resource management, and the effects of global climate change. Environmental scientists bring a systems approach to the analysis of environmental problems. Key elements of an effective environmental science include the ability to discover space, and time relationships, as well as quantitative analysis. Such a broad, complex and interdisciplinary field holds much potential for the application of data mining and integration methods and also poses many challenges to existing data-analytics methods, as discussed in *Data Analysis and Statistics for Geography, Environmental Science & Engineering*, Miguel F. Acevedo, CRC Press, 2012.

In Chapter 19, Blower et al. examine a category of environmental science research that is rarely described, which we shall call '*interactive research*'. In this mode, the scientist is aiming to explore new ideas and perform rapid data analysis tasks in order to find productive future directions. The knowledge delivery step is particularly important, as it is critical to use effective visual-izations.

- **Humanities**. E-Humanities has established itself as an integral part of vari-ous national and international e-Science programmes. There are members of a new generation of researchers in the humanities who are aware how new technologies and vast stores of digitized materials, that previous humanities scholars did not have, are changing the general understanding of the liberal arts. The emerging field of e-Humanities is probably best understood as an umbrella term covering a wide range of activities, from online preservation and digital mapping to data mining and the use of geographic information sys-tems. It is also an emerging domain for using high-performance computing and high-capacity storage resources.

  The arts and humanities e-Science initiative in the UK has successfully shown, in more than ten projects, that new e-Science tools and methodologies can help arts and humanities scholarship. The German TextGrid project is a significant investment into enabling traditional e-Humanities activities, such as the collaborative creation of critical editions within a shared-data envi-ronment. There are similar initiatives in the Netherlands, France and other European countries, as well as in the USA. The European DARIAH infras-tructure (Digital Research Infrastructure for the Arts and Humanities) attempts to bring together many of these national initiatives, in a light-weight and fed-erated way, so that researchers can work with a large but cohesive body of research materials.

  In Chapter 20, Aschenbrenner et al. review this progress and the challenges that lie ahead to enable more researchers in the Arts and Humanities to reap the benefits of their growing wealth of digital data.

- **Engineering and transport**. There are different data-mining applications in engineering for example: (i) analysis of simulation output, where data mining can complement visualization; (ii) identification of coherent structures in tur-bulence; (iii) understanding the effect of design parameters by investigating dependence of output data on input parameters; (iv) verification and valida-tion by comparison between simulations, operational data and experiments; (v) refining the physics model; and (vi) diagnostics and maintenance. To min-imize maintenance costs throughout an engine's life cycle, engineers must obtain knowledge gained from maintenance histories of similar products dur-ing the design phase of new products. This will help engineers identify parts most likely to be problematic throughout the engine's entire life cycle.

  Recently, diagnostic data-mining research was addressed by many engi-neers. The aim is to understand the data and/or to find causes of problems and actionable knowledge in order to solve those problems. This type of data mining is crucial for engineering, manufacturing and scientific applications.

  Several data-mining research results achieved in engineering, especially those arising in maintenance and diagnostics, can be ported to the transporta-tion domain, where the scientists are now able to collect real-time data on traffic conditions and instantaneously analyze that data to shape strategies that minimize delays and congestion.

In Chapter 21, Jim Austin discusses the development of data-intensive methods in engineering-diagnostics research over the last ten years, centered on the lessons learned through a number of large national-scale UK projects. The work was primarily undertaken within the UK e-Science programme and is focused on the analysis of large and complex data, mainly time-series data from engineering and science. The initial work was based on applying artificial neural networks to large data obtained by monitoring vibrations on aero-engines. His group then applied their time-series feature-detection technology to a range of other data sources. The chapter then considers a wider range of transport applications.

- **Zoology and ecology**. Data-intensive research begins to enter new fields like zoology, a branch of biology which relates to the animal kingdom, including the structure, embryology, evolution, classification, habits, and distribution of all animals, both living and extinct. We have very little information about the interactions amongst species and the influence that environmental factors, such as rain, earthquakes, predator invasions, and so on, have on the behavior of a particular group of birds. Recently, several successes have been reported, for example, applying data-mining techniques to the problem of acoustic recognition of bird species in conjunction with the existing deployment of sensor networks.

  In Chapter 22, Kelling et al. introduce results achieved by zoology-focused research using data mining within the DataOne project. The aim is to determine the patterns of species occurrence through time and space, and understand their links with features of the environment, taking account of the uncertainties and varied densities of observation. These are also central themes in ecology. This project involves data- and compute-intensive modeling running on the TeraGrid platform.

18

Data-Intensive Methods in Astronomy

Thomas D. Kitching
*Institute of Astronomy, University of Edinburgh, Edinburgh, UK
and Mullard Space Science Laboratory, University College London, Dorking, UK*

Robert G. Mann
Institute of Astronomy, University of Edinburgh, Edinburgh, UK

Laura E. Valkonen
School of Informatics, University of Edinburgh, Edinburgh, UK

Mark S. Holliman
Institute of Astronomy, University of Edinburgh, Edinburgh, UK

Alastair Hume
EPCC, University of Edinburgh, Edinburgh, UK

Keith T. Noddle
Institute of Astronomy, University of Edinburgh, Edinburgh, UK

18.1 INTRODUCTION

Similar to many other scientific disciplines, astronomy is undergoing a revolution in data availability. Fundamentally, this is driven by developments in detector

The DATA Bonanza: Improving Knowledge Discovery in Science, Engineering, and Business, First Edition.
Edited by Malcolm Atkinson, Rob Baxter, Michelle Galea, Mark Parsons, Peter Brezany, Oscar Corcho,
Jano van Hemert, and David Snelling.
© 2013 John Wiley & Sons, Inc. Published 2013 by John Wiley & Sons, Inc.

technologies, which allow astronomers to capture more bits of information per second of telescope time. As the quantity of data increases, so does the science that is possible, and observational astronomy is undergoing a fundamental change. Most telescope time used to be allocated in blocks of a few nights to an astronomer undertaking a modest observational program, targeting a sample of his/her favorite class of objects, but, nowadays, more time is dedicated to large, systematic sky surveys. These may be awarded several hundred nights of observing time over several years—or, increasingly, undertaken on purpose-built survey telescopes—and may generate tens or hundreds of terabytes of data. The pipeline processing of this data, to remove its instrumental signatures and produce "science-ready" data products, and the analysis of those products are both very data-intensive processes, and astronomy is becoming increasingly dependent on the computational infrastructure needed to support them.

In this chapter, we first briefly outline, in Section 18.2, the concept of the virtual observatory as a science response to this growing wealth of astronomical data and the increasing requirement to answer scientific questions using astronomical data from multiple sources. Then we describe two examples of data-intensive applications from astronomy. The first, described in Section 18.3, centers on running classification algorithms on two existing sky survey databases to generate a catalog of quasars, while the second, in Section 18.4, outlines the derivation of constraints on cosmological parameters via weak gravitational lensing, which is one of the main science drivers for the next generation of sky surveys. This pair of examples illustrates some of the problems faced by modern astronomy, which require the development of new data-intensive methods and the availability of a computational infrastructure on which to run them. It is the rate of development of these methods which is likely to dictate the pace of astronomical discovery in the coming two decades.

18.2   THE VIRTUAL OBSERVATORY

As publicly available astronomical archives grow in volume and number, it is becoming ever less feasible for individual astronomers to access and download entire datasets to their own workstations for processing and analysis. Moreover, most archives only contain data collected by one particular instrument, for example, a ground-based infrared telescope or an X-ray satellite, in formats unique to that instrument. Since much of modern astrophysics is now interested in comparisons between data from different instruments, the interoperability of such datasets has become increasingly important, and this is being addressed by the global virtual observatory (VO) movement. The main goals of the various VO projects that are taking shape within the world-wide astronomy research community are, therefore, to not only provide easy access to distributed data sources but also to develop the standards and protocols needed to achieve interoperability and scalability of those heterogeneous resources.

These standards are developed under the aegis of the International Virtual Observatory Alliance (IVOA[1]) that now comprises 19 members (national and regional VO projects) who together publish more than 10,000 data resources through VO registries. The work of the IVOA is driven by twice-yearly "Interop" meetings at which working groups develop the variety of standards needed to make the world's astronomical data resources interoperable. This process has, so far, progressed more than two dozen standards to the highest level of "IVOA Recommendation" and a further dozen or so are being developed toward that point. While the IVOA is formally a federation of VO projects, the open nature of the Interops and other IVOA procedures means that any interested party can participate in the standards development process, and the process itself remains responsive to the emergence of new scientific requirements and new technology trends.

18.3 DATA-INTENSIVE PHOTOMETRIC CLASSIFICATION OF QUASARS

18.3.1 Motivation

Quasars are the highly energetic cores of galaxies where matter is falling into black holes, releasing prodigious quantities of energy in the process. The unusual brightness of these objects allows them to be seen from great distances making quasars very important probes of cosmology. As their name implies, quasars (quasi-stellar radio sources) are starlike in appearance and distinguishing them from stars requires information from the distribution of their light across the electromagnetic spectrum. The spectra of stars show the classic curve of blackbody radiation, with temperatures of $T \sim 10^{3-4}$ K, whereas the highly energetic processes occurring within the cores of galaxies result in a significantly different spectral shape for the radiation emitted by quasars. The observed spectrum of a distant quasar also differs from that of the light it emitted, both because of the redshifting it has experienced because of the quasar's great distance and because of the effects of the intergalactic matter it has passed through before reaching Earth.

Spectral information is, therefore, essential for the identification of quasars, but spectroscopic measurements that map out the entire spectrum of radiation, are time-consuming and expensive compared to broadband photometric measurements that provide a single measurement of the total radiation in a given wavelength range: the higher spectral resolution of the spectroscopic observation means that the telescope needs to be pointed toward the sky for much longer, in order to obtain a sufficiently high signal-to-noise ratio in spectroscopic measurements, than for photometry. Spectroscopy is also done on an object-by-object basis, whereas photometry can capture all objects within a given area at once. A compromise can be reached by sampling the spectrum, taking broadband photometric measurements at a number of different wavelengths: the more samples you can take, the closer

[1] www.ivoa.net, accessed January 2013.

you can get to recovering the real spectrum and the more accurately you can distinguish quasars from stars. Quasar catalogs have, therefore, traditionally been based on multiband photometric surveys that identify quasar candidates and these are confirmed through follow-up spectroscopy: most starlike objects are, indeed, stars (not quasars), so it is essential to perform this filtering stage, lest huge amounts of telescope time be wasted on taking spectra of what turn out to be stars.

As photometric sky surveys grow in size—the largest have measurements for $\sim 10^9$ objects—the follow-up spectroscopy of quasar candidates has become prohibitively expensive, and so, interest has turned to determining whether quasars can be classified accurately and efficiently using photometric data alone. This work was pioneered by Richards et al. [1] who applied a Bayesian classifier to five-band photometric data from the Sloan Digital Sky Survey (SDSS) and showed that through training on a subset of SDSS objects spectroscopically identified as quasars, the classifier could identify quasars as accurately from photometric data alone as is possible from spectroscopic data (a small fraction of quasar candidates yield poor or unclassifiable spectra), thereby removing the requirement for follow-up spectroscopy completely.

18.3.2 Using Multiphotometric Surveys

While the work of Richards and collaborators (most recently in Richards and Deo [2]) has shown that the five SDSS bands, all in the optical region of the spectrum, can be used to classify point sources into stars and quasars with a reasonable degree of accuracy, recent studies have revealed that adding more data points, in the form of infrared wavelength bands, can further improve the accuracy and efficiency of the classification algorithms [3–5] and can also increase the detection rates of quasars with unusual spectra [3, 6–8]. A data-intensive experiment was, therefore, conducted to combine near-infrared photometry from the UK Infrared Deep Sky Survey (UKIDSS) with SDSS optical data and then to undertake a classification similar to that of Richards et al.

18.3.3 The Sky Survey Data

The latest public SDSS data release, DR7 [9], includes a database containing the sky coordinates and photometric measurements of 450 million distinct astronomical objects that have been detected in the SDSS images taken in five different optical wavelength bands, known as the u-, g-, r-, i-, and z-bands, and covering one-quarter of the sky. UKIDSS is the near-infrared counterpart to the SDSS and the latest public data release of its large area survey (LAS) contains photometric measurements for almost 60 million distinct objects at four different infrared wavelengths, known as the Y-, J-, H-, and K-bands. Many of the objects appear in both the SDSS and UKIDSS databases, while others may only appear in one, being too faint to be detected in the other.

18.3.4 Quasar Classification Algorithms

Typical quasar-classification algorithms begin by cross matching the catalogs to identify the objects that appear in both catalogs; for example, the sky coordinates for each object in one catalog are matched against all of those in the other catalog, using geometric functions to search within a small radius around the target coordinates. Once the counterparts have been identified, their location in the multiparameter space (defined by the u-, g-, r-, i-, z-, Y-, J-, H-, and K-band data) can be used to classify the objects into stars or quasars. The classification can be based on theoretical models of quasar spectra, which predict quasar brightnesses in each of the bands or can be based on empirical data from known quasars. As well as the photometric catalog of all of the detected objects, the SDSS database also contains a table of 120,000 known quasars, which have been confirmed using spectroscopic follow-up observations and can be used as training data for data-mining algorithms [10, 11].

18.3.5 The Quasar Classification Workflow

The first task in the experiment was to generate the merged optical/infrared catalog from the separate SDSS and UKIDSS databases. The experiment was conducted on the ADMIRE test bed (discussed in other chapters of this book) and used copies of both datasets hosted in Edinburgh, but the parent SDSS database is, in fact, hosted in the United States, and production analyses would generally have to be undertaken on geographically distributed databases. This is now becoming possible, thanks to the VO.

A significant step along the path to a fully integrated "VO on your desktop" would be for a researcher to be able to query two or more heterogeneous distributed sources as if they were a single database. This has, in fact, been achieved using the ADMIRE data-intensive platform, which in turn exploits the distributed query processing functionality of OGSA-DAI.[2]

The SDSS and UKIDSS databases both expose a Table Access Protocol (TAP) interface; TAP is an IVOA standard for publishing tabular datasets to the VO, and we use the TAP implementation provided by the DataSet Access (DSA) Web service developed by AstroGrid, the United Kingdom's VO project. The first step toward the goal of classifying quasars is to create an OGSA-DAI view of the SDSS and UKIDSS databases, making these two distributed databases appear as a single TAP interface to the user, as demonstrated in Figure 18.1.

The workflow for generating the merged optical/near-infrared catalog contains the following steps:

1. The user sends a query expressed in the Astronomical Data Query Language[3] (ADQL) to the TAP interface of the DSA service fronting the virtual federated

---

[2]www.ogsadai.org.uk accessed January 2013.
[3]www.ivoa.net/Documents/latest/ADQL.html accessed January 2013.

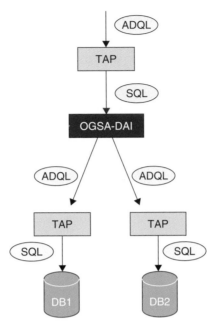

Figure 18.1   *The data-integration stage of the quasar classification process is performed by using OGSA-DAI to create a virtual federation of the SDSS and UKIDSS databases (the arrows indicate the requests to initiate data streams that then flow in the other direction).*

database, specifying a spatial join between the SDSS PhotoObj and UKIDSS lasSource tables which record the positions, shapes, brightnesses, and other properties of celestial sources detected in the optical and near-infrared sky surveys, respectively.

2. The DSA server translates this ADQL query into SQL and passes it onto OGSA-DAI.

3. OGSA-DAI's Distributed Query Processor (DQP) analyzes the query and generates from it a query plan. On the basis of that, the OGSA-DAI sends ADQL queries to the TAP services for the SDSS and UKIDSS databases to create an input stream from each.

4. Each TAP service then translates that ADQL query into the appropriate dialect of SQL for its database and passes it to the database via JDBC.

5. The TAP services stream their results to OGSA-DAI.

6. OGSA-DAI reads the two streams and joins them.

7. OGSA-DAI streams the result to the TAP service representing the virtual federated database, which then passes it to the desired output location.

This TAP-to-OGSA-DAI-to-TAP-to-Database chain has been implemented and tested, although some work remains to automate the extraction by OGSA-DAI of the database metadata through a TAP metadata query and to ensure that OGSA-DAI can handle all of the extensions to standard SQL that are included in ADQL. In this experiment, the queries involved the `PhotoObj` and `DR5QuasarCatalog` tables of SDSS, containing 453,846,233 and 77,429 rows, respectively, and the `lasSource` table in UKIDSS, which has 58,060,655 rows.

In addition to running queries over distributed databases, OGSA-DAI supports workflows that combine "activities," that can include an appropriately wrapped Web service, making possible the situation shown in Figure 18.2, where the OGSA-DAI service receives the data from the two databases and passes them onto a data-mining service, and then deposits the results in VOSpace, a distributed storage service which astronomers use for work in progress, all within the control of an OGSA-DAI workflow (the scope of which is indicated by the dashed line).

While the photometric classification of quasars is a very specific application for the future data-mining aspect of this work, the aim of this initial exercise, from the OGSA-DAI perspective, has been to demonstrate how its DQP functionality could be used to integrate generic TAP-enabled data resources. This approach could in theory be applied to any datasets that the DSA software is able to translate, with no extra work required on the part of the providers of the distributed resources.

18.4 PROBING THE DARK UNIVERSE WITH WEAK GRAVITATIONAL LENSING

Astronomical amounts of data will be required over the next decade in an effort to understand the dark Universe (dark energy and dark matter) that constitutes over 95% of the content of the Universe but the nature of which is entirely unknown.

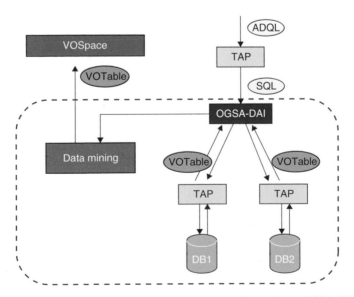

Figure 18.2 *Mining distributed virtual observatory data archives using an OGSA-DAI workflow.*

18.4.1 Gravitational Lensing

Of particular interest for dark Universe studies are wide-field (large area) imaging surveys of the sky. These experiments aim to create optical and near-infrared images of the sky over large contiguous areas with very high resolution (e.g., CFHTLS,[4] VST-KIDS,[5] DES,[6] Pan-STARRS,[7] Euclid [13], and LSST[8]). The data volume is expected to increase by an order of magnitude over the next decade as larger telescopes are employed for increasingly longer timescales gathering such data (Fig. 18.3).

In order to ascertain the nature of these dark components of the Universe, cosmologists need to distinguish between competing models and measure indicative cosmological parameters to sufficient accuracy. This high-level constraint places subpercent requirements on both the statistical accuracy of the observables and on the level of systematic contamination. This in turn leads to a requirement on the amount of raw data and on processing requirements. Figure 18.4 shows a schematic representation of how predictions on the level at which models will need to be tested leads to data size and processing requirements.

These imaging data will allow very faint and distant galaxies to be resolved. The imaging of very faint resolved galaxies is crucial for dark Universe studies, as their observed shapes are very slightly distorted (of the order of a 1% change in the brightness of an object) through the gravitational lensing effect of the intervening

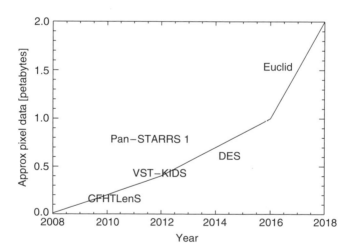

Figure 18.3 *A representation of the imaging data volume (axis Y), the product of area and number of imaging bands, increase over the next decade (axis X). Figures are a product of the area observed and number of wavelengths that each experiment plans to create [12].*

[4]www.cfht.hawaii.edu/Science/CFHLS accessed January 2013.
[5]www.astro-wise.org/projects/KIDS accessed January 2013.
[6]www.darkenergysurvey.org accessed January 2013.
[7]pan-starrs.ifa.hawaii.edu/public accessed January 2013.
[8]www.lsst.org/lsst accessed January 2013.

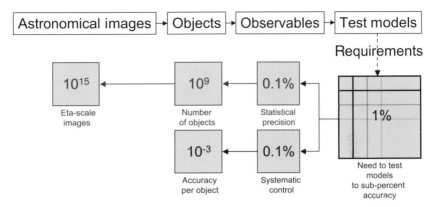

Figure 18.4 *In cosmology, we use objects (galaxies) detected in astronomical images to generate observable functions that depend on the cosmological model we wish to test. To test models to percent accuracy requires subpercent statistical accuracy on parameter estimation and a similar level of systematic control. These statistical and systematic requirements in turn require extremely large datasets and very high precision data analysis techniques.*

dark-matter distribution. Gravitational lensing has been identified [14 16] as the method with the highest potential for dark Universe discovery. However, it is a particularly data-intensive method for the following reasons:

- Billions of objects are needed to statistically measure the gravitational lensing effect.
- High resolution images of billions of objects result in peta-scale raw data products.
- The lensing effect on an individual object needs to be determined to within 1 part in 10^{-3} accuracy; current methods for this are CPU intensive.
- The images also contain an unknown and spatially varying convolution kernel[9] that must be estimated from stars within an image.

Additional challenges for gravitational lensing measurements are that images are pixelized and a typical galaxy is observed at a signal-to-noise ratio of only 5–10 (see GREAT08/GREAT10 in [12,17]). Figure 18.5 shows the most significant processes that contribute toward the galaxy images we observe. The convolution kernel affects both galaxies and stars, but as stars do not experience the lensing effect, they can be used to determine the amount of smoothing.

18.4.2 Gravitational Lensing Data

The process through which raw image data are manipulated to enable gravitational lensing science presents multiple data-intensive steps that cover a variety of

---

[9]A convolution kernel is a function that acts to blur an image. In astronomical images, this function varies in time (between exposures) and across the field of view.

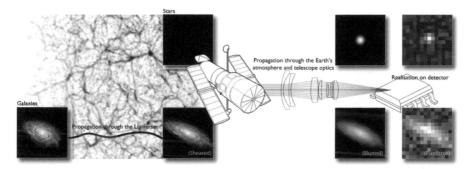

Figure 18.5 *The gravitational lensing effect induced by the dark matter structure in the Universe induces a small distortion (shear) in observed shapes of galaxies, as their light propagates through the Universe. There is a further convolution due to the Earth's atmosphere and the telescope optics. The final images are also noisy and pixelated. Stars do not experience the lensing effect and can be used to estimate the convolution kernel [12]. Source: Hubble outline and images courtesy of NASA.*

potential solutions (Fig. 18.6). The raw data are provided by astronomical instruments as a series of images, or "exposures." Each exposure must be processed individually because of the heterogeneous nature of systematic instrument effects and because the convolution kernel is a function of exposure time and spatial coordinates.

The initial raw data are processed and cleaned; this is an I/O and CPU-intensive process. However, each image can be processed individually for some steps. The convolution kernel must then be estimated from the cleaned data, and the kernel and images given to the algorithm that performs the lensing analysis. The lensing analysis stage is CPU intensive but is also trivially parallelizable, as each object can be analyzed independently (this is not true for the convolution kernel estimation). Finally, the resultant catalog is tested for inconsistencies using a variety of cross checks. There may also be multiple algorithms at each of the previous stages, which typically result in multiple (tens of) data processing loops.

The current state-of-the-art gravitational lensing pipeline can produce science-ready catalogs over a time scale of weeks using off-the-shelf hardware (a few hundred CPUs). Scaling this up toward the next generation of experiment that will deliver orders of magnitude more data (and will require an order of magnitude more accuracy) will require optimization at every stage. The science analysis itself presents a data-mining challenge, where giga-scale catalogs need to be processed. Techniques that allow a visualization of the next generation of data product do not yet exist.

18.4.3 Gravitational Lensing Challenges

In order to test models that can potentially explain the dark energy and dark matter that account for 95% of the Universe, cosmologists require high fidelity optical

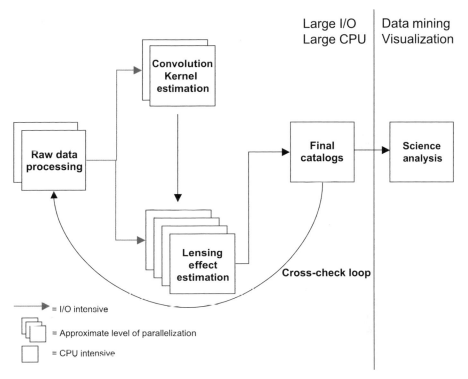

Figure 18.6 *A typical gravitational-lensing pipeline that goes from raw images to science-ready catalogs. The input data are heterogeneous as a result of the instrument and environment in which the images are taken. The requirements on each stage in the chain are heterogeneous in terms of data throughput, CPU, and parallelization requirements. The science analysis itself is a data-mining and visualization challenge.*

and near-infrared imaging of billions of galaxies, identified from peta-byte scale images so that the gravitational lensing effect from each galaxy can be measured.

Each stage in the gravitational lensing data analysis chain presents unique challenges. Foremost are the very large amount of heterogeneous data and complex multimode data processing elements, each of which can be optimized in a variety of ways, some stages requiring fast I/O, some stages requiring large CPU resources, and each stage having varying amounts of parallelizability.

Algorithms to perform each of the data processing stages must be refined, optimized, and developed for the next generation of experiment. The GRavitational lEnsing Accuracy Testing (GREAT) program is a PASCAL[10] challenge to the computer science and astronomical communities, which provides a simulation environment in which new algorithms for lensing measurement and convolution kernel estimation can be developed.

[10]pascallin2.ecs.soton.ac.uk/Challenges accessed January 2013.

18.5 FUTURE RESEARCH ISSUES

The ADMIRE quasar-classification experimental workflow has been handcrafted by several of the software engineers responsible for developing the OGSA-DAI software, together with other experts in the details of the TAP standard and Astro-Grid's DSA software. The ultimate goal must be to provide an infrastructure where a research astronomer can perform an equivalent analysis without requiring expert knowledge of the infrastructural software that underpins it. This will require a lot of additional work: to simplify the definition of the virtual federated database and the implementation of a TAP interface to it, to automate the extraction of the database metadata required for OGSA-DAI's DQP to generate sensible query execution plans, to implement more efficient joins within OGSA-DAI capable of handling the large data volumes produced by realistic queries on astronomical databases, and to provide a flexible infrastructure within which the researcher can specify the analysis algorithm to be run on the merged catalog.

The gravitational lensing scenario is further from concrete realization but is equally pressing as it will form the core of the science to come from several forthcoming sky surveys. It will require the development of sophisticated new algorithms for lensing measurement and convolution kernel estimation, as well as the optimization of pipeline code to run these analyses effectively on large-scale hardware deployments.

More generally, the astronomical community requires a framework for running data analysis routines within the data center: this is already being planned for LSST [14], but it is far from clear how the required functionality can be provided as a general utility for the research community.

18.6 CONCLUSIONS

In this chapter, we have highlighted the data-intensive opportunities and challenges presented by rare object classification and high precision cosmology. In particular, with upcoming surveys, the demands that cosmological model testing will place on both the precision and throughput require an order of magnitude change in the way that data are processed. This is exemplified in gravitational lensing experiments that require very high accuracy measurements and systematic control on pixel and catalog-level products.

Finally, in order to calibrate and test any pipelines and to correctly assess the impact of systematics, cosmological simulations will be required. The challenge in creating these simulations, peta-scale N-body and hydrodynamical codes, and in analyzing them, where thousands of simulations will be required to calibrate each dataset, is even an order of magnitude larger than analyzing the data itself.

For hundreds of years, progress in astronomy has been limited by the speed of advance of the technologies needed to capture the light from celestial sources, but we are now entering a phase in which it is the development of computational techniques that is the limiting factor. The next generation of sky surveys is designed to address some of the most fundamental questions in science at present, but they will only be able to answer them if supported by computational technologies and techniques capable of manipulating the huge volumes of (often distributed and heterogeneous) data produced by the coming generation of sky survey instruments. This will test the ingenuity of computer scientists every bit as much as astronomers, and it is clear that the collaboration between the two communities will become ever more necessary and, it is to be hoped, ever more beneficial to both sides.

Acknowledgments

This work was supported in part by the Euro-VO AIDA project, the framework of the FP7 eInfrastructure Scientific Research Repositories initiative (project RI2121 104). T. Kitching was supported in this by a Royal Astronomical Society 2010 Fellowship and a PASCAL 2 Challenge Grant (GREAT10).

REFERENCES

1. G. T. Richards, A. D. Myers, A. G. Gray, N. R. Riegel, R. C. Nichol, R. J. Brunner, A. S. Szalay, D. P. Schneider, and S. F. Anderson, "Efficient photometric selection of quasars from the sloan digital sky survey: 100,000 $z < 3$ quasars from data release one," *Astrophysical Journal Supplement Series*, vol. 155, pp. 257–269, 2004.

2. G. T. Richards and R. P. Deo, "Eight-dimensional mid-Infrared/optical bayesian quasar selection," *Astrophysical Journal*, vol. 137, pp. 3884–3899, 2009.

3. K. Chiu, G. T. Richards, P. C. Hewett, and N. Maddox, "The optical and near-infrared properties of 2837 quasars in the United Kingdom Infrared Telescope Infrared Deep Sky Survey," *Monthly Notices of the Royal Astronomical Society*, vol. 375, pp. 1180–1188, 2007.

4. G. T. Richards, A. D. Myers, A. G. Gray, N. R. Riegel, R. C. Nichol, R. J. Brunner, A. S. Szalay, D. P. Schneider, and S. F. Anderson, "Efficient photometric selection of quasars from the sloan digital sky survey. II. 1,000,000 quasars from data release 6," *Astrophysical Journal Supplement Series*, vol. 180, pp. 67–83, 2009.

5. X. B. Wu and Z. Jia, "Quasar candidate selection and photometric redshift estimation based on SDSS and UKIDSS data," *Monthly Notices of the Royal Astronomical Society*, vol. 406, pp. 1583–1594, 2010.

6. D. J. Mortlock, M. Patel, S. J. Warren, et al., "Discovery of a redshift 6.13 quasar in the UKIRT infrared deep sky survey," *Astronomy & Astrophysics*, vol. 505, pp. 97–104, 2009.

7. N. Maddox, P. C. Hewett, S. J. Warren, and S. M. Croom, "Luminous K-band selected quasars from {UKIDSS}," *Monthly Notices of the Royal Astronomical Society*, vol. 386, pp. 1605–1624, 2008.

8. B. P. Venemans, R. G. McMahon, S. J. Warren, et al., "The discovery of the first luminous $z \sim 6$ quasar in the UKIDSS Large Area Survey," *Monthly Notices of the Royal Astronomical Society*, vol. 376, pp. 76–80, 2007.

9. K. N. A. Abazajian, J. K. Adelman-McCarthy, M. A. Agueros, et al., "The seventh data release of the sloan digital sky survey," *Astrophysical Journal Supplement Series*, vol. 182, pp. 543–558, 2009.

10. R. D'Abrusco, G. Longo, and N. A. Walton, "Quasar candidates selection in the Virtual Observatory era," *Monthly Notices of the Royal Astronomical Society*, vol. 396, pp. 223–262, 2009.

11. D. Gao, Y. X. Zhang, and Y. H. Zhao, "Support vector machines and kd-tree for separating quasars from large survey data bases," *Monthly Notices of the Royal Astronomical Society*, vol. 386, pp. 1417–1425, 2008.

12. T. Kitching, A. Amara, G. Mandeep, et al., "Gravitational lensing accuracy testing 2010 (GREAT10) challenge handbook," *Annals of Applied Statistics*, vol. 5, pp. 2231–2263 September 2011.

13. A. Refregier, A. Amara, T. D. Kitching, A. Rassat, R. Scaramella, J. Weller, and Euclid Imaging Consortium, "Euclid Imaging Consortium Science Book," *ArXiv e-prints*, 2010.

14. Z. Ivezic, J. A. Tyson, E. Acosta, et al., "LSST: from science drivers to reference design and anticipated data products," version 2.0.9 of June, 2011, available from http://lsst.org/lsst/overview/.

15. J. A. Peacock, P. Schneider, G. Efstathiou, J. R. Ellis, B. Leibundgut, S. J. Lilly, and Y. Mellier, "ESA-ESO Working Group on "Fundamental Cosmology," tech. rep., European Space Agency, 2006.

16. A. Albrecht, G. Bernstein, R. Cahn, W. L. Freedman, J. Hewitt, W. Hu, J. Huth, M. Kamionkowski, E. W. Kolb, L. Knox, J. C. Mather, S. Staggs, and N. B. Suntzeff, "Report of the Dark Energy Task Force," *ArXiv Astrophysics e-prints*, 2006.

17. S. Bridle, J. Shawe-Taylor, A. Amara, et al., "Handbook for the GREAT08 Challenge: an image analysis competition for cosmological lensing," *Annals of Applied Statistics*, vol. 3, pp. 6–37, 2009.

19

The World at One's Fingertips: Interactive Interpretation of Environmental Data

Jon Blower, Keith Haines, and Alastair Gemmell

Reading e-Science Centre, University of Reading, Reading, UK

19.1 INTRODUCTION

In the environmental sciences, the use of visualization techniques is vital for understanding the ever-increasing volume and diversity of data that are being produced by Earth-observing systems and computer simulations. The primary purpose of visualization is to gain insight [1, 2], but the majority of current tools in wide use are not adequate for achieving this.

- The time and effort required to generate visualizations is far too great. Scientists must grapple with technical details such as the interpretation of

The DATA Bonanza: Improving Knowledge Discovery in Science, Engineering, and Business, First Edition.
Edited by Malcolm Atkinson, Rob Baxter, Michelle Galea, Mark Parsons, Peter Brezany, Oscar Corcho, Jano van Hemert, and David Snelling.

a diverse array of file formats and metadata conventions simply for the purpose of reading data from files. Kelvin Droegemeier, professor of mesoscale meteorology at the University of Oklahoma, once stated that PhD students and postdoctoral researchers often end up spending a large majority of their time on these low-level tasks (personal communication) and his experience is by no means unique. This crippling overhead means that visualizations are commonly only the end result of an analysis, rather than playing a key role— as they should—in the whole scientific process, from hypothesis generation to conclusion [3].

- In order to generate and develop new ideas, users must be able to explore data interactively, which requires a different type of visualization from the static plots that are currently the main outcomes of scientific visualization.

- Visualizations, once generated, usually retain no link to their source data or the method that produced them. These images, not the data, become the primary artifacts of scientific collaboration, more by virtue of convenience than their inherent value. They are shared, perhaps contained within journal papers, presentation slides, or emails, within the scientific community and the recipient cannot easily retrieve the source data in order to perform a new analysis or interpretation.

Visualization in itself is, therefore, more complex and yet more limited than it should be, and the complexity increases hugely when many different data sources must be brought together to attack a problem. In fact, only rarely is a single, homogeneous dataset adequate for gaining new insight. Studies of model validation, ground truthing of remote sensing data, quality control, and data assimilation all rely on the ability to synthesize diverse data sources, yet few tools aid the scientist sufficiently to allow him or her to focus on the scientific question at hand, rather than the considerable challenges of the information technology.

In this chapter, we discuss the current practices and emerging new methods of environmental data visualization, exploration, and intercomparison in the particular context of the "fluid earth sciences," namely meteorology, oceanography, and climate science. The discussion is also highly relevant to other areas of study of the Earth system, particularly where large, multidimensional datasets are involved. We begin by providing an overview of the many varieties of data with which scientists must get to grips, and the characteristics and capabilities of the tools that are in current common use. We describe the current state of informatics and infrastructure that underpin current tools and methods. We explain some new approaches in the form of specific software applications and infrastructures, ranging in complexity from visualization-only systems to those that support quantitative processing and intercomparison, highlighting the scientific applications and the recent technological advances that have enabled them. We conclude by speculating as to future developments in the field, and what the scientific and technical communities must achieve in order to fulfill this vision.

19.2   THE CURRENT STATE OF THE ART

This section provides a report on the state of the art, which introduces the starting position of our project and represents the initial inputs that have driven the project effort.

19.2.1   Current Data Volumes

Almost every modern scientific discipline now complains of a "data deluge," in which the volume of data available to the community grows exponentially or worse [4], and the environmental sciences are no exception. The Earth is monitored—incompletely of course—by a vast, diverse, and growing array of instruments. Three thousand autonomous floats roam the oceans [5], each providing vital information about the ocean interior every 10 days, giving roughly 10,000 new hydrographic profiles each month. Every day, satellites provide nearly 2 million observations (1 million of sea surface temperature, 0.8 million of sea ice concentration, and 40,000 of sea level) that are assimilated into operational ocean forecasting models. Innumerable weather observations of various kinds record winds, temperatures, humidity, and many other quantities besides, from the Earth's surface to the upper atmosphere. Earth-observing satellites sense a huge range of properties from soil moisture, through land cover and ocean salinity to atmospheric chemistry. Another kind of instrument--the supercomputer—captures as best it can our understanding of the physics, chemistry, and biology of the whole Earth system and produces large-scale integrated information about the planet as a whole, filling in the gaps in the past observational record as well as giving some capability to predict the future.

Numerical modeling activities produce even more voluminous datasets. For example, the Coupled Model Intercomparison Project (CMIP)[1] collects numerical simulations of the Earth's climate from a number of modeling institutions worldwide. Its results form a vital part of the scientific evidence base underpinning the assessment reports (ARs) of the Intergovernmental Panel on Climate Change (IPCC)[2]. The volume of data managed in each iteration of CMIP has grown rapidly, from less than 1 TB in its early phases to 36 TB for CMIP3. The next iteration (CMIP5[3]) that will underpin the Fifth Assessment Report, is expected to involve 2.5 PB of managed data, which will be distributed among the world's data centers [6]. This growth is driven by increases in the spatial resolution of models and the simulation of an ever-increasing array of Earth system components, including the oceans, atmosphere, ice sheets, and carbon cycle.

---

[1]cmip-pcmdi.llnl.gov
[2]www.ipcc.ch
[3]There was no CMIP4. The version numbers of CMIP have now been aligned with those of the IPCC's Assessment Reports. Therefore, AR5 will be based on CMIP5 and so on.

19.2.2 Data Diversity

All these diverse data sources possess their own intrinsic value that is multiplied when data from different sources can be combined. For example, in CMIP5, there will be an attempt to initialize many of the climate models with Earth Observation data collected from global observing systems to allow, for the first time, the prediction of climate changes in the near term of a year to a decade, much as weather forecast services at present use models of the atmosphere to predict weather over 1 day to 2 weeks ahead.

The volume and diversity of data with which the environmental scientist must work is clear to see. To these concerns organizational problems can be added: datasets are produced by a large number of organizations worldwide. In the case of operational weather forecasting, there is a large degree of agreement and harmonization as to how data are distributed on the Global Telecommunications System [7]. However, in other, smaller, communities, groups often develop their own approach to data management and dissemination.

19.2.3 Current Research Practice

Many scientists typically perform studies with one or two datasets in which they are expert, but they will not have had time to familiarize with using the full range of available data. The technical difficulties of finding, accessing, and interpreting these diverse sources of data remain key barriers to scientific progress. The degree to which these obstacles truly limit enquiry very much depends on the manner of the research in question. For example, if a scientist knows in advance that he must rigorously and painstakingly sift through datasets X and Y, which are already familiar to them, in order to address specific questions P and Q, then the overhead of accessing data and converting it to a useful form may be tolerably low compared with the total duration of the work. Nevertheless, despite the appearance often given retrospectively by scientific papers (and prospectively by proposals), scientific research cannot usually be planned accurately in advance. New lines of enquiry spontaneously emerge as a result of new data or new ideas, and unfruitful directions are abandoned frequently in the course of a real project. Easy access to the ever-growing array of datasets can, therefore, be a real spur to the generation of new ideas. We are aiming, therefore, at a much more interactive mode of data analysis and exploration.

The analytical weapons in the armory of a typical environmental scientist include hand-coded programs (in languages such as C, C++, and Fortran), problem-solving environments (including MATLAB, Octave, and IDL [8]), and high-level scripting languages (e.g., Python and R), in addition to the ubiquitous spreadsheets. Hand-coded programs are often employed in cases in which performance is important, and/or datasets are large, although the effort required by the scientist is usually high, and there is a very slow cycle of work involving coding, compiling, running, and debugging. Software packages such as MATLAB and IDL, and increasingly the general-purpose scripting languages, provide high-level functions and libraries that can greatly reduce the amount of time required to arrive at a result, sometimes at the expense of some performance. Workflow engines such as Taverna [9], Kepler [10], and XBaya [11] provide a graphic programming environment in which users perform data analysis by the assembly of high-level modules or blocks. Computational steering [12] is not yet widely used in environmental science.

19.2.4   Current Support for Interaction

How many of these solutions can support our desire for greater interaction with data? The low-level programs are not usually interactive, requiring a considerable turnaround time. The problem-solving environments and scripting languages are commonly termed "interactive" because they remove the need for the compilation step and give new results line by line; however, the plots they produce are almost always static, and the script must be edited and rerun in order to alter the visualization. Workflow engines are usually not very much different from high level programming languages in this respect, although some graphic programming environments such as LabView permit true interactivity by instantly responding to changes in their inputs without requiring manual rerunning of the program. Spreadsheets do provide a truly interactive mode of operation, in which plots and charts instantly change if their input data are altered; however, spreadsheets are not usually a suitable engine for processing large geographic datasets that characterize the environmental sciences.

Driven in part by a recognition of this gap in tooling, together with a desire to combine environmental science data with those from other sources, there is a great deal of current interest in the use of Geographic Information Systems (GIS) in environmental science [13–18]. Historically, the GIS ecosystem has been populated by a small number of costly, mutually incompatible commercial tools. These tools have been designed for applications that usually deal with two-dimensional, land-based data. As such, these tools are sometimes used scientifically in areas such as remote sensing and hydrology, but very little in the fluid earth sciences. Putting aside concerns of cost, the main reason is a fundamental impedance mismatch: these sciences are concerned with three-dimensional processes that evolve rapidly in time and would, therefore, require a four-dimensional GIS. The process of "upgrading" from two to four dimensions is far from straightforward, involving essentially a complete rethinking of GIS tools and services. Nevertheless, the standard GIS technique of overlaying georeferenced data from different sources is an extremely powerful one, although only a few environmental science tools support it in a convenient manner.

Some desktop tools such as NASA World Wind [19] and the Unidata Integrated Data Viewer [20] provide powerful interactive visualization techniques and overlaying capabilities but require the user to download and understand large and complex applications, even for performing simple tasks (Fig. 19.1). There is a niche in the ecosystem waiting to be filled by easy to use, responsive, interactive visualization applications that make it very easy to perform simple (yet extremely useful) visualization tasks.

(a)

(b)

(c)

(d)

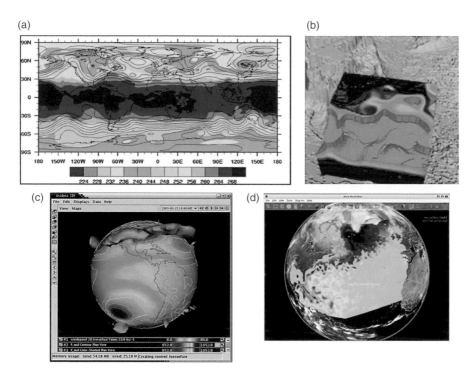

Figure 19.1 Screenshots of visualizations produced using a number of currently available tools. (a) A typical static graphic from a problem-solving environment such as MATLAB or IDL; (b) A Silicon Graphics 3D interactive visual exploration environment; (c) The NASA World Wind virtual globe; and (d) An interactive graphic from the Unidata Integrated Data Viewer (image courtesy UCAR/Unidata). Although powerful, systems such as these often present a steep learning curve to users. GIS tools, even"scientifically oriented" ones such as World Wind, typically possess limited support for exploring all facets of four-dimensional environmental data.

19.2.5 Neogeography Tools

A new generation of GIS, based on lightweight, open tools, components, and standards in place of the existing proprietary, heavyweight tools, is emerging. Inspired by intuitive, easy-to-use tools such as Google Maps and Google Earth, and coordinated by international bodies such as ISO and the Open Geospatial Consortium (OGC),[4] these "neogeography" approaches bring GIS techniques within the reach of the mass market that of course includes scientists [21]. These tools are characterized by fast, fluid-user interaction and a focus on simple visualization; analytical functions are rarely present.

We consider that, for the case of interactive data exploration, concerns of performance, intuitiveness, and user engagement tend to outweigh the desire for sophistication in data processing. We, therefore, argue that a new generation of

[4]www.opengeospatial.org.

"4D GIS" tools, based on the principles of neogeography, open standards, and user-friendliness, is required to gain greater insight from the environmental data deluge. These new tools will not replace existing approaches but rather complement them [1].

19.3 THE TECHNICAL LANDSCAPE

Any scientific tool naturally requires access to data and the ability to interpret them. Fortunately, the past decade or two has seen great strides in harmonizing digital data in the environmental sciences, although much work remains to be done. This section briefly summarizes the state of the art in environmental informatics and infrastructure, as these necessarily underpin developments in end-user tooling.

19.3.1 Data Formats and Standards

Two main aspects of the technical landscape concern us particularly here: the means of accessing data and the means of encoding them. Starting with the problem of encoding, we observe that it would be almost impossible in practical terms to develop tools that visualize and bring together diverse datasets if each and every data provider chose a different digital file format. Historically, this has not been far from the truth, but in recent years, there has been a gradual convergence around a relatively small number of well-known formats. Still, there remain some broad differences between communities; the ocean and climate modeling communities are standardizing around the NetCDF format [22], meteorologists have long adopted the World Meteorological Organization's standard GRIB format [23], the satellite community tends to use HDF [24], whereas the *in situ* data community is moving from *ad hoc* text formats to formats such as NetCDF and standardized flavors of semistructured text files. The GIS community uses a different suite of formats, notably shapefiles and GeoTIFFs.

19.3.2 Metadata Formats and Standards

The file-format ecosystem, therefore, remains diverse, and this presents a considerable challenge to the tool developer. Thankfully, the trend is very firmly in the direction of harmonization, and the NetCDF format is rapidly becoming a de facto standard for many communities, being a relatively simple yet portable binary file format that is supported by a suite of tools and libraries in a number of popular programming languages. NetCDF is itself entirely domain-agnostic, consisting essentially of a means to encode multidimensional arrays and their attributes and must, therefore, be augmented by community-specific metadata standards to ensure correct semantic interpretation. Metadata are embedded in the file, therefore, files can be entirely self-describing. In the case of environmental science, the predominant conventions are provided by the Climate and Forecast (CF) community [25]. Although the CF conventions are well developed for gridded data (including model data and high level satellite products), conventions for nongridded data (e.g., *in situ* observations) are only just emerging. Nevertheless, the combination of CF and NetCDF provides, perhaps, the best hope for data harmonization across the environmental sciences and is at the time of writing under discussion as a candidate OGC standard, which will promote its interoperability with GIS tools.

For purposes of contrast with other communities, it is worth noting that relational database systems are not in wide use in the fluid earth sciences, except for the purposes of storing metadata. The relational model is a poor match for gridded data, although there is some use of array-oriented databases such as Rasdaman [26] and the Barrodale Grid DataBlade [27] for specialist applications. Having said this, each NetCDF file can be thought of as a mini database in its own right, supporting efficient (but limited) queries of data arrays, including slicing and subsetting.

19.3.3   Data Access Standards

Turning to the problem of accessing and sharing data across networks, two main approaches are in current use: bulk file transfer and Web services. File-transfer mechanisms include the typical examples of HTTP(S), (s)FTP, and, increasingly, GridFTP. More interesting—and much more important for the problem of interactive visualization—is the case of Web service mechanisms. Web services provide an extra layer of intelligence and convenience, freeing the user from the need to understand how data are physically stored. Users request just the data they require in the format they want, with all of the subsetting and reformatting operations being performed invisibly on the server. Data files (e.g., a collection of files representing a number of time steps in a weather forecast model run) can be aggregated into virtual datasets [28], turning a set of three-dimensional fields into a single logical four-dimensional hypercube that can be subsetted along any of its dimensions.

Interestingly, the use of Web services[5] in ocean science dates back to several years before the term "Web services" was coined. In 1992, the OPeNDAP Web service protocol [30] (then called DODS, the Distributed Oceanographic Data System) was conceived, then implemented a year or two later. Nearly two decades on, a great many Earth-science datasets are made available via OPeNDAP, which provides a very convenient means of reading remotely held data, and subsets thereof. OPeNDAP's data model is a superset of that of NetCDF, meaning that NetCDF data can be transmitted with little or no loss of fidelity. The most important practical feature is that tools and libraries have developed to such an extent that programs designed to read data from local NetCDF files can be trivially adapted to read remote data via OPeNDAP. The e-Infrastructure then becomes almost invisible. The combination of CF, NetCDF, and OPeNDAP therefore provides a solid base for a great deal of scientific work on large, distributed data [31, 32]. OPeNDAP, similar to NetCDF, is domain agnostic and could be adopted outside the earth sciences.

---

[5]We take a broad definition here to include all services that use Web technology, without restricting ourselves to SOAP-based services (www.w3.org/TR/soap) or RESTful ones [29].

The OGC publishes a suite of standard Web service specifications for serving all kinds of geographic data [33]. They are not specifically designed for scientific data but can be used to give an "interoperability layer" between scientific data and GIS tools. These standards are intended to encompass a wide range of use cases and communities and are, therefore, very general, requiring considerable specialization within individual communities. Blower et al. [34], for example, discuss the advantages of these standards and the difficulties in applying them to the ocean community. Nevertheless, we shall see that these standards can work alongside existing technologies to deliver part of the toolchain required to support interactive visualization and exploration.

19.4   INTERACTIVE VISUALIZATION

The past two decades or so have, therefore, laid the foundations for the next generation of interactive tools. Although a great deal of work remains to be done, the increased harmonization of data and metadata and the ability to create entirely "self-describing" data files, together with the ability to access huge stores of remotely held data as if they were on the user's desktop, mean that tools can emerge which free the scientist from the low level technical tasks that tend to soak up so much valuable time. By coupling this e-Infrastructure with easy-to-use interfaces for geographic data exploration, we can begin to create a whole new suite of compelling, interactive tools that place visualization at the heart of the scientific process instead of at its endpoint.

19.4.1   Introducing Godiva2

We focus here on the Godiva2 system [35] that allows multidimensional, gridded environmental data—mostly numerical-model output, and also satellite data and interpolated observations—to be explored using only a Web browser in a "Google Maps-like" interface (Fig. 19.2). Overviews of data can be generated very quickly, from which the scientist can select particular features to investigate in more detail by pointing and clicking on the map. This approach follows the Visual Information Seeking Mantra: "Overview first, zoom, and filter, then details on demand" [36], which is widely accepted as good practice for guiding users through large and complex datasets. This smooth zooming between spatial scales, from global to local and vice versa, together with the ability to change the area of interest simply by clicking and dragging the map, is now commonplace in consumer Web-mapping applications such as Google Maps and MapQuest, but Godiva2 is one of the first tools to apply this principle systematically to the visualization of complex environmental science data.

Godiva2 has seen very wide adoption, particularly in the ocean science community, and also in meteorology and climate science. It is a client-server system in which the client is a browser-based, Javascript-driven application built around the

(a)   (b)

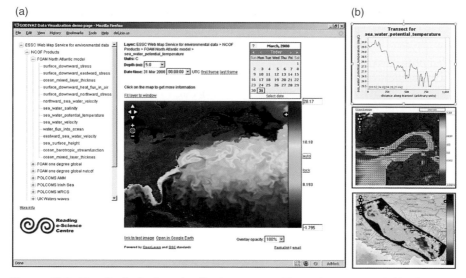

Figure 19.2   *The Godiva2 data visualization system. The main map panel (a) allows the selection of variables (such as temperature and sea surface height) from a number of datasets. Visualizations are displayed very quickly, accurately overlaid on the interactive map, which can be panned and zoomed to investigate features. Data can be explored in four dimensions, through alteration of the elevation and time of the currently displayed map, as well as the generation of many different plot types (b) through simple pointing and clicking. Tasks that are very tedious in many existing tools are made automatic and intuitive, including the display of velocity fields (c), the generation of animations and the handling of data on distorted grids (d).*

open-source OpenLayers mapping library [37]. The server is a Java Web application that converts data into images on the fly in response to Web service requests from the client. The server implements the OGC Web Map Service (WMS [38]) specification—and is, therefore, interoperable with several GIS tools—and also includes a number of nonstandard extensions in order to support the needs of scientists.

The key features of Godiva2 are:

- The user interface updates very quickly in response to user input. The user can pan and zoom through the map view, change the time and elevation, and alter the color scale with the minimum number of mouse clicks. This is the key to a truly interactive and exploratory user experience.

- Exploration of data in many slices through multidimensional space is possible: time-series plots and animations (which feedback shows is crucial to many users) can be generated far more easily than with many current systems. Vertical sections (i.e., "curtains") of data can be extracted and plotted by drawing an arbitrary (perhaps even dog-legged) line on the map with the mouse, providing a near-unique capability for examining complex three-dimensional structures in the data. The generation of these arbitrary vertical sections using traditional tools is sufficiently tedious that it is currently rarely done.

- Images and plots are generated very rapidly by the server, even for large, high resolution datasets or those with complex grids [39]. Existing visualization packages tend to scale up poorly in terms of performance when faced with large or complex datasets.

- The ability to read many different data file formats, including CF-NetCDF, GRIB, and HDF, through Unidata's Common Data Model, is an abstraction that is embodied in the Java NetCDF libraries. Users do not have to concern themselves at all with the low-level process of reading data from files, or the process of converting between geographic coordinates and data array indices: these processes occur entirely on the server.

- Data from many different physical locations can be brought together in a single portal; again, this is invisible to the user. Remote datasets are accessed by the Godiva2 server using OPeNDAP [40].

- The visualization can be shared with colleagues by sharing (e.g., by email) a "permalink" that contains all of the information needed to recreate the current view. Colleagues can load the visualization and then customize it or adapt it to answer their own questions.

19.4.2 Experience with Godiva2

Godiva2 focuses purely on visualization and currently lacks any capability to perform analyses. Nevertheless, adoption is widespread. The primary users are perhaps scientists who wish to diagnose the latest generation of ocean models: visualization is key here because the eye can pick out features that are missed by automated analysis tools. Godiva2 also acts as a simple catalog interface for environmental data infrastructures [41], allowing prospective customers to browse data interactively without the need for downloading large files. Importantly, the Godiva2 software is now integrated into the widely used THREDDS Data Server software [42], which has been adopted by data providers worldwide, and provides access to a huge number of datasets: each of these datasets can now be explored online directly in the Web browser. Some projects have adopted Godiva2 as a component in a larger infrastructure (e.g., IMOS [43]), using it to provide visualizations of model data that are "mashed up" alongside observations. The system has also been used in education and training [44], as it provides students with a rare opportunity to interact with real data, something that is usually beyond the scope of undergraduate programs because of the technical challenges of working with data.

The shift of "intelligence" from the client to the server changes the economics of the deployment. Compared with simple file-sharing systems such as FTP, the server must perform a great deal more work. There are, therefore, concerns over the scalability of systems such as these, and deployment infrastructures must be carefully designed to maintain performance for multiple simultaneous users. Caching is generally very difficult in this case, because the underlying datasets may change; furthermore, data can be turned into images in many different ways and it is relatively unlikely that two users will choose the same parameters. When tested under heavy load, the Godiva2 server can be either I/O- or CPU-bound, depending on usage patterns (repetitive usage tends to lead to CPU-bound behavior [45]). (Only images are transferred across the network; these are relatively small compared with the data themselves and, therefore, bandwidth is not usually a limiting factor.) Mitigation strategies in operational deployments tend to be somewhat costly, involving the use of fast disks, data replication, and load balancing. It is, therefore, not a trivial task for a data provider to make such a system available operationally for the benefit of its users. These concerns—and others—are crucial in any considerations of future, more ambitious, cloud-based systems for data analysis (Section 19.6).

19.5 FROM VISUALIZATION TO INTERCOMPARISON

Although interactive browsing of individual datasets holds a great deal of scientific value in itself, this value is greatly increased if multiple datasets can be brought together. Many studies in environmental science rely on the ability to intercompare diverse data sources, in order to validate model predictions against observations and to combine different data sources to provide a "best estimate" of the state of a complex system (this latter process is known as *data assimilation* [46, 47]). All of the difficulties highlighted above with using traditional tools for simple visualization are multiplied when multiple datasets are brought into play. Tools designed for a particular community are often ill-suited for handling data produced by other communities, meaning that the scientist must spend time on tedious and error-prone processes of data conversion and manipulation in order to ingest data into their tool of choice.

We briefly describe here two data-intercomparison applications that adhere to the same principles as Godiva2—chiefly interactivity and the hiding of technical details from users—but extend the capabilities in different ways.

19.5.1 ECOOP Web Portal

The European project ECOOP (European COastal sea OPerational observing and forecasting system) brought together 71 partners including providers of coastal-ocean data from all over Europe. The coastal oceans are of crucial societal and economic value, and it is, therefore, extremely important to understand them and predict their behavior. In the project, data from all of the operational forecast models were harmonized in an agreed format (CF-NetCDF) and provided through OPeNDAP services. A customized Godiva2 site [41] was set up to act as a Dynamic Quick View system, providing project partners and end users with a means to browse rapidly through the entire data holdings.

A particularly novel aspect of the technical developments within ECOOP was the fusion of these forecast models with marine observations from moored buoys, floats, and ship-borne instruments. These observations had been cast into a common format in a previous project (SEPRISE [48]) and the ECOOP project gathered these observations and made them available through an OGC Web feature service. A new

Web portal was then created that allowed, for the first time, model and observation data from the entire project to be combined using only a Web browser [40]. The aim of the portal was to produce a system that allows users to explore data and assess the strengths and weaknesses of the various models in terms of their ability to match observations. Figure 19.3 demonstrates the Web portal in action.

This capability is simple yet highly effective, quickly revealing areas of disagreement between models and observations, and driving improvements in models. (There is a social element at work here too: when an accessible and easy-to-use Web site makes it possible for anyone to find these disagreements, there is an extra incentive for the modeling community to resolve them.) Perhaps unexpectedly, when there is disagreement it is not always the model that requires correction. In Figure 19.3, the initial discrepancy is caused by a metadata error in the observation record, which was found using this tool and corrected. It is very hard for automated quality-control systems to pick up this kind of problem, so it is vital that scientists be able to explore data rapidly to discover issues and correct them.

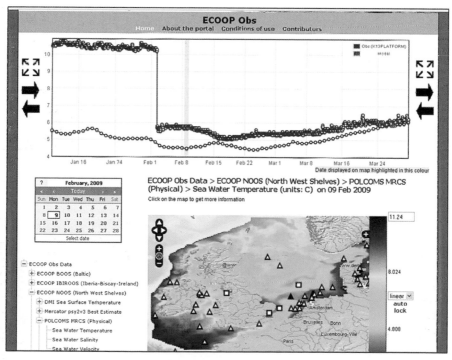

Figure 19.3 Screenshot of the ECOOP Web portal, displaying results from a numerical model of the UK shelf seas together with a number of locations of marine instruments (triangles and squares on the map). By clicking on a particular instrument location, an interactive time-series plot is generated showing the measurement from the instrument together with the prediction of the model. The time-series plot can be panned and zoomed with data values being revealed on mouseover. The apparent discrepancy between the model and observation in late January was caused by a metadata error in the instrument record, which had previously gone unnoticed by automated quality-control checks.

19.5.2 OceanDIVA

The Ocean Data Intercomparison and Visualization Application (OceanDIVA [49]) provides a capability to compare datasets not just visually but quantitatively. The scientific use case is similar to that of the ECOOP portal, namely, the improvement of numerical forecast models by challenging them with observations. However, instead of comparing observations individually in response to user commands, OceanDIVA performs tens of thousands of comparisons and provides an interactive means of browsing the results, this time using a virtual globe (Google Earth) as the visualization platform instead of the Web browser.

The ENSEMBLES dataset [50] of ocean observations contains millions of hydrographic profiles that are measurements of ocean temperature, salinity, and other quantities at a number of points from the surface down to depths of 2 km or more. These profiles give vital information about the state of the ocean depths, which until recently were very sparsely sampled. This dataset is very widely used for testing and constraining numerical models that ingest (or assimilate) the data in order to give a better estimate of the overall state of the oceans. OceanDIVA provides a simple means for scientists to compare these hydrographic profiles with a number of numerical models, which are accessed through NetCDF files or OPeNDAP services. Again, we note that the harmonization of the underlying data sources is critical: without this, OceanDIVA would only be able to work with a very limited number of datasets, considerably reducing its value and reusability. The user selects the datasets to be compared, together with the geographic region and time period of interest, using a Web-based, menu-driven interface and results are produced in KML format [51], a simple XML format (and OGC standard) for geographic data, which is understood by many "neogeography" tools such as Google Earth [51, 52]. Figure 19.4 illustrates the result of such an analysis.

(a)   (b)

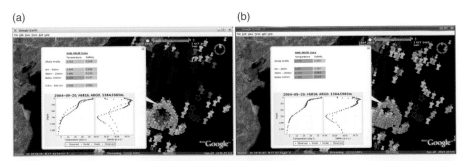

Figure 19.4   A study of data assimilation using the OceanDIVA tool that employs Google Earth as an interactive visualization platform. Two numerical models, one "control run" (a) and one "assimilation run" (b) are compared with the ENSEMBLES database of ocean observations. Red pins represent poor fits between models and observations according to a user-selected criterion, while green pins represent good fits. OceanDIVA quickly reveals geographic areas in which fits are systematically poor, and the user can click on individual observations to examine plots that reveal more details about how the misfits vary with depth in the ocean (pop-up balloons). The assimilation run has ingested some observational data, whereas the control run does not. As might be expected, the assimilation run produces a better fit to observations.

Again, this system is simple but effective and is driving real improvements in the models themselves. The capability to gain an overview of the system and quickly drill down to detailed results is crucial for helping scientists to focus their attention on the areas that most require it and explore new ideas and hypotheses.

19.6   FUTURE DEVELOPMENT: THE ENVIRONMENTAL CLOUD

The applications above demonstrate the value of interactivity in the gaining of insight from environmental data. However, the applications focus on a limited set of capabilities and have been custom developed to support particular needs. How can these principles be extended to provide a more general data analysis capability and encompass more use cases? How can scientists bring new datasets into these systems, and how can access rights be preserved?

Through the use of Web services, we have already seen that the applications discussed above can be extended to bring in new sources of data and to make outputs (e.g. visualizations) available to a variety of different clients. The key to developing a truly flexible, extensible, and generic capability is surely to extend this idea to its logical conclusion by considering that all of the components of the system, including data feeds, data processing routines, and plotting routines, should be made available as services. This is essentially the vision of the "Environmental Cloud": a suite of well-defined components that can be rapidly assembled to solve a problem. The job of each component is to hide from the user any unnecessary technical details, including the format (and even the physical location) of the data involved.

The MashMyData project [53, 54] is taking initial steps toward achieving this vision. MashMyData is an infrastructure that brings together secure feeds from data centers and data-processing facilities such as clusters behind an interactive, map-driven, browser-based user interface (Fig. 19.5). Users can upload their own data to their private workspace and compare them with various sources of external data. An illustrative use case proceeds as follows.

- An ocean biogeochemist has proxy measurements of ocean temperature derived from isotopic ratios of oxygen in the shells of marine microorganisms. He or she wishes to compare these measurements with various data sources from models and *in situ* observations.
- He or she logs on to the system (using OpenID) and uploads the data to his/her workspaces in a format with which they are familiar (typically comma-separated values exported from Excel). The data immediately appear plotted on the interactive map.
- He or she selects an external dataset with which the comparison is to be made. This dataset is held securely at the British Atmospheric Data Centre (BADC) and is also plotted on the interactive map. This overlaying immediately gives a very quick visual comparison.

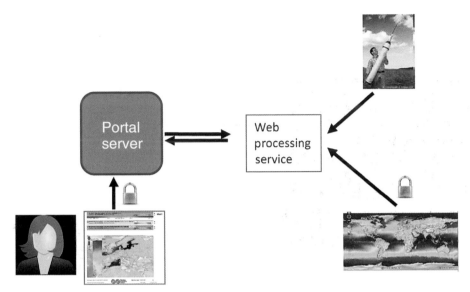

Figure 19.5 *Overview of the MashMyData infrastructure. The user (bottom left) uploads data to be compared with data held on public servers (top right) or secure data centers (bottom right). Results of the comparison are displayed in the Web portal on a multilayer interactive map. The intercomparison tasks are performed on a cluster, with jobs submitted and monitored through a Web processing service interface. Data feeds from the data centers require authentication, and so the user's credentials must pass to the Web processing service that retrieves data on a user's behalf. This "delegation problem" is very challenging in an interactive Web environment.*

- He or she selects an area of the globe using a rubber band tool and clicks "Compare." He or she is presented with a menu of possible comparison algorithms, from which he or she chooses "root-mean-square misfit."
- The processing job is submitted through an OGC Web processing service (WPS [55]) interface and performed at a cluster at BADC (minimizing data transfer time for the external dataset), generating a new dataset representing the misfits between his/her data and the external data.
- The misfits are plotted on the interactive map and made available for download.
- The system, invisibly to the user, records the entire process that generated the end result, linking the result to its parent data and processing algorithms.

The choice of the WPS protocol as the means of submitting the processing job is noteworthy. The WPS standard is becoming increasingly widely adopted in environmental sciences as a simple yet powerful tool for job submission and monitoring. WPS services tend to have a low overhead and can run synchronously, which is very important for quick jobs such as those that characterize the Mash-MyData use cases: this means that the scheduling overhead does not dominate the run time and results can be retrieved quickly.

This use case presents many technical challenges of various types, but the most challenging and pervasive one is that of security. As Figure 19.5 shows, the external data (held under access control at BADC) are not retrieved directly by the user but by the Web portal server and the WPS instance, which saves the user from having to download large datasets. How then can the user's credentials be applied to the data-transfer operations so that the BADC knows that the user is entitled to access the data? The MashMyData project is investigating two solutions, based, respectively, on Grid proxy certificates and OAuth.[6] This situation is quite generic, and the results of this investigation are likely to have a wide impact on future infrastructures of this type in environmental science and beyond.

The findings of MashMyData (itself only a brief proof-of-concept study) will be more widely applied, particularly, in the high profile NERC[7] Environmental Virtual Observatory Pilot project (EVOp [56]). This will investigate important practical problems in hydrology, including diffuse pollution, and will require many stakeholders in academia and government agencies to have the ability to run hydrological models and validate them against observations. The infrastructure will extend Mash-MyData by permitting the running of (perhaps long-running) models "in the cloud," following the vision of the model Web [57].

19.7 CONCLUSIONS

We have seen that one way of coping with the environmental data deluge is to develop a new approach to working with data. A more interactive, exploratory approach to data visualization and processing will become a powerful means to extract more insights during data-intensive research, complementing (and perhaps, in some instances, replacing) existing tools based on traditional programming, scripting, and batch-mode processing. The approach can be followed in both desktop and Web-based tools, and both have their advantages and disadvantages. The user can ingest his/her own data more easily into a desktop tool, but Web-based tools are highly convenient and portable, requiring no downloading of software or datasets.

Other scientific communities have reached similar conclusions and have also investigated new toolsets with considerable success, such as the analysis of complex social networks through interactive visualization tools [58]. We may extract from these studies (and the ones outlined previously in this chapter) a set of ingredients that are essential for developing these tools.

- Datasets that are harmonized or standardized sufficiently to permit a considerable degree of automated processing: In the fluid earth sciences, we are able to automatically reason how data are referenced to space and time, which is

[6]http://oauth.net/, accessed August 2011.
[7]UK Natural Environment Research Council

essential for GIS-style overlaying and coplotting. Deeper levels of semantic inference are active topics of current research [59].

- Routines and infrastructures that permit the extraction and visualization of data in (near) real time, permitting interactive exploration. This requires distributed infrastructures that are closer to the Web than the Grid, as interactive tasks require low overhead and synchronous responses. However, scalability then becomes a key issue, which is why cloud infrastructures, with their potential for elastically scaling up and down in response to usage patterns, are under active investigation [18].

- For Web-based systems, we require an approach to data security that permits a user to delegate his or her authority to a remote system to access data on his or her behalf. Without this, any secure data must pass directly through the user's own machine, creating a bottleneck and lessening the value of the "cloud" approach.

We have noted that both the NetCDF file format and the OPeNDAP Web service protocol are extremely important, particularly for the encoding and sharing of model simulation data. However, neither of these technologies is at all specific to the environmental sciences, and other communities could easily adopt these approaches if their data are suitable. We predict that the use of NetCDF and OPeNDAP will continue to grow outside the fluid earth sciences into other fields.

Finally, we have been careful to say that these new interactive tools are complementary to the existing workhorses of Fortran, MATLAB, and so forth. A key future technical challenge will be to invent means to link these approaches together, allowing the scientist to perform initial exploration in an interactive tool, then segue smoothly into a problem-solving environment (or perhaps workflow engine) in order to perform more detailed analysis.

Acknowledgments

The authors gratefully acknowledge the support of the European Commission (MERSEA, ECOOP, and MyOcean projects) and the Natural Environment Research Council (MashMyData project). The work of key technology providers is also much appreciated: these include OPeNDAP Inc, the Open Geospatial Consortium, and UCAR's Unidata program (supported by the National Science Foundation), which provides the NetCDF tools and the Integrated Data Viewer.

REFERENCES

1. D. A. Keim, "Information visualization and visual data mining," *IEEE Transactions on Visualization and Computer Graphics*, vol. 8, no. 1, pp. 1–8, 2002.

2. S. K. Card, J. Mackinlay, and B. Shneiderman, *Readings in Information Visualization: Using Vision to Think*. Morgan Kaufmann, February 1999.

3. P. Fox and J. Hendler, "Changing the equation on scientific data visualization," *Science*, vol. 331, pp. 705–708, 2011.

4. Editorial, "Community cleverness required," *Nature*, vol. 455, no. 7209, p. 1, 2008.

5. H. J. Freeland, D. Roemmich, S. L. Garzoli, P. L. Traon, M. Ravichandran, S. Riser, V. Thierry, S. Wijffels, M. Belbèoch, J. Gould, F. Grant, M. Ignazewski, B. King, B. Klein, K. A. Mork, B. Owens, S. Pouliquen, A. Sterl, T. Suga, M. Suk, P. Sutton, A. Troisi, P. J. Vèlez-Belchi, and J. Xu, "Argo - a decade of progress," in *Proceedings of OceanObs' 09: Sustained Ocean Observations and Information for Society* (J. Hall, D. Harrison, and D. Stammer, eds.), vol. 1 of *ESA* Publication WPP-306, Venice, Italy, European Space Agency, 2010.

6. J. T. Overpeck, G. A. Meehl, S. Bony, and D. R. Easterling, "Climate data challenges in the 21st century," *Science*, vol. 331, pp. 700–702, 2011.

7. World Meteorological Organization, "Global Telecommunication System," http://www.wmo.int/-pages/prog/www/TEM/GTS/index_en.html. Accessed 28th April 2011.

8. I. Visual Information Solutions, "IDL," http://www.ittvis.com/language/en-us/product sservices/-idl.aspx. Accessed 1st May 2011.

9. Taverna, "Taverna Workflow Management System," http://www.taverna.org.uk. Accessed 28th April 2011.

10. "Kepler", http://www.kepler-project.org/.

11. K. K. Droegemeier, "Transforming the sensing and numerical prediction of high-impact local weather through dynamic adaptation," *Philosophical Transactions of the Royal Society A: Mathematical, Physical and Engineering Sciences*, vol. 367, pp. 885–904, 2009.

12. J. Brooke, P. Coveney, J. Harting, S. Jha, S. Pickles, R. Pinning, and A. Porter, "Computational steering in RealityGrid," in *Proceedings of the UK e-Science Meeting* (S. Cox, ed.), Nottingham, pp. 885–888, 2003. Publisher: EPSRC Sept 2003, ISBN 1-904425-11-9.

13. S. Nativi, B. Blumenthal, T. Habermann, D. Hertzmann, R. Raskin, J. Caron, B. Domenico, Y. Ho, and J. Weber, "Differences among the data models used by the geographic information systems and atmospheric science communities," in *Proceedings of the American Meteorological Society 20th Interactive Image Processing Systems Conference*, January 2004.

14. S. Nativi, J. Caron, B. Domenico, and L. Bigagli, "Unidata's common data model mapping to the ISO 19123 data model," *Earth Science Informatics*, vol. 1, no. 2, pp. 59–78, 2008.

15. S. Nativi and B. Domenico, "Enabling interoperability for digital earth: earth science coverage access services," *International Journal of Digital Earth*, vol. 2, pp. 79–104, 2009.

16. K. E. Grossner, M. F. Goodchild, and K. C. Clarke, "Defining a digital earth system," *Transactions in GIS*, vol. 12, no. 1, pp. 145–160, 2008.

17. R. Vijay, D. R. Satapathy, B. Nimje, S. Nema, S. Dhurve, and A. Gupta, "Development of GIS-based environmental information system: an indian scenario," *International Journal of Digital Earth*, vol. 2, no. 4, pp. 382–392, 2009.

18. J. D. Blower, "GIS in the cloud: implementing a Web map service on Google app engine," in *Proceedings of COM.Geo, The 1st International Conference and Exhibition on Computing for Geospatial Research & Applications*, Washington, DC, ACM, pp. 1–4, 2010.

19. NASA, "NASA World Wind," http://worldwind.arc.nasa.gov. Accessed 28th April 2011.

20. Unidata, "Integrated Data Viewer," http://www.unidata.ucar.edu/software/idv/. Accessed 28th April 2011.

21. Editorial, "Think global," *Nature*, vol. 439, p. 763, February 2006.

22. Unidata, "Network Common Data Form (netCDF)," http://www.unidata.ucar.edu/software/netcdf/. Accessed 28th April 2011.

23. World Meteorological Organization, "GRIB (GRIdded Binary) format," http://www.wmo.int/pages/prog/www/WMOCodes.html. Accessed 28th April 2011.

24. T. H. Group, "Hierarchical Data Format," http://www.hdfgroup.org/. Accessed 28th April 2011.

25. "NetCDF Climate and Forecast (CF) metadata conventions," http://www.cfconventions.org/. Accessed 28th April 2011.

26. P. Baumann, "Large-Scale earth science services: a case for databases," in *Advances in Conceptual Modeling - Theory and Practice* (J. Roddick, V. Benjamins, S. Si-said Cherfi, R. Chiang, C. Claramunt, R. Elmasri, F. Grandi, H. Han, M. Hepp, M. Lytras, V. Mišic, G. Poels, I. Song, J. Trujillo, and C. Vangenot, eds.), vol. 4231 of *Lecture Notes in Computer Science*, pp. 75–84, Springer, Berlin/Heidelberg, 2006. DOI: 10.1007/11908883_11.

27. B. Computing Services, "The Grid DataBlade-a database extension for manipulating gridded data," http://www.barrodale.com/bcs/bcs-grid-datablade. Accessed 28th April 2011.

28. J. Blower, F. Blanc, R. Clancy, P. Cornillon, C. Donlon, P. Hacker, K. Haines, S. Hankin, T. Loubrieu, S. Pouliquen, M. Price, T. Pugh, and A. Srinavasan, "Serving GODAE data and products to the ocean community," *Oceanography*, vol. 22, no. 3, pp. 70–79, 2009.

29. R. T. Fielding and R. N. Taylor, "Principled design of the modern Web architecture," *ACM Transactions on Internet Technology*, vol. 2, no. 2, pp. 115–150, 2002.

30. OPeNDAP Inc., "OPeNDAP (Open-source Project for a Network Data Access Protocol)," http://www.opendap.org. Accessed 1st May 2011.

31. R. P. Signell, S. Carniel, J. Chiggiato, I. Janekovic, J. Pullen, and C. R. Sherwood, "Collaboration tools and techniques for large model datasets," *Journal of Marine Systems*, vol. 69, pp. 154–161, 2008.

32. L. S. Froude, "Storm tracking with remote data and distributed computing," *Computers & Geosciences*, vol. 34, no. 11, pp. 1621–1630, 2008.

33. Open Geospatial Consortium, "OGC standards and specifications," http://www.open geospatial.-org/standards. Accessed 28th April 2011.

34. J. Blower, S. Hankin, R. Keeley, S. Pouliquen, J. de la Beaujardiere, E. V. Berghe, G. Reed, F. Blanc, M. Gregg, J. Fredericks, and D. Snowden, "Ocean data dissemination: new challenges for data integration," in *Proceedings of OceanObs' 09: Sustained Ocean Observations and Information for Society* (J. Hall, D. Harrison, and D. Stammer, eds.), vol. 1 of *ESA* Publication WPP-306, Venice, Italy, European Space Agency, 2010.

35. J. Blower, K. Haines, A. Santokhee, and C. Liu, "GODIVA2: interactive visualization of environmental data on the Web," *Philosophical Transactions of the Royal Society A*, vol. 367, pp. 1035–1039, 2009.

36. B. Shneiderman, "The eyes have it: a task by data type taxonomy for information visualizations," in *IEEE Symposium on Visual Languages*, Los Alamitos, CA, IEEE Computer Society, p. 336, 1996.

37. "OpenLayers," http://www.openlayers.org. Accessed 28th April 2011.

38. Open Geospatial Consortium, "Web map service," http://www.opengeospatial.org/stand ards/wms. Accessed 1st May 2011.

39. J. D. Blower and A. Clegg, "Fast regridding of complex geospatial datasets," in *Proceedings of COM.Geo, the 2nd International Conference on Computing for Geospatial Research & Applications*, Washington, DC, 2011.

40. A. L. Gemmell, R. M. Barciela, J. D. Blower, K. Haines, Q. Harpham, K. Millard, M. R. Price, and A. Saulter, "An ECOOP Web portal for visualising and comparing distributed coastal oceanography model and in-situ data," *Ocean Science Discussions*, vol. 8, no. 1, pp. 189–218, 2011.

41. "ECOOP Dynamic Quick View site," http://www.resc.reading.ac.uk/ecoop. Accessed 1st May 2011.

42. Unidata, "TDS (THREDDS Data Server)," http://www.unidata.ucar.edu/software/tds/. Accessed 28th April 2011.

43. "Integrated Marine Observing System," http://www.imos.org.au/. Accessed 28th April 2011.

44. M. Mineter, "ncWMS for UM data," https://www.wiki.ed.ac.uk/display/cesdwiki/[-4]nc WMS+for+UM+data. Accessed 8th May 2011.

45. J. D. Blower, A. Gemmell, G. H. Griffiths, K. Haines, A. Santokhee, and X. Yang, "ncWMS: a Web Map Service implementation for the visualization of multidimensional gridded environmental data," submitted to Environmental Modelling and Software, 2012.

46. W. Lahoz, B. Khattatov, and R. Menard, eds., *Data Assimilation: Making Sense of Observations (First Edition)*. Springer, 2010.

47. R. Swinbank, V. Shutyaev, and W. A. Lahoz, eds., *Data Assimilation for the Earth System*, vol. 26 of *NATO Science Series: IV: Earth and Environmental Sciences*, 2003.

48. "SEPRISE (Sustained, Efficient Production of Required Information SErvices)," http://www.-seprise.eu/. Accessed 28th April 2011.

49. A. Gemmell, G. Smith, K. Haines, and J. Blower, "Validation of ocean model syntheses against hydrography using a new Web application," *Journal of Operational Oceanography*, vol. 2, pp. 29–41, 2009.

50. T. E. Project, "ENSEMBLES," http://ensembles-eu.metoffice.com/. Accessed 1st May 2011.

51. Google, "KML Documentation," http://code.google.com/apis/kml/documentation/. Accessed 8th May 2011.

52. J. Blower, A. Gemmell, K. Haines, P. Kirsch, N. Cunningham, A. Fleming, and R. Lowry, "Sharing and visualizing environmental data using virtual globes," in *Proceedings of the UK e-Science Meeting*, Nottingham, pp. 102–109, September 2007.

53. "The MashMyData Project," http://www.mashmydata.org/. Accessed 28th April 2011.

54. A. Gemmell, J. Blower, P. Kershaw, S. Pascoe, and A. Stephens, "Mashmydata: combining and comparing secure environmental data on the Web," in preparation, 2011, http://www.esciencecentral.co.uk/docs/2010.AHM.MMD.pdf. Accessed February 2013.

55. Open Geospatial Consortium, "Web processing service," http://www.opengeospatial.org/stand-ards/wps. Accessed 1st May 2011.

56. "Environmental Virtual Observatory pilot," http://www.environmentalvirtualobservatory.org/. Accessed 8th May 2011.

57. G. Geller and W. Turner, "The model Web: a concept for ecological forecasting," in *Geoscience and Remote Sensing Symposium, 2007. IGARSS 2007. IEEE International*, pp. 2469–2472, 2007.

58. A. Perer and B. Shneiderman, "Integrating statistics and visualization: case studies of gaining clarity during exploratory data analysis," in *Proceeding of the Twenty-Sixth Annual SIGCHI Conference on Human Factors in Computing Systems*, CHI '08, New York, ACM, pp. 265–274, 2008. ACM ID: 1357101.

59. C. Rueda, L. Bermudez, and J. Fredericks, "The MMI ontology registry and repository: a portal for marine metadata interoperability," in *OCEANS 2009, MTS/IEEE Biloxi - Marine Technology for Our Future: Global and Local Challenges, Biloxi, Mississippi*, pp. 1–6, March 2010.

20

Data-Driven Research in the Humanities—the DARIAH Research Infrastructure

Andreas Aschenbrenner

State and University Library Göttingen, Gottingen, Germany

Tobias Blanke

Digital Research Infrastructure in the Arts and Humanities,
Centre for e-Research, King's College London, London, UK

Christiane Fritze and Wolfgang Pempe

State and University Library Göttingen, Göttingen, Germany

20.1   INTRODUCTION

E-Humanities has established itself as an integral part of various national and international e-Science programs. Among these, the arts and humanities e-Science initiative in the United Kingdom[1] has successfully shown, in over 10 projects,

[1]www.ahessc.ac.uk, verified January 2013.

The DATA Bonanza: Improving Knowledge Discovery in Science, Engineering, and Business, First Edition.
Edited by Malcolm Atkinson, Rob Baxter, Michelle Galea, Mark Parsons, Peter Brezany, Oscar Corcho,
Jano van Hemert, and David Snelling.

that new e-Science tools and methodologies can help arts and humanities scholarship. The German TextGrid project[2] is a significant investment into enabling traditional e-Humanities activities, such as the collaborative creation of critical editions within a distributed data-sharing environment. There are similar initiatives in the Netherlands, France, and other European countries, as well as in the United States.

Projects in these initiatives often have as a starting point that humanities are rapidly developing from a data-poor research domain into a largely data-rich domain. The large European digitization programs for cultural heritage around the Europeana project[3] will reach 20 million objects soon. Many projects have developed in recent years to explore new methodologies to enable humanities research using the significantly increased number of records of past and contemporary human societies. Activities in the UK arts and humanities e-Science program included agent-based modeling for the analysis of past societies and the use of data-mining technologies to create faceted browsing interfaces to more traditional support of markup work.

The European DARIAH infrastructure (Digital Research Infrastructure for the Arts and Humanities)[4] attempts to bring together many of these national initiatives in a light weight and federated way, so that researchers can work with a large but cohesive body of research materials. The DARIAH will be as decentralized as possible, empowering individual contributors (e.g., researchers, national centers, thematic centers) to work with and within the DARIAH community and to shape its features to their needs. Each contribution adds to DARIAH and is linked via DARIAH's architecture of participation.

At the same time, collaboration across the borders of individual centers requires the use of common technologies for authentication or federation of archive contents. The DARIAH activities will, therefore, include:

- services and tutorials to help existing humanities data archives link their systems into the DARIAH network;
- software and consultancy/training packages that support emerging data centers in establishing their own technology environment;
- an interoperability layer that will connect data centers;
- a means of linking into DARIAH for countries or disciplines that do not yet have e-Humanities infrastructure and cannot afford it in the near future; and
- best practices and guidelines for individual researchers which foster data interoperability and preservation across the DARIAH network.

The DARIAH has been funded to build a virtual bridge between the various e-Humanities infrastructures. It is funded to bring together all aspects of national

---

[2] www.textgrid.de, verified January 2013.
[3] www.europeana.eu, verified January 2013.
[4] www.dariah.eu, verified January 2013.

infrastructures from research activities to technological support. As in all research infrastructures, its work will, therefore, not just be technology oriented but mainly concentrated on community engagement and integration. This range of focus also applies to the technology solutions it will offer to deliver the DARIAH network. Figure 20.1 summarizes the technical interoperability framework behind DARIAH. In panel (a), two pillars for interoperability of (i) meta/data and (ii) services glue the decentralized DARIAH environment together. Each pillar has different levels of interoperability: (i) *meta/data interoperability* can range from a metadata federation on the lowest level, to semantically deep integration of research data; (ii) *service interoperability* may simply link external reference data sources or may provide compute workspaces (for processing research data). The graph on panel (b) zooms in on the interoperability of research archives (c.f. data pillar, deep integration). Other than query- or harvesting-based approaches (e.g., OAI-PMH), this framework suggests state updates (CRUD: create, read, update, delete) through notifications. Together with core data formats, this framework links decentralized archives on a physical, logical, and conceptual layer for semantically deep integration.

In this chapter, we analyze how such an infrastructure can support diverse needs of highly distributed European researchers of arts and humanities. In particular, we focus on how we can support what we would call large scale, data-driven humanities, that is, research that is based on the close examination of research materials from resources that are scattered across diverse repositories. Contrary to Anderson [1], we do not understand data driven humanities to be the end of theory, but a process of a close relationship between theory and examination of research materials.

It is the thesis of this chapter that the large variety of humanities research is not the problem. Instead, we argue that the fact that *research collections are*

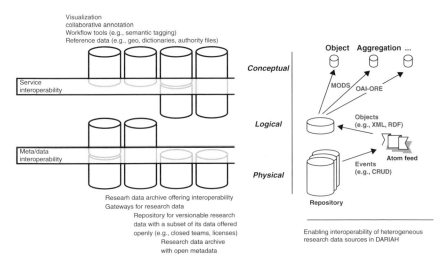

Figure 20.1   *DARIAH technical interoperability framework (a), with a close-up on data interoperability (b).*

often scattered across different sites and cannot be easily retrieved and embedded in infrastructures is the dominating challenge. There are indeed many similarities between the different humanities research activities. They often involve common philosophical and historical approaches. Our contribution will look at the problem of shared e-Humanities services for data analysis, which we see as a first step to systematically enhanced tools and methodologies for data-driven humanities. We look at how we can provide a view onto these collections using on-demand indexing of their textual content.

Section 20.2 introduces the reader to the tradition of digital humanities, as we do not expect a detailed background knowledge of the field[5]. Section 20.3 continues by describing the specifics of data involved in the arts and humanities before we describe our case study to analyze large amounts of data in the humanities in Section 20.4. Here, we cover the DARIAH experiment to prepare an infrastructure to deploy virtual research environments on the European e-Infrastructure.

20.2 THE TRADITION OF DIGITAL HUMANITIES

For over 60 years, humanities research has been experimenting with computers. In the past, there have generally been two kinds of interest in the use of computers for humanities. The first one, and still the most dominant one, is to build infrastructures to support humanities research. Because the traditional infrastructure for humanities has been the libraries, it is no wonder that humanities researchers developed an interest relatively early in building and running digital libraries. Many successful digital library projects are directly linked to humanities research. Examples include the Oxford text archive,[6] founded in the 1970s, the Perseus Digital Library founded in 1987 to collect and make available data for the study of ancient Greece,[7] while the former Arts and Humanities Data Service (AHDS) in the United Kingdom collected and preserved arts and humanities research data for over 10 years until its funding ended in 2008.[8] Projects such as Perseus and the AHDS have been the exemplar ones—not just for humanities.

The second main interest in computer-supported humanities research has been in developing new methodologies. Humanities researchers realized relatively early that computers are symbol-manipulating machines rather than pure calculators. As symbol-manipulating machines, computers lend themselves to many traditional

---

[5]Being fully aware that there is no common understanding of the difference, or rather the relationship, between the two terms "e-Humanities" and "digital humanities" [2], we prefer to use the second one in a much broader sense of any computer-aided research in the humanities while "e-humanities" is seen in close analogy with "e-Science" as "the systematic development of research methods that exploit advanced computational thinking" (www.rcuk.ac.uk/escience).

[6]ota.ahds.ac.uk, verified January 2013.

[7]www.perseus.tufts.edu, verified January 2013.

[8]www.ahds.ac.uk, verified January 2013.

humanist activities such as text analysis. Specialized research centers have developed[9] which are embedded in larger humanities schools. They research methods and tools for humanities research and support the more specialized computing needs in the various humanities departments, from archaeology to languages. The DARIAH is also an attempt not only to connect these into a network of centers, but also as a technical network. In this chapter, we concentrate on our work to integrate and develop research tools for text-centric resources. The DARIAH has also run various experiments to support object-centric research in the arts and humanities. For instance, we developed a research portal to discover monuments for archaeological research in our ARENA2 demonstrator (muninn.york.ac.uk/arena2). Overall, there is a large body of work that supports the e-Science needs in archaeology [3] or shared infrastructures to support retrieval and analysis of large image files (www.sheffield.ac.uk/hri/projects/projectpages/did_images).

Next to generic tools such as those that support bibliographic analysis or word processing—a recent example is the widely used Zotero tool[10]—specialized tools from the community have been developed to help with concordance analysis or optical character recognition [4]. More radical improvements can be expected from advanced e-Science technologies used in the analysis of the material under consideration. Further statistical analysis of research materials and, therefore, data-driven humanities—as we know it from many other application domains such as information retrieval or text mining—had previously been limited as the necessary computing infrastructure to support such work did not exist, or if it existed, it was not available for use by humanities researchers. According to early research in humanities computing, literary analysis using computers [5] would hugely benefit from unlimited access to high quality, digitized texts and from the ability to redefine the statistical analysis on-the-fly. E-Science infrastructure will help implement a more substantial shift here.

As an example of why a more powerful infrastructure is needed to support data-driven humanities, consider that many humanities scholars are language experts. It is, therefore, one of the requirements of any advanced language analysis tool to present not just the results of its processing but also the intermediate steps, which in turn requires more advanced and research-driven computational analyses. Together with aggregating context information such as workflows, services, and scripts, this makes it possible to recapture how the results were achieved [6]. E-Humanities researchers often express the need to transform the underlying statistical algorithms "interactively" by changing parameters and constraints in them. In this way, they can follow their particular interest by experimenting with the outcome of the analysis, and therefore, gain better insights into the structures of the text.

In many cases, humanities research is an iterative process, combining automatic data processing with human interaction, for instance, preparing a critical edition via

---

[9]See www.arts-humanities.net/noc for a list of such centers in Great Britain and Ireland. For an international overview, see digitalhumanities.org/centernet/centers, verified January 2013.
[10]www.zotero.org, verified January 2013.

the machine-driven collation of the transcriptions of two (or more) text witnesses—and the subsequent intellectual process of editing the results in order to produce a critical apparatus. Another desirable example is the creation of linguistic corpora: searching and finding appropriate texts according to certain criteria and algorithms (automatic preselection versus human choice)—using (Web) services such as those provided by GATE[11] or WebLicht[12] for the automatic linguistic annotation (e.g., tokeniser + lemmatiser + POS tagging) of that corpus—and the subsequent "manual" disambiguation if high quality annotation.

Deep semantic annotation remains a process for which human input is essential. As early as the 1990s, the first larger collaborative annotation projects emerged, gathering scholars around digital corpora. Examples included the Helsinki Corpus of Neo-Assyrian texts[13] with the subproject *The Prosopography of the Neo-Assyrian Empire*,[14] which was based on the analytic work of many volunteers from around the world, or—somewhat later—the HyperNietzsche Project.[15] HyperNietzsche sees itself as a *"research instrument that [...] allow[s] a delocalized community of specialists to work in a cooperative and cumulative manner and to publish the results of their work worldwide on the Internet"*[16] based on the digitized primary sources from Nietzsche, which were made available online for the first time. In the meantime, more infrastructures and projects[17] have evolved, providing so-called virtual research environments (VREs) for both accessing digital resources and services for processing them—as well as enabling collaborative annotation and editing of the (intermediate) results.

The observant reader would have noticed that we imply already, while describing large-scale interaction with data in the humanities, a certain type of data, which are documents. These can be either text-based documents, for which established statistical analysis processes exist, or multimedia-oriented ones, for which computational analysis is more difficult. The next section describes this particular type of "data."

20.3 HUMANITIES RESEARCH DATA

In the humanities, there are many document-type collections that are exposed via searchable Web sites. Examples from Europe include

- the British National Corpus[18];

---

[11] gate.ac.uk, verified May 2011.
[12] weblicht.sfs.uni-tuebingen.de/englisch/weblicht.shtml, verified January 2013.
[13] www.helsinki.fi/science/saa/cna.html, verified.
[14] www.helsinki.fi/science/saa/pna.html, verified.
[15] *Nietzsche Source*, www.nietzschesource.org, verified.
[16] www.hypernietzsche.org/doc/presentation/en, verified January 2013.
[17] e.g., Alfalab (virtualknowledgestudio.nl/current-projects/alfalab), eAQUA (www.eaqua.net), MONK (www.monkproject.org) TextGrid (www.textgrid.de), and TEXTvre (textvre.cerch.kcl.ac.uk) verified January 2013.
[18] www.natcorp.ox.ac.uk, verified.

- the COSMAS Portal[19]; and
- the German Text Archive.[20]

These document collections are all characterized by heterogeneous sets of textual resources, where the individual items are relatively small in size, and the challenge in presenting the collections lies in the number of items involved rather than their individual size. We would also claim that once the problem of retrieval and discovery of such datasets is solved, then inherent similarity between them could be better analyzed.

In the various fields of humanities, there are numerous datasets, often small and isolated, that would be of great utility if the information they contained could be integrated. In the humanities, researchers work more commonly with text-centric XML, essentially text documents, marked up as XML, to capture document structure, and some additional metadata [5]. Here, it is often more important to find sufficient relevant information in the texts so that standard document retrieval techniques can be applied and adopted to deal with the specifics of handling additional structural constraints [7].

The report [8] points to persistent differences between humanities research and the sciences, especially in the type of collections and resources that are commonly subsumed under the concept of data. Structured data is used relatively little, except in some areas of historical research, and data as it is traditionally understood in the sciences, that is, the results of measurements and the lowest level of abstraction for the generation of scientific knowledge, even less so. Although one can expect the amount of structured information to increase in the near future, as fields such as linguistics and archaeology continue to produce large amounts of more scientifically oriented data, it remains true that the core research material for humanities, as found in the archives of human knowledge, are texts and other types of unstructured information. These can be texts or facsimiles and also more recently advanced multimedia recordings of human activities.

At the same time, with these kinds of resources, it is also not surprising that in terms of pure size, the data deluge has long arrived in the humanities. Let us take as an example the recently funded and DARIAH-supported European Holocaust Research Infrastructure (EHRI).[21] The EHRI partner Yad Vashem, which has been collecting photocopies of relevant material from many different institutions in Europe, uploaded a selection of more than 5 million documents and photographs online. It has recently introduced an online bibliography for Holocaust literature that contains 117,000 titles in 54 languages. Its archives contain 550 TB of digitized material and its databases contain over 600 GB of structured information on Holocaust victims. Governments in the Task Force for International Cooperation on

---

[19]www.ids-mannheim.de/cosmas2—enabling access to currently 109 corpora of mostly contemporary German Texts (www.ids-mannheim.de/cosmas2/projekt/referenz/korpora.html) verified.
[20]www.deutschestextarchiv.de, verified January 2013.
[21]www.ehri-project.eu, verified January 2013.

Holocaust Education, Remembrance, and Research (ITF) have agreed to encourage *"all archives to make their holdings on the Holocaust more widely accessible,"* which means we will see a rapid growth of these kinds of materials in the near future.

Because in recent years Holocaust research has created a large quantity of digital material that represents a significant investment, both in terms of public funding and of intellectual effort in a general sense, Holocaust research (and contemporary history and the humanities in general) is faced with a data deluge that is the result of two complementary developments. Firstly, old analog data in humanities is being transformed into digitized forms. Here, the data deluge does not just apply to heritage information from museums and so on in general but to more research-oriented resources too. Particularly, in the domain of Holocaust research, it has long been recognized that this research data deluge is a reality. In the US debate on an integrated humanities research infrastructure, Holocaust archives are the most commonly used example to justify large investments in cyber infrastructure for the humanities [3]. Here, in particular, the 200 TB of the oral history collection of Holocaust survivors funded by the Spielberg foundation is contrasted with the current 120 TB of the Sloan Digital Sky Survey.

Such comparisons that point to the fundamentally document-oriented nature of humanities data might make useful points about the general relationship between science and humanities datasets. They, however, often obscure the fundamentally more important challenge on how to give researchers quality access to these datasets. For humanities, this challenge is rooted in the inherent complexity and inconsistency of databases, as it is mainly generated by humans directly. The integration of data items into arts and humanities research is nontrivial, as different languages and complicated semantics underlie the archives of human reports. Holocaust and other humanities research data are highly contextual, the interpretation depending on relationships with other resources and collections which are not necessarily available digitally.

- Formats are very diverse for both data and metadata. The databases that contain these documents rarely follow standardized database schemas, so typically any two schemas will be different. Moreover, the use of markup can vary significantly for semistructured material, and data modeling of unstructured material is only just emerging. Some communities may facilitate convergence through standardization, but stylistic variation may occur even when standards are adopted.
- Transforming archives to standard form is infeasible; resources are normally allocated to new material, particularly the intellectual effort that is required. In addition, scholars fear that there is a risk of losing important information or introducing artifacts as a result of the transformation.
- Resources are not easily available for use; they may be locked away on local or departmental machines, or "published" on a Web site in a way that is not particularly usable by a researcher. Even when a resource is available, it is

often available only in isolation and rarely has sufficient metadata about its origin and context.

• Resources may be owned by different communities and subject to different rights; the scholars who created them may be unwilling to accept anything that affects the integrity of the original resources; and eventually research on data inherently depends on where the data stems from and how the data was created. Consequently, any integration initiative must respect this autonomy of the communities and track the authenticity of the resources, if it is to be successful.

Figure 20.2 explains how we try to address these challenges within the specific context of digital arts and humanities communities, and their resources. Our attempts to build interoperability between arts and humanities resources are based on a set of well-defined services to address infrastructure, data, and service interoperability. As Figure 20.2 demonstrates, we think we need to answer the challenge of diversity in resources not with one large infrastructure solution that fits all sizes of resource, but with dedicated services to address specific challenges. To this end, we plan to collaborate closely with associated projects. These include CLARIN (www.clarin.eu), the other humanities ESFRI (The European Strategy Forum on Research Infrastructures) project focused on linguistic resources, project Bamboo (www.projectbamboo.org), InterEdition (www.interedition.eu), and general infrastructure-related projects such as the European Grid Initiative (www.egi.eu) and the Open Archives Initiative (www.openarchives.org).

The next section briefly discusses a use case to illustrate the general points of services that enable research work with complex and heterogeneous resources. The use case is based on one of the early DARIAH experiments on how to set up a central infrastructure to support e-Humanities research.

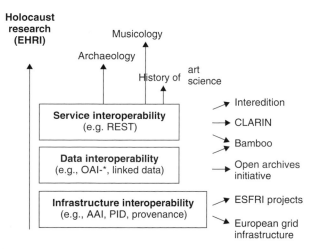

Figure 20.2 Sketch of the landscape of DARIAH context with communities from arts and humanities to the top (including EHRI), and some sample associated projects to the right.

20.4   USE CASE

As is the case for most ESFRI[22] projects, the DARIAH went into production in 2011, starting to build the services that it will run during its operational phase. Until the end of 2010, it was funded by the European Commission to prepare for this production phase; it developed various policy documents, conducted experiments, and drew up blueprints for the future architecture. In this section, we describe one of those experiments that closely related to data-driven humanities based on documents in humanities archives.

The DARIAH sees itself as a service to provide a platform to enable other research projects in arts and humanities to realize their architecture as efficiently and as quickly as possible. We will try to keep interfaces simple so that other research projects are able to concentrate on the services that serve their particular research needs. The DARIAH provides core and stable infrastructure services that have proven to be useful across community environments. The first ones will include services for persistent identification (PID) and authentication (AAI), the minimum glue to ensure interaction between bespoke services.

20.4.1   A Document Integration

As one of the first collaborations, we work with the EHRI.[23] The EHRI only started its work in November 2010, but some parts of the collaboration have already become clear. Services we aim to build together include persistent identifiers and authentication services, as well as an archive in a box that will help EHRI members to set up their own archives easily. This should ensure that the digital memory of this important part of European history will be distributed widely across Europe.

This chapter concentrates on those services that provide central research services for environments such as EHRI that rely on a large number of small archives containing images and text-based resources. Already in the DARIAH preparation phase, we tried to prepare the work with such archives with one of our national community demonstrators. The JISC-funded and DARIAH-supported VRE project gMan[24] attempted to build a research environment for everyday data-driven research in humanities. It aimed to show that large amounts of small archives of human records can be integrated on demand to provide specific views of datasets, which correspond to specific research interests.

20.4.2   A Data Integration Experiment

Considering the diversity and heterogeneity of datasets in the humanities, as described in Section 20.3, integrating collections poses major challenges. This is especially the case if you require an integrated view onto those collections

---

[22]ec.europa.eu/research/infrastructures, verified January 2013.
[23]www.ehri-project.eu, verified January 2013.
[24]gman.cerch.kcl.ac.uk, verified January 2013.

which corresponds to the way current researchers work. There is a wide range of researchers working with digital methods in the humanities, ranging from highly specialized semantic annotations in community standards such as the TEI (Text Encoding Initiative.[25]) to the use of standard online research tools such as integrated library catalogs and Google Scholar. In the gMan experiment, we wanted to address those humanities researchers who work toward a more specialized usage of digital collections within their communities, but who are not satisfied with standard search and retrieval tools. We wanted to cater for a community that would like to create specific views on datasets using multilingual text-based indexes, which they want to create on demand for various collections. gMan addressed services that would enable more general purpose humanities research activities, such as integrating and organizing the heterogeneous and often unstructured digital resources, and support for active reading processes [9] through advanced discovery facilities.

For the experiment, we focused on Classics collections as one of the more advanced communities in the e-Humanities. The following datasets were brought together in our experiments.

- The Heidelberger Gesamtverzeichnis (HGV) der griechischen Papyrusurkunden Aegyptens, a collection of metadata records for 65,000 Greek papyri from Egypt.[26]
- Project Volterra, a database of Roman legal texts, currently in the low tens of thousands but very much in progress, stored in a series of themed tables in Microsoft Access.[27]
- The Inscriptions of Aphrodisias (IoA), a corpus of about 2,000 ancient Greek inscriptions from the Roman city of Aphrodisias in Asia Minor, published in TEI XML.[28]

From the beginning, this experiment aimed to go beyond creating another specialized VRE and to explore new research opportunities. That is why we concentrated on the text-based resources that humanities researchers most commonly work with. The above datasets are good examples of typical document collections in the humanities. IoA, for instance, uses advanced XML markup to capture document structure and additional metadata. Volterra employs a database to store Roman legal texts. The database structure offers explanations of the structure of the documents. Researchers search such resources for further investigation based on loose criteria of relevance, for example, by searching for all of the Roman legal texts in one resource containing information on punishments that are also mentioned in papyri from another resource. They are, therefore, not served by general purpose search tools such as Google.

[25]www.tei-c.org, verified January 2013.
[26]www.rzuser.uni-heidelberg.de/~gv0/gvz.html, verified January 2013.
[27]www.ucl.ac.uk/history2/volterra/pv2.htm, verified January 2013.
[28]insaph.kcl.ac.uk, verified.

Google also does not generally index deep-Web resources. The Volterra texts, for instance, are hidden from search engines in a standard MySQL database. So, we needed an environment that would allow on-demand generation of index resources according to specific research views and to be able to integrate deep-Web resources and to support the researchers with further tools and services. Our work investigated how (digital) archival content can be delivered to humanities researchers more effectively, independently of the location and implementation of that content, and with special facilities provided for customizing the retrieval, management, and manipulation of the content. We investigated how the UK and European research infrastructure can be exploited to support data-driven, collaborative research in the humanities by using the gCube environment [10], which was developed by the EU-funded D4Science project.[29] The gCube allows virtual research communities to deploy VREs on demand by making use of the shared resources of the European research infrastructure and provides services that match closely the sort of information organization and retrieval activities that we identified as being typical in humanities research.

In our experiment, research communities, organized in a virtual organization for Classics, were able to upload the three example collections into the D4Science environment. To this end, the metadata in the resources had to be mapped onto a standard schema in the D4Science environment. Researchers were supported in this task by an effective archival import service that offered standard workflows to import data into D4Science, which could be customized using a simple scripting language. The same environment also allows researchers to set up various text-based indexes for the collections that generate specific research-relevant views onto the collections. The XML fields can be merged or ignored, and indexes can be recreated.

Using the imported collections, researchers could then deploy specific virtual research environments to work on specific research questions, by combining the data resources that their virtual organization has access to with tools and services that support interaction with the underlying data. Various search and browse tools offer access to the collections using keywords or geo-locations as entry points. Finds can be brought together in so-called virtual collections that assemble references to items in existing collections. These virtual collections and the items in them can in turn be shared among the group of researchers that come together in the VRE. Other tools and services include a report writing tool, as well as several annotation services. Further information on gMan and its experiments can be found in [11].

We believe that gMan offered unique insights into the possibilities of a centralized infrastructure to support VREs. The experiment was only possible as we could obtain computational resources on demand from the European research infrastructure via EGI. gMan was only the beginning of the future exploitation in the humanities of research infrastructures originally designed for the sciences.

---

[29] www.d4science.eu, verified January 2013.

20.5 CONCLUSION AND FUTURE DEVELOPMENT

In the future, new technologies will have to prove that they can be embedded in everyday humanities research. The question will be how to move the technologies to the mainstream of research. gMan was a first step in this direction. Next to the generic retrieval services that gMan delivered, we will need to establish ways of convincing everyday researchers that the extraction of facts from large document collections means more than something somebody else might also do. To this end, it is important to find ways of generating out of these numbers new discourses and stories, just as current discourses and stories in the arts and humanities are based on exchanging and comparing discourses. In computing terms, it is essential to regenerate unstructured information from the structured information.

The generation of this unstructured information from structured information is one of the first major future research challenges. Another research challenge is the further customization of the existing retrieval technologies toward humanities' needs. Dictionaries, gazetteers, and other authoritative lists play an important role in these technologies that most often rely on complementing statistical processes with pattern matching of key terms. The problem for humanities research here is that these key terms often have a time axis attached to them. Names of places are good examples. Everybody knows that they change over time and depend on socioeconomic developments. However, generating authority files is costly, especially if historical changes of key terms are taken into account. The compilation of toponym lists that are applicable to certain historically or geographically limited text corpora, including variant spellings, is a research topic in its own right. Humanities often lack the kind of resources to maintain such authority lists. Novel ways of setting them up and maintaining them need to be found. Here, Web 2.0 technologies (social networks, crowd sourcing) can help, provided mechanisms for training volunteers and monitoring quality can be found.

Also in the humanities, data-intensive research naturally implies the processing of huge amounts of data. This could be many small text files in the case of text mining or linguistic analysis, or (not so many) large files with facsimiles in the case of optical character recognition (OCR). Thus, humanities have to make use of high throughput and high performance computing, where the dispersion of data turns out to be a significant bottleneck. One way to handle this problem is to keep instances of the necessary services (which need to be executed in parallel) on the same nodes as the data. Another, not yet approved, way is to send the services to the data. Any of these solutions has to draw on grid or cloud technologies.

Acknowledgments

This work is has been partially funded by the European Commission in the context of the DARIAH preparation (FP7) project as well as by UK (JISC) and German (BMBF) national funders.

REFERENCES

1. C. Anderson, "The end of theory: the data deluge makes the scientific method obsolete," *Wired Magazine*, vol. 16.07, June 2008.

2. T. Blanke, A. Aschenbrenner, M. Küster, and C. Ludwig, "No claims for universal solutions," in *E-Science '08: Proceedings of the IEEE e-Humanities Workshop*, IEEE Computer Society, 2008.

3. J. Unsworth, *"The Draft Report of the American Council of Learned Societies Commission on Cyberinfrastructure for Humanities and Social Sciences,"* 2006.

4. M. Bryant, T. Blanke, M. Hedges, and R. Palmer, "Open source historical OCR: the OCRopodium project," in *Research and Advanced Technology for Digital Libraries* (M. Lalmas, J. Jose, A. Rauber, F. Sebastiani, and I. Frommholz, eds.), vol. 6273 of *Lecture Notes in Computer Science*, Ch. 72, pp. 522–525, Springer, 2010.

5. M. Nentwich, *Cyberscience: Research in the Age of the Internet*. Vienna: Austrian Academy of Science Press, 2003.

6. S. Bechhofer, D. De Roure, M. Gamble, C. Goble, and I. Buchan, "Research objects: towards exchange and reuse of digital knowledge," http://imageweb.zoo.ox.ac.uk/pub/2010/Proceedings/-FWCS2010/05/Paper5.pdf, 2010.

7. T. Blanke, M. Hedges, and S. Dunn, "E-Science in the arts and humanities—From early experimentation to systematic investigation," in *E-Science '07: Proceedings of the Third IEEE International Conference on e-Science and Grid Computing*, IEEE Computer Society, 2007.

8. C. L. Palmer, L. C. Teffeau, and C. M. Pirmann, *"Scholarly Information Practices in the Online Environment: Themes from the Literature and Implications for Library Service Development. Report commissioned by OCLC Research,"* www.oclc.org/programs/publications/reports/2009-02.pdf, 2009.

9. J. Kircz, *"E-based Humanities and e-Humanities on a SURF platform,"* tech. rep., SURF-DARE, 2004.

10. L. Candela, D. Castelli, and P. Pagano, "On-demand virtual research environments and the changing roles of librarians," *Library Hi Tech*, vol. 27, no. 2, pp. 239–251, 2009.

11. T. Blanke, L. Candela, M. Hedges, M. Priddy, and F. Simeoni, "Deploying general-purpose virtual research environments for humanities research," *Philosophical Transactions of the Royal Society A*, vol. 368, no. 1925, pp. 3813–3828, 2010.

21

Analysis of Large and Complex Engineering and Transport Data

Jim Austin

Department of Computer Science, University of York, York, UK

21.1 INTRODUCTION

This chapter discusses the development of data-intensive methods in research over the last 10 years, centered on the lessons learned through a number of large, national-scale UK projects. The work was primarily undertaken within the UK e-Science program [1] and is focused on the analysis of large and complex data, mainly time-series data from engineering and science. The initial work was based on applying artificial neural networks to large data; this then moved to apply the lessons learned to general methods. The work has demonstrated two key requirements of systems that need to handle large volumes of data.

- Data are typically too large to move to allow them to be processed, requiring the need to move the computation needed to process the data and not the data.

The DATA Bonanza: Improving Knowledge Discovery in Science, Engineering, and Business, First Edition.
Edited by Malcolm Atkinson, Rob Baxter, Michelle Galea, Mark Parsons, Peter Brezany, Oscar Corcho, Jano van Hemert, and David Snelling.

- Methods to process the data need to be optimized to handle large data. One reasonably good approach to this is to design the methods to recognize the bottlenecks in computer systems.

This chapter gives a number of example problems that have demonstrated how this can be achieved.

21.2 APPLICATIONS AND CHALLENGES

Our work has centered on the general domain of diagnostics and prognostics and the need to process data from complex and valuable assets. Typical examples are gas turbines used for aircraft and power generation, as well as transport assets, such as trains and complex transport infrastructures. Typically, data come from a number of sources and must be integrated into a single view to allow the correct conclusions to be drawn.

Considering aircraft engines first, the challenge has been to identify possible "maintenance events," that is, events in the engine, which will require action, in the near or distant future. Typically, engines are run on a fixed service schedule, implying inefficiencies and extra costs for servicing engines that do not require it. Prognostics and diagnostics are needed to detect issues on an as-needed basis. To do this, data can be collected from each engine. An example is the Rolls-Royce Trent engine (Fig. 21.1). Typical data volumes can exceed 1 GB per engine per long-haul flight. The challenge is to not only detect events in this data but also manage the data. In the Distributed Aircraft Maintenance Environment (DAME) project [2], we examined this problem and developed an example platform that led to other applications.

Our analysis showed that the data would be arriving at airports all over the world, some with very limited Internet connections. As it was necessary to undertake analysis after each aircraft had landed by comparing data from aircraft in different locations, undertaking this task was a challenge. To solve the problem, we needed to process the data at the airport, rather than moving the data. This prompted the development of the Pattern Match Controller (PMC) [3] architecture, a technology that allows us to search data spread over a number of geographically distinct computer systems. The technology allows integration of the data search over different locations, that is, the comparison of events recorded in one engine at one location with data from other engines at other locations.

The problem domain involved identification of problems with the engine using the data from the engine. This consisted of various pressures, temperatures, speeds, and so on, as well as vibration data. Companies typically have a model of the engine that allows them to check if the engine parameters are all correct and the underlying reason for any discrepancies. However, the vibration data were more problematic. No models were available to identify the underlying cause of unusual vibrations, meaning that diagnosing a problem was an issue. To overcome this, we looked at how a search engine based on neural networks could be used to check for unusual

Figure 21.1 *Rolls-Royce Trent 500 engine © Rolls-Royce plc.*

engine vibrations against a library of stored examples. The stored examples would be examples from other engines and the earlier life of the engine in question under known engine conditions against the vibration patterns that would be produced. The challenge was to deal with the large volumes of data in these patterns in time to allow the aircraft to take off. Our work that developed the Signal Data Explorer technology to assist this is described later in this chapter.

This problem also extended to power generation, as turbines are often used as backup generators to coal- and oil-based power stations, allowing fast delivery of extra power at very short notice. These need to be monitored in the same way as aero engines. The challenge here was to widen the analysis to lower-cost assets that might be associated with the equipment, such as pumps and valves. The problem was driven by the cost of modeling the normal behavior of the asset. Modeling is typically an expensive and time-consuming process. If an asset is of low value, it may not justify the cost of developing a model of normal and abnormal operation. In addition, every time the asset is altered, its characteristics can alter, meaning renewal of the model. This leads to the need for an online modeling system that can be used autonomously at low costs that can adapt to new conditions and work on large volumes of data. To meet this challenge, we developed the AURA (Advanced Uncertain Reasoning Architecture) alert methods described later [4].

Our final example concerns traffic data. All cities have complex traffic networks and typically use sophisticated data-logging and display systems. Such systems collect data from thousands of "loop" sensors, which are buried in the road, and which allow the system to monitor the traffic flow along roads. While these sensors allow traffic lights to respond to events, the data can also be used to spot events (e.g., accidents) in the network and suggest how these may be overcome. Within the Freeflow project, the challenge has been to detect road-flow information that indicates problems. This example poses the same challenge as the vibration data, modeling the events is complex and expensive, and new and unknown events can occur regularly. Our solution [5] has been to use a high speed search to recognize previously seen events and report that the same events have occurred again. To do this, we have applied our AURA-based, neural-network methods that can recognize and learn new events quickly.

These examples show a common set of needs. Data are large and arrive at regular intervals. The response is needed within short timescales to deal with the issue and the required analysis changes rapidly. An added factor has been that experts are often available to manually spot the events, but the data scales overwhelm their availability, requiring the need to reuse their knowledge automatically on the large data.

21.3 THE METHODS USED

The general framework for processing large data developed in our work is shown in Figure 21.2. Typically, data arrive locally to the asset and are stored in a local database. Because the data we use are typically time-series data, there are challenges in storing them in a conventional database. The normal approach is to store each value and its time stamp as a row in a database table. Although this allows easy access to individual items, analysis over time on the data can be very slow, as many accesses are needed to the database. To overcome this, we prefer to store the data in a flat file, as time–value pairs. These data are then loaded into our search engine as described next. Note that data can be incomplete, contain errors, and lack any annotation.

To allow processing to be undertaken at high rates, our search engine, AURA [6], and associated preprocessing are loaded on each node. AURA is, conceptually, constructed around a central component, a large binary matrix, where each column is a data sample and each row is a measurement value on a parameter from the

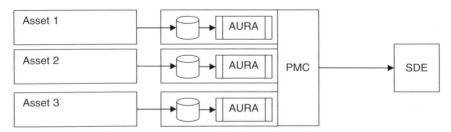

Figure 21.2 *The general framework used in our research. The assets supply data to local nodes, which contain the AURA pattern-matching system. The Pattern Match Controller (PMC) manages communication between the system and the desktop controller signal data explorer (SDE).*

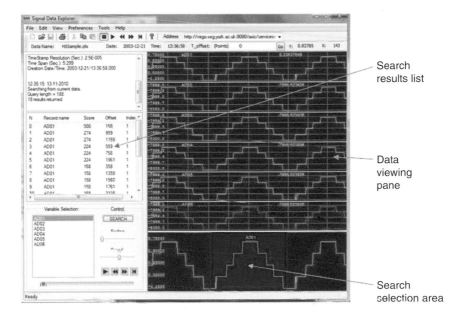

Search
results list

Data
viewing
pane

Search
selection area

Figure 21.3 *Screenshot of the Signal Data Explorer (SDE).*

asset. Methods allow a new data sample to be input and stored in the matrix and unknown data samples to be matched to the data very quickly.

Above the nodes we developed a system, called *Pattern Match Controller* [7], that manages requests from a front-end application that allows search requests to be managed. The user interfaces to the system via a desktop application, Signal Data Explorer, that allows local viewing of the data as well as controlling the search process.

The applications described in the previous section use different combinations of the elements as given in Figure 21.3. The main structure of this system was developed in the above mentioned DAME project for Rolls-Royce engines.

The front-end component, SDE, is shown in Figure 21.3 [8]. The tool allows a user to not only enter *ad hoc* queries to search the data but also contains a "task planner" that allows the user to set up and store previously used search settings across multiple parameters. This functionality allows users to set up standard search queries for known patterns representing, for instance, previous patterns of faults. The tool has many viewing options, allowing users to manipulate data from the data stored on the remote or local computers. There are, in effect, four levels of search:

1. Use the human eye to view the data via the flexible display screens—in particular, the system allows quick zooming into data items, allowing a user to see the overall structure, select an area of interest, and then zoom into the details. This allows casual exploration of the data.

2. Use a sample from the current data to search across all other time series, allowing the user to compare different events in the current or historical data.

3. Use a template of a single time-series pattern stored in a pattern library and search the current data for this event, allowing simple known events to be searched for.

4. Use the "task planner" to look for multiple events over multiple time series.

The SDE allows users to add search capabilities. There are a number of simple search functions built into the tool. Underpinning our search capability is the AURA that has already been briefly mentioned. This is a set of binary, neural-network methods designed to learn rapidly and to be applied to large complex datasets. The methods cover signals, text, and graphs, although our focus here is on signals.

Recently, we have added the ability to search for novel events using a new method called "AURA alert" [4]. Using AURA's ability to store and match large amounts of data, the method allows a user to quickly build a model of the time-series data. The method takes a sample at each time interval across the time series and stores these in the AURA memory. This may be done continually. As each sample is time stamped, it may be deleted or archived after some time period. The new data arriving from the asset are fed into the system and checked to see if they match any data in the store. If they do, the asset is noted as working correctly. However, if the example does not match any example sufficiently well, then the system may alert the user. In practice, this is only done if it happens repeatedly over a period of time. The user may also require that samples follow the same order of occurrence as they did during storage.

An example from the system is shown in Figure 21.4. The example shows a system with six variables recorded from a gas turbine. The plots show how the asset is behaving in monitoring mode. The bottom trace shows when the signals are unlike any seen before, by going "low."

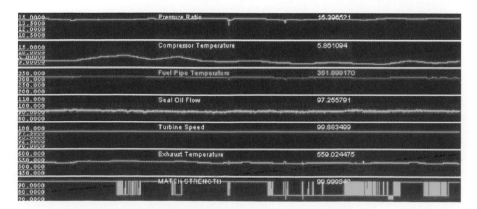

Figure 21.4   The raw data from six variables and the AURA alert matching strength (bottom).

The application to road networks uses a similar approach to AURA alert [9]. In this case, the system supplies traffic-flow information. When an event occurs, the operators indicate to the system what this is and the action (intervention) to be taken to overcome the effect of the event. To allow this to be applied again in future, the system records the set of parameters in AURA at the point of the event, along with the "intervention," that is, the action to be taken if this event happens again. The system is then used to continuously monitor the traffic flow. When an event occurs, the AURA system responds with the known event, triggering an intervention. To reduce the load on the AURA system, a preprocessor is used, which detects if an abnormality has occurred, but not what that is. When the road network is seen as abnormal, AURA is then used to locate the problem. A major issue that the approach overcomes is the scale of the network, containing thousands of sensors. The system has been combined into an intelligent decision support system (IDS) and tried out in the UK cities of York and London. In York, it has been used to monitor transport links into the city. In London, the area around Hyde Park Corner has been monitored. Surprisingly, the results of the work outperform other classifiers such as multilayer perceptron (MLP) [10] and support vector machine (SVM) [9].

In all the applications above, the data often have items missing. For example, a system can suffer dropouts due to sensor failure or communication loss. It is not sufficient for the system to stop working in these cases. The system must continue to report but with a reduced confidence to indicate that data are missing. The AURA methods have the implicit ability to deal with missing data, which makes them ideal for these problems. This ability arises from the way data are dealt with in the neural network. The inputs to the network consist of binary values derived from the input data. The bits that are set to zero indicate "do not care states" while those at one indicate "known data" values. The system adds any new data that correlate with "known data." If a data item is missing, the system has reduced evidence for a match. This is unlike other methods that do not have an unknown state input.

One of the major features of the AURA methods is their scalability on large datasets. The methods are designed to accept a small loss in accuracy while giving a large gain in processing time. Hodge [11] has found that the methods outperform conventional methods in terms of greatly improved speed with only a small loss in accuracy. With time-series analysis, where there can be many tens of search values, AURA gives a valuable increase in performance. Added to this, the methods are very amenable to memory (RAM) operation, again adding to the performance. The AURA software library [2] has many methods incorporated, which allow us to manage binary data very efficiently.

Our work still has to deal with data removal and optimization of the memory. The existing AURA technology operates well across a range of applications. However, the accuracy only meets the accuracy of other methods that do prolonged training in a few cases. Our work has still to understand how to optimize the memory for better accuracy.

In summary, the applications require systems that meet the following overarching requirements:

- Data are continually changing, therefore analysis algorithms should be able to adapt to the changes.
- The user's knowledge is important and must be captured.
- The systems must extend the user's capability, not replace them.
- Data often have items missing, changed, or added. This requires appropriate data preprocessing methods.

The approach described here meets these requirements in real-world applications.

21.4 FUTURE DEVELOPMENTS

Our ultimate aim is to provide a versatile and usable system for rapidly analyzing and exploring large distributed data. To do this, we have recently developed a platform, CARMEN, for sharing software and data across institutions (Software as a Service, SaaS). The CARMEN[1] system [12] is a versatile platform for researchers working in electrophysiology in neuroscience. It incorporates SDE to allow it to visualize and search electrophysiology data. SDE is currently loosely incorporated into CARMEN as is shown in Figure 21.5. CARMEN serves the SDE tool with files to be visualized. Currently, the search process is undertaken locally on the user's PC, using buffered data from the server.

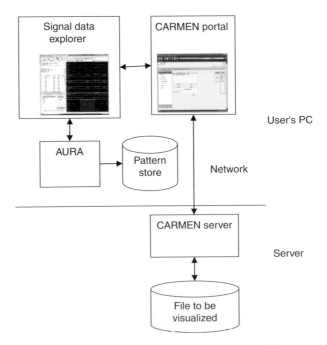

Figure 21.5 The interaction between SDE, the CARMEN portal, AURA, and data to search.

[1] www.carmen.org.uk, accessed February 2013.

We are now incorporating our data management layer to allow the search to be done on the CARMEN portal. The CARMEN platform has been prototyping a workflow engine. The engine allows users to bring together a set of services to analyze the data. One application would be to apply feature selection and filtering before the AURA alert is applied. An additional capability that CARMEN adds is the secure sharing of data and services. Users are given the ability to share with a set of individuals, or publicly, a fundamental requirement in many domains.

21.5 CONCLUSIONS

The chapter has shown how a scalable pattern-matching technology has been applied successfully to a number of complex and challenging diagnostic and prognostic problems. These methods may be applied in many fields. We have applied them in the rail and medical fields, as well as in those described above. It has highlighted the two key issues identified at the beginning of the chapter that moving large data is not practical and that systems that deal with large data need to be engineered to do so. The development of the Signal Data Explorer for visualizing the data, the Pattern Match Controller for managing the data and the AURA alert for spotting events, all underpinned by AURA, provide an advanced platform for diagnostics and prognostics. The technology has been highly successful and is being taken to market through the group's spin-off company, Cybula Ltd. (www.cybula.com), where applications in oil and gas, power, and renewable technologies (wind turbines) are being developed. The methods described here are a start to solving the hard problems involving large data. However, many issues surrounding these problems remain to be addressed. For example, with the advent of cloud computing, the opportunity to host the application on the cloud arises. This is a challenge as the systems may not host data and computer resources at the same place. Another issue is how to increase trust in the effectiveness of the system to solve the problem. Uniquely, AURA allows the user to trace the reasons why it has found a match in the data. Using this capability, it should be possible to raise trust in the platform, something we are now looking at. Finally, we have found that diagnostic and prognostic systems involve large numbers of different people, each with their own requirements from the system. Adapting the operation of the system to address these needs is a key. Again, we are now looking at how this can be supported.

Acknowledgments

The work described here has involved many people, universities, and companies. In particular, I would like to thank the support of Grant Brewer, Julian Young, and John McAvoy at Cybula Ltd., Colin Ingram and Paul Watson at the University of Newcastle, and Lesley Smith at Stirlang University. The members of the team at York University: Vicky Hodge, Tom Jackson, Mark Jessop, Martyn Fletcher, Bojian

Liang, Mike Weeks, Aaron Turner, Mark Hewitt, and Prof. Mike Smith. We recognize the support of EPSRC in the CARMEN, Freeflow, DAME, and BROADEN projects, as well as BBSRC in CARMEN and DFT, and TSB in Freeflow and BROADEN.

REFERENCES

1. A. J. G. Hey and A. E. Trefethen, "The UK e-science core programme and the grid," *Future Generation Computer Systems*, vol. 18, pp. 1017–1031, 2002.

2. J. Austin, R. Davis, M. Fletcher, T. Jackson, M. Jessop, B. Liang, and A. Pasley, "DAME: searching large data sets within a grid-enabled engineering application," *Proceedings of the IEEE - Special Issue on Grid Computing*, vol. 93, pp. 496–509, 2005.

3. T. Jackson, M. Jessop, A. Pasley, and J. Austin, "Searching against distributed data using a Web service architecture," Challenges of Large Applications in Distributed Environments, 2005.

4. J. Austin, G. Brewer, T. Jackson, and V. Hodge, "AURA-Alert; the use of binary associative memories for condition monitoring applications," in *Proceedings of Condition Monitoring, Stratford upon Avon*, 2010.

5. R. Krishnan, V. Hodge, J. Austin, J. Polak, and J. Lee, "On identifying spatial traffic patterns using advanced pattern matching techniques," in *Transportation Research Board (TRB) 89th Annual Meeting*, 2010.

6. J. Austin, *RAM Based Neural Networks, Advances and Application*. World Scientific Publishing Co. Ltd, 1997.

7. J. Austin, T. Jackson, M. Fletcher, M. Jessop, P. Cowley, and P. Lobner, "Distributed aircraft engine diagnostics," in *The Grid: Blueprint for a New Computing Infrastructure*, Ch. 5 (2nd edition). Morgan Kaufmann, 2004.

8. M. Fletcher, T. Jackson, M. Jessop, and B. Liang, "The signal data explorer: a high performance grid based signal search tool for use in distributed diagnostic applications," in *CCGrid 2006–6th IEEE International Symposium on Cluster Computing and the Grid*, 2006.

9. V. J. Hodge, M. Smith, and J. Austin, "Data, intelligent decision support and pattern matching," in *XIII Euro Working Group on Transportation*, 2009.

10. N. Ye, *The Handbook of Data Mining*. Lawrence Erlbaum Associates, 2003.

11. V. Hodge and J. Austin, "A binary neural k-nearest neighbour technique," in *Knowledge and Information Systems*, Ch. 8, pp. 276–292, Springer-Verlag, 2005.

12. L. Smith et al., "The CARMEN e-science pilot project: neuroinformatics work packages," in *Proceedings of the UK e-Science All Hands Meeting 2007*, 2007.

22

Estimating Species Distributions—Across Space, Through Time, and with Features of the Environment

Steve Kelling, Daniel Fink, Wesley Hochachka, and Ken Rosenberg

Cornell Lab of Ornithology, Cornell University, Ithaca, New York, USA

Robert Cook

Environmental Sciences Division, Oak Ridge National Laboratory, Oak Ridge, Tennessee, USA

Theodoros Damoulas

Department of Computer Science, Cornell University, Ithaca, New York, USA

Claudio Silva

Department of Computer Science, Polytechnic Institute of New York, Brooklyn, New York, USA

William Michener

DataONE, University of New Mexico, Albuquerque, New Mexico, USA

The DATA Bonanza: Improving Knowledge Discovery in Science, Engineering, and Business, First Edition.
Edited by Malcolm Atkinson, Rob Baxter, Michelle Galea, Mark Parsons, Peter Brezany, Oscar Corcho, Jano van Hemert, and David Snelling.
© 2013 John Wiley & Sons, Inc. Published 2013 by John Wiley & Sons, Inc.

22.1   INTRODUCTION

Determining the patterns of species occurrence through time and space and understanding their links with features of the environment are central themes in ecology [1]. Now more than ever, such research is essential for understanding the impact that humans have on Earth's natural systems, and for developing science-based management policies to address those impacts. But ecological patterns are exceedingly complex and can progressively reveal more variation the larger the spatial scales across which they are studied [2]. Animal migration, for example, is among the most complex and dynamic natural phenomenon on the planet. In North America, billions of birds of more than 400 species migrate annually, often traveling thousands of miles between breeding and nonbreeding areas. A multitude of factors influence bird migration and many of the most critical factors become apparent only when studied at sufficiently large spatial scales [3–5]. For example, stochastic processes, such as unanticipated juxtapositions of weather during migration or variations in suitable habitat availability along bird migration routes, can have a profound influence on the annual patterns of migration [6, 7].

Identifying the factors that influence species distributions is challenging and requires examining multiple facets of species' natural history and their relationships with the complex and variable environments in which they live. At least initially, this is best done by exploring a large number of potential associations between observations of species occurrence and the multitude of factors that may affect their occurrence. However, given the large number of potential associations that need to be examined, traditional expert-centered parametric analyses become unfeasible, and new analysis procedures are required [8]. What is required is a new data-intensive research paradigm in biodiversity studies where occurrence patterns emerge from the relationships among large and diverse volumes of data using techniques tailored to the discovery of complex patterns in high dimensional data [9]. Using data-intensive approaches, scientists can analyze larger and more complex systems efficiently and complement more traditional scientific processes of hypothesis generation and experimental testing, and in so doing refine our understanding of the natural world [10].

Data-intensive science requires a management and research environment that supports the entire data life cycle, from acquisition, storage, management, and integration to data exploration, analysis, visualization, and other computing and information processing services. Over the past year, a working group consisting of computer scientists, domain researchers, programmers, and analysts met to identify and develop data-intensive procedures that could serve as exemplars in the creation of DataONE (www.dataone.org). DataONE is a United States National Science Foundation (NSF)-funded initiative to develop the cyberinfrastructure that makes environmental data available from atmospheric, ecological, hydrological, and oceanographic sources, provides secure and long-term data preservation, and engages scientists, land managers, policy makers, students, educators, and the public in the use of these data via active accession and exploration mechanisms for intuitive analysis and visualization.

This chapter reports the results of this working group. For this project, we identify the dynamic habitat relationships of hundreds of species of birds across North America through the assembly, exploration, analysis, and visualization of data using examples based on the synthesis and modeling of large datasets collected across multiple scientific domains.

22.1.1 Identifying Working Group Outcomes

The working group developed a data-intensive approach for discovery, access, exploration, analysis, and visualization of the annual patterns of bird occurrence across North America. Our ecologically-motivated goal was to understand the environmental drivers associated with the annual patterns of species' populations across continent-sized areas. We divided the relevant analysis components into the following high level steps:

- *Data Discovery, Access, and Synthesis:* identifying data sources and preparing them for analysis.
- *Model Development:* advancing species distribution modeling.
- *Managing Computational Requirements:* handling computationally intensive models.
- *Exploring and Visualizing Model Results:* describing tools for data exploration and visualization.
- *Examples of Results:* providing new information on continent-scale patterns in bird migration.

What follows is a detailed description of each step leading to the successful completion of the project.

22.2 DATA DISCOVERY, ACCESS, AND SYNTHESIS

Over the past decade, increasing access to biological databases has made them a valued resource in scientific investigations. For example, genomics data is doubling annually and exceeded 5 PB in 2009 [11]. Now, environmental data are becoming increasingly available in the United States via federal agencies (e.g., National Aeronautics and Space Administration (NASA), United States Geological Survey (USGS), National Oceanic and Atmospheric Administration (NOAA) and Department of Energy (DOE)) and other global initiatives (e.g., Global Biodiversity Information Facility, Knowledge Network for Biodiversity, and Avian Knowledge Network (AKN)). Access to these data is providing new research opportunities in ecology [8, 12–19]. Using a data-intensive science approach, the research focuses on synthesizing data from multiple sources, such as organism observations, (i.e., the response of interest, which we will call the "input" data) and links these with a multitude of "drivers," covariates potentially associated with the occurrence of the organism. For our study, numerous hurdles had to be overcome to link observations of birds with covariates such as climate, physical environment, and anthropogenic factors. Data had to be standardized in multiple ways (e.g., scale, units, spatial and temporal resolutions, and file formats) and then joined into a common data structure. This process was incredibly time-consuming, certainly the longest aspect of our project.

Data access and synthesis are a multistep process [20]. First, the analyst needs to discover and access the required input (i.e., species occurrence) and covariable data. New data appropriate for analysis may need to be generated through preanalysis of multiple datasets. Next, data must be synthesized into an interoperable dataset. Finally, all data must be processed for analysis and visualization. Given the time and diverse skills required to accomplish these processes, the informatics community must improve the services that perform these steps and allow domain investigators to search, retrieve, and store content in a persistent infrastructure as easily as storing and accessing data on local disk space.

22.2.1   Discovery and Access to Input Data Sources — Species Occurrence Data

For the current project, a dataset was identified, which provided year-round and continent-wide bird occurrence data. Fortunately, a significant volume of bird observation data for North America has been organized in a standard format and made available through the Avian Knowledge Network (AKN) [21]. Data from eBird [22] were selected. eBird is a volunteer-based bird monitoring project that gathers high quality bird observations [19] from a global network of contributors. For the current study, eBird data gathered in the United States from 2004 to 2009 were used (Fig. 22.1).

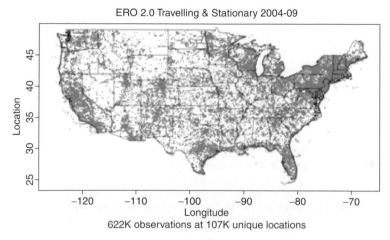

Figure 22.1 *Locations of submission of bird observations to eBird between 2004 and 2009. More than 20 million observations were gathered through 622,000 checklist submissions from over 107,000 unique locations.*

22.2.2 Discovery and Access to Data Sources — Driver Data

One of the major challenges in building the data resource necessary for this analysis was identifying and then calibrating the different data sources into a standard functional format. While input data are often readily available to the researcher and maintained in accessible domain-centric repositories (e.g., AKN), finding and then accessing driver data is more difficult and time-consuming. For example, the researcher must first identify what driver data were required for the study. Then they must find sources of that data, which is difficult and often found serendipitously, because no central data-discovery repository is available. For example, in the current study, researchers identified the need for information on the physical conditions, boundaries, flow, and related characteristics of surface waters. Specifically, this hydrographic data are required to estimate the distance from water where bird observations were made, an important variable for estimating species occurrence. But multiple searches via the Internet and other means could not identify a suitable hydrography dataset. It was not until one-on-one discussions with individual researchers occurred that a suitable dataset was obtained.

On the basis of our experience, we recommend a metadata repository of earth observational data that is derived from many disciplines, both biotic (e.g., genomic, cellular, physiology, morphology, biodiversity, populations, communities, ecosystems, etc.) and abiotic (e.g., hydrology, geospatial, weather, climate, etc.) data. The purpose of this repository would be to provide a consistent and reliable means of discovery and access to data. Metadata information should include information about how to access specific data and specific details about the content and how they are stored.

22.2.3 Access to Data Sources

The primary goal of a data user is to handle all of their data requirements as efficiently as possible. Unfortunately, this is far from the norm, and from our experience we estimated that as much as 90% of the analyst's time was spent in data preparation. The major issue is that the data sources are tremendously complex and stored in unique file formats that limit data interoperability and accessibility. Specifically, synthesizing and integrating data that vary in their expression and granularity of spatial and temporal dimensions, amongst other dimensions of heterogeneity (units, error tolerance, etc.), is a tedious process that must be done manually, which effectively limits their use in analysis.

22.2.4 Data Interoperability

Data-intensive research often tackles broad and complex questions that require the integration of data gathered across multiple domains. Conceptually, this integration is possible because all observations are derived from similar processes; they all represent a measurement of an attribute of some object made within a particular context [20]. The context is the set of conditions under which the measurements were made, such as the time, date, and location of the observation. The attributes are some characteristics of the object such as type of organism, temperature, behavior, or sensor output. The measurement describes the process in which the attributes were collected. To take advantage of these observation similarities requires clarification of interobservational relationships, which would lead to a common observational data model [23]. This observational data model could enhance data discovery, interoperability, analysis, and management throughout the data life cycle. Unfortunately, while a number of observational data models and ontologies have been developed [24], no one model has been adopted by the broader community.

22.2.5 Data Accessibility

Gaining access to data can be challenging for two primary reasons: (i) many domain scientists are not trained in accessing and managing large datasets and (ii) many data centers do not provide efficient access to data. To overcome this requires innovative thinking about user needs, data download processes, and access control. For example, in the current study, researchers wanted to include remotely sensed environmental data collected by the moderate resolution imaging spectroradiometers (MODIS) on board NASA's Terra and Aqua satellites. The remote sensing data of MODIS are useful for viewing terrestrial, atmospheric, and ocean phenomenology at regional, continental, and global scales. While MODIS data were available, collecting the volume of data needed for this project proved difficult. Specifically, the size and format of the archived MODIS data tiles made them difficult to access and use. To overcome this challenge, the Oak Ridge National Laboratory Distributed Active Archive Center (ORNL DAAC) for biogeochemical dynamics developed a series of Web-based MODIS data subsetting tools to improve ease of use of MODIS data. The ORNL DAAC tools allow users to examine MODIS time-series data for relatively few ($\sim$1500 sites) or small ($<$200 km $\times$ 200 km) field sites. Unfortunately, these tools did not scale well to the large number of sites (more than 100,000) and continental scales required in the present study. Realizing this shortcoming, the ORNL DAAC modified their Web tools to allow us to submit the geocoordinates of multiple locations in large batches, and time-series MODIS data for each location were processed at the ORNL DAAC. This modification shortened the duration of MODIS data preparation from 6 months to 6 weeks.

22.2.6 Data Synthesis

In the present study, we needed to associate locations where bird observations were made with a multitude of environmental variables, which required linking observations in space and time (Fig. 22.2). While intuitively this appears straightforward, it is a tedious and error-prone task. First, the analyst must determine the format in which data are stored. While metadata that describe the provenance attributes of the datasets were helpful, our experience indicated that this was not sufficient to allow us to synthesize datasets. Specifically, typical descriptive metadata were not sufficient to adjust the nonuniformity in data gathering procedures, spatial processing,

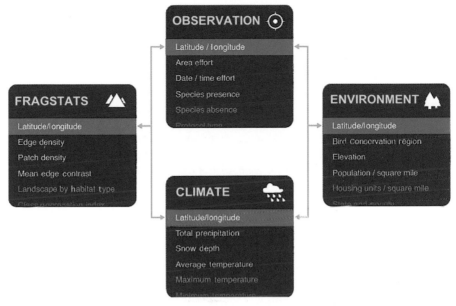

Figure 22.2 *Multidimensional data warehouse for bird occurrence. Data were stored in a star schema consisting of an event table that contains information from observations of birds, and multiple predictor tables. Tables were linked using latitude and longitude.*

and measurement outcomes across multiple data resources. Second, many environmental variables are static, in that they are derived from environmental snapshots tied to a specified time frame, while bird observations were made throughout the entire year. Third, each of the datasets used in the current study were stored in different spatial or temporal resolutions; bird observations were stored as discrete points, while many land cover, climate, and anthropogenic datasets were provided as a two-dimensional surface of contiguous cells (grid). These different extents had to be rectified to create a new dataset, and careful data manipulation was required to ensure that the range of values found in the new dataset matched those of the discrete datasets. For example, the MODIS data tiles had to be associated with discrete locations where bird observations were made. This was done by projecting the latitude and longitude of the bird observations onto the grid coordinate system of the MODIS data. Then the MODIS value at the location of the bird observation was extracted.

22.2.7 Preanalysis

Before running the model, additional data processing is often required. For example, landscape and land cover statistics were run to describe the habitats and habitat configuration at each location where bird observations were made. We computed FRAGSTATS metrics to estimate the spatial heterogeneity, and the extent of individual landscape cover types around each observation site [25]. Information about land cover and habitat were computed from raster data obtained from the National Land Cover Dataset (NLCD) (www.mrlc.gov/nlcd.php). We extracted land cover information from the raw 2001 NLCD database for grids centered on each location where bird observations were gathered. Since the ideal neighborhood size depends on the species under consideration, we repeated this process for three different spatial extents: 2.25 hectares, 225 hectares, and 22,500 hectares around each location. These extents were selected to cover local ecological processes at small, medium, and large ranges. This land cover matrix was then used as input to the FRAGSTATS program [25] to generate land cover classifications. Fourteen landscape-level FRAGSTATS metrics, such as habitat patch size and edge density for each patch, were calculated for each spatial extent around each location where bird observations were gathered.

22.2.8   Data Products

The result of data processing, preanalysis, and synthesis was a new dataset. For the current study, all of the data were stored in a star schema data warehouse [26]. Our warehouse is multidimensional and consists of an event table (i.e., the information detailing the observation of a bird) and multiple driver tables (Fig. 22.2). The data warehouse is available through the AKN Web site [19].

22.3   MODEL DEVELOPMENT

Our goal was to describe the environmental drivers associated with patterns of species' occurrence across broad landscapes. For example, the ability to quantify the association between physical and environmental features and bird occurrence has multiple applications such as identifying the mechanisms by which climate change may alter the timing of birds' migrations. Even now, relatively little is known about the temporal dynamics of broad-scale occurrence patterns for many common North American birds. Therefore, we chose to model these bird occurrence patterns using an automatic, semiparametric modeling approach to facilitate the rapid exploration of migrations across a broad set of species with highly variable migration strategies.

To accomplish our goals, we used the spatiotemporal exploratory model (STEM) [16]. STEM was designed to be a highly automated, multiscale predictive model geared specifically to discover seasonal and regional patterns in data. Spatiotemporal variation in habitat associations are captured by combining a series of separate but overlapping submodels that describe the distribution within a relatively small area and time window. By associating environmental inputs with observed patterns of bird populations, STEM, similar to many predictive models, provides a formalized framework to harness available data and reveal detailed patterns of distribution. We use this predictive framework to "fill-in" the sparsely distributed bird observation data from eBird, using the habitat associations learned by STEM to make predictions at unobserved locations across the country. In addition, this

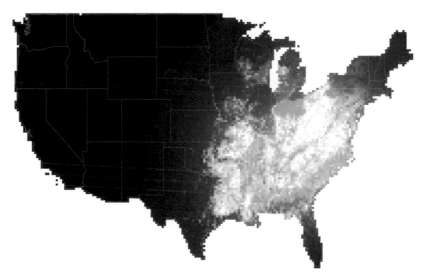

Figure 22.3 *Spatiotemporal exploratory distribution model of Acadian flycatcher (Empidonax virescens). It breeds in the southeastern United States, with the northern extension of its range barely reaching New England. In southeastern swamps, they like groves of American holly while in the Appalachians they can be found in cool, wet hemlock ravines. Distribution models for many species using eBird data, including Acadian flycatcher, achieve monthly AUC scores above 0.85 during periods of species residency in the United States denoting high model accuracy that is confirmed by domain experts.*

framework is used to control important sources of bias present in the observed data. By standardizing all predictions as if they were made by a single observer making consistent observations (e.g., all observations made during a standard time period), we removed many important sources of bias from our predictions, essentially "cleaning" our data as we "filled" in the gaps. Figure 22.3 shows the predicted probability of occurrence for Acadian flycatcher (*Empidonax virescens*) during the breeding season of 2009 after controlling for observational effort across the continental United States. Map results for a number of species can be seen on the eBird Web site (ebird.org/content/ebird/news/ebird-animated-occurrence-maps).

22.4   MANAGING COMPUTATIONAL REQUIREMENTS

The STEM modeling approach is computationally intensive because of the volume and spatial extent of the data. Each of the thousands of locations where bird predictions were made provides information on species' presence or absence and how this relates to hundreds of driver variables. Using an "in-house" computing system running a STEM model for a single species requires 3–4 days using a single computer processor core, and generating the fine scale predictions (i.e., at roughly 1 million points throughout the lower 48 states of the United States) required an additional 7 days. Because we wanted to conduct analyses for hundreds of species, the "in-house" approach was not feasible and we had to develop an alternative strategy for data processing and model analysis.

Fortunately, our analysis technique can be treated as a parallel computing problem, even for a single species, and we adapted our methods to run in a high performance computing infrastructure: the US National Science Foundation-funded XSEDE (www.xsede.org) [27]. The major challenges in running STEM on the XSEDE were the requirements for access to a large quantity of random access memory (RAM) for each processor core, and the need for fast Input/Output (I/O) operations for writing thousands of files to disk (approximately 100,000 files per species). To overcome the RAM challenge required the STEM code to be divided into a number of subtasks, in our case treating each species' analysis as 10 subtasks organized in a master–worker architecture that synchronized the execution. We ran analyses for 125 species of birds on the XSEDE's "Lonestar" system (Dell Linux Cluster) as 250 subtasks within a single job submission. Each subtask was run using half of a "Lonestar" node (two cores) in order to secure availability of the 3.85 GB of RAM per subtask out of a node total of 7.7 GB. Completing the analysis in batches of data from 25 bird species, therefore, required the use of 250 processors (500 cores) and processing was completed in 6 h. It is worth noting that owing to the massively parallel nature of the STEM models, we can analyze hundreds of species in the same computational time (6 h) on a large high performance system such as those in XSEDE ("Lonestar" has 5200 cores and other systems, such as "Ranger," currently have 62,976 cores).

The second challenge imposed by the heavy I/O operations was tackled via a "staging" process where the I/O process was broken down into steps operating at the level of individual computational nodes. During the "stage-in" subprocess, relevant data layers and STEM analysis code were sent to individual nodes for a specific species and subtask. From that point onward, the master–worker execution took over, spawning the subtasks for model fitting and prediction in alignment with which species-specific subtasks were planned for each node (2 per node). On completion of its work, the 20,000 files per node were written with local I/O operations to avoid overloading the main "Lonestar" file system and were then compressed and assembled back for storage, with output from each set of 25 species yielding 2.5 million data files (for 25 species) containing the ensemble fitted models and the overall spatiotemporal predictions from STEM.

After the model analysis was completed, the results had to be transferred to a data repository. Every species analysis generated large amounts of output, and transfer rates had to be carefully monitored to ensure that no serious bottlenecks would throttle back the transfer rate or exceed the temporary storage available on "Lonestar."

22.5   EXPLORING AND VISUALIZING MODEL RESULTS

Our analysis approach is exploratory [8, 9] and requires that model results can be intuitively and efficiently explored, analyzed, and visualized so that patterns in the data can be easily revealed. Owing to the large volume of data generated from running the STEM models, innovative measures for data management, exploration, and visualization are required. To illustrate the scale of the model results data management challenge, running a STEM model on a single species generated almost 4 GB of output data (compressed), and analysis of data from 500 species would generate almost 2 TB of data. This volume of data will be generated annually.

The most successful way of exploring complex models and large volumes of model result data is through visualizations of low dimensional model summaries. These summaries (e.g., maps or partial-dependence plots) provide intuitive representations of how the input variable or response depends on one or a small set of predictors. In addition, it is often the case that the most interesting effect of a driver variable(s), such as climate change or human activity, may only be observable in smaller regions of the data space; not only restricted geographical regions, but also subsets of time (e.g., effects could vary seasonally). Hence, computational processes need to summarize the model for many such "slices" of the data space. Thus, a major challenge is to efficiently scale up summary computation for use in exploring patterns along a larger number of putatively important dimensions that include spatial and temporal patterning. We believe that computational summaries are necessary when the goal is to facilitate examination of output as an interactive process, unhindered by long response times for creation of each new set of summaries.

While cyberinfrastructure advances are fostering more inquiry-based, data-intensive exploration, the exploratory nature of the modeling and the massive quantity of model output does not eliminate the human from the analysis loop. On the contrary, the more computational summaries a scientist can explore, the greater the chance to find interesting patterns that lead to new hypotheses and ultimately to scientific discovery. Thus, human expertise is required to discover the structure of a complex model and create the interpretations needed for scientific publications, Web sites, and project reports. For these reasons, scientific workflow software provides a platform to support the necessary processes to gather, organize, annotate, visualize, and explore data. This requires the cyberinfrastructure to support the inherently exploratory analysis and visualization tasks, and maintain provenance of the intermediate and final results. Stemming from the French word *provenir* ("to come from"), provenance means the origin, or the source, of something, or the history of an object's ownership or location. The provenance (also referred to as the *audit trail* and *lineage*) of a digital object contains information about the process and data used to derive the object and provides important documentation that is key to preserving data, to determining the data's quality and authorship, and to reproduce as well as validate the results. Subsequently, we briefly summarize our ideas for creating interactive exploration of model output.

We believe that exploration of model output will be most productive if the analyst is able to seamlessly document and refer to their progression through the course of exploration (i.e., the provenance of their conclusions) and if the process of challenging their assumptions is facilitated. Notably, there must be support for reflective reasoning, which in turn requires *the ability to store temporary results, to make inferences from stored knowledge and to follow chains of reasoning backward and forward, sometimes backtracking when a promising line of thought proves to be unfruitful* [28]. To this end, we are incorporating the VisTrails workflow system as the main tool to support our computational tasks, including data analysis and visualization.

VisTrails is an open-source, freely available tool and has been used in a variety of scientific domains. It combines and substantially extends useful features of visualization and scientific workflow systems [29]. Similar to visualization systems, VisTrails makes advanced scientific visualization techniques available to users allowing them to explore and compare different visual representations of their data. Similar to scientific workflow systems, VisTrails enables the composition of workflows that combine specialized libraries, distributed computing infrastructure, and Web services. As a result, users can create complex workflows that encompass important steps of scientific discovery, from data gathering and manipulation to complex analyses and visualizations, all integrated in one system. But in contrast to these systems, VisTrails transparently tracks detailed provenance of the exploratory process: the steps followed and data derived in the course of an exploratory task [30, 31]. This includes provenance of data products (e.g., visualizations, plots), the workflows that produced these products and their relationships, and the executions of these workflows.

Besides enabling reproducible results, VisTrails leverages provenance information through a series of operations and intuitive user interfaces that aid users to collaboratively analyze data. Figure 22.4 shows an example of an exploratory visualization using VisTrails with project-relevant data. Each node in the history tree in the center of the figure (i.e., vistrail or visual trail) corresponds to a workflow and a line between two nodes corresponds to changes applied to transform the parent workflow into the child (e.g., through the addition of a module or a change to a parameter value). The tree-based representation supports reflective reasoning: users can navigate workflow versions in an intuitive way, undo changes but not lose any results, visually compare multiple workflows, show their results side by side in a visual spreadsheet, and examine the actions that led to a result [30]. In addition, the system has native support for parameter sweeps, the results of which can also be displayed on a spreadsheet [30].

VisTrails addresses important usability issues that have hampered a wider adoption of workflow and visualization systems. It provides a series of operations and user interfaces that simplify workflow design and use, including the ability to create and refine workflows by analogy, the ability to query workflows by example, and the automatic generation of recommendations for completions as users interactively construct and refine their workflows [32, 33].

22.6   ANALYSIS RESULTS

Our goal was to determine which environmental features impact where a species will and will not occur, and accurately describe species' distributions and habitat

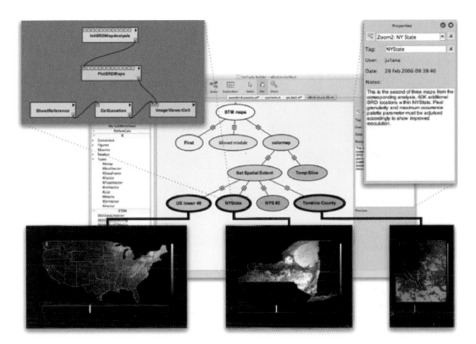

Figure 22.4 *Exploratory visualization for studying patterns of species occurrence across three geographical extents derived from STEM species distribution analysis using VisTrails. At the center, the version tree provides a visual trail of the exploratory process. Each node corresponds to a workflow and its associated results. The hierarchical structure captures the series of refinements the different workflows went through during an exploratory task. While provenance is captured transparently, users can also add annotations to the individual workflows (top right) that details the issues they encountered or their reasoning in analyzing the results.*

associations throughout the entire year. Here, we demonstrate how by taking a data-intensive science approach we can (i) accurately describe seasonal changes in species' distributions, (ii) identify regional differences in organisms' migratory movements, and (iii) discover seasonal differences in habitat associations.

Our combination of data and analysis techniques produce very accurate models of species distributions. Figure 22.5 displays the predicted distribution of breeding prevalence of occurrence and habitat preferences of the Indigo Bunting (*Passerina cyanea*) and Chimney Swift (*Chaetura pelagica*), two species with similar breeding ranges. Comparisons of these predictions closely match with prior knowledge of these species, indicating high accuracy of our models. Quantitative measures of breeding season predictive performance confirm this qualitative assessment, with predictive accuracies of 83% and 88% and AUC[1] scores of 0.88 and 0.84 for Indigo Bunting and Chimney Swift, respectively. We emphasize that the distribution maps

---

[1]The AUC is a commonly used measure of predictive accuracy that measures a model's ability to discriminate between positive and negative observations.

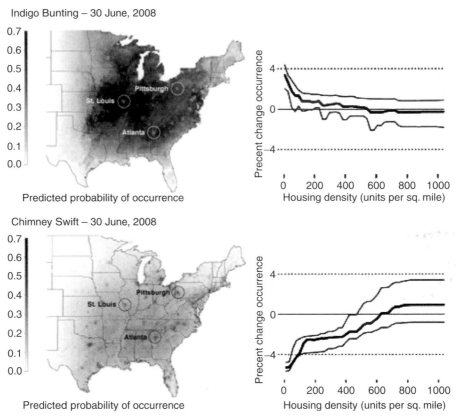

Figure 22.5 *Predicted probability of occurrence and partial dependence on housing density for Indigo Bunting (a and b) and Chimney Swift (c and d) for June 30, 2008. Although both species have similar, widespread distributions across eastern United States, the fine-scale differences around major urban centers is striking. The Indigo Bunting has relatively low occurrence rates in urban centers while the Chimney Swift has high occurrence rates. We note three major urban centers (Pittsburg, St. Louis, and Atlanta) and provide the partial effect estimates of housing density to highlight these differences.*

are habitat based and not simple interpolations. This can be seen by contrasting partial effects of human housing density in urban centers (Fig. 22.5).

22.7 CONCLUSION

Data-intensive science is a new paradigm in scientific research and is becoming increasingly prevalent as data become organized, discoverable, and accessible. As we have described, this approach provides the opportunity for novel descriptions of the world—more detailed and extensive than previously possible. The opportunity now to discover patterns in massive quantities of data promises empirical scientific study of increasingly more complex and comprehensive systems.

A major goal of data-intensive analyses is discovering patterns in the data that account for potentially complicated relationships between multiple sources, such as observations of an organism with a multitude of "drivers," covariates potentially associated with the occurrence of the organism. Conventional analyses of ecological data are geared toward hypothesis confirmations that require specific, detailed input in the form of parametric models. But when candidate sets of important environmental drivers number in the tens, if not hundreds, new exploratory data analysis tools emerging from the fields of machine learning, data mining, and statistics are required to automatically identify patterns in large and complex environmental data sources. But many obstacles must be overcome for data-intensive science to become broadly accessible to a wide community.

Data access and synthesis are the most difficult challenges to overcome in a data-intensive environment. First discovering and then processing data requires multiple steps, and many data resources are difficult to discover and hard to access. Efficient tools to synthesize these data must be made available. We strongly feel that the diverse skills necessary in performing data synthesis at present requires the informatics community to provide services that perform these steps more efficiently.

In a data-intensive setting, even relatively simple models are often complicated by the large numbers of driver variables. This requires an analysis approach that allows intuitive and efficient integration of data so that it can be explored, analyzed, and visualized, ensuring that patterns are easily revealed. Thus, knowledge discovery in a data-intensive environment requires the careful balance between human and machine expertise, where visualizations of low dimensional model summaries are provided in a logical, intuitive, and interactive format, so that interesting patterns can be discovered based on the user's background knowledge. We believe that new developments in scientific workflows provide an essential part of exploration visualization and analysis in a data-intensive science.

In conclusion, our work in the scientific exploration analysis and visualization working group for DataONE has developed novel methods to explore, analyze, and visualize observations and equip scientists and students with the technologies that provide the ability to follow the journeys of birds across continents. The continent-scale models of bird migration developed for this project provide the opportunity to visualize bird population dynamics over time and space and predict responses to environmental change at spatial and temporal scales here-to-fore unimaginable. Newly developed Web-accessible workflow software makes it possible for students and professionals to intuitively access massive biodiversity datasets without knowing how to manipulate databases or write code. Such developments are rapidly transforming the ways land managers, conservation scientists, and students investigate conservation issues affecting individual species to entire taxonomic groups on local to global scales.

Acknowledgments

This work was funded by the Leon Levy Foundation, Wolf Creek Foundation, and the National Science Foundation (Grant Numbers OCI-0830944, CCF-0832782,

ITR-0427914, DBI-1049363, DBI-0542868, DUE-0734857, IIS-0748626, IIS-061 2031, IIS-1050422, IIS-0905385, IIS-0746500, and CNS-0751152.).

REFERENCES

1. J. M. Scott, P. J. Heglund, and M. L. Morrison, eds., *Predicting Species Occurrences: Issues of Accuracy and Scale*. Island Press, 2002.

2. B. A. Maurer and M. L. Taper, "Connecting geographical distributions with population processes," *Ecology Letters*, vol. 5, no. 2, pp. 223–231, 2002.

3. S. A. J. Gauthreaux and C. G. Belser, "Radar ornithology and biological conservation," *The Auk*, vol. 120, no. 2, pp. 266–277, 2003.

4. M. Schaub, F. Liechti, and L. Jenni, "Departure of migrating European robins, from a stopover site in relation to wind and rain," *Animal Behaviour*, vol. 67, no. 2, pp. 229–237, 2004.

5. A. P. Tøttrup, K. Thorup, and C. Rahbek, "Patterns of change in timing of spring migration in North European songbird populations," *Journal of Avian Biology*, vol. 37, no. 1, pp. 84–92, 2006.

6. K. P. Able, "How birds migrate: flight behavior, energetics, and navigation," in *Gatherings of Angels: Migrating Birds and Their Ecology* (K. P. Able, ed.), pp. 11–27, Cornell University Press, 1999.

7. I. Newton, "Bird migration," in *Handbook of the Birds of the World* (J. D. Hoyo, A. Elliott, and D. A. Christie, eds.), vol. 13, pp. 15–47, Lynx Edicions, 2008.

8. W. M. Hochachka, R. Caruana, D. Fink, M. A. Munson, M. Riedewald, D. Sorokina, and S. Kelling, "Data-mining discovery of pattern and process in ecological systems," *Journal of Wildlife Management*, vol. 71, no. 7, pp. 2427–2437, 2007.

9. S. Kelling, W. M. Hochachka, D. Fink, M. Riedewald, R. Caruana, G. Ballard, and G. Hooker, "Data-intensive science: a new paradigm for biodiversity studies," *BioScience*, vol. 59, no. 7, pp. 613–620, 2009.

10. A. J. G. Hey, S. Tansley, and K. Tolle, eds. *The Fourth Paradigm: Data-Intensive Scientific Discovery*. Microsoft Research, 2009.

11. C. Southan and G. Cameron, "Beyond the Tsunami: developing the infrastructure to deal with life sciences data," in *The Fourth Paradigm: Data Intensive Scientific Discovery* (A. J. G. Hey, S. Tansley, and K. Tolle, eds.), pp. 117–124, Microsoft Research, 2009.

12. K. E. Fabricius and G. De'ath, "Environmental factors associated with the spatial distribution of crustose coralline algae on the Great Barrier Reef," *Coral Reefs*, vol. 19, no. 4, pp. 303–309, 2001. DOI: 10.1007/s003380000120.

13. R. Caruana, M. Elhaware, A. Munson, M. Riedewald, and D. Sorokina, "Mining citizen science data to predict prevalence of wild bird species," in *Proceedings ACM SIGKDD International Conference on Knowledge Discovery and Data Mining*, pp. 909–915, 2006.

14. D. R. Sheldon, M. A. S. Elmohamed, and D. Kozen, "Collective inference on Markov models for modeling bird migration," in *Neural Information Processing Systems*, 2007.

15. J. Elith and J. R. Leathwick, "Species distribution models: ecological explanation and prediction across space and time," *Annual Review of Ecology, Evolution, and Systematics*, vol. 40, no. 1, pp. 677–697, 2009.

16. D. Fink, W. M. Hochachka, D. Winkler, B. Shaby, G. Hooker, B. Zuckerberg, M. A. Munson, D. Sheldon, M. Riedewald, and S. Kelling, "Spatiotemporal exploratory models for large-scale survey data," *Ecological Applications*, vol. 20, no. 8, pp. 2131–2147, 2010.

17. S. J. Phillips, M. Dudík, C. H. G. J. Elith, A. Lehmann, J. Leathwick, and S. Ferrier, "Sample selection bias and presence-only distribution models: implications for background and pseudo-absence data," *Ecological Applications*, vol. 19, no. 1, pp. 181–197, 2009.

18. D. Sorokina, R. Caruana, M. Riedewald, W. M. Hochachka, and S. Kelling, "Detecting and interpreting variable interactions in observational ornithology data," in *ICDM Workshops '09*, pp. 64–69, 2009.

19. M. A. Munson, R. Caruana, D. F. Fink, W. M. Hochachka, M. I. Iliff, K. V. Rosenberg, D. R. Sheldon, B. L. Sullivan, C. L. Wood, and S. Kelling, "A method for measuring the relative information content of data from different monitoring protocols," *Methods in Ecology and Evolution*, vol. 1, no. 3, pp. 263–273, 2010.

20. S. Kelling, *Significance of Organism Observations—Data Discovery and Access in Biodiversity Research*. GBIF, 2008. http://www.gbif.org/informatics/primary-data/types-of-primary-biodiversity-data/observational-data/, accessed January 2013.

21. M. J. Iliff, L. Salas, E. R. Inzunza, G. Ballar, D. Lepage, and S. Kelling, "The Avian Knowledge Network: a partnership to organize, analyze, and visualize bird observation data for education, conservation, research, and land management," in *Proceedings of the Fourth International Partners in Flight Conference: Tundra to Tropics*, pp. 365–373, 2009.

22. B. L. Sullivan, C. L. Wood, M. J. Iliff, R. E. Bonney, D. Fink, and S. Kelling, "eBird: a citizen-based bird observation network in the biological sciences," *Biological Conservation*, vol. 142, no. 10, pp. 2282–2292, 2009.

23. J. Madin, S. Bowers, M. Schildhauer, S. Krivov, D. Pennington, and F. Villa, "An ontology for describing and synthesizing ecological observation data," *Ecological Informatics*, vol. 2, pp. 279–295, 2007.

24. L. Lefort, P. Barnaghi, L. Bermudez, M. Compton, O. Corcho, S. Cox, R. Castro, J. Graybeal, C. Henson, A. Herzog, K. Janowicz, D. L. Phuoc, H. Neuhaus, and K. Page, "W3C Incubator Group Report—review of Sensor and Observation ontologies," tech. rep., W3C, 2010, www.w3.org/2005/Incubator/ssn/wiki/Incubator_Report#Review_of_Sensor_and_Observation_ontologies, accessed January 2013

25. K. S. McGarigal, A. Cushman, M. C. Neel, and E. Ene, "FRAGSTATS: Spatial Pattern Analysis Program for Categorical Maps," 2002. www.umass.edu/landeco/research/fragstats/frag-stats.html, accessed January 2013.

26. M. McGuirea, A. Gangopadhyay, A. Komlodi, and C. Swan, "A user-centered design for a spatial data warehouse for data exploration in environmental research," *Ecological Informatics*, vol. 3, no. 4–5, pp. 273–285, 2008.

27. E. Marris, "Birds Flock Online: supercomputer time will help ornithologists make ecological sense of millions of records of bird sightings," *Nature*, 2010. DOI: 10.1038/news.2010.395.

28. D. A. Norman, *Things that Make Us Smart: Defending Human Attributes in the Age of the Machine*. Addison-Wesley, 1993.

29. L. Bavoil, S. P. Callahan, P. J. Crossno, J. Freire, and H. T. Vo, "VisTrails: enabling interactive multiple-view visualizations," in *IEEE Visualization 2005*, pp. 135–142, 2005.

30. J. Freire, C. T. Silva, S. P. Callahan, E. Santos, C. E. Scheidegger, and H. T. Vo, "Managing rapidly-evolving scientific workflows," in *International Provenance and Annotation Workshop (IPAW), LNCS 4145*, pp. 10–18, Springer Verlag, May 2006.

31. S. B. Davidson, S. C. Boulakia, A. Eyal, B. Ludascher, T. M. McPhillips, S. Bowers, M. K. Anand, and J. Freire, "Provenance in scientic workflow systems," *IEEE Data Engineering Bulletin*, vol. 30, no. 4, pp. 44–50, 2007.

32. C. E. Scheidegger, H. T. Vo, D. Koop, J. Freire, and C. T. Silva, "Querying and creating visualizations by analogy," *IEEE Transactions on Visualization and Computer Graphics*, vol. 13, no. 6, pp. 1560–1567, 2007.

33. D. Koop, C. E. Scheidegger, S. P. Callahan, J. Freire, and C. T. Silva, "VisComplete: automating suggestions for visualization pipelines," *IEEE Transactions on Visualization and Computer Graphics*, vol. 14, no. 6, pp. 1691–1698, 2008.

Part VI

The Data-Intensive Future

The DATA Bonanza: Improving Knowledge Discovery in Science, Engineering, and Business, First Edition.
Edited by Malcolm Atkinson, Rob Baxter, Michelle Galea, Mark Parsons, Peter Brezany, Oscar Corcho,
Jano van Hemert, and David Snelling.
© 2013 John Wiley & Sons, Inc. Published 2013 by John Wiley & Sons, Inc.

23

Data-Intensive Trends

Malcolm Atkinson and Paolo Besana

School of Informatics, University of Edinburgh, Edinburgh, UK

This chapter commences with a review of what we have learnt about data-intensive methods and their potential power. It then identifies the current research that should be observed by those who wish to further develop data-intensive strategies. This leads to insights regarding the future of research, industry, and society.

23.1 REPRISE

23.1.1 The Data Bonanza

The drivers of data-intensive change are the pervasive use of digital technology to capture and transmit information in just about every walk of life, and almost ubiquitous connectivity. Advances in device technology and commoditization of digital products have led to digital devices becoming cheaper and hence more numerous, while expensive digital products become ever faster and ever more sensitive. Both developments increase the available data. The growing reach of digital communications and steadily increasing bandwidths in many connection technologies increase the opportunity to gather, collate, and aggregate data. These factors make the growth of available data possible, but that growth would stall without a commensurate benefit.

The DATA Bonanza: Improving Knowledge Discovery in Science, Engineering, and Business, First Edition.
Edited by Malcolm Atkinson, Rob Baxter, Michelle Galea, Mark Parsons, Peter Brezany, Oscar Corcho, Jano van Hemert, and David Snelling.
© 2013 John Wiley & Sons, Inc. Published 2013 by John Wiley & Sons, Inc.

Pioneering businesses in the fossil-fuel and pharmacological industries have shown the power of integrating data, typically by using data-warehousing and advanced database technology to cope with their scale and heterogeneity. Other industries, commerce and Internet services, for example, have shown the power of managing, analyzing, and presenting data to steer business strategy, react rapidly to changing customer behavior, and design new business products—some also use management and presentation of data as their value to customers. Contemporaneously, scientific research has learned to handle growing volumes of data in biology, Earth sciences, astronomy, particle physics, and medical research. There, new results have been achieved by bringing together more data to understand rare events and data from more sources to understand complex phenomena. In all branches of engineering, new strategies are emerging for the use of data for the lifetime of products, to inform their design and maintenance. This combination of the growing availability of data and demonstrated value of data to benefit business, commerce, research, and diagnosis is a positive feedback loop. This we call the *data bonanza*.

Chapters 1 and 2 introduced the factors that power the data bonanza, with key examples and statistics. Chapters 14–22 illustrated the diversity of those potential benefits and some of the methods by which they are achieved in eight distinct application domains. For example, Chapter 16 showed how digital microscopy is leading to new biological insights, and Chapter 18 showed how the new resolving power of the latest sky surveys can lead to maps of the invisible dark matter that dominates the visible universe. Both of these depend on advances in data-intensive methods and show benefits that are stimulating yet more data collection and analysis.

23.1.2   The Digital Revolution and Data-Intensive Methods

This growing data bonanza is just one aspect of a turbulent, worldwide *digital revolution* described in Chapters 1 and 2. Because it is spreading at Internet speed, it is potentially the most significant that humankind has experienced. We are in its early stages and its eventual path is hard to predict. What is certain is that it will change human behavior, have a dramatic impact on society, government, and business, and impact virtually everything we humans do. In such a turbulent and unpredictable context, well-informed and agile responses to new opportunities and threats have premium value. At present, this is manifest in the search for answers to challenges such as husbanding scarce resources, feeding the world's population, and ameliorating climate change [1]. Good exploitation of data is key to understanding these challenges, to formulating effective strategies, and to implementing effective policies and plans. An increase in the use of data-driven methods in research has two positive effects:

- A direct effect of accelerating, or even enabling, discovery, and of improving confidence in the results

- Expanding the cohort of people adept at exploiting data, who may then engage their skills for other local, regional, and global causes.

Frequently, the required results are achieved by multidisciplinary teams collaborating for extended periods. Members of these teams spend considerable effort locating and understanding the data needed, transforming them into a form that makes a subset of the data useful for their goals, integrating that data with other data collected from their own observations or other sources, and then analyzing the composite data collection to discover informative patterns that provoke hypotheses, to detect interesting anomalies that hint at new phenomena, to calibrate models, or to test theories. Whether the context is business, research, government, or healthcare, this set of activities centered around data often involves many iterations as the phenomena and data are explored and understood. Where aspects of handling data is a major part of an overall task, we designate that task *data intensive*.

This book argues that as a result of the data bonanza, more and more aspects of governmental, organizational, and individual activity will contain substantial dataintensive tasks. There are already many opportunities to exploit data that are not properly pursued and the growth in data, both increasing volume and increasing diversity, will expand those opportunities. Leaders and strategists will recognize these opportunities and wish to pursue them. The public will see strategy, policy, planning, and action being well founded on data-driven evidence in some domains and expect similar evidence development in everything they consider important; for example, the care of the elderly, their own well being, their work, and ameliorating risk in their environment. Consequently, there will be accelerated demand for people to undertake data-intensive tasks. This will require more people with the relevant skills than will emerge naturally through the educational impact of data-driven research flowing into curricula.

A campaign is needed before this shortage becomes a crisis. It needs the following three elements:

- Partitioning of the conceptual and intellectual space to make the skills requirements more tractable
- Well-articulated *data-intensive methods* that are cost and time effective, and straightforward to apply
- An affordable and easily accessed set of data and computational services that are well adapted for data-intensive tasks.

23.1.3 Divide and Conquer

The data-intensive challenges throw up considerable complexity when considered as a whole from the application's viewpoint through to the underpinning computational, statistical, and technological issues. Within today's interdisciplinary teams, this is addressed by assembling diverse skills and experience and by allocating responsibilities within a team. To meet tomorrow's much larger number of dataintensive activities, the requirement for composite skills and division of labor needs a recognized framework. On the basis of the natural foci of interest and on practical limits to the scope of skills that can be acquired by a sufficient cohort, we recognize three broad categories.

The *domain experts* have their focus in their field of application. They understand and are well trained in that field's knowledge, skills, and practices. They know which issues are important. They can make judgments about sources and quality of domain-specific data. They can progressively formulate and sharpen the questions that lead toward meeting their overall challenge. They can judge the quality of evidence needed to produce actionable results. They understand how the results should be presented to influence the relevant audience. They can guide a campaign taking into account the legal and ethical issues of their field.

The *data analysis experts* have their focus on extracting information from data that is relevant to defined targets and meets evidential criteria. They may be experts in methods appropriate to a group of cognate domains or in a group of mathematical, statistical, or computational methods. They will be adept at specifying the stages of data access, data cleaning, data preparation, data analysis, and result aggregation. They may have skills in the effective visualization of result data. They often contribute algorithms and workflows.

The *data-intensive engineers* build, organize, operate, and optimize the data-handling and computational machinery that provides a platform that efficiently enables the data-intensive processes needed to meet the challenges. They will include people with system, architectural and business model skills, who shape sustainable and economic provision. They will include software engineers who build the interfaces, middleware, tools, and data-management systems in which the applications, algorithms, workbenches, portals, and workflows run. A new skill is emerging here, of using data-intensive methods to analyze workloads and operational data, in order to optimize the ways in which data and computation are provided. In other words, computing provision is also an application domain where data-intensive engineers use data-intensive methods to analyze workloads and operations, in order to manage them and improve configurations and subsequent design.

The primary purpose of this division is to make it feasible to become skilled and effective in each category. There are exceptional research leaders who span these aspects of data-intensive research, but they are *exceptional*. To meet future demand, a realistic expectation is to develop cohorts for each category, through education, training, and experience.

A secondary advantage is that the domain experts can choose where they find the other capabilities they need from a recognizable and competitive community that may be organized academically or as businesses. The other categories may gain the opportunity to supply to more domains and increase their effectiveness while amortizing more widely the cost of developing and providing their data-intensive capabilities.

This does not circumvent the high value of long-term alliances, and it certainly still requires excellent collaboration and communication. One aspect of the categorization is that it clarifies which topics each pair needs to converse about. In this book, we suggest a language and a graphical notation to facilitate those conversations.[1] We anticipate that this will trigger more thought about the nature of the concepts, the choice of notations, and the educational pathways to equip each category of expert. Of course, specialisms will remain within each category, and their internal communication and collaboration will still require attention.

23.1.4 Data-Intensive Methods and Patterns

There are recurrent patterns in data-intensive processes and in working procedures at many levels. These reappear within data intensive projects and across projects. For example, at the highest level, we see patterns such as the following:

- The selection of data sources, including those under the control of the project and those made available by external organizations. The arrangement of access to the data and then extraction and transport of relevant subsets. Preparation of the data through pipelined stages such as format translation, cleaning, normalization, filtering, sampling, and integration. Analysis of these composed data and production of result data plus quality control data, preparation for presentation and visualization, domain-expert judgment, leading to approval, retention, cataloguing, and archiving of the results.
- Repeated application of processes such as the above example, to handle new data, to explore variations in any aspect of the data-discovery processes, and iteration toward goals, such as sufficient evidence quality.
- Tracking of the provenance of derived data so that data-intensive processes may be reexamined, so that problems may be diagnosed, credit may be properly attributed, and evidence may be backed up with arguments about how it was obtained.

Similarly, at a more detailed level, we see patterns such as the following:

- The use of multiple arrangements, protocols, and data-movement methods to bring the data into the context of the study, with varying amounts of data warehousing and intermediate data reuse.
- The development of data identification methods, so that such reuse and the provenance tracking can be undertaken reliably.
- The use of compression to achieve economy in data transport and data storage and the use of encryption for privacy.
- The co-location of stages of data preparation pipelines to minimize data-handling costs between stages.
- The use of random partitions of data for training and calibrating models, and the remainder for testing them.

---

[1] Although we do not suggest that it is suitable for direct use by most domain experts, we would expect the majority to use graphical editors or prepackaged workflows.

- Repetition to explore parameter spaces, to assess analysis reliability, and to optimize estimates of parameters.
- The use of parallel farms of computation and data resources to accelerate processes, for example, to run multiple data preparation pipelines, to perform repetitions concurrently or to perform all-meets-all tasks.
- The use of steering, whereby an expert is presented with intermediary results, and chooses whether to continue a process, to adjust parameters and then continue, or to abandon it in order to start afresh.

As we approach the actual execution of tasks on communication, computation, and storage infrastructures, patterns such as the following become evident:

- Validation of requests to perform processes, often encoded as workflows, to verify consistency, that the submitter has the authority and credit to access the data and use the platform, and the availability of the data and resources.
- Transformation of the request, including partitioning into subprocesses that are delegated to other parts of a distributed platform.
- Assignment of tasks based on suitability of the components for the subprocesses, for example, delivering data-intensive processes to machinery where I/O bandwidth is in an appropriate ratio with CPU power.
- Mapping from logical components, both data and code, to physical instances that have the same properties and that are in some way optimally chosen.
- Graph transformations to accelerate tasks or reduce their costs, for example, by moving data-reduction stages nearer to data sources and by introducing parallel data paths.
- Monitoring to detect and recover from failures and to provide information for recovery and future optimizations.
- Aspect-programming style additions to workflows to introduce provenance tracking, monitoring, and recovery.

All of the above patterns, and many others, are introduced and often repeatedly encountered in the earlier chapters of this book. We have also seen them in a wide range of other contexts during the past decade, and they are widely reported and analyzed in the literature that we have cited. Nevertheless, they are often still faced *ab initio* by each data-intensive project and each organization that seeks to exploit its new data-enabled opportunities. Such wastefully repeated solutions are only affordable during the pioneering phase. As we move toward pervasive use of data-intensive methods, we need commonly reused solutions for two reasons. One, as they are reused, they become well tested and more reliable. Two, this will accelerate the paths to solving data-intensive challenges and save unnecessary costs. Systematic description of common data-intensive patterns—there are many more than those listed above—is a key first step to their recognition. This will lead to a better understanding of their use and advances in their implementation. We have used functional descriptions to initiate such developments.

23.1.5 A Computational Environment for Data-Intensive Tasks

The prevalent method of supporting data-intensive work at present is to assemble the software on existing services. For example, in an academic project, the work is performed on an existing high performance computing system or cluster provided by the academic institution or a national service, whereas, in a company, it may use its existing IT systems, their established database services, or an appropriate Cloud service. There are notable exceptions. For example, Google has designed its whole infrastructure of multiple data centers around making data-driven processes economically sustainable. Similarly, some researchers have developed specialized clusters, well tuned to data-intensive work (Section 4.7.1), while organizations, such as EBI, wwPDB, and IRIS have built data services around their large collections of curated data.[2]

The current status is similar to the curate's egg—good in parts. We introduced a three-level architecture to stimulate the development of a more cohesive, flexible, and sustainable environment for data-intensive problem solving. The three levels are revisited subsequently.

The *tool level* includes all of the places at which people work when solving data-intensive problems. These will provide appropriate virtual work environments for each group of domain experts. Such environments present all of the data, the data catalogs, metadata, methods, tools, workflows, and libraries needed by those experts in a consistent manner informed by their standards and working practices. The idea is that all of the assets needed to address their data-intensive problems are ready to hand and easy to use in combination with each other. As there are many disciplines and many ways of working, there will be a great diversity of requirements, virtual problem-solving environments, data sources, metadata practices, and tools to support work at this level. It will grow as each group of data users invests in developing an effective environment for their work and evolve as those groups gather data, invent methods, and revise their tools.

The *canonical level* will become a standardized, precisely defined means of communicating everything that is required between the other two levels. To facilitate adoption, it will be defined incrementally with a slow rate of change, so that investments in its use are worthwhile. This interposed standard is to protect investment above from the perpetual innovation in the technology providing data-intensive computing below, which is then more advantageous as existing solutions do not need to be reworked. The properties of this canonical form will be kept as minimal as possible while delivering the required power, but it will inevitably grow in complexity, as the communities above and below demand extra capability. Judicious management, as exercised by W3C for HTML and HTTP, will balance the need for stability against the pressure for new functionality.

The *enactment level* includes the digital communications, data handling, storage and computational resources, the middleware, software services, workflow management systems, component libraries, and resource management mechanisms

---

[2]www.ebi.ac.uk, www.wwpdb.org, and www.iris.edu, respectively.

that enable the tasks and processes to be accomplished. They are heterogeneous, distributed, diverse, and rapidly evolving, as they are driven by technological progress and business innovation. It is desirable that multiple providers at this level offer alternatives for availability and performance, to stimulate competition and to adapt to changing mixtures of work.

This approach should do for data what Tim Berners-Lee's initiative did for documents [2]. Before the introduction of a number of browsers (the tools level), a canonical form—HTTP and HTML (the canonical level)—and Web servers (the enactment level), there were systems for obtaining documents, but they were each isolated, different, and often complex to use. His initiative, particularly the protocol and format for communication between the two diverse levels, initiated the explosive growth of a world-wide phenomena. Without that canonical form of communication, it was not worthwhile investing in tools[3] because they did not reach enough document sources as they were specific to each document source. Similarly, it was not worthwhile investing in providing widespread access to digital documents as very few people, mainly professional librarians, would access them. Since their initial introduction in 1990, every level of the Web has become more complex, sophisticated, and powerful because of 20 years of W3C carefully managing the evolution of the canonical communication standards. This enabled them to keep step with growing user and provider requirements, but they did not change so rapidly as to undermine investment.

We now need to do the same for data, but data are more complex than documents, and hence the invention and introduction of a *lingua franca* for communicating about data is more challenging. It is clear that it would be beneficial and lead to the same kind of positive feedback in investment, convenience, and exploitation that Tim Berners-Lee achieved. Our initial stab is incomplete, and yet it may stimulate thought along similar or quite different lines to trigger a comparable impact. As there are far more data than documents and as there are far more dynamic effects at work, a much greater critical mass adoption will be needed. However, as data carry so much information about so many topics of critical importance to individuals and organizations, the breakthrough will have an even greater transformative impact.

In the following section, we review activity from the viewpoints of the three categories of data-intensive workers. We suggest places to look for those who wish to update the ideas in this book in terms of subsequent research or products. It is hard to give advice to domain experts as progress in their own field, enabled by innovative use of data, will be where the issues most important to them will be addressed. For the other two categories of workers, we are able to point to current research groups that are likely to continue to be relevant and product developments that we expect to be influential. Such attempts to foretell the importance of current R&D are prone to omissions and misjudgments, so we ask readers to treat this section with caution and to search diligently for other relevant work, such as the recent publication on data-intensive distributed computing [3].

---

[3]Such as the original graphical browser, Mosaic (www.ncsa.illinois.edu/Projects/mosaic.html), which added features such as icons, pictures, and bookmarks to make browsing easy for the nonexpert.

23.2 DATA-INTENSIVE APPLICATIONS

One of the first questions that skeptical readers may raise is whether the problems discussed in this book will be solved by technology in a few years and, therefore, whether the techniques presented are only temporary patches before definitive technological solutions emerge. In fact, the technological solutions are temporary patches, as the problem is shifting and technology tries to keep up. The identification of patterns and of abstract models for dealing with all aspects of data tackles the problem at a deeper level as they remain valid in the area above the shifting threshold of what is problematic to handle.

Skeptical readers are supported in their doubts by the history of computing. In 2001, 12 years ago, CPUs were single core, hard disks of 80 GB were considered large and expensive. Local networks of 100 Mb/s were at the higher end of the market, and 10 Mb/s was still common.[4] The USB 1.1 was spreading and allowed a transfer rate of 12 Mb/s between computers and external devices such as external drives containing data. Handling a dataset of 100 GB was a relatively large problem that required careful consideration. Fast forward 5 years, and external hard disks easily reach 250–300 GB, USB 2.0, with a theoretical bandwidth of 480 Mb/s, has become common and multicore CPUs are replacing single-core CPUs even on laptops. Handling 100 GB datasets becomes easily tractable.

Skeptical readers accept that currently dealing with 10 TB starts to be problematic, and more than 100 TB is challenging. However, they note that technologies are already appearing to deal with these volumes. Intel has introduced a hard disk controller for solid-state disks (SSD) able to deal with 6 Gb/s. Gigabit connection is becoming common. So they reason that within a few years what is problematic now will become easy.

Data-intensive applications are challenging in different dimensions: the heterogeneity of the applications, the volume of data, the complexity and heterogeneity of the data being processed, the statistical sensitivity required, and so on. They are and will remain demanding in skills for choosing, handling, interpreting, and presenting data. These critical skills are already in short supply and without well-targeted action, shortages of these skills deprive countries, companies, and societies of the potential benefits from data.

23.2.1 Heterogeneity of Applications

In astronomy, images from optical and radio telescopes are stored and processed to refine the model of the universe. In microscopy, robotic experiment execution means that thousands of experiments can be performed in a single array and millions of images are taken every day. In medicine, resolution of diagnostic imaging is continuously increasing and remote health care with digitally assisted living[5] is

---

[4]Reminder: "b" denotes "bit" and "B" denotes "byte"; it takes roughly 10 bits to transmit a byte because of network protocol overheads.
[5]www.side.ac.uk

starting to expand, bringing with it large amounts of data that may need urgent, reliable, and safe interpretation. In seismology, arrays of digital seismometers store data continuously.

Data-intensive applications are not limited to science: early large databases were developed for tracking transactions at very high rates, for example, at eBay and Amazon, and for customer relationship management applications. Commercial companies can exploit the data bonanza, and the possibilities provided by cheap and easily connected sensors, such as those registering the movement of radio-frequency identification (RFID)-tagged items. For example, the water companies in London follow in real time the usage of water in the network, and adapt flow, and intervene when there are problems before customers are even aware of them. Similarly, the idea behind the smart grid for electricity [4] is based on adaptive behavior and requires real-time data collection of local consumption and problems. In finance, high frequency trading works on a stream of data about shares from stock exchanges, evaluating the actions based on a sliding window of statistical infor- mation, and triggering decision algorithms. Similarly, credit card companies use fraud-detection systems to analyze card transactions to detect suspicious patterns that may imply malicious uses and of the cards [5, 6].

23.2.2   Volume of Data

The volume of data is increasing. In astronomy, the Sloan Digital Sky Survey (SDSS) [7] started in 1992 when it aimed at publishing, for public consumption, 35 TB of raw data from optical telescopes, together with a catalog of 5 TB. It took 16 years to finish and its data archive contains 5 PB of data. The space telescope EUCLID is planned for the year 2017, 25 years after this earlier attempt. Its planned lifetime is 6 years, during which it will send high resolution images with the goal of mapping the geometry of the dark Universe by analyzing how light is deviated by gravitational effects (Chapter 18). It will generate 1 TB of primary data a day for 6 years, for a total of 2.2 PB of data, nearly 100 times more *primary data* than in the SDSS project—we may expect a similar scale up of derived data and catalogs as occurred for SDSS. The LOFAR project[6] will cover the period 2012– 2017. Large and expensive radio telescope dishes are replaced by many lower cost dipoles that require no mechanical movement; the selected observing directions are steered electronically in milliseconds. It aims at scanning a large portion of the sky over low radio frequencies. The theoretical output is 1.6 TB/s, yielding 38 PB/day of raw data. However, filtering at the source is necessary as the connections from each site are 10 Gb/s. Even more impressive, although further in the future, is the square kilometer array (SKA) radio telescope,[7] planned to start taking data in 2020; it will produce more data per day than the entire current daily Internet traffic.

[6]www.lofar.org
[7]www.skatelescope.org

For 30 years, the EISCAT (European Incoherent Scatter) has studied the interaction between the Sun and the Earth as revealed by disturbances in the magnetosphere and the ionized parts of the atmosphere (these interactions also give rise to the spectacular aurora) by operating three radar systems in Northern Scandinavia. Its next phase, EISCAT3D,[8] will build and operate a high powered, very large synthesized aperture radar capable of detecting signals as low as 10^{-18} W. It will have multiple steerable beams synthesized with multiple antennae and will use tens of thousands of antennae per receiver in a manner similar to LOFAR. It will be able to scan the sky for phenomena and obtain 20 parameters per voxel in a 3D space with high resolving power at multiple frequencies in all three dimensions. It will record the dynamics of these phenomena, and hence needs a very high data collection rate. It will receive about 25 PB of raw observational data per day and will derive 200 TB of derived data products per year, holding an active 100 TB of recent data for alternative analyses. It is expected to operate for 30 years and data products will be stored for at least 10 years.

Digital seismometers appeared less than 20 years ago and revolutionized the way of doing seismology. The use of these digital seismometers reduced their cost, resulting in a transition from sparse networks orientated toward detection and analysis of strong events to continuous records from dense networks of hundreds or thousands of recorders. Over the same period, there has been a move from focusing on analyzing events to the use of continuous waveforms—see Chapter 17. There are projects that cover entire regions with arrays of seismometers. For example, the United States has a network of 2,630 sensors in a lattice that covers two-thirds of the country. The Earthscope project[9] that collects data from the USArray network and from other networks throughout the world currently receives 21 TB of data every year. In Europe, the EIDA project[10] aims at interconnecting the archives of seismographic data that collect streams from seismometers distributed over the territory. The VERCE project[11] is building a coherent virtual research environment for seismologists with the aim of making it convenient to analyze the large collections of seismic data and to compare observational data with data from simulations to refine the models of seismic phenomena and tectonic plate dynamics.

These examples show that there is no foreseeable let up in the growth of data collected. We believe that although details may vary, the growth in data collected will pervade all businesses, governments, and most walks of life, such as healthcare and emergency services.

23.2.3 Complexity and Heterogeneity

The challenges arising from data volumes are often outweighed by the complexity of data and algorithms, by the multiplicity of data sources that must be integrated,

[8] www.eiscat3d.se
[9] www.earthscope.org
[10] www.webdc.eu
[11] www.verce.eu

by physical limits, for example, maximum radiation doses for medical images, on the availability of data, and on the criticality or urgency of the applications. These are subsequently illustrated.

Remote and mobile healthcare and digitally assisted living will enable an increasing portion of older people to remain independent and to live at home for much longer. The medical domain is complex; for example, owing to physical, ethical, and economic constraints, not all of the necessary information is available when decisions need to be made. Automated systems need to balance the risk of errors against the need to filter irrelevant events from those significant events that require immediate intervention. They need to deliver adequate security and privacy, achieve continuous availability, and escalate processing to engage appropriate medical expertise sufficiently rapidly when a life-threatening emergency may be involved. This is a prime example of a context where appropriate portrayal of the information is essential.

Clinical trials, fundamental for evaluating therapies and tools, are expensive. One of the main bottlenecks is the recruitment of appropriate subjects; on one side there are thousands of active trials, and on the other there are possibly millions of patients whose conditions are starting to be stored in electronic form. The EHR4CR project[12] aims to design and demonstrate a scalable and cost-effective approach to interoperability between Electronic Health Record systems (EHRs) and Clinical Research, integrating data from different sources in different countries, with varying local and national stakeholders under various legal frameworks. There remains a considerable challenge in balancing the ethical considerations with the imperative to make best use of existing data in order to improve well-being as rapidly as possible. In these medical examples, the challenge of dealing with all the modalities of medical data, the human values, and the national, regional, and institutional variations are multiplied by the number and diversity of individual cases.

In environmental sciences, one common problem is connecting sensors to allow the transmission of data. Once the problem of connectivity is solved, it is possible to deploy sensors that are able to measure many different aspects of the environment. In the Fish4Knowledge project,[13] cameras are located in the Taiwanese reef in order to study the presence and the behavior of fish and correlate them with other environmental measures, such as water temperature and currents. The Okinawa Institute of Science and Technology coordinates an extensive system of reef observing projects.[14] In this case, algae grow rapidly on camera enclosures reducing image quality until a diver cleans them; consequently, permitted dive time limits a combination of image quality and quantity.

In the Integrated Carbon Observing System (ICOS),[15] there is a plan to collect data from marine observations, atmospheric observations, and ecosystem

[12]www.ehr4cr.eu
[13]www.fish4knowledge.eu/
[14]www.oist.jp
[15]www.icos-infrastructure.eu

monitoring for a period of 20 years. Euro-ARGO[16] is part of a global effort that started in 2,000 to deploy submersible robots to obtain a multidecade time series of observations of all of the oceans. Each of the 3,000 robots operates on an approximately 10-day cycle, submerging to various depths to collect observations, then surfacing to transmit them via satellite to ground stations. They handle about 100,000 uploads, each of a few tens of kilobytes, per year, but robots are replaced every 3 years and each new generation observes more variables. There are six catalogs based on different metadata standards[17] for accessing the collected data from a single global repository, the Global Ocean Observing System (GOOS). Wide use is made of NetCDF and SeaDataNet.[18] The European Multidisciplinary Seafloor Observatory (EMSO)[19] will have 12 long-term sea-floor observatories, collecting diverse forms of environmental, ecological, and geophysical data over decades. To cope with this open-ended diversity, it adopts a strong commitment to ISO19136.[20] They also engage with SeaDataNet. They need to support scientific, governmental, and industrial use of their facilities and data in conjunction with cognate projects, such as KM3Net, EPOS, ECOS, SIOS, Euro-ARGO, and OceanSITES.[21] Here, we see the intrinsic complexity of observing Earth's systems, there are so many interacting phenomena, multiplied by the political complexities of establishing multinational observing and integrating systems, exacerbated by sensitivities over the interpretation of results.

23.2.4 Data Integration

The LIFEWATCH project[22] focuses on the integration challenge to record and understand biodiversity. To this end, it plans to provide integrated access to data from 30 different data sources, each of which is itself an aggregator of data from many sources [8].[23].

What is clearly emerging is the challenge of complexity and diversity—coping with the changing and diverse data collected. This is compounded by the challenge

---

[16] www.euro-argo.eu

[17] European Directory of Marine Organisations (EDMO), European Directory of Marine Environmental Data (EDMED), European Directory of Marine Environmental Research Projects (EDMERP), Cruise Summary Reports (CSR), and European Directory of the Initial Ocean-Observing Systems (EDIOS).

[18] gosic.org/ios/GOOS-Main-page.htm, www.unidata.ucar.edu/software/netcdf, and www.seadatanet.org

[19] www.emso-eu.org

[20] www.iso.org/iso/iso_catalogue/catalogue_tc/catalogue_detail.htm?csnumber=32554

[21] Neutrino telescope www.km3net.org, European Plate Observing System www.epos-eu.org, European Ecological Citizens' Organisation for Standardisation www.ecostandard.org, Svalbard Integrated Arctic Earth Observing System www.sios-svalbard.org, and www.oceansites.org, respectively.

[22] www.lifewatch.eu

[23] For example, from the European Biodiversity Observation Network (EBONE), www.ebone.wur.nl/uk; from the Group on Earth Observations: Biodiversity Observation Network (GEOBON), www.earthobservations.org/geobon.shtml; the European Distributed Institute of Taxonomy (EDIT) under the aegis of CETAF, cetaf.biodiv.naturkundemuseum-berlin.de/activities.php; EVOLTREE, www.evoltree.eu; and Species 2000, www.sp2000.org and www.4d4life.eu. These are just the first five; the full list can be found on pages 12–18 of [8]

of coordinating sufficiently to enable data from multiple observation campaigns to be used together. We introduced GEOSS, OGC, and INSPIRE in Chapter 2 as contexts in which development, selection, and adoption of standards are fostered to enable data integration in the sciences concerned with the Earth and its biota. The endeavor to enable ever wider interdisciplinary research has to leave freedom for rapid local innovation in pursuit of new observing methods and advances of understanding. The key strategy is to agree on interchange formats, to establish registries of the data that can be federated, and to ensure linkable semantics by agreeing on common terms and their controlled use. Examples of interchange formats and common geospatial frameworks have already been given. Another aspect of today's campaign is the development of agreed ontologies that denote key concepts scientists wish to match across their independent activities—these are potentially more useful when the registries map their metadata to RDF and participate in the Linked Open Data campaign.[24] [9] For example, the LIFEWATCH project has identified 11 specific controlled vocabularies needed for its integration task [10].

Such specific vocabularies are used in conjunction with more widely adopted ontologies, such as the SWEET ontology developed by NASA for physical units, FOAF for human networking, and the various Dublin Core for attribution metadata.[25] The development of sufficient agreements for data to be integrated across project, discipline, and national boundaries is itself a major undertaking and requires an organizational context as well as social and economic commitment. However, it has the benefit of forcing a discussion that leads to better understanding of adopted concepts as well as providing terms on which information can be reliably matched. Both aspects may benefit a discipline, although in the short term they may divert the attention of leading researchers if they are to gain sufficient quality. It is then necessary to have distributed query systems behind the tools used to access the integrated view. These query systems have to cope with multiple representations of metadata and access protocols and convert queries so that they exploit the standardized terms correctly, for example, consult appropriate authorities to match synonyms.

The use of controlled vocabularies and standardized metadata is composed with the standards for the representation of data. For example, where geospatial data are in use, the ISO19000 standards come into play together with ongoing efforts in GEOSS, at OGC, and in implementing the INSPIRE directive. Data that are denoted by large-scale and multiscale matrices will use standards, such as NetCDF and HDF5, while images will use the standards for their community, such as DICOM in medicine. The diversity of standards, the complexity of individual standards, and the cost of converting existing investments to comply, combine to ensure that while we may develop islands of consistency, and reference points where data can be cross-linked between those islands, heterogeneity will prevail. Skill and ingenuity will always be needed to cross boundaries and to link data that come

[24]www.w3.org/2012/ldp
[25]sweet.jpl.nasa.gov/ontology, www.foaf-project.org, and dublincore.org, respectively.

from independent domains. But as the data volumes grow and the occasions on which such boundary crossing is needed increase, this skill cannot be found and deployed to deliver a one-off solution each time. Mechanisms that reuse the skill and insights automatically should be developed—these may integrate expert opinion gleaned from networks of domain experts as they work and redeploy that knowledge semi-automatically [10]. Those mechanisms must themselves be discoverable and subject to scrutiny and revision [11].

In the medium term, we can envisage well-developed virtual research environments that hide the details of data sources and compute resources, but which present in one consistent framework the methods, tools, metadata, data, libraries, and e-Infrastructure services *for a given discipline*. These will have capabilities for preserving and managing the intermediate data and unpublished results, as well as associated research objects, for each user. This composition will probably be prepared for each subdiscipline drawing on a larger universe of discourse for the full discipline that will invariably overlap with aspects of cognate fields. Although it will be presented in a form that is tuned to the culture and education of the target subdiscipline, it will still be a rich and general purpose work environment. Consequently, individuals will shape a view that contains material relevant to their current project using personalization facilities. These will include not only dynamic filtering of concepts and components on display but also standard compositions of the initial components that match their current work requirements. These will sometimes be shared among coworkers, to accelerate induction and align effort. There is, therefore, a constant interplay between these specialization tendencies that increase diversity and the larger-scale efforts to cross discipline, project, and cultural boundaries. This will be partially resolved in the longer term, as education introduces to each discipline (often global) conceptual and practical standards, so that the comfortable working environment and the global standards for integration are better aligned. But the tension between local pressures to specialize and global pressures to standardize will never entirely vanish. When people collect data, they are focused on the challenges of acquiring and organizing their data and on the purposes driving the initial collection. They often do not have the time and opportunity to think about future linking. The potential for other uses and the significance of the work done is usually recognized much later.

There are good reasons for groups of subjects making as much of their e-Infrastructure and virtual research environment common when they can. It amortizes the cost of building and maintaining the facilities and accelerates the rate at which they are polished and become reliable. It also makes it feasible to work across disciplines, more easily bringing other data, methods, and tools into a working environment. It takes brave researchers, even after preparation for such boundary-crossing work, to venture into the added complexity; as we saw above, the complexity within a field of study can easily be daunting. But many of today's challenges require these conceptual expeditions.

Similarly, most workers can work effectively with details of the underpinning computational provision hidden, such as distribution, heterogeneity, and ownership of data, storage, computers, and networks. But a few, often the individuals who pioneer new approaches, need to be able to explore and exploit relevant detail. As the engineering improves and the resource provision becomes more widely shared, the occasions on which such details need to be exposed are reduced.

It will always remain the case that individuals or businesses will make dramatic advances by spotting a new way of relating data between different domains because they have a new insight about the relationships in the real world that those data represent. Similarly, innovative engineers and researchers will spot new ways of supporting existing data-intensive processes or new methods for discovering knowledge from data.

REFERENCES

1. J. Sulston (chair), P. Bateson, N. Biggar, C. Fang, S. Cavenaghi, J. Cleland, J. Cohen, P. Dasgupta, P. M. Eloundou-Enyegue, A. Fitter, D. Habte, S. Harper, T. Jackson, G. Mace, S. Owens, J. Porritt, M. Potts, J. Pretty, F. Ram, R. Short, S. Spencer, Z. Xiaoying, and E. Zulu, "People and the planet," The Royal Society Science Policy Centre report 01/12 DES2470. The Royal Society, 2012.

2. T. Berners-Lee and M. Fischetti, *Weaving the Web—The Original Design and Ultimate Destiny of the World Wide Web by its inventor*. HarperBusiness, 2000.

3. T. Kosar, *Data Intensive Distributed Computing: Challenges and Solutions for Large-scale Information Management*. IGI Global, 2012.

4. G. Reitenbach, "Smart Grid 2011: more than meters," *Power Magazine*, 5 pages, http://www.powermag.com/smart_grid/Smart-Grid-2011-More-than-Meters_3265.html, accessed January 2013, 2011.

5. P. K. Chan, W. Fan, A. L. Prodromidis, and S. J. Stolfo, "Distributed data mining in credit card fraud detection," *IEEE Intelligent Systems*, vol. 14, pp. 67–74, 1999.

6. R. J. Bolton and D. J. Hand, "Statistical fraud detection: a review (with discussion)," *Statistical Science*, vol. 17, no. 3, pp. 235–255, 2002.

7. K. N. A. Abazajian, J. K. Adelman-McCarthy, M. A. Agueros, et al., "The seventh data release of the sloan digital sky survey," *Astrophysical Journal Supplement*, vol. 182, pp. 543–558, 2009.

8. H. Hummel and P. van Avesaath, "LIFEWATCH report on data and research network strategy II," tech. rep., LIFEWATCH, 2012.

9. T. Berners-Lee, "Testimony of Sir Timothy Berners-Lee, CSAIL Decentralized Information Group, Massachusetts Institute of Technology, Before the United States House of Representatives Committee on Energy and Commerce Subcommittee on Telecommunications and the Internet Hearing on the 'Digital Future of the United States: Part I—The Future of the World Wide Web'," tech. rep., MIT, 2007.

10. A. Garcìa-Silva, O. Corcho, H. Alani, and G.-P., Asuncóin, "Review of the state of the art: discovering and associating semantics to tags in folksonomies," *The Knowledge Engineering Review*, vol. 27, pp. 57–85, 2012.

11. C. Bizer, T. Heath, and T. Berners-Lee, "Linked data—the story so far," *International Journal on Semantic Web and Information Systems (IJSWIS)*, vol. 5, no. 3, pp. 1–22, 2009.

24

Data-Rich Futures

Malcolm Atkinson

School of Informatics, University of Edinburgh, Edinburgh, UK

In this chapter, we first focus on the technological and business trends that are shaping data-intensive infrastructures; this includes a selection of ongoing research. We then consider some of the economic and social forces at play, shaping the future of data use. We conclude with a call to arms, asking practitioners and educators to take up the challenge of establishing and ensuring standards in order that data may be used reliably and that decisions based on data may be well founded.

We see emerging a data infrastructure. Trying to predict its future is probably as challenging as it would have been for the builders of Victorian canals to predict the railways, highways, hydrofoils, aircraft, and wind-harnessing eco-transport of today's still evolving transport infrastructure. We are probably at a similarly early stage and equally unable to be clairvoyant, but we will try, informed by the growth of other infrastructures, to predict some key aspects of the data infrastructure in decades to come. Of course, it is even harder to predict the new activities, human responses, and economic consequences as infrastructure supporting a data-rich society emerges.

An infrastructure grows and evolves depending on a society's perceived needs and on that society's ability to pay for it. But the advent of the infrastructure generates ideas and capabilities, transforming those expectations and the ability of the economy to pay. Contemporaneous changes in the neighboring infrastructures yield

The DATA Bonanza: Improving Knowledge Discovery in Science, Engineering, and Business, First Edition.
Edited by Malcolm Atkinson, Rob Baxter, Michelle Galea, Mark Parsons, Peter Brezany, Oscar Corcho,
Jano van Hemert, and David Snelling.

ideas and competition: this further influences the direction of local infrastructures. As we have seen earlier, data flows around the world at Internet speeds, so there is also a direct coupling of the decisions that influence the data infrastructure's development. Regulation and standardization tends to follow the more major infrastructure changes but may then constrain local and detailed developments. We will identify some of the forces at work here.

In conjunction with the developing data, infrastructure is an evolution of social, economic, and governmental behavior. Early examples have been observed in this book and in the cited literature. Current use of data is limited either to innovators or to the packaged data-driven services—predominantly Internet businesses. Innovators are a very small proportion of the numbers who will use a successful idea once it is established. The initial businesses tend to focus on immediate gain. We know from other examples of a capability becoming available that, if it is useful and attractive, it will soon be much more widespread and diverse, but can we say more than that? Economic viability and business success can often depend on capturing the "long tail," that is, expanding the user base, quickly [1].

The anticipated dependence on a data infrastructure, the growth in the use of data to underpin decisions from the personal to the global and from life-critical to trivial, and the potential for malevolent interference mean that there will be an obligation to operate responsibly and ethically. This will be as important as it is for any other aspect of business, innovation, and government that can jeopardize life and humanity. But it will be as difficult here as it is elsewhere to work out the safe methods, the balances between different benefits and threats, and the assignment of control to appropriate scales, organizations, and individuals. In the rapidly changing world of the digital revolution it will be challenging to keep up. We must prepare our culture through education and communication for that challenge. We must develop professional behavior that helps in the implementation of safe data infrastructures and ethically, economically, and socially beneficial data use.

24.1   FUTURE DATA INFRASTRUCTURE

An infrastructure grows dynamically and is shaped by many forces as it grows. For example, transport networks were never designed as a total entity and then built; there was a period of building canals, a period of building railways, and a period of building roads. As these happened, early investments were sometimes integrated and sometimes abandoned. Railways were typically linked with major ports, but airports were constructed where there was space, and later connected by better roads and new rail links. The driving initiatives were sometimes commercial and sometimes governmental. Consistency emerged from a mix of personal leadership, organizational dominance, and international negotiation; technical prowess alone was no guarantor of success. Consistency is never complete. When a mode of transport was overtaken, its decline in use led to its closure or repurposing. We may expect similar multidirectional forces to buffet and shape the path of data infrastructure.

There are already major data infrastructures including the following:

- The global networks of data centers underpinning Internet businesses including their delivery of customer-attracting data and advertisements. These include major investments in online entertainment, including games, broadcasting, and social networking.
- The major collections of R&D data in engineering, mining, fossil fuel, and pharmaceutical companies.
- The operational data for companies at all scales, linked with their R&D data in many cases.
- The administrative data used by governmental processes from city to national and international scales in most countries.
- The rapidly handled data streams to support early warning systems, such as those that generate alerts for epidemics, hurricanes, tornados, floods, earthquakes, tsunami, and failures in food and water supply.
- The reference data collections and current observational or experimental data in many research disciplines. These often hold historical data that may be gathered via continuous monitoring systems, such as those for the above-mentioned alerts, and provide reference data and research opportunities for improving the timing and precision of alerts. This synergy between observation for practical purposes with collection of data for research increases the value of collecting, curating, and exploiting data.
- The delivery of online entertainment over the Internet with 49.2% of US peak-time Internet traffic, primarily contributed via Netflix and BitTorrent with 22.2% and 21.6% of the 24-h data-traffic average in the United States [2].
- The mechanisms for collecting operational data and acting on it underpinning most delivery of services by utilities, such as electrical power, water and sewerage, transport, and logistics and communications. These often have to span companies and administrative borders.
- The current agreements, sometimes underpinned by standards, for sharing or interchanging data at many scales in many domains of business, government, and research. These vary between those that are established and unchallenged to those that are fighting for dominance in a sea of competitors. Even the most established will vary in their level of implementation.
- Current support for campaigns in Earth sciences, research infrastructure, media, communications, and engineering, where there is sharing of data, information, and knowledge, often on a global scale, with a framework for agreeing on how the data standards and data infrastructure should evolve. These last as long as there is a sufficient consensus that the campaign has priority and, therefore, investment continues.

The above incomplete list illustrates that today's data infrastructure is already diverse as a result of its independent growth from many starting points and with many different models of finance and governance. It is instructive to note that data infrastructure grows at different scales. The data infrastructure for sharing information within a car or an aircraft is emerging in each of those contexts, at present shaped by the leading manufacturers. But as they have many digital equipment suppliers contributing to their final products, they need a model and standards to make the evolving set of data-generating and data-consuming components a feasible engineering proposition. At an intermediate scale, the data for the construction and operation of a building is pooled among the architects, engineers, construction companies, and regulators during construction, and some aspects are handed on to the building's operators, subsequent maintenance, and emergency services— at least that is the emerging model, although only elements of it are in place for a minority of buildings at present [3, 4]. At a global scale, we have already reported the arrangements for sharing biological data via the wwPDB consortium for interchanging model data for the Intergovernmental Panel on Climate Change's modeling campaigns, and the effort of GEOSS to provide a framework for integrating all Earth observation. The INSPIRE directive provides an example at the continental scale.

The role of infrastructure also varies in its time scale. For example, the precrash system on a Toyota Prius is taking data from multiple cameras and millimeter wavelength radar to sense external risks and driver condition [5]. The shared information from these sources is needed only for seconds. In contrast, the observations of natural phenomena, such as the Earth's environment or the cosmos, are valuable almost indefinitely, as extended time series allow the study of longer-term phenomena and more accurate characterization of trends. The building information systems and deployed engine monitoring that we have seen earlier have intermediate timescales associated with the lifetime of the man-made item they observe. The current engine-control systems deployed in many cars retain significant events to the next service or breakdown.

24.1.1   Data Technology Innovation

A key factor in infrastructure is the underpinning technology. We list here a few of the current technologies that are significant and are likely to improve in ways that change the feasibility and economics of data infrastructure.

- Balanced scalable hardware that is based on data bricks with appropriate Amdahl ratios in order to increase the amount of data-intensive work that can be accomplished with a given amount of energy [6–11].
- Distributed server farms, with distributed replicating file systems, such as those underpinning the Internet companies and Cloud computing providers [12, 13]. Key factors from the economic viewpoint are the reduction of operational costs, such as electricity, equipment and system management, and procurement in bulk. Technical factors include adequate security, maximizing memory residence for hot data, and large numbers of independent data paths,

carefully balanced with storage and computation provision for the experienced workloads [14–18].

- Message queuing and reliable delivery services, such as implementations of AMQP,[1] including RabbitMQ, StormMQ, and Apache Qpid.[2] Advanced scheduling and coordination systems using message passing such as Dryad [19] and Swift [20]. They manage large workloads, monitor operations, and accommodate planned changes. They complete large runs irrespective of partial failures and maintain continuous availability.

- Models for organizing data-intensive computation that combine many parallel paths on large numbers of independent nodes, such as the mapreduce pattern and its refinements [21–23], distributed join and all-meets-all algorithms, and distributed query algorithms [24, 25]. The open source Storm technology[3] used by Twitter, is capable of continuously processing streams of data, redistributing load and handling failures, with support for virtually any graph of interconnections and interfaces to existing queuing and database systems.

- Distributed structured memory systems, such as BigTable [26], hbase,[4] htable [22, 27], Sector & Sphere [16], and Cassandra,[5] that propagate a shared view of updates. Advances in distributed cache-coherence protocols to increase scalability trade tolerated discrepancies against speed and cost [28].

- Advanced database systems, such as SciDB,[6] [29, 30] MonetDB[7] [31, 32], and RASDAMAN [33] and commercial systems, such as Microsoft SQL-Server, Vertica, and Oracle. These progressively integrate analytic algorithms, increase their scale and speed, and simultaneously extend the types of data, such as multidimensional arrays, images, and time series, whose properties they accommodate and exploit [9, 34–36]. In some cases, these access data in files, while still in their original format, such as HDF5, NetCDF, and SEED[8] [37]. Incremental translation into database formats when data are touched by map reduce algorithms can also bring about savings [38]. Most scientific DBMSs also support nontransactional, mostly append, updates, as these are faster and the updates can be organized and if necessary reapplied using the primary data in many data-intensive contexts. Concomitant developments add the ability to use sophisticated algorithms, exploiting special hardware, highly developed algorithmic libraries and parallelism, within queries [39–41]. Faster algorithms for graph queries will open up new ways of studying relationships in data [42–44]. Advances in XML-query methods will allow better use of metadata and of the research data encoded in XML [45].

---

[1] www.amqp.org
[2] www.rabbitmq.com, stormmq.com, and qpid.apache.org respectively.
[3] storm-project.net
[4] hbase.apache.org
[5] cassandra.apache.org
[6] www.scidb.org
[7] www.monetdb.org
[8] Used for seismometer traces.

- Support for handling very large bodies of data [46] with combined use of multiple forms of data, for example, HDF5 plus relational, relational plus formatted binary file, relational, XML, and RDF. The convenience with which combined data can be accessed, analyzed, and managed will be critical [47].

- Indexing systems that accelerate the access patterns of required analyses and are well suited to both large data and specific data organizations and patterns, for example, the access to time series of states from very large multidimensional simulations [48].

- Archival systems for combinations of data and metadata with mechanisms for trading rate of data loss against costs and for ensuring compliance with governance rules [46]. The Data Curation Centre (DCC)[9] develops digital-data curation policy and good-practice guides, and maintains an up-to-date view of ongoing R&D in this field. Technology for archiving has been developed by many groups, iRODS [49] is a recent example. Current operational examples of digital library systems that contain data and metadata include DataCite, ePrints, dLibra, and D-Space.[10] Examples of projects that are developing archiving and its application have been mentioned from Chapter 2 onward; the following are further examples: DataONE, the Data Conservancy, the EU Alliance for Permanent Access to the Records of Science (APA), Planets, CASPAR, DRIVER and Driver II, Digital Preservation Europe (DPE), and D4Science.[11]

- Workflow languages well adapted to composing data and computational tasks, which are platform independent and well supported with comprehensive libraries and optimizing enactment systems. Easily understood, higher-level specialized languages will enable specific patterns of use and specific domains of application to be described succinctly. These have been discussed in many chapters, and an overview of current R&D was presented in Section 3.8.

The above list illustrates the diversity and complexity of the many technological lines of development that will lead to improved infrastructure for data-intensive computation. There are two important caveats. First, scale issues are not always the dominant priority. Urgent response, continuity of connection with sensors, agile accommodation of change in complex heterogeneous data, and facilitation of existing work practices are just a few examples of sometimes overriding priorities. In the on-board vehicle data systems introduced above, reliability and fidelity will outweigh other factors. Second, incremental and interacting developments within the most comprehensive list may be overtaken by a, as yet unanticipated, new technology.

[9] www.dcc.ac.uk
[10] datacite.org, eprints.org, dlibra.psnc.pl, and dspace.org, respectively.
[11] dataone.org, dataconservancy.org, www.alliancepermanentaccess.eu, www.planets-project.eu, www.casparpreserves.eu, www.driver-repository.eu, www.driver-support.eu, www.digitalpreservationeurope.eu, and www.d4science.eu, respectively.

24.1.2 Data Methods Innovation

The developing infrastructure will be used by a steadily improving repertoire of methods for discovery of knowledge from data. These new methods will depend on contributions from several lines of research.

- Improved statistical methods that underpin the inferences and characterizations used in data-intensive analyses. This will include advances in the way that these statistical processes are formulated [50].
- Automation of data cleaning and quality control [51–53].
- New analytic techniques; for example, analyzing streaming data, yielding approximations, or larger-scale analyses [54, 55]. A good compendium on the foundations that underpin data mining is provided by Bishop [56].
- Innovative methods for displaying, and allowing interaction with, results to improve understanding and enhance precision when people act on the information [57]. The Web site datavisualization.ch provides up-to-date news and examples of design and visualization methods.
- New algorithms implementing methods, techniques, and visualizations; these may use fewer resources or deliver results faster [58–60].
- Advanced forms of description, of data, concepts, and methods, that allow automation to handle detail and that facilitate agile use of compositions of data and algorithms with at least partial validation of appropriate composition and application [61].
- Notations that are easier to use, more expressive, and more powerful, for specifying the knowledge discovery process at each stage from formulating the problem, through data acquisition and preparation to analysis and presentation.

There is an interplay between developments at this level and the advances in data-intensive infrastructure discussed above. It is beneficial to enhance this relationship. The domain specialists who want results and who thereby justify the resources will predominantly interact with the evolving capabilities at the method level. These capabilities are built by the efforts of data analysis experts. The providers of data-intensive infrastructure depend on the quality of the families of methods developed by data analysis experts to attract the users with real problems, who may then make the infrastructure financially viable. Therefore, it behooves these providers to establish good development environments in which groups of data analysis experts can build data analytic libraries. These would need to include the statistical and linear-programming libraries that these workers traditionally use. But it must also include good diagnostic and performance analysis tools and facilitate transport of implementations between versions of the infrastructure. The infrastructure provider may develop, or fund the development of, initial libraries to initiate the process, but it is also necessary to provide an open-ended framework that encourages the addition of new methods, techniques, algorithms, and visualizations. Interworking with existing technology and with contemporary algorithmic advances on which data analysis builds must be well supported.

24.1.3   Virtual Environments Innovation

It is also important to provide a virtual research environment, or more generally a *virtual work environment*, that brings together and consistently presents all of the data, methods, descriptions, and tools that each community of data-intensive users requires. There is a combination of research issues to be addressed here, each of which at present probably receives too little attention.

- Study using ethnographic and computationally supported observation of the working practices to better understand the requirements and the groupings within each field of deployment. This is, of necessity, to be a long-term process, as the response to new methods and tools, beyond the atypical enthusiastic pioneer groups, has to be well understood.
- Collation of the ethical and legal issues pertinent in each field across institutional, regional, and national boundaries. Again, longitudinal investigations are needed as the advent of new data-intensive opportunities will invoke change in attitudes and laws. Indeed, the improved understanding developed through these studies may be helpful in shaping the legal changes and in reformulating ethical guidelines.
- Development of frameworks and tools to accelerate construction and adaptation of the virtual working environments, including identification and provision of common underpinning elements, such as personalization and short-term storage of work in progress with configurable controlled access.
- Development of common visual forms and metaphors to help worker mobility and to reduce interpretation errors. These may also facilitate the adventurous worker who undertakes integration of concepts, methods, and data across the conventional boundaries of disciplines, organizations, and working practices. As mentioned above, these are important pioneers and innovators, who should be supported. However, the "long tail" of traditional workers does much of the critical spade work for that innovation and for applications of the new methods. They use data-intensive facilities in large numbers, often on a daily basis. Hence, attracting and supporting the "long tail" is key to making data-intensive services and tools financially viable. They have to be provided with an appropriate virtual work environment that makes them feel comfortable as they do their work.

The success of data-intensive R&D, measured by influence, take up, or income, will almost certainly depend more on the investment in the design and appeal of these virtual work environments than on anything else.[12] Without the appeal

---

[12]Long-term collaboration of domain and data analysis experts with data-intensive engineers, *walking a path together* is necessary for pioneering new methods and demonstrating their power. But those pioneers are motivated by novelty and creativity; they tolerate a working context that would not suit normal workers. Observation and support of pioneering behavior yields few benefits when designing for typical workers.

of good design, the take up will languish. Who will be the "Apple Inc." of data workplaces?

24.2   FUTURE DATA ECONOMY

As reported in Chapter 2, the annual production of data already greatly exceeds the total global storage capacity. This might suggest that data production will no longer grow. This is far from the truth; the mechanization and automation of work, the advances in the sensitivity of digital sensors, their increasing speed, and growing ubiquity will continue to accelerate the generation of data. Commercial pressures will drive some of this growth; for example, the latest microscopes for Perkin Elmer will allow biologists and biochemists scanning for medically effective compounds to collect thousands of images where they once collected one, and to do this hundreds of times per day, per microscope.[13] The desired acceleration of drug discovery and research into processes in living organisms can only be realized if the resulting higher rates of data are successfully exploited as fast as they are obtained. The same argument applies to capturing more data from any environmental, business, engineering, healthcare, or research context—unless the expected benefit can be derived by processing data at comparable speed, the investment in data collection capacity will be futile. At present, some leaders invest in improved data collection in the hope that the data processing can be economically expanded to yield the benefit. As we have seen, this is both technically and intellectually challenging to achieve. Unless data-intensive R&D keeps pace and the results are accessible to the chief technologists advising those leaders, the (in)ability to conduct the data analyses at comparable speeds will limit innovation. Those making the investment in data collection will need to understand that they must balance investment in all steps from data acquisition to knowledge presentation if they are to get the best return on their investment. Some may claim that the extra data are not needed, as smart sampling will suffice. For rare events, subtle effects, and unanticipated discoveries, sampling is not sufficient, although it should be used when it is known to yield adequate answers. With or without sampling, the benefits depend on people with the relevant insights and skills. Their training and their time must be part of the investment.

Investors in data infrastructure frequently focus on the costs of instruments for observation, laboratory equipment and time for experiments, and computational time for simulations. However, as Jim Gray pointed out in 2007, the software costs invariably dominate before the benefit is obtained from the data [62]. These are often seriously underestimated. Software is the primary fabric for constructing highways from data to knowledge. Investment in software often lasts much longer than it does in hardware, and a good software infrastructure can accumulate value

---

[13]Quantitatively, their microscopes were initially using 96 well plates, then 384 well plates, and now 3,840 well plates. The resolution for each well plate has gone from 512×512 to $4,096\times4,096$ per image, and the number of channels from 1 to 4. An overall increase by a factor of $>10,000$.

as it is polished and adapted. Nevertheless, understanding the true cost of software is difficult. Its initial construction is often dwarfed by lifetime maintenance costs, and it is hard to predict which of the hundreds of tools and libraries that emerge to handle new data are the ones that warrant long-term support. It is usually necessary to allow a quasi-organic selection process to filter out the weaker elements, but this does not lead to integrated and consistent elements that make building and running specific data-to-knowledge highways easier. We know we have to make this construction easier. It remains a research challenge for computer scientists to find the best ways of doing this. This will then leave researchers just writing the idiosyncratic code that stitches facilities together—setting the route for the data-to-knowledge journey—that reflects their research goals.

At present, much effort is spent on data wrangling. The data users find data and manually organize its movement, often by "sneaker net,"[14] to machines where they can manipulate them. Automating that movement will save users learning how to organize and manage data movement, and it will also yield a track of where copies of data are held. This gives two benefits: the use of data can be better identified, allowing the benefit of collecting and handling data to be recognized, and it makes possible the reduction of data movement, as locally available copies can be reused. When data are large, their transport has a high cost, in which case it is often better to bring data-reducing steps close to the data and ship their derivatives. This requires innovation in automating the partitioning of the work and shipping the appropriate fragments to their data's context. It also requires security, safety, and accounting that takes account of the real costs and allows the data provider to afford the support of the shipped-in code. In today's infrastructure, this only happens within organizations or a few disciplines; it is a challenge to engineer it across administrative boundaries for every data provider and user.

Data often come in different formats from each source, sometimes these formats are hard to discover or interpret. So data users spend a great deal of time understanding the formats and then finding or writing code to translate the data to the form they need for the next stage of their data-to-knowledge journey. Many data users that we talked to, whether using data from observations, experiments, or simulations, in industry and academia, said that this was taking more than half, and in some cases, >80% of their time [63]. Not a good use of creative minds. We can do better; the OMERO project,[15] for example, works with microscope manufacturers so that OMERO's image management software is prepared to take the format from each new microscope. OMERO then incorporates translation software, Bio-Formats,[16] which translates between all known biological image formats, so that OMERO users can easily invoke translation steps. Standard annotation, which described the data formats, would complete the process by eliminating the need for biologists to learn and remember when such translations are necessary.

---

[14]Where humans take disks to the data source, load them with data, and carry them to the data's destination, where the data are copied again. A labor-intensive and vulnerable procedure that poses many problems.
[15]www.openmicroscopy.org
[16]loci.wisc.edu/software/bio-formats

Surely, we can do even better in each discipline. The cost of understanding which formats are produced and which formats are required, and of manually inserting the necessary translation steps, could be largely eliminated. It is reasonable to expect each piece of equipment or software that produces data to also provide accurate information about the format and interpretation of that data. Similarly, every software element can be explicit about what format it requires. This also applies to each piece of translation software. Then it should be possible to discover automatically when translation is necessary and to insert the necessary translators automatically, seeking user advice only when information may be lost or the choice of translator is not clear. Initially, the many-to-many space of possible translations may look intractable, but as experts steer paths between incoming formats, a knowledge base of preferred choices and trusted translators will be built. If that knowledge is pooled, the popular data-translation routes will soon be well charted and costly hand-crafted solutions will become rare. The Taverna and myExperiment projects have explored this idea for many biological services and data-processing steps [64].

Social factors are likely to alter the economic balance, at least where health and wellbeing are concerned. The population will see individual successes, such as the accurate assessment of natural or man-made hazards, the support of individuals in assisted independent living, or the data-driven improvements in diagnosis and treatment in healthcare. They will then expect these successes to be repeated reliably in normal practice. This translation from pioneering to widespread production requires much engineering and business investment, although it can amortize costs over larger communities. It rarely proceeds as fast as people would wish it to.

People now expect convenient interaction between their personal devices. Sharing contacts, calendars, reminders, music, and images between smartphones and laptops is a standard convenience. Our cars and personal phones exchange information; soon we will expect to set the car's GPS target to where we took a particular picture, or ask it to remember an observation, as we spot something of interest, and add it to our relevant database when we get home, complete with time and location. But the next step will be to expect the building and car systems to interact. We will ask our GPS to take us to an address, and then click the option "Park." The car will dialogue with the building or nearby buildings and streets to find a parking slot as we approach. If it is in a building, the map to the now tentatively allocated parking bay will be loaded to the car and updated if someone else grabs the bay. The building's cameras will check whether the car is expected and the car's collision avoidance system will be supplied with enough data to navigate safely to the bay. If there is a parking charge, the on-board computer will use any credit authority we have authorized it to use. Our smartphone will be loaded with the walk to our destination, a reminder as to when the parking expires and a recommended route back. This interplay between systems initially motivated by other purposes illustrates the continuing challenge of making data available across boundaries. The typical user would like that to be unnoticeable—it just works. The moment it starts working, they will expect it everywhere and will not be happy if a data exchange error results in their car scraping a wall.

As the digital revolution is a global phenomenon traveling at Internet speed, some effects propagate quickly, as can be seen by the uptake of digital phones, digital displays, and social networking. But these are by no means uniform global phenomena; some societies trail, while others have amazing coverage. Inevitably, these differences will generate expectations, and ultimately growth in the currently less-fortunate communities will drive further demand, again extending and increasing the pressure for effective data-intensive services, infrastructure, and methods.

There are many reasons for keeping and curating data. For example, to allow judicial review of life critical decisions, to challenge the interpretation of data as they affect policy, business practices, or scientific conclusions, as a reference framework for other data, and to provide a foundation for further research and innovation. But data curation has significant costs, not just for reliable persistent storage, but for quality control, professional support for access, interpretation, use, and enhancement, and capture of additional contextual information that is needed to preserve the utility of the data. Once curated collections of reference material have been built, they potentially benefit very wide communities—we have seen earlier examples where these are global. But it is difficult to recover costs from the whole of those communities. On the other hand, many researchers in academia and business will have built their practices on the assumption of these reference collections remaining available, and it would be catastrophic for their work were a reference-data service on which they depend to terminate.

In many cases, the cost of collecting data is very high, and failure to retain them or their key derivatives would be wasteful. In some cases, the data record transient and nonrepeatable phenomena. Where those phenomena may be correlated by some natural time series, their loss may significantly reduce potential knowledge discovery. Where the data are based on experiments and on sampling phenomena that do not change with time, the cost of retaining rather than reacquiring data can be calculated. This comparison is not straightforward, as it is necessary to understand the value of the data's availability via a reference site as well as its preservation versus recapture costs.

Looking at the way data are used, we also see economic effects. For example, the cost of random accesses to large volumes of data are very high compared with serial scans. Consequently, there is an advantage to making lower volume data available as proxy for the large volumes if that will satisfy many users. We see this in the various abstractions of the data from a particle collision in a large accelerator. We see that it is also in the catalogs of astronomical objects (Chapter 18), where entries in the catalog denote a derived representation of the original observation that is sufficient for many astronomers' purposes. There are two factors at work here. One, the user of the catalog is saved from having to understand all of the processes to derive the astronomical parameters and from the time waiting for the data access and derivation. Two, the provider of astronomic data is able to use much more data to calibrate the derivation and to avoid supporting the costs of randomly and repeatedly doing this derivation. But there is a danger that the derivation will become "the truth," whereas it is a derivation that may be challenged.

Data providers often support researchers revisiting the primary data to carry out rederivation, but as that is both technically difficult and potentially expensive, they usually introduce a requirement for further authorization. When those researchers find new popular properties, these may be added to later catalogs to avoid the cost of lots of requests to revisit primary data randomly. Since it is well understood how to present and optimize access to catalogs, their use will grow in every discipline. As each discipline's data collections become larger and more complex, the economic value of catalogs will grow, both as a conceptually simpler access model and as a way of saving computational costs. As time passes, the contents of each catalog will reflect more of what its user community needs.

We have seen in this section that there are many aspects to the *full cost* of data, from acquisition, through the production of standard data products such as catalogs, analysis for specific purposes, and curation to reuse or discard. It is clearly beneficial to balance the investment along this entire path so as to get the best returns. However, as the use of data from multiple sources and the interdependence between resources develops, understanding the costs and benefits becomes ever more complex. It is a research challenge to develop adequate economic models to predict the longer-term benefits and the full long-term costs of data. The decision makers who invest in major programs of data collection or who plan new observational systems should use such a model to help them act wisely.

24.3   FUTURE DATA SOCIETY AND PROFESSIONALISM

Finally, we look at how society may react to the data bonanza, including the propensity for dependence and overexpectations. This has implications for the professional practices that data-intensive workers should adopt. We conclude with a call to arms to develop the foundations for those professional practices.

In their personal lives, many people handle more and more data; for example, capturing more with their cameras and smartphones. They also use more data with the GPS route finders and their reference data collections in their smartphones—to identify birds and plants, to know the geology of the region in which they stand, to verify fascinating facts, to find synonyms, to translate phrases, and to organize their tourism, to give just a few examples. They are also comfortable with supplying data for many transactions, from booking travel to completing tax returns, and frequently use Internet services for searches and social networking. They handle textual data, map, and video data. The majority take the data in the form offered by their devices, apps, and services. Only a minority will collate, transform, or integrate data. Even fewer will collect data as evidence—they will typically be citizen scientists, for example, those making the bird observations in Chapter 22, or activists planning to challenge a local or national decision. In these latter cases, people often belong to a society or group that helps in developing and teaching the methods and in funding the development of supporting tools.

It is challenging to try to predict how this will change in the future. Will personal tools and services for integrating and analyzing data become popular? We can remember people saying browsers would only be used by librarians and spread-sheets by accountants.[17] It is easy to ridicule such negative remarks, but there have always been those who foresaw changes in the way people use information. Although his envisioned "memex" was mechanical, Vannevar Bush's anticipation, in *As we may think* in 1945, of links, bookmarks, and hypertext, to mark paths through information space was incredibly farsighted [65]. Similarly, Ted Nelson's recognition of the power of hypertext, in *Literary Machines*, included an extensive vision of the ways in which people would interact with computer-supported infor-mation [66]. Jim Gray, in his talk to the NRC-CSTB[18] in 2007, *On e-Science: A transformed scientific method*, where he introduced *The Fourth Paradigm*, had a clear vision of a world where it was easy to use research data and research papers in combination [62]. To quote:

> The goal is to have a world in which all of the science literature is online, all of the science data is online, and they interoperate with each other. Lots of new tools are needed to make this happen.

We believe that implementing Jim Gray's vision is critical for the future. It needs to be taken further, as we describe subsequently. The research world has to interact effectively with the rest of society if it is to deliver its full value. As Steven Chu, U.S. Secretary of Energy and a Nobel Laureate, said, "We seek solutions. We don't seek—dare I say this?—just scientific papers anymore." [67]. The translational step from research to action requires that the science and the societal context are integrated so that ideas and information flow both ways. This leads to the addition of public and commercial documents and data to Jim Gray's easily accessed milieu. It also requires us to engage the public with the data and the processes used to go from data to knowledge. First, because if they are engaged, they are more likely to trust the work of researchers and business, and to agree that the resources and methods used are justified. Second, their direct engagement is valuable scrutiny and prepares them to be more receptive when the knowledge produced requires them to act. To get them engaged requires that they see immediate benefits.

If the wider public is to share directly in the power of data, they will need much better tools for collecting, creating, finding, accessing, aggregating, analyz-ing, providing, and presenting data. It will require a step change in the ways in which data are handled. For example, all data sources will need to describe their available data and terms of use in such a way that services and agents acting on behalf of the user will be able to find it based on content criteria, be able to assess cost, quality, and statistical properties, and be able to interpret the formats and representation to automatically deliver the data in the right form to the next step. All of the familiar requirements for saving histories, making bookmarks, saving

---

[17]They are widely used by very large numbers of people for planning, data organization, and data sharing. Many of the data gatherers listed above use spreadsheets for their records, as the visual interface is easy to understand. As the groups advance, they may migrate to shared databases, but often they still use spreadsheets as their data-handling, data-integrating, and data analysis framework.

[18]National Research Council nationalacademies.org/nrc, Computer Science and Telecommunications Board sites.nationalacademies.org/CSTB/index.htm.

partial results in a form for personal or group use, and good metaphors with icons that have an intuitively sensible affordance will be needed. Today's analytic methods would need to be packaged, with automatic but safe selection of their control parameters, and good explanations of the validity and applicability of their results. These systems would need to trade inferential power for safety, understandability, and affordability. The visualization phase would have good defaults for each form of data and analysis, with easy controls to adjust the resulting dynamic visualizations. The challenge, as it was for Mosaic, is to come up with a pragmatic initial choice of function and presentation that exploits already familiar interfaces and user behaviors—perhaps extending the spreadsheet metaphor, as it is already widely used for data handling. The new, personal data browser has to work with a non-ideal world initially, as only a few data sources would have the necessary properties. Would those be based on Linked Open Data? Are additional descriptive conventions needed? Clearly, data browsers would need to understand popular data that are already widely used, such as geospatial information, transport timetables, and language data.

Adoption would probably commence with people who already use data in their work or hobbies just as it began with people who already used computers when Mosaic made the Web accessible. These might include citizen scientists, enthusiasts for sport statistics, and activists in campaigns where their (re)interpretation of data might help. But it would soon become much more general. It could include manipulation of consumer comparisons to make better purchasing decisions, running one's own usage history, and known family events into the expenditure model. It could include taking the data from the domestic appliances and vehicles and analyzing these to better understand consumption and the impact of different maintenance providers. It could include analysis of personal health data in comparison with available public data to understand the trade-offs in risks and outcomes when considering medical interventions or choice of medical practices. It could include analysis of local and national government benefits vis-à-vis personal circumstances. As multiple uses of the data browser proceeded, they would build a personal data collection and a tuned relationship with the tools and external data services. A crucial value is for the user to feel that they now control and understand that personal model and that it enables them to choose how to interpret governmental, commercial, and public data. They may choose to share some of it, with their family or friends perhaps, and so will need fine-grained controls that they understand. Everything that the data browser could do can be done at present, but at present, it is such hard work that virtually no one does it. Two key steps are necessary: the emergence of the first attractive data browser, simple enough to understand, powerful enough to support personal decision making; and education, most probably initially through popular media, about the ways in which you can use data to make better life decisions. There is already early evidence of data browsers in specific application domains that may indicate how more generic data browsers may emerge.

- Googlemaps and GoogleEarth initiated a framework for browsing geospatial data, as described in Chapter 19. Google Fusion Tables lets you discover, visualize, expand, and share data tables (with charting tools for presentation).[19]

- Tableau[20] provides desktop tools and servers for business intelligence based on multisourced data.
- Datamarket[21] provides data from multiple suppliers for reuse in businesses.
- Stat4you[22] publishes collections of data in a common format.
- Infochimps[23] provides a data-handling infrastructure on the cloud with skills and tools for data integration and analysis.

Such an uptake of the data browser would have two positive feedback effects. Understanding of the value of data as a foundation for well-informed policy and decisions would develop and the payoff for making data available sufficiently described and compliant would result in most data providers joining the club. The former should have the effect of insisting that professional, commercial, and governmental decisions have properly used the relevant available data and, perhaps, a better understanding of the limits of the data—we revisit this with an example. The latter should benefit the users in businesses, particularly small businesses, as the self-description and automated data adaptation would remove a huge impediment and chore when combining data they need. Here, we see the effect of introducing a well-engineered highway from data to knowledge stimulating the industries that use it. This in turn would make it easier to make well-founded decisions based on data and would accelerate all the research and knowledge businesses. It also heightens the need for professionalism; not claiming the data provides backing for a decision when it does not, not claiming the data has been properly prepared and carefully used, when it has not, and so on. Most importantly, it requires that practitioners provide a link to the source data and the methods used when they present results or suggest action. It requires that data honestly reflect what they purport to represent. It requires ethical behavior; not using privileged access to data to the detriment of others or for personal gain. Some of these issues may need revised legal frameworks, as data and information will, like financial assets, be a crucial asset that can be, deliberately or carelessly, mismanaged.

The most sensitive domains demanding professional treatment of data are those where people's lives are at stake: healthcare, emergency response, and military operations are prime examples. A recent case in Italy will illustrate some of the issues. Seismologists, in this case at the Instituto Nationale di Geofisica e Vulcanologia (INGV),[24] observe incoming seismic data for two purposes: to generate estimates of the hazard from earthquakes using the historical record and models, and, when an earthquake occurs, to identify its properties and notify relevant emergency response services so that they may deploy appropriately. The hazard data are presented as maps of the probability of earthquakes above a chosen

[19] www.google.com/fusiontables   and   developers.google.com/chart/interactive/docs/spread sheets.
[20] www.tableausoftware.com
[21] datamarket.com
[22] www.stat4you.com
[23] www.infochimps.com
[24] www.ingv.it

magnitude occurring in a given duration, e.g. 10 or 50 years. These maps are used to classify the earthquake risk in terms agreed by the Italian government. This agreed risk estimate determines the legally required building regulations and emergency response plans. The trigger for an emergency response is transmitted formally by telephone to each emergency response center after a duty seismologist has agreed that the interpretation of data from seismometers is a valid indication of a high magnitude earthquake and there is an emergency. Public communication is also automatically generated at that point. The characterization of the seismic event is then refined.[25]

For the earthquake in question, L'Aquila M 6.16th April 2009 (Italy), in a region identified as having a high seismic hazard since 1915, there were 309 deaths, 1,600 injured, and 65,000 made homeless [69]. Several citizens formally requested that a local prosecutor investigate. L'Aquila's chief prosecutor concluded that he had gathered enough evidence in June 2011, and as a result, seven Italian scientists and government officials were charged with manslaughter for failing to warn of the impending earthquake. Seismologists worldwide leapt to the seismologists' defense explaining the impossibility of predicting specific earthquakes. Seismologists had acted professionally when preparing the estimates of hazard in the region and when identifying and characterizing the initial earthquake. But this leaves a moot point about the effectiveness of the seismologists' communications on these matters. The local inattention to the long-term hazard warnings suggests that it was not taken sufficiently seriously, and blame for this can perhaps be attributed to both parties, although formally the local authority and builders should have implemented the safeguards against structure collapses. The immediate communication to emergency services was effective, but the long-term importance of hazard estimates may have been less effective. In consequence, the INGV now has an outreach program, for example, on YouTube, Twitter, and through schools, so that the public better understands the hazard warnings as well as preparing them for seismic events [70].

The above example is one of many where we see the emerging need for professional behavior in all aspects of extracting knowledge from data. Those doing the extraction not only have a responsibility to derive the best knowledge they can from the data in a timely manner but also have a responsibility to deliver it in a form that can be acted on professionally by the recipients. Conversely, the recipients of the information have to understand its data-as-evidence foundation and treat it with appropriate seriousness. If this is a critical channel of communication, as in the emergency response scenario, there is a professional obligation on both the producer and receiver of information to prepare the way for such communication, learning about each other's constraints and issues, appreciating inevitable uncertainties, and developing shared vocabularies, images, notations, and procedures. It is as important to ensure that public harm is avoided through the misuse or misinterpretation of data, as it was to ensure that railway passengers were not killed by

---

[25]The following timescale is typical of detection and information refinement: 3 s: first station detects P wave, event identification, and initial location; 6 s: first station records 3 s of wave allowing initial magnitude estimation; 7 s: four stations triggered, refined location; 12 s: four stations observed > 3 s P wave, refined magnitude estimate; 30 s: all stations trigger, final location; 2 min: full trace at all stations: magnitude estimation—from [68]. Consequently, communication and decisions are compressed into a short period.

exploding boilers in the early days of steam. Engineering had to develop responsible codes of practice and ways of recognizing when engineers were sufficiently trained to be trusted. They had to develop the role of consulting engineers, who could represent clients or the public and review the designs and practice of other engineers. Accident enquiries and legislation backed this up.

Now, all of those responsible for engineering and operating highways from data to knowledge need to develop a similar professionalism. All of those responsible for the quality of collected data must accurately document and maintain its quality. All of those responsible for inferring information and knowledge from the available data must take responsibility for and accurately represent the quality of their results. All of those building technology to enable these inferences and the management of data must ensure that their software and systems do an accurate job and that the limits of the technology are properly described. All of those presenting that information must take responsibility for communicating it, so that the recipients' responses are appropriate. All of those acting on the received information have an obligation to act on it appropriately. Such interlocking responsibilities need to be developed by the relevant professional bodies. They need to work with the educational establishments to ensure that the emerging semitrained professionals have the correct foundations to undertake the roles in the handling and use of data. They need to work with the employers to ensure proper professional development leading to trustworthy and competent data handling, data use, data presentation, and data interpretation.

Society faces many extreme challenges. Better exploitation of data will improve societies' chances of prospering. Professional behavior is necessary to maximize this potential and to avoid the pitfalls of misinterpretation. As we strive to realize Jim Gray's vision of all data and all research papers being easily used together, and to extend that into business and society, we must also strive to build the educational, ethical, and legal framework for using data honestly, fairly, safely, and effectively.

REFERENCES

1. C. Anderson, *The Longer Long Tail: How Endless Choice is Creating Unlimited Demand*. Random House Business Books, 2009.

2. Sandvine, "Global Internet Phenomena Report: Spring 2011," tech. rep., Sandvine Intelligent Broadband Networks, 2011.

3. *"Construction Project Information Committee, Collaborative Production of Architectural, Engineering and Construction Information, Code of Practice,"* British Standard 1192:2007, British Standards Institute, 2008.

4. T. Beach, Y. Rezgui, O. Rana, and M. Parashar, "Governance model for cloud computing in building information management," *Philisophical Transactions of the Royal Society A*, 2012.

5. "Toyota and safety," tech. rep., Toyota, 2012.

6. G. Bell, J. Gray, and A. S. Szalay, "Petascale computational systems: balanced cyberinfrastructure in a data-centric world," *IEEE Computer*, vol. 39, no. 1, pp. 110–112, 2006.

7. A. S. Szalay, G. Bell, J. vanden Berg, A. Wonders, R. C. Burns, D. Fay, J. Heasley, A. J. G. Hey, M. A. Nieto-Santisteban, A. R. Thakar, C. van Ingen, and R. Wilton, "GrayWulf: scalable clustered architecture for data intensive computing," in *Hawaii International Conference on Systems Sciences*, pp. 1–10, 2009.

8. A. S. Szalay, G. C. Bell, H. H. Huang, A. Terzis, and A. White, "Low-power amdahl-balanced blades for data intensive computing," *ACM SIGOPS Operating Systems Review*, vol. 44, no. 1, pp 71–75 2010.

9. A. Thakar, A. S. Szalay, K. Church, and A. Terzis, "Large science databases - are cloud services ready for them?" *Scientific Programming*, vol. 19, no. 2–3, pp. 147–159, 2011.

10. A. S. Szalay, "Extreme data-intensive scientific computing," *Computing in Science and Engineering*, vol. 13, no. 6, pp. 34–41, 2011.

11. M. L. Kersten and S. Manegold, "Revolutionary database technology for data intensive research," *ERCIM News*, no. 89, 2012.

12. S. Ghemawat, H. Gobioff, and S.-T. Leung, "The google file system," in *ACM Symposium on Operating Systems Principles*, pp. 29–43, 2003.

13. K. Hwang, J. Dongarra, and G. C. Fox, *Distributed and Cloud Computing: From Parallel Processing to the Internet of Things*. Morgan Kaufmann, 2011.

14. Y. Gu and R. L. Grossman, "Sector: a high performance wide area community data storage and sharing system," *Future Generation Computer Systems*, vol. 26, no. 5, pp. 720–728, 2010.

15. R. L. Grossman, Y. Gu, J. Mambretti, M. Sabala, A. S. Szalay, and K. P. White, "An overview of the Open Science Data Cloud," in *High Performance Cloud Computing*, pp. 377–384, 2010.

16. Y. Gu and R. L. Grossman, "Toward efficient and simplified distributed data intensive computing," *IEEE Transactions on Parallel and Distributed Systems*, vol. 22, no. 6, pp. 974–984, 2011.

17. B. Trushkowsky, P. Bodík, A. Fox, M. J. Franklin, M. I. Jordan, and D. A. Patterson, "The SCADS director: scaling a distributed storage system under stringent performance requirements," in *Proceedings of FAST '11: Conference on File and Storage Technologies*, USENIX, 2011.

18. S. Patil and G. Gibson, "Scale and concurrency of GIGA+: file system directories with millions of files," in *Proceedings of the 9th USENIX Conference on File and Stroage Technologies*, FAST'11, pp. 13–13, Berkeley, CA, USENIX Association, 2011.

19. M. Isard, M. Budiu, Y. Yu, A. Birrell, and D. Fetterly, "Dryad: distributed data-parallel programs from sequential building blocks," in *Proceedings of the Second ACM SIGOPS/EuroSys European Conference on Computer Systems 2007*, pp. 59–72, ACM, 2007.

20. M. Wilde, I. Foster, K. Iskra, P. Beckman, Z. Zhang, A. Espinosa, M. Hategan, B. Clifford, and I. Raicu, "Parallel scripting for applications at the petascale and beyond," *Computer*, vol. 42, no. 11, pp. 50–60, 2009.

21. J. Dean and S. Ghemawat, "MapReduce: simplified data processing on large clusters," *Communications of the ACM*, vol. 51, no. 1, pp. 107–113, 2008.

22. T. White, *Hadoop: The Definitive Guide*. O'Reilly, 2009.

23. M. Stonebraker, D. Abadi, D. J. DeWitt, S. Madden, E. Paulson, A. Pavlo, and A. Rasin, "MapReduce and parallel DBMSs: friends or foes?" *Communications of the ACM*, vol. 53, no. 1, pp. 64–71, 2010.

24. B. Dobrzelecki, A. Krause, A. Hume, A. Grant, M. Antonioletti, T. Alemu, M. P. Atkinson, M. Jackson, and E. Theocharopoulos, "Integrating distributed data sources with OGSA-DAI DQP and views," *Philisophical Transactions of the Royal Society A*, vol. 368, no. 1926, pp. 4133–4145, 2010.

25. C. B. Aranda, M. Arenas, and Ò. Corcho, "Semantics and optimization of the SPARQL 1.1 federation extension," in *ESWC (2)* (G. Antoniou, M. Grobelnik, E. P. B. Simperl, B. Parsia, D. Plexousakis, P. D. Leenheer, and J. Z. Pan, eds.), vol. 6644 of *Lecture Notes in Computer Science*, pp. 1–15, Springer, 2011.

26. F. Chang, J. Dean, S. Ghemawat, W. C. Hsieh, D. A. Wallach, M. Burrows, T. Chandra, A. Fikes, and R. E. Gruber, "Bigtable: a distributed storage system for structured data," *ACM Transactions on Computer Systems*, vol. 26, no. 2, pp. 1–26 2008.

27. S. Nishimura, S. Das, D. Agrawal, and A. E. Abbadi, "MD-HBase: A Scalable Multidimensional Data Infrastructure for Location Aware Services" in *Mobile Data Management (1)* (A. B. Zaslavsky, P. K. Chrysanthis, D. L. Lee, D. Chakraborty, V. Kalogeraki, M. F. Mokbel, and C.-Y. Chow, eds.), pp. 7–16, IEEE, 2011.

28. D. Kossmann, T. Kraska, and S. Loesing, "An evaluation of alternative architectures for transaction processing in the Cloud," in *SIGMOD Conference*, pp. 579–590, ACM, 2010.

29. The SciDB team, "Overview of SciDB: large scale array storage, processing and analysis," in *SIGMOD'10*, ACM, 2010.

30. E. Soroush, M. Balazinska, and D. Wang, "ArrayStore: a storage manager for complex parallel array processing," in *SIGMOD'11*, ACM, 2011.

31. M. Ivanova, N. Nes, R. Goncalves, and M. L. Kersten, "MonetDB/SQL meets Sky-Server: the challenges of a scientific database," in *Scientific and Statistical Database Management*, p. 13, 2007.

32. S. Idreos, F. Groffen, N. Nes, S. Manegold, K. S. Mullender, and M. L. Kersten, "MonetDB: two decades of research in column-oriented database architectures," *IEEE Data Engineering Bulletin*, vol. 35, no. 1, pp. 40–45, 2012.

33. P. Baumann, "Large-Scale earth science services: a case for databases," in *Advances in Conceptual Modeling - Theory and Practice* (J. Roddick, V. Benjamins, S. Si-Said Cherfi, R. Chiang, C. Claramunt, R. Elmasri, F. Grandi, H. Han, M. Hepp, M. Lytras, V. Mišic, G. Poels, I. Song, J. Trujillo, and C. Vangenot, eds.), vol. 4231 of *Lecture Notes in Computer Science*, pp. 75–84, Springer, Berlin/Heidelberg, 2006. 10.1007/11908883_11.

34. F. J. Alexander, A. Hoisie, and A. S. Szalay, "Big data [guest editorial]," *Computing in Science and Engineering*, vol. 13, no. 6, pp. 10–13, 2011.

35. K. Kanov, E. A. Perlman, R. C. Burns, Y. Ahmad, and A. S. Szalay, "I/O streaming evaluation of batch queries for data-intensive computational turbulence," in *Proceedings of the 25th International Conference on High Performance Computing Networking, Storage and Analysis, Super Computing 2011* (S. Lathrop, J. Costa, and W. Kramer, eds.), p. 29–38, ACM, 2011.

36. Y. Zhang, M. L. Kersten, M. Ivanova, and N. Nes, "SciQL, bridging the gap between science and relational DBMS," in *Proceedings of the 15th Symposium on International Database Engineering & Applications (IDEAs)*, ACM, pp. 124–133, 2011.

37. M. Ivanova, M. L. Kersten, and S. Manegold, "Data vaults: a symbiosis between database technology and scientific file repositories," in *Proceedings of the 24th International Conference on Statistical and Scientific Database Management (SSDBM)* (A.

Ailamaki and S. Bowers, eds.), vol. 7338 of *Lecture Notes in Computer Science*, pp. 485–494, Springer, 2012.

38. A. Abouzied, D. Abadi, and A. Silberschatz, 'Access-driven data transfer from raw files into database systems," in *Big Data 2012*, 2012.

39. L. Dobos, A. S. Szalay, J. A. Blakeley, T. Budavari, I. Csabai, D. Tomic, M. Milo-vanovic, M. Tintor, and A. Jovanovic, "Array requirements for scientific applications and an implementation for Microsoft SQL server," in Baumann et al. (71), pp. 13–19, 2011.

40. E. Givelberg, A. S. Szalay, K. Kanov, and R. C. Burns, "MPI-DB, a parallel database services software library for scientific computing," in *EuroMPI* (Y. Cotronis, A. Danalis, D. S. Nikolopoulos, and J. Dongarra, eds.), vol. 6960 of *Lecture Notes in Computer Science*, pp. 339–341, Springer, 2011.

41. R. Goncalves and M. L. Kersten, "The data cyclotron query processing scheme," *ACM Transactions on Database Systems*, vol. 36, no. 4, pp. 1–35, 2011.

42. W. Fan, J. Li, S. Ma, N. Tang, and Y. Wu, "Adding regular expressions to graph reachability and pattern queries," *Frontiers of Computer Science*, vol. 6, no. 3, pp. 313–338, 2012.

43. W. Fan, "Graph pattern matching revised for social network analysis," in *ICDT* (A. Deutsch, ed.), pp. 8–21, ACM, 2012.

44. W. Fan, J. Li, S. Ma, N. Tang, and W. Yu, "Interaction between record matching and data repairing," in *SIGMOD Conference* (T. K. Sellis, R. J. Miller, A. Kementsietsidis, and Y. Velegrakis, eds.), pp. 469–480, ACM, 2011.

45. W. Fan, J. X. Yu, J. Li, B. Ding, and L. Qin, "Query translation from XPATH to SQL in the presence of recursive DTDs," *VLDB Journal*, vol. 18, no. 4, pp. 857–883, 2009.

46. A. Shoshani and D. Rotem, *Scientific Data Management: Challenges, Technology and Deployment*, *Computational Science Series*, Chapman and Hall/CRC, 2010.

47. S. J. Lynden, Ò. Corcho, I. Kojima, M. Antonioletti, and C. B. Aranda, "Open standards for service-based database access and integration," in *Grid and Cloud Database Management* (S. Fiore and G. Aloisio, eds.), pp. 3–21, Springer, 2011.

48. G. Lemson, T. Budavari, and A. S. Szalay, "Implementing a general spatial indexing library for relational databases of large numerical simulations," in *SSDBM* (J. B. Cushing, J. C. French, and S. Bowers, eds.), vol. 6809 of *Lecture Notes in Computer Science*, pp. 509–526, Springer, 2011.

49. M. Conway, R. Moore, A. Rajasekar, and J.-Y. Nief, "Demonstration of policy-guided data preservation using iRODS," in *POLICY*, pp. 173–174, IEEE Computer Society, 2011.

50. P. Teetor, *R Cookbook* (*First Edition*). O'Reilly, 2011.

51. W. Fan and F. Geerts, "Capturing missing tuples and missing values," in *Proceedings of the twenty-ninth ACM SIGMOD-SIGACT-SIGART symposium on Principles of database systems* (J. Paredaens and D. V. Gucht, eds.), pp. 169–178, ACM, 2010.

52. W. Fan, J. Li, N. Tang, and W. Yu, "Incremental detection of inconsistencies in distributed data," in *proceedings of the 28th IEEE International Conference on Data Engineering (ICDE)* (A. Kementsietsidis and M. A. V. Salles, eds.), pp. 318–329, IEEE Computer Society, 2012.

53. W. Fan and F. Geerts, "Uniform dependency language for improving data quality," *IEEE Data Engineering Bulletin*, vol. 34, no. 3, pp. 34–42, 2011.

54. A. Bifet, G. Holmes, R. Kirkby, and B. Pfahringer, "MOA: massive online analysis," *Journal of Machine Learning Research*, vol. 11, pp. 1601–1604, 2010.

55. A. Rajaraman and J. D. Ullman, *Mining of Massive Datasets*. Cambridge University Press, 2011.

56. C. M. Bishop, *Pattern Recognition and Machine Learning (Information Science and Statistics)*. Springer, 2007.

57. J. Steele and N. Iliinsky, *Beautiful Visualisation: Looking at Data Through the Eyes of Experts*. O'Reilly, 2010.

58. T. Segaran and J. Hammerbacher, *Beautiful Data: The Stories Behind Elegant Data Solutions*. O'Reilly, 2009.

59. I. H. Witten, E. Frank, and M. A. Hall, *Data Mining: Practical Machine Learning Tools and Techniques (Third Edition)*. Morgan Kauffman, 2011.

60. P. K. Janert, *Data Analysis with Open Source Tools*. O'Reilly, 2011.

61. A. Gomez-Perez, O. Corcho, and M. Fernandez-Lopez, *Ontological Engineering: with examples from the areas of Knowledge Management, e-Commerce and the Semantic Web. First Edition (Advanced Information and Knowledge Processing)*. Springer, 2004.

62. J. Gray, "Jim Gray on e-Science: a transformed scientific method," in *The Fourth Paradigm: Data Intensive Scientific Discovery* (S. T. Tony Hey and K. Tolle, eds.), pp. xix–xxxiii, Microsoft Research, 2009.

63. M. Atkinson and D. D. Roure, "Realising the power of data-intensive research," tech. rep., National e-Science Centre, 2010.

64. D. De Roure, C. Goble, and R. Stevens, "The design and realisation of the myExperiment virtual research environment for social sharing of workflows," *Future Generation Computer Systems*, vol. 25, pp. 561–567, 2009.

65. V. Bush, "As we may think," *The Atlantic Monthly*, 8 pages, July 1945, www.theatlantic. com/magazine/archive/1945/07/as-we-may-think/303881/1, accessed January 2013.

66. T. Nelson, *Literary Machines: The Report on, and of, Project Xanadu Concerning Word Processing, Electronic Publishing, Hypertext, Thinkertoys, Tomorrow's Intellectual Revolution, and Certain other Topics Including Knowledge, Education and Freedom*. Mindful Press, 1981.

67. J. Dozier and W. B. Gail, "The emerging science of environmental applications," in *The Fourth Paradigm* (S. T. Tony Hey and K. Tolle, eds.), pp. 13–19, Microsoft Research, 2009.

68. A. Zollo, "The challenge of time: from early warning to accurate estimates," *Presentation at Global challenges for seismological data analysis workshop*, Erice, Italy, May 2012.

69. M. Cocco, "Responsibility and liability of scientists: the case of the L'Aquila earthquake," *Presentation at Global challenges for seismological data analysis workshop*, Erice, Italy, 2012.

70. E. Casarotti, V. Lauciani, A. Piersanti, and G. Selvaggi, "INGV terremoti: tools to improve the communication on earthquakes," *Presentation at Global Challenges for Seismological Data Analysis* workshop, Erice, Italy, 2012.

71. P. Baumann, B. Howe, K. Orsborn, and S. Stefanova, eds., *Proceedings of the 2011 EDBT/ICDT Workshop on Array Databases, Uppsala, Sweden, March 25, 2011*. ACM, 2011.

Appendix A

Glossary

Michelle Galea and Malcolm Atkinson

School of Informatics, University of Edinburgh, Edinburgh, UK

ACRM Analytical Customer Relationship Management, use of an organization's operational data to enable the measurement, analysis, and optimization of its customer relationships.

ADFL Athena Data Flow Language.

ADMIRE The European Union Framework Programme 7 project "Advanced Data Mining and Integration Research for Europe" ADMIRE ICT 215024.

ALADIN A meteorological prediction model used to determine temperature, surface pressure, specific humidity, and other physical variables.

API Application Program Interface, an inter-software communication specification used for accessing functionality or services from programs.

Azure Microsoft Windows platform for cloud computing.

BADC British Atmospheric Data Centre.

BBSRC UK Biotechnology and Biological Sciences Research Council.

BGS British Geological Survey.

BPEL (or WS-BPEL) Web Services Business Process Execution Language, a Web services-based language for specifying business processes.

cloud computing A business model for enabling the delivery as a service of shared computing resources such as CPUs, networks, storage, and applications to multiple users.

The DATA Bonanza: Improving Knowledge Discovery in Science, Engineering, and Business, First Edition.
Edited by Malcolm Atkinson, Rob Baxter, Michelle Galea, Mark Parsons, Peter Brezany, Oscar Corcho, Jano van Hemert, and David Snelling.

component   One of the computational elements involved in a data-intensive or computational process, such as application codes, scripts, workflows, services, catalogs, registries, data collections, data resources, functions, gateways, libraries, PEs, PE instances, format definitions, and types.

CRISP-DM   A description of the six phases of data mining recognized by the Cross Industry Standard Process for Data Mining, a forum of data-mining systems vendors, and application developers.

CRM   Customer Relationship Management is a strategy that defines an organization's business operations for building and managing its relationships with customers.

DAGMan   Directed Acyclic Graph Manager is a Pegasus engine used for executing workflows on available compute resources.

data   Any digitally encoded information that can be stored, processed, and transmitted by computers. It consists of text files, database records, images, video sequences, and recordings.

data-analysis expert   An expert in building or using knowledge discovery methods in a data-rich environment.

data collection   A collection of data, e.g. a file, list of files, a relational table, a set of relational tables, an XML document, an RDF database, etc. that are intended to be used together.

data-intensive   An adjectival phrase that denotes that the item to which it is applied requires attention to the properties of data, and to the ways in which data are handled.

data-intensive architecture   An architecture to organize data-intensive business, processes, and systems.

data-intensive computing   Computing that necessitates attention to any relevant property of data which includes their volumes, distributed locations, and the heterogeneity of their formats and storage structures.

data-intensive engineer   An expert in designing, providing, tuning, operating, and improving the use of computational platforms for data-intensive tasks.

data-intensive platform   The invariably distributed infrastructure of hardware, software, services, and operational procedures that provides a context for data-intensive computation.

data integration   The process of combining data residing at different sources and providing the user with a unified view of these data. This process emerges in a variety of situations both commercial (when two similar companies need to merge their databases) and scientific (combining research results from different repositories) domains.

data mining   The process of automatically extracting patterns from data using techniques such as classification, association-rule mining, and clustering.

database management system (DBMS)   Software designed for the purpose of managing databases.

data-intensive virtual machine (DIVM) An abstraction for the computational environment (i.e. the layers of software and hardware) in which a processing element instance runs during enactment.

DICOM Digital Imaging and Communications in Medicine is a file format standard for viewing and distributing medical images such as CT and MRI scans.

DISPEL Data-Intensive Systems Process Engineering Language is a workflow composition language for data-intensive applications. See Appendix B for DISPEL related definitions.

distributed computing The collective use of distributed resources, including data and applications, to solve a computational problem.

DOE US Department of Energy.

domain expert A person who is skilled in a particular field of research or decision making.

DQP Distributed Query Processing, an example of a data integration component, providing a declarative access to distributed data resources.

Dublin Core Metadata vocabularies to support interoperable solutions for the discovery and management of resources.

EDIM1 Edinburgh Data-Intensive Machine 1, a University of Edinburgh experimental architecture for data-intensive computing.

e-Infrastructure The ICT element of a research infrastructure, a distributed collection of data, storage, and compute resources, interconnected by digital communications and organized to serve a common purpose.

enactment The execution of a workflow on a computational platform; this generally involves coordinated use of multiple and often heterogeneous communication, data and compute resources.

enactment level The lower part of the data-intensive architecture, containing all the technology and services that enable data-intensive processes to be enacted. It provides the environment for and is managed by data-intensive engineers.

EPSRC UK Engineering and Physical Sciences Research Council.

e-Science Sustained research in any discipline conducted by widely distributed, often inter-disciplinary collaborations and enabled by advances in informatics and e-Infrastructures.

ESFRI European Strategy Forum on Research Infrastructures.

European Bioinformatics Institute (EBI) Bioinformatics research institute providing data and other services and is a part of the European Molecular Biology Laboratory (EMBL).

exabyte (EB) 10^{18} or 1,000,000,000,000,000,000 bytes.

gateway A software subsystem, typically at the middleware level, that accepts requests for computational and data-handling tasks. It vets those requests to establish whether they are valid, e.g. are syntactically and semantically consistent, and are authorized. Requests that are not validated are rejected. Requests that are accepted are passed to other software systems, at the same or other locations, for execution.

GEO   Group on Earth Observations.

GEOSS   Global Earth Observation System of Systems.

gigabyte (GB) 10^9 or 1,000,000,000 bytes.

GrayWulf   Scalable clustered architecture for data-intensive computing.

grid   A system concerned with the integration, virtualization, and management of services and resources in a distributed, heterogeneous environment that supports collections of users and resources (virtual organizations) across traditional administrative and organizational domains (real organizations).

grid computing   A computing model that treats all resources as a collection of manageable entities with common interfaces to such functionality as lifetime management, discoverable properties, and accessibility via open protocols.

GridFTP   Grid File Transfer Protocol is an extension of the standard FTP for use with grid computing.

Hadoop   A software framework used to support data-intensive computing, enabling applications to run on distributed computers and data.

HDF5   A data format specification with supporting libraries and tools for managing large volumes of numerical data.

high performance computing (HPC)   Use of powerful processors, high-speed networks, and parallel supercomputers for running computationally intensive applications.

HTML   HyperText Markup Language.

HTTP   HyperText Transfer Protocol.

INSPIRE   Infrastructure for Spatial Information in Europe, an EU directive aimed at enabling the access, sharing and re-using of spatial data for governance and policy making purposes.

integrated development environment (IDE)   Also known as Interactive Development Environment, a software system designed for supporting software writing, often including a source code editor, a debugger, and build automation tools.

IPCC   Intergovernmental Panel on Climate Change.

IRIS   Incorporated Research Institutions for Seismology.

iRODS   integrated Rule-Oriented Data System is an open source software for managing large collections of distributed data and metadata.

JISC   UK Joint Information Systems Committee.

Kepler   Open source scientific workflow management system.

KDD   Knowledge Discovery in Databases is the process of discovering useful knowledge in collections of data, iterating over several stages as necessary such as data selection, pre-processing, transformation, mining, and interpretation and evaluation.

KNIME   Open source data analytics and integration platform.

linked open data (LOD)   A W3C community initiative aimed at interlinking freely available data on the Web.

mapreduce   Programming model for distributed processing of large volumes of data on clusters of computers.

MATLAB   High level language for technical computing from MathWorks.

Meandre   Semantic-driven data-intensive workflow execution environment.

megabyte (MB) 10^6 or 1,000,000 bytes.

metadata   Data that describes data. Metadata may include references to schemas, provenance, and information quality.

massive online analysis (MOA)   A software environment comprising a collection of machine learning algorithms and tools for the mining of large-volume data streams.

MonetDB   Open source column-store database management system.

myExperiment   Collaborative virtual research environment for sharing scientific workflows.

NetCDF   Network Common Data Form, a set of interfaces, libraries, and machine-independent formats for the creation, access, and sharing of array oriented data.

OGSA-DAI   Open Grid Services Architecture-Data Access and Integration, an open source product for distributed data access and management.

omics   In biology, informally refers to a field of study ending in -omics, such as genomics, transcriptomics, and proteomics.

ontology   In computer science it is a formal, explicit specification of a shared conceptualization.

Open Geospatial Consortium (OGC)   An international consortium establishing and promoting standards for the sharing of location and geospatial data.

ORFEUS   Observatories and Research Facilities for EUropean Seismology.

Pegasus   Workflow management service, mapping, and executing workflows on available compute resources.

petabyte (PB) 10^{15} or 1,000,000,000,000,000 bytes.

portal   In the context of knowledge discovery a tool designed for a particular group of domain experts that can be used via their browsers; it enables them to establish their identity and rights, and to pursue conveniently a set of tasks for which the portal is designed.

PostgreSQL   Also known as Postgres, an open source object-relational database management system supporting most structured query language (SQL) constructs.

processing element (PE)   A software component that encapsulates a particular functionality and can be used to construct a workflow.

processing element instance   An instance of a processing element that is executed during a workflow enactment.

R   A free language and environment used for statistical computing and graphics.

RapidMiner   Open source system for data mining.

RASDAMAN   RASter DAta MANager, database management system for multi-dimensional arrays.

RDF   Resource Description Framework is a language for representing information about resources in the World Wide Web.

research infrastructure   The collection of equipment, resources, organizations, policies, and community support that enables a particular discipline to conduct research. Normally, this refers to the advanced facilities that enable frontier research, such as the research infrastructures endorsed by ESFRI.

registry   A persistent store of definitions and descriptions of data-intensive components and their relationships in order to facilitate discovery, sharing, and consistent use.

repository   In the context of the data-intensive architecture explored in this book, a repository is a central store holding software definitions, other shared code, and data, that supports distributed concurrent access, update, and version management.

RFID   Radio Frequency IDentification.

SCiDB   Open source data management and analytics software for scientific research.

SCUFL   Simple Conceptual Unified Flow Language, language used by Taverna for defining workflows.

semantic Web   An evolving extension of the World Wide Web in which Web content can be expressed not only in natural language, but also in a form that can be understood, interpreted, and used by software agents, thus permitting them to find, share, and integrate information more easily.

SPARQL   A query language for RDF.

SSD   Solid-State Drive.

SVG   Scalable Vector Graphics, a W3C XML file format for defining vector graphics.

Taverna   Open source scientific workflow management system.

terabyte (TB) 10^{12} or 1,000,000,000,000 bytes.

tools level   The upper part of the data-intensive architecture containing all of the portals and tools for supporting domain experts and most of the development tools that support data-analysis experts.

Trident   Microsoft workflow management system.

Triana   An open source software for data analysis, which includes text and signal and image processing.

URI   Unified Resource Identifier.

virtual organization   A collection of geographically dispersed people and institutions working together on a topic of common interest and sharing resources within an agreed management structure.

virtual research environment (VRE)   A presentation of (ideally all of) the resources, a researcher may need in a consistent and easily used form. These resources include catalogs, data, metadata, libraries, tools, workflows, programs, services, visualization systems, and research methods.

VisTrails   Scientific workflow management system for data exploration and visualization.

W3C   World Wide Web Consortium is an international community of member organizations and the public that works to define and promote standards for Web technologies.

Web service   A software system designed to support interoperable machine- or application-oriented interaction over a network.

Weka   Open source machine learning data software for data mining.

workflow   A process of composed data-handling tasks, computational tasks, and human interactions intended to implement a research method or established working practice.

wrapper   A design pattern where a piece of code allows computational or data-handling components to work together that normally could not because of incompatible interfaces.

wwPDB   worldwide Protein Data Bank.

XML   Extensible Markup Language.

zettabyte (ZB) 10^{21} or 1,000,000,000,000,000,000,000 bytes.

ZigZag   Language used by Meandre for describing the directed graphs that define workflows.

Appendix B

DISPEL Reference Manual

Paul Martin

School of Informatics, University of Edinburgh, Edinburgh, UK

The Data-Intensive Systems Process Engineering Language (DISPEL) is a workflow composition language for distributed data-intensive applications. Tasks are modeled as data streams flowing through processing elements, charting workflow graphs. Graphs can be submitted to gateways; a gateway refers to a registry in order to identify suitable implementations of workflow components before delegating their execution to available resources. DISPEL is imperative and statically-typed, with strict, call-by-value evaluation of expressions.

Preamble

Language constructs are described within this reference in Extended Bachus–Naur Form. Whitespace between tokens is only necessary to distinguish tokens and is consumed on parsing. Productions enclosed within special sequences (demarked by ?) are lexical constructs that do not permit whitespace within them except where explicitly specified. Productions are ordered by precedence.

The DATA Bonanza: Improving Knowledge Discovery in Science, Engineering, and Business, First Edition.
Edited by Malcolm Atkinson, Rob Baxter, Michelle Galea, Mark Parsons, Peter Brezany, Oscar Corcho, Jano van Hemert, and David Snelling.
© 2013 John Wiley & Sons, Inc. Published 2013 by John Wiley & Sons, Inc.

Lexical primitives. Lexical primitives used in productions are described as POSIX basic regular expressions below:

```
       character = .
          letter = [A-Za-z]
       uppercase = [A-Z]
       lowercase = [a-z]
           digit = [0-9]
 escape-sequence = \\[tbnrf'"\\]
     end-of-line = \\[nr]
```

Comments. Scripts can contain comments that will be ignored upon parsing. Two types of comment exist — single-line comments and multi-line comments:

```
comment = ? "//" { character - end-of-line } end-of-line ?
        | ? "/*" { character - "*/" } "*/" ? ;
```

Comments are considered to be a form of whitespace for grammatical purposes.

B.1   WORKFLOW MODEL

A DISPEL workflow is an abstract network of processing elements through which data can be streamed in order to perform some data-intensive task.

- A *processing element* (PE) describes a persistent computational entity. Every PE has a number of connection interfaces through which data is either consumed or produced. Data is streamed between PE instances via connections made between output and input interfaces.
- A *connection* streams data from one output interface to at least one input interface. A connection is established by linking an output to an input and is given additional channels by linking additional inputs to the original output. Data streamed through a connection is replicated across all of its channels.

Workflows are produced by DISPEL scripts. A script is executed by submitting it to a *gateway*. The gateway interprets the script and exporting and importing the workflow components to and from its associated *registry*. Interpretation results in the construction of a workflow graph, which can then be used to coordinate the deployment of tasks onto a suitable enactment platform.

B.1.1   Workflow Graphs

The workflow(s) constructed by a DISPEL script are described by an annotated directed graph constructed incrementally during interpretation. In a workflow graph, nodes have interfaces to which edges (connections) can be attached:

- *PE* nodes represent PE instances; each node records the type of PE used and its configuration and has a number of input and output interfaces as described by its connection signature. PE nodes are created upon instantiation of PE instances.
- *Stream* nodes represent data streams defined in the script itself and injected directly into a workflow; each node has a single output interface [§ B.3.1.3].
- *Sink* nodes represent data-sinks; each node permits a single inbound connection. Sink nodes are created whenever a connection is asserted, which goes to any of the sink types described in § B.1.3 below.
- *External* nodes represent data sources or data destinations external to the workflow; external inputs have a single output interface while external outputs have a single input interface. This is applicable only to internal workflows within composite PEs [§ B.4.9].

Each node in a workflow graph has a number of input and output interfaces through which to consume and produce data. Each interface can have a *structural* [§ B.3.2] and a *domain* [§ B.3.3] type, constraining the syntactic structure and semantic meaning respectively of data elements passed through it. A connection can only carry data that exists in the intersection of its interfaces' structural and domain types.

There are three kinds of PE from the perspective of a DISPEL gateway. *Primitive* PEs are PEs that can be directly implemented by the gateway. *Composite* PEs are PEs which can be implemented as a composition of other PEs. *Abstract* PEs are PEs for which no implementation exists; abstract PEs cannot be instantiated until implemented as a primitive or composite PE using a constructor [§ B.4.18].

Connections created without nodes to connect both ends are *untethered*. Sub-graphs need not be connected; isolated sub-graphs represent independent workflows and can be submitted to a gateway separately or collectively. Sub-graphs with untethered connections cannot be submitted. The workflow graph for a DISPEL script is initially empty. PE constructors produce their own independent workflow graphs.

B.1.2 Streaming

A data stream is a sequence of data elements that can be channeled in series through a connection in a workflow. Data elements can be arbitrarily complex, but must have a recognizable structural type. Data streamed through a connection can be assumed to consist of literal values and tokens. Tokens are used to describe the logical structure of streamed content:

SoS / EoS denotes the start / end of the stream.

SoA / EoA denotes the start / end of an array of values.

SoL / EoL denotes the start / end of a list of values.

SoD / EoD denotes the start / end of a dictionary of values.

NmD (no-more-data) is a special token, streamed *back* through a connection to request the cessation of streaming.

Dictionary elements [§ B.3.1.5] are streamed key then value. Each PE instance has its own data requirements that affect consumption and production of data; buffering of data within connections is handled automatically by the enactment platform so as to ensure steady data-flow.

B.1.3   Data Sinks

Data can be streamed out of a workflow via a data-sink. There are four built-in data-sink types:

discard immediately disposes of any data streamed into it.

error writes any data streamed into it to a locale specified by the gateway for error output.

warning writes any data streamed into it to a locale specified by the gateway for warning output.

terminate acts as discard, but immediately sends back a NmD token upon receiving any data.

Sinks error and warning should not be expected to be able to handle large volumes of data. Conventional results should be retrieved from a workflow by streaming them to a suitable PE instance, which can perform external operations.

B.1.4   Submission

Upon submission of a workflow sub-graph, PE nodes will be assigned implementations in accordance with information from the registry associated with the chosen gateway. Stream nodes will be implemented by anonymous PEs that will generate the desired streams. Composite PE nodes [§ B.4.9] will be replaced by their internal workflows; the connections within the internal workflow assigned to the composite PE's interfaces will be mapped to its connections in the external graph [§ B.4.18]. Any new nodes introduced will be assigned implementations recursively until a flattened workflow graph is created composed only of primitive components. All components of a flattened sub-graph will then be deployed for enactment regardless of graph connectivity.

B.1.5   Termination

A workflow terminates when all of its components terminate. A PE instance terminates when all output connections close, all input connections close, or it terminates itself. When a PE terminates, the EoS (end-of-stream) token is sent through any open output connections and a special token NmD (no-more-data) is sent back through any open input connections.

A connection is closed upon streaming an EoS token. Individual channels within a connection will be closed if a NmD token is sent back through the channel from its exit interface. If all channels are closed in this way, then the connection as a whole will close, passing back a NmD token through its entry interface. Note that a connection channel will continue to stream data until the NmD token is received and recognized.

B.2 SCRIPT COMPOSITION

A DISPEL script is composed of a series of statements to be executed in sequence:

```
compilation-unit = statement-block { statement-block } ;
```

Scripts are often partitioned into statement blocks delimited by braces:

```
statement-block = statement | "{" { statement-block } "}" ;
```

Statement blocks can be nested; a statement is considered to be within every statement block it physically resides between the delimiters.

B.2.1 Namespaces

Logical entities such as variables and types are given identifiers:

```
identifier = ? ( letter | "_" ) { letter | digit | "_" } ? - keyword ;
```

The entity referred to by a given identifier is determined by the local *namespace*. A mapping between identifier and entity is inserted into the namespace whenever a statement introduces an entity and is removed at the end of the innermost statement block within which that statement resides. More recent mappings override older ones until removed. Each DISPEL script has its own namespace, as does each function, PE type and PE constructor.

Some entities have sub-components. These components can be accessed by prefacing their identifiers with a reference to their parent entities:

```
reference = { reference "." }
            ( identifier | function-call ) [ "[" expression "]" ] ;
```

Entities can be referenced by their identifiers, or by a suitable function call [§ B.4.17]. Array elements require that their index be specified [§ B.3.1.4].

B.2.2 Registered Entities

PE types, structural types, domain types, PE constructors and functions can be exported (registered) and then imported into different scripts. Registered entities are arranged hierarchically into packages. Any registered entity can be referred to without being imported into the namespace by prefacing its identifier with that of its parent package:

```
registered-entity = package-name "." identifier ;
```

Being hierarchical, package names are sequences of identifiers describing the path from a root package to a desired sub-package:

```
package-name = { identifier "." } identifier ;
```

Thus `registered-entity` is a kind of `reference`. Any node in the hierarchy can contain any number of entities and sub-packages.

B.2.3 Variable Declaration

A variable is an entity that can store a value or set of values during execution of a script:

```
variable = { variable "." } ( identifier | array-element ) ;
```

Some entities have internal variables that can be referred to by prefixing their identifiers with that of the parent entity; elements of an array are accessed by affixing to the array identifier an integer expression reducing to an index [§ B.3.1.4]. A variable declaration introduces one or more new identifiers into the namespace representing variables of a given language type [§ B.3.1]:

```
declaration = language-type identifier [ "=" expression ]
                    { "," identifier [ "=" expression ] } ;
```

Each variable can be immediately assigned the value of a corresponding expression [§ B.2.4]. This value must be of the same type as the variable.

B.2.4 Expressions

An expression describes an operation that reduces upon evaluation to a value of a particular type:

```
expression = literal-value | reference
           | "(" expression ")"
           | cast-expression
           | initialization
           | assignment
           | dictionary-assignment
           | ternary-expression
           | logical-expression
           | arithmetic-expression ;
```

Expressions apply suitable operators to literals, variable references and function calls [§ B.2.4.7]. Operations can be nested, and their default precedence manipulated using parentheses. Expressions can also be decomposed by the language type of the value to which they reduce (e.g. `integer-expression`, `stream-expression`).

B.2.4.1 Casting

A cast can be performed to change the type of the value an expression reduces to by prefixing the expression with the desired type:

```
cast-expression = "(" language-type ")" expression ;
```

An `Integer` can be cast into a `Real` and vice versa (returning the floor of the real value). A `String` can be cast into either an `Integer` or a `Real` if an integer or real literal is embedded between the string quotes:

```
castable-string = ? '"' { escape-sequence | " " }
    [ "-" ] digit { digit } [ "." digit { digit } ]
                   { escape-sequence | " " } '"' ? ;
```

A cast from `String` to `Integer` will be the floor of any embedded real value. A reference to a PE instance can be cast into any PE type which its actual PE type is a subtype of [§ B.3.1.6].

B.2.4.2 Initialization

Instances of arrays and PEs require initialization before they can be referred to:

```
initialization = array-initialization | PE-initialization ;
```

Array initialization is described in § B.3.1.4, PE initialization in § B.3.1.6.

B.2.4.3 Assignment

A variable assignment changes the value stored within a variable by application of a suitable assignment operator [§ B.2.4.7]:

```
assignment
    = variable ( "=" | "+=" | "-=" | "*=" | "/=" | "%=" ) expression
    | ( "++" | "--" ) variable
    | variable ( "++" | "--" ) ;
```

The value of any expression must be of the same type as the variable. When used within an expression, an assignment returns a value based on the assignment operator used.

B.2.4.4 Ternary operator

The ternary operator can be used to make conditional expressions:

```
ternary-expression
    = boolean-expression "?" expression ":" expression ;
```

While the first operand must reduce to a value of type `Boolean`, the other operands can be of any same type.

B.2.4.5 Logic   Logical operations reduce to `Boolean` values. Comparisons can only be performed between operands of the same type while disjunctions, conjunctions and negations can only be performed on operands of type `Boolean` [§ B.2.4.7]:

```
logical-expression = expression ( "==" | "!=" ) expression
                   | expression ( "<=" | ">=" | "<" | ">" ) expression
                   | expression "||" expression
                   | expression "&&" expression
                   | "!" expression ;
```

PE instances are only considered equal if the two given identifiers refer to the same entity. Comparison checks are performed in accordance with the rules for each type [§ B.3.1]. Disjunction and conjunction are non-strict; the second operand will only be evaluated if necessary to determine the value of whole expression.

B.2.4.6 Arithmetic   Arithmetic operations can be performed on expressions, which reduce to values of type `Integer` and `Real` — or `String` and `Stream` for string and stream concatenation, respectively [§ B.2.4.7]:

```
arithmetic-expression = expression ( "+" | "-" ) expression
                      | expression ( "*" | "/" | "%" ) expression
                      | ( "+" | "-" | "++" | "--" ) expression ;
```

Both operands in any binary operation must reduce to the same type.

B.2.4.7 Operators   All valid assignment operators are described in Table B.1 in order of descending precedence. Likewise, all valid expression operators are described in Table B.2.

B.2.5 Annotations

Annotations are used to provide additional information about a given entity:

```
annotations = annotation { "," annotation } ;
```

An annotation is a key-value pair where the value must reduce to a string literal and the key is a special identifier preceded by an @ symbol:

```
annotation = descriptor "=" expression ;

descriptor = ? "@" { letter | digit | "_" } ?
```

TABLE B.1 Assignment Operators

var ++	Increments the value assigned to var by one; returns the unincremented value (Integer and Real variables only).
var --	Decrements the value assigned to var by one; returns the undecremented value (Integer and Real variables only).
++ var	Increments the value assigned to var by one; returns the incremented value (Integer and Real variables only).
-- var	Decrements the value assigned to var by one; returns the decremented value (Integer and Real variables only).
var = exp	Assigns the value of exp to var; returns that value (both operands must be of the same type).
var += exp	Appends the value of exp to that of var; returns the concatenation (both operands must be Strings or both Streams).
var +⁻ exp	Adds the value of exp to that of var; returns the sum (both operands must be Integers or both Reals).
var -= exp	Subtracts the value of exp from that of var; returns the difference (both operands must be Integers or both Reals).
var *= exp	Multiplies the value of var by that of exp; returns the product (both operands must be Integers or both Reals).
var /= exp	Divides the value of var by that of exp; returns the quotient (both operands must be Integers or both Reals).

Annotations wield no influence in DISPEL, but may be used to pass information to the enactment platform or as an additional mode of documentation. Annotations can be attached to any registerable entity [§ B.4.4] during specification or registration and to PE instances [§ B.3.1.6]; all annotations are recorded upon registration regardless of provenance.

B.3 TYPE SYSTEM

DISPEL has three type systems: *language* types refer to the types of variables in scripts; *structural* types refer to the syntactic structure of data elements streamed between PE instances; *domain* types refer to the semantic (principally ontological) meaning assigned to data elements.

B.3.1 Language Types

Each variable has a language type that restricts the set of values that can be attributed to it:

```
language-type = primitive-type | reference-type ;
```

Variables of primitive types store literal values:

```
primitive-type = "Boolean" | "Integer" | "Real" | "String" ;
```

TABLE B.2 Expression Operators

`++ exp`	Increments the value of `exp` by one; if `exp` is a variable, then the value assigned to `exp` will be incremented by one (`Integer` and `Real` only).
`-- exp`	Decrements the value of `exp` by one; if `exp` is a variable, then the value assigned to `exp` will be decremented by one (`Integer` and `Real` only).
`- exp`	Negates the given expression (`Integer` and `Real` only).
`! exp`	Evaluates to the logical negation of the operand (`Boolean` only).
`exp * exp`	Multiplies both operands together (both operands must be `Integers` or both `Reals`).
`exp / exp`	Divides the left operand by the right (both operands must be `Integers` or both `Reals`).
`exp % exp`	Returns the remainder when the left operand is divided by the right (both operands must be `Integers` or both `Reals`).
`exp + exp`	Concatenates two expressions such that the left operand precedes the right (both operands must be `Strings` or both `Streams`).
`exp + exp`	Sums the values of two expressions (both operands must be `Integers` or both `Reals`).
`exp - exp`	Subtracts the right operand from the left (both operands must be `Integers` or both `Reals`).
`exp < exp`	Evaluates whether or not the left operand is less than the right operand (comparables only).
`exp > exp`	Evaluates whether or not the left operand is greater than the right operand (comparables only).
`exp <= exp`	Evaluates whether or not the left operand is less than or equal to the right operand (comparables only).
`exp >= exp`	Evaluates whether or not the left operand is greater than or equal to the right operand (comparables only).
`exp == exp`	Equality check.
`exp != exp`	Inequality check.
`exp && exp`	Evaluates the logical conjunction of both operands (boolean only).
`exp || exp`	Evaluates the logical disjunction of both operands (boolean only).
`exp ? exp : exp`	Returns the middle operand if the left operand is `true`; otherwise, the right operand is returned.

Variables of reference types store references to objects. These references are internal values, which can be copied from one variable to another without replicating the object being referred to:

```
reference-type = "Connection" | "Stream" | array-type
               | dictionary-type | language-identifier ;
```

References cannot be directly manipulated. `language-identifier` is a kind of `identifier` for constructed types such as PEs defined using `Type` declarations [§ B.4.5] or imported from a registry [§ B.4.3].

B.3.1.1 Primitive types An expression of a primitive type will reduce to literal value, which can be stored within any variable of that type. Each primitive type has its own set of literals:

```
literal-value = boolean-literal | integer-literal | real-literal
              | string-literal ;
```

A Boolean can be true or false:

```
boolean-literal = "true" | "false" ;
```

An Integer can be any integer number:

```
integer-literal = [ "-" ] ? digit { digit } ? ;
```

A Real can be any decimal number:

```
real literal = [ "-" ] ? digit { digit } [ "." digit [ digit } ] ? ;
```

A String can be any sequence of characters:

```
string-literal
    = ? '"' { escape-sequence | character - ( '"' | '\' ) } '"' ? ;
```

Strings can contain escape characters that represent non-printable elements such as carriage returns and tabs, as well as double-quotes themselves.

B.3.1.2   *Connections*

A Connection is a reference to a connection. A value can only be assigned to a Connection variable by instantiating a PE, which it is an interface of [§ B.3.1.6], passing it to a connection declaration [§ B.4.8] or assigning another Connection variable to it. An interface of a PE instance cannot be assigned another Connection variable.

B.3.1.3   *Streams*

A Stream is a reference to either a sequence of primitive literals and stream tokens, or a stream comprehension describing such a sequence. A sequence can be constructed by assigning a Stream variable a concatenation of streamable expressions and stream tokens [§ B.1.2], or a stream literal:

```
stream-literal = "|-" [ streamable-expression
                { "," streamable-expression } ] "-|" ;
```

A streamable-expression is a kind of expression which reduces to a primitive value or to a reference to an instance of a streamable constructed type. A constructed type instance is streamable if it contains only primitive values or references to streamable constructed type instances. Alternatively, a Stream variable can be assigned a stream comprehension:

```
stream-comprehension
    = "|-" "repeat" ( "enough" | integer-expression ) "of"
      ( streamable-expression | "(" streamable-expression
      { "," streamable-expression } ")" ) "-|" ;
```

A comprehension repeat expression of sequence describes a recurring sequence. If streamed through a connection [§ B.4.8], sequence should repeat expression times, or if expression is enough, until a NmD token is received by the source. Expressions within comprehensions are evaluated upon execution as normal; comprehensions themselves are computed incrementally when streamed.

B.3.1.4 Arrays

An array variable stores a reference to an array. An array is an ordered list of values of the same type, indexed numerically by offset. An array is constructed by affixing [] to the type of its elements:

```
array-type = language-type "[" "]" ;
```

A multidimensional array can be created by constructing an array of arrays. An array must be initialized before it can be referred to, by assigning an array literal or specifying the array size:

```
array-initialization = "{" [ expression { "," expression } ] "}"
                     | "new" language-type "[" integer-expression "]"
                     { "[" integer-expression "]" } ;
```

An array literal is an ordered sequence of expressions of the expected type equal in length to the array to which it is assigned; the value of each expression is assigned to the corresponding array element. A multidimensional array must be initialized in a single statement by specifying the array size of each nested array in sequence.

Once an array has been initialized, values can be freely assigned to its elements. An array element is referred to by affixing to a reference to the array an expression that reduces to the index of the desired element:

```
array-element = reference "[" expression "]" ;
```

Thus array-element is itself a kind of reference. Indices start at zero and increment by one for each element after the first.

B.3.1.5 Dictionaries

A dictionary variable stores a reference to a dictionary, an unordered composition of labeled values of different language-types. A dictionary is constructed by declaring its constituent elements within <> brackets:

```
dictionary-type
    = "<" [ language-type-group { ";" language-type-group } ] ">" ;

language-type-group = language-type identifier { "," identifier } ;
```

Specification of elements of the same type can be grouped together. Each element has its own identifier, which must be unique within the dictionary. Elements can be assigned values individually, or collectively:

```
dictionary-assignment = "<" [ identifier "=" expression
                        { "," identifier "=" expression } ] ">" ;
```

A dictionary assignment is a mapping of expressions to specific entities in the dictionary; not all entities need be assigned values in a single assignment. Individual elements in a dictionary are accessed by affixing their identifiers to a reference to the dictionary:

```
dictionary-element = reference "." identifier ;
```

Thus `dictionary-element` is itself a kind of `reference`. A dictionary without elements is denoted by the empty dictionary `<>`.

B.3.1.6 Processing elements

A PE specification is considered within DIS-PEL to be a constructed type. A new PE type can be constructed using a `Type` declaration [§ B.4.5] where:

```
PE-type-constructor
    = ( "PE" "(" { stype-declaration ";" } { dtype-declaration ";" }
                connection-signature ")" | PE-type )
      [ "with" ( configuration [ "," annotations ] | annotations ) ] ;
```

A PE type is described by its connection signature or by adapting an existing PE type; thus `PE-type` is a kind of `language-identifier`. A connection signature describes a PE's connection interfaces as a dictionary of inputs linked to a dictionary of outputs:

```
connection-signature = interfaces "=>" interfaces ;

interfaces = "<" [ interface-group { ";" interface-group } ] ">" ;
```

Each input and output connection interface is an augmented `Connection` or `Connection` array declaration with the optional addition of a structural type [§ B.3.2], a domain type [§ B.3.3] and any number of connection modifiers:

```
interface-group
    = "Connection" [ "[" "]" ]
      [ ":" structural-type ] [ "::" domain-type ]
      { modifier } identifier { "," identifier } ;
```

Connection modifiers are used to modify the behavior of connection interfaces.

```
modifier = modifier-id [ "(" expression { "," expression } ")" ] ;
```

Some modifiers take parameters — these parameters are listed in parentheses immediately after the modifier. All valid `modifier-ids` are described in Table B.3.

TABLE B.3   Connection Modifiers

after	Used to delay the consumption of data through one or more connections. *[Requires a list of predecessors.]*
compressed	Used to compress data streamed out of the modified connection or to identify the compression used on data being consumed when applied to an output or an input interface respectively. *[Requires a compression scheme.]*
default	Used to specify the default input streamed through a connection should input be otherwise left unspecified. *[Requires a stream expression; input only.]*
encrypted	Used to encrypt data streamed out of the modified connection or to identify the encryption scheme used on data being consumed when applied to an output or an input interface respectively. *[Requires an encryption scheme.]*
initiator	Used to identify connections which provide only an initial input before terminating. Inputs maked initiator are read to completion before reading from inputs not so marked. *[Input only.]*
limit	Used to specify the maximum number of data elements a connection will consume or produce before terminating. *[Requires a positive integer value.]*
locator	Used where the modified connection indicates the location of a resource to be accessed by the associated PEI (which might influence the distribution of the workflow upon execution). *[Input only.]*
lockstep	Indicates that one data element must be streamed through every interface in the modified array before another element can be streamed through any of them. *[Connection arrays only.]*
permutable	Indicates that a given array of inputs can be read from in any order without influencing the outputs of the PEI. *[Input connection arrays only.]*
preserved	Indicates that data streamed through the modified connection should be recorded in a given location. *[Requires a URI, or goes to a default location.]*
requiresDtype	Dictates that upon instantiation, the specific domain type of the modified connection must be defined.
requiresStype	Dictates that upon instantiation, the specific structural type of the modified connection must be defined.
roundrobin	Indicates that a data element must be streamed through each interface in the modified array in order, one element at a time. *[Connection arrays only.]*
successive	Indicates that each interface of the modified array must terminate before the next one is read. *[Connection arrays only.]*
terminator	Causes a PEI to terminate upon the termination of the modified connection alone (rather than once all inputs or all outputs have terminated).

If an interface omits an explicit structural type, then it is of type Any; if it omits an explicit domain type, then it is of type Thing. Interfaces with the same structural type, domain type and connection modifiers can be grouped together as normal for dictionary elements. An instance of a PE must be created before it can be connected to a workflow:

```
PE-initialization = "new" PE-type [ "with" ( configuration
                    { "," annotations } | annotations ) ] ;

configuration = configurable { "," configurable } ;
```

The length of a `Connection` array can be defined for PE instances. Connection interfaces can also be redefined, adding new connection modifiers or restricting their structural and domain types:

```
configurable = [ identifier "." ] "length" "=" expression
   | [ identifier "as" ] [ interface-type ] { modifier } identifier ;
```

Only existing interfaces can be redefined in this way; interfaces can be renamed however by declaring `old` as ... `new`, where `old` is the original interface identifier and `new` is its replacement. A PE's interfaces are identified within the local namespace for the duration of the statement, allowing interfaces to be referred to without prefix.

A PE variable may only store a reference to an instance of a PE that is a subtype of the variable's type. A PE `Child` is a subtype of PE `Parent` if and only if any instance of `Child` can replace an instance of `Parent` in any workflow:

- Each input interface of `Parent` must have a structural and domain type that are sub-types of those of an input interface of `Child` with the same name [§ B.3.2.5, B.3.3.3]. If `Child` has any additional input interfaces, then they must each have a `default` property.
- For each output interface of `Parent`, `Child` must have an output interface of the same name with structural and domain types that are sub-types of those of `Parent`'s interface.

B.3.2 Structural Types

Every connection has a structural type that restricts the set of values that can be streamed through it:

```
structural-type = "Any" | simple-stype | compound-stype ;
```

Interfaces of type `Any` can stream any data value. Interfaces of simple types stream unstructured literal values:

```
simple-stype = "Boolean" | "Integer" | "Real" | "String" | "Byte" ;
```

Interfaces of compound types stream structured data, which is composed of data with their own structural types:

```
compound-stype = array-stype | list-stype | dictionary-stype
                 | constructed-type ;
```

Aliases for compound types are defined using `Stype` declarations [§ B.4.6] or imported from a registry [§ B.4.3].

B.3.2.1   *Simple types* Any data element can be decomposed into one of five data types.

- A `Boolean` element can be true or false.
- An `Integer` element is any whole number.
- A `Real` element is any number.
- A `String` element is any fragment of text.
- A `Byte` element is a single byte of binary data.

DISPEL does not assume a particular representation of primitive structural types — this is handled by the gateway.

B.3.2.2   *Arrays* An array is an ordered list of values of the same structural type. An array is described by affixing `[]` to the type of its elements:

```
array-stype = structural-type "[" "]" ;
```

A multidimensional array can be created by describing an array of arrays. An array is streamed by first sending the `SoA` token followed by size of the array; each element of the array is then streamed in turn, finishing with the `EoA` token. Note that the size of an array is not specified with a script, but is determined during execution of a workflow.

B.3.2.3   *Lists* A list is an array of unspecified size. A list is described by embedding the type of its elements within `[]` brackets:

```
list-stype = "[" structural-type "]" ;
```

A list is streamed by first sending the `SoL` and then sending each element of the list in turn, finishing with the `EoL` token.

B.3.2.4   *Dictionaries* A dictionary is an unordered set of labeled values of different structural types. A dictionary is described by declaring its constituent elements within `<>` brackets:

```
dictionary-stype = "<" [ "rest" | structural-type-group
                  { ";" structural-type-group } [ ";" "rest" ] ] ">" ;

structural-type-group = structural-type identifier { "," identifier } ;
```

Specification of elements of the same type can be grouped together. If an interface is only concerned with some of the values in a dictionary, then only the identifiers for those values of interest need be specified, followed by the `rest` keyword. `rest` must be the final component of a dictionary and represents zero or more unidentified data elements. A dictionary is streamed by first sending the SoD token and then sending each element of the dictionary in turn, label then value, finishing with the EoD token.

B.3.2.5 Sub-typing Whether or not a structural type ST' is a subtype of another structural type ST ($ST' \sqsubseteq ST$) is determined by the following rules:

- $\forall$ ST. $ST \sqsubseteq Any$.
- $\forall$ ST. $ST \sqsubseteq ST$.
- $[ST'] \sqsubseteq [ST]$ if and only if $ST' \sqsubseteq ST$.
- $ST'[] \sqsubseteq ST[]$ if and only if $ST' \sqsubseteq ST$.
- $< ST'_1\ id'_1\ ;\ \ldots\ ;\ ST'_m\ id'_m > \sqsubseteq < ST_1\ id_1\ ;\ \ldots\ ;\ ST_n\ id_n >$ if and only if $m = n$ and, after sorting identifiers according to a standard scheme, $id'_i = id_i$ and $ST'_i \sqsubseteq ST_i$ for all i such that $1 \le i \le n$.
- $< ST'_1\ id'_1\ ;\ \ldots\ ;\ ST'_m\ id'_m > \sqsubseteq < ST_1\ id_1\ ;\ \ldots\ ;\ ST_n\ id_n ;\ rest >$ if and only if $m \ge n$ and there exists a permutation of identifiers $id'_1, \ldots, id'_m$ such that $id'_i = id_i$ and $ST'_i \sqsubseteq ST_i$ for all i such that $1 \le i < n$.

B.3.3 Domain Types

Every connection interface has a domain type that ascribes a semantic interpretation to the data streamed through it:

```
domain-type = "Thing" | domain-identifier | domain-descriptor
            | domain-array | domain-list | domain-dictionary ;
```

Thing is the super-type of all domain types, and is implied where no domain type is specified. A domain-identifier is an identifier representing a domain descriptor or constructed domain type [§ B.4.7].

B.3.3.1 Domain descriptors A domain descriptor is a direct reference to an element in an ontology:

```
domain-descriptor =
    ? '"' character - ( '"' | '\' ) { character - ( '"' | '\' ) }
      ":" character - ( '"' | '\' )
        { character - ( '"' | '\' ) } '"' ? ;
```

A domain descriptor is a domain namespace identifier [§ B.4.2] prefixing an ontology element name. Domain descriptors can be substituted for domain type identifiers when specifying the domain type of a connection interface [§ B.3.1.6].

B.3.3.2 Compound domain types Compound domain types can be described in the same form as for structural types:

```
domain-array = domain-type "[" "]" ;

domain-list = "[" domain-type "]" ;

domain-dictionary = "<" [ "rest" | domain-group { ";" domain-group }
                        [ ";" "rest" ] ] ">"

domain-group = domain-type identifier { "," identifier } ;
```

The structure of a domain type must correspond to the structure of the structural type assigned to the same interface; it is permissible however for a simple domain type to correspond to a compound structural type.

B.3.3.3 *Sub-typing*   Whether or not a domain type DT' is a subtype of another domain type DT ($DT' \sqsubseteq DT$) is determined by the following rules:

- $\forall$ DT. DT $\sqsubseteq$ Thing.
- $\forall$ DT. DT $\sqsubseteq$ DT.
- $DT' \sqsubseteq DT$ if DT' represents an ontology element `"o:x"`, DT represents an ontology element `"o:y"` and x is a subtype of y according to ontology o.
- $[DT'] \sqsubseteq [DT]$ if and only if $DT' \sqsubseteq DT$.
- $DT'[\,] \sqsubseteq DT[\,]$ if and only if $DT' \sqsubseteq DT$.
- $< DT'_1 \; id'_1 \; ; \; \ldots \; ; \; DT'_m \; id'_m > \; \sqsubseteq \; < DT_1 \; id_1 \; ; \; \ldots \; ; \; DT_n \; id_n >$ if and only if $m = n$ and, after sorting identifiers according to a standard scheme, $id'_i = id_i$ and $DT'_i \sqsubseteq DT_i$ for all i such that $1 \leq i \leq n$.
- $< DT'_1 \; id'_1 \; ; \; \ldots \; ; \; DT'_m \; id'_m > \; \sqsubseteq \; < DT_1 \; id_1 \; ; \; \ldots \; ; \; DT_n \; id_n ; \; rest >$ if and only if $m \geq n$ and there exists a permutation of identifiers $id'_1, \ldots, id'_m$ such that $id'_i = id_i$ and $DT'_i \sqsubseteq DT_i$ for all i such that $1 \leq i \leq n$.

B.4 STATEMENTS

A DISPEL script is built from simple and compound statements executed in series:

```
statement = package-statement | namespace-statement | import-statement
          | registration | declaration ";" | assignment ";"
          | ltype-declaration | stype-declaration | dtype-declaration
          | connection-declaration | composition | if-statement
          | switch-statement | while-statement | for-statement
          | break-statement | continue-statement | function
          | function-call ";" | return-statement | PE-constructor
          | submission ;
```

Compound statements include statement blocks that are themselves executed in series during execution of the overall statement.

B.4.1 package statement

A statement block can be associated with a particular package, automatically adding entities registered within that package to the namespace for the extent of that statement block:

```
package-statement = "package" package-name statement-block ;
```

package associates the enclosed statement block with the given package then executes it. If the package statement is already associated with a package, then the association is overridden within the enclosed statement block. The package referred to need not exist prior to execution of the statement.

B.4.2 namespace statement

Identifiers can be conferred to outside ontologies, allowing references to elements within those ontologies:

```
namespace-statement = "namespace" identifier string-literal ";" ;
```

namespace maps an identifier to the given ontology URI in the local namespace, permitting the use of domain descriptors prefixed with that identifier [§ B.3.3.1].

B.4.3 import statement

A use statement imports the given registered entities into the namespace, obviating the need to preface their identifiers with those of their parent package:

```
import-statement = "use" package-name "."
        ( identifier | "{" identifier { "," identifier } "}" ) ";"
```

Multiple entities from the same package can be imported simultaneously. Entities within package dispel.lang are imported into the namespace automatically at the beginning of every script for its full extent.

B.4.4 register statement

A register statement registers one or more entities:

```
registration = "register" identifier { "," identifier }
                    [ "with" annotations ] ";" ;
```

Each entity will be registered within the package associated with the register statement with the annotations provided. If no such package exists, then register cannot be invoked. If an entity with the same identifier already exists within the package associated with the register statement, then that entity will be overridden.

If a function [§ B.4.17] or PE constructor [§ B.4.18] is registered, then its namespace information will also be recorded so as to permit the import of entities upon which it depends. If any such entities are unregistered, then they will be registered automatically prior to registration of the dependent entity with no additional configuration.

B.4.5   Type declaration

New constructed language types can be defined using `Type` declarations:

```
ltype-declaration
    = "Type" language-identifier "is"
        ( language-type "with" annotations | PE-type-constructor ) ";" ;
```

A constructed type can simply be an alias for an existing language type (usually a compound type like a dictionary), or it can describe a new abstract PE type [§ B.3.1.6]. The identifier for the new type will be inserted into the local namespace.

B.4.6   Stype declaration

An `stype` declaration allows the creation of aliases for compound structural types:

```
stype-declaration = "Stype" structural-identifier "is" structural-type
                    "with" annotations ";" ;
```

The identifier for the new type is added to the local namespace. If declared within a PE type specification [§ B.3.1.6] and attributed to any interface of that PE, then any unification of the declared type with another type in a connection [§ B.4.8] will result in a commensurate unification with all instances of the declared type used in other interfaces of that PE instance.

B.4.7   Dtype declaration

A `Dtype` declaration derives a new domain type from an existing type:

```
dtype-declaration
    = "Dtype" domain-identifier ( "is" domain-type
    [ "represents" domain-descriptor ]
    | "represents" domain-descriptor ) "with" annotations ";" ;
```

The identifier for the new type is added to the local namespace. A constructed domain type can be directly associated with an element in an ontology — any compound type constructed using the new domain type will be assumed to be a compound involving the represented element, and likewise any subtype relation with the domain type will be assumed to describe an equivalent relationship with the element. As with structural types, declaring a domain type within a PE type specification will create sympathy between interfaces attributed that domain type [§ B.4.6].

B.4.8   Connections

A connection declaration forms a new connection or adds a channel to an existing connection:

```
connection-declaration = ( reference | stream-expression )
                         "=>" ( reference | data-sink ) ";" ;
```

By default, a declaration entry => exit merges two connections in the local workflow graph referred to by two Connection variables entry and exit. Two connections can merge provided that at least one connection is untethered at its source; the new connection will inherit the union of both parents' channels, the intersection of both parents' structural and domain types [§ B.3.2.5 and § B.3.3.3] and be referred to by both entry and exit. Alternatively, entry can be a Stream, in which case a connection emitting from a stream node will be created and merged with exit. Finally, exit can be a data-sink [§ B.1.3]:

```
data-sink = "discard" | "error" | "warning" | "terminate" ;
```

A connection directed to a sink node will be created and merged with entry.

B.4.9 Processing Element Composition

A PE composition statement creates a new composite PE by applying a PE constructor [§ B.4.18] to an abstract PE:

```
composition = "PE" "<" PE-type ">" PE-type "=" constructor-call ";" ;
```

A statement PE<AbstractPE> CompositePE = constructor(...) will apply constructor constructor to abstract PE AbstractPE, creating a new (composite) PE type CompositePE which can be instantiated. The connection signature of AbstractPE must match that used by constructor.

B.4.10 if conditional

An if statement only permits the execution of a statement block if a given boolean expression evaluates as true:

```
if-statement = "if" "(" boolean-expression ")" statement-block
               [ "else" statement-block ] ;
```

An optional else clause can provide an alternative statement block to execute if the given expression is false; otherwise, execution will skip to the next unenclosed statement.

B.4.11 switch conditional

A switch statement partitions a statement block — different partitions are executed based on the evaluation of a given expression:

```
switch-statement = "switch" primitive-expression "{"
                   { "case" literal-value ":" { statement } }
                   [ "default" ":" { statement } ] "}" ;
```

Partitions are marked by case markers, each associated with a literal denoting a particular value of the given expression; execution will proceed from the first matching marker until the end of the statement block unless redirected. If no matching case is found, then execution will proceed from the default marker should one exist or immediately after the statement block otherwise.

B.4.12 `while` iterator

A `while` iterator repeats the execution of a given statement block while a given boolean expression evaluates as `true`:

```
while-statement = "while" "(" boolean-expression ")" statement-block ;
```

If the expression becomes (or is initially) `false`, execution resumes immediately after the iterator.

B.4.13 `for` iterator

A `for` iterator describes a repetition based on a regular update of a control variable:

```
for-statement
    = "for" "(" declaration ";" boolean-expression ";"
              assignment ")" statement-block ;
```

Prior to attempting to execute a statement block, the given variable declaration is executed. The statement block is executed if the given boolean expression is `true` and is re-executed until it becomes `false`, at which point execution resumes immediately after the iterator. After each iteration (if any), the given assignment is executed.

B.4.14 `break` statement

A `break` statement forces execution of an iterator or `switch` statement to end:

```
break-statement = "break" ";" ;
```

Execution is resumed immediately after the innermost iterator or `switch` statement in which `break` is located should one exist.

B.4.15 `continue` statement

A `continue` statement forces execution of an iteration to end:

```
continue-statement = "continue" ";" ;
```

`continue` can only be invoked within an iterator. Execution skips ahead to the next iteration of the innermost iterator in which `continue` is located provided that the iteration condition holds; otherwise execution resumes immediately after the iterator.

B.4.16 `submit` statement

A `submit` statement submits (part of) the local workflow graph for enactment:

```
submission = "submit" [ identifier { "," identifier } ] ";"
```

submit submits all nodes of the local workflow graph connected to at least one of the PE instances provided, or the entire graph if no instance is provided. Submission cannot be performed within a PE constructor; submission of nodes with untethered connections will fail.

B.4.17 Functions

A function is a parameterized statement block describing a recurring execution pattern:

```
function = ( "void" | language-type ) identifier parameter-tuple
            statement-block ;
```

A function is not executed immediately, but is instead invoked on demand as often as required. A function consists of a return type, an identifier (inserted into the local namespace), a set of parameters and a statement block. The return type must be a valid language type, or void. A tuple of variable declarations without assignments form the function parameters:

```
parameter-tuple = "(" [ language-type identifier
                  { "," language-type identifier } ] ")" ;
```

Each function has its own namespace, consisting of the local namespace at the end of the statement block in which the function is defined, extended with its parameter set.

A function is invoked using its identifier and a tuple of values; these values correspond and are assigned to the function's parameters for the duration of the invocation:

```
function-call = identifier "(" [ expression { "," expression } ] ")" ;
```

The function is executed within its own namespace. A function can be invoked as a statement or as a part of an expression unless void: if invoked as a statement, then execution will continue from immediately after the statement upon completion; If invoked within an expression, the function call will reduce to the value returned by the function and execution of the expression will resume upon completion.

If a function is not void, then it must return a value of its return type, which a call to the function will then reduce to within any expression. This is ensured by including a return statement within the function:

```
return-statement = "return" [ expression ] ";" ;
```

A return statement of this kind may only be included within a function. It immediately ends execution of a function, returning the value which the provided expression reduces to should one be provided — which must be the case if the function is not void. If the function is not void, a return statement must be executed within a function before the end of the function.

B.4.18   Processing Element Construction

A PE constructor is a parameterized statement block used to specify an internal workflow graph with which to implement instances of composite PEs.

```
PE-constructor = "PE" "<" PE-type ">" identifier parameter-tuple
                 statement-block ;
```

A PE constructor consists of a reference to an abstract PE, identifier (inserted into the local namespace), parameter tuple and statement block. It has its own namespace, consisting of the local namespace at the end of the statement block in which constructor is defined, extended with its parameter set. The constructor's own statement block is not executed immediately, but upon every act of PE composition which uses the constructor [§ B.4.9].

A PE constructor is invoked using its identifier and a tuple of values; these values correspond and are assigned to the constructor's parameters for the duration of the invocation.

```
constructor-call = PE-type "(" [ expression { "," expression } ] ")" ;
```

The constructor is executed within its namespace, producing an internal workflow graph distinct from the local graph at point of invocation. A PE constructor must invoke a special `return` statement before it terminates:

```
PE-return = "return" "PE" "(" "<" interface-assignments ">" "=>"
                             "<" interface-assignments ">" ")" ";"

interface-assignments = [ interface "=" connection
                          { "," interface "=" connection } ] ;
```

Every interface of the constructor's abstract PE type must be assigned a connection in the internal workflow such that no untethered connections remain.

Appendix C

Component Definitions

Malcolm Atkinson and Chee Sun Liew

School of Informatics, University of Edinburgh, Edinburgh, UK

This appendix contains a list of all of the DISPEL elements used in the book. They are organized by packages, as shown in the first table. The second table is an alphabetic listing of these components. Column 1 gives the component's identifier, column 2 its kind, and column 3 the full package name in which it is defined. The detailed definitions and descriptions for each of these components can be found at www.dispel-lang.org/.

Alphabetic List of Packages

Package	Comments
book.examples	general purpose DISPEL examples used early in the book
book.examples.brainimaging	used to introduce domain types
book.examples.dispel	an early simple introductory example
book.examples.euroexpress	gene expression from images examples
book.examples.geography	structural type examples used in DISPEL manual
book.examples.math	prime number example in DISPEL manual
book.examples.oceanography	used to introduce domain types

(Continued)

The DATA Bonanza: Improving Knowledge Discovery in Science, Engineering, and Business, First Edition.
Edited by Malcolm Atkinson, Rob Baxter, Michelle Galea, Mark Parsons, Peter Brezany, Oscar Corcho, Jano van Hemert, and David Snelling.
© 2013 John Wiley & Sons, Inc. Published 2013 by John Wiley & Sons, Inc.

Alphabetic List of Packages (*Continued*)

Package	Comments
`book.examples.seismology`	used for introductory running example
`dispel.core`	general-purpose processing elements normally available as standard
`dispel.datamining`	data-mining processing elements normally available as standard
`dispel.db`	database processing elements normally available as standard
`dispel.files`	file processing elements normally available as standard
`dispel.lang`	mandatory foundational types and processing elements always part of a DISPEL implementation
`dispel.textmining`	standard text-mining processing elements normally available as standard
`dispel.util`	general-purpose processing elements normally available as standard

Alphabetic Table of DISPEL Components

Identifier	Kind	Package
`AllConsistentPairs`	PE	`book.examples`
`AllIntegerPairs`	PE	`book.examples`
`AllMeetsAllSymmetricCorrelator`	PE	`book.examples.seismology`
`AllPairs`	PE	`book.examples`
`ArchivedTraceDescription`	Dtype	`book.examples.seismology`
`bexd`	namespace	`book.examples.math`
`BinaryCombiner`	PE	`dispel.core`
`BinaryMerge`	PE	`dispel.core`
`Boolean`	Type	`dispel.lang`
`BrainScan`	Dtype	`book.examples.brainimaging`
`BulkMover`	PE	`dispel.core`
`Byte`	Type	`dispel.lang`
`ByteSegment`	Stype	`dispel.files`
`Char`	Type	`dispel.lang`
`CleanAndValidate`	PE	`book.examples`
`CohortStudy`	Dtype	`book.examples.brainimaging`
`Combiner`	PE	`dispel.core`
`correlateAll`	Function	`book.examples.seismology`
`CorrelationTraceDescription`	Dtype	`book.examples.seismology`

Alphabetic Table of DISPEL Components (*Continued*)

Identifier	Kind	Package
CorrFarm	PE	book.examples.seismology
CorrHandler	PE	book.examples.seismology
CorrTraceMD	Stype	book.examples.seismology
Count	PE	book.examples
DataDeliveryReceipt	PE	dispel.core
db	namespace	dispel.db
DBoolean	Dtype	dispel.lang
DByte	Dtype	dispel.lang
DBURI	Dtype	dispel.db
Deliver	PE	dispel.lang
Detector	PE	book.examples
DChar	Dtype	dispel.lang
DInteger	Dtype	dispel.lang
dispel	namespace	dispel.lang
DPixel	Dtype	dispel.lang
DReal	Dtype	dispel.lang
DString	Dtype	dispel.lang
DTime	Dtype	dispel.lang
Error	Stype	dispel.lang
ErrorMessage	Dtype	dispel.lang
EventTime	Dtype	dispel.lang
FileDescriptor	Stype	dispel.core
FilePath	Dtype	dispel.db
FileSegment	Dtype	dispel.files
FileSystem	Dtype	dispel.db
fillStringArgs	Function	dispel.util
Filter	PE	book.examples
GeoPosition	Stype	book.examples.oceanography
GetFromHTTP	PE	dispel.files
Identifier	Dtype	book.examples.brainimaging
Integer	Type	dispel.lang
Java	Dtype	dispel.lang
JavascriptScript	Dtype	dispel.lang
ListCombiner	PE	dispel.core
ListConcatenate	PE	dispel.core
ListMerge	PE	dispel.core
ListSample	PE	dispel.core
ListSplit	PE	dispel.core
ListToStream	PE	dispel.core
lockSQLDataSource	Function	book.examples.dispel

(*Continued*)

Alphabetic Table of DISPEL Components (*Continued*)

Identifier	Kind	Package
LongitudinalStudy	Dtype	book.examples.brainimaging
makeAllMeetsAll	Function	dispel.core
makeAllMeetsAllSelfJoin	Function	dispel.core
makeAllMeetsAll-SymmetricCorrelator	Function	book.examples.seismology
makeCorrelationPipeline	Function	book.examples.seismology
makeCorrFarm	Function	book.examples.seismology
makeDataExtractQuery	Function	book.examples.seismology
makeCorrHandler	Function	book.examples.seismology
makeMwayCombiner	Function	dispel.core
makeMwayMerge	Function	dispel.core
makeResponder	Function	book.examples.seismology
makeSieveOfEratosthenes	Function	book.examples.math
MedicalImage	Dtype	book.examples.brainimaging
Merge	PE	dispel.core
NotYetDone	PE	book.examples.seismology
Observation	Stype	book.examples.oceanography
ObservationTrack	Stype	book.examples.oceanography
PairNotYetDone	PE	book.examples.seismology
PairToCorrelate	Dtype	book.examples.seismology
ParallelSQLQuery	PE	dispel.db
Pause	PE	dispel.core
PEInstanceID	Dtype	dispel.lang
Pixel	Type	dispel.lang
Position	Stype	book.examples.oceanography
PostToHTTP	PE	dispel.files
PreparedTraceDescription	Dtype	book.examples.seismology
PrimeFilter	PE	book.examples.math
PrimeGenerator	PE	book.examples.math
ProgramScript	Dtype	dispel.lang
ProgrammableFilterProject	PE	dispel.core
ProgrammableFilterProject-Distinct	PE	dispel.core
ProgrammableJoin	PE	dispel.core
ProgrammableSort	PE	dispel.core
ProgressReport	Stype	dispel.core
PythonScript	Dtype	dispel.lang
RandomListSplit	PE	dispel.core
RDBTuple	Dtype	dispel.db
ReadFile	PE	dispel.files
ReadPartFile	PE	dispel.files

Alphabetic Table of DISPEL Components (*Continued*)

Identifier	Kind	Package
Real	Type	dispel.lang
ReliableBulkMover	PE	dispel.core
ReliableDataDeliveryReceipt	PE	dispel.core
ReliableParallelSQLQuery	PE	dispel.db
ReliableProgrammableFilter- ProjectCount	PE	dispel.core
ReliableReadFile	PE	dispel.files
ReliableSQLInsert	PE	dispel.db
ReliableWriteFile	PE	dispel.files
Responder	PE	book.examples.seismology
Results	PE	dispel.lang
RubyScript	Dtype	dispel.lang
RuleFP	Stype	dispel.core
RuleFPD	Stype	dispel.core
Sample	PE	dispel.core
SBoolean	Stype	dispel.lang
SByte	Stype	dispel.lang
Scan	Dtype	book.examples.brainimaging
SChar	Stype	dispel.lang
SeismicCorrelator	PE	book.examples.seismology
SeismicStacker	PE	book.examples.seismology
seismo	namespace	book.examples.seismology
SInteger	Stype	dispel.lang
Sort	PE	dispel.core
SortRule	Dtype	dispel.core
SphericalPosition	Stype	book.examples.oceanography
SPixel	Stype	dispel.lang
Split	PE	dispel.core
SQLError	Stype	dispel.db
SQLErrorMessage	Dtype	dispel.db
SQLInsert	PE	dispel.db
SQLInsertStatement	Dtype	dispel.db
SQLParameterizedQuery	PE	dispel.db
SQLParameterizedUpdate	PE	dispel.db
SQLQuery	PE	dispel.db
SQLQueryStatement	Dtype	dispel.db
SQLScript	Dtype	dispel.lang
SQLStatement	Dtype	dispel.db
SQLUpdateStatement	Dtype	dispel.db
SQLToTupleList	PE	book.example.dispel

(Continued)

Alphabetic Table of DISPEL Components (*Continued*)

Identifier	Kind	Package
SReal	Stype	dispel.lang
StreamToList	PE	dispel.core
SString	Stype	dispel.lang
STime	Stype	dispel.lang
String	Type	dispel.lang
Submittable	PE	dispel.lang
Survey	Stype	book.examples.oceanography
SymmetricCombiner	PE	dispel.core
Terminator	PE	dispel.lang
Time	Stype	book.examples.oceanography
Time	Type	dispel.lang
timeToString	Function	dispel.util
Trace	Stype	book.examples.seismology
TraceDescription	Dtype	book.examples.seismology
TraceLocations	Stype	book.examples.seismology
TracePair	Stype	book.examples.seismology
TracePreparer	PE	book.examples.seismology
TraceMD	Stype	book.examples.seismology
TraceStandardiser	PE	book.examples.seismology
Transform	PE	book.examples.seismology
TupleBuild	PE	dispel.core
TupleBurst	PE	dispel.core
TupleRowSet	Dtype	dispel.db
URI	Dtype	dispel.lang
Warning	Stype	dispel.lang
WarningMessage	Dtype	dispel.lang
WriteFile	PE	dispel.files
WritePartFile	PE	dispel.files

Index

The DATA Bonanza: Improving Knowledge Discovery in Science, Engineering, and Business, First Edition.
Edited by Malcolm Atkinson, Rob Baxter, Michelle Galea, Mark Parsons, Peter Brezany, Oscar Corcho, Jano van Hemert, and David Snelling.
© 2013 John Wiley & Sons, Inc. Published 2013 by John Wiley & Sons, Inc.

WILEY SERIES ON PARALLEL AND DISTRIBUTED COMPUTING
Series Editor: Albert Y. Zomaya

Parallel and Distributed Simulation Systems / Richard Fujimoto

Mobile Processing in Distributed and Open Environments / Peter Sapaty

Introduction to Parallel Algorithms / C. Xavier and S. S. Iyengar

Solutions to Parallel and Distributed Computing Problems: Lessons from Biological Sciences / Albert Y. Zomaya, Fikret Ercal, and Stephan Olariu (*Editors*)

Parallel and Distributed Computing: A Survey of Models, Paradigms, and Approaches / Claudia Leopold

Fundamentals of Distributed Object Systems: A CORBA Perspective / Zahir Tari and Omran Bukhres

Pipelined Processor Farms: Structured Design for Embedded Parallel Systems / Martin Fleury and Andrew Downton

Handbook of Wireless Networks and Mobile Computing / Ivan Stojmenović (*Editor*)

Internet-Based Workflow Management: Toward a Semantic Web / Dan C. Marinescu

Parallel Computing on Heterogeneous Networks / Alexey L. Lastovetsky

Performance Evaluation and Characteization of Parallel and Distributed Computing Tools / Salim Hariri and Manish Parashar

Distributed Computing: Fundamentals, Simulations and Advanced Topics, *Second Edition* / Hagit Attiya and Jennifer Welch

Smart Environments: Technology, Protocols, and Applications / Diane Cook and Sajal Das

Fundamentals of Computer Organization and Architecture / Mostafa Abd-El-Barr and Hesham El-Rewini

Advanced Computer Architecture and Parallel Processing / Hesham El-Rewini and Mostafa Abd-El-Barr

UPC: Distributed Shared Memory Programming / Tarek El-Ghazawi, William Carlson, Thomas Sterling, and Katherine Yelick

Handbook of Sensor Networks: Algorithms and Architectures / Ivan Stojmenović (*Editor*)

Parallel Metaheuristics: A New Class of Algorithms / Enrique Alba (*Editor*)

Design and Analysis of Distributed Algorithms / Nicola Santoro

Task Scheduling for Parallel Systems / Oliver Sinnen

Computing for Numerical Methods Using Visual C++ / Shaharuddin Salleh, Albert Y. Zomaya, and Sakhinah A. Bakar

Architecture-Independent Programming for Wireless Sensor Networks / Amol B. Bakshi and Viktor K. Prasanna

High-Performance Parallel Database Processing and Grid Databases / David Taniar, Clement Leung, Wenny Rahayu, and Sushant Goel

Algorithms and Protocols for Wireless and Mobile Ad Hoc Networks / Azzedine Boukerche (*Editor*)

Algorithms and Protocols for Wireless Sensor Networks / Azzedine Boukerche (*Editor*)

Optimization Techniques for Solving Complex Problems / Enrique Alba, Christian Blum, Pedro Isasi, Coromoto León, and Juan Antonio Gómez (*Editors*)

Emerging Wireless LANs, Wireless PANs, and Wireless MANs: IEEE 802.11, IEEE 802.15, IEEE 802.16 Wireless Standard Family / Yang Xiao and Yi Pan (*Editors*)

High-Performance Heterogeneous Computing / Alexey L. Lastovetsky and Jack Dongarra

Mobile Intelligence / Laurence T. Yang, Augustinus Borgy Waluyo, Jianhua Ma, Ling Tan, and Bala Srinivasan (*Editors*)

Advanced Computational Infrastructures for Parallel and Distributed Adaptive Applicatons / Manish Parashar and Xiaolin Li *(Editors)*

Market-Oriented Grid and Utility Computing / Rajkumar Buyya and Kris Bubendorfer (*Editors*)

Cloud Computing Principles and Paradigms / Rajkumar Buyya, James Broberg, and Andrzej Goscinski

Energy-Efficient Distributed Computing Systems / Albert Y. Zomaya and Young Choon Lee (*Editors*)

Scalable Computing and Communications: Theory and Practice / Samee U. Khan, Lizhe Wang, and Albert Y. Zomaya

The DATA Bonanza: Improving Knowledge Discovery in Science, Engineering, and Business / Malcolm Atkinson, Rob Baxter, Michelle Galea, Mark Parsons, Peter Brezany, Oscar Corcho, Jano van Hemert, and David Snelling *(Editors)*